LIVING LITURGY™

LIVING LITURGY™

Spirituality, Celebration, and Catechesis for Sundays and Solemnities

Year A • 2020

Brian Schmisek
Katy Beedle Rice
Diana Macalintal

LITURGICAL PRESS
Collegeville, Minnesota

www.litpress.org

Cover design by Monica Bokinskie. Art by Ned Bustard (pages 1–16, 101–10, 174–224), Emanuel Franco-Gómez, OCarm (cover and pages 21–38, 69–96, 147–70), and Tanja Butler (pages 43–64, 113–42, 228–58).

ISSN 1547-089X

ISBN 978-0-8146-4421-8 ISBN 978-0-8146-4446-1 (ebook)

CONTENTS

CONTRIBUTORS

Brian Schmisek is professor and dean of the Institute of Pastoral Studies at Loyola University Chicago. Prior to coming to Chicago in 2012, he was the founding dean of the School of Ministry at the University of Dallas. His published works include *The Rome of Peter and Paul: A Pilgrim's Handbook to New Testament Sites in the Eternal City* (Pickwick), *Ancient Faith for the Modern World: A Brief Guide to the Apostles' Creed* (ACTA), *Resurrection of the Flesh or Resurrection from the Dead: Implications for Theology* (Liturgical Press), and many other books coauthored for biblical study, and articles.

Katy Beedle Rice is a catechist and writer who lives with her husband and three children in Boise, Idaho. She is a formation leader for the National Association of the Catechesis of the Good Shepherd, training catechists who work with children ages three through six. Rice is also a contributing preacher for the Dominican Podcast *the Word* (https://word.op.org), writes for Celebration Publications, a division of the National Catholic Reporter Publishing Company, and blogs about motherhood, ministry, and the Eucharist at blessedbrokenshared.blogspot.com.

Diana Macalintal has served as a liturgist, musician, author, speaker, and composer for the last twenty-five years, and her work can be found in *Give Us This Day* and many other publications. She is the author of *The Work of Your Hands: Prayers for Ordinary and Extraordinary Moments of Grace*, *Joined by the Church, Sealed by a Blessing: Couples and Communities Called to Conversion Together*, and *Your Parish* Is *the Curriculum: RCIA in the Midst of the Community* (Liturgical Press). Macalintal is a cofounder of TeamRCIA.com with her husband, Nick Wagner.

PREFACE

Renewal

This is the third year since Liturgical Press gave a new look and feel to this popular resource, and the second year with this writing team. We are proud of the text with its engaging artwork and updated design, and we look forward to its use in parishes and faith settings throughout the world. We authors have incorporated feedback that we've received as we promote these materials throughout the year. But some things remain the same. As last year, we followed the structure established by Sr. Joyce Ann Zimmerman, CPPS, director of the Institute for Liturgical Ministry (now closed, unfortunately), and Sr. Kathleen Harmon, SNDdeN, concerning the "Focusing the Gospel," "Connecting the Gospel," and "Connecting the Responsorial Psalm" sections. Producing these materials has been for us a "work of faith and labor of love" (1 Thess 1:3). We hope that shows.

Artwork

The updated artwork continues to receive positive reviews, and so we are happy to say Liturgical Press brought back the three artists from the 2018 and 2019 editions: Deborah Luke, Tanja Butler, and Ned Bustard. The artwork for this edition, like previous editions, is new and original.

Reflecting on the Gospel and Living the Paschal Mystery

According to what we have learned, the most frequented part of the book remains "Reflecting on the Gospel," followed by "Living the Paschal Mystery." Sr. Joyce Ann designed it this way, and we should not be surprised that it remains the case. Brian Schmisek wrote these pieces again, as he did last year, with that in mind. In this year of Matthew, we hear distinct themes of mercy. His gospel has been called "the church's gospel" in part because his is the only gospel to use the word "church." Aside from that, he gives us the Our Father, the Sermon on the Mount, the leadership role of Peter, the connection between words and action, some unique parables, and the demands of discipleship. Jesus teaches often in this gospel about end-times judgment (often punctuated with violent imagery). Some of these readings can be especially challenging.

Focusing the Gospel, Connecting the Gospel, Connecting the Responsorial Psalm, Prompts for Faith Sharing, and Homily Points

Katy Beedle Rice made her debut with this work last year, and she returns again, writing much of the material for pages 2–3 each week. As a mother, wife, and catechist, her insights are germane, to the point, and especially well written.

Liturgy

Diana Macalintal brings both broad and deep experience coupled with knowledge of the liturgy to this work aptly named "Living Liturgy." We are grateful that she returns for a third year, with fresh commentary and good advice for professional liturgists and volunteer ministers alike.

Purpose

The three authors for this book, Brian, Katy, and Diana, continue to retain its original and primary purpose: "to help people prepare for liturgy and live a liturgical spirituality (that is, a way of living that is rooted in liturgy), opening their vision to their baptismal identity as the Body of Christ and shaping their living according to the rhythm of paschal mystery dying and rising. The paschal mystery is the central focus of liturgy, of the gospels, and of this volume." We are humbled and privileged to be carrying on this task. We hope this work with its artful imagery assists many in living a liturgical spirituality. We are open to feedback and look forward to hearing from you about this renovated home for *Living Liturgy*™.

SEASON OF ADVENT

SPIRITUALITY

GOSPEL ACCLAMATION
Ps 85:8

℟. Alleluia, alleluia.
Show us, Lord, your love;
and grant us your salvation.
℟. Alleluia, alleluia.

Gospel

Matt 24:37-44; L1A

Jesus said to his disciples:
"As it was in the days of Noah,
so it will be at the coming of the Son of Man.
In those days before the flood,
they were eating and drinking,
marrying and giving in marriage,
up to the day that Noah entered the ark.
They did not know until the flood came and carried them all away.
So will it be also at the coming of the Son of Man.
Two men will be out in the field;
one will be taken, and one will be left.
Two women will be grinding at the mill;
one will be taken, and one will be left.
Therefore, stay awake!
For you do not know on which day your Lord will come.
Be sure of this: if the master of the house
had known the hour of night when the thief was coming,
he would have stayed awake
and not let his house be broken into.
So too, you also must be prepared,
for at an hour you do not expect, the Son of Man will come."

Reflecting on the Gospel

"Stay awake!" These words in the Gospel of Matthew today strike us to the core as we begin the Advent season. These words also foreshadow the disciples' struggle during the agony in the garden. The call to stay awake presumes that we might be dozing off, idling our time away. Disciples must be ready at all times without resorting to a false sense of security.

Jesus tells his audience that as it was in the time of Noah, so shall it be at the coming of the Lord. In Noah's day, human beings went steadily on their way, unaware and apparently unconcerned that something larger was at work. Yet, "the flood came and carried them all away." Jesus tells his listeners that the Son of Man will come when we do not expect it. These words were written for Matthew's community, which might have grown complacent during the intervening decades between Jesus' time on earth and the composition of the gospel. But these same words are for us, even two thousand years later. Rather than expecting a cataclysmic event like the flood of Noah or something apocalyptic, we might consider our own death, which may come when we least expect it.

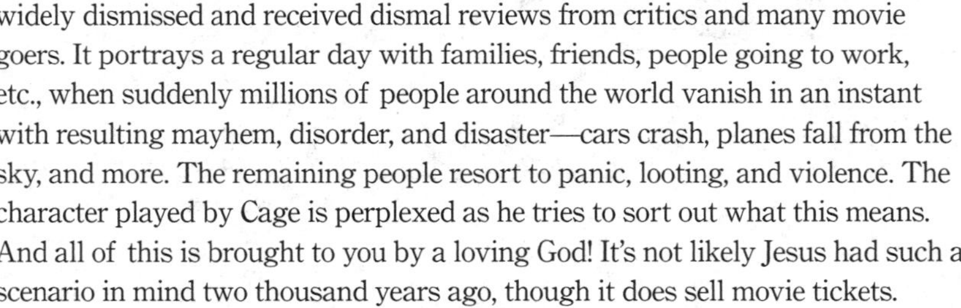

Unfortunately, some preachers and many others take the imagery in this gospel passage literally. There was even a 2014 movie that depicts the events from Matthew's gospel in graphic detail. The film, *Left Behind* starring Nicolas Cage, was widely dismissed and received dismal reviews from critics and many movie goers. It portrays a regular day with families, friends, people going to work, etc., when suddenly millions of people around the world vanish in an instant with resulting mayhem, disorder, and disaster—cars crash, planes fall from the sky, and more. The remaining people resort to panic, looting, and violence. The character played by Cage is perplexed as he tries to sort out what this means. And all of this is brought to you by a loving God! It's not likely Jesus had such a scenario in mind two thousand years ago, though it does sell movie tickets.

Perhaps there is a reason biblical literalism, also known as a fundamentalist approach to Scripture, is referred to as "a kind of intellectual suicide" by the Pontifical Biblical Commission (*The Interpretation of the Bible in the Church*, 35). As Catholics, we recognize the theological truth conveyed in these gospel stories are much more profound than that portrayed in a 2014 action/horror film. When we reduce the message of Christ to crashing planes and big explosions, we may be fairly sure we are no longer on sound footing.

In sum, we must be prepared for the coming of the Son of Man, when we meet our own personal end (death). And with respect to that day, none of us knows when it might be. It will come as a thief in the night. Therefore, we should not grow weary, but instead "stay awake!"

Living the Paschal Mystery

The transformation that happens with the paschal mystery reaches out to us in our daily lives. Any tendency to become lethargic is thwarted by a resounding call to "stay awake!" The mystery of Christianity, the life, death, resurrection, and ongoing life of Jesus animates us so we are no longer complacent. We are not carried away by the latest thriller or a glittering spectacle. Our life in Christ makes us rooted in God's vision of the world. We see the world through new lenses. We are prepared for anything that might come, even our own death. In a state of preparation, then, we are alert, aware, and awake. The metamorphosis on the horizon approaches. It is coming, though we know not when.

Focusing the Gospel

Key words and phrases: [S]tay awake!

To the point: We enter Advent with a clarion call to attention. The patterns of our lives continue from one season to the next, and yet, on this first day of December and first day of Advent, we are called to pause and attune all of our senses to what really matters: Christ present in our midst and the kingdom of heaven being built here and now.

Connecting the Gospel

to the second reading: St. Paul echoes Jesus' call to "stay awake" in his letter to the Romans. He tells them, "[I]t is the hour now for you to awake from sleep." Both the gospel reading from Matthew and this portion of St. Paul's letter are examples of eschatological literature found within the Bible. This genre deals with subjects concerning the end of mortal existence, most specifically death and judgment. Because we have a limited amount of time upon the earth, we can always be assured that, as St. Paul says, each moment "our salvation is nearer now than when we first believed" (Rom 13:11; NABRE). Adding to our mortality is the uncertainty of human life; not only will our lives come to an end, but we never know which day might be our last.

to experience: Advent calls us to confront both the gift and the anxiety of our mortality. We do not have unlimited time to spend our days in a stupor of half-living. Instead, we are invited to "put on the armor of light" and become the Christ-bearers we are called to be.

Connecting the Responsorial Psalm

to the readings: In the first reading, the prophet Isaiah foresees a time when the temple in Jerusalem ("the mountain of the Lord's house") shall not only belong to God's chosen people, but to all the peoples of the world. For "[a]ll nations shall stream toward it" in search of divine wisdom and guidance. Our psalm tells us why the temple, "the house of the Lord," has the ability to attract all the peoples of the world—this is a house of joy, one that promises unity, a place of peace and justice, and what nation doesn't long for these things?

to psalmist preparation: We have entered into the time of Advent, and although we might associate the color purple with a time of penance, fasting, and preparation, we are called to joyfully journey toward the feast of Christmas and the fullness of the kingdom of God. The responsorial psalm calls us to "go rejoicing to the house of the Lord." Is your parish a place that elicits joy?

PROMPTS FOR FAITH-SHARING

Advent is a season for preparation. Amid the physical preparations for Christmas, how would you like to prepare spiritually for the feast of Christ's nativity?

The first reading from Isaiah foretells a time when the people will beat their swords into plowshares—turning instruments of war into those of cultivation. How do you already live this call to peace? How might you embrace this call more fully?

In the second reading, St. Paul invites the Romans to "throw off the works of darkness / and put on the armor of light." What spiritual practices strengthen you to live in the light of Christ?

In the gospel Jesus urges the disciples to "stay awake! / For you do not know on which day your Lord will come." What is Jesus calling you to "wake up" to this Advent?

Model Penitential Act

Presider: On this First Sunday of Advent we come before the Lord with hopeful hearts and joyful spirits, and ask him to once again send his light to illuminate the darkness in our lives . . . *[pause]*

Lord Jesus, you call us to walk in the way of peace: Lord, have mercy.
Christ Jesus, you are the light that dispels the darkness: Christ, have mercy.
Lord Jesus, you hold the world in love and offer salvation to all: Lord, have mercy.

Homily Points

• Before the invention of electricity, for thousands of years our ancestors followed the rising and setting of the sun in their daily rhythms. Now, in this time of artificial lighting, it is easy to divorce ourselves from the motion of the sun across the horizon. We can stay up late into the night reading a captivating story or watching a new TV show, only to hit the snooze button and pull our eye shades tighter to block out the sunlight peeking through the blinds of our bedroom window the next morning.

• In the gospel today Jesus gives the command "stay awake!" Later in Matthew's gospel he will tell the parable of the ten bridesmaids (Matt 25:1-13) who are entrusted with keeping watch for a delayed bridegroom. When the bridegroom arrives, the five young women with lamps burning brightly are invited to join in the wedding feast. In today's first and second reading we hear more imagery of this light that leads to the kingdom of God. St. Paul urges the Romans to "throw off the works of darkness / and put on the armor of light." Isaiah calls the people of Israel to "walk in the light of the Lord!"

• In the northern hemisphere, the season of Advent coincides with the darkest time of the year. As we look ahead to the feast of Christmas, when we celebrate the light of God coming into the world in the mystery of the incarnation, we might ponder, what is it that helps us to heed Jesus' call to stay awake? When we let the light of God shine in our lives, we are compelled to waken to the reality of what is—to confront the darkness inside ourselves and the darkness in our world. And then to recommit to being people of light.

Model Universal Prayer (Prayer of the Faithful)

Presider: Strengthened by the word of God, let us confidently bring our needs before the Lord.

Response: Lord, hear our prayer.

For bishops, priests, and religious leaders, may they lead the people of God to true conversion and repentance this Advent season . . .

For leaders of nations, may they embrace the vision of the prophet Isaiah for a peaceful world in which swords are turned into plowshares . . .

For those who suffer in the darkness of mental illness and addiction, may the light of Christ ease their burdens and foster healing and hope . . .

For this parish, may we dedicate this Advent season to righteous deeds that embody the light and peace of Christ . . .

Presider: God of peace, your love and care envelop all creation. Hear our prayers that, formed by your word and nourished by your Body and Blood, we might become instruments of your creative will. We ask this through Christ our Lord. **Amen.**

COLLECT

Let us pray.

Pause for silent prayer

Grant your faithful, we pray, almighty God,
the resolve to run forth to meet your Christ
with righteous deeds at his coming,
so that, gathered at his right hand,
they may be worthy to possess the heavenly Kingdom.
Through our Lord Jesus Christ, your Son,
who lives and reigns with you in the unity of the Holy Spirit,
one God, for ever and ever. **Amen.**

FIRST READING

Isa 2:1-5

This is what Isaiah, son of Amoz,
saw concerning Judah and Jerusalem.
In days to come,
the mountain of the LORD's house
shall be established as the highest mountain
and raised above the hills.
All nations shall stream toward it;
many peoples shall come and say:
"Come, let us climb the LORD's mountain,
to the house of the God of Jacob,
that he may instruct us in his ways,
and we may walk in his paths."
For from Zion shall go forth instruction,
and the word of the LORD from Jerusalem.
He shall judge between the nations,
and impose terms on many peoples.
They shall beat their swords into plowshares
and their spears into pruning hooks;
one nation shall not raise the sword against another,
nor shall they train for war again.
O house of Jacob, come,
let us walk in the light of the LORD!

RESPONSORIAL PSALM
Ps 122:1-2, 3-4, 4-5, 6-7, 8-9

℟. Let us go rejoicing to the house of the Lord.

I rejoiced because they said to me,
"We will go up to the house of the LORD."
And now we have set foot
within your gates, O Jerusalem.

℟. Let us go rejoicing to the house of the Lord.

Jerusalem, built as a city
with compact unity.
To it the tribes go up,
the tribes of the LORD.

℟. Let us go rejoicing to the house of the Lord.

According to the decree for Israel,
to give thanks to the name of the LORD.
In it are set up judgment seats,
seats for the house of David.

℟. Let us go rejoicing to the house of the Lord.

Pray for the peace of Jerusalem!
May those who love you prosper!
May peace be within your walls,
prosperity in your buildings.

℟. Let us go rejoicing to the house of the Lord.

Because of my brothers and friends
I will say, "Peace be within you!"
Because of the house of the LORD, our God,
I will pray for your good.

℟. Let us go rejoicing to the house of the Lord.

SECOND READING
Rom 13:11-14

Brothers and sisters:
You know the time;
it is the hour now for you to awake from sleep.
For our salvation is nearer now than when we first believed;
the night is advanced, the day is at hand.
Let us then throw off the works of darkness
and put on the armor of light;
let us conduct ourselves properly as in the day,
not in orgies and drunkenness,
not in promiscuity and lust,
not in rivalry and jealousy.
But put on the Lord Jesus Christ,
and make no provision for the desires of the flesh.

CATECHESIS

About Liturgy

The urgency of the Gospel: In his last public address before succumbing to cancer, Joseph Cardinal Bernardin of Chicago said, "A dying person does not have time for the peripheral or the accidental . . . To say it quite boldly, it is wrong to waste the precious gift of time given to us, as God's chosen servants, on acrimony and division" (*A Moral Vision for America*, ed. John P. Langan). This is the urgency we get from today's readings as well.

At its beginning, Advent insists we look to the end. Advent prepares us not only for the first coming but also the second coming of Christ at the end of time (cf. Universal Norms on the Liturgical Year and the General Roman Calendar 39). Therefore, let us make Advent less like a sentimentalized Christmas card and more like a dying person's call to action, for those suffering on the brink of death have precious little time. We must act now to live the gospel on their behalf.

Let this urgency be present in your preaching, intercessions, music choices, and environment. Most especially, let radical hospitality and reconciliation be how you "put on the armor of light" (second reading).

About Initiation

The sacrament of the liturgical year: Sacraments are specific moments when we most clearly recognize God's grace acting in our lives through prescribed rituals. These rituals make visible how God is saving us. Small "s" sacraments are also perceptible moments of grace. These may be more intimate encounters with God that are unique for each person. In this sense, we can call the liturgical year a sacrament revealing the mystery of God's love for us.

When we think of time this way, it is no longer abstract, neutral, or meaningless. Every moment of our lives, whether filled with joy or grief, is an opportunity to encounter God's presence. All these moments of grace gathered into a lifetime have the potential to reveal the mystery of God. We know this because God's visible presence in Jesus entered human history to consecrate all human time.

For this reason, the church takes seriously the sacramentality of time. It is also why the length of the catechumenate should be long enough so that the catechumens "are properly initiated into the mysteries of salvation" (RCIA 76).

Don't rush God's time. Let time do its sacred work of gradually drawing your catechumens to the heart of God.

About Liturgical Music

The importance of beginnings: My piano teacher always emphasized the importance of good beginnings in performance. How you approached the piano, acknowledged the audience, placed your hands on the keys, allowed space for silence, and breathed before that first note—all these were as important as the piece itself. They signaled the value of the performance and prepared both performer and audience to fully enter the experience of the music.

What we do at Sunday Mass is not a concert. Yet the same disciplines for good beginnings still apply. At the beginning of Mass, especially in Advent, give space for silence. Complete any rehearsals and setup at least ten minutes before Mass starts so you can be present to the people and prepare yourself for prayer. If you offer a spoken greeting to the assembly before Mass, do it with respect for them and a sense of the dignity of the work you are about to do together. Before the season begins, reflect on the profound ministry we do to lead people in prayer. Give thanks and ask the Spirit to bless this new year of service to God's people.

SPIRITUALITY

GOSPEL ACCLAMATION
Luke 3:4, 6

℟. Alleluia, alleluia.
Prepare the way of the Lord, make straight his paths:
all flesh shall see the salvation of God.
℟. Alleluia, alleluia.

Gospel Matt 3:1-12; L4A

John the Baptist appeared,
preaching in the desert of Judea
and saying, "Repent, for the kingdom of heaven is at hand!"
It was of him that the prophet Isaiah had spoken when he said:
A voice of one crying out in the desert,
Prepare the way of the Lord,
make straight his paths.
John wore clothing made of camel's hair
and had a leather belt around his waist.
His food was locusts and wild honey.
At that time Jerusalem, all Judea,
and the whole region around the Jordan
were going out to him
and were being baptized by him in the Jordan River
as they acknowledged their sins.

When he saw many of the Pharisees and Sadducees
coming to his baptism, he said to them,
"You brood of vipers!
Who warned you to flee from the coming wrath?
Produce good fruit as evidence of your repentance.
And do not presume to say to yourselves,
'We have Abraham as our father.'
For I tell you,
God can raise up children to Abraham from these stones.

Continued in Appendix A, p. 261.

Reflecting on the Gospel

Though today is December 8 when we might expect the solemnity of the Immaculate Conception, it happens to fall on a Sunday. Therefore, the Second Sunday of Advent is what we celebrate today. We will commemorate the Immaculate Conception tomorrow. And for this Advent Sunday we hear the fiery preaching of John the Baptist, introduced for the first time in the Gospel of Matthew.

It almost goes without saying that John the Baptist is Jewish, and he is preaching to fellow Jews. But because he is considered a Christian saint, it's possible to overlook that he is a Jewish prophet calling the Jewish people to repentance, as prophets had done for centuries before. He directly confronts the Pharisees and Sadducees, name-calling them a "brood of vipers." They are not to rest assured in their being part of the chosen people of God, the children of Abraham. For God can raise up children of Abraham from the stones. This message is so stark it nearly needs to be recast to our own day for those of us who might feel secure in our Christian or Catholic identity. We can hear John telling us that God can make Christians from the stones. There is no inherent value or guarantee of salvation simply by being Christian. Such a statement is shocking. But John would say something more is demanded. We are to repent, for the kingdom is at hand.

The people confessed their sin and were baptized for repentance. Even this, however, is only a foreshadowing of the one who is to come, for he will baptize "with the Holy Spirit and fire." It can be easy to overlook the "fire" with which the one mightier than John will baptize. But the fire will consume the chaff. The baptism John imagines is apocalyptic and judgmental.

We are familiar with the stories of John the Baptist and his preaching. But when we read them with careful attention to detail, new meaning pops from the page. Let us not grow complacent in the face of such a baptism. John's baptism only prefigures that of Jesus, the mightier one. An interior renewal is called for. Resting in our identity as chosen by God, even as a Christian, is not enough.

Living the Paschal Mystery

As human beings we desire consistency, predictability, and stability. Though it's good to experience new things, not many of us thrive on doing new things all the time. Our lives may be punctuated by difference, but regularity reigns. Even the liturgical cycle of readings is regulated, and each Advent we read from John the Baptist's fiery preaching.

Even so, it's good for us to be shaken up a bit and jostled from our regular routine, as John the Baptist is doing today. We are reminded that we need to repent, turn away from selfish interests and turn toward God. This interior renewal is nothing less than a dying to self and rising with Christ, the paschal mystery. What regular routines do we need to abandon? From what in our lives do we need to turn away? What does turning toward God look like in our own time and place, in the midst of the relationships we have? Going to church, being Catholic, or knowing about God is not enough. An interior reorientation toward God and the values of his kingdom is demanded.

Focusing the Gospel

Key words and phrases: He will baptize you with the Holy Spirit and fire.

To the point: In last week's gospel we heard Jesus' own words from the end of his ministry. Today we turn backward to John the Baptist's witness to Jesus near the beginning of Matthew's gospel, preparing the people for this one who will come to baptize them with the Holy Spirit and fire. In the season of Advent, the light of our candles burn brighter each week. May we pray for the fire of this season to purify us and prepare us to welcome the risen Christ into our hearts anew at Christmas.

Connecting the Gospel

to the first and second readings: The Spirit with which Jesus comes to baptize, as proclaimed by John the Baptist in the gospel, is described in the prophet Isaiah's words from the first reading. The Spirit Jesus gives is one that seeks to anoint us in wisdom, understanding, counsel, strength, knowledge, and fear of the Lord (sometimes translated as wonder and awe in God's presence). And it is only through calling on these gifts that we can live in true Christian community with one another. In the second reading St. Paul describes this type of community when he urges the Romans to "think in harmony with one another, / in keeping with Christ Jesus, / that with one accord you may with one voice / glorify the God and Father of our Lord Jesus Christ."

to experience: We receive this Spirit at baptism and are strengthened in its gifts at confirmation, but every day of our Christian life we can call upon this Spirit to refine us in God's fiery love and lend us the spiritual ability most needed at that moment as we endeavor to build the kingdom of God.

Connecting the Responsorial Psalm

to the readings: Our responsorial psalm paints us a picture of the kingdom of God: "Justice shall flourish in his time, and fullness of peace forever." In the first reading Isaiah prophesies that the one to come shall have justice as "the band around his waist." This justice is the force that hears the cries of the poor and bears good fruit in the lives of those who live by its dictates. The harsh words John the Baptist has for the Pharisees and the Sadducees is a warning for anyone in a position of religious leadership. Later in Matthew's gospel, Jesus will describe the principal fault of these religious leaders by stating, "They tie up heavy burdens [hard to carry] and lay them on people's shoulders, but they will not lift a finger to move them" (23:4; NABRE).

to psalmist preparation: What enables you, as ministers who lead the people of God in worship and song, to minister from a place of humility, formed by justice and peace?

PROMPTS FOR FAITH-SHARING

Which gift of the Spirit (wisdom, understanding, counsel, strength, knowledge, or fear of the Lord) from today's first reading are you in need of most in your life right now?

The responsorial psalm tells us, "Justice shall flourish in his time, and fullness of peace forever." What ministries within your parish or diocese are seeking to establish a more just and peaceful world? How might you be called to participate in this work?

In the second reading, St. Paul urges us to "[w]elcome one another, then, as Christ welcomed you." When and where have you received this kind of welcome? What difference did it make in your life?

In the gospel, John the Baptist describes Jesus as holding a "winnowing fan in his hand," ready to gather the wheat and burn the chaff of his harvest. We know Jesus is both perfectly just and perfectly merciful. In your spiritual life are you more apt to focus on Jesus' justice or his mercy? Why do you think this is?

Model Penitential Act

Presider: In today's gospel John the Baptist tells us, "Repent, for the kingdom of heaven is at hand!" For the times we have not lived lives worthy of God's kingdom of justice and peace, let us ask for forgiveness . . . *[pause]*

Lord Jesus, you hear the cries of the poor and afflicted: Lord, have mercy.
Christ Jesus, you are the source of true justice and peace: Christ, have mercy.
Lord Jesus, you call us to continual conversion: Lord, have mercy.

Homily Points

• As we prepare for the feast of Christmas, often thought of (and advertised) as one of the happiest and most joyful times of the year, we hear some of the most challenging gospel passages. Today's ends with the ominous warning that Jesus comes with "winnowing fan in his hand," ready to "clear his threshing floor / and gather his wheat into his barn, / but the chaff he will burn with unquenchable fire." Despite the starkness of this language, St. Paul assures us in his letter to the Romans that all of the Scriptures have been written with one purpose in mind, so "we might have hope."

• Where do we find hope in this gospel? Perhaps it is the hope of redemption. John the Baptist preaches repentance to the people of his day, and they respond by acknowledging their sins and being cleansed in the Jordan River. Even the Pharisees and Sadducees whom John calls "a brood of vipers" are not turned away from this redemption. Instead they, too, are invited to this baptism of repentance in order to give up their prideful ways and "produce good fruit."

• In December 2014 Pope Francis began his annual address to the Roman Curia by clarifying what we really celebrate at Christmas: "It is our encounter with God who is born in the poverty of the stable of Bethlehem in order to teach us the power of humility." John the Baptist tells us the one who is coming "will baptize you with the Holy Spirit and fire." With hope, we could consider this fire as a purifying flame ready to free us from the crippling effects of pride and beckoning us to embrace the humility of Christ.

Model Universal Prayer (Prayer of the Faithful)

Presider: With hope in God's mercy and trust in his everlasting love, let us bring our prayers before the Lord.

Response: Lord, hear our prayer.

For the church throughout the world, may all her members joyfully take up the work of preparing the way of the Lord . . .

For civic leaders, may they be strengthened in their desire to serve the common good and in so doing, reject all worldly power and pride . . .

For the poor and afflicted within war-torn communities, may they receive the support and resources necessary to rebuild their lives in safety and peace . . .

For those gathered around this altar table, endowed with the gifts of the Holy Spirit, may we proclaim God's love to all in word and deed . . .

Presider: God of compassion and love, your Spirit strengthens us with wisdom and understanding. Hear our prayers that we might await the coming of your son, Jesus, in joyful hope. We ask this through Christ our Lord. **Amen.**

COLLECT

Let us pray.

Pause for silent prayer

Almighty and merciful God,
may no earthly undertaking hinder those
who set out in haste to meet your Son,
but may our learning of heavenly wisdom
gain us admittance to his company.
Who lives and reigns with you in the unity
of the Holy Spirit,
one God, for ever and ever. **Amen.**

FIRST READING

Isa 11:1-10

On that day, a shoot shall sprout from the stump of Jesse,
and from his roots a bud shall blossom.
The spirit of the LORD shall rest upon him:
a spirit of wisdom and of understanding,
a spirit of counsel and of strength,
a spirit of knowledge and of fear of the LORD,
and his delight shall be the fear of the LORD.
Not by appearance shall he judge,
nor by hearsay shall he decide,
but he shall judge the poor with justice,
and decide aright for the land's afflicted.
He shall strike the ruthless with the rod of his mouth,
and with the breath of his lips he shall slay the wicked.
Justice shall be the band around his waist,
and faithfulness a belt upon his hips.
Then the wolf shall be a guest of the lamb,
and the leopard shall lie down with the kid;
the calf and the young lion shall browse together,
with a little child to guide them.
The cow and the bear shall be neighbors,
together their young shall rest;
the lion shall eat hay like the ox.
The baby shall play by the cobra's den,
and the child lay his hand on the adder's lair.
There shall be no harm or ruin on all my holy mountain;
for the earth shall be filled with knowledge of the LORD,
as water covers the sea.
On that day, the root of Jesse,
set up as a signal for the nations,
the Gentiles shall seek out,
for his dwelling shall be glorious.

RESPONSONSORIAL PSALM

Ps 72:1-2, 7-8, 12-13, 17

℟. (cf. 7) Justice shall flourish in his time,
and fullness of peace for ever.

O God, with your judgment endow the king,
and with your justice, the king's son;
he shall govern your people with justice
and your afflicted ones with judgment.

℟. Justice shall flourish in his time, and fullness of peace for ever.

Justice shall flower in his days,
and profound peace, till the moon be no more.
May he rule from sea to sea,
and from the River to the ends of the earth.

℟. Justice shall flourish in his time, and fullness of peace for ever.

For he shall rescue the poor when he cries out,
and the afflicted when he has no one to help him.
He shall have pity for the lowly and the poor;
the lives of the poor he shall save.

℟. Justice shall flourish in his time, and fullness of peace for ever.

May his name be blessed forever;
as long as the sun his name shall remain.
In him shall all the tribes of the earth be blessed;
all the nations shall proclaim his happiness.

℟. Justice shall flourish in his time, and fullness of peace for ever.

SECOND READING

Rom 15:4-9

Brothers and sisters:
Whatever was written previously was written for our instruction,
that by endurance and by the encouragement of the Scriptures
we might have hope.
May the God of endurance and encouragement
grant you to think in harmony with one another,
in keeping with Christ Jesus,
that with one accord you may with one voice
glorify the God and Father of our Lord Jesus Christ.

Continued in Appendix A, p. 261.

About Liturgy

The peaceable kingdom: Isaiah's reading today beautifully describes the messianic dream of the day that the ideal king comes to reign. Creatures that have long been enemies will live together as neighbors, their children at peace. Would that this be our own dream for our communities!

This worldwide peace may seem impossible in these contentious days of conflict, racism, and prejudice. Yet for those of us who are Christians, a primary focus of Advent is the kingdom of God, which we pray to come every time we pray the Lord's Prayer. By keeping this vision of the peaceful reign of God ever before us, we can take small steps toward making that vision a reality in our lives.

One place we rehearse these small steps is at our Sunday gathering. At the Sunday assembly, we can practice judging not by appearance or hearsay (cf. Isa 11:3) but with justice, especially for those afflicted and outcast. This begins simply by greeting the stranger seated next to, in front of, or behind us. Do not wait to be invited to do so by parish leadership; make it a habit and discipline on your own. This small step will train your eye to see God's kingdom that is already here.

About Initiation

Way of faith and conversion: The opening words of the Rite of Christian Initiation of Adults summarize what this entire process is: "The rite of Christian initiation presented here is designed for adults who, after hearing the mystery of Christ proclaimed, consciously and freely seek the living God and enter the *way of faith and conversion* as the Holy Spirit opens their hearts" (RCIA 1, emphasis added). It is a path, a road, or, in John the Baptist's words today, "the way of the Lord." The RCIA is not a schedule of classes; it is a journey on which one meets Christ and grows in that relationship. Attend to how you structure this process so it truly is a path of conversion and not merely a classroom syllabus. The destination of initiation is not complete knowledge of the tenets of faith but a total change in one's way of life, that is, repentance. Therefore, measure conversion not through written tests or oral exams but in verifiable actions and attitudes that show that inquirers are becoming more and more like Christ, through "conversion in mind and in action . . . sufficient acquaintance with Christian teaching as well as a spirit of faith and charity" (RCIA 120).

About Liturgical Music

Moderation and anticipation: John the Baptist's call to repent reminds us of Advent's penitential nature. In both Lent and Advent, we express this through moderation in the liturgy, in particular through the retrained use of instruments. In Lent this moderation is taken to its penitential fullness through the directive that states that organ and other instruments are allowed "only in order to support the singing," with some exceptions (General Instruction of the Roman Missal 313). In Advent, however, this penitence is more akin to heightened attentiveness, similar to the anticipation felt on the eve of one's wedding. Thus, the church recommends that in Advent "the use of the organ and other musical instruments should be marked by a moderation suited to the character of this time of year, without expressing in anticipation the full joy of the Nativity of the Lord" (GIRM 313).

This anticipatory moderation can be expressed through the use of simpler instrumentation. For example, if your ensemble includes a full roster of keyboard, solo instruments, guitar, and percussion, experiment with using only guitar or only percussion on some pieces. Try this with the acclamations used each Sunday of the season.

GOSPEL ACCLAMATION
cf. Luke 1:28

℟. Alleluia, alleluia.
Hail, Mary, full of grace, the Lord is with you;
blessed are you among women.
℟. Alleluia, alleluia.

Gospel Luke 1:26-38; L689

The angel Gabriel was sent from God
to a town of Galilee called Nazareth,
to a virgin betrothed to a man named Joseph,
of the house of David,
and the virgin's name was Mary.
And coming to her, he said,
"Hail, full of grace! The Lord is with you."
But she was greatly troubled at what was said
and pondered what sort of greeting this might be.
Then the angel said to her,
"Do not be afraid, Mary,
for you have found favor with God.
Behold, you will conceive in your womb and bear a son,
and you shall name him Jesus.

Continued in Appendix A, p. 261.

See Appendix A, pp. 261–262, for the other readings.

Reflecting on the Gospel

Angels are a popular topic today, just as they have been popular throughout history. Many modern books about angels sell well, and a number of them can be found in the self-help section! Artwork, paintings, sculptures, books, and more portray these heavenly beings. Even though many of us imagine angels, very few people would agree on precisely what angels are. Ask two friends about angels and you will likely hear three or more conflicting ideas. The appearance of an angel (what an angel looks like) is often left to the mind or imagination of the reader, and today's reading from Luke is a good case in point.

Luke's story of the annunciation, not the immaculate conception, is our gospel reading. Nowhere in the Scriptures do we have an account of Mary being conceived, and therefore there is no account of her being conceived without sin, which is the feast we celebrate today. Instead, in the Gospel of Luke we have the story of the annunciation, the news announced to Mary by an angel that she was to be the mother of Jesus.

In movies and TV series, the angel of the annunciation is depicted in a variety of ways, sometimes as a light from offscreen (as in Franco Zeffirelli's *Jesus of Nazareth* [1977]) or other times in a more graphic way much as a human being (as in *The Nativity Story* [2006]). But Luke does not describe the angel Gabriel. The reader is left to fill in the details. We do not even know what time of day it was. And other than Nazareth, a small Galilean village, we don't know where Mary was when this happened. Was this at home? On the road? In a field? Luke does not tell us. So it is interesting to ask ourselves how many details we have naturally filled in after hearing the story. The way we fill in these details conveys much about our own theological perspectives. Luke is content to say the angel Gabriel was sent from God to Nazareth. The subsequent conversation between Gabriel and Mary set the course of human history.

Still, we celebrate today the Immaculate Conception, the purity of Mary from the moment she herself was conceived. The theological mysteries we proclaim are worthy of reflection, thought, prayer, and conversation with other Christians.

Living the Paschal Mystery

The paschal mystery encompasses all of creation, so that even much of the New Testament speaks of angels and other immaterial beings. The thought world of antiquity shapes our own, so in the liturgy, too, we mention angels. The imagined drama of "good angels" and "fallen angels" has been the realm of speculative theology for centuries and makes for popular works of fiction today. But it would be a mistake to travel too far down that path without considering the message of the angel Gabriel today. Gabriel is sent by God to Nazareth to announce to Mary her role in salvation history. She cooperates and thus becomes a model of discipleship for the ages.

We, too, are invited to cooperate with the work of God in history, dying to our own personal wants and desires. Our cooperation means rising to a new life with Christ.

Focusing the Gospel

Key words and phrases: Hail, full of grace!

To the point: Gabriel's first words to Mary identify her as "full of grace." Even before Jesus is conceived within her womb, she is already filled with God's favor. Gabriel's naming speaks to each of us as well—how God looks at each one of us in love and wonder and sees the core of our being, created in his own image, full of grace. Can we claim this identity for ourselves?

Model Penitential Act

Presider: On this feast of the Immaculate Conception, we ponder Mary's proclamation: "May it be done to me according to your word." Let us ask for healing for the times our own faith in God's goodness has wavered . . . *[pause]*

Lord Jesus, you are Son of God and son of Mary: Lord, have mercy.

Christ Jesus, your kingdom endures forever: Christ, have mercy.

Lord Jesus, you chose us before the foundation of the world and call us to holiness: Lord, have mercy.

Model Universal Prayer (Prayer of the Faithful)

Presider: Through the intercession of Mary, mother of God and our mother, let us bring our prayers before the Lord.

Response: Lord, hear our prayer.

For the church spread throughout the world, may we continue to grow in holiness and grace following the example of Mary's complete trust in God . . .

For all of creation from plants to human beings, may life flourish upon the earth and bring glory to God . . .

For pregnant mothers and their unborn children, may they receive compassionate care and the support to thrive and deliver safely . . .

For all gathered here, may we cast off the shackles of fear and learn to trust God more and more each day . . .

Presider: God of Mary, the angel Gabriel proclaims that with you, "nothing will be impossible." Hear our prayers that, renewed in faith and strengthened in love, we might go forth to bring Christ to others. We ask this through Jesus Christ, our brother. **Amen.**

About Liturgy

Honoring Mary in the liturgy: In any celebration of the Eucharist, our focus is always on Christ, through whom and by whose Spirit we give praise to the Father. As we are the people of God, this is "our duty and salvation" (Eucharistic Prayer II). It is also Mary's. Although she "far surpasses all creatures, both in heaven and on earth" (*Lumen Gentium* [LG] 53), she is still "one with all those who are to be saved" (LG 53).

On days when we honor the Blessed Mother, keep Christ at the center of the Eucharist. In your church environment, highlight any statues, windows, or artwork depicting Mary. If you have images of St. Anne and Joachim, Mary's parents, highlight them as well since they are indirectly connected to this solemnity. In music, choose settings of the *Magnificat*, Mary's own song of praise to God, over songs that praise Mary. In the homily, reflect on the various places in the Mass where we recall Mary's special role in the church: in the *Confiteor*, Creed, and the eucharistic prayer. Avoid adding extraneous prayers, such as the rosary or Hail Mary. These are more appropriate outside of the Mass.

COLLECT

Let us pray.

Pause for silent prayer

O God, who by the Immaculate Conception of the Blessed Virgin
prepared a worthy dwelling for your Son,
grant, we pray,
that, as you preserved her from every stain
by virtue of the Death of your Son, which you foresaw,
so, through her intercession,
we, too, may be cleansed and admitted to your presence.
Through our Lord Jesus Christ, your Son,
who lives and reigns with you in the unity of the Holy Spirit,
one God, for ever and ever. **Amen.**

FOR REFLECTION

- As the model disciple, Mary shows us the way to live a life completely devoted to Christ. How would you like to emulate Mary more fully in this coming year?
- St. Paul writes to the Ephesians, "[W]e were also chosen, / destined in accord with the purpose of the One." What specific purpose do you think God has for your life? How are you living out this purpose?

Homily Points

- Today's first reading tells us how sin came into the world. Adam and Eve, who were created in the image of God for communion with God, are now hiding from their creator. When God calls out, "Where are you?" Adam explains why he is hiding: "I was afraid, because I was naked." Experiencing shame for the first time, Adam does what most human beings think they can do at some point—hide from the one who knows and loves them best.
- In Mary we find the antidote for this fear that distances us from God. In her book *The Reed of God,* English theologian Caryll Houselander proclaims, "There is only one cure for fear—trust in God. That is why the beginning of Christ's being formed in us consists in echoing Our Lady's *fiat,* it is a surrender, a handing over of everything to God."

SPIRITUALITY

GOSPEL ACCLAMATION
Isa 61:1 (cited in Luke 4:18)

℟. Alleluia, alleluia.
The Spirit of the Lord is upon me,
because he has anointed me
to bring glad tidings to the poor.
℟. Alleluia, alleluia.

Gospel Matt 11:2-11; L7A

When John the Baptist heard in prison of the works of the Christ,
he sent his disciples to Jesus with this question,
"Are you the one who is to come,
or should we look for another?"
Jesus said to them in reply,
"Go and tell John what you hear and see:
the blind regain their sight,
the lame walk,
lepers are cleansed,
the deaf hear,
the dead are raised,
and the poor have the good news proclaimed to them.
And blessed is the one who takes no offense at me."

As they were going off,
Jesus began to speak to the crowds about John,
"What did you go out to the desert to see?
A reed swayed by the wind?
Then what did you go out to see?
Someone dressed in fine clothing?
Those who wear fine clothing are in royal palaces.
Then why did you go out? To see a prophet?
Yes, I tell you, and more than a prophet.
This is the one about whom it is written:
Behold, I am sending my messenger ahead of you;
he will prepare your way before you.
Amen, I say to you,
among those born of women
there has been none greater than John the Baptist;
yet the least in the kingdom of heaven is greater than he."

Reflecting on the Gospel

John the Baptist's presence features prominently in the gospel today. Though we are in the midst of Jesus' ministry and John is in prison, he has a question for the would-be Christ: "Are you the one who is to come / or should we look for another?" Though it might be surprising to us, it seems as though Jesus did not fit the expectations of John the Baptist! Two thousand years later, we see these figures through the eyes of faith and so it can be difficult to place ourselves in the context of their day.

John the Baptist had been preaching fiery judgment, imminent wrath. Last week's gospel itself states this message quite plainly. In John's mind, the one to come would baptize with the Holy Spirit and with fire. The winnowing fan is in his hand. The chaff will be burned in an unquenchable fire. But then John is arrested and imprisoned, and Jesus begins preaching and doing mighty deeds. There is not the judgment that John expected. Thus, he sends his own disciples from his imprisonment with an astonishing question for Jesus. Had John gotten it wrong? Is Jesus the one? Or is there another?

For his part, Jesus does not respond with a simple "yes" or "no" answer. He responds by sending John's disciples back to him with a report of what they have seen and heard. Jesus reviews some of his deeds in alluding to the prophet Isaiah. He then concludes with an ominous beatitude that seems to be addressed to John directly: "Blessed is the one who takes no offense at me."

In the Gospel of Matthew we do not have a story of John and Jesus as cousins, as Luke would have it. Instead, Matthew tells us something that might be closer to the historical picture. Perhaps John misunderstood Jesus and his mission. Perhaps John even took offense at what Jesus was preaching and what he was doing. Jesus' words and actions were not what John had expected.

Jesus reminds the one who baptized him that among other things, the deaf hear, the dead are raised, and the poor have the good news preached to them. This is the mission of the Christ sent by God. Though John is greater than any person, the least in the kingdom of God is greater than he. Nowhere does it say how John responded to this beatitude addressed specifically to him. That silence speaks volumes. Jesus' mission is proclaiming this kingdom and creating it. Let us not take offense at his priorities, even if they are not our own. Instead, let us align ourselves with the Christ sent by God, assisting in proclaiming and creating the kingdom in our own day and time.

Living the Paschal Mystery

Expectations can be lofty things and it is disappointing when we see someone fall short or when we ourselves fall short. Then again, how often are we held to expectations beyond our ability or opposed to our own priorities? If and when we fail to meet the expectations of others, especially when we've had no say in those expectations, the fallout may be significant. Not many of us like to be told what we need to do or how we need to do it. So it is incumbent upon us not to lay unrealistic or uninformed expectations on others either.

Today we learn about John's expectations for Jesus, the one he baptized. John was likely offended at Jesus' behavior and preaching because it was not what he had foretold. The disconnect was so great that John wondered if there was someone else who was to come. This is a good reminder for us to temper our expectations of others. We are ultimately responsible for ourselves, not anyone else. We can let God raise up in others the special gifts, talents, and abilities given to them. We would do well to let die any desire to control others through the expectations we might place on them.

Focusing the Gospel

Key words and phrases: "Are you the one who is to come, / or should we look for another?"

To the point: John's disciples approach Jesus with one of the quintessential questions of life: "Is this it?" How are we supposed to know when we have arrived when we don't know the signposts for where we're going? Jesus gives them to us. The kingdom is in our midst when "the blind regain their sight, / the lame walk, / lepers are cleansed, / the deaf hear, / the dead are raised, / and the poor have the good news proclaimed to them." This is the kingdom that Jesus proclaims in word and deed and to which he invites us. As we journey onward toward Christmas, the great feast of the Incarnation, let us rededicate ourselves to incarnating the life of Jesus and the kingdom of God in our words and actions.

Connecting the Gospel

to the first reading: The gospel and the first reading act almost as a call and response. The disciples of John go to Jesus and ask, "Are you the one who is to come, / or should we look for another?" In the first reading we find an answer to this question. The prophet Isaiah proclaims to the people in exile, "Here is your God, / he comes with vindication; / with divine recompense / he comes to save you." God's saving action can be seen in the flowers that bloom in the desert and in the healings of the blind, the lame, and the deaf.

to experience: In all things our God brings life from death, healing from illness, light from darkness. Often these saving actions can be missed when our focus is overwhelmed by the other realities of the world crowding in. Where do you see God's saving action taking place here and now in your own life?

Connecting the Responsorial Psalm

to the readings: Today's psalm gives us a litany of the Lord's saving actions that mirror closely the words of Jesus to John's disciples and the proclamation of the prophet Isaiah to the people of Israel: "Here is your God, / he comes with vindication; / with divine recompense / he comes to save you." The psalmist names God as the one who feeds the hungry, frees captives, protects the vulnerable, and in all ways, "raises up those who [are] bowed down." These are the markers of discernment that Jesus points to for John's disciples on their quest to discover if he is the one they have been waiting for. Jesus' saving actions reveal him to be the incarnate Son of the living God, who has been the champion of his people throughout history.

to psalmist preparation: This week, take time each evening to pause and consider where throughout the day you have encountered the saving action of God who "keeps faith forever."

PROMPTS FOR FAITH-SHARING

Looking at the world, your community, and your own life, where could you say, "Here is [our] God!" as the prophet Isaiah proclaims to the people of Israel?

The psalmist tells us, "The Lord gives sight to the blind." We look upon the world from our own perspective and sometimes this can blind us to the needs and concerns of others. Who is God wishing to open your eyes to?

The first words from today's second reading from the letter of St. James are "[b]e patient, brothers and sisters." When in your life have you been blessed through embracing patience?

The disciples of John the Baptist ask Jesus, "Are you the one who is to come, / or should we look for another?" In our culture, what do you think are the greatest temptations that lead us to turn our gaze from Christ and to search for fulfillment elsewhere?

Model Penitential Act

Presider: In today's gospel John's disciples ask Jesus, "Are you the one who is to come, / or should we look for another?" For the times we have looked elsewhere instead of focusing our gaze on Christ, let us ask for mercy and pardon . . . *[pause]*

Lord Jesus, you came to proclaim good news to the poor: Lord, have mercy.
Christ Jesus, you open eyes blinded by fear and anger: Christ, have mercy.
Lord Jesus, you call us to new life: Lord, have mercy.

Homily Points

• Today's second reading from the letter of St. James encourages us to adopt a difficult spiritual practice: patience. Patiently waiting is challenging whether we are expecting overdue medical test results, are awaiting an admissions letter from the school of our dreams, or are longing for the fullness of the kingdom of God. In a letter to a friend, Pierre Teilhard de Chardin muses, "We are quite naturally impatient in everything to reach the end without delay." Indeed, we could say it is a hallmark of a person of faith to be anxious to reach the time that has been promised by Jesus and the prophets when there will be no more war, pain, suffering, hunger, or mourning. We want the kingdom of God to be established in the here and now.

• While this longing for God's kingdom is a theme of the season of Advent, we must not stop there but also embrace the slow work required to bring about this kingdom. Chardin tells his friend that in our anxiety, we should often "like to skip the intermediate stages." This is where patience enters. St. James uses the image of the farmer who "waits for the precious fruit of the earth, / being patient with it / until it receives the early and the late rains."

• We cannot force growth or compel other natural processes to adapt to our expedited timelines. Instead, like the farmer, we are called to the work of cultivation and to nourish the kingdom of God in every single small and seemingly insignificant act of loving-kindness and compassion. Our mysterious God, who exists beyond human comprehension, is present wherever those who are "bowed down" are raised up and those who suffer are healed. Through action and word, we can pray, "Lord, let your kingdom come!"

Model Universal Prayer (Prayer of the Faithful)

Presider: In this third week of Advent, we pause amidst the preparation intrinsic to this season to rejoice in God's saving action within our own lives. With gratitude for all he has done, we bring our prayers before the Lord.

Response: Lord, hear our prayer.

For the church, may it constantly look beyond itself to see and minister to Christ present in the poor and struggling on the peripheries of society . . .

For all the nations of the world, may they be fortified to provide for the needs of the ailing and the disabled . . .

For the poor hidden within our own communities, may we see their need and affirm their preciousness in the sight of God . . .

For all gathered in this place as we continue this Advent journey, may our joy in Christ grow ever stronger . . .

Presider: Faithful God, you never cease to offer healing and love to the downtrodden, weary, and afflicted. Hear our prayers that, revived by your life-giving Word, we might venture forth to speak your love to the world. Through Christ our Lord. **Amen.**

COLLECT

Let us pray.

Pause for silent prayer

O God, who see how your people
faithfully await the feast of the Lord's
Nativity,
enable us, we pray,
to attain the joys of so great a salvation
and to celebrate them always
with solemn worship and glad rejoicing.
Through our Lord Jesus Christ, your Son,
who lives and reigns with you in the unity
of the Holy Spirit,
one God, for ever and ever. **Amen.**

FIRST READING

Isa 35:1-6a, 10

The desert and the parched land will
exult;
the steppe will rejoice and bloom.
They will bloom with abundant flowers,
and rejoice with joyful song.
The glory of Lebanon will be given to
them,
the splendor of Carmel and Sharon;
they will see the glory of the LORD,
the splendor of our God.
Strengthen the hands that are feeble,
make firm the knees that are weak,
say to those whose hearts are frightened:
Be strong, fear not!
Here is your God,
he comes with vindication;
with divine recompense
he comes to save you.
Then will the eyes of the blind be opened,
the ears of the deaf be cleared;
then will the lame leap like a stag,
then the tongue of the mute will sing.

Those whom the LORD has ransomed will
return
and enter Zion singing,
crowned with everlasting joy;
they will meet with joy and gladness,
sorrow and mourning will flee.

RESPONSORIAL PSALM

Ps 146:6-7, 8-9, 9-10

℟. (cf. Isaiah 35:4) Lord, come and save us.
or:
℟. Alleluia.

The LORD God keeps faith forever,
secures justice for the oppressed,
gives food to the hungry.
The LORD sets captives free.

℟. Lord, come and save us.
or:
℟. Alleluia.

The LORD gives sight to the blind;
the LORD raises up those who were bowed down.
The LORD loves the just;
the LORD protects strangers.

℟. Lord, come and save us.
or:
℟. Alleluia.

The fatherless and the widow he sustains,
but the way of the wicked he thwarts.
The LORD shall reign forever;
your God, O Zion, through all generations.

℟. Lord, come and save us.
or:
℟. Alleluia.

SECOND READING

Jas 5:7-10

Be patient, brothers and sisters,
until the coming of the Lord.
See how the farmer waits for the precious fruit of the earth,
being patient with it
until it receives the early and the late rains.
You too must be patient.
Make your hearts firm,
because the coming of the Lord is at hand.
Do not complain, brothers and sisters, about one another,
that you may not be judged.
Behold, the Judge is standing before the gates.
Take as an example of hardship and patience, brothers and sisters,
the prophets who spoke in the name of the Lord.

CATECHESIS

About Liturgy

Signs of true worship: In last Sunday's first reading from Isaiah, we saw a vision of God's reign in which those who were once enemies dwelt together in peace. This week's vision, also from Isaiah, depicts what true worship looks like when all the earth takes part. The desert and the dry places "exult"; the grasslands "rejoice" and bloom in "joyful song" (Isa 35:1-2). These are liturgical actions and elements! In God's reign, all creation will be united in praise to God who comes to save us. The church's liturgy is a premier sign of that salvation.

Now take note of the result of true worship: blind eyes are opened; deaf ears hear; stiff legs and backs bend in dance; the silent sing. True worship is not an action done for itself but on behalf of those most in need, for it must result in relationships made right. Thus, we recall St. John Paul II's words about what makes the Eucharist authentic: "[B]y our mutual love and, in particular, by our concern for those in need we will be recognized as true followers of Christ. This will be the criterion by which the authenticity of our Eucharistic celebrations is judged" (*Mane nobiscum Domine* 28).

About Initiation

Signs of salvation: Jesus' response to John the Baptist's question gives us the signs to look for of God's saving action in the world. When we see these things happening, in particular, when the "poor have the good news proclaimed to them" (Matt 11:5), we know that the reign of God is at hand.

The initiation of adults is a process that starts when an adult hears the mystery of Christ proclaimed and responds by freely seeking a new way of life on the path of faith (cf. RCIA 1). Along this way, we are to look for signs of salvation, markers that reveal to us God's saving deeds in the lives of these inquirers. For those who are unbaptized, the first signs we look for are listed in RCIA 42: start of a spiritual life, fundamental Christian teachings have been planted, "first faith," initial conversion, intention to change, first stirrings of repentance, beginnings of prayer, "a sense of the Church," and the beginnings of friendship with Christians.

As soon as an inquirer enters into your community, begin to look for these signs that they are ready to take the next public step of faith through the Rite of Acceptance.

About Liturgical Music

Suggestions: For most Catholics, Advent is incomplete without singing the traditional song "O Come, O Come Emmanuel." It is typically sung during the last nine days of the season. However, today's *Gaudete* or "rejoice" Sunday provides the perfect opportunity to sing this piece if you have not already been using it as a seasonal song throughout Advent. Take care to truly express the joy in the text by not taking too slow a tempo and by showing that joy on your own face when you sing. The restrictions to instrumentation mentioned in last Sunday's liturgical music commentary can rightly be lifted slightly for today's celebration. So consider adding percussion or finger cymbals to bring out the message of the refrain. Tony Alonso's setting of this refrain in "Come, Emmanuel" (GIA), using text by Gabe Huck in the verses, is a great alternative to the traditional setting that still enables full participation by the assembly in the familiar refrain.

For a communion procession, consider *Psallite*'s gorgeous refrain "Be Patient, Beloved" (Liturgical Press). The assembly sings a beautiful text derived from the second reading, while the verses dwell on the signs of God's saving love all around us.

SPIRITUALITY

GOSPEL ACCLAMATION
Matt 1:23

℟. Alleluia, alleluia.
The virgin shall conceive, and bear a son,
and they shall name him Emmanuel.
℟. Alleluia, alleluia.

Gospel

Matt 1:18-24; L10A

This is how the birth of Jesus Christ came about.
When his mother Mary was betrothed to Joseph,
but before they lived together,
she was found with child through the Holy Spirit.
Joseph her husband, since he was a righteous man,
yet unwilling to expose her to shame,
decided to divorce her quietly.
Such was his intention when, behold,
the angel of the Lord appeared to him in a dream and said,
"Joseph, son of David,
do not be afraid to take Mary your wife into your home.
For it is through the Holy Spirit
that this child has been conceived in her.
She will bear a son and you are to name him Jesus,
because he will save his people from their sins."
All this took place to fulfill what the Lord had said through the prophet:
Behold, the virgin shall conceive and bear a son,
and they shall name him Emmanuel,
which means "God is with us."
When Joseph awoke,
he did as the angel of the Lord had commanded him
and took his wife into his home.

Reflecting on the Gospel

On this Fourth and final Sunday of Advent we have a story about Joseph told by Matthew. There are so few stories where Joseph is even named in the New Testament that it is good to read this one carefully. Interestingly, we have no words from Joseph in this story or any other in the New Testament. He is a quiet but righteous man, doing what is right in the sight of God.

Thus, Joseph's desire to end the relationship with Mary quietly upon finding out that she is with child is in keeping with his character. Technically, Mary could be exposed to the law, which would mean a death sentence. But Joseph is not that kind of person. He is content instead to handle this matter discreetly. Such was his intention before the appearance of an angel in a dream.

As Luke tells the story, an angel by the name of Gabriel appeared to Mary. But in Matthew's story an unnamed angel appears to Joseph in a dream. The two stories are not necessarily contradictory and, in fact, many find them complementary. But each evangelist is relating his story on its own terms. Neither seems to have been aware of the other. That is, Luke had not read Matthew, and Matthew had not read Luke.

The appearance of an angel in Joseph's dream is enough to change his mind. He takes his wife into his home in Bethlehem (not Nazareth, as Luke has it). Later the child will be born there, at the home. Again, this is not Luke's story of the family in Nazareth going to Bethlehem for the census. Matthew's story has no census; Joseph and Mary live in their home in Bethlehem where Mary will soon give birth.

On this Fourth Sunday of Advent the stage is set for Christmas morning, the nativity of our Lord. A discreet, quiet man who does what is right in the sight of God has taken the pregnant Mary into his home as his wife. What was a scandal worthy of death under the law has been directed by an angel in a dream into safety and security for the woman and her unborn child. God is doing something new.

Living the Paschal Mystery

"Ready or not here we come" is a phrase repeated often in the game of hide and seek, and it is a phrase appropriate for this Fourth Sunday of Advent. Christmas will be here soon whether we are ready or not. And as Christmas is the celebration of the birth of a child, we see that this phrase is appropriate for that too. Many parents reach a sometimes-startling conclusion that the baby will be here whether they are ready or not.

Our Advent has undoubtedly been spent in preparation. But no matter how much preparation we've done, there's likely more we could do. In the end, the day is going to come whether we are ready or not. Despite all of our planning or lack of thereof, soon the celebration will begin. In these remaining days, let us die to anything that takes our focus and attention away from the reason for the preparation. The Christ Child is about to be born. Life has profound meaning. Ready or not, Christmas is coming.

Focusing the Gospel

Key words and phrases: *Emmanuel,* / which means "God is with us."

To the point: The angel's message for Joseph affects his life not only practically ("do not be afraid to take Mary your wife into your home") but also spiritually. In Matthew's gospel, Joseph is the one who receives the angelic proclamation of Jesus' identity. The baby growing inside the womb of his betrothed, a child he will protect and support and share daily life with, is also the Promised One, the Savior. In Joseph we find a model for living life in Christ in ways big and small, from heavenly revelations to the minutiae of household chores and everyday family interactions. Joseph may not speak a word in the gospels, but his actions say it all: "Yes, Lord, thy will be done."

Connecting the Gospel

to the first reading: In the first reading we see another man in need of reassurance about the plan of God for his life. King Ahaz and his people are fearful when they hear that the armies of Syria and Israel are setting out to conquer Judah. God sends the prophet Isaiah to convince Ahaz to trust the Lord instead of turning to the mighty nation of Assyria for protection. Isaiah addresses Ahaz with words very similar to those spoken to Joseph in the gospel, "Take care to remain calm and do not fear" (Isa 7:4; NABRE). Unlike Joseph, Ahaz does not trust the Lord, and instead of asking for a sign from God, he decides to entrust himself and his people to the power of the Assyrians. The prophecy given to Ahaz is repeated at the end of today's gospel: "Behold, the virgin shall conceive and bear a son, / and they shall name him Emmanuel, / which means 'God is with us.'"

to experience: The gospel writer invites us to see within Jesus the greatest sign of God's presence among us. We, too, are instructed to "take care to remain calm and do not fear" for the Lord of life is with us.

Connecting the Responsorial Psalm

to the readings: Today's responsorial psalm proclaims, "Let the Lord enter; he is king of glory." This psalm is sung to the one who created the earth and sky, who "founded" the oceans and "established" the rivers. And yet, we also sing this hymn to the child of Bethlehem, growing within his mother's womb, vulnerable to the perceptions of a society that sees him as something shameful, a baby conceived out of wedlock.

to psalmist preparation: The three figures in today's readings (Ahaz, king of Judah; Paul, "a slave of Christ Jesus"; and Joseph, the husband of Mary) are invited to have radical trust in the Lord. From resisting the protection offered by a powerful nation, to proclaiming Jesus Christ in hostile territory and fostering a child not his own, these men are asked to reject the safe choice and instead trust in the God of the unexpected. Where is God asking for this trust in your life?

PROMPTS FOR FAITH-SHARING

In today's readings the prophet Isaiah and the angel of the Lord call upon Ahaz and Joseph to trust in the mysterious workings of God. Where is the God of life calling you to greater trust?

In St. Paul's letter to the Romans, he says that he has been "called to be an apostle and set apart for the gospel of God." How would it change your life to intentionally view it as "set apart" for the glory of God?

In the gospel, Matthew explains that the birth of Jesus would fulfill the prophecy from the first reading that *"the virgin shall conceive and bear a son, / and they shall name him Emmanuel."* Matthew adds an explanation of the term Emmanuel, "which means 'God is with us.'" When in your life have you most vividly experienced God's presence?

In the gospel we hear the familiar phrase "[D]o not be afraid." Where do you see fear affecting your family, community, or society at large?

Model Penitential Act

Presider: In today's gospel the angel of the Lord tells Joseph, "[D]o not be afraid to take Mary your wife into your home." For the times fear has kept us from following God's will for our lives, let us turn to God for mercy . . . *[pause]*

Lord Jesus, you call us to holiness: Lord, have mercy.
Christ Jesus, you fulfill the prophecies of old: Christ, have mercy.
Lord Jesus, you are Emmanuel, God with us: Lord, have mercy.

Homily Points

• First-time parents soon realize after the birth of a baby that no matter how intentional and thorough their preparations have been, things often do not go according to plan. Their child will turn their lives upside down in ways both beautiful and trying. We see this lived out in the infancy narratives of Matthew and Luke. From Jesus' conception through the Holy Spirit, to his birth among the animals in Bethlehem, Mary and Joseph model a deep faith and trust in God, the one who told them through an angel, "Do not be afraid" (Luke 1:30 and Matt 2:20; NABRE).

• In Advent, we enter into the preparation of an expectant parent. We prepare our homes and hearts to celebrate anew the birth of Jesus, God with us. And just like parents waiting for the birth of a child, we must prepare ourselves to let go of expectations and control in the life of faith. In St. Paul's letter to the Romans, he introduces himself as "a slave of Christ Jesus, / called to be an apostle and set apart for the gospel of God." From the moment Paul is struck down on the road to Damascus, his life is not his own. In choosing to follow Jesus he begins an extraordinary (and at times harrowing) adventure that will take him from Israel to Rome spreading the good news of Jesus' birth, death, and resurrection to everyone he meets.

• This baby, whose birth we celebrate on December 25, is a gift for us and for the whole world, but we are also a gift for the baby. Like St. Paul, as Christians we are called to live lives "set apart" for the gospel, lives turned upside down by our own encounter with Emmanuel, God present in our midst.

Model Universal Prayer (Prayer of the Faithful)

Presider: Confident in God's trustworthiness and constant care, we offer up all of our needs to the Lord.

Response: Lord, hear our prayer.

For the church, may it be a steadfast sign of God's presence throughout the world . . .

For peacemakers and diplomats, may they guide nations toward the peaceful resolution of conflicts and to crafting a society free of fear . . .

For the outcasts of society, may they, and all who interact with them, know their value in the sight of God . . .

For this community as it seeks to follow the one who is called Emmanuel, God with us, may we never stop growing in faithfulness . . .

Presider: God of prophesy and promise, you constantly send your people reminders of your love and care. Attune our eyes and ears to see and hear your gifts of self in all of creation. We ask this through Christ, our Lord. **Amen.**

COLLECT

Let us pray.

Pause for silent prayer

Pour forth, we beseech you, O Lord,
your grace into our hearts,
that we, to whom the Incarnation of Christ your Son
was made known by the message of an Angel,
may by his Passion and Cross
be brought to the glory of his Resurrection.
Who lives and reigns with you in the unity of the Holy Spirit,
one God, for ever and ever. **Amen.**

FIRST READING

Isa 7:10-14

The LORD spoke to Ahaz, saying:
Ask for a sign from the LORD, your God;
let it be deep as the netherworld, or high as the sky!
But Ahaz answered,
"I will not ask! I will not tempt the LORD!"
Then Isaiah said:
Listen, O house of David!
Is it not enough for you to weary people,
must you also weary my God?
Therefore the Lord himself will give you this sign:
the virgin shall conceive, and bear a son,
and shall name him Emmanuel.

RESPONSORIAL PSALM
Ps 24:1-2, 3-4, 5-6

℟. (7c and 10b) Let the Lord enter; he is king of glory.

The LORD's are the earth and its fullness;
the world and those who dwell in it.
For he founded it upon the seas
and established it upon the rivers.

℟. Let the Lord enter; he is king of glory.

Who can ascend the mountain of the LORD?
or who may stand in his holy place?
One whose hands are sinless, whose heart is clean,
who desires not what is vain.

℟. Let the Lord enter; he is king of glory.

He shall receive a blessing from the LORD,
a reward from God his savior.
Such is the race that seeks for him,
that seeks the face of the God of Jacob.

℟. Let the Lord enter; he is king of glory.

SECOND READING
Rom 1:1-7

Paul, a slave of Christ Jesus,
called to be an apostle and set apart for the gospel of God,
which he promised previously through his prophets in the holy Scriptures,
the gospel about his Son, descended from David according to the flesh,
but established as Son of God in power
according to the Spirit of holiness
through resurrection from the dead,
Jesus Christ our Lord.
Through him we have received the grace of apostleship,
to bring about the obedience of faith,
for the sake of his name, among all the Gentiles,
among whom are you also, who are called to belong to Jesus Christ;
to all the beloved of God in Rome, called to be holy.
Grace to you and peace from God our Father
and the Lord Jesus Christ.

About Liturgy

Decorating for Christmas: Long before today, you hopefully have already decided on your liturgical environment for the Christmas season. However, before you place that first poinsettia, be sure you have read the guidelines for seasonal decorations at paragraphs 124 and 125 in the United States bishops' document Built of Living Stones: Art, Architecture, and Worship. Here are some points from these paragraphs.

Decorate the entire worship space and not just the sanctuary. Include the spaces of the assembly, entryways and doors, and outside the church building.

The goal of the seasonal environment is "to draw people to the true nature of the mystery being celebrated rather than being ends in themselves" (124). Don't let decorations distract from the main ritual focal points of the Mass.

Stick with natural flowers, plants, and wreaths. Use real candles instead of electrical candles or oil-filled containers resembling wax candles.

Keep access to liturgical areas clear. The altar "should remain clear and freestanding, not walled in by massive floral displays or the Christmas crib, and pathways in the narthex, nave, and sanctuary should remain clear" (124).

Finally, maintain your Christmas environment until the end of the Christmas season, which is the Baptism of the Lord on January 12, 2020 (see 125).

About Initiation

About names: In today's gospel and first reading, we hear about the giving of the name "Emmanuel." In the initiation process, one's name bears special significance. At the Rite of Acceptance, the assembly formally hears each person's name, and at the Rite of Election, those to be elected offer their names to the bishop. At their initiation, they are baptized and confirmed with their given name.

In years past, many Catholics followed the practice of choosing a saint's name for confirmation, and parents were required to baptize their child with a Christian name. The revised Code of Canon Law in 1983 removed this requirement. Today, the rites for Christian initiation recommend that persons use their given names for these rites as long as they are not "foreign to a Christian mentality" (Code of Canon Law 855). The *Catechism of the Catholic Church* says it beautifully: "God calls each one by name. Everyone's name is sacred. The name is the icon of the person. It demands respect as a sign of the dignity of the one who bears it" (2158).

About Liturgical Music

Las Posadas: Every English-speaking choir is probably familiar with "O Come, O Come, Emmanuel," traditionally sung during the last part of Advent. There is another Advent musical tradition that is becoming more familiar, especially in communities with families of Mexican heritage. *Las Posadas* is a nine-day devotion celebrated in Mexican Catholic neighborhoods during the days leading up to Christmas. A central element of this devotion is a traditional song, "Las Posadas," which means "the inns." A group of participants representing Joseph and the pregnant Mary stands outside a designated home where they sing the first verse of the song, which asks for shelter. Another group inside the home sings the second verse, denying their request. Then both groups continue on to other homes, repeating the process, singing several verses until they all come to the last home. There the group within welcomes all the pilgrims with a joyful song and fiesta.

Although the traditional song is in Spanish Oregon Catholic Press provides a bilingual version of "Las Posadas" that would be a simple way to introduce this beautiful devotion to English-speaking choirs.

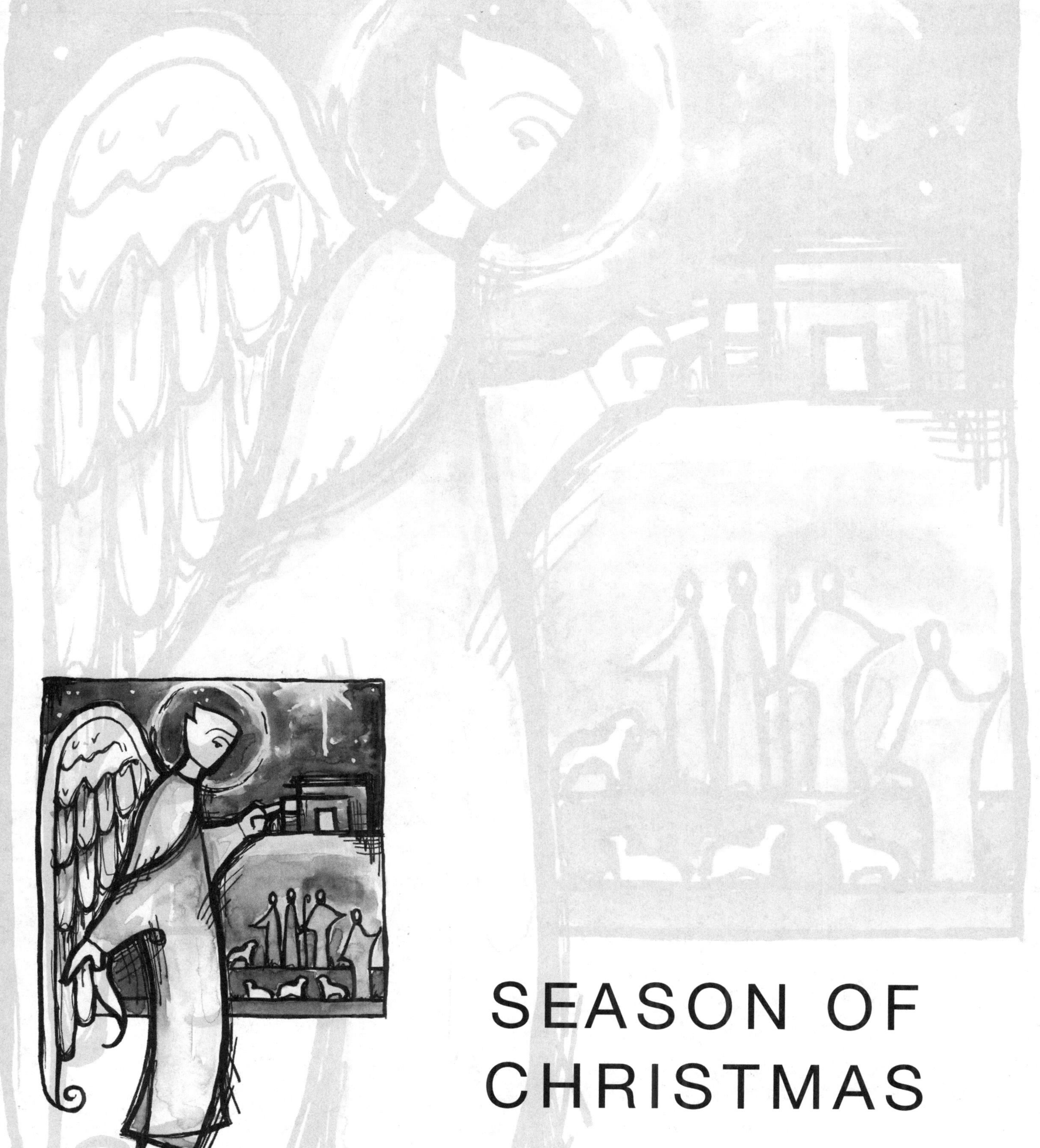

SEASON OF CHRISTMAS

This is the one who became human in a virgin. . . .
This is the lamb that was silent.
This is the one who was born of Mary,
that beautiful ewe-lamb.

—Melito of Sardis, *Peri Pascha*, 70–71

SPIRITUALITY

The Vigil Mass

GOSPEL ACCLAMATION

℟. Alleluia, alleluia.
Tomorrow the wickedness of the earth will be destroyed:
the Savior of the world will reign over us.
℟. Alleluia, alleluia.

Gospel

Matt 1:1-25; L13ABC

The book of the genealogy of Jesus Christ,
the son of David, the son of Abraham.

Abraham became the father of Isaac,
Isaac the father of Jacob,
Jacob the father of Judah and his brothers.
Judah became the father of Perez and Zerah,
whose mother was Tamar.
Perez became the father of Hezron,
Hezron the father of Ram,
Ram the father of Amminadab.
Amminadab became the father of Nahshon,
Nahshon the father of Salmon,
Salmon the father of Boaz,
whose mother was Rahab.
Boaz became the father of Obed,
whose mother was Ruth.
Obed became the father of Jesse,
Jesse the father of David the king.

David became the father of Solomon,
whose mother had been the wife of Uriah.
Solomon became the father of Rehoboam,
Rehoboam the father of Abijah,
Abijah the father of Asaph.

Continued in Appendix A, p. 262, or
Matt 1:18-25 *in Appendix A, p. 263.*

See Appendix A, p. 263, for the other readings.

Reflecting on the Gospel and Living the Paschal Mystery

Key words and phrases: "[Y]ou are to name him Jesus, / because he will save his people from their sins."

To the point: The first part of the gospel reading is the genealogy of Jesus. The list of names can seem long, especially when we're anticipating the joys of Christmas. And yet, each year, these names are read aloud on this night; there must be a reason. Within the family tree of Jesus we find some shocking ancestors. Non-Jews, adulterers, and others of questionable moral character are named alongside great patriarchs and matriarchs, and heroes of Israel's past. And the last name added to the list is "Jesus, who is called the Christ." The angel tells Joseph, "[Y]ou are to name him Jesus, / because he will save his people from their sins."

To ponder and pray: Jesus is born into the world as we know it, full of wonder and beauty, as well as corruption and darkness. His family tree might look like ours, with members we are proud to claim and others we wish we could forget about. And yet, in being born into the messiness of humanity and history, Jesus claims all of it and redeems it, for indeed, he is "God with us."

SPIRITUALITY

Mass at Midnight

GOSPEL ACCLAMATION
Luke 2:10-11

℟. Alleluia, alleluia.
I proclaim to you good news of great joy:
today a Savior is born for us,
Christ the Lord.
℟. Alleluia, alleluia.

Gospel

Luke 2:1-14; L14ABC

In those days a decree went out from Caesar Augustus
that the whole world should be enrolled.
This was the first enrollment,
when Quirinius was governor of Syria.
So all went to be enrolled, each to his own town.
And Joseph too went up from Galilee from the town of Nazareth
to Judea, to the city of David that is called Bethlehem,
because he was of the house and family of David,
to be enrolled with Mary, his betrothed, who was with child.
While they were there,
the time came for her to have her child,
and she gave birth to her firstborn son.

Continued in Appendix A, p. 264.

See Appendix A, p. 264, for the other readings.

Reflecting on the Gospel and Living the Paschal Mystery

Key words and phrases: She wrapped him in swaddling clothes and laid him in a manger, Glory to God in the Highest

To the point: The reading from Luke at the Midnight Mass is sublime, yet popular. Even the 1965 Peanuts Christmas special, *A Charlie Brown Christmas,* features this gospel passage, read by the character Linus. The master storyteller Luke enraptures us with the story of Jesus' birth. The simple clause "because there was no room for them at the inn" has inspired innumerable artists, homilists, theologians, and more. But Luke says no more about that episode than those few simple words. He says much more about the shepherds, the angel, and the multitude of the heavenly host. The few verses of this gospel reading light up our imagination, touching on key themes for Luke, such as Jesus as Savior, Jesus as food for the world (laid him in a *manger*), and the situation of the Christ-event at a particular time and place (with mention of Quirinius and the town of Bethlehem). How appropriate that we read this story of the shepherds keeping the night watch at our Midnight Mass.

To ponder and pray: Midnight by definition is a time of darkness, the middle of the night. And yet, it is during this time that light enters the world by the birth of the Christ, the Savior. Such a stark contrast is not by accident in the Gospel of Luke or in our liturgy tonight. We recall how God brings life from death, joy from sadness, and light from darkness. When we face moments of darkness in our own lives, let us recall the Christian faith that is at our core, that sees the birth of a child during the night watch as a profound moment of grace.

SPIRITUALITY

Mass at Dawn

GOSPEL ACCLAMATION
Luke 2:14

℟. Alleluia, alleluia.
Glory to God in the highest,
and on earth peace to those
on whom his favor rests.
℟. Alleluia, alleluia.

Gospel

Luke 2:15-20; L15ABC

When the angels went away from them to heaven,
the shepherds said to one another,
"Let us go, then, to Bethlehem
to see this thing that has taken place,
which the Lord has made known to us."
So they went in haste and found Mary and Joseph,
and the infant lying in the manger.
When they saw this,
they made known the message
that had been told them about this child.
All who heard it were amazed
by what had been told them by the shepherds.
And Mary kept all these things,
reflecting on them in her heart.
Then the shepherds returned,
glorifying and praising God
for all they had heard and seen,
just as it had been told to them.

See Appendix A, p. 265, for the other readings.

Reflecting on the Gospel and Living the Paschal Mystery

Key words and phrases: The infant lying in the manger, Mary kept all these things/reflecting on them in her heart

To the point: Luke tells the story from the point of view of the shepherds who had been keeping the night watch. After the angelic apparition and the announcement of the birth of the Savior, the shepherds go in haste and find just what had been told to them. Salvation has come in the person of an infant. New life, new human life, is certainly a cause of joy. And in this case, Mary herself is said to have kept these matters in her heart. We hear nothing about Joseph other than that he was there.

To ponder and pray: The shepherds who feature so prominently in today's gospel are nameless, foreshadowing the scores of disciples, members of the crowds, and various onlookers that Jesus will attract throughout his short life. Where do we find ourselves in such a picture? Do we seek Jesus this morning because of an angelic apparition? Or because someone else told us about him, much like the shepherds told many others? Or are we the evangelizers, drawing others to the Savior? This child, Jesus, is destined to be the rise and fall of many. What will be our role in this drama?

SPIRITUALITY

Mass during the Day

GOSPEL ACCLAMATION

℟. Alleluia, alleluia.
A holy day has dawned upon us.
Come, you nations, and adore the Lord.
For today a great light has come upon the earth.
℟. Alleluia, alleluia.

Gospel

John 1:1-18; L16ABC

In the beginning was the Word,
and the Word was with God,
and the Word was God.
He was in the beginning with God.
All things came to be through him,
and without him nothing came to be.
What came to be through him was life,
and this life was the light of the human race;
the light shines in the darkness,
and the darkness has not overcome it.

A man named John was sent from God.
He came for testimony, to testify to the light,
so that all might believe through him.
He was not the light,
but came to testify to the light.
The true light, which enlightens everyone,
was coming into the world.
He was in the world,
and the world came to be through him,
but the world did not know him.
He came to what was his own,
but his own people did not accept him.

But to those who did accept him
he gave power to become children of God,
to those who believe in his name,
who were born not by natural generation
nor by human choice nor by a man's decision
but of God.

Continued in Appendix A, p. 265, or
John 1:1-5, 9-14 *in Appendix A, p. 265.*

See Appendix A, p. 266, for the other readings.

Reflecting on the Gospel and Living the Paschal Mystery

Key words and phrases: In the beginning. And the Word became flesh and made his dwelling among us.

To the point: It is no coincidence that the opening words of John's prologue proclaimed at Christmas, "In the beginning" (John 1:1), are the same words we hear at the Easter Vigil in the story of creation from Genesis. John's theological hymn begins the evangelist's gradual revelation of Christ's identity, from divine Word spoken from the beginning, to Word made flesh in the life of Jesus, to Word of life breathed from the cross from the Son's spirit commended back to the Father with whom he is one from the beginning.

Christmas is intimately tied to Easter, for the incarnation is the beginning of the resurrection. In this christological descent of the Word spoken on the first day of creation—"Let there be light" (Gen 1:3)—we are taken up in the Son's ascent to the Father, "that we may share in the divinity of Christ, who humbled himself to share in our humanity" (collect, Nativity of the Lord, Mass during the Day). This is how God saves us: through our very humanity. We need not reject the world in order to see God and know God's presence. Rather, we dwell more deeply into it with the grace we have received as God's children, just as the Word dwelt among us in grace and truth. Thus will we be taken up in Christ to see God's glory in our midst.

To ponder and pray: The gospel of Christmas Day is not what most normally think of as the "Christmas story," a conflation of Jesus' birth from the gospels of Matthew and Luke. There are no shepherds, but there is the Good Shepherd whose feet upon the mountains bring good news. There is no star, but the Light, which no darkness can overcome. We hear no hosts of angels, but the Word made flesh through whom God spoke clearly and fully. No babe, meek and mild, do we gather around but the very imprint of God's being in whom we are gathered to become children of God.

Christmas Day soothes with no bedtime lullabies nor amuses with innocent pageants. Rather, in the harsh light of day, when all the world's brokenness is laid bare, we hear the sentinels weep for joy at the announcement of "peace." Song is heard among the ruins of our relationships made right. For in *this* beginning, with *this* birth, we, too, are re-created again.

Today reminds us that Christmas is more than a child's story. It is the narrative that rewrites our story, saying to all that, in God's eyes, humanity is worth saving, not from afar, but in the midst of our darkness. Out of love for us, our God is born into the suffering of our human weakness that we may know the freedom of dying to our sinfulness and rising to new life in Christ.

Model Penitential Act

Presider: As we prepare to enter into the mystery of the incarnation, God become human to dwell among us, let us pause and offer to God our very selves, our triumphs as well as our failings, trusting in God's infinite mercy . . . *[pause]*

Lord Jesus, you are the light that illuminates all darkness: Lord, have mercy.

Christ Jesus, you are the baby wrapped in swaddling clothes and placed in a manger: Christ, have mercy.

Lord Jesus, you are true God and true man: Lord, have mercy.

Model Universal Prayer (Prayer of the Faithful)

Presider: With ever-growing trust in our God, who took on flesh to dwell among us, let us bring our needs before the Lord.

Response: Lord, hear our prayer.

For God's holy church, may it faithfully proclaim the good news of Jesus' birth to all people . . .

For those who govern nations, may they humbly use the authority that has been granted them to protect the vulnerable and promote the common good . . .

For all the people of the world who, like Mary and Joseph, are in need of shelter and safety, may they find welcome, care, and compassion . . .

For all those gathered in this place, may we be illumined by the light of Christ and inspired to bring this light with us wherever we go . . .

Presider: God of eternal light and life, you promised through the prophets to send a savior to your people, and in Jesus we see the fulfillment of this promise. Hear our prayers that in celebrating the feast of his Nativity, the darkness in our own lives will be dispelled. Through Christ our Lord. **Amen.**

About Liturgy

Returning to basic: If you've been preparing liturgy or music for a while, the details of the Christmas Day liturgies and the Christmas season may seem pretty familiar or even rote. If you feel this way, reviewing the basics of this season can help you renew your wonder and ensure that you're on the right track with your preparations. Here are some key points.

On Christmas Day and throughout the season, the Gloria should be sung and not recited. Use familiar Christmas music and Mass settings throughout to unify the entire season.

The normal liturgical color for Christmas is white, but the General Instruction of the Roman Missal, 346, allows other colors, especially gold or silver, on more solemn or festive days. These colors can help connect the seasons of Christmas and Easter, the two most important times of the liturgical year. (Remember that Christmas is a season that stretches to the end of the Baptism of the Lord, January 12, 2020.)

Pay more attention to the "Word made flesh" in how you reverence the Book of the Gospels and treat other books containing the Scriptures.

COLLECT

(from the Mass during the Day)

Let us pray.

Pause for silent prayer

O God, who wonderfully created the dignity of human nature
and still more wonderfully restored it,
grant, we pray,
that we may share in the divinity of Christ,
who humbled himself to share in our humanity.
Who lives and reigns with you in the unity of the Holy Spirit,
one God, for ever and ever. **Amen.**

FOR REFLECTION

- In Luke's narrative of Jesus' birth (proclaimed at the Mass at midnight and Mass at dawn), we find many characters who occupy different roles in the nativity story. From Mary, who ponders all these things in her heart, to the shepherds who rush in haste to find the baby, to the indifferent city that closes its doors to the expectant couple, where do you see yourself? Which role(s) have you played in this story and which role would you like to play?
- Each of the four Christmas liturgies (vigil, midnight, dawn, and day) has its own set of readings. Which Christmas gospel speaks most to your faith at this moment in time?

Homily Points

- At the beginning of the Liturgy of the Eucharist, after the gifts of bread and wine have been brought forth to the altar, the priest or deacon prepares the chalice by filling the vessel with wine and then adding a small drop of water, while saying the prayer, "By the mystery of this water and wine / may we come to share in the divinity of Christ / who humbled himself to share in our humanity." This is the mystery of the incarnation boiled down to its essential core.
- Our God redeems and saves us through his son who enters into our humanity and rests his head in the manger of Bethlehem. And even now, he calls to us to join him in divine life. Within the water and wine mingled together, we find a sign of our union with God, the one who desires to be with us, the one who is called Emmanuel.

SPIRITUALITY

GOSPEL ACCLAMATION
Col 3:15a, 16a

℟. Alleluia, alleluia.
Let the peace of Christ control your hearts;
let the word of Christ dwell in you richly.
℟. Alleluia, alleluia.

Gospel Matt 2:13-15, 19-23; L17A

When the magi had departed, behold,
the angel of the Lord appeared to Joseph in a dream and said,
"Rise, take the child and his mother, flee to Egypt,
and stay there until I tell you.
Herod is going to search for the child to destroy him."
Joseph rose and took the child and his mother by night
and departed for Egypt.
He stayed there until the death of Herod,
that what the Lord had said through the prophet might be fulfilled,
Out of Egypt I called my son.

When Herod had died, behold,
the angel of the Lord appeared in a dream
to Joseph in Egypt and said,
"Rise, take the child and his mother and go to the land of Israel,
for those who sought the child's life are dead."
He rose, took the child and his mother,
and went to the land of Israel.
But when he heard that Archelaus was ruling over Judea
in place of his father Herod,
he was afraid to go back there.
And because he had been warned in a dream,
he departed for the region of Galilee.
He went and dwelt in a town called Nazareth,
so that what had been spoken through the prophets might be fulfilled,
He shall be called a Nazorean.

Reflecting on the Gospel

It's likely that in our own minds we've conflated the nativity stories of Luke and Matthew into one. But reading Matthew on his own terms reveals something fascinating. In Matthew's telling, Joseph and Mary had a home in Bethlehem, where Jesus was born. The magi eventually found their way to the home to find the *child* Jesus (not the infant). And now Joseph takes the *child* and his mother into Egypt. Only after Herod had died did Joseph have the courage to return. Even then, he was inspired by an angel in a dream! And he did not return to Bethlehem, but instead made his way to Nazareth.

For Matthew, this entire episode fulfills Scripture in a number of ways. The evangelist quotes from the Old Testament frequently, showing precisely how the actions of the Holy Family fulfill holy writ. But beyond a literal fulfillment of sacred text, Matthew's story of the Holy Family's flight into Egypt is essentially a story of refugees. Matthew states clearly that Joseph was afraid. He feared the authorities and what might happen if he and his family were apprehended. This is no mere artistic rendering, painting, or sculpture of an exhausted family, such as we might see with the caption "flight into Egypt." The fears were real, and the danger proximate. The Holy Family crossed boundaries into Egypt to escape the authorities. Upon Herod's death, the coast was not clear, only clear enough to leave Egypt and settle somewhere else. So that is precisely what they did. Joseph, Mary, and the child left Egypt. Instead of settling in Bethlehem, their home, they made a home in Nazareth. The shifting, perhaps chaotic early years of Jesus' life speak to a reality that millions unfortunately face, and have faced throughout human history.

In our modern world, we are witnessing a magnitude of migration of peoples not seen since World War II. As Christians we might ask ourselves how do we treat these people? Can we see the Holy Family in their plight? Or are they merely scofflaws, evading the authorities? It can be one thing to look with pity on the Holy Family and their flight into Egypt. We admire the artistic representations of this biblical story. But what of the lived reality of this biblical story in the lives of so many in our world today? May we as followers of this child refugee, this migrant Holy Family, recognize that same presence today and, in so doing, act on their behalf.

Living the Paschal Mystery

Domesticating the gospel happens far too frequently. It's difficult to read or hear these stories fresh or in a new way when we are so familiar with them. But with today's gospel we are reminded of the reality that Joseph, Mary, and the child Jesus were political refugees. They feared for their lives, as Herod had massacred the innocents. The Holy Family found safety and refuge in a foreign country. Though Jesus was Emmanuel, danger was present and must have seemed a specter shadowing the Holy Family. We know that Jesus will ultimately lose his life at the hands of the state. Is it any wonder that the gospel message was so popular with the outcast and marginalized?

As we live the paschal mystery, we are called to let go of the domestication of the gospel and allow it to speak to the realities we face. Let us, as disciples, identify with the outcast, marginalized, and afflicted, for that is how the Holy Family lived. In so doing, we will suffer and die in this struggle only to be raised to new life.

Focusing the Gospel

Key words and phrases: Joseph rose and took the child and his mother by night / and departed for Egypt.

To the point: Matthew's gospel continues to focus on the actions of Joseph in the birth, infancy, and childhood of Jesus. On the Fourth Sunday of Advent, we read how Joseph is visited in a dream by the angel of the Lord urging him to accept Mary, his betrothed, and the child she carries by the Holy Spirit into his home. In today's gospel Joseph continues to listen to God's commandments, spoken to him in dreams, and to act. His unquestioning trust in God, even through uncertainty and fear, protects the child Jesus and his mother.

Connecting the Gospel

to the first reading: Today's gospel gives us a glimpse into Jesus' childhood in which he is not the main actor. Instead, it is up to his foster father, Joseph, and his mother, Mary, to make decisions about his life and to protect him. In the first reading from Sirach the writer counsels us in the right relationship of family life in which father, mother, and children all honor and respect each other. How amazing to contemplate that God, in choosing to be born as a baby, also fulfilled these requirements, submitting to the decisions of his mother and foster father. In Matthew's gospel, the words that end the passage today are the final verses about Jesus' childhood. The gospel story continues in chapter 3 with the preaching of John the Baptist and the beginning of Jesus' adult ministry.

to experience: Although only a small portion of the Gospels of Matthew and Luke are devoted to Jesus' infancy and childhood, how does reflecting on these "hidden years" of Jesus' life affect your faith and experience of family?

Connecting the Responsorial Psalm

to the readings: Today's psalm paints an idyllic picture of the family life waiting for those "who fear the Lord and walk in his ways." While we know that there is no guarantee of creating this type of family (spouse and children) based on our faith alone, we also know that we are all a part of the holy family of God. As St. Paul reminds us in his letter to the Colossians, God's holy family is brought together whenever people "put on . . . compassion, kindness, humility, [and] gentleness" in their dealings with one another.

to psalmist preparation: In your ministry as a cantor, how do you help to create the holy family of God within your parish? When have you been most grateful for this parish family in your life?

PROMPTS FOR FAITH-SHARING

The responsorial psalm proclaims, "Blessed are those who fear the Lord and walk in his ways." Fear of the Lord has also been translated as having "wonder and awe in God's presence." Which translation do you like better? What do each of the phrases "fear of the Lord" and "wonder and awe in God's presence" mean to you?

In the second reading St. Paul urges the Colossians, "Let the word of Christ dwell in you richly." How do you make space for this living Word to deeply penetrate your heart?

St. Paul also urges the people to "let the peace of Christ control your hearts." Where do you find peace in your daily life?

In the gospel reading today Mary, Joseph, and Jesus face extreme peril. What has been the most difficult experience you have encountered as a member of your family? What helped you make it through this time?

Model Penitential Act

Presider: In the Holy Family we find a model of love, service, and unity. Let us pause to ask Mary, Joseph, and Jesus to intercede for us for the times we have failed to imitate them . . . *[pause]*

Lord Jesus, you call us to live within the communion of the Holy Family: Lord, have mercy.

Christ Jesus, you show us the way of humility, gentleness, and patience: Christ, have mercy.

Lord Jesus, you desire to bring us your peace: Lord, have mercy.

Homily Points

• The main actor in today's gospel is Joseph, Jesus' foster father. After receiving a warning that King Herod intends to search for Jesus and destroy him, Joseph immediately sets out for Egypt with Mary and her toddler son, a sojourn which biblical scholars speculate could have lasted anywhere from a few weeks to a few years.

• During this time the Holy Family would have encountered many people, from fellow travelers on the road, to patrolling soldiers, and the Jewish community in Egypt. Few, if any, of these people probably knew they were interacting with the Messiah, the Mother of God, and a great saint, fleeing from persecution and seeking safety in a foreign land. Although only Joseph's actions of faithfulness and care are documented in the Gospel of Matthew, we can ponder the countless people who might have helped this refugee family.

• Oftentimes we might think of the Holy Family as an isolated unit of three, sufficient unto themselves, and yet, we know that all families must interact with the broader society; it would have been no different for Mary, Joseph, and Jesus. As children of God, we are all called to belong to this Holy Family. And when we act with the "compassion, kindness, humility, gentleness, and patience" that St. Paul writes about, we manifest this family wherever we go. Although the people who reached out to the Holy Family during their time in Egypt might not have known whom they were helping, we do. Later in Matthew's gospel, Jesus will tell his followers, "Whatever you did for one of these least brothers of mine, you did for me" (25:40; NABRE). How might we greet all whom we meet as beloved brothers or sisters in the Holy Family of God?

Model Universal Prayer (Prayer of the Faithful)

Presider: Through the intercession of the Holy Family, we bring our prayers before our Lord.

Response: Lord, hear our prayer.

For the church throughout the world, that it might continue to grow in holiness, compassion, kindness, humility, gentleness, and patience . . .

For people all over the world who are engaged in peaceful resistance of corrupt political regimes, may they be strengthened in their work for peace and justice . . .

For refugees and those seeking political asylum, may they be granted safe passage and hospitable welcome in a new land . . .

For those of us gathered around this altar table, may we recognize Christ in the stranger and welcome him within our midst . . .

Presider: God of the vulnerable and marginalized, wherever there is suffering, you are present. Hear our prayers that we might bring your healing and love to the broken places within our families, communities, and throughout the world. We ask this through Christ our Lord. **Amen.**

COLLECT

Let us pray

Pause for silent prayer

O God, who were pleased to give us
the shining example of the Holy Family,
graciously grant that we may imitate them
in practicing the virtues of family life and
in the bonds of charity,
and so, in the joy of your house,
delight one day in eternal rewards.
Through our Lord Jesus Christ, your Son,
who lives and reigns with you in the unity
of the Holy Spirit,
one God, for ever and ever. **Amen.**

FIRST READING

Sir 3:2-6, 12-14

God sets a father in honor over his
children;
a mother's authority he confirms over
her sons.
Whoever honors his father atones for sins,
and preserves himself from them.
When he prays, he is heard;
he stores up riches who reveres his
mother.
Whoever honors his father is gladdened
by children,
and, when he prays, is heard.
Whoever reveres his father will live a long
life;
he who obeys his father brings comfort
to his mother.

My son, take care of your father when he
is old;
grieve him not as long as he lives.
Even if his mind fail, be considerate of
him;
revile him not all the days of his life;
kindness to a father will not be forgotten,
firmly planted against the debt of your
sins
—a house raised in justice to you.

RESPONSORIAL PSALM

Ps 128:1-2, 3, 4-5

℟. (cf. 1) Blessed are those who fear the Lord and walk in his ways.

Blessed is everyone who fears the LORD,
who walks in his ways!
For you shall eat the fruit of your
handiwork;
blessed shall you be, and favored.

R. Blessed are those who fear the Lord
and walk in his ways.

Your wife shall be like a fruitful vine
in the recesses of your home;
your children like olive plants
around your table.

R. Blessed are those who fear the Lord
and walk in his ways.

Behold, thus is the man blessed
who fears the LORD.
The LORD bless you from Zion:
may you see the prosperity of
Jerusalem
all the days of your life.

R. Blessed are those who fear the Lord
and walk in his ways.

SECOND READING

Col 3:12-21

Brothers and sisters:
Put on, as God's chosen ones, holy and
beloved,
heartfelt compassion, kindness,
humility, gentleness, and patience,
bearing with one another and forgiving
one another,
if one has a grievance against another;
as the Lord has forgiven you, so must
you also do.
And over all these put on love,
that is, the bond of perfection.
And let the peace of Christ control your
hearts,
the peace into which you were also
called in one body.
And be thankful.
Let the word of Christ dwell in you richly,
as in all wisdom you teach and
admonish one another,
singing psalms, hymns, and spiritual
songs
with gratitude in your hearts to God.
And whatever you do, in word or in deed,
do everything in the name of the Lord
Jesus,
giving thanks to God the Father through
him.

Wives, be subordinate to your husbands,
as is proper in the Lord.
Husbands, love your wives,
and avoid any bitterness toward them.
Children, obey your parents in everything,
for this is pleasing to the Lord.
Fathers, do not provoke your children,
so they may not become discouraged.

or Col 3:12-17

See Appendix A, p. 266.

CATECHESIS

About Liturgy

Rethinking "cry rooms": The Dogmatic Constitution on the Church (*Lumen Gentium*) says, "The family is . . . the domestic church" (11). The Christian household is the most basic visible expression of the church and a fundamental place where we foster unity with Christ and with one another.

Yet, many common parish practices inadvertently separate families when they come together to pray on Sundays. One of these practices is the misuse of "cry rooms."

Having a space where parents or guardians can attend to the needs of infants and young children is a practical and hospitable necessity. But "cry rooms" should not be viewed as rooms where those who need them are expected to participate in worship. It is nearly impossible to truly participate in liturgy in these kinds of rooms! It would be more hospitable to families and more authentic to the spirit of communion to encourage parents to keep their children with them in the main assembly and to nurture a culture of welcome and communal support of parents among all the parishioners. Then, provide a quiet, comfortable, and beautiful space where parents can care for their child temporarily until they are ready to return to the assembly.

About Initiation

A Catholic calendar: As we approach the end of the calendar year, this is a good opportunity to introduce catechumens and candidates to a Catholic approach to time. As we said in *About Initiation* for the First Sunday of Advent, the liturgical year is a sacramental way to encounter God's presence in our lives. Help them create their own Catholic calendar that will encourage them to mark the significant moments in their own life where they encounter the mystery of Christ.

Using a blank calendar or a Catholic calendar provided by your parish for 2020, have them highlight some important days. The most important day for Catholics is always Sunday because it is the Lord's Day. The next is Easter Sunday, which is the premier Sunday of the entire year. Then follow the seasons of Easter and Christmas. After highlighting the other holy days and solemnities, have them mark your parish's feast day, their name days or patron saint days, baptismal anniversaries if they are baptized, and, for catechumens, the day they entered the order of catechumens. Include wedding anniversaries, death anniversaries of loved ones, and birthdays. Help them learn about any saints whose feasts fall on these significant personal days.

About Liturgical Music

Intergenerational ministry: Many parishes will have a children's choir or a youth choir that serves at specific Masses. These are wonderful ways to foster participation in the liturgy among our younger members of the church. However, these can also become ways we "segregate" children or youth from the rest of the assembly. At worst, they may even promote a performance mentality to music ministry where parents and the assembly see these as photo or video opportunities. Or children are asked to cantor even if they are not well-trained or suitable for that role.

A better way to encourage participation among children on a regular basis every Sunday is to get their entire family involved in liturgical ministry. Instead of a children-only choir, consider forming a family choir where parents and their children serve together. Children can still be highlighted as a *schola cantorum*, taking leadership during certain verses or songs. Also, children and parents trained for musical leadership can cantor together during the psalm or other songs. This is also a good way to prepare children to serve alone as cantors and song leaders.

GOSPEL ACCLAMATION
Heb 1:1-2

℟. Alleluia, alleluia.
In the past God spoke to our ancestors through
the prophets;
in these last days, he has spoken to us through
the Son.
℟. Alleluia, alleluia.

Gospel Luke 2:16-21; L18ABC

The shepherds went in haste to Bethlehem and found Mary and Joseph,
and the infant lying in the manger.
When they saw this,
they made known the message
that had been told them about this child.
All who heard it were amazed
by what had been told them by the shepherds.
And Mary kept all these things,
reflecting on them in her heart.
Then the shepherds returned,
glorifying and praising God
for all they had heard and seen,
just as it had been told to them.

When eight days were completed for his circumcision,
he was named Jesus, the name given him by the angel
before he was conceived in the womb.

See Appendix A, p. 267, for the other readings.

Reflecting on the Gospel

We begin the secular New Year with the solemnity of Mary, the Mother of God. Mary's role in the life of Jesus was paramount, as is the role of any mother in a child's life, even in absence. We can imagine the lessons Jesus learned from his mother, who was chosen by God for this relationship. In the same Gospel of Luke from which we read today, we learn that Mary has a heart for the poor, the downtrodden, and the neglected when we hear her *Magnificat*. This was the spirit that animated her before Jesus was born; we can imagine it animated and influenced him too.

By referring to Mary as "Mother of God," we are echoing a term from the fifth-century christological debates about the nature of Jesus. Theologians at the time wondered about Jesus' identity. Was he merely Christ or could he be referred to as "God"? More precisely, was Mary the Mother of the Christ, or could she be referred to as the "Mother of God" or, in Greek, *theotokos* (God-bearer)? This was not an easy question, and it captured the imagination of some of the church's best thinkers of the time. Eventually, as we can surmise, the church came to consider it acceptable to refer to Mary as *theotokos* (God-bearer/Mother of God). It should be remembered that though it's certainly a Marian title, the title says more about Jesus and his identity than it does about Mary.

When we consider Jesus' role and identity through the lens of Mary, we often gain a new insight into his personhood. It's much like when we meet someone for the first time, get to know that person better, and eventually meet his or her family, we gain a deeper, more profound understanding of that person. Something similar happens when we explore the role of Mary in the life of Jesus. Her influence upon him was profound. And we know from Luke that Mary was present at many of the events in Jesus' life—and even after his earthly life when she was present with the disciples.

Today, let us renew our appreciation for Mary and her role in the life of Jesus, and by extension may we renew our appreciation for all mothers and the role they play in the life of their children.

Living the Paschal Mystery

"The apple doesn't fall far from the tree" is an expression we use to speak of how a child mimics or emulates the behavior of a parent. The same could be said of Jesus and his relationship with his mother and father, Mary and Joseph. Each of his parents instilled in him a profound respect for God, care for the poor, and concern for the lowly. Though Jesus was raised in the small town of Nazareth (likely a few hundred people), he imbibed the religious values of his parents and lived them out in a dramatic way. Jesus was no divine puppet who knew everything but kept it hidden lest others detect his identity. Instead, Luke tells us that Jesus "grew and became strong" and he "advanced [in] wisdom and age and favor before God and man" (Luke 2:40, 52; NABRE).

This is a good reminder that we can allow ourselves and others to grow in wisdom. None of us has all the answers; we rely on others for advice. The role of a parent is critical in this respect and doesn't end when we reach adulthood. Let us continue to set aside our own hubris and pride, being open to the influence of others who can help us grow in wisdom and knowledge. In that way, we continue to be children of God, apples who do not fall far from the tree.

Focusing the Gospel

Key words and phrases: [T]hey made known the message / that had been told them about this child.

To the point: What an amazing scene we encounter in today's gospel. Mary and Joseph, who have been told about Jesus' identity through their own angelic experiences, now have the good news proclaimed to them by a group of Bethlehem shepherds. Mary's response is to reflect on the shepherd's words in her heart. Mary not only physically carries the word of God within her womb and brings it to birth, she continues to nurture this Word inside of her, her whole life long. How might we follow Mary's example of quiet reflection?

Model Penitential Act

Presider: We gather on this solemnity of Mary, holy Mother of God, to listen to the words of Scripture and to be fed at the table of the Lord. Let us prepare our hearts and minds by recalling the places in our lives where we require God's healing and mercy . . . *[pause]*

Lord Jesus, you call us to walk by the light of salvation: Lord, have mercy.
Christ Jesus, you are the Son of God and son of Mary: Christ, have mercy.
Lord Jesus, you heal us by your holy name: Lord, have mercy.

Model Universal Prayer (Prayer of the Faithful)

Presider: Through the intercession of Mary, Mother of God, Queen of Peace, and model disciple, let us bring our prayers before the Lord.

Response: Lord, hear our prayer.

For members of the church throughout the world, inspired by Mary's example, may we also ponder deeply the mystery of the incarnation in our hearts . . .

For places in the world shattered by war, may the light of God's hope and peace overcome the darkness of violence . . .

For children living in poverty, may they receive the resources and care they need to grow and thrive . . .

For all gathered here on this day, may our words and actions proclaim the good news of Jesus Christ to all we meet . . .

Presider: God of light and life, you give us Mary as a spiritual mother and model disciple to show us the way to your son, Jesus. Hear our prayers that we might emulate Mary in word and deed. We ask this through Christ, our Lord. **Amen.**

About Liturgy

Octaves: In liturgical terms, an octave is the eighth day after a major solemnity or feast. It can also refer to the time beginning from a major solemnity and inclusive of the days after it until the eighth day. Sunday is the premier "octave" in that it is the "eighth day" of the Lord's Day. Today's solemnity of Mary is the eighth day after Christmas and completes the octave of Christmas.

The practice of octaves was introduced in the fourth century to mark the eight days of celebration after the dedication of major churches. Over time, annual octaves were included, starting with an octave of Easter, Pentecost, and Christmas. Eventually, the liturgical calendar included at least eighteen octaves in addition to octaves for each region's patron saint! Today, there are two octaves that are celebrated in the liturgical calendar: Easter and Christmas. Each day of these octaves is observed as a solemnity.

An octave signifies the world-changing, overwhelming joy that cannot be contained by just one day. With eight days of jubilee, we savor the new life we have found in Christ who, by being born of Mary, transformed all creation.

COLLECT

Let us pray.

Pause for silent prayer

O God, who through the fruitful virginity of
Blessed Mary
bestowed on the human race
the grace of eternal salvation,
grant, we pray,
that we may experience the intercession of her,
through whom we were found worthy
to receive the author of life,
our Lord Jesus Christ, your Son.
Who lives and reigns with you in the unity of
the Holy Spirit,
one God, for ever and ever. **Amen.**

FOR REFLECTION

- In the first reading Aaron and his sons are given the ministry of blessing the people. Who do you bless in your prayer life and who blesses you?
- The responsorial psalm includes the phrase "may [God] let his face shine upon us." What image does this bring to mind for you? How have you experienced God's face shining in your life?
- In today's gospel we find both examples of proclaiming the good news and of receiving it. Which role are you most comfortable in as a Christian: proclamation of the word of God or meditation upon that word?

Homily Points

- Today is the eighth day of our celebration of the mystery of the incarnation. The readings for Advent and Christmas are full of the contrast between light and dark. At the Midnight Mass we read the words from the prophet Isaiah, "The people who walked in darkness / have seen a great light."

- In today's gospel we focus on the response of the shepherds watching their flocks by night whose darkness was pierced by the "glory of the Lord." In haste, they go to find the one who would later proclaim, "I am the light of the world" (John 8:12; NABRE) and then leave "glorifying and praising God / for all they had heard and seen." Let us, too, walk as people who have had our darkness enlightened by Christ.

SPIRITUALITY

GOSPEL ACCLAMATION
Matt 2:2

℟. Alleluia, alleluia.
We saw his star at its rising
and have come to do him homage.
℟. Alleluia, alleluia.

Gospel

Matt 2:1-12; L20ABC

When Jesus was born in Bethlehem of Judea,
in the days of King Herod,
behold, magi from the east arrived in Jerusalem, saying,
"Where is the newborn king of the Jews?
We saw his star at its rising
and have come to do him homage."
When King Herod heard this,
he was greatly troubled,
and all Jerusalem with him.
Assembling all the chief priests
and the scribes of the people,
he inquired of them where the Christ was to be born.
They said to him, "In Bethlehem of Judea,
for thus it has been written through the prophet:
And you, Bethlehem, land of Judah,
are by no means least among the rulers of Judah;
since from you shall come a ruler,
who is to shepherd my people Israel."
Then Herod called the magi secretly
and ascertained from them the time of the star's appearance.
He sent them to Bethlehem and said,
"Go and search diligently for the child.
When you have found him, bring me word,
that I too may go and do him homage."

Continued in Appendix A, p. 267.

Reflecting on the Gospel

The story of the Epiphany, or the visitation of the magi, is told only in Matthew. But like many other elements of the Nativity story, we've likely combined this in our mind with Luke's story too. So it's helpful to read this in the context of Matthew's gospel for he makes pertinent theological points. It's easy to read into the story, however, imagining that *three kings* bring the infant Jesus presents. But in reality, the number of magi is not given. We typically imagine three because of the number of gifts they brought. Also, the three are thought of as "kings," even though that word doesn't appear here either. Matthew calls them "magi," which were a class of Zoroastrian priests from Persia (modern-day Iran). And though we likely imagine the infant Jesus, he is called a "child" here (akin to a toddler).

The gifts themselves represent royalty, and the magi represent Gentiles. This tells us that even Gentiles come and worship Jesus, prefiguring the conclusion of the gospel, when the risen Lord will give the commandment to go out to all the nations (Gentiles) teaching them and baptizing them. Finally, the fact that the magi find the child Jesus (rather than the infant) is significant too, as Herod will order the slaughter of the male children based on when the star initially appeared. So it's good for us to read the story carefully, gleaning the theological insights that Matthew means to impart.

This story gives us many points to consider. One might be the fact that Gentiles (considered "the other") come to worship Jesus. Herod needs to ask his advisors about the prophecy when those from Persia (Gentiles) are seeking out the child on their own. We, too, might be open to the other, those who come to the truth and to the person of Jesus on their own accord or by following their own stars. We know that by the end of the gospel, this is Jesus' intention too, that his teachings are not restricted to a few, but are open to all. This is the same gospel that will tell us that not everyone who says, "Lord, Lord" will enter the kingdom of heaven. Instead, entry is only for those who do the will of the Father. And the will of the Father is that we act mercifully, much like the magi of the gospel today.

Let us then read the story carefully, with attention to detail. Matthew, the evangelist and theologian, has much to tell us about the great teacher and child-king Jesus.

Living the Paschal Mystery

The magi in today's gospel represent all those who are not part of the "in" crowd. These foreigners who do not know Jesus come to worship him before anyone else. They recognize in the signs of nature that something significant has happened, and they seek it out. Those who should know their own Scriptures missed something that Zoroastrian priests perceived.

We can ask ourselves, too, what we might miss when signs are right in front of our eyes. What is God doing in our midst? Is it something that others—foreigners, those not part of the "in" crowd—notice, but it escapes our attention? Let us die to our preconceived notions and surety in knowing the Lord, and be open to what God has in store for us. God is doing something new. There is an epiphany under way. May we have eyes to see and ears to hear.

Focusing the Gospel

Key words and phrases: And behold, the star that they had seen at its rising preceded them, / until it came and stopped over the place where the child was.

To the point: The magi undertake an extraordinary journey. Their two-year sojourn comes to its conclusion in Bethlehem, where they find the toddler Jesus with his mother. What was it about this child that led them to proffer him their gifts of gold, frankincense, and myrrh and to prostrate themselves in worship? As the first Gentile disciples of Christ, the magi model radical trust in the God of creation who reveals his son to them through the light of a star.

Connecting the Gospel

to the first and second readings: In a way, the journey of the magi is foretold in the first reading from the prophet Isaiah where the people of Israel are told, "Nations shall walk by your light." Jesus, the light of the world, is revealed by the brightness of a star that leads foreigners to the land of Israel and to the savior born there. In seeking to unite all people to himself, Jesus unifies those who were once separate. St. Paul proclaims in his letter to the Ephesians, "[T]he Gentiles are coheirs, members of the same body, / and copartners in the promise of Christ Jesus through the gospel."

to experience: In Christianity we are called to renounce the idea that the world is divided into "us" and "them." All people are invited to walk in the light of the star of Bethlehem. While our journeys of faith might take us along different routes, the same God of creation, manifested to us in his Son, Jesus Christ, awaits us with arms stretched wide to gather the entire world to himself.

Connecting the Responsorial Psalm

to the readings: Today's psalm offers a vision of kings traveling from far-off lands to pay tribute to the king of Israel who will bring about justice and peace in his time. When we consider a king, we might think of a palace, riches, servants, and luxury. This is not what the magi found when they traveled from afar to seek the "newborn king of the Jews." Instead, the child and his mother dwell in a simple house in Bethlehem. And yet, the magi offer gifts and prostrate themselves in worship.

to psalmist preparation: God, the King, comes to us in the ordinary form of a toddler in the small town of Bethlehem. The word "epiphany" means manifestation or revelation. Where do you find God manifested or revealed in your life?

PROMPTS FOR FAITH-SHARING

In the first reading, the prophet Isaiah tells the people of God, "Nations shall walk by your light." How do you see God's church acting as a light in the world today?

As evident in the second reading from St. Paul's letter to the Ephesians, the early church struggled to form a unified community made up of both Gentiles and Jews. Within your own parish community, what groups struggle to live in communion with each other? How might God be calling you to work toward unity?

Within the gospel reading today, nature itself, in the form of a star, proclaims the birth of Jesus, the Son of God. From your own encounters with the natural world, what have you gleaned about the God of creation?

The magi find the newborn king they seek, not in a palace but in a humble house in Bethlehem. Where do you find Christ's light and love in the ordinary?

Model Penitential Act

Presider: In the first reading, the prophet Isaiah proclaims, "Rise up in splendor, Jerusalem! Your light has come." On this feast of Epiphany let us greet Jesus Christ, the light of the world, and invite him to illuminate the darkness within our lives . . . *[pause]*

Lord Jesus, you call all nations and peoples to walk in your light: Lord, have mercy.
Christ Jesus, you are the source of true justice and profound peace: Christ, have mercy.
Lord Jesus, you fulfill the words of the prophets: Lord, have mercy.

Homily Points

• In a little over six months, on the Twenty-First Sunday in Ordinary Time, we will read the gospel where Jesus asks his disciples, "Who do you say that I am?" (Matt 16:15). If our central desire as Christians is to deepen our relationship with Christ, this question offers us a lens through which to read and reflect on all the gospel readings throughout our church year. Who do we profess Jesus to be? And what is revealed anew to us through the word of God when we encounter him in the Scriptures?

• On the feast of the Epiphany we look to Jesus particularly as the manifestation and revelation of the living God. When we read the gospel closely, we are given many details about this child who is sought by the magi. The prophets proclaim that he will be both a ruler and a shepherd for the people of Israel. The star that leads these foreigners to Bethlehem shows us that he is for all people, not just those whose heritage he shares.

• Through his humble birth Jesus enters into our reality, God become truly human. This is the king whom the magi prostrate themselves before, a toddler at home in the small village of Bethlehem with his mother, Mary. The revelation of Christ to each of us is not a once-and-for-all event, but one that continues throughout our lives. Along each step of the journey, we might formulate a different answer to the question echoing in our hearts from the one who cannot be contained or defined by human intellect: "Who do you say that I am?" Like the magi may we continue to follow the stars in our lives that lead us closer and closer to Jesus' divine presence within the holy and the ordinary.

Model Universal Prayer (Prayer of the Faithful)

Presider: With faith in the God of glory and justice, let us bring our needs and desires before the Lord.

Response: Lord, hear our prayer.

For the ministers of the church throughout the world, may their dedication to welcoming and encountering those of other faiths grow ever stronger . . .

For members of the diverse religions of our world, may respectful dialogue promote peace and harmony for all . . .

For children worldwide, especially those caught in the crosshairs of violence and war, may they know protection and safety, and experience healing from trauma . . .

For all gathered here, may we seek to manifest Jesus, the light of the world, through lives well lived and love poured out . . .

Presider: God of creation, through the shining of a star, you revealed your son's birth to the magi. Hear our prayers that we, too, might be attentive to your light shining in the darkness. We ask this through Christ our Lord. **Amen.**

COLLECT

Let us pray.

Pause for silent prayer

O God, who on this day
revealed your Only Begotten Son to the nations
by the guidance of a star,
grant in your mercy
that we, who know you already by faith,
may be brought to behold the beauty of your sublime glory.
Through our Lord Jesus Christ, your Son,
who lives and reigns with you in the unity of the Holy Spirit,
one God, for ever and ever. Amen.

FIRST READING

Isa 60:1-6

Rise up in splendor, Jerusalem! Your light has come,
the glory of the Lord shines upon you.
See, darkness covers the earth,
and thick clouds cover the peoples;
but upon you the LORD shines,
and over you appears his glory.
Nations shall walk by your light,
and kings by your shining radiance.
Raise your eyes and look about;
they all gather and come to you:
your sons come from afar,
and your daughters in the arms of their nurses.

Then you shall be radiant at what you see,
your heart shall throb and overflow,
for the riches of the sea shall be emptied out before you,
the wealth of nations shall be brought to you.
Caravans of camels shall fill you,
dromedaries from Midian and Ephah;
all from Sheba shall come
bearing gold and frankincense,
and proclaiming the praises of the LORD.

RESPONSORIAL PSALM
Ps 72:1-2, 7-8, 10-11, 12-13

℟. (cf. 11) Lord, every nation on earth will adore you.

O God, with your judgment endow the king,
and with your justice, the king's son;
he shall govern your people with justice
and your afflicted ones with judgment.

℟. Lord, every nation on earth will adore you.

Justice shall flower in his days,
and profound peace, till the moon be no more.
May he rule from sea to sea,
and from the River to the ends of the earth.

℟. Lord, every nation on earth will adore you.

The kings of Tarshish and the Isles shall offer gifts;
the kings of Arabia and Seba shall bring tribute.
All kings shall pay him homage,
all nations shall serve him.

℟. Lord, every nation on earth will adore you.

For he shall rescue the poor when he cries out,
and the afflicted when he has no one to help him.
He shall have pity for the lowly and the poor;
the lives of the poor he shall save.

℟. Lord, every nation on earth will adore you.

SECOND READING
Eph 3:2-3a, 5-6

Brothers and sisters:
You have heard of the stewardship of God's grace
that was given to me for your benefit,
namely, that the mystery was made known to me by revelation.
It was not made known to people in other generations
as it has now been revealed
to his holy apostles and prophets by the Spirit:
that the Gentiles are coheirs, members of the same body,
and copartners in the promise in Christ Jesus through the gospel.

CATECHESIS

About Liturgy

The liturgy as an epiphany: Epiphany is not merely a celebration of a past event. Yes, we recall the magi who followed the star and studied the signs of the times to find the Christ Child. We commemorate their homage of the newborn king by gifts of gold, frankincense, and myrrh. And we memorialize their courage to change their path and resist the injustice of worldly rulers.

However, if today's solemnity remains only an ancient story, we miss the greater epiphany that the Spirit reveals to us every time we are gathered and sent from our Sunday Eucharist. Our liturgical journey from baptism until our final return home to God's kingdom is an epiphany. It is a lifelong opportunity for us to not only follow Christ's light but also make known to all generations what has been revealed in Christ—that the promise of salvation is given to all people. Entrusted with the light of Christ, we bring the gift of ourselves to the feet of Christ, and from that posture of praise and thanksgiving, we are sent, changed, to live a new way and called to glorify God by our lives.

About Initiation

We exist to evangelize: In his apostolic exhortation On Evangelization in the Modern World, Blessed Paul VI said, "Those who have received the Good News and who have been gathered by it into the community of salvation can and must communicate and spread it . . . Evangelizing is in fact the grace and vocation proper to the Church, her deepest identity. She exists in order to evangelize" (13–14).

The first period of the RCIA is officially titled the period of evangelization and precatechumenate. That title is important because it reminds us of what this period and this entire process are about. The first step in making disciples is not an interview or a series of inquiry sessions. It's evangelization! We proclaim the gospel, through our actions and words, to those who have never heard of Jesus or do not know that there is hope and meaning in life through Christ. The reason we do this is not so they can become experts in Catholicism but so they can become "copartners in the promise" (second reading) and evangelizers themselves of the good news of Christ to others who long to hear that message.

About Liturgical Music

Music ministers as evangelists: If we take Blessed Paul VI's quote above seriously, then the core purpose of music ministry is evangelization. We do this namely through leadership of musical prayer that enables the gathered assembly to participate fully in the communal rites of the church. Yet whatever approach we use, the core purpose of why we do this must always be there.

Singers and musicians may be excellent at performing their music, but they cannot authentically evangelize through their music unless they are living their faith in all aspects of their lives. You can begin to help them do this by making sure music rehearsals include prayer and some reflection or sharing of faith, even if it is brief. Schedule a retreat day for music ministers that helps them return to the focus of their ministry, which is announcing the good news of Christ by their very lives. Teach them to reflect on the meaning of the words they sing and their implications for how we are to live as disciples. Music leaders should also strengthen their own faith-sharing disciplines. A good start is simply to pray each day that God will give you an opportunity to share your faith with another person.

SPIRITUALITY

GOSPEL ACCLAMATION
cf. Mark 9:7

℟. Alleluia, alleluia.
The heavens were opened and the voice of the Father thundered:
This is my beloved Son, listen to him.
℟. Alleluia, alleluia.

Gospel

Matt 3:13-17; L21A

Jesus came from Galilee to John at the Jordan
to be baptized by him.
John tried to prevent him, saying,
"I need to be baptized by you,
and yet you are coming to me?"
Jesus said to him in reply,
"Allow it now, for thus it is fitting for us
to fulfill all righteousness."
Then he allowed him.
After Jesus was baptized,
he came up from the water and behold,
the heavens were opened for him,
and he saw the Spirit of God descending like a dove
and coming upon him.
And a voice came from the heavens, saying,
"This is my beloved Son, with whom I am well pleased."

Reflecting on the Gospel

Have you ever heard a story and then retold it to make it "better"? Maybe it was a question of timing, or introductions, or clarifying motivation. There are many ways stories are told and retold, and often they do get better in the retelling. This is what happens in today's gospel when we hear Matthew's version of the baptism of Jesus by John. The story Matthew had at hand was from Mark. There, John is said to have preached a baptism of repentance for the forgiveness of sins. So one question naturally arises: why would (sinless) Jesus undergo baptism for the forgiveness of sins? Also, Matthew has an entire infancy narrative with Joseph and Mary privy to his identity, something entirely absent from Mark's version. Thus, in Mark the heavenly voice says, "You are my beloved son" (addressed to Jesus). Not so in Matthew, where the heavenly voice says, "This is my beloved son." In Matthew, the voice is not for Jesus' sake but for the crowds. In these and in many other ways Matthew has improved the story—made it "better."

The theological sophistication Matthew demonstrates is significant. He recognizes that John baptizing Jesus is a theological quandary. Thus, Matthew includes the exchange between these two. John protests and recognizes that he is the one who should be baptized by Jesus. Jesus does not match the apocalyptic vision John has been preaching. Instead, Jesus is mixing with sinners, those truly in need of baptism. In short, John objects to this state of affairs. But Jesus holds his ground and proposes that they proceed to fulfill "righteousness," which means something like fulfilling what has been prophesied. The salvific intent of God has been foretold in the Scriptures. Each now is to play a designated part.

The command "Allow it now" by Jesus is followed by the straightforward "Then he allowed him." This, too, echoes ancient Scripture whereby God would command and it would be followed. For example, in Genesis when God said to Abram, "[G]et up and go," Abram "got up and went." This is a classic "command-execution" formula.

Ultimately, the gospel passage we read today is not so much about the baptism of Jesus as it is about the revelation of Jesus' identity to John and the others. Even the passive voice phrase "After Jesus was baptized" is only one word in Greek. Matthew spends much more time on the revelation of Jesus' identity, the spirit of God, and the voice from heaven. As with so many episodes in the gospel, we would do well to focus on the theological insights conveyed by the author.

Living the Paschal Mystery

Baptism is an ancient practice with some roots in the Essene community and in the ministry of John. Many of those ancient Jewish people who felt a need to repent of sin and experience forgiveness were baptized by John in the Jordan. How strange then that Jesus, too, went to John to be baptized. This has been a theological quandary ever since. Each evangelist handles the matter in a slightly different way, with the Gospel of John skipping the baptism altogether, so that John simply testifies to Jesus as the Lamb of God!

Baptism will be the way new members, too, are grafted on to this people of God, in imitation of Jesus himself. At the conclusion of Matthew's gospel, Jesus commands the Eleven to go to the nations (Gentiles) and make disciples by baptizing them.

We see baptism then as a dying to a former way of life and living now for God. Once baptized we are welcomed into the family of God, living a life in the spirit, the same spirit that animated the ministry of Jesus. On this feast of the baptism, let us recall the meaning of our own baptism and live lives worthy of that call.

Focusing the Gospel

Key words and phrases: "I need to be baptized by you, / and yet you are coming to me?"

To the point: In this one question we encounter the entire "scandal of the incarnation." Why would the divine creator of the world take on mortal flesh? Why would the sinless one partake in a baptism of repentance? Why would the master of the universe kneel to wash his disciples' feet? And why would he remain on the cross to suffer a painful and agonizing death? Our surprise might match that of John the Baptist, and yet here on the banks of the Jordan River we find Jesus revealing once again that within himself there is no separation between the human and the divine. And so, of course, we find the Savior of the world among the sinners in order to fulfill all righteousness.

Connecting the Gospel

to the second reading: The second reading from the Acts of the Apostles comes immediately before the baptism of Cornelius, a Roman centurion, who has sent for Peter to come to his house and speak to him about Jesus. In the verses before this reading Peter has a vision in which God proclaims that all foods are now clean. In speaking to Cornelius, Peter equates his vision of all categories of foods as clean with all categories of people: "God has shown me that I should not call any person profane or unclean" (10:28; NABRE). Cornelius and his household accept Peter's testimony about Jesus and even as he continues to speak, "the Holy Spirit fell upon all who were listening to the word." Peter asks the Jewish Christians who have accompanied him to Cornelius's house, "Can anyone withhold the water for baptizing these people who have received the Holy Spirit even as we have?" (10:45, 47; NABRE).

to experience: In entering the waters of the Jordan for his baptism, Jesus sanctifies them. Baptism's holy waters continues to call us and all people to new life in Christ.

Connecting the Responsorial Psalm

to the readings: In the responsorial psalm, the image of water is evoked twice. We hear that "the voice of the Lord is over the waters, / the Lord, over vast waters." And then that "[t]he Lord is enthroned above the flood." The first image reminds us of the waters of creation when "a mighty wind" swept over the waters (Gen 1:2; NABRE). The second of the great flood that washes creation clean again in the time of Noah. Both of these moments are referred to in the Rite of Baptism when the water in the font is blessed. The presider prays, "At the very dawn of creation your Spirit breathed on the waters, making them the wellspring of holiness. The waters of the great flood you made a sign of the waters of baptism, that make an end of sin and a new beginning of goodness" (54).

to psalmist preparation: In our everyday life, water cleanses and sustains us. How do you celebrate, remember, and renew the cleansing, sustaining power of your own baptism?

PROMPTS FOR FAITH-SHARING

Each year we celebrate the feast of the Baptism of the Lord, an important moment in Jesus' life and a transition to his public ministry. How do you celebrate the anniversary of your own baptism?

The first reading from the prophet Isaiah seems to contain an oxymoron—the Lord's chosen one will "bring forth justice to nations" while "not crying out, not shouting, / not making his voice heard in the street." Who models this quiet, nonviolent justice for you?

In the Acts of the Apostles, Peter ends his summary of Jesus' ministry by stating, "He went about doing good / and healing all those oppressed by the devil, / for God was with him." How does your family and parish community continue to carry out the ministry of Jesus?

After Jesus is baptized, a voice from the heavens proclaims, "This is my beloved Son, with whom I am well pleased." From this place of "belovedness" Jesus begins his public ministry. How would it change your ministry if you were to hear the voice of God proclaim to you each day, "You are my beloved in whom I am well pleased"?

Model Rite for the Blessing and Sprinkling of Water

Presider: After Jesus' baptism in the Jordan River, a voice from the heavens proclaims, "This is my beloved Son, with whom I am well pleased." May this holy water remind us of the joy of our own baptism and strengthen us to live out our lives filled with the love of Jesus . . . *[pause]*

[*continue with* The Roman Missal, *Appendix II*]

Homily Points

• Today's feast of the Baptism of the Lord marks the end of the Christmas season within our liturgical year. Tomorrow will be the first Monday of Ordinary Time. Today's feast also marks a transition in the life of Jesus from his quiet, family life in Nazareth to the active years of his public ministry. It is telling that in the life of Christ the vast majority of his years were occupied with the tasks of everyday living: working as a carpenter, eating meals with his family, praying in the synagogue, and making pilgrimages to worship in the temple in Jerusalem.

• In the Christmas season, we might have also experienced a time of "being" instead of "doing." With the chaos of Christmas preparation over, hopefully these last few weeks have been a time to spend with family and friends and to live out the joy of the incarnation, to grow closer to Emmanuel, God with us.

• Beginning tomorrow, as we enter Ordinary Time, we are invited to begin to integrate what we have experienced throughout this holy season. What have you encountered in the gospels of Christmas, the feast of the Holy Family, the solemnity of Mary, Epiphany, and the Baptism of the Lord that has touched your life in a new and different way? And as you continue your life in the world through work or school or community service and interaction, how can you bring what you have experienced with you? In the waters of our own baptism we were anointed priest, prophet, and king, and assured of our own "belovedness" as a daughter or son of the living God. How is God calling you to live out this belovedness in your own public ministry?

Model Universal Prayer (Prayer of the Faithful)

Presider: Confident in God's grace and trusting in his mercy, we dare to bring our needs before the Lord.

Response: Lord, hear our prayer.

For God's holy church, may it continue Jesus' ministry by constantly doing good works and offering healing to those oppressed in body, mind, and spirit . . .

For places in the world infected by the scourge of slavery, exploitation, and human trafficking, may God raise up just leaders and advocates to effect change . . .

For all who profit from the oppression of others, may the God of mercy show the way of repentance and right relationship with all . . .

For all gathered here, renewed by the grace of our own baptism, may we be rooted in our true identity as beloved children of God . . .

Presider: God of justice and peace, you sent your son, Jesus, to show us the way of your kingdom where the vulnerable are safeguarded and sinners are redeemed. Hear our prayers that, emboldened with your divine hope and grace, we might bear witness to your endless mercy. We ask this through Christ our Lord. **Amen.**

COLLECT

Let us pray

Pause for silent prayer

Almighty ever-living God,
who, when Christ had been baptized in the
River Jordan
and as the Holy Spirit descended upon
him,
solemnly declared him your beloved Son,
grant that your children by adoption,
reborn of water and the Holy Spirit,
may always be well pleasing to you.
Through our Lord Jesus Christ, your Son,
who lives and reigns with you in the unity
of the Holy Spirit,
one God, for ever and ever. **Amen.**

FIRST READING

Isa 42:1-4, 6-7

Thus says the LORD:
Here is my servant whom I uphold,
my chosen one with whom I am pleased,
upon whom I have put my spirit;
he shall bring forth justice to the
nations,
not crying out, not shouting,
not making his voice heard in the street.
A bruised reed he shall not break,
and a smoldering wick he shall not
quench,
until he establishes justice on the earth;
the coastlands will wait for his teaching.

I, the LORD, have called you for the victory
of justice,
I have grasped you by the hand;
I formed you, and set you
as a covenant of the people,
a light for the nations,
to open the eyes of the blind,
to bring out prisoners from confinement,
and from the dungeon, those who live in
darkness.

RESPONSORIAL PSALM
Ps 29:1-2, 3-4, 9-10

℟. (11b) The Lord will bless his people with peace.

Give to the LORD, you sons of God,
give to the LORD glory and praise,
give to the LORD the glory due his name;
adore the LORD in holy attire.

℟. The Lord will bless his people with peace.

The voice of the LORD is over the waters,
the LORD, over vast waters.
The voice of the LORD is mighty;
the voice of the LORD is majestic.

℟. The Lord will bless his people with peace.

The God of glory thunders,
and in his temple all say, "Glory!"
The LORD is enthroned above the flood;
the LORD is enthroned as king forever.

℟. The Lord will bless his people with peace.

SECOND READING
Acts 10:34-38

Peter proceeded to speak to those gathered
in the house of Cornelius, saying:
"In truth, I see that God shows no partiality.
Rather, in every nation whoever fears him
and acts uprightly
is acceptable to him.
You know the word that he sent to the Israelites
as he proclaimed peace through Jesus Christ, who is Lord of all,
what has happened all over Judea,
beginning in Galilee after the baptism
that John preached,
how God anointed Jesus of Nazareth
with the Holy Spirit and power.
He went about doing good
and healing all those oppressed by the devil,
for God was with him."

About Liturgy

The dignity of baptism: When the Christmas season officially ends with a commemoration of a moment in the life of the adult Jesus, it reminds all of us that Christmas is not simply about a baby. The incarnation is more than just a beautiful manger scene. Christmas recalls the inauguration of Christ's mission to the world, a mission that will require of Jesus (and of us) to make difficult choices for the sake of God's kingdom. In Jesus' life, and in ours as his followers, that mission began with baptism.

Today's feast is an opportune moment for all of us to recall the dignity of our baptism. Baptism is the sacramental beginning of a life of missionary discipleship and the doorway to all the sacraments. It is what makes us full and complete members of Christ's body.

Let us be aware of anything we do or say that may lessen the dignity of the baptized or communicate that one needs something more than baptism to be recognized as members of God's holy priesthood: "By Baptism they share in the priesthood of Christ, in his prophetic and royal mission . . . Baptism gives a share in the common priesthood of all believers" (*Catechism of the Catholic Church* 1268).

About Initiation

Doorway to the sacraments: The *Catechism of the Catholic Church* says that baptism is "the door which gives access to the other sacraments" (1213). Most of the people we work with in RCIA are already baptized but are uncatechized and preparing to celebrate confirmation and Eucharist. Or, they are baptized in other Christian traditions and are being received into the Full Communion of the Catholic Church. In our parishes, we also may have young people preparing to be confirmed or to celebrate First Communion. You also probably have a few couples who are preparing for marriage or maybe even a person entering the process for ordination. No doubt, you also have baptized Catholics in need of reconciliation or anointing of the sick.

Today's feast is an opportune time to help all these baptized members of the common priesthood of believers recall and give thanks for their baptism. You might encourage presiders to include the sprinkling rite and a renewal of baptismal promises in today's liturgies. If you have persons who are ready, today may also be a good day to celebrate the Rite of Reception of Baptized Christians in the Full Communion of the Catholic Church.

About Liturgical Music

Christmas into Ordinary Time: For most people, it will feel strange to still hear Christmas songs at today's Mass in the middle of January! Yet that is the countercultural beauty of our liturgical year. The way we observe time as Christians shapes our outlook into the world. Christ's birth was not for just one day but for all time. Most important, our commemoration of his birth always includes his mission as an adult. So look for Christmas songs that turn our attention toward the work of salvation that we see in the life of the adult Christ.

Some suggestions: A familiar carol that helps us recall the mission of Christ is "Good Christian Friends, Rejoice" (traditional) with its reminder that Christ was born to save. Another traditional hymn is "Songs of Thankfulness and Praise" whose text refers to the three manifestations of Christ: to the magi, at the Jordan, and at the wedding at Cana. A lovely contemporary carol is "Wood of the Cradle" by Francis Patrick O'Brien (GIA). The text connects Christmas to Easter by linking the manger and the cross, places where we are fed by the Word made flesh.

ORDINARY TIME I

SPIRITUALITY

GOSPEL ACCLAMATION
John 1:14a, 12a

℟. Alleluia, alleluia.
The Word of God became flesh and dwelt among us.
To those who accepted him,
he gave power to become children of God.
℟. Alleluia, alleluia.

Gospel

John 1:29-34; L64A

John the Baptist saw Jesus coming toward him and said,
"Behold, the Lamb of God, who takes away the sin of the world.
He is the one of whom I said,
'A man is coming after me who ranks ahead of me
because he existed before me.'
I did not know him,
but the reason why I came baptizing with water
was that he might be made known to Israel."
John testified further, saying,
"I saw the Spirit come down like a dove from heaven
and remain upon him.
I did not know him,
but the one who sent me to baptize with water told me,
'On whomever you see the Spirit come down and remain,
he is the one who will baptize with the Holy Spirit.'
Now I have seen and testified that he is the Son of God."

Reflecting on the Gospel

Most children love magicians; they love to see them perform at birthday parties, events, and special shows. Magicians sometimes say they are more properly called "illusionists," because that title more closely reflects what they actually do. They perform illusions rather than magic. We might say they are creating the illusion of magic. We think we see something, maybe a rabbit pulled from a hat or a card that disappears, but it is only an illusion.

In reading today's gospel from John, we may think Jesus is baptized. But when we look at the story more carefully, we see that there's no baptism at all. The story is about John the Baptist, but his role is not to baptize Jesus. Instead, it is to testify to Jesus—a testament that, namely, Jesus is the Son of God. This title is significant for the Gospel of John, and it appears in the closing verse of the gospel (prior to the epilogue): "[T]hese [things] are written that you may come to believe that Jesus is the Christ, the Son of God, and that through this belief you may have life in his name" (20:31; NABRE).

So what John the Baptist testifies to in the beginning, that Jesus is the Son of God, is the entire purpose of the gospel. And all of this is done without Jesus being baptized. We would need the other gospels to learn that Jesus was indeed baptized by John. This gospel gracefully omits that detail.

In addition to this narrative sleight of hand, the Gospel of John also claims that Jesus "existed before" John the Baptist. The prologue makes this clear in identifying the word of God in the beginning, and that the Word was made flesh. But here we have pre-existence on the lips of the Baptist himself. No other gospel is quite so explicit about this theological point. And the Baptist continues by saying the only reason he was baptizing at all was to give testimony to this one who "might be made known to Israel."

When we read the Gospel of John, let's pay special attention to the words he uses and the theological claims he makes. Otherwise, we might miss the essential truth and mistake it with a glance of an illusion. We are so familiar with these stories and the gospels, we can see what we already "know" and miss a deeper insight.

Living the Paschal Mystery

St. Paul tells us that we have been baptized into Christ's death (Rom 6:3). Mark speaks of John's baptism of repentance for the forgiveness of sins, which Jesus also underwent (Mark 1:4, 9). But John the Baptist appears in the Fourth Gospel not to baptize Jesus, but to testify to him. Baptism, this foundational sacrament of water, has a multiplicity of meanings and interpretations in the New Testament and also for us today. When we dip our fingers into the holy water at church, we are reminded that we have been baptized into Christ's death, with the forgiveness of sins. Then we, as his followers, are to testify to him in the world. Our belief in Jesus as the Son of God gives life in his name. We live this life having undergone the paschal mystery in our own baptism from death to new life.

Focusing the Gospel

Key words and phrases: "Behold, the Lamb of God, who takes away the sin of the world."

To the point: Written last of all the gospels, John's word could be considered the fruit of the longest reflection on the person and mission of Jesus, the Christ. From the very first chapter, the evangelist tells us who Jesus is: "the Lamb of God, who takes away the sin of the world." At the very beginning of Jesus' ministry, John the Baptist alludes to its completion on the wood of the cross, where Jesus, the sacrificial lamb, becomes the ultimate paschal sacrifice to deliver the people from death, just as the blood of the lamb caused the angel of death to pass over the households of the Hebrew people living in slavery in Egypt.

Connecting the Gospel

to the first and second readings: Along with proclaiming Jesus as the Lamb of God, John the Baptist also tells us what this Lamb has come to the earth to do: "baptize with the Holy Spirit." The first and second readings show us what this baptism will enable and call us to. Through the prophet Isaiah, God tells the people of Israel, "I will make you a light to the nations." Speaking to the Corinthians, St. Paul proclaims "you . . . have been sanctified in Christ Jesus, called to be holy." To be holy, to be a light, are not things that people can cause by the force of their own will. Only through the power of the Holy Spirit can our intentions to follow in the footsteps of Jesus, the Lamb of God, be fulfilled.

to experience: Baptism is an image of immersion, to be completely submerged in a substance and then to emerge as a new creation. In the baptism that Jesus confers we are invited to view our lives as plunged into the holy and surrounded by the light and life of God.

Connecting the Responsorial Psalm

to the readings: Throughout the history of salvation, God has called upon human collaborators to work with him in building the kingdom of God on the earth. In today's responsorial psalm, "Here am I, Lord; I come to do your will," we find the response we can imagine must please the Lord above all others, a ready and willing partner to be God's hands, heart, and love in the world. In the first reading the people of Israel are invited to take on this role, to be the servant through whom God shows his glory, and a light that will reach out to all nations. In the gospel, John the Baptist is the one who heralds the Son of God's presence, and in the second reading St. Paul tells the Corinthians that now it is they who have been sanctified and are "called to be holy."

to psalmist preparation: God's work, and ours, has not yet been completed. We are the ones who are now invited to tell the Lord, "Here I am, I come to do your will."

PROMPTS FOR FAITH-SHARING

Once again, we have entered into Ordinary Time following the season of Christmas. While Lent, Advent, Christmas, and Easter all have their own themes and practices, sometimes Ordinary Time can seem, well, ordinary. How would you like to keep this time of living and growing in faith?

Speaking through the prophet Isaiah, God tells the people of Israel, "I will make you a light to the nations, / that my salvation may reach the ends of the earth." Where is light most needed now in the world? How might the church seek to be this light in darkness?

The psalmist sings, "I have waited, waited for the Lord." Patience is a difficult spiritual virtue to cultivate. How do you "wait on the Lord" and what practices help you in times where patience is required?

In his greeting to the church in Corinth, St. Paul reminds the people that they have been sanctified and called to holiness. Who models holiness for you in everyday life?

Model Penitential Act

Presider: In today's gospel, John the Baptist tells his disciples that Jesus is the Lamb of God who takes away the sins of the world. To prepare our hearts and minds to encounter Jesus in word and sacrament, let us offer up to him the burden of our own sins and ask for healing and mercy . . . *[pause]*

Lord Jesus, you are the Lamb of God, who takes away the sins of the world: Lord, have mercy.

Christ Jesus, in you we are sanctified and called to holiness: Christ, have mercy.

Lord Jesus, Son of God, you baptize us in the Holy Spirit: Lord, have mercy.

Homily Points

• Only two and a half weeks have passed since New Year's Day, with its tradition of making resolutions. You could say our innately human desire for transformation and transcendence can be seen in this practice. And yet, research reveals that by the end of January, around 40 percent of those who made resolutions will already have broken them. While we might look at this figure as proof of the futility of trying to turn over a new leaf, the second reading from St. Paul's letter to the Corinthians offers another perspective.

• Having heard of factions, dissent, and some immorality within the church in Corinth, St. Paul writes a letter to the community urging them to remember who they are: disciples of Christ "who have been sanctified" and are "called to be holy." Rather than condemning or berating the erring community, Paul speaks to them as brothers and sisters in faith and issues anew the call to conversion.

• Our own path to holiness might involve many different twists and turns. In five more weeks, on the second Sunday in Ordinary Time and the last Sunday before the season of Lent (another time of resolutions and promises), the gospel from Matthew will urge us to "be perfect, just as your heavenly Father is perfect." We might wonder, why did Jesus give us a commandment we were bound to fail at? And we *will* fail if we try to fulfill it on our own. Only through the healing of the Lamb of God and the strength that comes by his baptism in the Holy Spirit can we hope to live out these words fully. And then, when we fail, to listen for the voice of God telling us who we really are: holy and sanctified and called to start anew.

Model Universal Prayer (Prayer of the Faithful)

Presider: Nourished and strengthened by the word of God, we now bring our petitions before our Lord, knowing he hears and answers all our prayers.

Response: Lord, hear our prayer.

For the entire people of God, may they be inspired by the witness of holy men and women throughout the ages to embrace the universal call to holiness . . .

For officials in elected office throughout the world, may they be strengthened to lead lives of integrity and service while promoting the common good . . .

For family members and caregivers of those struggling with addiction, may they receive the support and resources necessary to care for themselves as they extend care and mercy to others . . .

For all gathered here, may we echo the words of today's psalm with hearts sanctified by the Holy Spirit, "Here am I, Lord; I come to do your will" . . .

Presider: Heavenly Father, our strength and our hope, you never cease to call all people to holiness. Hear our prayers that, baptized with the Holy Spirit and sealed in grace, we might embody your light, justice, and mercy in lives well lived. We ask this through Christ our Lord. **Amen.**

COLLECT

Let us pray.

Pause for silent prayer

Almighty ever-living God,
who govern all things,
both in heaven and on earth,
mercifully hear the pleading of your people
and bestow your peace on our times.
Through our Lord Jesus Christ, your Son,
who lives and reigns with you in the unity of the Holy Spirit,
one God, for ever and ever. **Amen.**

FIRST READING

Isa 49:3, 5-6

The LORD said to me: You are my servant,
Israel, through whom I show my glory.
Now the LORD has spoken
who formed me as his servant from the womb,
that Jacob may be brought back to him
and Israel gathered to him;
and I am made glorious in the sight of the LORD,
and my God is now my strength!
It is too little, the LORD says, for you to be my servant,
to raise up the tribes of Jacob,
and restore the survivors of Israel;
I will make you a light to the nations,
that my salvation may reach to the ends of the earth.

RESPONSORIAL PSALM
Ps 40:2, 4, 7-8, 8-9, 10

℟. (8a and 9a) Here am I, Lord; I come to do your will.

I have waited, waited for the LORD,
  and he stooped toward me and heard
    my cry.
And he put a new song into my mouth,
  a hymn to our God.

℟. Here am I, Lord; I come to do your will.

Sacrifice or offering you wished not,
  but ears open to obedience you gave me.
Holocausts or sin-offerings you sought not;
  then said I, "Behold I come."

℟. Here am I, Lord; I come to do your will.

"In the written scroll it is prescribed for
    me,
to do your will, O my God, is my delight,
  and your law is within my heart!"

℟. Here am I, Lord; I come to do your will.

I announced your justice in the vast
    assembly;
  I did not restrain my lips, as you, O
    LORD, know.

℟. Here am I, Lord; I come to do your will.

SECOND READING
1 Cor 1:1-3

Paul, called to be an apostle of Christ
    Jesus by the will of God,
  and Sosthenes our brother,
  to the church of God that is in Corinth,
  to you who have been sanctified in
      Christ Jesus,
    called to be holy,
  with all those everywhere who call upon
      the name of our Lord
    Jesus Christ, their Lord and ours.
Grace to you and peace from God our
    Father
  and the Lord Jesus Christ.

CATECHESIS

About Liturgy

Week of prayer for Christian unity: During the octave of days between January 18 and 25, the worldwide church each year marks a week of prayer for Christian unity. Pope Benedict XV made this practice, first observed in 1908 by a small group of Roman Catholics and Episcopalians, a universal observance in the Roman Catholic Church in 1916. Since then the church has encouraged Christians around the world to observe this week in prayer for visible unity among all Christians. Be sure to include an intercession in today's Masses for increased dialogue and work toward unity among all Christians.

A return to the ordinary: Many liturgical ministers might be breathing a collective sigh of relief. Finally, we're done with Christmas! Our return to Ordinary Time may mean a return to simpler liturgies in comparison to the previous weeks, but it doesn't mean a settling for ordinariness. When it comes to the Sunday gathering of the assembly in its weekly memorial of the paschal mystery, nothing is ordinary! Remember that "ordinary" in Ordinary Time refers not to the quality of the liturgies but to the ordering of weeks between the seasons of Advent/Christmas and Lent/Easter.

About Initiation

"Converts": Sometimes, one might hear someone use the term "convert" to describe a person who becomes Catholic, whether or not that individual was previously baptized. Even some former Protestants who are now Catholic might self-identify as converts to Catholicism.

As we mark the annual week of prayer for Christian unity, let us always remember that "convert," both theologically and pastorally, should be used to describe only those persons who had never been baptized but now live the Christian faith by their baptism. The United States bishops explain that "the term 'convert' should be reserved strictly for those converted from unbelief to Christian belief and never used of those baptized Christians who are received into the full communion of the Catholic Church" (National Statutes for the Catechumenate 2).

Baptism is always about conversion to Christ. One who is already baptized, whether Catholic or Protestant, has already been converted to Christ. That fundamental orientation to Christ should always be respected in our language and actions—even if the person is not practicing that faith or living it well—because baptism is always God's initiative. It is not we who chose Christ but Christ who chose us.

About Liturgical Music

Doing God's will: In our liturgical music repertoire, we have many well-loved settings of today's responsorial psalm refrain, and this particular psalm is often assigned in the liturgical year and for various rites. For music ministers, how do we take this psalm's meaning to heart?

Read carefully the text of the verses. Although the text is from the psalmist's perspective, the main actor and initiator is God. The psalmist waits for God and listens for God's call. The psalmist does not speak his own words but those placed in his mouth by God. And that message from God is one of justice.

When we think of doing music, we often speak about it as *our* ministry or call, and indeed it is. Yet, carrying out God's will often requires us to do and say things that we do not choose but that are given to us by God to do and announce. Ministry, ultimately, is not ours but God's. Let us approach that call to do God's will with joy, humility, and even a bit of trepidation—for God's will is often not the one we would choose for ourselves.

SPIRITUALITY

GOSPEL ACCLAMATION
cf. Matt 4:23

℟. Alleluia, alleluia.
Jesus proclaimed the Gospel of the kingdom
and cured every disease among the people.
℟. Alleluia, alleluia.

Gospel Matt 4:12-23; L67A

When Jesus heard that John had been arrested,
he withdrew to Galilee.
He left Nazareth and went to live in Capernaum by the sea,
in the region of Zebulun and Naphtali,
that what had been said through Isaiah the prophet
might be fulfilled:
Land of Zebulun and land of Naphtali,
the way to the sea, beyond the Jordan,
Galilee of the Gentiles,
the people who sit in darkness have seen a great light,
on those dwelling in a land overshadowed by death
light has arisen.
From that time on, Jesus began to preach and say,
"Repent, for the kingdom of heaven is at hand."

As he was walking by the Sea of Galilee, he saw two brothers,
Simon who is called Peter, and his brother Andrew,
casting a net into the sea; they were fishermen.
He said to them,
"Come after me, and I will make you fishers of men."
At once they left their nets and followed him.
He walked along from there and saw two other brothers,
James, the son of Zebedee, and his brother John.

Continued in Appendix A, p. 267, or
Matt 4:12-17 *in Appendix A, p. 267.*

Reflecting on the Gospel

Though it's the Third Sunday in Ordinary Time, we now begin reading from the Gospel of Matthew. Last week of course we read from the Gospel of John. But liturgically we are in Cycle A, when we read mostly from Matthew, also known as "the church's Gospel." Matthew gives us so many familiar passages, and critical passages as well, that it might be difficult to imagine the church without the influence of this gospel. In fact, this gospel is the only one even to use the word "church." Even more, the version of the "our Father" that we pray comes from Matthew. The Sermon on the Mount with the eight Beatitudes is in Matthew. Jesus' promise to build the church on the rock that is Peter, is in Matthew.

And as Matthew used Mark as a source, he seems to have reproduced nearly all of his gospel, about 600 of the 661 verses by the count of most scholars. Because nearly all of Mark is found in Matthew, Matthew became the favored gospel between the two. Why read the shorter version (Mark) when the longer one essentially included Mark and much more?

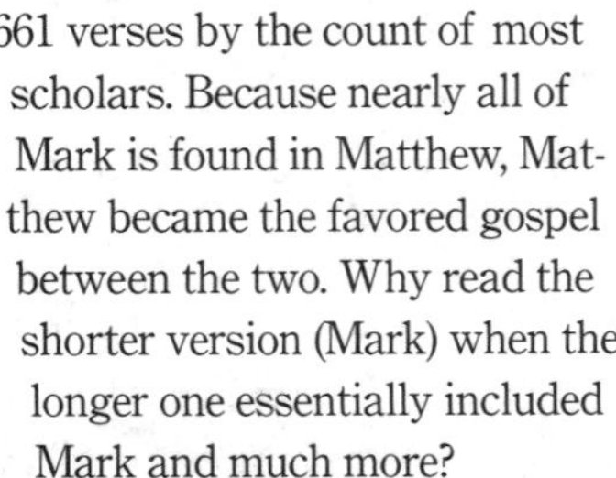

Today, in the story of the call of the first disciples, we see an example of Matthew lengthening the stories that he inherited from Mark. He introduces the story by explaining that Jesus withdrew to Galilee upon learning that John had been arrested. Matthew tells us that this fulfilled Scripture. Mark says no such thing. Further, Matthew tells us that Jesus went to live in Capernaum, as though he might have had a house there. This seems to be a story of a young man striking out on his own after leaving the small town he called home.

The remainder of the story, with the calling of the two sets of brothers, generally follows Mark. But this example demonstrates how Matthew has made the story "better." He gives a rationale for Jesus' withdrawal into Galilee, into Capernaum. And this move actually fulfills Scripture in the eyes of Matthew. As we continue to read from Matthew this liturgical year, we will pay close attention to some unique elements of his theological insight.

Living the Paschal Mystery

Jesus called the disciples near the beginning of his ministry. And he called them two by two, the brothers Simon and Andrew, and James and John. These were fishermen, in some ways the ancient equivalent of today's highly skilled blue-collar workers. They worked with their hands, as even the "mending their nets" indicates. At the invitation of Jesus, they all leave behind their way of life to follow him.

Modern calls to discipleship are scarcely so dramatic. But the imagery presented in Matthew speaks to us when we imagine putting away prior commitments that tend to disintegrate in the face of an invitation from Jesus. We may hear the same call to put aside the tedious, monotonous, quotidian activities that mark our lives and enter into a new relationship with him. This relationship will ultimately lead to a putting away of our entire selves, a dying to ourselves, so that we might rise with him. And that is the paschal mystery. At this, the beginning of Jesus' ministry, we hear the call to follow him to the point of forsaking our very selves. In so doing, we will be raised to new life with him.

Focusing the Gospel

Key words and phrases: "Repent, for the kingdom of heaven is at hand."

To the point: Today's gospel begins with Jesus hearing the news of John the Baptist's arrest and responding by leaving the region of Judea where John's ministry was located to return to Galilee. In John the Baptist's life, Jesus would have seen the risks and dangers of his mission lived out. As the forerunner of the Lord, John preaches repentance and suffers his own martyrdom at the hands of a corrupt person fearful of what this preaching demanded of him in his own life. While it might seem like Jesus is retreating, this is not the case and in Capernaum his words, "Repent, for the kingdom of heaven is at hand," echo the exact refrain of John when he began preaching in the desert of Judea (Matt 3:2).

Connecting the Gospel

to the second reading: In the second reading St. Paul chides the Corinthians for the divisions that threaten to splinter their fledgling Christian community. And he points to the source of their unity, Christ. It is telling that the first action Jesus makes after proclaiming that the kingdom of heaven is at hand is to recruit followers. These disciples will help him as they become "fishers of men." Eventually, it will be up to this group of close friends to take on the work of spreading the good news of God's kingdom to every nation of the earth. They are only able to do it through the power of the Holy Spirit and the unity of the Christian family.

to experience: At times, we can become focused on the personal aspects of faith, but both Jesus and Paul remind us that we are not saved by ourselves; we are saved in community, as the Body of Christ, called to be one.

Connecting the Responsorial Psalm

to the readings: Imagery of light echoes throughout the first reading, the gospel, and the responsorial psalm. We sing together, "The Lord is my light and my salvation." What does this mean? How is Jesus like a light for us? Isaiah gives us a clue when he prophesies, "The people who walked in darkness / have seen a great light." There is an immense difference between trying to walk in darkness and walking in light. In darkness we are unaware of where our steps are taking us or what dangers and obstacles might be in our path. In the gospel these words of the prophet are changed slightly to tell us, "[T]he people who sit in darkness have seen a great light / on those dwelling in a land overshadowed by death / light has arisen." To *sit* in darkness conjures an image of hopelessness and despair. We are consumed by the darkness that covers us and see no way of escape. Within this state it is easy to see how one might become "overshadowed by death," a term that could mean despair or loss of hope and joy.

to psalmist preparation: How do you experience Jesus as "light" and "salvation"?

PROMPTS FOR FAITH-SHARING

The psalm for today proclaims, "The Lord is my light and my salvation; / whom should I fear?" Where does fear most often creep into your life? How might you hand that fear over to God?

In his letter to the Corinthians, St. Paul chides the community for the rivalries and dissensions that threaten to tear it apart. How does your parish community deal with divisions and disagreements? How might God be calling your parish to grow in this area?

The symbolism of light and darkness is highlighted in today's first reading and gospel passage, and indeed, all throughout the sacred Scriptures. When you consider light and darkness, what images spring to mind? How do these images help you to understand Jesus and salvation history?

Jesus begins his preaching with the words, "Repent, for the kingdom of heaven is at hand." Where do you find the kingdom of heaven in the here and now?

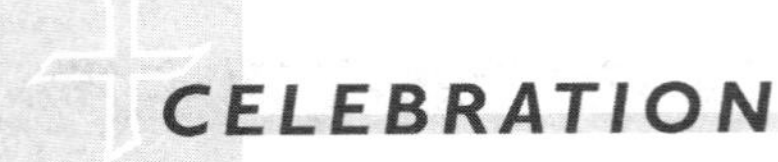

CELEBRATION

Model Penitential Act

Presider: In today's gospel Jesus calls two sets of brothers to join him in his work of proclaiming the kingdom of God. Immediately the brothers leave family and livelihood to follow him. Let us ask for pardon and healing so that we, too, might follow the Lord of life with single-hearted love . . . *[pause]*

Lord Jesus, you fulfill the words of the prophets: Lord, have mercy.

Christ Jesus, you are the light of the world and the salvation of the peoples: Christ, have mercy.

Lord Jesus, you call us to leave everything else behind and follow you: Lord, have mercy.

Homily Points

• In today's gospel we find the first words and the first actions of Jesus within his public ministry. In a way we could say these provide us, in miniature, the core of Jesus' message and his method. The gospel tells us, "From that time on, Jesus began to preach and say, / 'Repent, for the kingdom of heaven is at hand.'" This is a theme we will hear again and again throughout the gospels. Jesus constantly preaches the kingdom of God in his parables, in his moral teachings, and through his actions of healing and reconciliation.

• The preaching of Jesus calls us most immediately to two things: a metanoia, or conversion, in which we turn from that which leads us away from the fullness of life Jesus is offering, and a realization that the kingdom of God is here in our midst. There is no need to delay; if the kingdom is "at hand," we are to live lives worthy of the kingdom in the here and now.

• If Jesus' message is the imminence of God's kingdom, his method is one of collaboration. Jesus' first action within his public ministry is to call four fishermen to join him, inviting them to become "fishers of men." We might expect Jesus, as the Son of God, to be completely sufficient unto himself, and he certainly could have taken this route. But just as God has sought out human collaborators throughout the history of salvation, Jesus does the same. Building and preaching this kingdom is not something he is interested in doing alone. Jesus' message and method continue up to our own moment in history, leading us to ask, how is Jesus calling us to collaborate with him in continuing this work of building and preaching God's kingdom of love and justice on earth?

Model Universal Prayer (Prayer of the Faithful)

Presider: With complete trust, Jesus' first disciples—Peter, Andrew, James, and John—leave behind all that they know to follow Jesus. Emulating their faith, let us bring our petitions before the Lord.

Response: Lord, hear our prayer.

For those who preach the good news of Jesus throughout the world, may they follow Christ with fidelity and serve him with joy . . .

For lawmakers and government officials, may they strive to pass legislation that supports the dignity of all people . . .

For the safety of fishermen and those who make their living on the sea, may they find safe harbor and calm waters . . .

For all gathered here, may we be granted the courage and strength to answer the call of Jesus in our lives . . .

Presider: Heavenly Father, our light and our salvation, you sent your son into the world to usher in the kingdom of heaven here and now. Hear our prayers that we might dedicate our lives to building this kingdom where all are welcome and your peace and justice reign. We ask this through Christ our Lord. **Amen.**

COLLECT

Let us pray.

Pause for silent prayer

Almighty ever-living God,
direct our actions according to your good pleasure,
that in the name of your beloved Son
we may abound in good works.
Through our Lord Jesus Christ, your Son,
who lives and reigns with you in the unity of the Holy Spirit,
one God, for ever and ever. **Amen.**

FIRST READING

Isa 8:23–9:3

First the LORD degraded the land of Zebulun
and the land of Naphtali;
but in the end he has glorified the seaward road,
the land west of the Jordan,
the District of the Gentiles.

Anguish has taken wing, dispelled is darkness:
for there is no gloom where but now there was distress.
The people who walked in darkness
have seen a great light;
upon those who dwelt in the land of gloom a light has shone.
You have brought them abundant joy
and great rejoicing,
as they rejoice before you as at the harvest,
as people make merry when dividing spoils.
For the yoke that burdened them,
the pole on their shoulder,
and the rod of their taskmaster
you have smashed, as on the day of Midian.

CATECHESIS

RESPONSORIAL PSALM
Ps 27:1, 4, 13-14

℟. (1a) The Lord is my light and my salvation.

The LORD is my light and my salvation;
whom should I fear?
The LORD is my life's refuge;
of whom should I be afraid?

℟. The Lord is my light and my salvation.

One thing I ask of the LORD;
this I seek:
to dwell in the house of the LORD
all the days of my life,
that I may gaze on the loveliness of the LORD
and contemplate his temple.

℟. The Lord is my light and my salvation.

I believe that I shall see the bounty of the LORD
in the land of the living.
Wait for the LORD with courage;
be stouthearted, and wait for the LORD.

℟. The Lord is my light and my salvation.

SECOND READING
1 Cor 1:10-13, 17

I urge you, brothers and sisters, in the name of our Lord Jesus Christ,
that all of you agree in what you say,
and that there be no divisions among you,
but that you be united in the same mind and in the same purpose.
For it has been reported to me about you, my brothers and sisters,
by Chloe's people, that there are rivalries among you.
I mean that each of you is saying,
"I belong to Paul," or "I belong to Apollos,"
or "I belong to Cephas," or "I belong to Christ."
Is Christ divided?
Was Paul crucified for you?
Or were you baptized in the name of Paul?
For Christ did not send me to baptize but to preach the gospel,
and not with the wisdom of human eloquence,
so that the cross of Christ might not be emptied of its meaning.

About Liturgy

Discerning one's call to ministry: Last Sunday, John the Baptist testified to Jesus' election by the Spirit to do the Father's will. This Sunday, that appointment to mission is given by Jesus to the first disciples and, by extension, to us. We see a pattern: In the work of announcing the reign of God, we do not volunteer our service; we are chosen for it, and then we respond.

Our participation in the church's liturgy is the way God transforms and strengthens those he has chosen—the baptized—that they may announce God's reign to the world. Liturgical ministry is always at the service of the people of God and their mission in Christ. Its goal is never for one's glorification or personal satisfaction.

As we invite and train new liturgical ministers for service, keep in mind that we are not asking for volunteers or simply filling gaps with anyone willing to help. Rather, we are calling forth fellow disciples to take on a great responsibility in the work of Christ. Therefore, make those invitations with a discerning heart and the seriousness it requires. Pray for wisdom. Then seek out those who show they are ready to respond with total commitment to do God's will.

About Initiation

Rite of Acceptance: The Rite of Acceptance into the Order of Catechumens is the first public ritual in the Rite of Christian Initiation of Adults. It is celebrated for unbaptized persons who are entering into a conversion process for baptism and have been deemed ready to begin training for Christian discipleship. Ideally, a parish would set aside two or three times during the year to celebrate it, if needed (see RCIA 18).

Winter Ordinary Time and this Sunday, in particular, with its gospel reading are good times for this significant ritual. The rite ritualizes God's call to the seekers and their response to that call by following the Gospel of Jesus. As the name describes, this rite enters a person into an official order of the church, that of catechumens. From then on, they have rights to the church's blessings and prayers as well as responsibilities to advance the mission of Christ. Therefore, discern well who is truly ready to answer this call to discipleship.

If you celebrate this rite today, the new catechumens normatively would not be baptized this Easter because they are expected to be in formation for at least one full liturgical year (see National Statutes for the Catechumenate 6).

About Liturgical Music

Divisions and rivalries: At some point in the life of any community, divisions and maybe even rivalries will appear. We see the early church dealing with this in today's second reading. It happens, too, in music ministry.

It used to be common to have one music director for a parish who oversaw the musical leadership for the entire community. Today, however, many parishes have several different persons, choirs, or ensembles taking on musical leadership at the community's various Masses without a common director to unite them or help them work together.

Even if this is your situation, you can still work toward more collaboration and unity among all the music ministers. Strive to instill a culture of shared ministry. Instead of saying, "I belong to the 5:30 p.m. Mass" or "I'm in the contemporary choir," music ministers should see and speak of themselves as *one* music ministry serving the parish. Rehearse together at times. Eat, play, and pray together often. Leaders can gather regularly to do faith-sharing and planning together. Even if you cannot have a common repertoire or leadership, you can still be united in mind, heart, and purpose.

SPIRITUALITY

GOSPEL ACCLAMATION
Luke 2:32

℟. Alleluia, alleluia.
A light of revelation to the Gentiles
and glory for your people Israel.
℟. Alleluia, alleluia.

Gospel

Luke 2:22-40; L524

When the days were completed for their purification
according to the law of Moses,
Mary and Joseph took Jesus up to Jerusalem
to present him to the Lord,
just as it is written in the law of the Lord,
Every male that opens the womb shall be consecrated to the Lord,
and to offer the sacrifice of
a pair of turtledoves or two young pigeons,
in accordance with the dictate in the law of the Lord.

Now there was a man in Jerusalem
whose name was Simeon.
This man was righteous and devout,
awaiting the consolation of Israel,
and the Holy Spirit was upon him.
It had been revealed to him by the Holy Spirit
that he should not see death
before he had seen the Christ of the Lord.
He came in the Spirit into the temple;
and when the parents brought in the child Jesus
to perform the custom of the law in regard to him,
he took him into his arms and blessed God, saying:
"Now, Master, you may let your servant go
in peace, according to your word,
for my eyes have seen your salvation,
which you prepared in sight of all the peoples,
a light for revelation to the Gentiles,
and glory for your people Israel."

Continued in Appendix A, p. 268, or
Luke 2:22-32 *in Appendix A, p. 268.*

Reflecting on the Gospel

When dealing with children or even with adults(!), it's good to keep things fair. We do not want to favor one over the other, for such is the breeding ground of jealousy and resentment. It is important to make sure that there is an even or equitable distribution.

Today's gospel is from Luke, who gives us more stories about women than any other gospel. In fact, often throughout the Gospel of Luke there is a story of a man paired with a story of a woman. And, in fact, we see this pairing today with Simeon and Anna.

Ideally, we will hear the "longer" version of the gospel today to include the story of Anna. There are so few stories of women in the gospels that it does not seem right to read only a portion of the story, in effect clipping out Anna, shortening it so that we hear only about Simeon rather than Simeon and Anna.

Joseph and Mary are fulfilling the obligations of Mosaic Law, the precepts of their faith. Both Simeon and Anna are in the temple, and each encounters the child Jesus—Simeon having been there at the prompting of the Spirit, and Anna because she never left the temple. Both are prophets, though Luke properly uses the feminine form, "prophetess," of Anna. Not only does Anna give thanks to God, but she also speaks about the child to those in her midst.

Luke sets this story in Jerusalem, in the temple, where Zechariah, the priest and father of John the Baptist, first learned that his wife, Elizabeth, would have a son. Jerusalem will also be the location where the gospel ends. Luke is geographically bookending his story as it were.

After Joseph and Mary leave the temple, having fulfilled the precepts of the law, they return to their home in Nazareth, and we never hear of Simeon and Anna again. Their respective prophecies continue themes from Luke that were sounded by Elizabeth and by Mary herself. Jesus is destined to be the rise and fall of many. The hungry will be filled and the rich will be sent away empty.

The gospel story for the presentation of the Lord is "rich" with theological significance and meaning. Luke gives us not only the perfunctory fulfillment of Mosaic Law, but also those actions accompanied by a prophet and by a prophetess. We would do well to read the story to include both Simeon and Anna, and not snub the significant role of a woman to save a few minutes during Mass.

Living the Paschal Mystery

It should go without saying that women figure prominently in some of the most remembered stories about Jesus, including his birth, death, and resurrection. And here today we have the story of his presentation, accompanied by the presence of Simeon and Anna. Many other stories about Jesus feature men so prominently that it seems only right to read today's gospel in its entirety. In so doing, we are reminded of something we know well: women speak the powerful words of God just as men do. In the Old Testament and in the New, women were prophets (prophetesses). When given the opportunity, let us showcase this too often neglected aspect of our rich faith. And in our own world, in our own day and age, let's listen attentively to the prophetesses in our own midst. Luke gives equal voice to the women. We would do well to follow his example.

Focusing the Gospel

Key words and phrases: "[M]y eyes have seen your salvation, / which you prepared in the sight of all the peoples: / a light for revelation to the Gentiles, / and glory for your people Israel."

To the point: Simeon's words in the temple tell us who this child is and who he is meant for. The gift of Jesus, God with us, is hailed in this gospel reading as "consolation," "Christ of the Lord," "salvation," "light," and "glory." Simeon ends his proclamation of praise, which the church treasures to this day in the *Nunc Dimittis* (The Canticle of Simeon), with the universal nature of Jesus' birth. This child, born in humble surroundings to an unknown peasant family, belongs not only to his mother and foster father, to his relatives, or even to his fellow countrymen. This child is light and glory for the whole world. With Simeon and Anna, let us lift our voices in praise!

Connecting the Gospel

to the first reading: In the lectionary, the first reading is chosen to correspond with the gospel. Sometimes the connections can be more obscure, but today's reading from Malachi seems to directly prophesy Simeon's fortuitous meeting with Jesus in the temple. Malachi writes, "[S]uddenly there will come to the temple / the Lord whom you seek, / And the messenger of the covenant whom you desire." Within this passage we have two active participants: the promised one who arrives at the temple, but also the one who waits and longs for his coming.

to experience: In Simeon and Anna we find models of patience and trusting faith in God's promises and goodness. Both have spent years upon years listening to God's word and waiting for God's revelation. Within the gospel passage their immense joy corresponds to the depth of their longing for this moment.

Connecting the Responsorial Psalm

to the readings: The readings today invite us to hold in tension multiple images of our Lord and Savior. The prophet Malachi paints a picture of the one who is coming as "refiner's fire," sent to purify the people. In the letter to the Hebrews, Jesus is the high priest who "expiate[s] the sins of the people" through his own body and blood. In the gospel, he is a helpless baby only a little over a month old, and in today's psalm he is the king of glory, a mighty warrior.

to psalmist preparation: Within our faith we can look at each of these images and we say, "[Y]es, this is our Lord," and yet, often as individual Christians we will find a particular way of looking at Jesus that resonates most within us. No single image, metaphor, or simile can encompass all aspects of Jesus, the Son of God, the second person of the Holy Trinity. Within today's readings, is there a way of considering Jesus that is new for you? How might this image deepen your relationship with Christ?

PROMPTS FOR FAITH-SHARING

The feast of the Presentation of the Lord is a traditional time to have candles blessed that will be used in the home throughout the coming year. On what occasions do you and your family light candles? How does the symbolism of the candle remind you of Jesus' presence?

Through the words of the prophet Malachi, God describes his messenger by saying, "[H]e is like the refiner's fire." When was a time in your life when you felt like you experienced this refining fire of God?

The letter to the Hebrews reminds us that Jesus is able to help us in times of testing, "[b]ecause he himself was tested through what he suffered." In your life of faith, how do you ask for Jesus' help when facing temptation?

In Simeon and Anna we find models of faith, patience, and prophecy. How are you being called in this moment in your life to exercise the spiritual gifts of Simeon and Anna?

CELEBRATION

Model Penitential Act

Presider: On this feast of the Presentation of the Lord, we greet Christ as Anna and Simeon greeted the infant Jesus in the temple, by claiming him as our savior, our consolation, our joy. Together with them, let us draw close to Jesus and humbly ask for his healing and mercy . . . *[pause]*

Lord Jesus, you are the revelation of the merciful love of God: Lord, have mercy.

Christ Jesus, you refine and purify the souls of all who come to you in faith: Christ, have mercy.

Lord Jesus, you are the king of glory and the messenger of God's covenant: Lord, have mercy.

Homily Points

• The feast of the Presentation of the Lord takes place forty days after Christmas and within it we find almost a second epiphany, or revelation of God. A few weeks ago, we pondered the identity of this child who was hailed by the magi as the divine king revealed by a star. Today, Simeon names Jesus salvation and light. Sometimes this feast is referred to as "Candlemas," due to the tradition of the faithful bringing candles to be blessed that will be used throughout the coming year. Some keep this tradition to this day, but in the Middle Ages particularly this was a major feast.

• We can imagine the depth of symbolism for the people of that time who brought their source of light in the darkness (candles) to be blessed as a reminder of the Light that illuminates all darkness. Whereas today we might see candles as something to enhance our prayer or elevate the atmosphere of a room, not so long ago they were absolutely essential to the workings of daily life.

• The imagery of Jesus as light is not unique to this feast. Jesus himself proclaims to the Pharisees in John's gospel, "I am the light of the world. Whoever follows me will not walk in darkness, but will have the light of life" (8:12; NABRE). Even in our modern society we quickly realize how essential light is when a natural disaster or equipment failure causes a power outage. Soon we are reaching for the tools of our ancestors to illuminate the world around us. Perhaps today's feast can lead us to ponder how Jesus has enlightened our own lives and also to consider how to welcome him as the source of true light for ourselves, our families, and our community in the year to come.

Model Universal Prayer (Prayer of the Faithful)

Presider: With trust in God's goodness, let us bring our petitions before the Lord, our salvation.

Response: Lord, hear our prayer.

For the church throughout the world, may it be purified in the refining fire of God's love so as to shine brightly as a light for all to see . . .

For leaders of nations, may they work tirelessly to lift up the disenfranchised, especially women and girls who are denied access to education and vocational opportunities . . .

For the elderly, infirm, and those nearing death, may they be encircled by the love of family and friends and find peace in God's constant care . . .

For all gathered here, may our eyes be opened to Christ in our midst as we seek to serve him in the least of our brothers and sisters . . .

Presider: God of light and glory, you reveal your son to Anna and Simeon as our salvation and Lord. Hear our prayers that his healing and purifying light might spread throughout the world and bring all people to complete joy and fullness of life. We ask this through Christ our Lord. **Amen.**

COLLECT

Let us pray

Pause for silent prayer

Almighty ever-living God,
we humbly implore your majesty
that, just as your Only Begotten Son
was presented on this day in the Temple
in the substance of our flesh,
so, by your grace,
we may be presented to you with minds
made pure.
Through our Lord Jesus Christ, your Son,
who lives and reigns with you in the unity
of the Holy Spirit,
one God, for ever and ever. **Amen.**

FIRST READING

Mal 3:1-4

Thus says the Lord GOD:
Lo, I am sending my messenger
to prepare the way before me;
and suddenly there will come to the temple
the LORD whom you seek,
and the messenger of the covenant whom
you desire.
Yes, he is coming, says the LORD of hosts.
But who will endure the day of his coming?
And who can stand when he appears?
For he is like the refiner's fire,
or like the fuller's lye.
He will sit refining and purifying silver,
and he will purify the sons of Levi,
refining them like gold or like silver
that they may offer due sacrifice to the
LORD.
Then the sacrifice of Judah and Jerusalem
will please the LORD,
as in the days of old, as in years gone by.

RESPONSORIAL PSALM
Ps 24:7, 8, 9, 10

℟. (8) Who is this king of glory? It is the Lord!

Lift up, O gates, your lintels;
reach up, you ancient portals,
that the king of glory may come in!

℟. Who is this king of glory? It is the Lord!

Who is this king of glory?
The LORD, strong and mighty,
the LORD, mighty in battle.

℟. Who is this king of glory? It is the Lord!

Lift up, O gates, your lintels;
reach up, you ancient portals,
that the king of glory may come in!

℟. Who is this king of glory? It is the Lord!

Who is this king of glory?
The LORD of hosts; he is the king of glory.

℟. Who is this king of glory? It is the Lord!

SECOND READING
Heb 2:14-18

Since the children share in blood and flesh,
Jesus likewise shared in them,
that through death he might destroy the one
who has the power of death, that is, the devil,
and free those who through fear of death
had been subject to slavery all their life.
Surely he did not help angels
but rather the descendants of Abraham;
therefore, he had to become like his brothers and sisters
in every way,
that he might be a merciful and faithful high priest before God
to expiate the sins of the people.
Because he himself was tested through what he suffered,
he is able to help those who are being tested.

About Liturgy

A feast of light: Occurring forty days after the Nativity of the Lord, today's feast is, for some cultures, the *true* end of the Christmas season. It is also a traditional day for blessing candles. These are taken home by the faithful to be lit during times of prayer and are used for the blessing of throats on St. Blaise Day, February 3.

Note that the Introductory Rites for this day are different from what is used in the usual Sunday. The Roman Missal gives two options for the entrance. In the first option, the entire assembly begins outside the church or in another building. Candles are given to every person and lit. (The week before, you might invite people to bring their own candles from home to be blessed.) After the sign of the cross and greeting, the priest leads a blessing over the candles. Then the entire assembly processes to the church. Once all are gathered inside, the Gloria is sung followed by the collect.

In the second option, a representative group of the faithful gathers at the doors of the church where the rest of the assembly can still be engaged in the rite. After the sign of the cross, greeting, and lighting, and the blessing of everyone's candles, the entrance procession begins as usual but concludes with the Gloria and collect, as in the first option. In both options, the Penitential Act is omitted.

About Initiation

Compline: Catechumens and candidates should be introduced to the variety of ways Catholics pray together. One important prayer form for all Christians is the "daily office" or Liturgy of the Hours. Some may be familiar with Morning Prayer (Lauds) and Evening Prayer (Vespers). However, others, including some Catholics, might never have heard of or prayed the liturgy for the last hour of the day, called Night Prayer or Compline, usually prayed just before bedtime.

The basic structure of Compline is similar to Morning or Evening prayer. It begins with the traditional opening dialogue from the office, followed by an examination of conscience to recall the events of the day. Then there are psalms, a brief reading, and a responsory dialogue. Compline always ends with the Canticle of Simeon, which we hear in today's gospel reading, and a concluding prayer. Often, the final song is a hymn to Mary, such as the "Salve Regina."

About Liturgical Music

Being prepared: Some music ministers might arrive at Mass today unaware that the feast of the Presentation of the Lord requires a different order for the Introductory Rites of the Mass (see above). Be sure you are prepared, and connect with your liturgy director or presider long before Sunday so everyone is on the same page. Depending on which option is chosen for the entrance, you may need to prepare processional music that can be sung unaccompanied. You will also want to know if your parish will invite the assembly to have their throats blessed during the Masses this Sunday, in anticipation of the memorial of St. Blaise. If individuals are invited to come forward for this blessing, you may need an additional processional song. The blessing of throats may take place after the Universal Prayer or as the concluding blessing of the Mass itself.

Today is also the perfect day to sing a setting of the Canticle of Simeon. It is the suggested processional song for today's entrance. Or you might use it as a sending forth song at the end of Mass. Psallite's "Christ Is the Light" (Liturgical Press) has a joyful refrain for the assembly and chanted verses of the canticle for the choir.

SPIRITUALITY

GOSPEL ACCLAMATION
John 8:12

℟. Alleluia, alleluia.
I am the light of the world, says the Lord;
whoever follows me will have the light
of life.
℟. Alleluia, alleluia.

Gospel

Matt 5:13-16; L73A

Jesus said to his disciples:
"You are the salt of the earth.
But if salt loses its taste, with what can it be seasoned?
It is no longer good for anything
but to be thrown out and trampled underfoot.
You are the light of the world.
A city set on a mountain cannot be hidden.
Nor do they light a lamp and then put it under a bushel basket;
it is set on a lampstand,
where it gives light to all in the house.
Just so, your light must shine before others,
that they may see your good deeds
and glorify your heavenly Father."

Reflecting on the Gospel

The gospel opens with the words "Jesus said to his disciples," thus giving us not only an account of something two thousand years ago, but something that is addressed to us today. There are two "you are" statements that cannot be missed. The metaphors are simple but sublime: "salt" and "light."

Jesus is telling his disciples as he tells us that we are the salt for the earth and the light of the world. What an impressive moniker! Are we up to it? Whether or not we deem the terms appropriate appellations, we are given those names nonetheless.

Jesus continues the metaphor in each case, spelling out some implications. With respect to salt, today we do not experience it losing its flavor. Scientifically speaking, sodium chloride is extremely stable. But in the ancient world, people were not buying table salt in convenient packaging at the grocery store. Instead, salt came from natural sources and its chemical composition included more than merely sodium chloride, which when exposed to water (rain, humidity, condensation) would have been removed, leaving only the crude remains. In other words, salt in antiquity was impure; in certain circumstances it could seem like it lost its taste. At that point it was not good for anything.

About light, this, too, is expressed in the ancient imagery of bushel baskets and lampstands. Of course, in antiquity a lamp would have meant burning oil, thus "light a lamp." Still the meaning of the metaphor is clear. Disciples are the light of the world. Their good deeds—that is, clothing the naked, feeding the hungry, and giving drink to the thirsty—should be seen by others. We disciples are not to do these good deeds for the sole purpose of being seen, but the deeds are to be done before others.

Even now, we consider an exemplar of this gospel passage to be someone like St. Mother Teresa, whose good deeds were seen by others who in turn gave glory to God. Mother Teresa was not doing this for her own benefit. She was motivated by love; she was a "light of the world." We, too, are called to be salt for the earth, the light of the world, performing deeds of justice and mercy, for we are disciples of Jesus. His words to the disciples are addressed to us.

Living the Paschal Mystery

Oftentimes it can be easy to read gospel stories of Jesus and the disciples without recognizing that we are disciples too. When Jesus speaks to his disciples, he is speaking to us. One prayer that is particularly apropos in this gospel is to exchange one's own name for "his disciples." So instead of reading, "Jesus said to his disciples," we read, "Jesus said to Kelly" or "Jesus said to Greg." Reading that passage over to oneself several times, replacing the text in this way, can give the gospel new meaning.

Essentially, we are Jesus' disciples and the words to his disciples apply equally to us. We are invited to be part of the paschal mystery with Christ. Let us journey with him and his disciples, learning from the ultimate teacher, whose destiny is known.

Focusing the Gospel

Key words and phrases: "[Y]our light must shine before others."

To the point: In today's gospel Jesus instructs the disciples, "[Y]our light must shine before others, / so that they may see your good deeds / and glorify your heavenly Father." Jesus' words are curious here. In this same Sermon on the Mount, Jesus will tell us, "Take care not to perform righteous deeds / in order that people may see them" (Matt 6:1; NABRE). We will read these words in a few weeks' time on Ash Wednesday. How do we reconcile these seemingly contradictory messages? Perhaps the key is the motivation for the deeds that make up a Christian life. They are not to be done for one's own glory or benefit, but instead to give all glory and honor to God through a life of loving service to others.

Connecting the Gospel

to the first reading: Jesus calls his disciples to be "the light of the world." In the first reading from Isaiah, we hear of exactly how this light will shine for the glory of the Lord when we feed the hungry, shelter the homeless, clothe the naked, and treat our brothers and sisters with compassion.

to experience: Of the many hallmarks of the saints, one seems to be a dedication to good works that naturally draw attention coupled with a desire to escape attention to oneself completely. During her acceptance speech for the 1979 Nobel Peace Prize, Mother Teresa said, "I personally am most unworthy . . . But I am grateful and very happy to receive [this award] in the name of the hungry, of the naked, of the homeless, of the crippled, of the blind, of the leprous, of all those people who feel unwanted." As disciples of Christ, we are called to a high standard—not only to do good works, but to do them selflessly as well.

Connecting the Responsorial Psalm

to the readings: To the imagery of light found in both the first reading and the gospel, the psalmist also highlights the firm foundation of the just. We are told that the upright one "shall never be moved" and that his heart is "firm" and "steadfast." In the gospel reading Jesus likens his disciples to a city on a hill that "cannot be hidden." The psalmist's characterization of the just one leads to another image; like a lighthouse "the just man is a light in darkness."

to psalmist preparation: Who has been an example of faith and a guiding light for you in times of darkness? How are you being called to be this light for others?

PROMPTS FOR FAITH-SHARING

The prophet Isaiah tells us it is only in works of mercy (feeding the hungry, sheltering the homeless, clothing the naked) that our light will shine before others. When have you personally experienced works of mercy bringing "light" to your life or the lives of others?

St. Paul writes to the Corinthians, "I resolved to know nothing . . . except Jesus Christ, and him crucified." What do these words mean to you?

In each of our lives, we have been given talents and abilities to use for the good of others. Is there a gift you have been hiding under a bushel basket, either consciously or unconsciously?

Often we hear the image of "light" in the Bible, but less so, salt. What do you think Jesus is implying about the spiritual life in calling for his disciples to be "salt of the earth"?

Model Penitential Act

Presider: In today's gospel Jesus tells us we are to be the light of the world and the salt of the earth. For the times we have failed to live up to this call, let us ask for mercy and healing . . . *[pause]*

Lord Jesus, you free the oppressed and renew the weary: Lord, have mercy.
Christ Jesus, in you our weakness finds strength: Christ, have mercy.
Lord Jesus, you offer us the light of life: Lord, have mercy.

Homily Points

• In today's gospel we enter into the Sermon on the Mount, which we'll continue to hear for the next two Sundays before entering into the season of Lent. In Matthew's gospel the section on the Sermon on the Mount begins, "When he saw the crowds, he went up the mountain, and after he had sat down, his disciples came to him. He began to teach them" (5:1-2; NABRE). This is the first time we hear of Jesus speaking to his disciples since calling the two sets of brothers (Simon and Andrew, James and John) away from their fishing boats and nets to follow him and become "fishers of men" (4:19; NABRE). Now Jesus tells them exactly how they will do this, by becoming "the light of the world" and "the salt of the earth."

• In its entirety, this sermon contains some of the most beloved (and also demanding) of Jesus' teachings. We are counseled to "stop judging" (7:1), "love your enemies" (5:44), and even "be perfect, just as your heavenly Father is perfect" (5:48).

• These moral teachings ask much more of us than merely following a list of rules or determining with black-and-white assurance that which is right and wrong. Instead of arbitrary guidelines, the Sermon on the Mount calls us to "a certain orientation of the whole person in life" (Sofia Cavalletti, *Religious Potential of the Child,* vol. 1). Only when our lives are directed toward the good of all and the love of God can we begin to fulfill the roles of salt and light. As we draw closer to the season of Lent, a time of conversion and realigning our lives to God, now is a good time to ask, "To whom or to what am I oriented?"

Model Universal Prayer (Prayer of the Faithful)

Presider: Trusting in God's promises and faithfulness, we bring our needs and the needs of our world before the Lord.

Response: Lord, hear our prayer.

For God's holy church, that in serving the homeless, poor, and oppressed it may live up to Jesus' call to be salt and light for the world . . .

For leaders of nations, may they work for the end of social and economic inequality based on race, gender, sexual orientation, and religion . . .

For those who have been falsely accused and unjustly imprisoned, may justice and truth prevail . . .

For all gathered here around the table of the Lord, may we be empowered to practice radical hospitality toward everyone we meet . . .

Presider: God of the poor and oppressed, in the voices of the prophets and the person of your son, you call us to care for our neighbor as our very self. Hear our prayers that through the work of our hands we might extend your care and compassion to those in need. We ask this through Christ our Lord. **Amen.**

COLLECT

Let us pray.

Pause for silent prayer

Keep your family safe, O Lord, with
unfailing care,
that, relying solely on the hope of
heavenly grace,
they may be defended always by your
protection.
Through our Lord Jesus Christ, your Son,
who lives and reigns with you in the unity
of the Holy Spirit,
one God, for ever and ever. **Amen.**

FIRST READING

Isa 58:7-10

Thus says the LORD:
Share your bread with the hungry,
shelter the oppressed and the homeless;
clothe the naked when you see them,
and do not turn your back on your
own.
Then your light shall break forth like
the dawn,
and your wound shall quickly be
healed;
your vindication shall go before you,
and the glory of the LORD shall be
your rear guard.
Then you shall call, and the LORD will
answer,
you shall cry for help, and he will say:
Here I am!
If you remove from your midst
oppression, false accusation and
malicious speech;
if you bestow your bread on the hungry
and satisfy the afflicted;
then light shall rise for you in the
darkness,
and the gloom shall become for you
like midday.

RESPONSORIAL PSALM
Ps 112:4-5, 6-7, 8-9

℟. (4a) The just man is a light in darkness to the upright.
or:
℟. Alleluia.

Light shines through the darkness for the upright;
he is gracious and merciful and just.
Well for the man who is gracious and lends,
who conducts his affairs with justice.

℟. The just man is a light in darkness to the upright.
or:
℟. Alleluia.

He shall never be moved;
the just one shall be in everlasting remembrance.
An evil report he shall not fear;
his heart is firm, trusting in the LORD.

℟. The just man is a light in darkness to the upright.
or:
℟. Alleluia.

His heart is steadfast; he shall not fear.
Lavishly he gives to the poor;
his justice shall endure forever;
his horn shall be exalted in glory.

℟. The just man is a light in darkness to the upright.
or:
℟. Alleluia.

SECOND READING
1 Cor 2:1-5

When I came to you, brothers and sisters,
proclaiming the mystery of God,
I did not come with sublimity of words or of wisdom.
For I resolved to know nothing while I was with you
except Jesus Christ, and him crucified.
I came to you in weakness and fear and much trembling,
and my message and my proclamation
were not with persuasive words of wisdom,
but with a demonstration of Spirit and power,
so that your faith might rest not on human wisdom
but on the power of God.

About Liturgy

Current events and the Mass: In the Mass, should we acknowledge current events affecting our community or world? Beyond generic intercessions, should more be said in the prayers or homily about divisive topics?

For some, the Mass is a retreat from the concerns of life, and they argue that secular issues have no place in the liturgy. Partisan politics certainly must be avoided. However, we cannot pretend that faith is lived in a vacuum removed from the human concerns of our day.

The incarnation teaches us that God entered into the very real and specific issues of the polis. The society in which Jesus and his first disciples lived was filled with political and systematic injustice. An oppressive social and religious system often privileged the powerful, despised the immigrant, and withheld support for the poor. Yet this was the very locus in which God's saving power was being revealed in Christ.

The question cannot be if there is a place for such topics in liturgy. The true question is, how could we give authentic worship to the Father if we do not name the world's wounds that long to be healed by Christ's light?

About Initiation

Training for justice: In paragraph 75 of the RCIA, the church gives us four areas of training for Christian life. All four areas are necessary in order to provide a complete catechesis for catechumens. These areas of discipleship are (1) study and profound awe and love for the Word and teaching of the church; (2) practice of living in community with Christians and sacrificing oneself for others; (3) learning to pray and be nourished by the prayer of the church; and (4) becoming apostolic witnesses and spreading the gospel by word and deed.

The marks of discipleship from this last area of training are what we hear in both the gospel and the first reading today. To be salt of the earth and light for the world are not just nice metaphors for what it means to be good Christians. Isaiah gives us the concrete actions we must take to be authentic disciples: give our food to the hungry; take into our homes and lives those without shelter or justice; give dignity to those who have been shamed; live in solidarity with one another. Practicing these acts of mercy is part of the curriculum for catechumens in order to become Jesus' disciples.

About Liturgical Music

Preparing for Lent: We are two and a half weeks away from the start of Lent! If you plan to introduce any new songs for the assembly to sing during Lent, these last two Sundays before Ash Wednesday are good times to begin teaching them to the assembly. Use the time before Mass to allow the assembly to hear the song and have them learn short sections of it. If appropriate, you can also schedule the song into the music for today's Mass, perhaps during those parts when the choir takes the lead in the singing, such as the preparation of gifts, or as a prelude or postlude. If the text of the song is not appropriate for these two Ordinary Time Sundays, then at least play the music instrumentally so the community begins to hear the melody.

In general, you want to keep new music for the assembly at a minimum, especially for the seasons of Lent/Easter and Advent/Christmas. When you do need to bring in a new assembly song, be sure to give your assemblies enough time to learn it several weeks before, so they can sing it fully at the liturgy. Also plan to use that song for several consecutive weeks so it becomes more familiar.

SPIRITUALITY

GOSPEL ACCLAMATION
cf. Matt 11:25

℟. Alleluia, alleluia.
Blessed are you, Father, Lord of heaven and earth;
you have revealed to little ones the mysteries of the kingdom.
℟. Alleluia, alleluia.

Gospel Matt 5:17-37; L76A

Jesus said to his disciples:
"Do not think that I have come to abolish the law or the prophets.
I have come not to abolish but to fulfill.
Amen, I say to you, until heaven and earth pass away,
not the smallest letter or the smallest part of a letter
will pass from the law,
until all things have taken place.
Therefore, whoever breaks one of the least of these commandments
and teaches others to do so
will be called least in the kingdom of heaven.
But whoever obeys and teaches these commandments
will be called greatest in the kingdom of heaven.
I tell you, unless your righteousness surpasses
that of the scribes and Pharisees,
you will not enter the kingdom of heaven.

"You have heard that it was said to your ancestors,
You shall not kill; and whoever kills will be liable to judgment.
But I say to you,
whoever is angry with his brother
will be liable to judgment;
and whoever says to his brother, 'Raqa,'
will be answerable to the Sanhedrin;
and whoever says, 'You fool,'
will be liable to fiery Gehenna.

Continued in Appendix A, p. 268, or Matt 5:20-22a, 27-28, 33-34a, 37 *in Appendix A, p. 269.*

Reflecting on the Gospel

The child was asked to clean his room before he could go out to play. He replied, "What's the least I have to do?" He wondered if making the bed would count, or if the floor had to be clean too. Do his clean clothes need to be put away, or only left in the laundry bin and tucked away in his closet? What about under his bed? Would that be checked, and would it have to be clean? The exasperated father wondered when the child would want a clean room for his own sake and not simply because the father had asked. Such an attitude on the part of the child is similar to what's on display in today's gospel.

To those people who want to be right with God, but wonder what is the minimum required to achieve that relationship, Jesus has an answer. Jesus takes certain aspects of the law of Moses and expands them. Rather than a command not to kill, Jesus says, do not grow angry. Rather than a command not to commit adultery, Jesus says not to look at another with lust. In other words, the Mosaic Law is not simply the bare minimum we need to do to be right with God. Instead, we need to go above and beyond the letter of the law if we are to be followers of Christ. Merely fulfilling the minimum is not enough.

When Jesus responds in this way, we may crave a return to the minimum! How can I keep myself from growing angry, which is a natural human response to perceived injustice? The standard Jesus sets may seem impossible to realize. The statement about plucking out one's eye is certainly hyperbole, and recognized as such by the early church. The standard established by Jesus fulfills the law rather than abolishing it. Jesus' teaching goes to the heart of the matter. His advice to let "yes" mean "yes" and "no" mean "no" is a clear statement to that effect. Disciples of Jesus speak the truth without equivocation.

So when we want to ask, "What's the least I have to do?" we may need to reconsider the question. When we desire a relationship with Christ for its own sake, and not simply because we've been somehow coerced, a life of faith flows naturally. We no longer count the minimum but instead live in a relationship of trust, fidelity, and love.

Living the Paschal Mystery

Living our lives as disciples of Jesus means that we follow a standard different from the world's standard. Jesus' injunction not to look on another with lust, or with anger, is a prime indication of that. In the ancient world (and even in the modern), it can seem easier to cover up a temptation so as not to deal with it. If looking on another causes lust, let's cover up the other or remove the other! But Jesus' response goes to the heart of a person. His response is not to cover up the temptation, but to challenge the person not to look on another with lust. Jesus places the responsibility on the individual, not on the object of temptation or anger. In this world there are things that will cause us anger. As disciples, we are not to harbor anger; we are not to harbor lust. Simply acting on these Christian precepts to eschew anger and lust will mark us as disciples, for we will be following a standard not of the world.

Focusing the Gospel

Key words and phrases: "Let your 'Yes' mean 'Yes,' and your 'No' mean 'No.'"

To the point: Jesus calls us to lead lives of integrity where we follow not only the letter of the law but, more important, its spirit. Involving more than simply the words we say, this integrity calls us to a whole-hearted living where all that we do and are reveals to whom we belong: the God of love revealed in Jesus Christ and communicated through the grace of the Holy Spirit.

Connecting the Gospel

to the first reading: The first reading from Sirach highlights the complete freedom of human beings in their relationship with God. Though God desires the good for us and all others, he does not compel us to do that which is right. Instead we are given the choice of whether to follow the commandments that lead to life or to reject them. In the gospel this choice is broken down even further. Are we interested in the bare minimum required from the laws laid forth in the Ten Commandments? If, therefore, we get through life without committing murder, entering adulterous relationships, or telling outright lies, have we lived up to our full potential?

to experience: In the first reading we hear that if we keep the commandments of God, we "shall live." In the Gospel of John, Jesus reveals that he has come to bring not only life, but life in abundance (10:10). This abundant life is offered to us in every moment, as we are given the opportunity to choose between love and hatred, light and darkness, life and death—not just to fulfill the requirement of the law of God, but to enter into the very life of God, which is love and light.

Connecting the Responsorial Psalm

to the readings: The psalmist proclaims, "Blessed are they who observe his decrees, / who seek him with all their heart." This whole-hearted living is what Jesus calls us to in the gospel and what the author of Sirach describes in the first reading. To live a "blessed" life can sometimes be interpreted as enjoying the gifts of friends, family, and material goods present in one's life. But in this psalm we are told that blessing comes from following God's laws. It is not that we are recompensed with external rewards when we live this way, but that living this way is its own reward.

to psalmist preparation: Created in the image of God, true peace, fulfillment, and purpose can only be found by delving deeply into the mystery of his love and grace, or as the psalmist says, "the wonders of your law." In your own walk of faith, how do you seek to keep the decrees of God with your whole heart?

PROMPTS FOR FAITH-SHARING

In the first reading the writer of the book of Sirach tries to convince his community that because God has given them free will, it is not possible to blame their sin on the "will of God." What role do you see personal responsibility taking in healing and reconciliation within your own family, parish, and community?

The psalmist tells us, "Blessed are they who observe [the Lord's] decrees, / who seek him with all their heart." Who has been a model for you in living a life of whole-hearted service to God?

Writing to the Corinthians nearly two thousand years ago, St. Paul says, "We speak a wisdom to those who are mature, / not a wisdom of this age." What is the wisdom the Christian tradition has to offer now to the age we find ourselves in?

In the gospel, Jesus urges his disciples to do more than simply follow the letter of the law. In your own spiritual life, what motivates you to grow in perfection each day?

CELEBRATION

Model Penitential Act

Presider: Today's gospel continues the Sermon on the Mount. Jesus counsels us to do more than follow the letter of the law by embodying its spirit of loving God and loving neighbor. Let us ask for God's mercy and forgiveness as we seek to keep this commandment in our own lives . . . *[pause]*

Lord Jesus, you embody the wisdom of God: Lord, have mercy.
Christ Jesus, you are the fulfillment of God's law: Christ, have mercy.
Lord Jesus, you lead us to the fullness of life: Lord, have mercy.

Homily Points

• This week we continue our journey toward Lent with another reading from Jesus' Sermon on the Mount. Jesus challenges his disciples to not only follow the letter of the law, but to fully embrace its spirit. Jesus warns against the pernicious effects of anger, lust, and dishonesty. Within these attitudes we find the seeds that, if left to grow, blossom into the bitter fruit of harm and destruction, and the breakdown of relationships where people are used, discarded, and duped instead of cherished and respected.

• These words of Jesus are straightforward and challenging, and call each of us to examine our own lives. Where have we let anger, lust, or dishonesty creep in? Have we told ourselves, "A white lie now and then doesn't make me untruthful"? Or rationalized our actions by thinking, "Of course I'm angry at my coworker; who wouldn't be with how they're acting?" Do we disregard reverence for other human beings through the media we consume, claiming, "It's impossible to avoid sexualized images, so why even bother?"

• Jesus' words call us to embrace a different way, a way of perfection and virtue. It's not easy, but it is worth it. And our Lord is always ready to forgive and help us start anew. As we draw closer to Lent, consider Jesus' warnings against anger, lust, and dishonesty. Where have these actions crept into your own life and how might this year's Lenten practices of fasting, almsgiving, and prayer help lead you closer to Christ?

Model Universal Prayer (Prayer of the Faithful)

Presider: In the Sermon on the Mount, Jesus calls us to lead lives of righteousness. Recognizing our reliance on God for all that is good, we entrust our needs and desires to the Lord.

Response: Lord, hear our prayer.

For the church throughout the world and especially all members who have been victims of sexual abuse, may their voices be heard and their wounds healed . . .

For nations of the world, may they come together in peace, combining resources to combat hunger, disease, and violence . . .

For families fractured and damaged by domestic abuse, may victims find safety and healing and abusers be led to conversion and repentance . . .

For all gathered here, with the help of Christ and each other, may we continue to grow in personal and communal holiness . . .

Presider: God of unfailing justice and mercy, through the voice of your son, Jesus, you call us to faithful discipleship. Hear our prayers that, strengthened by your Word and nourished by the Body and Blood of Christ, we might come to emulate him more fully. We ask this through Christ our Lord. **Amen.**

COLLECT

Let us pray.

Pause for silent prayer

O God, who teach us that you abide
in hearts that are just and true,
grant that we may be so fashioned by
your grace
as to become a dwelling pleasing to you.
Through our Lord Jesus Christ, your Son,
who lives and reigns with you in the unity
of the Holy Spirit,
one God, for ever and ever. **Amen.**

FIRST READING

Sir 15:15-20

If you choose you can keep the
commandments, they will save you;
if you trust in God, you too shall live;
he has set before you fire and water;
to whichever you choose, stretch forth
your hand.
Before man are life and death, good and
evil,
whichever he chooses shall be given
him.
Immense is the wisdom of the Lord;
he is mighty in power, and all-seeing.
The eyes of God are on those who fear
him;
he understands man's every deed.
No one does he command to act unjustly,
to none does he give license to sin.

RESPONSORIAL PSALM

Ps 119:1-2, 4-5, 17-18, 33-34

℟. (1b) Blessed are they who follow the law of the Lord!

Blessed are they whose way is blameless,
who walk in the law of the LORD.
Blessed are they who observe his decrees,
who seek him with all their heart.

℟. Blessed are they who follow the law of the Lord!

You have commanded that your precepts
be diligently kept.
Oh, that I might be firm in the ways
of keeping your statutes!

℟. Blessed are they who follow the law of the Lord!

Be good to your servant, that I may live
and keep your words.
Open my eyes, that I may consider
the wonders of your law.

℟. Blessed are they who follow the law of the Lord!

Instruct me, O LORD, in the way of your
statutes,
that I may exactly observe them.
Give me discernment, that I may observe
your law
and keep it with all my heart.

℟. Blessed are they who follow the law of the Lord!

SECOND READING
1 Cor 2:6-10

Brothers and sisters:
We speak a wisdom to those who are
mature,
not a wisdom of this age,
nor of the rulers of this age who are
passing away.
Rather, we speak God's wisdom,
mysterious, hidden,
which God predetermined before the
ages for our glory,
and which none of the rulers of this age
knew;
for, if they had known it,
they would not have crucified the Lord
of glory.
But as it is written:
*What eye has not seen, and ear has not
heard,*
*and what has not entered the human
heart,*
*what God has prepared for those who
love him,*
this God has revealed to us through
the Spirit.

For the Spirit scrutinizes everything, even
the depths of God.

About Liturgy

"Do the red, say the black" is a myth: You may have heard some people claim that they "only do the red and just say the black" when it comes to the liturgy, meaning they follow every single rubric (written in red) and never deviate from any of the assigned proper texts (written in black), spoken or sung.

A friend of mine who is a priest and a world-famous liturgist teaches seminarians how to lead the Mass. He told me that he cautions his students that no one ever follows *all* the liturgical rules *all* the time. It is simply impossible. Even the most rubric-minded priest, liturgist, musician, or liturgical committee will make mistakes. They will also make choices (sometimes unknowingly) that are outside the liturgical norms because of their own preferences, the needs of the assembly, or because the immediate situation requires it. My friend admitted that he doesn't follow every single jot and tittle either because that isn't the point of liturgy. Liturgy is a dynamic relationship between God and God's people. To be true to that, we must go beyond the law to its spirit.

Just as notes and words on a page do not become a song until they are sung, liturgy doesn't happen until rubrics and texts are joined to human tradition, need, and frailty and brought to life by those who are faithful to the spirit of the law that requires more of us than merely following rules.

About Initiation

Readiness for the Rite of Election: Although the bishop at the Rite of Election chooses the catechumens who are ready for initiation, he does not come to that decision on his own. Before the rite, "the bishop, priests, deacons, catechists, godparents, and the entire community . . . after considering the matter carefully, arrive at a judgment about the catechumens' state of formation and progress" (RCIA 121).

RCIA teams often get queasy when they think of making this judgment. Some just let the Holy Spirit decide, allowing all their catechumens onward to baptism. They might even justify this by saying, "Who are we to judge?"

My response to that is, "You are the baptized!" As the RCIA implies, it's our serious responsibility to be certain a person is ready to be a disciple before taking on the lifelong duty to live as one. It is the most pastoral thing we can do for them. As a colleague once said, you don't push someone out of a plane until you're certain that person knows the basics of skydiving!

Let's take our responsibility to discern a person's readiness with all the gravity and humility this sacred act requires. Pray for the Spirit's guidance. Use the criteria set forth in RCIA 120 and the three questions at RCIA 131B, and discern together with the individual catechumens, their sponsors, and those who know them best how far they have progressed in their journey. Finally, help everyone remember that saying "not yet" is not a rejection but an invitation to deeper conversion to Christ.

About Liturgical Music

Suggestions: Three familiar songs fit today's readings. David Haas's "Deep Within" (GIA) speaks of God's law written on our hearts and not on stone. This would be a fitting song for the upcoming Lenten season as well. Marty Haugen's "Eye Has Not Seen" (GIA) connects with today's second reading and truly helps place Scripture upon the assembly's lips. Finally, Bernadette Farrell's "Your Words Are Spirit and Life" (OCP) is a lilting paraphrase of Psalm 19 reflecting the joy given to the one who follows God's law.

SPIRITUALITY

GOSPEL ACCLAMATION
1 John 2:5

℟. Alleluia, alleluia.
Whoever keeps the word of Christ,
the love of God is truly perfected in him.
℟. Alleluia, alleluia.

Gospel Matt 5:38-48; L79A

Jesus said to his disciples:
"You have heard that it was said,
An eye for an eye and a tooth for a tooth.
But I say to you, offer no resistance to one who is evil.
When someone strikes you on your right cheek,
turn the other one as well.
If anyone wants to go to law with you over your tunic,
hand over your cloak as well.
Should anyone press you into service for one mile,
go for two miles.
Give to the one who asks of you,
and do not turn your back on one who wants to borrow.

"You have heard that it was said,
You shall love your neighbor and hate your enemy.
But I say to you, love your enemies
and pray for those who persecute you,
that you may be children of your heavenly Father,
for he makes his sun rise on the bad and the good,
and causes rain to fall on the just and the unjust.
For if you love those who love you,
what recompense will you have?
Do not the tax collectors do the same?
And if you greet your brothers only,
what is unusual about that?
Do not the pagans do the same?
So be perfect, just as your heavenly Father is perfect."

Reflecting on the Gospel

Today's gospel reading from Matthew picks up where we left off last week, in the midst of the Sermon on the Mount. Jesus' own preaching is on par with and actually fulfills the Mosaic Law, which came from God. Jesus' teaching authority is therefore equivalent to God, as Jesus says, "[Y]ou have heard that it was said . . . but I say to you . . ." The passive voice "it was said" refers to God's word through Mosaic Law. Jesus uses the active voice, first-person singular, in claiming his own teaching authority. To claim such authority would have been shocking to those who heard it. The words we have reflect not only Jesus' teaching but also Matthew the evangelist's reckoning that the authority of Jesus is paramount.

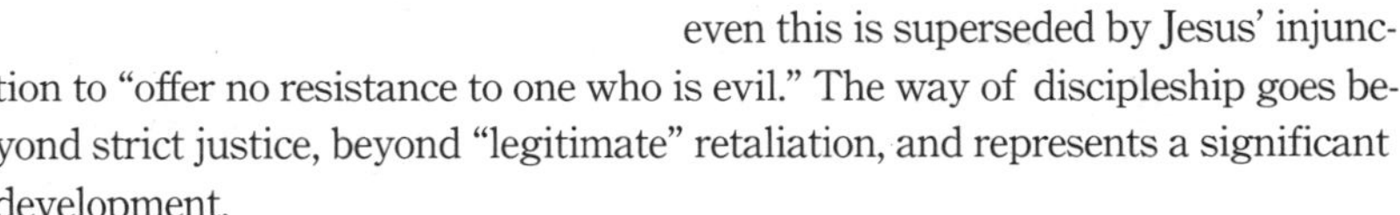

In the teachings from last week, Jesus goes to the heart of Mosaic Law, sometimes issuing commands that go beyond the mere letter of the law, such as prohibiting anger (rather than murder) and lust (rather than adultery). In this week's gospel, Jesus goes beyond the "law of retaliation" (eye for an eye, tooth for a tooth). The law of retaliation represented a development in its time (centuries prior to Jesus) by limiting retaliation to one for one rather than five for one. Yet, even this is superseded by Jesus' injunction to "offer no resistance to one who is evil." The way of discipleship goes beyond strict justice, beyond "legitimate" retaliation, and represents a significant development.

Something similar is at work in the next injunction Jesus issues, which is to pray for one's persecutors rather than hate them. All too often feelings of exclusion and division can rise up in the face of persecution, which is certainly understandable. Striking back in the face of persecution is a natural human response. But the way of Jesus calls his disciples to the lofty goal of praying for those persecutors. Few people have lived up to this ideal, but those who have are known for it, including Martin Luther King Jr., Mahatma Gandhi, and the Dalai Lama. If we treat with kindness only those who treat us with kindness, we are merely living the values of the world. Jesus demands that we are "perfect," meaning pure in our devotion to God. Then we will be known as his disciples.

Living the Paschal Mystery

Admiring Jesus is easy to do. He was a gifted teacher, who lived an ethical life. His sayings inspire us, to say nothing of his death and resurrection. Yet, merely admiring Jesus is not what we are called to do. As disciples, we are to follow him. The Sermon on the Mount, from which we read today, is addressed to Jesus' disciples. That is, the Sermon on the Mount is addressed to us. His words should certainly challenge us and our basic attitudes toward life. It's much easier to be evangelized by the modern culture with values of the world. And many of these values are not bad, such as treating with kindness those who treat us with kindness. But Jesus has another way. We are to pray for our persecutors. We are to turn the other cheek. In the face of such injunctions, we may choose to admire Jesus for his simple advice, while quietly concluding that is not the way the world works. Jesus would agree. He calls his disciples to be salt for the earth, leaven for the world. The conclusion of this journey is not "to get ahead" but to die on a cross. But then comes the promised resurrection. Such is the paschal mystery, which is to be lived, not merely admired.

Focusing the Gospel

Key words and phrases: "I say to you, love your enemies / and pray for those who persecute you."

To the point: Jesus tells us that, as Christians, we are not simply to eschew revenge, but instead to will and act for the good of our persecutors, tormentors, and enemies. How is this possible? In the Sermon on the Mount, Jesus offers the guidelines by which he will live his life of perfect, self-giving love and holiness. From the cross he will pray for his crucifiers: "Father, forgive them, they know not what they do" (Luke 23:34; NABRE). The teachings of Jesus are hard. They call us to strip away all hatred and anger in order to be the people we have been created to be, made in the image and likeness of the living God. And when it seems impossible, we can rely on Christ within us, the one who prayed for his executioners, to lead the way to forgiveness and healing.

Connecting the Gospel

to the first reading: In the first reading Moses speaks to the people on behalf of God, urging them to "[t]ake no revenge and cherish no grudge against any of your people." In the gospel, Jesus echoes these words and also provides a path for living out these injunctions. If we truly are to "love our enemy," then we must pray and act. Pray for those who persecute us and give to the one who seeks to take. In the face of enmity and cruelty, Jesus enjoins us to act with the overflowing love and compassion of God.

to experience: At times, it can seem impossible to forgive. When we have been hurt deeply, feelings of anger are natural. In these situations, it is only the grace of God that can give us the ability to respond with love.

Connecting the Responsorial Psalm

to the readings: The gospel offers us a seemingly impossible commandment: "[B]e perfect, just as your Heavenly Father is perfect." And it *is* impossible to fulfill on our own. As humans, we are not capable of perfection. Only through the merciful kindness of our Creator and Lord are we able to live into these words of Jesus. The psalmist reminds us that in God there is no need for fear. The one who made us "pardons all [our] iniquities, / heals all [our] ills." When we falter and fail, when we sin and wander, our God, in his perfect compassion, redeems us. Removing our transgressions and "crowning us with kindness."

to psalmist preparation: In striving to be like our heavenly Father, we are called to emulate God's kindness and mercy, to others and to ourselves. Is there a situation in your life that is calling out for mercy and compassion? How might you embrace the perfect love of God as you move forward?

PROMPTS FOR FAITH-SHARING

In Leviticus, God tells the people, "Though you may have to reprove your fellow citizen, / do not incur sin because of him." When do you think it becomes imperative for Christians to reprove their fellow citizens?

St. Paul writes to the Corinthians, "Do you not know that you are the temple of God, / and that the Spirit of God dwells in you?" What would our society look like if this truth, that the human body is holy, was revered?

In today's gospel Jesus tells us to "turn the other" cheek. What is your understanding of this phrase and how might you use this advice in a situation you are currently in?

Have you had an experience in your life where you practiced Jesus' commandment to "love your enemies"? What was the outcome?

Model Penitential Act

Presider: In today's readings we are called to be holy and perfect with the very holiness and perfection of God. Acknowledging our sinfulness, let us pause to ask for God's compassion and mercy . . . *[pause]*

Lord Jesus, you are rich in kindness and abounding in love: Lord, have mercy.
Christ Jesus, you redeem the sinner and pardon the transgressor: Christ, have mercy.
Lord Jesus, you show us the way of nonviolence and grace: Lord, have mercy.

Homily Points

- The first line of today's first reading and the last line of the gospel contain two very similar commandments. God tells Moses, "Speak to the whole Israelite community and tell them: / Be holy, for I, the Lord, your God, am holy." The gospel reading concludes with Jesus' words: "[B]e perfect, just as your heavenly Father is perfect." What apt readings for the final Sunday before our Lenten journey begins on Ash Wednesday.
  - Both these readings seem to guard against the divisions and fractions that can happen within a community where revenge, anger, and bitterness take root. God tells the people in the book of Leviticus, "Take no revenge and cherish no grudge against any of your people." Jesus goes even farther by urging his disciples to love their enemies and pray for their persecutors. To be holy and perfect seems to require being concerned for the "whole."
  - In his apostolic exhortation Rejoice and Be Glad, Pope Francis writes, "We are never completely ourselves unless we belong to a people. That is why no one is saved alone, as an isolated individual" (6). Sometimes when we consider the path of holiness, we think of personal piety and devotion. While these can be important aspects of individual spirituality, they are not our primary calling as Christians. Rather, as a people, together, we strive to be the Body of Christ in the world, offering love, compassion, and inclusion to all we meet. In our preparation for Lent today we might ponder, how can our prayer, almsgiving, and fasting be oriented to making our community more whole, holy, and perfect?

Model Universal Prayer (Prayer of the Faithful)

Presider: Trusting in our compassionate God who "makes the sun rise on the bad and the good, / and causes rain to fall on the just and the unjust," let us bring our needs, and those of our world, before the Lord.

Response: Lord, hear our prayer.

For our pope, bishops, and priests, may they be strengthened in holiness and inspired with love to carry out their ministry in joy . . .

For leaders of nations, may they work to promote the dignity and worth of all human lives, especially those most in need of mercy and forgiveness . . .

For those who have become consumed with thoughts of revenge, may their hearts be freed from bitterness and granted the ability to forgive . . .

For all gathered here, may we listen attentively to the word of God so as to grow in wisdom and understanding . . .

Presider: God of abounding mercy and grace, you call us to love our enemies and pray for our persecutors. Hear our prayers that, with your never-failing help, we might grow in holiness so as to project your merciful love into the world. We ask this through Christ our Lord. **Amen.**

COLLECT

Let us pray.

Pause for silent prayer

Grant, we pray, almighty God,
that, always pondering spiritual things,
we may carry out in both word and deed
that which is pleasing to you.
Through our Lord Jesus Christ, your Son,
who lives and reigns with you in the unity
of the Holy Spirit,
one God, for ever and ever. **Amen.**

FIRST READING

Lev 19:1-2, 17-18

The LORD said to Moses,
"Speak to the whole Israelite
community and tell them:
Be holy, for I, the LORD, your God, am
holy.

"You shall not bear hatred for your brother
or sister in your heart.
Though you may have to reprove your
fellow citizen,
do not incur sin because of him.
Take no revenge and cherish no grudge
against any of your people.
You shall love your neighbor as yourself.
I am the LORD."

RESPONSORIAL PSALM

Ps 103:1-2, 3-4, 8, 10, 12-13

℟. (8a) The Lord is kind and merciful.

Bless the LORD, O my soul;
and all my being, bless his holy name.
Bless the LORD, O my soul,
and forget not all his benefits.

℟. The Lord is kind and merciful.

He pardons all your iniquities,
heals all your ills.
He redeems your life from destruction,
crowns you with kindness and
compassion.

℟. The Lord is kind and merciful.

Merciful and gracious is the LORD,
slow to anger and abounding in
kindness.
Not according to our sins does he deal
with us,
nor does he requite us according to our
crimes.

℟. The Lord is kind and merciful.

As far as the east is from the west,
so far has he put our transgressions from us.
As a father has compassion on his children,
so the LORD has compassion on those who fear him.

℟. The Lord is kind and merciful.

SECOND READING
1 Cor 3:16-23

Brothers and sisters:
Do you not know that you are the temple of God,
and that the Spirit of God dwells in you?
If anyone destroys God's temple, God will destroy that person;
for the temple of God, which you are, is holy.

Let no one deceive himself.
If any one among you considers himself wise in this age,
let him become a fool, so as to become wise.
For the wisdom of this world is foolishness in the eyes of God,
for it is written:
God catches the wise in their own ruses,
and again:
The Lord knows the thoughts of the wise,
that they are vain.
So let no one boast about human beings,
for everything belongs to you,
Paul or Apollos or Cephas,
or the world or life or death,
or the present or the future:
all belong to you, and you to Christ, and Christ to God.

About Liturgy

***Praying for our enemies*:** Unfortunately, tragedies such as school shootings and other attacks upon innocent human beings are becoming more common in our society. When terrible things like these happen, we should be ready to include at least an intercession for those who were killed and have been affected by it.

However, if we are to take today's gospel reading to heart, we must also include prayers for those who commit such violence. For many of us, this is difficult and at times impossible, for good reason. Remember when the attacks upon the United States happened on September 11, 2001, it was almost considered treasonous to even think of praying for those who planned it and killed so many of our loved ones. And yet, that is exactly what Jesus calls his disciples to do: "I say to you, love your enemies and pray for those who persecute you" (Matt 5:44).

Look again at that command. Not only are we to pray for our enemies; we are to *love* them! Not just pray for God's mercy upon them but also treat them as our neighbor.

To be perfect as our Father is perfect is not to be indifferent toward those who hurt us. Rather it is to recognize that we belong to one another in Christ and we are not whole if we refuse to see that we are connected to one another, even in our pain and anger.

About Initiation

Rite of Sending: Parishes that have catechumens to send to the Rite of Election next Sunday may celebrate the optional Rite of Sending today. This rite shares some elements with the Rite of Election. In both, the catechumens are presented and godparents and assembly affirm their readiness through testimonies. However, whereas the Rite of Election takes place at the cathedral and is not optional, the Rite of Sending is a parish celebration and is optional. The biggest distinction is that only the bishop can make the "act of admission or election," which is the climax of the Rite of Election. There is no such act in the Rite of Sending. Finally, check with your diocese to see if the Book of the Elect is to be signed at the Rite of Election or if it is signed before then. If the latter, then the signing of the book may take place during the Rite of Sending.

About Liturgical Music

A day for Alleluias: This last Sunday before Lent is a perfect opportunity to sing as many "Alleluias" as we can before we put the word away for Lent, so to speak. Plan to end today's Masses with a rousing hymn filled with Alleluias. One good example is "Alleluia! Sing to Jesus," sung to the tune of Hyfrydol.

Also be sure to make the gospel procession and acclamation a bit more solemn on this Sunday. Perhaps work with the deacon or the priest to coordinate a longer processional route so that the assembly can fully reverence the presence of Christ in the gospels and your gospel acclamation can shine.

In some places, communities have observed the tradition of burying the Alleluia. Sometimes humorous, other times solemn, this practice ritualizes the coming fast from the Alleluia. Children and others decorate a banner or poster with the word "Alleluia" and place it in an urn or box. This is then buried or locked away until Easter when the Alleluia returns to our lips and song. This would be a wonderful way for your choirs to end the last rehearsal before Lent.

SEASON OF LENT

GOSPEL ACCLAMATION
See Ps 95:8

If today you hear his voice,
harden not your hearts.

Gospel Matt 6:1-6, 16-18; L219

Jesus said to his disciples:
"Take care not to perform righteous deeds
in order that people may see them;
otherwise, you will have no recompense from your heavenly Father.
When you give alms,
do not blow a trumpet before you,
as the hypocrites do in the synagogues and in the streets
to win the praise of others.
Amen, I say to you,
they have received their reward.
But when you give alms,
do not let your left hand know what your right is doing,
so that your almsgiving may be secret.
And your Father who sees in secret will repay you.

"When you pray,
do not be like the hypocrites,
who love to stand and pray in the synagogues and on street corners
so that others may see them.
Amen, I say to you,
they have received their reward.
But when you pray, go to your inner room,
close the door, and pray to your Father in secret.
And your Father who sees in secret will repay you.

"When you fast,
do not look gloomy like the hypocrites.
They neglect their appearance,
so that they may appear to others to be fasting.
Amen, I say to you, they have received their reward.
But when you fast,
anoint your head and wash your face,
so that you may not appear to be fasting,
except to your Father who is hidden.
And your Father who sees what is hidden will repay you."

See Appendix A, p. 269, for the other readings.

Reflecting on the Gospel

The ways of God can seem beyond us. Much of the Old Testament and even the New speaks to the inscrutable ways of God. But Jesus knew the ways of God and taught that to his disciples. This might be part of the reason Jesus was known as a teacher, and in the Gospel of Matthew is a teacher par excellence. His insights were so keen, so "spot on" that after his resurrection his disciples recognized that he had a special, divine quality about him that gave him this unique ability to teach God's ways. He was God's son.

Today's gospel reading comes from that inscrutable teaching moment known as the Sermon on the Mount. Here as Matthew depicts it, Jesus teaches and promulgates law as God had promulgated the law to Moses. Jesus' own teaching is on par with, and actually fulfills, the Mosaic Law. His lessons apply equally to the audience of his day as they do to us today. The three marks of our Lenten season—almsgiving, prayer, and fasting—are the objects of Jesus' teaching.

There can be a temptation for any religious person to be seen as religious, pleasing to God, and therefore pleasing to others. These sorts of people were prevalent in Jesus' day, as they are in our own. Yet, such actors are "hypocrites" in the eyes of Jesus or, more literally translated, "stage actors." The disciples of Jesus are told that the true audience of their almsgiving, prayer, and fasting is God, not fellow human beings. The disciples are certainly to give alms, fast, and pray, but not to make a show of it, as is too often the case.

Disciples are to give alms "in secret." Some in Jesus' day would toss coins in the street for the poor, making a show of their own generosity when the destitute would scamper for the loose change. Such "generous" figures already received their reward by being the object of praise by others. Far better to give secretly; the audience (God in heaven) knows what we do.

In like fashion, when we pray, we are to pray in secret. Though Jesus was not against group prayer or liturgical prayer, as the gospel elsewhere indicates, personal prayer is not dependent upon saying the right words or being in the right place. One's prayer to the Father should be an authentic expression, and wherever we are, we sanctify the place by our spiritual communion with God. We do not need to go somewhere special (temple, synagogue, church, tabernacle) to pray.

Finally, fasting is not to be done for show, but for the only audience that matters: our Father in heaven. In antiquity and even today, some proclaim their fast so others know how dedicated they are to God. Jesus tells us to put away such boasting and show. If we fast in such a way, we have already received our reward in the admiration of others. Instead, we should fast solely for God, who knows what we do.

So we can see how and why Jesus, God's son, was known as a teacher, whose teaching fulfilled Mosaic Law.

Living the Paschal Mystery

As we initiate our Lenten season with Ash Wednesday, we are dramatically reminded that our lives will come to an end. What remains of us on this earth are only ashes. By wearing this stark sacramental marking us as Christians today, we know that this life is but a prelude to another. Any quest for fortune and fame ought to be tempered with our call to give alms, fast, and pray.

In Jesus' teaching, the inscrutable ways of God are made clear, straightforward, and shockingly simple. Indeed, sometimes we might prefer a more complicated system to earn our way to God. But that is not the teaching of Jesus.

As disciples, children of the Father, we have only one audience, which is God in heaven. Let us act mercifully toward one another for the sake of God, not drawing attention to ourselves, but giving alms, fasting, and praying in a quiet, humble way, appropriate to this Lenten season and our lives as disciples.

Focusing the Gospel

Key words and phrases: [Y]our Father who sees in secret (what is hidden) will repay you.

To the point: This phrase is repeated three times in today's gospel. We are reminded that none of our actions are hidden from the gaze of our loving Father. Whether our deeds and intentions are for the good or not, they are witnessed by our creator. Today's gospel tells us that if our motivation is to please or impress others, our accomplishments and prayers are empty. It is only when our focus is on pleasing God alone that our lives of faith become fruitful and a blessing to us and others.

Model Universal Prayer (Prayer of the Faithful)

Presider: Having received ashes as a sign of our repentance and deep desire to return to God with our whole hearts, let us make our needs known to the Lord.

Response: Lord, hear our prayer.

For God's holy church, may the baptized members of the Body of Christ journey in grace and love with catechumens preparing for baptism . . .

For governments throughout the world, may they work in concert with each other to end hunger and ensure adequate health care for all . . .

For those living in poverty, especially children, the elderly, the disabled, and the mentally ill, may they receive support that respects their dignity and honors their gifts . . .

For all gathered here, by renewing our commitment to the practices of prayer, fasting, and almsgiving, may we be led to reconciliation with God and others . . .

Presider: God of all righteousness, you assure us that "now is an acceptable time . . . now is the day of salvation." Hear the prayers that we bring to you this day that in our observance of Lent we might draw closer to you. We ask this through Christ our Lord. **Amen.**

About Liturgy

Lent at home: One way to increase our appreciation of the church's communal liturgies during Lent (and throughout the year) may seem a bit counterintuitive. But when we pray more at home and observe personal devotions and spiritual practices each day, we become more ritual-oriented people and more fluent in the symbolic language of liturgy. Lent is an excellent time to begin! Start with the traditional disciplines of prayer, fasting, and almsgiving.

Build a dedicated prayer space at home with a cross, Bible, and candle. Pray there each day for one specific person or group you find difficult to love. Let yourself go hungry in some way each day and let those hunger pangs be reminders to pray for those who hunger not by choice. Finally, give a bit of yourself to another person in need each day: offer a word of kindness to someone in need; share your time when you are busy; give help to someone who cannot repay you.

As you practice these disciplines, bring these daily memories to the Sunday liturgy and see how much greater your Lenten joy may be.

COLLECT

Let us pray.

Pause for silent prayer

Grant, O Lord, that we may begin with holy fasting
this campaign of Christian service,
so that, as we take up battle against spiritual evils,
we may be armed with weapons of self-restraint.
Through our Lord Jesus Christ, your Son,
who lives and reigns with you in the unity of the Holy Spirit,
one God, for ever and ever. **Amen.**

FOR REFLECTION

- How will you fast this Lent?
- What practice of prayer will you take up in response to Jesus' invitation, "[W]hen you pray, go to your inner room, / close the door, and pray to your Father in secret"?
- Jesus encourages us to care for others through our secret almsgiving. How are you being called to give alms this Lent?

Homily Points

- Deep within each of us is a need and a desire to do better, to *be* better. In the first reading from the prophet Joel, the whole community is included in the urgent call to fast and repent. From the elderly, to the very young, from the bride and bridegroom with their reasons to rejoice, to the ministers of God who might consider themselves above such repentance—to each is issued the invitation: "[R]eturn to the Lord with your whole heart."

- Within community we find the strength and dedication to answer the call of the Lord, to be charitable, to fast, and to pray. As we begin this Lenten season, let us consider how we can support each other in these practices of repentance. May our actions be oriented for the glory of God alone, and may we trust in the one who sees in secret to build up our communities and make us a blessing to each other.

SPIRITUALITY

GOSPEL ACCLAMATION
Matt 4:4b

One does not live on bread alone,
but on every word that comes forth from
the mouth of God.

Gospel

Matt 4:1-11; L22A

At that time Jesus was
led by the Spirit
into the desert
to be tempted by the devil.
He fasted for forty days and
forty nights,
and afterwards he was
hungry.
The tempter
approached and
said to him,
"If you are the Son
of God,
command that these stones become
loaves of bread."
He said in reply,
"It is written:
One does not live on bread alone,
but on every word that comes
forth
from the mouth of God."

Then the devil took him to the holy city,
and made him stand on the parapet
of the temple,
and said to him, "If you are the Son
of God, throw yourself down.
For it is written:
He will command his angels
concerning you
and with their hands they will
support you,
lest you dash your foot against a
stone."
Jesus answered him,
"Again it is written,
You shall not put the Lord, your
God, to the test."

Continued in Appendix A, p. 270.

Reflecting on the Gospel

Temptations can be difficult to avoid! Even the Lord's Prayer concludes with the exhortation to "lead us not into temptation." But what is a temptation in the modern world? Sometimes, for people attempting to control their weight or lose weight, a temptation can be dessert or an especially delightful meal. For others who tend to procrastinate, a temptation can be a movie, a good book, some TV, or nearly anything else but the task at hand!

In today's gospel we learn that Jesus himself faces temptation, and not only one but three. The early church fathers recognized that these temptations were metaphorical for (1) the needs of the body, (2) one's relationship with the divine, and (3) one's own desire for power and glory. In each instance, of course, Jesus overcomes the temptation. He recognizes that one does not live on bread alone, that one does not put the Lord to the test, and that power and glory are not to be had by worshiping anything other than God.

If these temptations seem beyond us, we need only look more carefully at our own lives. Bodily needs, desires, and wants can easily overtake us. We are reminded that there is much more to life than food, clothes, shelter, a car, or any other physical thing. When we become captivated by sophisticated marketing and believe we must have the next best thing, we can take comfort in knowing that we do not live by bread alone. In other words, there is more to life than creature comforts or satisfying the needs of the body.

Not many of us will be tempted to throw ourselves down from a cliff to see if God's angels will catch us, but how many of us ask God for a sign or test God in another way? Jesus reminds us that we are not to test God. In times of stress, or prior to making a major decision, we want to know the right path and so we might place limitations or strictures on God and how God might interact with us. Such is not the way of Christ. Instead, we must live our lives without putting God to the test.

Finally, it may seem strange that Jesus would be tempted to worship the devil himself. But upon reading the story, we see that the temptation was "all the kingdoms of the world." The price for that was prostrating oneself before the devil. Jesus does not succumb. But what compromises do we make to get ahead in the world? Rarely, if ever, will we be tempted to prostrate ourselves before the devil. But we might be asked to neglect family or to choose power instead of the sanctity of a relationship.

In the end, temptation does not approach us as the devil incarnate. Christians have known this for centuries. The story in Matthew's gospel was meant to be understood broadly, addressing fundamental temptations of humankind for the self. In those circumstances, we rest in our baptism, knowing that our relationship with God is secure. As disciples of Christ, we are confident sons and daughters of God.

Living the Paschal Mystery

The pursuit of bodily pleasures, a God who acts on our behalf for our whims and desires, and our own accumulation of power are fundamental temptations for human beings. Food, shelter, and clothing are all necessary and good as a means of something more. But they are not ends in themselves. God is there by our side, but not as our enforcer. And power and glory are not ends in themselves either.

Today's gospel invites us to consider the human condition from the viewpoint of Christ who overcame temptation. Turning away bread is not so much about fasting as it is about recognizing that there is more to life than food. Our god is not the belly. When we come to the end of our lives, what will we have? With the power of Christ, let us overcome the temptation to see the value of our lives only in terms of the world. Instead, may we see with the eyes of faith that human relationships are good in and of themselves. Bonds formed in this way last through life eternal.

Focusing the Gospel

Key words and phrases: He fasted for forty days and forty nights

To the point: Throughout the Bible, many numbers are repeated over and over again, such as three, twelve, and forty. The rain of the flood fell for forty days and forty nights while Noah and his family took shelter in the ark. The Israelites wandered in the desert for forty years after leaving a life of slavery in Egypt and before entering into the Promised Land. In the book of Deuteronomy, Moses stays on Mount Sinai for "forty days and forty nights" before receiving the tablets of the law (9:9-10) and then again, forty more days and nights "prostrate before the Lord" (9:18) to atone for the people's worship of the golden calf. Forty signifies a time of trial and testing, purification and preparation for a closer walk with God. Each Lent we enter into our own forty days of purification and preparation before renewing our baptismal promises at Easter.

Connecting the Gospel

to the first reading: In the first reading and the gospel, we have two tales of temptation. In the garden of Eden, the serpent tempts the woman to eat of the fruit that God has forbidden, telling her that to do so will make her and her husband "be like gods." In the desert, the devil confronts Jesus, tempting the one who *is* both fully divine and fully human to create bread from stones, test God's care for him, and worship the devil in return for ruling the kingdoms of the world. In the first reading, Adam and Eve give in to temptation, eat of the forbidden fruit, and as a result have their eyes opened to sin within and around them. In the gospel, Jesus resists the temptations placed before him, remaining true to his nature, "though he was in the form of God, / [he] did not regard equality with God something to be grasped" (Phil 2:6).

to experience: The lie within temptation is that by going against the will of God, we might have a greater fullness of life. Only in resisting these temptations can true freedom and true abundance be found.

Connecting the Responsorial Psalm

to the readings: Today's psalm presents us with two truths: as human beings our relationship with God and others is marked by sin in some way, and God's mercy is great enough to wipe out the effects of sin and wash away all guilt. The second reading from St. Paul's letter to the Romans interprets the story of our first parents' sin saying, "[T]hrough one transgression / condemnation came upon us all." And then continues, referencing Jesus' victory over sin and death: "[S]o, through one righteous act, / acquittal and life came to all."

to psalmist preparation: In this season of Lent how are you being called to live deeply into the truth of your own sinfulness and the truth of God's overwhelming mercy?

PROMPTS FOR FAITH-SHARING

In the first reading from Genesis we hear the second creation story, where God creates man out of the earth and then blows into him "the breath of life." How do you experience the breath of God in your life?

The psalmist asks of God, "Give me back the joy of your salvation." When have you known this joy most fully in your life?

In the desert Jesus is tempted to sate his hunger, test God's love for him, and rule the kingdoms of the world by worshiping the devil. Which of these temptations (material goods, testing God, power and glory) is the one you struggle with the most?

Jesus responds to the devil's request to turn stone into bread by saying, "One does not live on bread alone, / but on every word that comes forth / from the mouth of God." How does God's word nourish and sustain you?

Model Penitential Act

Presider: In today's first reading we hear of how God formed Adam from the clay of the ground and then "blew into his nostrils the breath of life." For the times that our lives have not reflected the life of God, let us ask for pardon and mercy . . . *[pause]*

Confiteor: I confess . . .

Homily Points

• As Christians, we seek to imitate Christ. Sometimes this might seem impossible; how are we who are human to emulate the divine? Jesus shows us the way through how he lived out his own humanity. In the gospels of Lent we encounter this humanity of Jesus. On this first Sunday of Lent our gospel focuses on Jesus' forty days and nights in the desert fasting and praying. At the end of this time, we are told, "[H]e was hungry." On the Third Sunday of Lent we hear how Jesus, "tired from his journey" through Samaria, sits down at a well. On the Fifth Sunday, Jesus weeps at the tomb of his friend Lazarus, and on Palm Sunday we encounter the most human experience of all: Jesus dies.

• Each year, Lent beckons us to enter into the dynamism of human weakness and divine care. On Ash Wednesday we smeared our foreheads with a sign of repentance and mortality. We are invited to take up the practices of prayer, almsgiving, and fasting to bring us back into right relationship with God and with each other. And yet, this focus on our sin is not meant to overwhelm or discourage us, but rather to highlight even more the compassionate and bountiful mercy of God who sent his son to live among us and to feel hunger, fatigue, and even fear and despair in the garden of Gethsemane.

• The paschal mystery reminds us that the only way to greater life is through death. Let us ask God for the grace and strength necessary to die to the temptations we face daily and to look to Jesus to show us the way to live out our own humanity centered in the love of God.

Model Universal Prayer (Prayer of the Faithful)

Presider: In the gospel reading we are reminded that "[o]ne does not live on bread alone, / but on every word that comes forth / from the mouth of God." Trusting in God's providence and care, let us bring our needs before him.

Response: Lord, hear our prayer.

For all who exercise authority within the church, may they be strengthened against every temptation and sanctified in grace . . .

For governments throughout the world, may they humbly serve the people in their care and work tirelessly to promote justice and peace . . .

For those struggling with addictions, may they receive the support, strength, and grace necessary to resist temptation . . .

For all gathered here around the table of the Lord, through our prayer, fasting, and almsgiving may we be brought to Easter joy . . .

Presider: God of abundant grace and never-ending mercy, you sent your son to dwell among us and show us the pathway to life everlasting. Hear our prayers that we might be renewed in spirit and cleansed of all sin. We ask this through Christ our Lord. **Amen.**

COLLECT

Let us pray.

Pause for silent prayer

Grant, almighty God,
through the yearly observances of holy Lent,
that we may grow in understanding
of the riches hidden in Christ
and by worthy conduct pursue their effects.
Through our Lord Jesus Christ, your Son,
who lives and reigns with you in the unity of the Holy Spirit,
one God, for ever and ever. **Amen.**

FIRST READING

Gen 2:7-9; 3:1-7

The LORD God formed man out of the clay of the ground
and blew into his nostrils the breath of life,
and so man became a living being.

Then the LORD God planted a garden in Eden, in the east,
and placed there the man whom he had formed.
Out of the ground the LORD God made various trees grow
that were delightful to look at and good for food,
with the tree of life in the middle of the garden
and the tree of the knowledge of good and evil.

Now the serpent was the most cunning of all the animals
that the LORD God had made.
The serpent asked the woman,
"Did God really tell you not to eat
from any of the trees in the garden?"
The woman answered the serpent:
"We may eat of the fruit of the trees in the garden;
it is only about the fruit of the tree
in the middle of the garden that God said,
'You shall not eat it or even touch it, lest you die.'"
But the serpent said to the woman:
"You certainly will not die!
No, God knows well that the moment you eat of it
your eyes will be opened and you will be like gods
who know what is good and what is evil."
The woman saw that the tree was good for food,
pleasing to the eyes, and desirable for gaining wisdom.

So she took some of its fruit and ate it;
and she also gave some to her husband,
who was with her,
and he ate it.
Then the eyes of both of them were
opened,
and they realized that they were naked;
so they sewed fig leaves together
and made loincloths for themselves.

RESPONSORIAL PSALM

Ps 51:3-4, 5-6, 12-13, 17

℟. (cf. 3a) Be merciful, O Lord, for we have sinned.

Have mercy on me, O God, in your
goodness;
in the greatness of your compassion
wipe out my offense.
Thoroughly wash me from my guilt
and of my sin cleanse me.

℟. Be merciful, O Lord, for we have sinned.

For I acknowledge my offense,
and my sin is before me always:
"Against you only have I sinned,
and done what is evil in your sight."

℟. Be merciful, O Lord, for we have sinned.

A clean heart create for me, O God,
and a steadfast spirit renew within me.
Cast me not out from your presence,
and your Holy Spirit take not from me.

℟. Be merciful, O Lord, for we have sinned.

Give me back the joy of your salvation,
and a willing spirit sustain in me.
O Lord, open my lips,
and my mouth shall proclaim your praise.

℟. Be merciful, O Lord, for we have sinned.

SECOND READING

Rom 5:12-19

Brothers and sisters:
Through one man sin entered the world,
and through sin, death,
and thus death came to all men,
inasmuch as all sinned—
for up to the time of the law, sin was in
the world,
though sin is not accounted when there
is no law.
But death reigned from Adam to Moses,
even over those who did not sin
after the pattern of the trespass of
Adam,
who is the type of the one who was to
come.

Continued in Appendix A, p. 270, or
Rom 5:12, 17-19 *in Appendix A, p. 270.*

CATECHESIS

About Liturgy

Twofold character of Lent: It's clear that Lent is a penitential season. However, that's just half the story. Lent has a twofold character. First, it is a time to recall or prepare for baptism. That is why we celebrate so many of the rites from the Rite of Christian Initiation of Adults during Lent. All the baptized assist those preparing to be initiated by "joining the catechumens in reflecting on the value of the paschal mystery and by renewing their own conversion" (RCIA 4). In Lent, we renew our conversion to Christ, particularly through prayer, fasting, and almsgiving.

Recollecting our baptism leads us to the second character of the season. As members of the baptized, we realize that we have not always lived up to our baptismal promises. Our actions and attitudes do not always reflect our faith in the Father, in Jesus, or in the Holy Spirit. Those preparing for baptism may have their moments of doubt as well. For them and for the baptized, penance, especially through more attentive listening to the word of God and fervent prayer, helps us reorient our lives to Christ and dispose us to celebrate his death and resurrection.

About Initiation

Purification and enlightenment: The third period of the RCIA, the period of purification and enlightenment, usually coincides with Lent. For both those preparing for baptism and for the faithful, this is a time for spiritual recollection and "more intense spiritual preparation, consisting more in interior reflection than in catechetical instruction" (RCIA 139). Therefore, the gatherings you have with catechumens, elect, and candidates during this period should have a qualitatively different feel from those of the period of the catechumenate. Your sessions during Lent should seem more like a retreat or holy hour than a class or lecture. The content should focus more on interior preparation and outward signs of faith than on academic knowledge or catching up on topics. An easy way to shift your Lenten RCIA gatherings is to look at what your parish is doing for Lent. You will probably find Stations of the Cross, soup suppers, penitential services, and increased outreach to the poor happening somewhere in your parish or diocese. Tap into these Lenten activities, and use them in place of some of your RCIA gatherings for the season.

About Liturgical Music

The power of the human voice: In "About Liturgical Music" for the Second Sunday of Advent, we reflected on the restrained use of musical instruments during penitential seasons. The General Instruction of the Roman Missal calls for moderation during Advent. However, for Lent, it says, "[T]he playing of the organ and musical instruments is allowed only in order to support the singing. Exceptions, however, are Laetare Sunday (Fourth Sunday of Lent), Solemnities, and Feasts" (313).

There is great power in the unaccompanied human voice. When an entire assembly sings together a cappella, they often sound louder than when they are accompanied by instruments. This may be because the individuals singing can hear themselves and one another better. Because unaccompanied singing is a vulnerable act, each person unconsciously relies on the other singers in the assembly. When you know your voice is needed by others, you may be inspired to stronger participation. Finally, the sounds in a space resonate even more in unison with unaccompanied singing by the assembly.

If your assembly has never sung without accompaniment before, Lent may be the perfect time to try a few songs or responses with the human voice as the main instrument. Use the organ or keyboard just to get them started and intermittently to keep them on pitch.

SPIRITUALITY

GOSPEL ACCLAMATION

cf. Matt 17:5

From the shining cloud the Father's voice is heard:
This is my beloved Son, hear him.

Gospel Matt 17:1-9; L25A

Jesus took Peter, James, and John his brother,
and led them up a high mountain by themselves.
And he was transfigured before them;
his face shone like the sun
and his clothes became white as light.
And behold, Moses and Elijah appeared to them,
conversing with him.
Then Peter said to Jesus in reply,
"Lord, it is good that we are here.
If you wish, I will make three tents here,
one for you, one for Moses, and one for Elijah."
While he was still speaking, behold,
a bright cloud cast a shadow over them,
then from the cloud came a voice that said,
"This is my beloved Son, with whom I am well pleased;
listen to him."
When the disciples heard this, they fell prostrate
and were very much afraid.
But Jesus came and touched them, saying,
"Rise, and do not be afraid."
And when the disciples raised their eyes,
they saw no one else but Jesus alone.

As they were coming down from the mountain,
Jesus charged them,
"Do not tell the vision to anyone
until the Son of Man has been raised from the dead."

Reflecting on the Gospel

The church gives us Matthew's story of the transfiguration on this Second Sunday of Lent. We are reminded of our faith, which proclaims resurrection from the dead. The Lenten season will culminate with Triduum and then Easter Sunday. The transfiguration gives the disciples and us a foretaste of the kingdom, and a reminder of Jesus' divine glory.

Moses and Elijah represent the Law and the Prophets. These two majestic figures in Israelite history each received a revelation from God on Mount Horeb (Sinai). Together they stand as pillars of Judaism, which Jesus himself fulfills.

Peter, as spokesperson for the group, expresses a desire to build three tents, "if you wish." This nod to Jesus is a Matthean addition, absent in Mark. By placing this conditional phrase on the lips of Peter, his boldness is subtly subdued.

Before Peter can finish, the divine presence is made manifest in the cloud and the heavenly voice. The disciples hear the words that accompanied Jesus at his own baptism: "This is my beloved Son, with whom I am well pleased." Only now, the imperative phrase "listen to him" is added. The disciples react with fear, falling prostrate and worshiping. Only by the touch of Jesus are they raised up again, to find that they are alone with him. The vision is no more.

This remarkable event surely emboldened the disciples in their faith, while it also seized them with fear. This mountaintop experience meant even more after the resurrection when the words of Jesus became clear.

The gospel today reminds us of our ultimate end, which is to be with Jesus in the heavenly realm. With such knowledge, cares of the world may wash away. Even a desire to commemorate such an event, as Peter desired to build three tents, are as nothing when compared to the experience itself. We have a foreshadowing of eternal glory. Let us continue to follow Jesus down the mountain, learning from him the entire way, knowing that the ultimate resurrection requires undergoing death itself.

Living the Paschal Mystery

Jesus fulfills the Law and the Prophets. This statement of faith is represented by the vision in today's gospel where Jesus is present with Moses (Law) and Elijah (Prophets). The story comes from Mark, which Matthew has changed slightly. Matthew clearly refers to this as a "vision," a term which is absent in Mark. This vision shows Jesus in his heavenly, divine glory. This is why Peter offers to make three tents, a term that recalls the abode of the divine.

The disciples are warned not to say anything of this vision "until the Son of Man has been raised from the dead." For the Gospel of Matthew, like later theologians, there is a link between understanding and believing, and conversely between believing and understanding. The vision was a foretaste of the heavenly kingdom, where Jesus will reign with God forever and ever. But before that point is reached, Jesus must be raised from the dead, a statement which presupposes his death. There can be no eternal life with God without death. Such is the paschal mystery.

Focusing the Gospel

Key words and phrases: "Rise, and do not be afraid."

To the point: In the transfiguration, Peter, James, and John are given a glimpse of what is to come in the resurrection. Jesus appears before them with face shining like the sun and clothes "as white as light." At first they are delighted by the sight, but when a voice speaks to them from the cloud, they fall prostrate in fear and again we find these words on the lips of Jesus: "Do not be afraid." Soon they will follow Jesus to Jerusalem where he will undergo suffering and persecution that will lead to death on a cross. And yet, this is not the end. What he spoke on the mountain of transfiguration remains true; do not be afraid, even when confronted with death, for life is stronger.

Connecting the Gospel

to the second reading: Writing to Timothy, St. Paul references God's grace "made manifest / through the appearance of our savior Christ Jesus." On the mountaintop in today's gospel, Peter, James, and John are given a new vision of Christ in the transfiguration. The man they have known as friend and teacher is now radiant, his face shining like the sun. This moment quickly passes, however, and soon they are returning down the mountain with Jesus beside them, looking as he did before.

to experience: The image of Jesus as glorified and radiating the light of God is a true one, just as the image of him bloodied and broken on the cross is true. The way we consider and think about Christ affects how we live our lives as his disciples. Which image of Jesus (the teacher, the wonder worker, the glorified one, the crucified) comes most easily to you in prayer? Which image are you called to spend time with as your relationship with Christ deepens?

Connecting the Responsorial Psalm

to the readings: Today's responsorial psalm paints a picture of God's mercy placed upon us, almost as if we could wear it as a cloak or shield. In the transfiguration, Jesus appears to Peter, James, and John in clothing as "white as light." We might consider the event in our own lives when we, too, wore clothing that covered us in the light of God. In the white baptismal garment we were proclaimed "a new creation" clothed in Christ.

to psalmist preparation: As we continue journeying toward the feast of Easter and the moment when we renew our own baptismal promises, how do you experience yourself as clothed in the mercy and love of Christ?

PROMPTS FOR FAITH-SHARING

In the first reading Abram is called to go forth from his family and homeland to a new place the Lord will reveal. When in your faith life have you been called to leave what was comfortable and familiar to embark into the unknown?

The psalmist proclaims, "Upright is the word of the Lord, / and all his works are trustworthy." How have you experienced the trustworthiness of God?

In the second reading St. Paul urges Timothy, "Bear your share of hardship for the gospel." When have you experienced hardship in your life as a Christian?

On the mountaintop the disciples hear a voice from the cloud proclaiming, "This is my beloved Son, with whom I am well pleased; / listen to him." In prayer, how do you spend time listening to God?

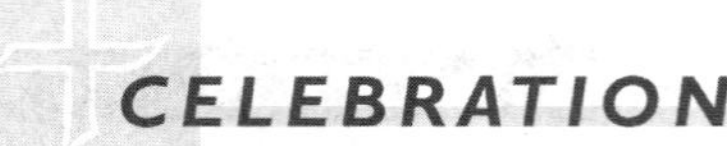

Model Penitential Act

Presider: In today's gospel Peter, James, and John hear a voice from a cloud tell them, "This is my beloved Son, with whom I am well pleased; / listen to him." Let us pause to ask for God's mercy for the times we have not been attentive to his voice . . . *[pause]*

Confiteor: I confess . . .

Homily Points

• Tradition tells us that Paul wrote his second letter to Timothy in prison before his execution in Rome. Within it he offers encouragement to Timothy in his own work as a pastor and missionary. Paul is not concerned or disheartened that his own mission could be considered unsuccessful by the eyes of the world. A few verses later in this letter he will tell Timothy, "You know that everyone in Asia deserted me" (1:15). Paul urges Timothy to remain strong, writing, "Remember Jesus Christ, raised from the dead, a descendant of David: such is my gospel, for which I am suffering, even to the point of chains, like a criminal" (2:8-9).

• Today's short reading from Paul's letter to Timothy could be read as a mission statement for all Christians. We are called to "bear [our] share of hardship for the gospel" and to lead a "holy life." In the life of Jesus and the saints, we see how this mission statement is lived out. Often the word of God is met with obstacles and sometimes outright derision and rejection. The one who proclaims it can expect to encounter these as well. The road we walk on leads to Calvary.

• Despite discouragements and failures, as Christians we are called to perseverance and to holiness. In all things we are to meet anger with love, darkness with light, and sin with mercy. This is not easy, and yet to be holy is to be "set apart" and to live our lives in such a way that it is obvious to whom we belong. As we continue on our Lenten journey, what are the hardships within your own life that you are being called to bear for the sake of the gospel? How are the Lenten practices of fasting, almsgiving, and prayer leading you to holiness?

Model Universal Prayer (Prayer of the Faithful)

Presider: Nourished and strengthened by the word of God, let us bring our needs, and the needs of our world, before the Lord.

Response: Lord, hear our prayer.

For members of the church throughout the world, may our ears be attuned to the voice of God calling us to fullness of life . . .

For leaders of nations as they consider how to build up their own countries, may they also commit to helping those stricken by natural disasters and poverty . . .

For refugees, migrants, and immigrants, who, like Abraham, have left all they know, may they find welcome, support, and meaningful employment . . .

For all gathered here, may the eyes of our hearts be healed to see Christ in all his glory and to serve him within the poor . . .

Presider: God of glory and might, like Peter, James, and John, we, too, stand before your son, Jesus, in awe and wonder. Hear our prayers that by listening to his voice and following his example, we might draw nearer to you each day. We ask this through Christ our Lord. **Amen.**

COLLECT

Let us pray.

Pause for silent prayer

O God, who have commanded us
to listen to your beloved Son,
be pleased, we pray,
to nourish us inwardly by your word,
that, with spiritual sight made pure,
we may rejoice to behold your glory.
Through our Lord Jesus Christ, your Son,
who lives and reigns with you in the unity
of the Holy Spirit,
one God, for ever and ever. **Amen.**

FIRST READING

Gen 12:1-4a

The LORD said to Abram:
"Go forth from the land of your kinsfolk
and from your father's house to a land
that I will show you.

"I will make of you a great nation,
and I will bless you;
I will make your name great,
so that you will be a blessing.
I will bless those who bless you
and curse those who curse you.
All the communities of the earth
shall find blessing in you."

Abram went as the LORD directed him.

RESPONSORIAL PSALM
Ps 33:4-5, 18-19, 20, 22

℟. (22) Lord, let your mercy be on us, as we place our trust in you.

Upright is the word of the LORD,
and all his works are trustworthy.
He loves justice and right;
of the kindness of the LORD the earth is full.

℟. Lord, let your mercy be on us, as we place our trust in you.

See, the eyes of the LORD are upon those who fear him,
upon those who hope for his kindness,
to deliver them from death
and preserve them in spite of famine.

℟. Lord, let your mercy be on us, as we place our trust in you.

Our soul waits for the LORD,
who is our help and our shield.
May your kindness, O LORD, be upon us
who have put our hope in you.

℟. Lord, let your mercy be on us, as we place our trust in you.

SECOND READING
2 Tim 1:8b-10

Beloved:
Bear your share of hardship for the gospel
with the strength that comes from God.

He saved us and called us to a holy life,
not according to our works
but according to his own design
and the grace bestowed on us in Christ Jesus before time began,
but now made manifest
through the appearance of our savior Christ Jesus,
who destroyed death and brought life and immortality
to light through the gospel.

CATECHESIS

About Liturgy

Prayer over the people: Typically, the blessing given at the end of Mass is the very brief and simple form, "May almighty God bless you, the Father, and the Son, and the Holy Spirit" (Roman Missal [RM] 141). However, on certain days and occasions, there is a prescribed solemn blessing that uses a three-part structure or an assigned short text called the prayer over the people (see RM 142). These prayers over the people are simpler in form than the solemn blessing, but are longer than the brief blessing above.

For each Sunday of Lent there is an assigned prayer over the people. These blessings are not optional and the text should not be changed, since they correspond to the readings of the day, especially in Cycle A. For example, the prayer over the people for the Second Sunday of Lent refers to the glory of the transfigured Christ, "whose beauty he showed in his own Body, to the amazement of his Apostles."

You'll find the prescribed texts for these prayers on their respective page for each Sunday of Lent in the Roman Missal. Note that there is a suggested prayer over the people for each weekday of Lent, but these are optional and the simple blessing may be used in its place.

About Initiation

Sacrament of Penance: Sometimes, RCIA teams wonder if catechumens are supposed to celebrate reconciliation before their initiation. Although the answer may be clear, it's good to review our understanding of the sacraments and who celebrates them.

For those who are unbaptized, the only sacrament they can celebrate is baptism, for baptism is "the door which gives access to the other sacraments" (*Catechism of the Catholic Church* 1213). Therefore, catechumens cannot celebrate the sacrament of penance until after they are baptized.

For baptized candidates preparing for confirmation or Eucharist, or for those baptized in another Christian tradition preparing to be received into the full communion of the Catholic Church, they should celebrate the sacrament of penance as part of their formation and "they should be encouraged in the frequent celebration of this sacrament" (National Statutes for the Catechumenate 27 and 36) during their preparation. Reconciliation should be celebrated at a time distinct from their reception or celebration of the other sacraments.

Everyone, whether baptized or not, should participate in penitential practices and, especially during Lent, in the non-sacramental penitential liturgies of the parish.

About Liturgical Music

Silence: As musicians, we have influence not only over the music in a liturgy but also, to some extent, over the silences. There are six prescribed silences we are to observe in every Eucharist: during the penitential act; after "Let us pray," in the collects; after each reading; after the homily; after Communion if a song of praise is not sung; and before the Mass begins (see General Instruction of the Roman Missal 45). You don't have control over all these moments, but you can certainly influence the length and quality of the silences during the penitential act if you are singing it, after the first and sometimes the second readings, and before the liturgy.

The silences don't need to be very long, but they do need to be intentional. One way to make them intentional is to observe stillness during each of them. Train your music ministers to be still during the silences. Don't use the silence as a time to turn pages or adjust instruments. Enter into each silence with deep prayer and focus. Inform other liturgical ministers, and ask them to assist by also observing stillness and silence at these six moments in the Mass.

SPIRITUALITY

GOSPEL ACCLAMATION
cf. John 4:42, 15

Lord, you are truly the Savior of the world;
give me living water, that I may never thirst again.

Gospel John 4:5-42; L28A

Jesus came to a town of Samaria called Sychar,
near the plot of land that Jacob had given to his son Joseph.
Jacob's well was there.
Jesus, tired from his journey, sat down there at the well.
It was about noon.

A woman of Samaria came to draw water.
Jesus said to her,
"Give me a drink."
His disciples had gone into the town to buy food.
The Samaritan woman said to him,
"How can you, a Jew, ask me, a Samaritan woman, for a drink?"
—For Jews use nothing in common with Samaritans.—
Jesus answered and said to her,
"If you knew the gift of God
and who is saying to you, 'Give me a drink,'
you would have asked him
and he would have given you living water."
The woman said to him,
"Sir, you do not even have a bucket and the cistern is deep;
where then can you get this living water?
Are you greater than our father Jacob,
who gave us this cistern and drank from it himself
with his children and his flocks?"

Continued in Appendix A, p. 271, or
John 4:5-15, 19b-26, 39a, 40-42 *in Appendix A, p. 272.*

Reflecting on the Gospel

Though we are in Cycle A, the Gospel of Matthew, the Third Sunday of Lent (as well as the Fourth and the Fifth) bring us readings from the Gospel of John, marking the "scrutiny Sundays." These gospel readings precede the "scrutinies" (examinations) of adult catechumens and candidates that take place after the homily. Even when the scrutinies take place in Cycle B or Cycle C, the readings from the Gospel of John are used. (See "About Liturgy" for more on the scrutinies.) The stories from the Gospel of John that make up the three scrutiny Sundays are the woman at the well, the man born blind, and the raising of Lazarus from the dead. In each story there are those who gradually come to believe in Jesus. The titles used for Jesus are significant in each.

Today we accompany Jesus as he meets the woman at the well. The setting is the Samaritan town of Sychar (Shechem), noteworthy because of its association with the patriarch Jacob (Gen 33:18; 48:22; Josh 24:32), though the Old Testament never mentions the well of Jacob. Samaritans were not considered by Judeans to be truly Jewish, as they worshipped not at the temple (which was in Judea) but at Shechem ("on this mountain"). Jesus tells the woman that there will come a time (considered fulfilled at the time of the writing of the Gospel of John) "when true worshipers will worship the Father in Spirit and truth." No longer will it matter whether one is at a particular place for worship.

The woman recognizes that Jesus is a prophet, and Jesus himself eventually reveals to her that he is the Messiah, the Christ. Even so, she does not initially refer to him with that title herself. Instead, she goes back to her townspeople claiming that she met someone who could be the Christ. Because of her word, many of the townspeople believed in him. After Jesus stayed with them for some time, many more came to believe in him, hearing him for themselves. They then claim to know that "he is the savior of the world." Though this is a common term in Luke and Paul, this is the only instance of Jesus being called "Savior" during his public ministry in the Gospel of John.

Thus we have a gradual coming to faith in the encounter at the well. The woman recognizes Jesus as a prophet and senses he could even be the Christ. She immediately evangelizes, spreads the good news to her townspeople. Some come to believe on her word alone, but more come to believe upon hearing Jesus for themselves. Such an encounter leads them to proclaim him as "Savior." Certainly, much more could be said about this multivalent reading, but for the scrutiny Sundays, it seems appropriate to focus on the experience of coming to faith in Jesus.

Living the Paschal Mystery

Each of us came to faith through someone else. Each of us can recall hearing about Christ from another person who likely meant something to us. The woman at the well shared her experience with the townspeople. Many believed upon hearing, and many more heard for themselves and believed. Even the process of believing or, rather, coming to faith is gradual. Terms like "prophet" give way to "Christ" and ultimately (in this story) to "Savior." Later in the Gospel of John still more titles will be used. Jesus cannot be encapsulated by one title or in one encounter. The initial experience leaves the woman and the townspeople wanting more. Such is the life of faith. We do not have a once-and-for-all encounter. But a relationship with Jesus unfolds over time, ever deepening, ever revealing, until we encounter the cross and the exaltation. These mysteries we will ponder throughout our lives and share them with others, who will also ponder the same. The life of faith is shared reflection on the paschal mystery.

Focusing the Gospel

Key words and phrases: "My food is to do the will of the one who sent me / and to finish his work."

To the point: On the first Sunday of Lent, we listened to Matthew's gospel where Jesus responds to the devil's temptation to turn stone into bread by saying, "One does not live on bread alone, / but on every word that comes forth / from the mouth of God." Today we hear a counterpart to this statement in the Gospel of John. Not only is listening to God's word necessary nourishment, we are also fed when we are about the work of God and following his will.

Connecting the Gospel

to the first reading: God provides water for a thirsting people in today's readings. In the first reading this is physical water that Moses draws forth from the rock to quench the thirst of the people in the desert. In the gospel it is a deeper thirst, no less real, that Jesus slakes, telling the Samaritan woman, "[W]hoever drinks the water I shall give will never thirst; / the water I shall give will become in him a spring of water welling up to eternal life."

to experience: We know that water is vital for life. Water makes up more than 60 percent of the adult human body. Whereas a human person can survive for several weeks or more without food, going more than a few days without water can be life threatening. In the exodus, the Israelites were given miraculous water from a rock to sustain them in the desert. Now, Jesus himself is the source of life-giving water. A few chapters following today's gospel, Jesus will announce to the gathered crowd, "Let anyone who thirsts come to me and drink" (7:37). The invitation stands for us today. What are you thirsting for?

Connecting the Responsorial Psalm

to the readings: Within the book of Psalms there are many places that use the imagery of a shepherd and sheep. In today's psalm we hear ourselves proclaimed as "the people [God] shepherds, the flock he guides." In the most beloved psalm about God as a shepherd (Psalm 23), we are told how we are cared for by the Lord: "In green pastures he makes me lie down; / to still waters he leads me; / he restores my soul" (23:2-3; NABRE). This is the same shepherd who produces water from a rock to satisfy the thirst of the Israelites on their journey to the Promised Land, and also the shepherd in today's gospel where Jesus tells the Samaritan woman that he is the source of living water, the only water that can quench thirst forever.

to psalmist preparation: Within a flock the sheep must know and follow the voice of their shepherd, lest they wander away from safety. How do you live out your relationship to God, the shepherd? Where do you hear his voice calling to you at this moment in your life?

PROMPTS FOR FAITH-SHARING

Have there been moments in your life where you, like the Israelites, questioned, "Is the Lord in our midst or not?" What helped you get through these times?

In his letter to the Romans, St. Paul rejoices that "the love of God has been poured out into our hearts / through the Holy Spirit who has been given to us." Where do you find this love flowing freely in your own life? Where are you being called to pour out more love?

Jesus tells the Samaritan woman, "[T]he hour is coming, and is now here, / when true worshipers will worship the Father in Spirit and truth." How do you seek to worship God in Spirit and truth?

Through the Samaritan woman's witness, her townspeople welcome Jesus into their village and eventually come to believe he is the savior of the world. In your life of faith, who have been the witnesses who have led you to relationship with Christ?

Model Penitential Act

Presider: In today's gospel the Samaritan woman tells her townspeople that Jesus "told me everything I have done." Let us turn to the one who knows all of our thoughts and deeds, both those that are charitable and righteous and those that are not, and ask for pardon and mercy . . . *[pause]*

Confiteor: I confess . . .

Homily Points

• Today's gospel story of Jesus' interaction with the Samaritan woman at the well is one of the longest we read during the liturgical year. Within it we find different scenes with distinct actions taking place. It can help to think of this moment in the Gospel of John as a scene from a play.

• Besides Jesus, the cast of characters include the Samaritan woman, the disciples, and the Samaritan townspeople. We could say that each person or group is struggling with the question of Jesus' identity. Who is this person? A Jewish teacher or, perhaps, something more? Both the Samaritan woman and the disciples treat Jesus as an ordinary human being at first, the woman questioning how he dares to ask her for a drink of water, and the disciples wishing to minister to his physical need for food. As a consequence of their interaction with him, however, the Samaritan woman and her townspeople come to a shocking revelation: they have not only encountered a human being, but also "the Messiah," "the Christ," "the savior of the world."

• The drama of our own lives as disciples centers on this same question, one Jesus asks of his followers in each of the Synoptic Gospels: "Who do you say that I am?" (Matt 16:15; Mark 8:29; Luke 9:20). The Samaritan woman and townspeople are only able to answer this question after spending time with Jesus. Despite having given up their livelihoods to follow Jesus, the disciples still have much to learn at this point in John's gospel. And this is true for us as well. The mystery of God revealed in Jesus invites us to go ever deeper into relationship as we ponder the question, "Who are you, Lord?"

Model Universal Prayer (Prayer of the Faithful)

Presider: In Jesus we find the living water that quenches the deepest thirsting of our souls. With gratitude for this gift and trust in God's love, let us bring our needs before the Lord.

Response: Lord, hear our prayer.

For pastors and pastoral ministers within the church, may their love of Christ and devotion to God's people grow with each passing day . . .

For nations of the world fractured by the sins of racism, segregation, and prejudice, may the Lord of life lead the way to healing and inclusion . . .

For those who are outcast or living on the fringes of society, may the larger community find ways to embrace and include those on the margins . . .

For all gathered here, may we drink deeply from the living water of word and sacrament and be emboldened to proclaim our joy to all we meet . . .

Presider: God, source of life and font of salvation, you have called us here to worship you in spirit and truth. Hear the prayers that we bring before you this day. May the living water of your grace cover us and all of creation. We ask this through Christ our Lord. **Amen.**

COLLECT

Let us pray.

Pause for silent prayer

O God, author of every mercy and of all goodness,
who in fasting, prayer and almsgiving
have shown us a remedy for sin,
look graciously on this confession of our lowliness,
that we, who are bowed down by our conscience,
may always be lifted up by your mercy.
Through our Lord Jesus Christ, your Son,
who lives and reigns with you in the unity of the Holy Spirit,
one God, for ever and ever. **Amen.**

FIRST READING

Exod 17:3-7

In those days, in their thirst for water,
the people grumbled against Moses,
saying, "Why did you ever make us leave Egypt?
Was it just to have us die here of thirst
with our children and our livestock?"
So Moses cried out to the LORD,
"What shall I do with this people?
A little more and they will stone me!"
The LORD answered Moses,
"Go over there in front of the people,
along with some of the elders of Israel,
holding in your hand, as you go,
the staff with which you struck the river.
I will be standing there in front of you on the rock in Horeb.
Strike the rock, and the water will flow from it
for the people to drink."
This Moses did, in the presence of the elders of Israel.
The place was called Massah and Meribah,
because the Israelites quarreled there
and tested the LORD, saying,
"Is the LORD in our midst or not?"

CATECHESIS

RESPONSORIAL PSALM
Ps 95:1-2, 6-7, 8-9

℟. (8) If today you hear his voice, harden not your hearts.

Come, let us sing joyfully to the LORD;
  let us acclaim the Rock of our salvation.
Let us come into his presence with thanksgiving;
  let us joyfully sing psalms to him.

℟. If today you hear his voice, harden not your hearts.

Come, let us bow down in worship;
  let us kneel before the LORD who made us.
For he is our God,
  and we are the people he shepherds, the flock he guides.

℟. If today you hear his voice, harden not your hearts.

Oh, that today you would hear his voice:
  "Harden not your hearts as at Meribah,
  as in the day of Massah in the desert,
where your fathers tempted me;
  they tested me though they had seen my works."

℟. If today you hear his voice, harden not your hearts.

SECOND READING
Rom 5:1-2, 5-8

Brothers and sisters:
Since we have been justified by faith,
  we have peace with God through our Lord Jesus Christ,
  through whom we have gained access by faith
  to this grace in which we stand,
  and we boast in hope of the glory of God.

And hope does not disappoint,
  because the love of God has been poured out into our hearts
  through the Holy Spirit who has been given to us.
For Christ, while we were still helpless,
  died at the appointed time for the ungodly.
Indeed, only with difficulty does one die for a just person,
  though perhaps for a good person one might even find courage to die.
But God proves his love for us
  in that while we were still sinners Christ died for us.

About Liturgy

Lengthy readings: Today and the following three Sundays have longer gospel readings than usual. Some parishes have made it a habit of inviting the assembly to be seated during these lengthy readings. This may seem to be a good pastoral adaptation done for the benefit of those who cannot stand for a very long time. However, the consequences may outweigh the perceived good.

There are two competing values at play: avoiding placing burdens on the assembly, especially on members who are weaker, and giving honor and reverence befitting the presence of Christ in the gospel. Both are worthy goals. Can both goals be achieved in a creative way other than simply asking everyone to be seated?

Attending to the elderly, the sick, parents caring for infants, and those unable to stand for long periods of time is a good intention, and we should make accommodations for those who need it. However, asking the entire assembly to be seated for the gospel, whether or not they need to, is not necessarily pastoral in this case. It eliminates any option for those who *do* want to stand and are able to; it catechizes poorly about sacrifice in relation to living the gospel and comfort in relation to the liturgy; and it devalues the normative posture of prayer and praise, which is standing, and misapplies the normative posture of teaching and being taught, which is sitting. Some argue that the assembly can pay better attention when they are seated. I would argue that sitting for the gospel enables more distraction because it is a more passive posture.

Of course, we should not place unreasonable burdens upon the assembly. Therefore, the better option for a typical assembly in which the majority are capable of standing even for lengthy periods of time is to ask everyone to remain standing and invite those who cannot do so, for whatever reason, to care for themselves and be seated as needed.

About Initiation

Scrutinies: Today and the following two Sundays call for the celebration of the scrutinies if you have elect present in your assembly. Remember that all three scrutinies are required. If your elect will miss one or two of these scrutinies for a serious reason, and they cannot be rescheduled later in the day or during the week, you must request dispensation from your bishop. See RCIA 20. Also, do not combine the scrutinies with the presentations of the Creed and the Lord's Prayer. Each of these rituals has prescribed readings that must be used and therefore cannot be celebrated within the same liturgy.

About Liturgical Music

Music during the Scrutinies: If your parish will celebrate the scrutinies today and the following two Sundays, you will need to plan for some additional music for this simple rite.

The first place for music is the intercessions for the elect. These are similar to the universal prayer, but chanting them with a sung assembly response heightens their solemnity. The second place for music is after the prayer of exorcism. A brief song may be sung here as a kind of acclamation of thanksgiving. A good option is the hymn "I Heard the Voice of Jesus Say" (KINGSFOLD). Use verse 2 this week, verse 3 next week, and verse 1 the following week to correspond to the gospel texts.

Do not be tempted to add music to the prayer of exorcism, especially during the laying on of hands. Silence during the laying on of hands is key to the ritual.

GOSPEL ACCLAMATION
Ps 84:5

Blessed are those who dwell in your house,
O Lord;
they never cease to praise you.

Gospel

Matt 1:16, 18-21, 24a; L543

Jacob was the father of Joseph, the husband of Mary.
Of her was born Jesus who is called the Christ.

Now this is how the birth of Jesus Christ came about.
When his mother Mary was betrothed to Joseph,
but before they lived together,
she was found with child through the Holy Spirit.
Joseph her husband, since he was a righteous man,
yet unwilling to expose her to shame,
decided to divorce her quietly.
Such was his intention when, behold,
the angel of the Lord appeared to him in a dream and said,
"Joseph, son of David,
do not be afraid to take Mary your wife into your home.
For it is through the Holy Spirit
that this child has been conceived in her.
She will bear a son and you are to name him Jesus,
because he will save his people from their sins."
When Joseph awoke,
he did as the angel of the Lord had commanded him
and took his wife into his home.

or Luke 2:41-51a *in Appendix A, p. 273.*

See Appendix A., p. 273, for the other readings.

Reflecting on the Gospel

St. Joseph is the patron saint of dreamers and workers; Pope Pius IX proclaimed him patron saint of the Catholic Church itself! Many parishes are named for him, and he is the patron of dioceses, countries, societies, and even a happy death. Though the gospels never record a word of what he said, his relationship as husband of Mary and legal father of Jesus meant that he provided for the Holy Family through his labor. Jesus' own skill as a woodworker was likely taught to him by Joseph.

The gospel reading from Matthew tells us how the birth of Jesus came about. Joseph is the main character in this story, as opposed to Mary in the Gospel of Luke. But it would be a mistake to believe that these stories need to be harmonized or blended together. Instead, each evangelist was writing an infancy narrative independently of the other, thus accounting for the differences (some irreconcilable) in each story.

In the Old Testament, the patriarch Joseph is the one who dreamed dreams and spoke with Pharaoh about impending years of plenty and years of famine. In Matthew's story, the namesake of this patriarch also dreams dreams. Because God communicated to Joseph in a dream, he has been called "the dreamer." In fact, Pope Francis prayed to St. Joseph on this Feast day in 2017, "[G]rant all of us the ability to dream because when we dream great things, good things, we draw near to God's dream, what God dreams about us" (Morning Meditation, Domus Sanctae Marthae Chapel, *L'Osservatore Romano* 13).

Living the Paschal Mystery

St. Joseph as the patron saint of dreamers and workers gives us the opportunity to consider how important each is in our society today, and especially for the spiritual life. Dreams may often be what keep us motivated and sustained for periods of time. Our daily work may or may not be meaningful, but it is a means of sanctification, of becoming holy. Though Joseph says not a word, we know he has a rich spiritual life, open to God's communication. And Joseph provides for his family, his loved ones, by means of his labor. Dreams on their own are not enough without dedication to daily tasks. Daily tasks are not enough without inspiration from our dreams.

As we look forward to undergoing the paschal mystery, may we keep in mind a balance between dreaming and working, letting one inform and inspire the other.

Focusing the Gospel

Key words and phrases: [H]e was a righteous man

To the point: The gospels of Luke and Matthew are the only ones who record any of the events within the life of St. Joseph. Even within these gospels we aren't told much about Jesus' foster father. We know he was a carpenter and also "a righteous man." The life of St. Joseph was mostly taken up with the everyday affairs of caring and providing for his family. In him we find an example for all of us within the ordinary rhythms of work and family life. Following in the example of St. Joseph, may our everyday tasks, chores, work, and play be filled with devotion to God and service of Christ.

Model Penitential Act

Presider: St. Joseph modeled discipleship in his role as foster father to Jesus. As we celebrate this solemnity, let us ask St. Joseph to pray for us that we might emulate him in the life of faith . . . [pause]

Lord Jesus, you are Emmanuel, God with us: Lord, have mercy.
Christ Jesus, you call us to faithfulness and trust: Christ, have mercy.
Lord Jesus, your kingdom shall endure forever: Lord, have mercy.

Model Universal Prayer (Prayer of the Faithful)

Presider: Together with St. Joseph, patron of the universal church, let us make our needs known to the Lord.

Response: Lord, hear our prayer.

For priests called to take on the role of spiritual fathers for their parishes, may they be strengthened in faith and purified in intention . . .

For laborers and workers throughout the world, may they be provided with safe working conditions and fair wages . . .

For all husbands and fathers, may they find joy in caring for their families and reassurance in the words of the gospel, "Do not be afraid" . . .

For all gathered here, may we continue to grow in faith, hope, and love through the intercession of Mary, Joseph, and all the saints . . .

Presider: God, Father of all, you called St. Joseph to be the spouse of the blessed Virgin Mary and the foster father of Jesus. Hear our prayers that we might follow in his footsteps by faithful commitment to those you have placed in our care. We ask this through Christ our Lord. **Amen.**

About Liturgy

Silent Joseph: In the gospels, we have so many wonderful words spoken by Mary to reflect upon. But with Joseph, we have nothing. Joseph, the father of Jesus, is silent in all the accounts about him. However, we have many examples of what Joseph *did* as a person of faith.

In a world inundated with texts, tweets, podcasts, and instant messages, silence is a revolutionary and countercultural act. Where debates rage over social media and each party rushes to make its points and its case with ever louder attacks, action, especially for the sake of those in need, speaks louder than words.

As those who care for the liturgy of our communities and strive to draw out the meaning of the rites in all its symbolic actions, let us ask St. Joseph to show us how to make our individual and communal actions this Lent speak clearly and loudly so that those who are afraid, in danger, and seeking Christ may find a steadfast example of faith in our deeds.

COLLECT

Let us pray.

Pause for silent prayer

Grant, we pray, almighty God,
that by Saint Joseph's intercession
your Church may constantly watch over
the unfolding of the mysteries of human salvation,
whose beginnings you entrusted to his faithful care.
Through our Lord Jesus Christ, your Son,
who lives and reigns with you in the unity of the Holy Spirit,
one God, for ever and ever. **Amen.**

FOR REFLECTION

- The readings lift up the faithfulness of David, Abraham, and Joseph. Where are you being strengthened or tested in faith?
- Today's psalm proclaims, "The promises of the Lord I will sing forever; / through all generations." How are you passing on the faith to future generations?
- Due to his experience of receiving revelations from God in dreams, St. Joseph has been called "the dreamer." What dream do you have at this moment for yourself, your family, or your parish community?

Homily Points

- We lift up the lives of the saints as models for Christian discipleship. Some saints left behind writings that give us further insight into their relationship with God. This is not the case for St. Joseph. Within the gospels Joseph remains silent. Instead, his actions are what speak of his devotion to God and his goodness to others.

- In Matthew's gospel Joseph is told to do something in a dream and immediately he awakes and complies. We hear of the first instance in today's gospel. When Herod dies, once again Joseph is notified by dream to bring his family back to Israel and then yet, again, to settle in Nazareth. Let us ask for the same resolve to immediately carry out what the Lord calls us to do.

SPIRITUALITY

GOSPEL ACCLAMATION
John 8:12

I am the light of the world, says the Lord;
whoever follows me will have the light of life.

Gospel

John 9:1-41; L31A

As Jesus passed by he saw a man blind from birth.
His disciples asked him,
"Rabbi, who sinned, this man or his parents,
that he was born blind?"
Jesus answered,
"Neither he nor his parents sinned;
it is so that the works of God might be made visible through him.
We have to do the works of the one who sent me while it is day.
Night is coming when no one can work.
While I am in the world, I am the light of the world."
When he had said this, he spat on the ground
and made clay with the saliva,
and smeared the clay on his eyes,
and said to him,
"Go wash in the Pool of Siloam"—
which means Sent—.
So he went and washed, and came back able to see.

His neighbors and those who had seen him earlier as a beggar said,
"Isn't this the one who used to sit and beg?"
Some said, "It is,"
but others said, "No, he just looks like him."
He said, "I am."

Continued in Appendix A, p. 274, or
John 9:1, 6-9, 13-17, 34-38 *in Appendix A, p. 275.*

Reflecting on the Gospel

The Fourth Sunday of Lent in Cycle A gives us the second gospel reading from John in as many weeks. Last week we read about the woman at the well. Next week is the raising of Lazarus from the dead. But this week we have Jesus healing the man born blind. The story is masterfully and artfully complex yet succinct. Drama abounds and intrigue develops with each verse. Fundamental themes and metaphors such as light versus darkness, sight versus blindness, knowing versus not knowing, and more, including willful ignorance in the face of demonstrable evidence, all are woven together in this gospel passage that is the source of tremendous insight and wisdom.

The story opens with popular wisdom of the day expressed by the disciples. Basically, they ask, "Whose fault is it?" that the man is blind. Jesus rejects such attribution, which parallels the attitudes he expresses in the Gospel of Luke. It is not that bad things happen to bad people. Such thinking, which infects many religious and non-religious people, is not new in our day. Jesus is far removed from any "prosperity gospel" (good things happen to those who are good), as it might be understood today.

After Jesus heals this blind person, those who knew him could not believe their own eyes! Indeed, they said it was not the same person. Only when the man who was formerly blind says that he is one and the same do the onlookers ask how this happened. The situation escalates quickly to the Pharisees when the reader is informed that all of this took place on a Sabbath, a holy day on which no work is to be done. This theological riddle puzzled the Pharisees, who viewed Jesus as a sinner because he did not keep the Sabbath. Yet how could a sinner make the blind see? When faced with such testimony from the man who had been blind, who proclaimed Jesus a prophet, it seems best to deny the testimony!

The story continues unfolding, as those who are considered learned deny straightforward evidence that is presented to them. Believing in Jesus would upend the worldview of those who profess to know the Scriptures and the ways of God.

Rather than see this only as an account of a sign that Jesus performed (Jesus performs "signs" rather than "miracles" in the Gospel of John), we would do well to ponder its application to us. How often do we reject plain evidence because it does not reconcile with what we "know" to be true? It is difficult to change one's mind, especially if that means changing many other attitudes and thoughts as well.

In today's gospel story, as in so many, Jesus takes the initiative. He creates cognitive dissonance in the minds and hearts of many, demanding that they make a decision for or against him. When do we face such encounters with Christ? What is our response? Do we deny what everyone can plainly see? Or do we undergo a change and enter into a new life with Christ?

Living the Paschal Mystery

Giving up habits and ways of thinking can be difficult. Imagine making a change to something simple, such as a banking account with direct deposit and automatic bill-pay. Once a structure has been established, linking accounts, deposits, and debits, it can be cumbersome to make a change, close the account, and open a new one. If we encounter such difficulty with a matter as simple as a bank account, imagine what we encounter—even at a subconscious level—when we change a way of thinking about something as central as religion, meaning, and purpose.

Focusing the Gospel

Key words and phrases: "I was blind and now I see."

To the point: Within today's gospel Jesus encounters both spiritual and physical blindness. In healing the man born blind, he gains a follower, while also deepening the animosity of the Pharisees who attribute his willingness to heal on the Sabbath to the actions of a sinner. Blinded by their fear and rigid interpretation of the law, the Pharisees are not able to see the man right in front of them for who he truly is: the Lord, the one who fulfills the prophecies of Isaiah by opening the eyes of the blind (Isa 35:5).

Connecting the Gospel

to the first and second readings: Both the first and second readings contain themes related to blindness. In searching for the next king of Israel, Samuel is urged to look beyond the exterior, for "[n]ot as man sees does God see, / because man sees the appearance / but the Lord looks into the heart." Today's second reading focuses on the contrast between the light of faith and the darkness of the unbeliever. St. Paul tells the Ephesians, "You were once darkness, / but now you are light in the Lord."

to experience: There are many different kinds of sight. While we might tend to think of physical sight as the most important, today's readings highlight spiritual sight as even more essential. We are invited as disciples of Christ to attune our eyes to those of the divine and to see as God sees, not distracted by outward appearance but focused on the heart. How would our world be different if the same emphasis that was placed on physical seeing was given to spiritual sight?

Connecting the Responsorial Psalm

to the readings: David is called in from the fields where he is tending the sheep to be presented to Samuel who anoints his head with oil that marks him as the next king of Israel. Tradition tells us that David, the shepherd, penned today's psalm to God, the ultimate Shepherd, who watches over and anoints all his sheep with his tender care. On the day of our baptism, we were anointed with the oil of salvation and claimed as Christ's own. The second reading from St. Paul harkens to baptism as well with his commandment to the Ephesians: "Live as children of light."

to psalmist preparation: Throughout the season of Lent we journey with the catechumens toward baptism and the renewal of our own baptismal promises. How do you strive to live as a child of light and an anointed one of God?

PROMPTS FOR FAITH-SHARING

Once again, in the first reading, we see God choosing the small or lowly (in this case the youngest of seven sons) to do the greatest work. Where in your life has something (or someone) considered small, humble, or lowly made a great impact?

Psalm 23 proclaims the beloved words, "The Lord is my shepherd; there is nothing I shall want." How have you experienced the abundance of God in your own life?

At the Easter Vigil we will renew our baptismal promises, the same ones that were recited on the day when we were baptized and we became "children of light," as St. Paul tells the Ephesians. How do you embrace this call to be a child of light?

In your life of faith, when have you had an experience of conversion or suddenly being able to "see" where before you had a spiritual "blind spot"?

Model Penitential Act

Presider: In today's second reading, St. Paul urges the Ephesians to "[l]ive as children of light." As we begin this celebration let us bring our sins and failings before the Lord, trusting in his mercy, love, and healing light . . . *[pause]*

Confiteor: I confess . . .

Homily Points

• Near the end of today's gospel, the Pharisees ask Jesus, "Surely we are not also blind, are we?" We could imagine the tone these religious leaders take as one of sarcasm or derision as they confront the son of a carpenter who dares consider himself someone who can speak with authority and perform wonders on behalf of God. Jesus' response to them almost comes out as a riddle: "If you were blind, you would have no sin; /but now you are saying, 'We see,' so your sin remains."

• The Pharisees are a perfect foil for the man born blind. Their lives have been devoted to studying the word of God and following his law with the utmost fidelity. In their society, and in ours today, people with this kind of devotion would be the ones we would expect to have the sharpest spiritual eyesight and to be trustworthy and able guides for others. And yet, in our gospel, they are upstaged by a man who was blind from birth, presumably illiterate, and considered sinful. In one day, this man gains both physical and spiritual sight when he responds to Jesus' self-revelation with the words, "I do believe, Lord."

• On this Laetare Sunday we pause our Lenten journey to celebrate that we are more than halfway to Easter. It is a good time to take a minute and assess the past three and a half weeks. How have we entered into this Lenten season? Are we growing in humility and spiritual sight? Rather than making us puffed up with our own importance, our practices of prayer, fasting, and almsgiving are ideally showing us a way of emptying ourselves in order to make room for God and others.

Model Universal Prayer (Prayer of the Faithful)

Presider: Secure in the knowledge that God is our shepherd, let us bring our prayers before the one who fulfills every need and satisfies every desire.

Response: Lord, hear our prayer.

For the God's holy church, through the Lord's healing and grace, may it be a beacon of light for the world . . .

For those in positions of power and authority throughout the world, may they use their influence to effect positive change and promote the common good . . .

For people living with disabilities, may our society become one that welcomes and celebrates diversity by recognizing and promoting the gifts each person brings . . .

For all gathered here, may we know the joy of Christ's healing touch and seek to be sources of healing for others . . .

Presider: God of justice and mercy, you call us to be children of light and to lead lives of righteousness, goodness, and truth. Hear our prayers that all corruption, darkness, and evil might be exposed and uprooted by the purifying light of Christ. We ask this through Christ our Lord. **Amen.**

COLLECT

Let us pray.

Pause for silent prayer

O God, who through your Word
reconcile the human race to yourself in a
wonderful way,
grant, we pray,
that with prompt devotion and eager faith
the Christian people may hasten
toward the solemn celebrations to come.
Through our Lord Jesus Christ, your Son,
who lives and reigns with you in the unity
of the Holy Spirit,
one God, for ever and ever. **Amen.**

FIRST READING

1 Sam 16:1b, 6-7, 10-13a

The LORD said to Samuel:
"Fill your horn with oil, and be on your
way.
I am sending you to Jesse of Bethlehem,
for I have chosen my king from among
his sons."

As Jesse and his sons came to the sacrifice,
Samuel looked at Eliab and thought,
"Surely the LORD's anointed is here
before him."
But the LORD said to Samuel:
"Do not judge from his appearance or
from his lofty stature,
because I have rejected him.
Not as man sees does God see,
because man sees the appearance
but the LORD looks into the heart."
In the same way Jesse presented seven
sons before Samuel,
but Samuel said to Jesse,
"The LORD has not chosen any one of
these."
Then Samuel asked Jesse,
"Are these all the sons you have?"
Jesse replied,
"There is still the youngest, who is
tending the sheep."
Samuel said to Jesse,
"Send for him;
we will not begin the sacrificial banquet
until he arrives here."
Jesse sent and had the young man brought
to them.
He was ruddy, a youth handsome to behold
and making a splendid appearance.
The LORD said,
"There—anoint him, for this is the one!"
Then Samuel, with the horn of oil in hand,
anointed David in the presence of his
brothers;
and from that day on, the spirit of the
LORD rushed upon David.

RESPONSONSORIAL PSALM
Ps 23:1-3a, 3b-4, 5, 6

℟. (1) The Lord is my shepherd; there is nothing I shall want.

The LORD is my shepherd; I shall not want.
In verdant pastures he gives me repose;
beside restful waters he leads me;
he refreshes my soul.

℟. The Lord is my shepherd; there is nothing I shall want.

He guides me in right paths
for his name's sake.
Even though I walk in the dark valley
I fear no evil; for you are at my side
with your rod and your staff
that give me courage.

℟. The Lord is my shepherd; there is nothing I shall want.

You spread the table before me
in the sight of my foes;
you anoint my head with oil;
my cup overflows.

℟. The Lord is my shepherd; there is nothing I shall want.

Only goodness and kindness follow me
all the days of my life;
and I shall dwell in the house of the LORD
for years to come.

℟. The Lord is my shepherd; there is nothing I shall want.

SECOND READING
Eph 5:8-14

Brothers and sisters:
You were once darkness,
but now you are light in the Lord.
Live as children of light,
for light produces every kind of goodness
and righteousness and truth.
Try to learn what is pleasing to the Lord.
Take no part in the fruitless works of darkness;
rather expose them, for it is shameful even to mention
the things done by them in secret;
but everything exposed by the light becomes visible,
for everything that becomes visible is light.
Therefore, it says:
"Awake, O sleeper,
and arise from the dead,
and Christ will give you light."

About Liturgy

Proclamation or acting? The vivid gospel readings for these Cycle A Sundays of Lent and especially the upcoming Passion readings often inspire some communities to "enact" the gospel stories as part of their liturgical proclamation. Sometimes this is done as a complete play with staging, costumes, and props. Other times, the theatrical elements are simpler, such as added gestures or multiple voices taking on character roles. Some have used other creative methods, such as having a single reader proclaim the gospel while a group visually acts out the scenes.

There is no doubt that people invest a lot of time, talent, creativity, and energy into preparing these dramatic renditions. Often, the parish youth get deeply involved in this project, and the moment can be intensely moving for the assembly.

However, these dramatic presentations, no matter how well done, overlook one critical element in the liturgical proclamation of the Word: the hearer's religious imagination. The same effect happens when we have read a great novel, visualizing all the characters and scenes with the mind's eye, then see the story adapted for stage or screen. Something shifts and is lost from that first intimate connection to the story through our imagination. It becomes less the story we imagined ourselves in and more someone else's version of the story presented to us. When theatrical elements are added to the primary, dual ritual action of proclamation and hearing, the full meaning of the Word can be restricted. Because God's word stirs the hearts of its hearers in different and unique ways, we should avoid possibly limiting the power of the Word proclaimed in the midst of the assembly. Instead let us ensure that those who proclaim these texts prepare well and proclaim them with meaning, sensitivity to their narrative format, care for the assembly, and, most especially, authentic faith in what they announce.

About Initiation

Rehearsing for the Easter Vigil: Soon, you will probably hold a rehearsal for those who will be participating in the Easter Vigil. One thing to keep in mind for this rehearsal (and for rehearsals of any of the RCIA rites throughout the year) is that the catechumens and candidates ideally should not be at the rehearsals. The reason for this is not to keep things secret or to make the rites a surprise. Rather, it is so they do not feel unnecessarily burdened with remembering everything they are to do—their cues, responses, where to stand, when to sit, etc. That is not their job! That is the job of their sponsors and godparents. They are the ones you want to rehearse thoroughly and well for the Easter Vigil (and the other rites) so that they can ritually carry out the expectation of their role: be a constant support and guide for their companions, reassuring them—in the liturgy and in life—that they are by their side.

About Liturgical Music

Laetare Sunday: At this midway point of Lent, called *Laetare* (or "rejoice") Sunday, we get a respite from the restrained moderation of the season. In addition to the lifting of the prohibition for flowers at the altar, the church also allows musical instruments to be played on this day (General Instruction of the Roman Missal 305, 313; *Paschale Solemnitatis* 25). Although we get a brief break from the sobriety of Lent, you will still want to observe the general self-control of the season and save the fullness of your musical arrangements for the Triduum and the Easter season.

GOSPEL ACCLAMATION
John 1:14ab

The Word of God became flesh and made his
dwelling among us;
and we saw his glory.

Gospel

Luke 1:26-38; L545

**The angel Gabriel was
sent from God
to a town of Galilee
called Nazareth,
to a virgin betrothed
to a man named
Joseph,
of the house of David,
and the virgin's name
was Mary.
And coming to her, he
said,
"Hail, full of grace!
The Lord is with
you."
But she was greatly
troubled at what was
said
and pondered what sort of greeting
this might be.
Then the angel said to her,
"Do not be afraid, Mary,
for you have found favor with God.
Behold, you will conceive in your womb
and bear a son,
and you shall name him Jesus.
He will be great and will be called Son
of the Most High,
and the Lord God will give him the
throne of David his father,
and he will rule over the house of
Jacob forever,
and of his Kingdom there will be no
end."**

Continued in Appendix A, p. 276.

See Appendix A, p. 276, for the other readings.

Reflecting on the Gospel

Today, March 25, we are nine months from the feast of the Nativity, Christmas, December 25. And so, we celebrate the Annunciation, when Mary became the mother of Jesus by means of her "yes" to the angel Gabriel. Of course, we do not know the actual date on which Jesus was born; therefore, we cannot know the date nine months prior to that. But once Christmas was established as December 25, the date of the annunciation, at least celebrated liturgically, is quickly and easily calculated.

The fact that the liturgical feasts of Christmas and the Annunciation have no precise historical dates should help us be informed about the nature of the gospel narrative itself. The theological significance of what we celebrate is much more important than when it is celebrated. And for the theological significance of this feast, the church reads from the Gospel of Luke, who tells the account with the central character of Mary who lives in Nazareth. Of course, this is different from the way Matthew tells the story, as his main character is Joseph, who is living in Bethlehem. Both stories have some incongruities and they are best left unreconciled with one another. Instead it is best to recognize that Luke's theology has something to convey, as does Matthew's.

Luke tells us that Mary cooperated in becoming the mother of Jesus. Even though she could not comprehend precisely how this would happen, she was open to the will of God as reflected in her *fiat* (the Latin term for "may it be done"). In presenting the story this way, Luke casts Mary as an ideal disciple.

Church fathers for centuries afterward contemplated just how significant her "fiat" was, in wondering how history would be different if she had said "no." Such is the realm of theological speculation. For us, we celebrate the annunciation to Mary nine months before we celebrate the birth of Jesus her son.

May we model our own discipleship on her, who was open to the will of God to such a degree that she became pregnant before marriage, facing the hostility and judgment such an act would entail in that culture.

Living the Paschal Mystery

Luke is the only gospel writer to use the term "plan of God" and it is something he continues in the Acts of the Apostles. Other evangelists use terms like "God's will," as Luke does in today's gospel. The term "plan of God" was a convenient way to speak of what God had done in Christ. Mary's role was one of an essential cooperator (a co-worker) in God's plan or will. Sometimes it can be important to look at events through another set of eyes or another point of view. Mary certainly had plans for her own life, but she let those go when she was invited to be a participant in God's plan. Each of us, too, has desires, plans, and goals for ourselves that we may need to set down in order to pursue God's will. When we are asked to die to our selves and to our own needs and wants to pursue something greater, may we be reminded of Mary's "fiat" and take inspiration from this first disciple.

Focusing the Gospel

Key words and phrases: "The Holy Spirit will come upon you, / and the power of the Most High will overshadow you."

To the point: In the annunciation we see the action of the Trinity at work. God, the Father, sends an angel to ask Mary to be the mother of the Savior.

When she questions how this will come about, the angel assures her it will be through the action of the Holy Spirit. In the three persons of the One God, we find a community of love working in harmony to bring about the incarnation, the full expression of Emmanuel, "God with us."

Model Penitential Act

Presider: On this feast of the Annunciation of the Lord, we celebrate the faith of Mary who told the angel, "May it be done to me according to your word." Let us, too, turn to God with this same trust and devotion to ask for his healing and pardon . . . *[pause]*

Lord Jesus, you are the Son of God and son of Mary: Lord, have mercy.
Christ Jesus, you fulfill the words of the prophets: Christ, have mercy.
Lord Jesus, you are the Lamb of God who takes away the sins of the world: Lord, have mercy.

Model Universal Prayer (Prayer of the Faithful)

Presider: Together with Mary, the mother of the Savior and our mother, let us bring our needs before the Lord.

Response: Lord, hear our prayer.

For all members of the universal church, may we grow in hope, faith, and love through the intercession of Mary . . .

For the world's diplomats and peacekeepers, with goodwill may they collaborate with each other in resolving conflicts and caring for those in need . . .

For pregnant mothers and the babies they carry, may they find welcome, care, and support within their families, communities, and countries . . .

For all gathered here, may we make Mary's prayer our own each day as we ask, "May it be done to me according to your word" . . .

Presider: Almighty and eternal God, in the incarnation you sent your son to be born of the Virgin Mary and to make his dwelling among us. Hear our prayers that emulating the trust and devotion of Mary, we, too, might be brought to eternal life. We ask this through Christ our Lord. **Amen.**

About Liturgy

Solemnities in Lent: The Annunciation of the Lord on March 25 is the second solemnity that may fall during the Lenten season (the first is the Solemnity of St. Joseph on March 19). Whenever these two dates occur on a Sunday of Lent, they are moved to the next possible date, usually the following Monday. The exception to this is when the Annunciation falls during Holy Week, Triduum, or the Easter octave. Then it is moved to the Monday of the Second Week of Easter.

This can seem pretty arbitrary at first, but there is good reason for these calendrical gymnastics. It makes it clear that the principal lens for all our celebrations is the paschal sacrifice of Jesus in his suffering, dying, and resurrection. The feasts of the saints and even the solemnities of the Lord give way to this central orientation.

On this day, the liturgical color is white, the Gloria and Creed are included, but we still refrain from singing the Alleluia.

COLLECT

Let us pray.

Pause for silent prayer

O God, who willed that your Word
should take on the reality of human flesh
in the womb of the Virgin Mary,
grant, we pray,
that we, who confess our Redeemer to be God and man,
may merit to become partakers even in his divine nature.
Who lives and reigns with you in the unity of the Holy Spirit,
one God, for ever and ever. **Amen.**

FOR REFLECTION

- In the first reading we are told that the child born of the Virgin will be named "Emmanuel, / which means 'God is with us!'" In your life as a Christian, how do you proclaim the good news of Jesus in word and deed?

- The responsorial psalm proclaims, "Here I am, Lord; I come to do your will." What is one action (big or small) you could undertake this week to collaborate in God's plan of love, justice, and peace for the world?

- Gabriel tells Mary, "[N]othing will be impossible for God." Where in your life are you in need of this radical hope in the God of possibilities?

Homily Points

- In the first creation story from Genesis, the world is created through the word of God (Gen 1:1-2:4a). Again and again this line is repeated: "Then God said: Let there be . . ." And whatever had been proclaimed from the mouth of God is instantly brought forth.

- Today we hear of a new creation, God with us, taking root in the womb of Mary and coming into the world. Again, it is God's word that brings this creation about, and also Mary's words of agreement. She proclaims, "May it be done to me according to your word." The word of God remains creative in our own time and place; how are we called to be collaborators with it?

SPIRITUALITY

GOSPEL ACCLAMATION
John 11:25a, 26

I am the resurrection and the life, says
the Lord;
whoever believes in me, even if he dies,
will never die.

Gospel
John 11:1-45; L34A

Now a man was ill, Lazarus from Bethany,
the village of Mary and her sister Martha.
Mary was the one who had anointed the Lord with perfumed oil
and dried his feet with her hair;
it was her brother Lazarus who was ill.
So the sisters sent word to Jesus saying,
"Master, the one you love is ill."
When Jesus heard this he said,
"This illness is not to end in death,
but is for the glory of God,
that the Son of God may be glorified through it."
Now Jesus loved Martha and her sister and Lazarus.
So when he heard that he was ill,
he remained for two days in the place where he was.
Then after this he said to his disciples,
"Let us go back to Judea."
The disciples said to him,
"Rabbi, the Jews were just trying to stone you,
and you want to go back there?"
Jesus answered,
"Are there not twelve hours in a day?
If one walks during the day, he does not stumble,
because he sees the light of this world.

Continued in Appendix A, p. 277, or John 11:3-7, 17, 20-27, 33b-45 *in Appendix A, p. 278.*

Reflecting on the Gospel

The church concludes the set of three Johannine readings during this Lenten season with the story of Lazarus being raised from the dead. We are reminded that two weeks ago we heard about the woman at the well. Last week Jesus made the man born blind to see. And today we have a sign of Jesus' identity par excellence: the raising from the dead. In the Gospel of John, Jesus performs signs rather than miracles, and there are precisely seven. The signs point to his true identity as incarnate Word of God, Light of the World, and the Author of Life. And the seventh and final sign, the raising of Lazarus is a fitting note on which to conclude the public ministry of Jesus. After this, the gospel story moves quickly to Holy Week and the events surrounding the Last Supper, Crucifixion, and Exaltation.

Today's gospel story is filled with misunderstanding, and one nearly has the sense that Jesus is getting frustrated with the disciples. But the misunderstanding is a narrative device that the evangelist uses to illustrate how Jesus' thoughts and ways of knowing are so much more than the disciples'. For example, even though Jesus was talking about Lazarus's death, the disciples took him literally in thinking that Lazarus was only asleep. Jesus tells them plainly that "Lazarus has died." He expresses gratitude that he was not there so that the disciples can believe (when he raises Lazarus from the dead). But even this is misunderstood by Thomas, who believes they are going to die with Jesus.

The misunderstanding continues with Martha's gentle scolding of Jesus when she claims that had Jesus been present, Lazarus would not have died. We recall that Jesus waited for two days after hearing the news of Lazarus being sick before he even went to see him! Jesus does not take the bait. He instead proclaims himself the resurrection and life. Martha, in another case of misunderstanding, says she knows that Lazarus will rise on the last day. (She does not understand that Jesus will raise him shortly.)

Even the crowd does not understand the identity of Jesus, for they wonder why the one who made the blind to see could not have prevented the death of Lazarus. It seems everyone is wholly unprepared for what Jesus has in mind, a resurrection from the dead, even though he proclaimed himself to be the resurrection and the life. Jesus' prayer to the Father is fundamentally one of thanksgiving and gratitude for the opportunity for those gathered to believe that Jesus is sent by God the Father.

With a command to come forth, Jesus speaks, and Lazarus rises from the dead. The author of life has power over death. And now many believe in him.

Living the Paschal Mystery

Such fundamental expressions of life and death are at the heart of today's gospel. Jesus deliberately was not present with Martha, Mary, and their brother Lazarus. It seems Jesus wanted to be sure Lazarus was understood to be dead, not merely sleeping or sick, so that Jesus could raise him from the dead. As a result, many began to believe in him—that he had been sent by the Father.

What do we believe about Jesus? Do we believe he is the author of life with power over death? Are there any people like Lazarus in our own lives who need to be raised to new life? Lazarus was a prefiguring of the resurrection. And yet, even Lazarus died again. Jesus' own resurrection is not a mere resuscitation, but a raising to new life, qualitatively different, never subject to death again. When we live with the promise of renewed life for eternity, we are living the promise of the paschal mystery.

Focusing the Gospel

Key words and phrases: "I am the resurrection and the life"

To the point: From the beginning of creation, death has been a part of life. In Lazarus we see this played out. As a mortal man, he grows sick and perishes. In raising Lazarus from death, Jesus shows that he is the Lord of life. Next week, on Palm Sunday, we will read the words from the passion according to Matthew, how at the moment of his own death, Jesus "cried out . . . in a loud voice, / and gave up his spirit." The one who proclaimed, "I am the resurrection and the life" humbles himself to the point of death on a cross. In raising Lazarus from the dead, Jesus foreshadows his own dying and rising. Unlike Lazarus, Jesus does not live to die again but is a new creation, the resurrected one who has passed through death and entered into even fuller life—life everlasting.

Connecting the Gospel

to the first reading: In the first reading, God, speaking through the prophet Ezekiel, tells his people, "I will open your graves / and have you rise from them." We could consider these words figuratively, and yet, in today's gospel, we find Jesus literally standing at a tomb and ordering, "Take away the stone . . . Lazarus, come out!" Lazarus emerges from his tomb, is unwrapped from his burial bands, and is set free to live anew.

to experience: As Christians, we live our lives to conform to the paschal mystery—the truth that from death comes life. Looking at today's readings from Ezekiel and the Gospel of John, we can ponder this mystery both literally (we will rise from death) and figuratively. We might ask, where are we being called forth from "tombs" within our own lives to embrace life anew?

Connecting the Responsorial Psalm

to the readings: Again, as in the First and Second Sundays of Lent, our responsorial psalm emphasizes God's mercy and power to redeem. Our hope in this mercy and redemption is to rival that of a "sentinel [waiting] for the dawn." What an apt image for our trust and belief in the one who promises to call us forth from our graves and offers us resurrected life in the face of death. Like a sentinel, we might at times grow weary in the watches of the night, and yet, we know that the dawn will break again and bring us into the light of a new day.

to psalmist preparation: In today's gospel Jesus tells Martha, "I am the resurrection and the life; / whoever believes in me, even if he dies, will live, / and everyone who lives and believes in me will never die. / Do you believe this?" What would your response to this question be?

PROMPTS FOR FAITH-SHARING

In the first reading from Ezekiel, God tells the people, "I will open your graves / and have you rise from them." What are the areas in your own life in need of God's life-giving touch?

Through Ezekiel, God proclaims, "I have promised, and I will do it." What promises of God do you hold fast to in your life?

In today's gospel we read our shortest Bible verse in English, "And Jesus wept." Why was it important for the gospel writer to include this detail? Does it affect your relationship with Jesus knowing he experienced human emotions?

Jesus reveals to Martha, "I am the resurrection and the life." How do you interpret these words?

Model Penitential Act

Presider: On this Fifth Sunday of Lent, we journey with Jesus to Bethany where he will raise his friend Lazarus from the dead. Let us bring before the Lord all the places in our own lives that are in need of his life-giving touch . . . *[pause]*

Confiteor: I confess . . .

Homily Points

• In today's gospel Thomas makes a shocking statement. When Jesus determines he will go to Bethany, Thomas says to the other disciples, "Let us also go to die with him." Though this might sound a little melodramatic, Thomas and the other disciples had reason to believe that their association with Jesus could ultimately end in their own violent deaths.

• Since Jesus barely escaped lynching by an angry mob on his last visit to Jerusalem, it seems foolhardy to return again. In today's gospel, Jesus enters Bethany, which we are told is "near Jerusalem," where he very publicly raises his friend Lazarus from death to life. This remarkable sign of Jesus' authority over everything, including death, leads directly to plans for his crucifixion by the chief priests and Pharisees.

• Within today's gospel we find life that is stronger than death, and a foreshadowing of the triumph over death that will happen in Jesus' resurrection. But the only way to this newness of life is through death and for all of their good intentions, when the religious leaders and crowds do finally carry out their plans to execute Jesus, every one of the Twelve, save the beloved disciple, are nowhere to be found. Discipleship requires this willingness to follow Jesus, even unto death (whether it be one of the many little deaths that make up a life, or the final and complete gift of self in the footsteps of the martyrs). Each Lent we trace Jesus' footsteps from the temptation in the desert and the beginning of his public ministry to his last breaths on the cross. Each year we say with Thomas, "Let us also go to die with him," for only in sharing this death do we arrive at the joy of Easter morning.

Model Universal Prayer (Prayer of the Faithful)

Presider: With Martha we proclaim, "You are the Christ, the Son of God," and so with faith bring our needs before the Lord.

Response: Lord, hear our prayer.

For catechists and all who share the faith with others, may their relationship with Jesus, the risen one, inspire and strengthen their ministry . . .

For legislators and officials in elected office, may they enact laws and support legislation that protects the dignity of life in all its stages . . .

For those mourning the loss of a loved one, may they know the comfort and care of Jesus who wept at the tomb of his friend Lazarus . . .

For all gathered here, may we bring to the Lord for healing all the places in our lives where death and darkness have crept in . . .

Presider: God, source of hope and life everlasting, you tell your people through the prophet Ezekiel, "I will open your graves / and have you rise from them." Hear our prayers that our faith in you might be strengthened and our lives transformed. We ask this through Christ our Lord. **Amen.**

COLLECT

Let us pray.

Pause for silent prayer

By your help, we beseech you, Lord our
God,
may we walk eagerly in that same charity
with which, out of love for the world,
your Son handed himself over to death.
Through our Lord Jesus Christ, your Son,
who lives and reigns with you in the unity
of the Holy Spirit,
one God, for ever and ever. **Amen.**

FIRST READING

Ezek 37:12-14

Thus says the Lord GOD:
O my people, I will open your graves
and have you rise from them,
and bring you back to the land of Israel.
Then you shall know that I am the LORD,
when I open your graves and have you
rise from them,
O my people!
I will put my spirit in you that you may
live,
and I will settle you upon your land;
thus you shall know that I am the LORD.
I have promised, and I will do it, says the
LORD.

RESPONSORIAL PSALM
Ps 130:1-2, 3-4, 5-6, 7-8

℟. (7) With the Lord there is mercy and
fullness of redemption.

Out of the depths I cry to you, O LORD;
LORD, hear my voice!
Let your ears be attentive
to my voice in supplication.

℟. With the Lord there is mercy and
fullness of redemption.

If you, O LORD, mark iniquities,
LORD, who can stand?
But with you is forgiveness,
that you may be revered.

℟. With the Lord there is mercy and
fullness of redemption.

I trust in the LORD;
my soul trusts in his word.
More than sentinels wait for the dawn,
let Israel wait for the LORD.

℟. With the Lord there is mercy and
fullness of redemption.

For with the LORD is kindness
and with him is plenteous redemption;
and he will redeem Israel
from all their iniquities.

℟. With the Lord there is mercy and
fullness of redemption.

SECOND READING
Rom 8:8-11

Brothers and sisters:
Those who are in the flesh cannot please
God.
But you are not in the flesh;
on the contrary, you are in the spirit,
if only the Spirit of God dwells in you.
Whoever does not have the Spirit of Christ
does not belong to him.
But if Christ is in you,
although the body is dead because of
sin,
the spirit is alive because of
righteousness.
If the Spirit of the One who raised Jesus
from the dead dwells in you,
the One who raised Christ from the dead
will give life to your mortal bodies also,
through his Spirit dwelling in you.

About Liturgy

Veiling statues and crosses: Older Catholics may remember going to church during Lent and seeing all the statues and crosses covered in purple cloth. In contemporary practice in the United States prior to Vatican II, churches were required to veil statues and crosses during the last two weeks of Lent, called Passiontide. Some parishes expanded that time frame to include the entirety of Lent, even though this was not the intent of the practice.

After Vatican II, the practice of veiling statues and crosses, if done at all, was left up to the decision of each country's conference of bishops. Most recently with the revised English translation of the third edition of the Roman Missal, the U.S. bishops have determined the following guideline and placed it in the Roman Missal as a rubric for the Fifth Sunday of Lent: "In the Dioceses of the United States, the practice of covering crosses and images throughout the church from this Sunday may be observed. Crosses remain covered until the end of the celebration of the Lord's Passion on Good Friday, but images remain covered until the beginning of the Easter Vigil."

It is important to note two things. First, this is an optional practice. And second, if a parish chooses to observe this practice, statutes and crosses cannot be veiled until the Fifth Sunday of Lent. Although Lent is a penitential season, it is not one that restricts us from the veneration of the saints in their images or of the cross in its glory. Rather, the practice of veiling statues and crosses during the final weeks of Lent helps us prepare for the fullness of joy at the Easter Triduum.

About Initiation

Presentation of the Lord's Prayer: During the fifth week of Lent, the community of the faithful presents the Lord's Prayer to the elect who will be baptized this Easter. (See RCIA 178-184.) This presentation is celebrated outside of the Sunday Mass, either at a Liturgy of the Word or a weekday Mass. The gospel reading assigned for this simple ritual is the reading from Matthew 6:9-13, in which Jesus teaches his disciples to pray. Therefore, do not try to combine this presentation with the third scrutiny celebrated at Mass today.

About Liturgical Music

Singing during the gospel proclamation: Some parishes have the practice of singing a short refrain interspersed throughout the long gospel readings of the Third, Fourth, and Fifth Sundays of Lent, Cycle A, and during the reading of the passion on Palm Sunday and Good Friday. Although there are a few published resources that provide original musical acclamations and recommended refrains for such use (and I have done the same practice myself), the liturgical documents do not expressly permit such an inclusion into the proclamation of the gospel.

Does lack of explicit permission automatically mean proscription of a practice not mentioned in the rubrics and laws? Not necessarily. Does this mean practices like these are allowed as long as the books don't forbid them? Not necessarily either. Liturgical law, rubrics, and ritual books are living documents and develop more organically than we might think. (See Paul Bradshaw's classic academic text *The Search for the Origins of Christian Worship: Sources and Methods for the Study of Early Liturgy* for a deep study on this topic.)

Liturgical decisions on nonessential elements such as occasional sung acclamations during the gospel reading should be a topic discussed with the liturgical leaders of your parish. This includes the presiders, deacons, music directors, and liturgical committees. Regardless of what you decide, remember this popular maxim: In essentials, unity; in doubtful matters, liberty; in all things, charity.

SPIRITUALITY

GOSPEL ACCLAMATION
Phil 2:8-9

Christ became obedient to the point of death,
even death on a cross.
Because of this, God greatly exalted him
and bestowed on him the name which is above
every name.

Gospel at the procession with palms

Matt 21:1-11; L37A

When Jesus and the disciples drew near Jerusalem
and came to Bethphage on the Mount of Olives,
Jesus sent two disciples, saying to them,
"Go into the village opposite you,
and immediately you will find an ass tethered,
and a colt with her.
Untie them and bring them here to me.
And if anyone should say anything to you, reply,
'The master has need of them.'
Then he will send them at once."
This happened so that what had been spoken through the prophet
might be fulfilled:
Say to daughter Zion,
"Behold, your king comes to you,
meek and riding on an ass,
and on a colt, the foal of a beast of burden."
The disciples went and did as Jesus had ordered them.
They brought the ass and the colt and laid their cloaks over them,
and he sat upon them.
The very large crowd spread their cloaks on the road,
while others cut branches from the trees
and strewed them on the road.

Continued in Appendix A, p. 279.

Gospel at Mass Matt 26:14–27:66; L38A
or Matt 27:11-54 *in Appendix A, pp. 279–281.*

Reflecting on the Gospel

Palm Sunday is a commemoration of highs and lows, exaltation and tragedy. We enter the church bearing palms singing Hosanna, and only minutes later we cry in unison, "Let him be crucified." The liturgical juxtaposition is certainly intended and representative of fickle humanity, not only during the events of Holy Week, but quite regularly, down into our modern era. Profound themes of betrayal, trust, friendship, power, and humility are present in the gospel reading from Matthew.

Who doesn't know what it's like to experience betrayal at the hand of a friend, for that is the very term Jesus uses of Judas Iscariot. Judas himself leads the authorities to Jesus for the price of thirty pieces of silver. Shortly thereafter he realizes the error of his ways and commits suicide. He was dead before Jesus was. Peter, too, betrayed Jesus but did not commit the ultimate act from which there is no return. The disciples who professed such devotion to Jesus only hours earlier folded quickly in the face of temptation. Jesus died alone, reviled even by those who were being crucified alongside him.

The taunts of the crowd sound like school yard bullies or even the rants of thugs. Their mocking requests for Jesus to come down from the cross and then they will believe are derisive. The attitude that says God can save him if he's really God's son is likewise sarcastic. Humanity itself is reflected in the crowd's behavior—in its willingness to put to death, after a sham trial, someone it turned on after only recently praising. There is a mob mentality at work and it should give us pause, not only for what happened in Jesus' day but for how such actions continue today. False testimony, deceit, betrayal, even physical force and violence leading to death are all prominently on display. The crowd, humanity itself, is only too eager to believe the worst, to mock, taunt, scourge, and kill the incarnation of love itself. Then, humanity has the gall to test God, telling God to rescue Jesus if he's really his son.

Of course, to be God's son means that Jesus trusts the Father to the point of enduring all things up to and including death. God's vindication will come not in bringing Jesus down from the cross, but in raising Jesus from the dead. God's ways are not human ways. We demand action from God that we can see with our own eyes. But there were no witnesses to the actual resurrection, only the risen Christ. The response demanded by God of humans is faith. When faced with deceit, lies, violence, and death, God has another way, and we are invited to enter into this new way of life.

Living the Paschal Mystery

Today's dramatic reading plunges us into the events of the paschal mystery. We undergo with Jesus betrayal, suffering, and eventual death. Like Jesus, we are called to remain faithful to God, ever trusting in his wisdom and providential care. To be God's son, Jesus demonstrates filial obedience and dedication to his mission to the point of death. Rather than shy away from the culmination of his ministry, Jesus faces it straightforwardly, knowing that it will result in a violent death. He places his confidence and trust in God himself, who will be true to his word, even when Jesus is on the cross.

The example of Jesus on this Palm Sunday inspires us to be true to God's will in our own lives. We are open to what God has in store, a resurrection from the dead that is new life. Such is the paschal mystery.

Focusing the Gospel

Key words and phrases: Jesus cried out again in a loud voice, and gave up his spirit.

To the point: In today's gospel reading, the Lord of life, the Son of God, does the humanly unthinkable: he surrenders to death. Matthew's gospel highlights Jesus' distress and also his complete fidelity to the Father as he prays, "[I]f it is not possible that the cup pass / without my drinking it, your will be done!" In Jesus' passion and death we find the method of God's wooing of humanity. It is not by force or coercion that our God calls us into covenant relationship. Instead, with extreme humility and nonviolence, Jesus offers himself, body and blood, for the healing of the world.

Connecting the Gospel

to the second reading: The second reading from St. Paul's letter to the Philippians is commonly believed to be an early Christian hymn to Jesus that Paul cites to make a point. Within its stanzas, we find a poetic retelling of the paschal mystery. The events that are detailed in the gospel are summarized here. Rather than refusing the cup of his passion and death, Jesus "humbled himself, / becoming obedient to death, / even death on a cross." Though our gospel today ends with the sealing of the tomb, the hymn from Philippians continues on to reveal the glory awaiting the one who was mocked by soldiers with a crown of thorns and taunted with shouts of "Hail, King of the Jews!" This is the Christ to whom "every knee should bend" and "every tongue confess" as Lord.

to experience: On the road to Calvary, Jesus shows us the way of humility and nonviolence. How do your own actions and words profess this Jesus as Lord of heaven and earth?

Connecting the Responsorial Psalm

to the readings: In our readings for today we go from the crowd's triumphant shouts of "Hosanna" to the silence of the tomb where Jesus's body is placed. We find the same contrast of triumph and despair in today's psalm, which begins "My God, my God, why have you abandoned me?" and ends with the psalmist calling on the assembly and all the descendants of Israel to praise the Lord and "give glory to him."

to psalmist preparation: Within the psalms we find all human emotions brought to God, from anger and despair, to love and trust. In Jesus' birth, life, death, and resurrection, God enters into the fullness of human emotion. We need not be afraid to bring all of who we are to our loving Father.

PROMPTS FOR FAITH-SHARING

In the first reading the suffering servant from Isaiah speaks: "The Lord has given me / a well-trained tongue, / that I might know how to speak to the weary / a word that will rouse them." What words of hope, promise, or challenge has the Lord given you to speak to others?

In the second reading from Paul's letter to the Philippians, we hear how Jesus "humbled himself" even "to the point of death." In your life, where have you encountered leadership through humility?

In the gospel for Palm Sunday we hear the words that are spoken over the bread and wine at each eucharistic celebration: "This is my body . . . This is my blood." In the Eucharist, as in his passion, death, and resurrection, Jesus gives all of himself to us. Looking ahead to Holy Week and the Triduum, what actions or practices might you embrace in response to this gift of the Lord?

Throughout the Lenten season we have prepared to enter into Holy Week by our practices of prayer, fasting, and almsgiving. How have your Lenten practices strengthened and nourished you this Lent?

CELEBRATION

Model Penitential Act

Presider: Today we gather to enter into the passion of the Lord and to bear witness to the moment of his death on a cross. Let us pause to seek God's mercy and healing that through this remembrance of the Lord's passion and death, we might be brought to the fullness of life . . . *[pause]*

Confiteor: I confess . . .

Homily Points

• The life of Christ begins and ends with infamy and persecution—from an unwed pregnancy and birth among the animals in Bethlehem to the flight into Egypt to escape a murderous King Herod. The gospel writers Matthew and Luke give us details of these stories that align Jesus with those on the margins of society.

• In Jesus' public ministry he is accused of being possessed by the devil (Matt 12:24; Luke 11:15) and is rejected by his hometown of Nazareth (Luke 4:14-30), where the crowd desires to throw him off the side of a hill. This is not the only time that those enraged by his words and actions will seek his life. In our gospel today, not only does Jesus undergo death, but also the cruelty of death on a cross. The Son of God, who was born in a place where animals were kept, is now crucified in the company of criminals.

• In today's gospel let us find both a comfort and a challenge. We believe in and worship a God who desires to be with us so completely that he would enter into the very basest and most heartbreaking of human experiences. And in entering into these experiences of rejection, violence, loneliness, and despair, he redeems them. When we find ourselves in such places, we find the Lord with us; this is the blessing. The challenge is that when we do not find ourselves in such places, when we are the comforted, the included, and the well-cared for, we are still called to meet our Lord in his passion and crucifixion. He is there with the outcast, the poor, the shamed, and the broken within our own families, communities, and world. May we be given eyes to see Jesus' face in those who suffer and hearts of tenderness to care for him there.

Model Universal Prayer (Prayer of the Faithful)

Presider: On the cross at Calvary, Jesus gave his life for the forgiveness of sins. Trusting in his compassion and love, let us bring our needs before the Lord.

Response: Lord, hear our prayer.

For the church, may it continue the ministry of Jesus by continually aligning itself with the poor, marginalized, oppressed, and vulnerable . . .

For nations torn apart by war and violence, may God raise up leaders who will work for lasting peace . . .

For those nearing death, may they know the peace of Christ and find physical and spiritual comfort through the care of others . . .

For all gathered here, may we seek to emulate the humility of Christ and proclaim God's love to the world in word and deed . . .

Presider: God of exceeding goodness, you sent your son, Jesus, to reveal your love for the world by his life, death, and resurrection. Hear our prayers that by the blood of Christ, we might be joined together with all creation in singing your praise. We ask this through Christ our Lord. **Amen.**

COLLECT

Let us pray.

Pause for silent prayer

Almighty ever-living God,
who as an example of humility for the human race to follow
caused our Savior to take flesh and submit to the Cross,
graciously grant that we may heed his lesson of patient suffering
and so merit a share in his Resurrection.
Who lives and reigns with you in the unity of the Holy Spirit,
one God, for ever and ever. **Amen.**

FIRST READING

Isa 50:4-7

The Lord GOD has given me
a well-trained tongue,
that I might know how to speak to the weary
a word that will rouse them.
Morning after morning
he opens my ear that I may hear;
and I have not rebelled,
have not turned back.
I gave my back to those who beat me,
my cheeks to those who plucked my beard;
my face I did not shield
from buffets and spitting.

The Lord GOD is my help,
therefore I am not disgraced;
I have set my face like flint,
knowing that I shall not be put to shame.

RESPONSORIAL PSALM

Ps 22:8-9, 17-18, 19-20, 23-24

℟. (2a) My God, my God, why have you abandoned me?

All who see me scoff at me;
they mock me with parted lips, they wag their heads:
"He relied on the LORD; let him deliver him,
let him rescue him, if he loves him."

℟. My God, my God, why have you abandoned me?

Indeed, many dogs surround me,
  a pack of evildoers closes in upon me;
they have pierced my hands and my feet;
  I can count all my bones.

℟. My God, my God, why have you
    abandoned me?

They divide my garments among them,
  and for my vesture they cast lots.
But you, O LORD, be not far from me;
  O my help, hasten to aid me.

℟. My God, my God, why have you
    abandoned me?

I will proclaim your name to my brethren;
  in the midst of the assembly I will
    praise you:
"You who fear the LORD, praise him;
  all you descendants of Jacob, give glory
    to him;
  revere him, all you descendants of
    Israel!"

℟. My God, my God, why have you
    abandoned me?

SECOND READING
Phil 2:6-11

Christ Jesus, though he was in the form
    of God,
  did not regard equality with God
  something to be grasped.
Rather, he emptied himself,
  taking the form of a slave,
  coming in human likeness;
  and found human in appearance,
  he humbled himself,
  becoming obedient to the point of
    death,
  even death on a cross.
Because of this, God greatly exalted him
  and bestowed on him the name
  which is above every name,
  that at the name of Jesus
  every knee should bend,
  of those in heaven and on earth and
    under the earth,
  and every tongue confess that
  Jesus Christ is Lord,
  to the glory of God the Father.

About Liturgy

Triumph and passion: "On Preparing and Celebrating the Paschal Feasts" (*Paschale Solemnitatis*) is the Vatican's document giving guidelines for Lent, Holy Week, the Triduum, and Easter. Regarding Passion Sunday, it says this day "joins the foretelling of Christ's regal triumph and the proclamation of the passion. The connection between both aspects of the paschal mystery should be shown and explained in the celebration and catechesis of this day" (28).

Triumph and passion are certainly the hallmarks of this day. Finding an appropriate balance between the two without bombast or melodrama while honoring your parish's unique character will be your challenge for this day and this entire week.

One way to help strike this balance is to recall that the underlying theme to every liturgy is the paschal mystery. Whether the simplest Ordinary Time Sunday or one of the principal liturgies of Holy Week, Christ's death *and* resurrection are always the focus. In the midst of the Lord's passion, we do not pretend that his resurrection did not happen; at the height of our praise and joy, we keep in mind the sacrifice of the cross. For each liturgical decision you make in your preparations for this week, ask yourself whether or not it reflects and communicates both the passion and the triumph of Jesus.

About Initiation

A week of preparation: This final week before their initiation should not feel like "business as usual" for the elect and their godparents. Help them observe each day of Holy Week in more intense and intentional prayer and fasting. Not everyone will be able to come to additional meetings or gatherings during this week, but you can encourage them to take extra time each day to reflect on how God has accompanied them thus far in their journey. Send them a text or an email message each day of Holy Week with a link to the day's readings and a brief note of encouragement. Include an intercession for the elect in the daily Masses and liturgies of Holy Week. Most especially, remind the elect and their godparents that on Holy Saturday, they should refrain from their usual routine and spend time in prayer and reflection in preparation for their initiation that night. RCIA 185–205 gives a possible outline for these preparation rites.

About Liturgical Music

Singing the Passion: Over the last few decades, many church communities have been rethinking the practice of giving the people of the assembly the "crowd" parts of the passion reading that are printed in popular missalettes and other aids. Critics of this practice claim that the division of texts in these resources often place the people in a negative light, and the necessity for them to follow along in the text adds a layer of "performance" upon what should be a focused and contemplative highlight of the Liturgy of the Word.

An alternative practice that many parishes have begun using is a chanted/sung setting of the passion gospels in which three cantors proclaim the reading. In fact, *Paschale Solemnitatis* says that the passion narrative "should be sung" (33) or read in this traditional way. The rubrics in the Roman Missal for Palm Sunday state that the passion may be read "by readers, with the part of Christ, if possible, reserved to a Priest" (21).

Robert Batastini has provided accessible chanted settings of the passion gospels bound in a ritual-ready book (GIA). Royce Nickel has also set St. Matthew's passion for three cantors and SAB choir, available for download at https://musicasacra.com/. Whether you have clergy capable of leading the sung proclamation, use a mix of lay and clergy singers, or have all three parts sung by lay cantors, both of these recommended settings would be worthy of your efforts.

EASTER TRIDUUM

I am the passover of your salvation, I am the lamb which was sacrificed for you, I am your ransom, I am your light, I am your savior, I am your resurrection, I am your king, I am leading you up to the heights of heaven, I will show you the eternal Father, I will raise you up by my right hand.

—Melito of Sardis, *Peri Pascha*, 103

Reflecting on the Triduum

The "Triduum," these three sacred days are unlike any other in the liturgical year for the Christian. They carry forward an echo of faith from centuries ago and then ripple through the year with their profound theological significance. The three days are not a reenactment of events from two thousand years ago, but they make the effects of that event present in our lives today. The Triduum is a touchstone of faith to which we return year after year.

On these three days we commemorate essential and everlasting elements of our incarnational spirituality, celebrating the death and resurrection of the author of life, the Word made flesh. This is too much for one liturgy or even one day. The movements of the sacred events take place over three days so that we may enter more fully into the mysteries we celebrate.

Holy Thursday commemorates the sign of service that Jesus gave us on that night of the Last Supper. He who came not to be served but to serve is our master who set an example for us. If the master served, we too must serve. Service is a constitutive element of following the one who served to the point of giving his life. Tragic themes of betrayal by a friend, a shared meal with the knowledge of betrayal, and the lure of money make this commemoration haunting in its near universal applicability.

On Good Friday we witness the cross; there is no eucharistic prayer, but only a significant Liturgy of the Word followed by Communion. As Christians have done for centuries, we pray for the world and for many other things. The prayers of intercession are accompanied by dramatic action and even movement. This day is unlike any other, and we leave the service in silence, alone with our thoughts.

After sunset on Saturday it's as though we cannot contain the Easter joy we know will be ours and we celebrate the resurrection. Readings of promise and salvation are punctuated by psalms of praise and exaltation. Easter lilies, lights, fire, bells, a Gloria—all signify that our Lord has risen, never to be subject to death again. Life has been transformed and will never be the same now that we have this existential promise of eternity with Christ.

The Triduum is too much for one liturgy or even one day. We are given three days to enter into this profound ancient mystery. Let's give ourselves the gift of not only preparing others for this experience, but undergoing it ourselves too.

Living the Paschal Mystery

The Triduum could be said to be the ultimate commemoration of the paschal mystery. In dramatic fashion, the Author of life is handed over to death by a friend for a few pieces of silver. Anyone who has been betrayed by another knows the hurt, pain, and loss of that experience, which is felt by the psalmist who says, "Even my trusted friend / who ate my bread, / has raised his heel against me" (Ps 41:10; NABRE). This psalm is quoted in the Gospel of John (13:18), and is certainly apropos. In addition to betrayal, we experience a sham trial, rigged "justice" that sends an innocent person to death. It is not too much of a leap to imagine those on death row today who have been exonerated because of DNA evidence. Unfortunately the condemnation of the innocent or not guilty is with us even today. The Triduum we celebrate is not only the paschal mystery that Jesus underwent, but it is being lived out in our midst today when people are betrayed and others sent to death. It's easy to look at Jesus as an unfortunate victim of betrayal and swift justice. But his experience should cause us to see all those who face similar action. When we do nothing, or cheer for vengeance, we are like those in the crowd on these days. The paschal mystery did not happen only once two millennia ago. It continues today. With eyes of faith we can see, and we have hope for an eternal future where God's justice truly reigns.

TRIDUUM

"Triduum" is an odd-sounding word that comes from a Latin term meaning "three days." These most sacred days begin Holy Thursday evening through Friday evening (day one), include Friday evening through Saturday evening (day two), and conclude with the Easter Vigil and Easter Sunday (day three). We recall that though the modern world (like ancient Rome) starts a day at midnight, the Jewish day starts at sundown. (And a day for the ancient Greeks started at sunrise!)

These three days are the most sacred of the year. And the pinnacle liturgical celebration of the Triduum is the Easter Vigil (General Norms for the Liturgical Year and the Calendar 19). Parishes sometimes begin this only an hour after sundown. It's as though the church can't wait to celebrate Easter.

SOLEMN PASCHAL FAST

Even though Lent officially ends with the Holy Thursday liturgy, that does not mean our Lenten fast ends too. Rather, the church keeps a solemn paschal fast on Good Friday and we are encouraged to keep it on Saturday as well, in anticipation of Communion at the Easter Vigil. Only then is our fast complete and the Easter season begun. "But the paschal fast must be kept sacrosanct. It should be celebrated everywhere on Good Friday, and where possible should be prolonged through Holy Saturday so that the faithful may attain the joys of Easter Sunday with uplifted and receptive minds" (The Constitution on the Sacred Liturgy 110).

GOSPEL ACCLAMATION
John 13:34

I give you a new commandment, says the Lord:
love one another as I have loved you.

Gospel John 13:1-15; L39ABC

Before the feast of Passover, Jesus knew
that his hour had come
to pass from this world to the Father.
He loved his own in the world
and he loved them to the end.
The devil had already induced Judas, son of Simon the Iscariot, to hand him over.
So, during supper,
fully aware that the Father had put everything into his power
and that he had come from God and was returning to God,
he rose from supper and took off his outer garments.
He took a towel and tied it around his waist.
Then he poured water into a basin
and began to wash the disciples' feet
and dry them with the towel around his waist.
He came to Simon Peter, who said to him,
"Master, are you going to wash my feet?"
Jesus answered and said to him,
"What I am doing, you do not understand now,
but you will understand later."
Peter said to him, "You will never wash my feet."
Jesus answered him,
"Unless I wash you, you will have no inheritance with me."
Simon Peter said to him,
"Master, then not only my feet, but my hands and head as well."
Jesus said to him,
"Whoever has bathed has no need except to have his feet washed,
for he is clean all over;
so you are clean, but not all."

Continued in Appendix A, p. 282.
See Appendix A, p. 282, for the other readings.

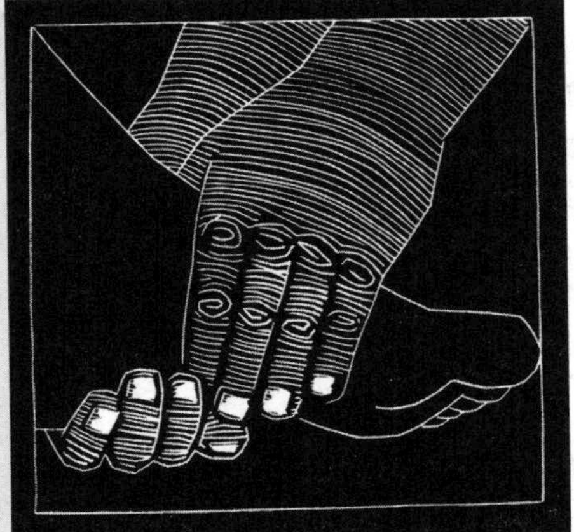

Reflecting on the Gospel and Living the Paschal Mystery

Key words and phrases: As I have done for you, you should also do; he poured water into a basin and began to wash the disciples' feet

To the point: To celebrate this Mass of the Lord's Supper, which commemorates the last meal Jesus had with his disciples, we read from the Gospel of John, which has a unique timeline for the event. The opening words of this gospel are often overlooked, but they indicate something critical. "Before the feast of Passover" tells the reader that this is not a Passover meal. The Synoptic Gospels, on the other hand, tell us that the Last Supper was a Passover meal. But in the Gospel of John, Jesus is dead by Passover. These two chronologies cannot be reconciled. And that is because ultimately the gospels convey theology rather than history. In fact, according to John's chronology, Jesus (the Lamb of God) is crucified at about the time the lambs are being slaughtered in preparation for the Passover meal later that evening. John is the only evangelist to use the title "Lamb of God" for Jesus, and it illustrates his unique theological perspective. Therefore, perhaps counterintuitively, there is no "institution of the Eucharist" during the Last Supper in this gospel. Instead, Jesus gives his disciples an outward sign of service, which they are to do also: wash one another's feet. Christian identity is marked by service. As Jesus the master has done, so should we also do.

To ponder and pray: As we begin to commemorate these sacred days, we call to mind the essential element of Christian identity, which is service. Perhaps more than prayer, liturgy, or other identifiable markers of our faith, we are called to imitate Jesus in service to others. As master, Jesus was not content to be served, but to serve. So let us, too, look for opportunities to be of service to our family, neighbors, friends, fellow parishioners, and any others who may need our help.

Model Penitential Act

Presider: With this celebration we enter into the holiest days of our Christian year. Let us pause to ask for God's mercy and healing as we seek to keep the Sacred Paschal Triduum with devotion and grace . . . *[pause]*

Lord Jesus, you are the Lamb of God: Lord, have mercy.
Christ Jesus, you show us the way of humility and service: Christ, have mercy.
Lord Jesus, you give us your body and blood as heavenly food: Lord, have mercy.

Model Universal Prayer (Prayer of the Faithful)

Presider: Confident in God's sacrificial love for us, let us bring before him our needs and the needs of our world.

Response: Lord, hear our prayer.

For bishops, priests, and deacons, in following the example of Jesus, may they offer humble service and care for those they shepherd . . .

For all throughout the world who suffer religious persecution, may they find safe harbor and protection . . .

For those who experience both physical and spiritual hunger, may they be provided nourishment to strengthen body, mind, and spirit . . .

For all gathered here, as the Body of Christ, may we strive to serve one another and all whom we encounter with humble, self-giving love . . .

Presider: God, our source of nourishment and strength, you have given us the eucharistic feast to draw us closer to you and to feed us with yourself. Hear our prayers that we who eat at this table might lead lives of gentle service and abounding love. We ask this through Christ our Lord. **Amen.**

About Liturgy

Washing of the feet: The *mandatum*, or washing of the feet, holds many different meanings. In it is reflected the role of the ministerial priesthood, which, along with the institution of the Eucharist, is commemorated in the Mass of the Lord's Supper (see Roman Missal [RM], Holy Thursday, 9). Set against John's gospel narrative of the Last Supper, in which there is no mention of bread and wine but rather only foot washing, this version of the Last Supper refers to the true meaning of communion, which is sacrifice and service for one another. Ultimately, this imitation of what Jesus, our Teacher and Lord, did for his disciples is a rehearsal in sharing Christ's love for us, "giving himself 'to the very end' for the salvation of the world" (Pope Francis). This is why the pope, on January 6, 2016, in a decree from the Congregation for Divine Worship and the Discipline of the Sacraments, officially changed the rubric regarding whose feet may be washed (RM, Holy Thursday, 11) from "The men who have been chosen…" to "Those who are chosen from amongst the people of God . . . ," making it clear that all, not only men, are called to this ritual act of Christian discipleship and love.

COLLECT

Let us pray.

Pause for silent prayer

O God, who have called us to participate
in this most sacred Supper,
in which your Only Begotten Son,
when about to hand himself over to death,
entrusted to the Church a sacrifice new for all
eternity,
the banquet of his love,
grant, we pray,
that we may draw from so great a mystery,
the fullness of charity and of life.
Through our Lord Jesus Christ, your Son,
who lives and reigns with you in the unity of
the Holy Spirit,
one God, for ever and ever. **Amen.**

FOR REFLECTION

- The psalm asks, "How shall I make a return to the Lord / for all the good he has done for me?" How are your words and actions a response to God's blessings?
- The second reading from Paul's first letter to the Corinthians gives us the oldest record of the Last Supper and the words Jesus spoke there. Why do you think Jesus gave us a meal as a way to remember him?
- In tonight's gospel Jesus gives us a model of service. When in the past year have you been served by others? When have you been the servant?

Homily Points

- On Holy Thursday we gather to commemorate the gift of the Eucharist within our lives. Today's readings point us to the gift of God, in bread and wine, and also calls us to be the Body and Blood of Christ for others.
- In eating Jesus' body and drinking his blood, we are intimately connected to our Lord. This partaking in the eucharistic feast requires that we act as he did. John's telling of the Last Supper highlights not the meal but the action of Jesus. Jesus tells his disciples at the Last Supper, and each of us, "I have given you a model to follow, / so that as I have done for you, you should also do."

GOSPEL ACCLAMATION
Phil 2:8-9

Christ became obedient to the point of death,
even death on a cross.
Because of this, God greatly exalted him
and bestowed on him the name which is above
every other name.

Gospel John 18:1–19:42; L40ABC

Jesus went out with his disciples
across the Kidron valley
to where there was a garden,
into which he and his disciples
entered.
Judas his betrayer also knew the
place,
because Jesus had often met
there with his disciples.
So Judas got a band of soldiers
and guards
from the chief priests and the
Pharisees
and went there with lanterns,
torches, and weapons.
Jesus, knowing everything that
was going to happen to him,
went out and said to them, "Whom are
you looking for?"
They answered him, "Jesus the Nazorean."
He said to them, "I AM."
Judas his betrayer was also with them.
When he said to them, "I AM,"
they turned away and fell to the ground.
So he again asked them,
"Whom are you looking for?"
They said, "Jesus the Nazorean."
Jesus answered,
"I told you that I AM.
So if you are looking for me, let these
men go."
This was to fulfill what he had said,
"I have not lost any of those you gave me."
Then Simon Peter, who had a sword,
drew it,
struck the high priest's slave, and cut
off his right ear.
The slave's name was Malchus.
Jesus said to Peter,
"Put your sword into its scabbard.
Shall I not drink the cup that the Father
gave me?"

Continued in Appendix A, pp. 283–284.
See Appendix A, p. 285, for the other readings.

Reflecting on the Gospel and Living the Paschal Mystery

Key words and phrases: "I AM"; "What is truth?"; "My kingdom does not belong to this world."

To the point: The gospel reading for the Good Friday liturgy is one of, if not the, longest readings of the liturgical year. Two chapters from the Gospel of John convey the drama of the passion and death of Jesus. The reading conveys theology, and we would do well to read it with that in mind. The author of life is put to death; truth itself is interrogated with the question "What is truth?" The dramatic events fulfill what was foretold in the prophets, foreseen by God, almost as though actors are playing parts, though each certainly has free will.

Though Jesus is called a king and is crucified as such, he claims his kingdom is not of this world. There is no room for violence (Peter's sword) on the part of his kingdom. Instead, he is crucified as the Lamb of God as the lambs are being slaughtered for the Passover meal later that evening. In the face of violence, Jesus submits. His values are not the values of the world. He does not fight back; he does not strike back harder than he is hit. Instead, he trusts in God, secure in his identity, knowing "I AM."

Unlike his disciples who fold under pressure (e.g., Peter's denial), Jesus is true to his identity and true to his mission to such a degree that Pilate ironically asks, "What is truth?"

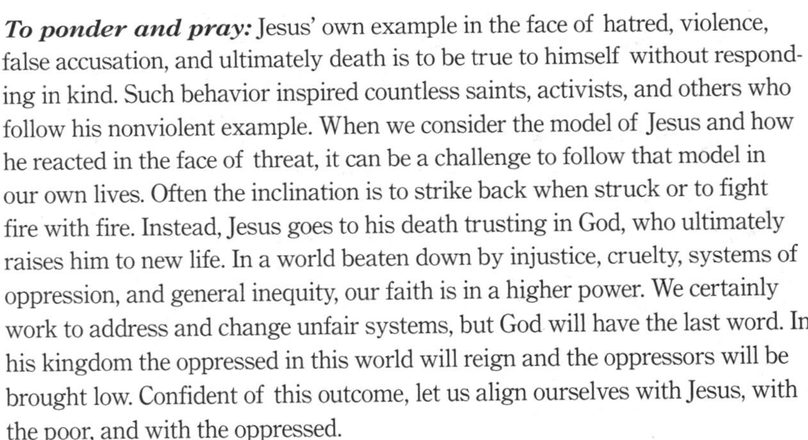

To ponder and pray: Jesus' own example in the face of hatred, violence, false accusation, and ultimately death is to be true to himself without responding in kind. Such behavior inspired countless saints, activists, and others who follow his nonviolent example. When we consider the model of Jesus and how he reacted in the face of threat, it can be a challenge to follow that model in our own lives. Often the inclination is to strike back when struck or to fight fire with fire. Instead, Jesus goes to his death trusting in God, who ultimately raises him to new life. In a world beaten down by injustice, cruelty, systems of oppression, and general inequity, our faith is in a higher power. We certainly work to address and change unfair systems, but God will have the last word. In his kingdom the oppressed in this world will reign and the oppressors will be brought low. Confident of this outcome, let us align ourselves with Jesus, with the poor, and with the oppressed.

About Liturgy

Adoration of the holy cross: At the very end of the Good Friday liturgy, we find the only time in any liturgical ritual when all are instructed to genuflect to something other than the Blessed Sacrament. Tonight, as we begin the silent vigil into Holy Saturday, we genuflect to the holy cross, the place where water and blood flowed to give us the water of life and the blood of salvation. (See the Roman Missal, The Passion of the Lord, 32.)

Let this gesture be slow and intentional, directed without question to the cross and nothing else. Then go one step further. With the same care given to preparing the place of repose for the Blessed Sacrament the night before, prepare a place for adoration of the cross where the faithful may remain in prayer. This place may even be the same place as was used for the Blessed Sacrament the night before (see *Paschale Solemnitatis* 71).

About Initiation

Dismissal of catechumens: Although there is no Eucharist at the liturgy of the passion of the Lord on this day, which would normally require the catechumens to be dismissed, there are, however, the solemn intercessions. These ten intercessions, with their highly structured format—announcement of the intention, invitation to kneel, silent prayer, invitation to stand, collect—constitute the fullest form of the universal prayers we have during the year. The universal prayer we pray at the Eucharist is, in essence, a simplified form of these Good Friday intercessions.

When catechumens are present at Mass, they are normally dismissed after the homily. The main reason they are dismissed is not because they cannot share in Communion but because they cannot yet pray the prayers that are assigned to the faithful. These are the Creed, the universal prayer, and the eucharistic prayer. These prayers will belong to them once they are baptized and enter into a new order, that of the apostolate of the faithful.

Keeping true to the purpose of the dismissal of catechumens, ideally catechumens (and the elect who will be baptized the following night) should be dismissed from the liturgy of the passion of the Lord after the homily and before the solemn intercessions. However, if this is not possible or for a serious reason, the catechumens may be invited to remain in the assembly, adapting the formulary found at RCIA 67C.

COLLECT

Let us pray.

Pause for silent prayer

Remember your mercies, O Lord,
and with your eternal protection sanctify your servants,
for whom Christ your Son,
by the shedding of his Blood,
established the Paschal Mystery.
Who lives and reigns for ever and ever. **Amen.**

or:

O God, who by the Passion of Christ your Son, our Lord,
abolished the death inherited from ancient sin
by every succeeding generation,
grant that just as, being conformed to him,
we have borne by the law of nature
the image of the man of earth,
so by the sanctification of grace
we may bear the image of the Man of heaven.
Through Christ our Lord. **Amen.**

FOR REFLECTION

- The letter to the Hebrews tells us, "Son though he was, he learned obedience from what he suffered." What have you learned through suffering?
- Jesus tells Pilate, "My kingdom does not belong to this world." How do you envision this kingdom that Jesus speaks of?
- Pilate asks Jesus, "What is truth?" How would you answer this question? What are the truths that you cling to in your life?

Homily Points

- Each Good Friday we enter into the passion story as portrayed by the Gospel of John. Jesus responds to a questioning Pontius Pilate, "You say I am a king. / For this I was born and for this I came into the world, / to testify to the truth." Jesus utters many truths in both word and action. Perhaps the most central truth is that life is stronger than death, love is stronger than hatred, and violence will not have the last word.

- Jesus says to Pilate, "Everyone who belongs to the truth, listens to my voice." Good Friday is a day of stillness, fasting, and prayer. We listen for the voice of the one who is truth echoing in our lives.

Gospel Matt 28:1-10; L41ABC

After the sabbath, as the first day of the week was dawning,
Mary Magdalene and the other Mary came to see the tomb.
And behold, there was a great earthquake;
for an angel of the Lord descended from heaven,
approached, rolled back the stone, and sat upon it.
His appearance was like lightning
and his clothing was white as snow.
The guards were shaken with fear of him
and became like dead men.
Then the angel said to the women in reply,
"Do not be afraid!
I know that you are seeking Jesus the crucified.
He is not here, for he has been raised just as he said.
Come and see the place where he lay.
Then go quickly and tell his disciples,
'He has been raised from the dead,
and he is going before you to Galilee;
there you will see him.'
Behold, I have told you."
Then they went away quickly from the tomb,
fearful yet overjoyed,
and ran to announce this to his disciples.
And behold, Jesus met them on their way and greeted them.
They approached, embraced his feet, and did him homage.
Then Jesus said to them, "Do not be afraid.
Go tell my brothers to go to Galilee,
and there they will see me."

See Appendix A, pp. 286–291, for the other readings.

Reflecting on the Gospel and Living the Paschal Mystery

Key words and phrases: "Do not be afraid . . . he has been raised from the dead."

To the point: The Gospel of Matthew presents Easter Sunday morning in a much more dramatic way than did the Gospel of Mark, which Matthew used as a source. In Matthew it's clear that the stone has been rolled away by an angel from heaven, whose appearance was not that of a mere mortal but of lightning. The guards, posted by Pilate himself, were left in a daze. The earth itself shook. And Jesus himself appeared to the women. What Mark related Matthew enhanced. Of course, both are Scripture, inspired by God, and authoritative, but we see the master evangelist at his craft when we compare the two accounts of Easter Sunday morning.

Significantly in Matthew, the risen Christ has appeared to Mary Magdalene and to "the other Mary." Women were the recipients of the first risen appearance, according to Matthew. They are told to relate the good news to the others—that Jesus is risen and they will see him in Galilee. Here it is not Peter or the Beloved Disciple, or the other disciples, who witness Jesus first. Mary Magdalene and the other Mary have that distinction. Jesus chooses those whom he wills. And we, too, are witness to his presence in the world.

To ponder and pray: We know from other stories in the gospels that the male disciples of Jesus dismissed the stories of the women who proclaimed, "He is risen" as nonsense (Luke 24:11). Even though the male disciples had been with Jesus and witnessed his ministry, when the women shared the good news, the men did not believe. We might like to think that we would act differently in their shoes or that we would have been among the first to believe. But the behavior of the disciples should cause us to ponder. Upon recognizing that Jesus has been raised to new life, we must recast all of our prior thinking. We have a promise of eternal life with him; death is not the ultimate end.

Model Universal Prayer (Prayer of the Faithful)

Presider: On this night of vigil and celebration, let us turn to the Lord in prayer, trusting in his everlasting love and abundant mercy.

Response: Lord, hear our prayer.

For the church, that in celebrating the paschal mystery of Jesus' death and resurrection it might be strengthened and purified to spread Christ's light in word and deed . . .

For the world, may the darkness of war, oppression, and injustice cease . . .

For all those in need of shelter on this holy night, may they find welcome and comfort . . .

For all gathered here, may the word of God take root within us and bear the fruits of faith, hope, and love . . .

Presider: God of glory, your son, Jesus, emerges triumphant from the tomb and urges his disciples to go and spread the news of his life that is stronger than death. Hear our prayers that we might carry the proclamation of the resurrection to all we meet. We ask this through Christ our Lord. **Amen.**

About Liturgy

Dispel the darkness and light up the night: Symbols should communicate clearly and truthfully what they mean. At the beginning of the Easter Vigil, the new fire symbolizes the "light of Christ rising in glory [to] dispel the darkness of our hearts and minds" (Roman Missal [RM], The Easter Vigil, 14).

The circular letter "On Preparing and Celebrating the Paschal Feasts" (*Paschale Solemnitatis*) says that the flames of the new fire "should be such that they genuinely dispel the darkness and light up the night" (82). A tiny fire in a barbecue grill does not adequately reflect Christ who breaks apart the darkness of death, nor does beginning before nightfall and true natural darkness for your region (see RM, The Easter Vigil, 3).

There are people in your community who not only can help you prepare an ample, blazing fire but also can make it burn efficiently and safely. These are your firefighters. When you enlist their help, you will also be engaging many more people in your community in the preparation and celebration of the Triduum.

COLLECT

Let us pray.

Pause for silent prayer

O God, who make this most sacred night radiant
with the glory of the Lord's Resurrection,
stir up in your Church a spirit of adoption,
so that, renewed in body and mind,
we may render you undivided service.
Through our Lord Jesus Christ, your Son,
who lives and reigns with you in the unity of
the Holy Spirit,
one God, for ever and ever. **Amen.**

FOR REFLECTION

- At the Easter Vigil, catechumens enter fully into the church through baptism, confirmation, and Eucharist. What are your memories of your own baptism, confirmation, and First Communion?
- After the blessing of the paschal candle, the priest lights it saying, "May the light of Christ rising in his glory / dispel the darkness of our hearts and minds." Where are you most in need of Christ's light?
- In the gospel reading Jesus tells the women, "Do not be afraid" but go and spread the word of his triumph over death. In word and deed how do you proclaim this good news?

Homily Points

- On this holy night we keep vigil. Meeting in darkness reminds us of the exodus event where Moses led the people to freedom from slavery by passing through the sea "just before dawn." It also hearkens to the event of the resurrection, occurring sometime in the night between Holy Saturday and Easter Sunday when the women arrived to find the tomb empty.
- These events, taking place in darkness, remind us of the power of light. St. Paul proclaims that in conforming our life to Christ's, we are no longer slaves to the darkness of sin. Instead, as we hear in the baptismal rite, we are "children of light." Just as tonight when we carried candles, lit from the paschal candle, may our lives always bear witness to the triumph of light over darkness.

GOSPEL ACCLAMATION
cf. 1 Cor 5:7b-8a

℟. Alleluia, alleluia.
Christ, our paschal lamb, has been sacrificed;
let us then feast with joy in the Lord.
℟. Alleluia, alleluia.

Gospel

John 20:1-9; L42ABC

On the first day of the week,
Mary of Magdala came to the tomb early in the morning,
while it was still dark,
and saw the stone removed from the tomb.
So she ran and went to Simon Peter
and to the other disciple whom Jesus loved, and told them,
"They have taken the Lord from the tomb,
and we don't know where they put him."
So Peter and the other disciple went out and came to the tomb.
They both ran, but the other disciple ran faster than Peter
and arrived at the tomb first;
he bent down and saw the burial cloths there, but did not go in.
When Simon Peter arrived after him,
he went into the tomb and saw the burial cloths there,
and the cloth that had covered his head,
not with the burial cloths but rolled up in a separate place.
Then the other disciple also went in,
the one who had arrived at the tomb first,
and he saw and believed.
For they did not yet understand the Scripture
that he had to rise from the dead.

or

Matt 28:1-10; L41A *in Appendix A, p. 292,*
or, at an afternoon or evening Mass
Luke 24:13-35; L46 *in Appendix A, p. 292.*

See Appendix A, p. 293, for the other readings.

Reflecting on the Gospel and Living the Paschal Mystery

Key words and phrases: [H]e saw and believed . . . he had to rise from the dead

To the point: That first Easter morning must have been a whirlwind of confusion, perplexity, and ultimately joy. According to John's gospel, Mary of Magdala was the first to find the tomb empty. Her reaction was not belief in the resurrection, but something more banal—that somebody had stolen the body. She immediately informs Peter and another disciple of her suspicion. That other disciple is thought to be the Beloved Disciple, aka "the disciple whom he [Jesus] loved." He is nameless throughout the Gospel of John, and there is no mention of this person in any other gospel. Yet he is portrayed as the model of discipleship, as we see that "he saw and believed," something not even Peter did upon witnessing the empty tomb.

Interestingly, the gospel passage ends on the note that these disciples did not yet understand the Scripture that he had to rise from the dead. After all this time with Jesus, and even finding the tomb empty, they still did not understand. Yet, the Beloved Disciple, at least, believed. Such a story gives hope to us who did not travel with Jesus or experience his historical ministry. If we have questions or experience a lack of understanding, we may be assured that the earliest disciples, the followers of Jesus himself, felt the same way even after the resurrection.

To ponder and pray: Much as it may sound surprising to us, the resurrection of Jesus seemed to be a surprise to his disciples. Mary of Magdala's first reaction is logical: the body was stolen. Peter and the Beloved Disciple see for themselves that the tomb is empty, but only one believes. They did not understand the Scripture. We are reminded that we live by faith and we seek understanding. Easter morning gives us our north star, the guiding light by which we live our lives. The death of Jesus was not his end. He was raised in a wholly unexpected way to new life. His destiny is ours; his new life will be shared by us who seek to follow him. On this Easter morning, may we be open to the unexpected ways that God may work in our lives.

Model Penitential Act

Presider: Christ has risen from the tomb and calls us to new life in him. In joy and thanksgiving, let us ask for his healing touch to free us from sin and lead us to everlasting life . . . *[pause]*

Lord Jesus, you are the anointed one of God: Lord, have mercy.
Christ Jesus, you are seated at the right hand of the Father: Christ, have mercy.
Lord Jesus, you have been appointed by God as judge of the living and the dead: Lord, have mercy.

Model Universal Prayer (Prayer of the Faithful)

Presider: Christ, our Savior, has conquered death and intercedes for us at the right hand of the Father. Let us bring our needs, and those of our world, before the risen Lord.

Response: Lord, hear our prayer.

For all disciples of the Lord, especially preachers and catechists, may they proclaim the good news of Jesus' resurrection with fervor and joy . . .

For the world, may the light of the risen Christ cover our planet and dispel the darkness of poverty, violence, and suffering . . .

For those suffering from mental, emotional, and spiritual illnesses, may Christ, the healer, bring comfort and hope . . .

For all gathered here, by renewing the promises of our baptism, may we be strengthened and purified to live as children of light . . .

Presider: God of life, in Christ's death and resurrection we are made new and become partakers in everlasting life. Hear our prayers that in keeping this Easter feast we might be renewed in the life of discipleship. We ask this through Christ our Lord. **Amen.**

About Liturgy

Pay attention to who is missing: The Triduum is the one time of the year that the entire local community is called to celebrate a single liturgical arc, spanning the Mass of the Lord's Supper, the Celebration of the Passion of the Lord, and the Easter Vigil.

The union of the entire parish at the highpoint of the liturgical year reflects the unity of the church and its communion with Christ. If members of the community are missing or left out, the Body of Christ is incomplete.

Who is missing from your Triduum assemblies? Among those preparing the liturgies and making liturgical decisions? Among the liturgical ministers and leaders? Whose languages and songs, rituals and devotions are missing? Are both young and elderly members present, seen, and serving in significant roles? Are women and men evenly represented in the ministries and in the music chosen throughout the Triduum?

Although you have just ended the busiest three days of the liturgical year, now is the time to write down your immediate thoughts on this year's Triduum, so that you can begin planning for next year's Triduum to be an even truer reflection of the unity of the Body of Christ.

COLLECT

Let us pray.

Pause for silent prayer

O God, who on this day,
through your Only Begotten Son,
have conquered death
and unlocked for us the path to eternity,
grant, we pray, that we who keep
the solemnity of the Lord's Resurrection
may, through the renewal brought by your Spirit,
rise up in the light of life.
Through our Lord Jesus Christ, your Son,
who lives and reigns with you in the unity of
the Holy Spirit,
one God, for ever and ever. **Amen.**

FOR REFLECTION

- In the psalm we hear, "The stone which the builders rejected / has become the cornerstone." God exalts the lowly and humbles the exalted. How do you live this in your own life?
- Today's gospel acclamation calls us to "feast with joy in the Lord." How does your family keep the Easter feast?
- We are told that upon entering the tomb, the Beloved Disciple "saw and believed." What has been your own journey to belief?

Homily Points

- The sign of Jesus' resurrection is the stone rolled back from the tomb. Mary Magdalene, assuming it was opened by thieves intent upon stealing Jesus' body, alerts the other disciples. In the Synoptic Gospels, the women who arrive on Easter morning worried that this stone will keep them from the one they love. But this is not the case.
- Nothing can keep us from God, not even death itself. It is not the force of human hands that removes the stone. It is the love of God. On Easter morning we come face-to-face with the empty tomb and know the proclamation of St. Paul: "neither death, nor life, nor angels, nor principalities, nor present things, nor future things, nor powers, nor height nor depth, nor any other creature will be able to separate us from the love of God in Christ Jesus our Lord" (Rom 8:38-39).

SEASON OF EASTER

SPIRITUALITY

GOSPEL ACCLAMATION
John 20:29

℟. Alleluia, alleluia.
You believe in me, Thomas, because you have seen me, says the Lord;
blessed are those who have not seen me, but still believe!
℟. Alleluia, alleluia.

Gospel John 20:19-31; L43A

On the evening of that first day of the week,
when the doors were locked, where the disciples were,
for fear of the Jews,
Jesus came and stood in their midst
and said to them, "Peace be with you."
When he had said this, he showed them his hands and his side.
The disciples rejoiced when they saw the Lord.
Jesus said to them again, "Peace be with you.
As the Father has sent me, so I send you."
And when he had said this, he breathed on them and said to them,
"Receive the Holy Spirit.
Whose sins you forgive are forgiven them,
and whose sins you retain are retained."

Thomas, called Didymus, one of the Twelve,
was not with them when Jesus came.
So the other disciples said to him, "We have seen the Lord."
But he said to them,
"Unless I see the mark of the nails in his hands
and put my finger into the nailmarks
and put my hand into his side, I will not believe."

Now a week later his disciples were again inside
and Thomas was with them.
Jesus came, although the doors were locked,
and stood in their midst and said,
"Peace be with you."

Continued in Appendix A, p. 293.

Reflecting on the Gospel

On this the Second Sunday of Easter the church gives us the only gospel reading that corresponds to the week after Easter, namely the story of "Doubting Thomas" (though he is never called that in the story). On the evening of Easter Sunday, Jesus makes his appearance to the disciples, though Thomas is absent. It is only one week later when Jesus appears again. During this intervening week, we might wonder what the other disciples said to Thomas, and we might wonder at Thomas's obstinacy in the face of their witness. Not only had Thomas experienced Jesus throughout his earthly ministry, but Thomas had the eyewitness testimony of his fellow disciples, his friends. Still, his lack of belief persisted. Only a personal experience of the risen Christ would melt away his doubt and unbelief. Such is a model of how individuals come to faith. Sometimes, like Thomas, despite all the evidence, testimony, and enthusiasm of believers, faith will never take root unless one personally encounters the risen Christ. Still, Jesus utters a beatitude that is meant for us, the reader: "Blessed are those who have not seen and have believed."

The gospel passage, and gospel itself, ends with an eloquent note from the author (though a later author added chapter 21!), stating explicitly the aim of the work: "that you may come to believe that Jesus is the Christ, the Son of God, and that through this belief you may have life in his name." With such an obvious conclusion, it does seem odd to find another chapter that begins with the disciples fishing. But as stated above, chapter 21 was written and added by a later author, as even the notes in the New American Bible indicate. The conclusion of today's story is a straightforward admission of the point of the gospel: belief in Jesus and life in his name. Twenty centuries later, and with our own reading of these very same words, it's safe the say the evangelist succeeded in his aim.

Finally, Jesus says at least twice that he brings peace. Such repetition is deliberate. The resurrection of Jesus gives us, his followers, peace. We are no longer subject to the buffeting winds of turmoil, drama, challenge, or turbulence. We may rest assured in the peace of Christ, knowing that there is life eternal. God is faithful. Violence, lawlessness, and collusion will not last. Instead, peace, love, friendship, and self-gift are eternal. The resurrection of Jesus and his lasting presence among his disciples are all the proof we need. Once we experience him for ourselves, there is no longer room for doubt.

Living the Paschal Mystery

After Jesus' death, the disciples were bewildered. Even Mary of Magdalen, the first to find the empty tomb, did not believe that Jesus was raised from the dead. Peter, too, upon seeing the empty tomb did not believe. As we heard in last week's gospel, only the unnamed Beloved Disciple believed without seeing. And in today's reading we hear how later that same evening on Easter, the remaining disciples (except Thomas) also came to believe upon seeing Jesus. Thomas stands in for all the second, third, and subsequent generations of Christians who know that Jesus suffered and died on a cross but did not experience the risen Christ in the way that the first disciples did. Even Thomas himself only believes upon seeing Jesus, which is when Jesus utters the beatitude meant for us.

We experience the suffering and death of Jesus when we encounter those tragedies in our own lives. We experience the resurrection of Jesus, too, when we are open to those encounters. Jesus, the source of life, continues to give life to his followers. On this Second Sunday of Easter, let us be aware of the occasions we have to experience not only the suffering and death of Jesus, but most especially his life and exaltation. In that way we live the paschal mystery more fully.

Focusing the Gospel

Key words and phrases: [T]hese are written that you might come to believe / that Jesus is the Christ, the Son of God.

To the point: In the last line of today's gospel reading, the evangelist tells us the motivation behind the words he has written—that his readers might come to belief. Unlike Thomas, who believes only after seeing the risen Jesus for himself, we encounter our Lord in other ways. Through the words of the gospel and the sacraments of the church, we are able to hear, see, and touch the one who calls us to live life abundantly. The gifts of the word of God and the sacraments have been passed down from generation to generation by the disciples of Jesus. They have been safeguarded and cherished by our ancestors in faith. May we now do our part so that others, too, might come to belief.

Connecting the Gospel

to the first reading: The reading from the Acts of the Apostles paints a picture of an idyllic Christian community where many members live together in unity, generosity, and self-giving. We know that the early Christian communities had their own struggles in living the life of faith. The epistles often encourage and sometimes even chastise these nascent churches to live justly and charitably. And yet, despite this, the Christian community grew and expanded.

to experience: In the gospel, the risen Lord greets his disciples and offers them the gift of his peace, and also the Holy Spirit in order to forgive sins. Only in Jesus, the source of peace and mercy, could these early Christian communities continue on the path of faith. In our own families and churches, we are sure to encounter the struggles that inevitably occur when trying to live in community with others. When this happens let us turn to Jesus and the Holy Spirit, praying that peace might reign and forgiveness flow freely.

Connecting the Responsorial Psalm

to the readings: This Second Sunday of Easter is also called Divine Mercy Sunday. In the gospel, Jesus encounters the disciples for the first time following their desertion of him during his passion and death. Instead of greeting them with reproach, he offers peace. The psalm for today also emphasizes the mercy of God. Three times in the first verse we hear the line repeated: "His mercy endures forever." Three is a number of fullness and completion in the Bible. As the responsorial proclaims, our God's love is everlasting.

to psalmist preparation: As you prepare to proclaim the mercy of God to the assembly, consider where you have received this mercy in your own life. How do you live a life of mercy and forgiveness?

PROMPTS FOR FAITH-SHARING

In the first reading from the Acts of the Apostles, we hear of an ideal Christian community in which communal life is lived to the fullest. Where has division crept into your family or parish community? How might you help to bring the peace of Christ to this situation?

Three times the psalmist calls for different groups to proclaim "[God's] mercy endures forever." On this Divine Mercy Sunday, how are you called to be a beacon of mercy for others?

In the first letter from St. Peter, the apostle writes that at times the believer "may have to suffer through various trials" like gold "tested by fire." When has your faith been tested?

Thomas believes in the resurrection only after seeing the risen Christ. Jesus tells him, "Blessed are those who have not seen and have believed." What are the events or experiences in your life that have brought you to belief?

Model Rite for the Blessing and Sprinkling of Water

Presider: In today's gospel the risen Christ appears to his disciples and offers them his peace. May these waters cleanse, purify, and strengthen us to bear Christ's peace to others . . . *[pause]*

[continue with The Roman Missal, *Appendix II]*

Homily Points

• On Easter Sunday we gathered to celebrate Christ's resurrection from the dead. Death itself could not keep our Lord from us; the tomb could not contain or squelch his love. Today, it is fear that stands between the disciples and the Lord. We hear that on the evening of the day of the resurrection, the disciples were gathered together in a room with locked doors, "for fear of the Jews." It was this fear that had caused them to flee on the night of Jesus' arrest.

• Just as the tomb could not keep Jesus in, the doors locked in fear cannot keep him out, and he suddenly stands in their midst. His first words to those who had deserted him during his passion might be considered surprising. He says to them, "Peace be with you." Not only does he bear no reproach, he entrusts the gathered disciples with a new mission: "As the Father has sent me, so I send you." Freed from their fear, the disciples are now called to bring this peace to others, specifically through the forgiveness of sins.

• Within our own lives we can recognize this pattern of the Lord at work. As human beings we will sin, fail, and even at times run away from our God and the work he has called us to do. And yet, with divine mercy, the Lord never ceases to call us back, offering peace to counteract our fear and forgiveness to wipe away our sins. As people who have received these gifts of peace and mercy, we are then sent forth to bear them to the world.

Model Universal Prayer (Prayer of the Faithful)

Presider: Trusting in the divine mercy of our creator and redeemer, let us bring our needs before the Lord.

Response: Lord, hear our prayer.

For God's holy church, may it be a beacon of Jesus' merciful love and a place of welcome for all . . .

For nations of the world, may leaders join together to provide and care for those suffering from natural disasters . . .

For those most in need of the mercy of God and the mercy of their fellow human beings, may Christ's peace restore and heal them . . .

For all gathered here, may we be strengthened to forgive those who have harmed us and to ask forgiveness of those we have harmed . . .

Presider: Creator God, through your son, Jesus, you have gifted us with your peace and your Holy Spirit. Hear our prayers that we might bear your peace and mercy to all we meet. We ask this through Christ our Lord. **Amen.**

COLLECT

Let us pray.

Pause for silent prayer

God of everlasting mercy,
who in the very recurrence of the paschal feast
kindle the faith of the people you have made your own,
increase, we pray, the grace you have bestowed,
that all may grasp and rightly understand
in what font they have been washed,
by whose Spirit they have been reborn,
by whose Blood they have been redeemed.
Through our Lord Jesus Christ, your Son,
who lives and reigns with you in the unity of the Holy Spirit,
one God, for ever and ever. **Amen.**

FIRST READING

Acts 2:42-47

They devoted themselves
to the teaching of the apostles and to the communal life,
to the breaking of bread and to the prayers.
Awe came upon everyone,
and many wonders and signs were done through the apostles.
All who believed were together and had all things in common;
they would sell their property and possessions
and divide them among all according to each one's need.
Every day they devoted themselves
to meeting together in the temple area
and to breaking bread in their homes.
They ate their meals with exultation and sincerity of heart,
praising God and enjoying favor with all the people.
And every day the Lord added to their number those who were being saved.

RESPONSORIAL PSALM

Ps 118:2-4, 13-15, 22-24

℟. (1) Give thanks to the Lord for he is good, his love is everlasting.
or: ℟. Alleluia.

Let the house of Israel say,
"His mercy endures forever."
Let the house of Aaron say,
"His mercy endures forever."
Let those who fear the LORD say,
"His mercy endures forever."

℟. Give thanks to the Lord for he is good, his love is everlasting.
or: ℟. Alleluia.

I was hard pressed and was falling,
but the LORD helped me.
My strength and my courage is the LORD,
and he has been my savior.
The joyful shout of victory
in the tents of the just.

℟. Give thanks to the Lord for he is good,
his love is everlasting.
or: ℟. Alleluia.

The stone which the builders rejected
has become the cornerstone.
By the LORD has this been done;
it is wonderful in our eyes.
This is the day the LORD has made;
let us be glad and rejoice in it.

℟. Give thanks to the Lord for he is good,
his love is everlasting.
or: ℟. Alleluia.

SECOND READING
1 Pet 1:3-9

Blessed be the God and Father of our Lord
Jesus Christ,
who in his great mercy gave us a new
birth to a living hope
through the resurrection of Jesus Christ
from the dead,
to an inheritance that is imperishable,
undefiled, and unfading,
kept in heaven for you
who by the power of God are
safeguarded through faith,
to a salvation that is ready to be
revealed in the final time.
In this you rejoice, although now for a
little while
you may have to suffer through various
trials,
so that the genuineness of your faith,
more precious than gold that is
perishable even though tested by
fire,
may prove to be for praise, glory, and
honor
at the revelation of Jesus Christ.
Although you have not seen him you love
him;
even though you do not see him now yet
believe in him,
you rejoice with an indescribable and
glorious joy,
as you attain the goal of your faith, the
salvation of your souls.

About Liturgy

Masses for neophytes: Having journeyed with the catechumens to their baptism, confirmation, and Eucharist at Easter, the community of the baptized now has a specific responsibility during the Easter season to these now-called neophytes, the newly initiated. The Rite of Christian Initiation of Adults (RCIA) says this: "During the period immediately after baptism, the faithful should take part in the Masses for neophytes, that is the Sunday Masses of the Easter season, welcome the neophytes with open arms in charity, and help them to feel more at home in the community of the baptized" (9.5).

Every Sunday Mass during the Easter season is designated a "Mass for Neophytes" when a neophyte is present. At these gatherings, your neophytes and their godparents should have special places in the assembly reserved for them (see RCIA 248). This is the only directive I know of in a ritual text that requires places of honor reserved for a member of the assembly aside from the minister. This tells you something about how significant the neophytes are in the life of the church!

Throughout Easter, you might invite the neophytes to continue wearing their white baptismal garments as a reminder to us—"old-phytes!"—of the dignity of our own baptism. The neophytes might also share a brief reflection with the assembly at an appropriate time during the Mass on the significance of their conversion to Christ. After each of these Masses, there should be a time for the community to gather with the neophytes for fellowship and conversation.

About Initiation

How to do mystagogy: RCIA teams often think that the period of mystagogy is a time for either more classes or getting neophytes to sign up for parish ministries. However, the RCIA describes this final period as a "time for the community and the neophytes together to grow in deepening their grasp of the paschal mystery and making it part of their lives" (244). The way they do this is threefold: meditating on the gospel, sharing in the Eucharist, and doing the works of charity. In other words, the way to do mystagogy with neophytes is to help them do what Christians do with other Christians: love the Word, celebrate the sacraments, and be witnesses of Christ in the world.

Today's first reading from Acts gives us concrete examples of what early Christians did to make the paschal mystery part of their lives. Go through that reading and list all the things the disciples did, and see how you can help your newly baptized do the same with your community.

About Liturgical Music

Helping neophytes pray the Eucharist: Music ministers might not realize it, but they have a role to play in helping the newly baptized deepen their grasp of the paschal mystery. Think about it. These former catechumens had been dismissed from the Mass after the homily for months, maybe years. Last week, their baptism was their first experience of the Liturgy of the Eucharist as members of the baptized! These Sundays of Easter will be the first time they will sing the acclamations to our great thanksgiving in the eucharistic prayer, the plea for mercy in the Lamb of God, and the communion song where they join their voices with others as they unite themselves to Christ and to one another. What an honor to be among the first to enable their song of praise to God!

You might not have much direct contact with the neophytes themselves, but your own prayer and ministerial life will be enhanced if you remember that the music you lead this Easter is teaching your neophytes how to give God thanks and praise in song. Remember them in prayer and think of them as you lead your assembly's singing.

SPIRITUALITY

GOSPEL ACCLAMATION

cf. Luke 24:32

℟. Alleluia, alleluia.
Lord Jesus, open the Scriptures to us;
make our hearts burn while you speak to us.
℟. Alleluia, alleluia.

Gospel Luke 24:13-35; L46A

That very day, the first day of the week,
two of Jesus' disciples were going
to a village seven miles from Jerusalem called Emmaus,
and they were conversing about all the things that had occurred.
And it happened that while they were conversing and debating,
Jesus himself drew near and walked with them,
but their eyes were prevented from recognizing him.
He asked them,
"What are you discussing as you walk along?"
They stopped, looking downcast.
One of them, named Cleopas, said to him in reply,
"Are you the only visitor to Jerusalem
who does not know of the things
that have taken place there in these days?"
And he replied to them, "What sort of things?"
They said to him,
"The things that happened to Jesus the Nazarene,
who was a prophet mighty in deed and word
before God and all the people,
how our chief priests and rulers both handed him over
to a sentence of death and crucified him.

Continued in Appendix A, p. 294.

Reflecting on the Gospel

Though we are celebrating the Third Sunday of Easter, the gospel story from Luke today has as its setting Easter Sunday. Emmaus was a small village not far from Jerusalem. Two disciples, one named Cleopas, were walking to Emmaus from Jerusalem when the risen Christ himself appears to them and accompanies them on their way. There is speculation that the unnamed disciple may have been a woman. When we are reminded that Luke has a special concern for women, often narrating a story about a woman before or after telling a story about a man, it seems likely that this unnamed disciple could have been a woman. Indeed, Conception Seminary in Missouri has an icon of this scene in which Jesus speaks with Cleopas and a female disciple. In any case, as Luke is not explicit about the identity of the other disciple, we should be open to possibilities.

As the two speak to Jesus and relate to him what happened, he in turn explains the Scriptures to them, causing their hearts to burn within them. Then, instead of continuing on his way, Jesus joins them and in explicit eucharistic language the gospel says, "[H]e took bread / said the blessing, / broke it, / and gave it to them." With that, in stunning Lucan language, Jesus vanished! Thus the disciples came to know him in the "breaking of the bread," illustrating vividly how subsequent Christians would come to know the risen Lord. So, when we break bread (in the Eucharist), we come to know the risen Christ.

With this experience, the two disciples race back to Jerusalem to report their encounter to the assembled others. The two are told that Jesus has also appeared to Simon, which according to Luke's gospel was the first appearance. The experience of coming to know him in the breaking of the bread is additional confirmation that Jesus lives eternally, building on the appearance of the risen Christ to Simon. Up to this point, for the assembled disciples, much like for us, they have only the testimony of Peter, Cleopas, and the other disciple. They also have reports of the empty tomb and of angels announcing that Jesus is alive. At this point in the story, the other disciples are relying on the testimony of others, and such is the Christian story. Disciples share the "good news" of Jesus being alive with one another. For those who have faith, the resurrection is a confirmation of God's activity on behalf of Jesus.

Living the Paschal Mystery

After Easter, the disciples come to know Jesus in the breaking of the bread. He is present among his followers as he was prior to his death and resurrection, but now, he is present in a new way. Of course, as Catholics, we see this clearly in the Eucharist, when we take bread, bless it, break it, and give it. The bread broken is Christ himself. He is our nourishment both spiritually and physically, metaphorically and actually. When we participate in the Eucharist, we call to mind his passion, death, and resurrection. We consume him who is the Bread of Life. When we want to know Jesus, we experience the Eucharist not merely by gazing at it, but by consuming it—for it is real food. In this way, we not only live but share in and become the paschal mystery.

Focusing the Gospel

Key words and phrases: [H]e interpreted to them what referred to him / in all the Scriptures. . . . [H]e took bread, said the blessing, / broke it, and gave it to them.

To the point: In the gospel story of the road to Emmaus, we find an image of our liturgy. On the road Jesus, the Word of God, interprets the Scriptures for the unwitting disciples. Then, when they arrive at their destination, he becomes the high priest who takes bread, blesses, breaks, and shares it with his companions. The disciples, nourished and empowered by the Word they have heard and the bread they have shared, rush out to share the good news of Jesus' resurrection with the rest of their community.

Connecting the Gospel

to the first reading: In the Acts of the Apostles, Peter attests to the resurrection of Jesus by proclaiming, "God raised him up, releasing him from the throes of death, / because it was impossible for him to be held by it." In today's gospel we see this Jesus, the one who has conquered death, quickly go about the work of restoring all who had been lost in the desertion during his passion and death, to full communion with him. The two disciples on the road to Emmaus are walking away from the empty tomb, which had already been proclaimed to them by the women. They have given up on their hope that Jesus could be the redeemer they longed for. Jesus meets them on the road, interprets the Scriptures for them, and is finally known to them in the breaking of the bread.

to experience: The Jesus that Peter announces, who cannot be held by death, is the one who continues to go about his Father's work of finding the lost and restoring them to communion. He continues to reach out to us in the Scripture and the sacraments; do we recognize his presence there?

Connecting the Responsorial Psalm

to the readings: Our responsorial psalm, "Lord, you will show us the path of life," seems to fit in well with today's gospel where Jesus joins the disciples on the road to Emmaus. The downcast disciples do not realize that they are on the road leading away from their salvation and the good news proclaimed by the empty tomb. Jesus joins them on the path they have chosen and slowly, through opening up the Scriptures and by sharing bread together, leads them to "abounding joy in [his] presence." After he has vanished from their midst, they immediately set out for Jerusalem on the same seven-mile road they journeyed earlier that day. But this time they are going toward their community with good news of their own to proclaim. This time they are on the path of life.

to psalmist preparation: How do you experience Jesus as walking beside you and leading you on the path of life?

PROMPTS FOR FAITH-SHARING

It is the Third Sunday of Easter. For the forty days of Lent we took up the practices of intentional prayer, fasting, and almsgiving. In Easter there are fifty days of celebration. How does your family or community continue to keep the Easter feast?

In the Acts of the Apostles, for the first time Peter stands before a crowd to proclaim the resurrection of Jesus, the Nazorean. Where do you find strength and courage when something new is required of you?

On the road to Emmaus we are told that Jesus "drew near and walked" with the disciples. In the life of discipleship, how do you perceive Jesus as walking alongside you?

The disciples describe their interaction with Jesus as one that caused their hearts to burn within them. What spiritual practices bring you closer to Jesus?

Model Rite for the Blessing and Sprinkling of Water

Presider: In today's gospel, two disciples recognize Jesus in the breaking of the bread. As we prepare to draw close to Jesus at the eucharistic feast, may this water remind us of the waters of baptism as they cleanse and restore us . . . *[pause]*

[continue with The Roman Missal, *Appendix II]*

Homily Points

• On the road to Emmaus, Jesus walks alongside two downcast disciples who do not recognize him. They are fixated on the dashing of their hopes that Jesus would be "the one to redeem Israel." Only through Jesus' interpretation of the Scriptures and breaking of the bread do they come to know him and have their faith rekindled. The disciples describe their experience with Jesus on the road to Emmaus as one in which "our hearts [were] burning within us." Earlier in Luke's gospel Jesus had told his disciples, "I have come to set the earth on fire, and how I wish it were already blazing!" (Luke 12:49; NABRE). It seems this fire is to start in the hearts of his disciples who will carry the blaze to others as the light of the risen Christ spreads throughout the world.

• The burning within their hearts spurs the disciples into action. Even though we are told that "the day is almost over" and night has most likely fallen, they "set out at once and returned to Jerusalem." This seven-mile journey would have been more dangerous at night, and yet the urgency of the good news they have to share will not let them wait.

• Within our eucharistic liturgy we also meet the risen Lord in the word of God and in the breaking of the bread. This encounter with the Lord is meant to make our own hearts burn with the joy and love of the gospel—joy that is too great not to be shared and love that will set the world on fire.

Model Universal Prayer (Prayer of the Faithful)

Presider: With faith in Jesus who meets us in the word of God and the bread and wine of the Eucharist, let us bring our needs before the Lord.

Response: Lord, hear our prayer.

For all members of the church, may we be renewed in our desire to draw close to the risen Lord and to walk with him always . . .

For politicians, legislators, and government officials, may mutual respect and care for humanity lead to fruitful dialogue in all areas of public life . . .

For those who have lost their way, may they find companions to walk alongside them with empathy and love, leading them to the path of life . . .

For all gathered here around the table of the Lord, may we know Jesus in the breaking of the bread and be nourished to serve him with fidelity . . .

Presider: Ever-living God, you call us here to be fed in Word and sacrament. Hear our prayers that we might be bread, broken and shared for others and the life of the world. We ask this through Christ our Lord. **Amen.**

COLLECT

Let us pray.

Pause for silent prayer

May your people exult for ever, O God,
in renewed youthfulness of spirit,
so that, rejoicing now in the restored glory
of our adoption,
we may look forward in confident hope
to the rejoicing of the day of resurrection.
Through our Lord Jesus Christ, your Son,
who lives and reigns with you in the unity
of the Holy Spirit,
one God, for ever and ever. **Amen.**

FIRST READING

Acts 2:14, 22-33

Then Peter stood up with the Eleven,
raised his voice, and proclaimed:
"You who are Jews, indeed all of you
staying in Jerusalem.
Let this be known to you, and listen to my
words.
You who are Israelites, hear these words.
Jesus the Nazorean was a man
commended to you by God
with mighty deeds, wonders, and signs,
which God worked through him in your
midst, as you yourselves know.
This man, delivered up by the set plan and
foreknowledge of God,
you killed, using lawless men to crucify
him.
But God raised him up, releasing him from
the throes of death,
because it was impossible for him to be
held by it.
For David says of him:
I saw the Lord ever before me,
with him at my right hand I shall not
be disturbed.
Therefore my heart has been glad and
my tongue has exulted;
my flesh, too, will dwell in hope,
because you will not abandon my soul to
the netherworld,
nor will you suffer your holy one to
see corruption.
You have made known to me the paths
of life;
you will fill me with joy in your
presence.

"My brothers, one can confidently say to you
about the patriarch David that he died
and was buried,
and his tomb is in our midst to this day.

But since he was a prophet and knew that
God had sworn an oath to him
that he would set one of his
descendants upon his throne,
he foresaw and spoke of the
resurrection of the Christ,
that neither was he abandoned to the
netherworld
nor did his flesh see corruption.
God raised this Jesus;
of this we are all witnesses.
Exalted at the right hand of God,
he received the promise of the Holy
Spirit from the Father
and poured him forth, as you see and
hear."

RESPONSORIAL PSALM
Ps 16:1-2, 5, 7-8, 9-10, 11

℟. (11a) Lord, you will show us the path of life. or: ℟. Alleluia.

Keep me, O God, for in you I take refuge;
I say to the LORD, "My Lord are you."
O LORD, my allotted portion and my cup,
you it is who hold fast my lot.

℟. Lord, you will show us the path of life.
or:
℟. Alleluia.

I bless the LORD who counsels me;
even in the night my heart exhorts me.
I set the LORD ever before me;
with him at my right hand I shall not be
disturbed.

℟. Lord, you will show us the path of life.
or:
℟. Alleluia.

Therefore my heart is glad and my soul
rejoices,
my body, too, abides in confidence;
because you will not abandon my soul to
the netherworld,
nor will you suffer your faithful one to
undergo corruption.

℟. Lord, you will show us the path of life.
or:
℟. Alleluia.

You will show me the path to life,
abounding joy in your presence,
the delights at your right hand forever.

℟. Lord, you will show us the path of life.
or:
℟. Alleluia.

SECOND READING
1 Pet 1:17-21

See Appendix A, p. 294.

CATECHESIS

About Liturgy

Rehearsing Emmaus: Today we hear the beloved story of the disciples on the road to Emmaus. This is a paschal mystery story of death to life, despair to joy, and inward focus to mission. We rehearse this story every time we celebrate the Eucharist.

Openness to the stranger: The change in the lives of the two disciples begins once they make space in their conversation for the stranger they meet along the road. There are strangers among us every Sunday whenever we gather for Mass. How do you make space in your life for them?

Word and sacrament: The disciples' recognition of the risen Christ in the breaking of the bread is intimately tied to their sharing of the Scriptures. Our breaking open of the Word through its proclamation, the homily, and response in intercession is the foundation for recognizing Christ in the breaking of the bread.

Seeing Christ in the absence: The moment of recognition takes place not while Jesus is visibly present but after he is no longer seen in the way the disciples expect. If we focus only on the presence of Christ in the consecrated bread and wine, we will miss Christ present right before us in the people of God gathered at the altar with us.

Return to the place of death with a message of hope: The disciples do not keep their newfound hope to themselves but go back to Jerusalem, where their despair began, and share the good news with others. The joy we find in the Eucharist is meant to be shared out in the world with those who need that joy the most.

About Initiation

New perception: The period of postbaptismal catechesis, or mystagogy, is when the neophytes are "introduced into a fuller and more effective understanding of mysteries through the Gospel . . . and above all through their experience of the sacraments" (RCIA 245). From this experience, they "derive a new perception of the faith, of the Church, and of the world" (245).

Just at the disciples on the road saw everything completely differently once they recognized Christ in the breaking of the bread, so, too, will the neophytes. For the disciples, their eyes were opened quite suddenly; for our neophytes, that new perception may come upon them more gradually.

This season is when your main goal with the neophytes is to help them participate fully in their encounter with Christ in the eucharistic celebration, then to break open that encounter with them. Ask them what they saw, heard, and felt in the breaking of the bread.

About Liturgical Music

Fraction of the Bread: The part of the Mass that follows the sign of peace is the Fraction Rite during which the *Agnus Dei*, or Lamb of God, is sung. This is one of the moments when the singing must coincide with the ritual action taking place. The General Instruction of the Roman Missal says, "This invocation accompanies the fraction of the bread and, for this reason, may be repeated as many times as necessary until the rite has been completed" (83).

To make the music and ritual action work together, begin the first invocation of the Lamb of God at the same moment that the presider breaks the first host. (You'll need to begin the introduction sooner.) Then keep repeating the litany as many times as needed until the presider is ready to say, "Behold, the Lamb of God." Remember that the text for these invocations is always "Lamb of God"; no other titles, such as "Jesus, Bread of Life," may be used.

SPIRITUALITY

GOSPEL ACCLAMATION
John 10:14

℟. Alleluia, alleluia.
I am the good shepherd, says the Lord;
I know my sheep, and mine know me.
℟. Alleluia, alleluia.

Gospel John 10:1-10; L49A

Jesus said:
"Amen, amen, I say to you,
whoever does not enter a sheepfold through the gate
but climbs over elsewhere is a thief and a robber.
But whoever enters through the gate is the shepherd of the sheep.
The gatekeeper opens it for him, and the sheep hear his voice,
as the shepherd calls his own sheep by name and leads them out.
When he has driven out all his own,
he walks ahead of them, and the sheep follow him,
because they recognize his voice.
But they will not follow a stranger;
they will run away from him,
because they do not recognize the voice of strangers."
Although Jesus used this figure of speech,
the Pharisees did not realize what he was trying to tell them.

So Jesus said again, "Amen, amen, I say to you,
I am the gate for the sheep.
All who came before me are thieves and robbers,
but the sheep did not listen to them.
I am the gate.
Whoever enters through me will be saved,
and will come in and go out and find pasture.
A thief comes only to steal and slaughter and destroy;
I came so that they might have life and have it more abundantly."

Reflecting on the Gospel

We are now in the Fourth Sunday of Easter and this week we do not have a resurrection appearance story. The church gives us instead this parable or, in the words of the gospel, a "figure of speech" from Jesus himself. Though the term is not used in these ten verses, this is the beginning of the "Good Shepherd" parabolic discourse. This section might be more properly called the "Gate" discourse, wherein Jesus says he is the gate through which the sheep enter and are saved. The distinction of Jesus as gate is significant and should not immediately be conflated with Jesus as Good Shepherd, which is stated explicitly later in this chapter. Here we see Jesus as the "Gate" with an accompanying image of the gatekeeper.

The images in this figure of speech are rooted in antiquity, or at least a different culture. A sheepfold, for example, is typically a small or low stone fence/wall that is open to the sky. The proper way to enter is via the gate. Thus, Jesus says the one who climbs over the stone wall is "a thief and a robber." The means to entry is the gate. Further, the sheep will hear the voice of the gatekeeper and follow him, but they do not recognize and will not follow the voice of strangers. Apparently, this imagery went over the heads of Jesus' audience so he said explicitly, "I am the gate."

The Fourth Gospel never uses the term "parable"; that is a term used in the Synoptic Gospels. As we saw above, the evangelist says that Jesus taught in a "figure of speech." Rather than parables, in the Fourth Gospel we might say Jesus speaks in "parabolic discourse." The difference might seem to be splitting hairs, but what it means is that rather than saying "the kingdom of heaven is like . . ." Jesus says, "I am . . ." So, for example, rather than saying, "[T]he kingdom of heaven is like a sheepfold and the gate through which the sheep enter and leave," Jesus says, "I am the gate." Similarly, Jesus will say in the Gospel of John, "I am the Good Shepherd," "I am the Vine," "I am the Way, the Truth, and the Life," or "I am the Resurrection." All of these are figures of speech and parabolic discourses.

We recall in this Easter season that Jesus is the gate through which we are saved. Jesus is the means by which we enter the sheepfold, paradise, heaven itself.

Living the Paschal Mystery

In the "figure of speech" in today's gospel, we are sheep whereas Jesus is the gate for the sheepfold. The imagery is simple and ancient. Here there is not "heaven" but instead a place of safety and security from the world with its dangers and threats. Even this place of safety is not entirely secure, as there are some thieves and robbers who would climb the fence, not entering through the gate. Our only "protection" from such dangers is that we would not follow their voice. This figure of speech should give us pause. Are we led astray by other voices in the culture—voices that might appeal to our preconceived ideologies or that would soothe us with simplistic and self-serving messages? Let us die to the other voices calling us away from gospel values. Let us know the gate through which we enter the sheepfold and not be called away by other voices.

Focusing the Gospel

Key words and phrases: "I came so that they might have life and have it more abundantly."

To the point: In speaking to the Pharisees, Jesus uses a "figure of speech" to help them understand his identity. He tells them, "I am the gate for the sheep." Rather than restricting the sheep, however, this gate protects them and also leads them to good pasture and abundant life. In the gospels, Jesus' arguments with the Pharisees usually have to do with their interpretation of the law. As righteous, religious leaders, the Pharisees are concerned with fidelity to the law, sometimes at the expense of mercy and charity to their fellow Jews. At one point Jesus accuses them, saying, "[The scribes and Pharisees] tie up heavy burdens hard to carry and lay them on people's shoulders, but they will not lift a finger to move them" (Matt 23:4; NABRE). Jesus' way is one of abundance and freedom in the love of God and neighbor.

Connecting the Gospel

to the second reading: In the second reading we also find the imagery of shepherds and sheep. St. Peter writes, "For you had gone astray like sheep, / but you have now returned to the shepherd and guardian of your souls." Peter highlights the protection offered by this shepherd, as well as his importance as a guide to keep the members of the church from going astray. Jesus' description of the shepherd who cares for the sheep is even more intimate. He says that this shepherd "calls his own sheep by name." Not only does the shepherd know the sheep as individuals, but the sheep also know their shepherd and can distinguish him from others, "because they recognize his voice."

to experience: Our covenant relationship with God is built both on God's call to us and on our response to God. To be sheep of God's pasture, we must attune our ears to the sound of his voice calling us to abundant life.

Connecting the Responsorial Psalm

to the readings: The abundant life Jesus offers to his disciples is illustrated beautifully in Psalm 23. With God as our Shepherd there is nothing we lack. Like a gracious host, the Lord sets a table before us and anoints our head with oil. It is no surprise the imagery of sheep and shepherds appears so frequently in the Bible. Shepherds keeping watch over their flock would have been a common sight in the land of Israel. Many of the patriarchs of ancient Israel were sheepherders, including Abraham, Isaac, and Jacob, not to mention King David (to whom this psalm is ascribed) and Moses, who meets God in the burning bush while "tending the flock of his father-in-law Jethro" (Exod 3:1; NABRE).

to psalmist preparation: Only a shepherd could fully understand the vulnerability of domesticated sheep when there is no one to guide them, or the relationship that can be built up between a shepherd and the flock he tenderly cares for. How do you experience God as a Shepherd?

PROMPTS FOR FAITH-SHARING

The psalmist sings, "The Lord is my shepherd . . . Beside restful waters he leads me; / he refreshes my soul." In what areas of your life are you in need of refreshment?

The second reading from the first letter of St. Peter reminds us that Jesus, "when he was insulted, he returned no insult; / when he suffered, he did not threaten." How do you follow Jesus' path of nonviolence?

In the gospel acclamation we hear the title for Jesus as "the good shepherd" who knows and is known by his sheep. How do you experience Jesus' shepherding care in your life?

Jesus tells the Pharisees that his sheep will not follow a stranger, "because they do not recognize the voice of strangers." What spiritual practices help you attune your ears to the voice of the Good Shepherd?

Model Rite for the Blessing and Sprinkling of Water

Presider: In today's gospel reading Jesus proclaims that he is the gate of the sheepfold through which we are saved. May this water remind us of the waters of baptism and our own birth into the sheepfold of the church . . . *[pause]*

[continue with The Roman Missal, *Appendix II]*

Homily Points

• In today's first reading, Peter invites those who have been listening to his testimony of Christ's death and resurrection to "[r]epent and be baptized . . . in the name of Jesus Christ for the forgiveness of your sins; / and you will receive the gift of the Holy Spirit."

• Throughout the fifty days of the Easter season, the whole church celebrates and prays with the newly baptized. For those of us who were baptized many years ago, this time calls us to revisit and remember the day of our own baptism and the many spiritual gifts we received that continue to sustain us. Looking at this sacrament from the lens of Psalm 23, we could say that in baptism Jesus refreshes our soul with living water, anoints our heads with the oil of salvation, and claims us as his own "to dwell in the house of the Lord for years to come."

• The technical term the church uses for the newly baptized is "neophyte," which means "new initiate." It comes from the Greek word *neophutos,* which can be translated literally as "newly planted." As every gardener knows, seeds placed within the ground require care and consideration. They will not grow without the nourishment of good soil, water, and sunlight. They also must be protected as they break open to put down deep roots before growing above the soil. The same is true in the life of faith. Today's gospel ends with Jesus' proclamation that he has "come so that [we] might have life and have it more abundantly." As we journey with the neophytes in our parish community, let us also be aware of the seed of faith within each of us and recommit ourselves to nourishing and protecting it so that it might bear abundant fruit.

Model Universal Prayer (Prayer of the Faithful)

Presider: With confidence in the Good Shepherd who sustains and guides us, let us bring our prayers to the Lord.

Response: Lord, hear our prayer.

For bishops and priests, may they follow in the footsteps of the Good Shepherd by serving their flocks with self-sacrificial love . . .

For places in the world lacking access to clean water, may efforts be prospered to find sources of drinking water and make them accessible to all . . .

For all who were recently baptized, may the abundance of the Holy Spirit continue to be poured out into their hearts . . .

For all gathered here, may our ears be attuned to the voice of the Good Shepherd, calling us to the fullness of life . . .

Presider: God of mercy and love, you sent your son, Jesus, to show us the pathway of abundant life. Hear our prayers that as the flock of the Good Shepherd, we might follow him with devotion all the days of our lives. We ask this through Christ our Lord. **Amen.**

COLLECT

Let us pray.

Pause for silent prayer

Almighty ever-living God,
lead us to a share in the joys of heaven,
so that the humble flock may reach
where the brave Shepherd has gone before.
Who lives and reigns with you in the unity
of the Holy Spirit,
one God, for ever and ever. **Amen.**

FIRST READING

Acts 2:14a, 36-41

Then Peter stood up with the Eleven,
raised his voice, and proclaimed:
"Let the whole house of Israel know for certain
that God has made both Lord and Christ,
this Jesus whom you crucified."

Now when they heard this, they were cut to the heart,
and they asked Peter and the other apostles,
"What are we to do, my brothers?"
Peter said to them,
"Repent and be baptized, every one of you,
in the name of Jesus Christ for the forgiveness of your sins;
and you will receive the gift of the Holy Spirit.
For the promise is made to you and to your children
and to all those far off,
whomever the Lord our God will call."
He testified with many other arguments,
and was exhorting them,
"Save yourselves from this corrupt generation."
Those who accepted his message were baptized,
and about three thousand persons were added that day.

RESPONSORIAL PSALM

Ps 23:1-3a, 3b-4, 5, 6

℟. (1) The Lord is my shepherd; there is nothing I shall want.
or: ℟. Alleluia.

The LORD is my shepherd; I shall not want.
In verdant pastures he gives me repose;
beside restful waters he leads me;
he refreshes my soul.

℟. The Lord is my shepherd; there is nothing I shall want.
or: ℟. Alleluia.

He guides me in right paths
for his name's sake.
Even though I walk in the dark valley
I fear no evil; for you are at my side
with your rod and your staff
that give me courage.

℟. The Lord is my shepherd; there is nothing I shall want.
or: ℟. Alleluia.

You spread the table before me
in the sight of my foes;
you anoint my head with oil;
my cup overflows.

℟. The Lord is my shepherd; there is nothing I shall want.
or: ℟. Alleluia.

Only goodness and kindness follow me
all the days of my life;
and I shall dwell in the house of the LORD
for years to come.

℟. The Lord is my shepherd; there is nothing I shall want.
or: ℟. Alleluia.

SECOND READING
1 Pet 2:20b-25

Beloved:
If you are patient when you suffer for doing what is good,
this is a grace before God.
For to this you have been called,
because Christ also suffered for you,
leaving you an example that you should follow in his footsteps.
He committed no sin, and no deceit was found in his mouth.

When he was insulted, he returned no insult;
when he suffered, he did not threaten;
instead, he handed himself over to the one who judges justly.
He himself bore our sins in his body upon the cross,
so that, free from sin, we might live for righteousness.
By his wounds you have been healed.
For you had gone astray like sheep,
but you have now returned to the shepherd and guardian of your souls.

About Liturgy

Christ the sheepgate: In today's gospel, Christ calls himself the gate through whom his sheep "come in and go out and find pasture." One important ritual symbol that is often overlooked is the door, or threshold, of the church. The church's doors symbolize the place where one enters into Christ's flock and from where one is sent on mission.

The threshold plays a role in several of our sacraments and rituals. It is where parents are welcomed with their infant for baptism and where seekers first enter into the order of catechumens as they cross the threshold into the household of God. Brides and grooms are met joyfully together at the church doors. At the end of life, Christians are welcomed there by the community for their final passover into eternal life. When a new church is dedicated, the local bishop unseals the doors for the people of that community. In Jubilee years, the doors of the major churches around the world serve as pilgrimage points where mercy is found. At significant moments, doors are locked, as at conclaves, and flung open as at the Year of Mercy.

What do the doors of your parish look like? Do they invite seekers to come in and disciples to go out in mission? Are they locked when they should be opened? Are they hard to find when the path to them should be made straight and plain?

About Initiation

The fundamental vocation: Baptism gives us our fundamental vocation of being apostles of Christ in whom we become priests, prophets, and kings: "From the fact of their union with Christ the head flows the laymen's right and duty to be apostles . . . If they are consecrated a kingly priesthood and a holy nation, it is in order that they may in all their actions offer spiritual sacrifices and bear witness to Christ all the world over" (Decree on the Apostolate of the Laity [AA] 3).

Sometimes we undervalue this fundamental vocation in relation to ordained ministry. How many times have you heard a layperson say he or she is "just helping Father," or, "A priest's blessing is better than mine. He should give the meal blessing"? Ordained ministry is certainly important and necessary for the life of the church, and there are indeed assigned roles and prayers only the ordained can do. But ordination does not make one a better or holier member of Christ's royal priesthood who is more capable of giving praise to God. The ministerial priesthood flows from the essential, fundamental vocation of the baptized and is "at the service of the common priesthood" (*Catechism of the Catholic Church* 1547). The apostolate of the laity "is so necessary within the Church communities that without it the apostolate of the pastors is often unable to achieve its full effectiveness" (AA 10).

Remind your neophytes and all the baptized of their inherent dignity as priests and of their mission to be apostles and prophets of Christ. All of us, lay and ordained, together are co-workers in the vineyard and servants of the Lord.

About Liturgical Music

Suggestions: We have many wonderful songs about Jesus as the Good Shepherd and various settings of Psalms 23 and 100. One aspect from today's readings that we might miss is the juxtaposition of titles for Jesus as shepherd who tends his flock, sheepgate that keeps it safe, *and* lamb slain for the life of the world. *Psallite* provides us a beautiful blending of these three images in "You Are the Shepherd" (Liturgical Press). The antiphon text is "You are the shepherd and you are the gate; you are the Lamb who was slain; you lay down your life so that we may have life, Jesus, the Lamb who was slain."

SPIRITUALITY

GOSPEL ACCLAMATION
John 14:6

℟. Alleluia, alleluia.
I am the way, the truth and the life, says the Lord;
no one comes to the Father, except through
me.
℟. Alleluia, alleluia.

Gospel John 14:1-12; L52A

Jesus said to his disciples:
"Do not let your hearts be troubled.
You have faith in God; have faith also in me.
In my Father's house there are many dwelling places.
If there were not,
would I have told you that I am going to prepare a place for you?
And if I go and prepare a place for you,
I will come back again and take you to myself,
so that where I am you also may be.
Where I am going you know the way."
Thomas said to him,
"Master, we do not know where you are going;
how can we know the way?"
Jesus said to him, "I am the way and the truth and the life.
No one comes to the Father except through me.
If you know me, then you will also know my Father.
From now on you do know him and have seen him."
Philip said to him,
"Master, show us the Father, and that will be enough for us."
Jesus said to him, "Have I been with you for so long a time
and you still do not know me, Philip?
Whoever has seen me has seen the Father.
How can you say, 'Show us the Father'?
Do you not believe that I am in the Father and the Father is in me?

Continued in Appendix A, p. 294.

Reflecting on the Gospel

As we continue to celebrate the Easter season, we hear another "parabolic discourse" from the Gospel of John. As we saw last week, John does not use the term "parable" in his gospel. Instead, he uses a number of "I am . . ." statements and we have another today: "I am the way and the truth and the life." In essence, this is similar to last week's gospel where Jesus said, "I am the gate" through which the sheep enter the sheepfold. Today Jesus says he is the way to the Father.

Embedded in this parabolic discourse are Jesus' additional sayings about his relation to the Father. We may forgive the disciples for being slightly confused. This passage alone inspired countless generations of theologians in their trinitarian work. Several times Jesus says he is in the Father and the Father is in him. He also says whoever has seen him (Jesus) has seen the Father and that he (Jesus) is going to the Father. And there is no mention of the Spirit!

Such metaphorical or poetic language is often the bane of modern mathematicians and engineers. The relationship between Jesus and the Father cannot be reduced to a mathematical formula; it is not an engineering problem. In the first verse of John's gospel he says, "In the beginning was the word, and the word was with God and the word was God." The Greek term for "with" is not the static *syn,* but the more dynamic *pros*, meaning something akin to "the word was in a dynamic relationship with God." This dynamic relationship is by definition not static. It is not reducible to quantifiable precision, as we might expect in a chemistry lab. Ultimately, we are dealing with imagery, metaphor, and analogy for the divine, which cannot be boxed up, packaged, and distributed in discrete packets of knowledge.

The gospel reading invites us to enter into this dynamic relationship between the Father and the Son, God and the Word. Once engaged, this dynamic relationship never ends, but only continues, often deepens, and typically challenges. By reading this parabolic discourse, may we be open to all that God has in store for us, by embracing the divine and casting aside any preconceived limitations on God and his goodness.

Living the Paschal Mystery

The opening words of today's gospel are addressed to the disciples, and we can imagine they are addressed to us as well: "Do not let your hearts be troubled. / You have faith in God; have faith also in me." These words were written to a community that did not have a history of trinitarian theology. Monotheism was in some ways challenged by Jesus' identity with the Father. We recall that Jesus was crucified for, among other things, blasphemy. The early Christians believed in Jesus. They had faith in Jesus. They also believed God and had faith in God. Centuries later, and after many disagreements and councils, trinitarian theology developed to a point where a common creed was held. But in the early church that was still distant.

In our own lives, we might be patient with ourselves and others who have difficulty with grandiose trinitarian concepts and instead root our knowledge of Jesus in the Scriptures and personal experience, for that is akin to what the early Christians did. Ultimately, Christianity is about service in the name of Jesus rather than knowledge in the name of Jesus. Therefore, we have faith in Jesus, as we have faith in God. We strive to die to ourselves in our own limited understanding, so that we might live to serve in his name. Such is the paschal mystery.

Focusing the Gospel

Key words and phrases: "I am the way and the truth and the life."

To the point: Jesus responds to Thomas's protest, "Master, we do not know where you are going; / how can we know the way?" by pronouncing that he himself is the way. This discussion takes place at the Last Supper, after the washing of the feet and before Jesus and the disciples go to the garden to pray. Both this week and next we will hear gospels from Jesus' discourse at the Last Supper. Jesus' words are difficult for the disciples to understand. As the disciples look back at these words from the point of view of the resurrection and ascension of the Lord, they come into focus. The kingdom of God, it seems, is not so much a place as a relationship with the dynamic in-dwelling trinity of God. The question is not "where?" but "who?" and the answer is Jesus.

Connecting the Gospel

to the second reading: In the second reading from the first letter of St. Peter, the faithful are invited into the same kind of relationship that Jesus and the Father share in the gospel reading. Those in the early church were not to consider themselves merely as a group of people who gather together to worship, but as "living stones" that make up a "spiritual house" and a "holy priesthood." This is only possible through the one who is the source of light and life, the one who told his followers, "I am the way and the truth and the life."

to experience: In our own parishes and church communities, it can be difficult to remember that it is not the buildings that animate and draw us together, but the Holy Spirit of God working in and uniting each one of us. Only by clinging to Jesus and the abundant life he offers can we hope to be "living stones" in God's church.

Connecting the Responsorial Psalm

to the readings: Our responsorial psalm prays, "Lord, let your mercy be on us, as we place our trust in you." In the gospel the disciples are called to place all of their trust in Jesus as their way to God, their pillar of truth, and their entry into abundant and ever-lasting life. This was a difficult thing to ask of them, especially on the night before Jesus' crucifixion. The words he spoke of where he was going and his relationship to the Father still baffled and confused most of the disciples. And yet even after their desertion of him during his passion and death, Jesus spends the time between his resurrection and ascension searching out and restoring those who had faltered. In his love and mercy, Jesus—our way, truth, and life—proves himself eminently trustworthy.

to psalmist preparation: The psalmist sings, "Upright is the word of the Lord, / and all his works are trustworthy." What events and experiences in your life have led you to trust in the Lord?

PROMPTS FOR FAITH-SHARING

Today's psalm proclaims, "[O]f the kindness of the Lord the earth is full." Where do you see the kindness of the Lord at work in the world?

In the second reading, St. Peter writes that we are all to consider ourselves as "living stones" and a "holy priesthood." Within your particular vocation (ordained or lay), how do you exercise your priesthood?

Jesus tells his disciples, "Do not let your hearts be troubled." Instead they are called to have faith in God and in him. Where have troubles entered into your life and how might you seek to turn them over to the Lord?

Jesus' description of his Father's house with many dwelling places is a comforting image for many. How do you interpret these words?

Model Rite for the Blessing and Sprinkling of Water

Presider: In today's gospel Jesus proclaims himself "the way, the truth, and the life." May this water cleanse our hearts and minds, and draw us into even deeper union with Christ . . . *[pause]*

[continue with The Roman Missal, *Appendix II]*

Homily Points

• On the night before he will be crucified, Jesus tells his disciples, "Do not let your hearts be troubled." Instead, he urges them to have faith in him and faith in God. Jesus seems to want to prepare the disciples for what is to come and the physical separation that will occur between them. He says, "I am going to prepare a place for you . . . I will come back again and take you to myself, / so that where I am you also may be."

• In next Sunday's gospel, Jesus will continue his reassurances to the disciples, even telling them, "I will not leave you orphans." He speaks of a time of complete communion when "you will realize that I am in my Father / and you are in me and I in you." In today's gospel Jesus speaks of "the Father who dwells in me" and also of the "many dwelling places" within "my Father's house."

• Often we might hear this gospel read at funeral or memorial liturgies. It is comforting to think that there is a place prepared for us in eternity to live in communion with God the Father, Son, and Holy Spirit. And yet, while we await this perfect unity with God, we are still called to dwell in the one in which "we live and move and have our being" (Acts 17:28; NABRE). It is only by dwelling within the Trinity that we might hope to become the "living stones" that St. Peter speaks of in his epistle. We are called to be at home in our God while also becoming spaces of welcome and refuge for others.

Model Universal Prayer (Prayer of the Faithful)

Presider: Jesus tells the disciples, "Do not let your hearts be troubled. / You have faith in God; have faith also in me." With confidence we express our needs to the Lord.

Response: Lord, hear our prayer.

For all the baptized, may we embrace our anointing as priests, prophets, and kings and seek to serve others through the use of our gifts . . .

For leaders of nations, may their decisions be guided by care for the most vulnerable within their societies, especially the elderly and the orphaned . . .

For those whose hearts are troubled through grief, depression, or despair, may they know comfort and find peace . . .

For all gathered here, may our words and actions testify to Jesus, the way, the truth, and the life, and invite others to know and follow him . . .

Presider: God, our strength and our shelter, your kindness fills the earth and causes all creation to sing your praise. Hear our prayers that as priests, prophets, and kings, we might spread the light of Christ to all we meet. We ask this through Christ, our Lord. **Amen.**

COLLECT

Let us pray.

Pause for silent prayer

Almighty ever-living God,
constantly accomplish the Paschal Mystery within us,
that those you were pleased to make new in Holy Baptism
may, under your protective care, bear much fruit
and come to the joys of life eternal.
Through our Lord Jesus Christ, your Son,
who lives and reigns with you in the unity of the Holy Spirit,
one God, for ever and ever. **Amen.**

FIRST READING

Acts 6:1-7

As the number of disciples continued to grow,
the Hellenists complained against the Hebrews
because their widows
were being neglected in the daily distribution.
So the Twelve called together the community of the disciples and said,
"It is not right for us to neglect the word of God to serve at table.
Brothers, select from among you seven reputable men,
filled with the Spirit and wisdom,
whom we shall appoint to this task,
whereas we shall devote ourselves to prayer
and to the ministry of the word."
The proposal was acceptable to the whole community,
so they chose Stephen, a man filled with faith and the Holy Spirit,
also Philip, Prochorus, Nicanor, Timon, Parmenas,
and Nicholas of Antioch, a convert to Judaism.
They presented these men to the apostles
who prayed and laid hands on them.
The word of God continued to spread,
and the number of the disciples in Jerusalem increased greatly;
even a large group of priests were becoming obedient to the faith.

RESPONSORIAL PSALM

Ps 33:1-2, 4-5, 18-19

℟. (22) Lord, let your mercy be on us, as we place our trust in you.
or: ℟. Alleluia.

Exult, you just, in the LORD;
praise from the upright is fitting.
Give thanks to the LORD on the harp;
with the ten-stringed lyre chant his praises.

℟. Lord, let your mercy be on us, as we place our trust in you.
or: ℟. Alleluia.

Upright is the word of the LORD,
and all his works are trustworthy.
He loves justice and right;
of the kindness of the LORD the earth is full.

℟. Lord, let your mercy be on us, as we place our trust in you.
or: ℟. Alleluia.

See, the eyes of the LORD are upon those who fear him,
upon those who hope for his kindness,
to deliver them from death
and preserve them in spite of famine.

℟. Lord, let your mercy be on us, as we place our trust in you.
or: ℟. Alleluia.

SECOND READING
1 Pet 2:4-9

Beloved:
Come to him, a living stone, rejected by human beings
but chosen and precious in the sight of God,
and, like living stones,
let yourselves be built into a spiritual house
to be a holy priesthood to offer spiritual sacrifices
acceptable to God through Jesus Christ.
For it says in Scripture:
Behold, I am laying a stone in Zion,
a cornerstone, chosen and precious,
and whoever believes in it shall not be put to shame.
Therefore, its value is for you who have faith, but for those without faith:
The stone that the builders rejected
has become the cornerstone,
and
A stone that will make people stumble,
and a rock that will make them fall.
They stumble by disobeying the word, as is their destiny.

You are "a chosen race, a royal priesthood,
a holy nation, a people of his own,
so that you may announce the praises" of him
who called you out of darkness into his wonderful light.

About Liturgy

Mother's Day: In the United States, this Sunday is Mother's Day. In the Book of Blessings, the church provides three sample intercessions that may be adapted and added to the universal prayer and a prayer over the people to bless mothers at the end of Mass. These are all good places to start when preparing ways to recognize mothers in your community. Take care, however, that the principal focus on Christ and the Easter mysteries is not overshadowed. In addition, you will want to be aware that there will be members in your assembly for whom this day may be very painful: those who have strained relationships with their own mothers that have never healed; those who long to be mothers but cannot for whatever reason; women who gave up children for adoption; those who take on the role of motherhood but are not recognized by that title, such as single fathers, godmothers, foster parents, and guardians not related by blood.

About Initiation

The "ministry" of neophytes: Easter is often a good opportunity for parishes to build on the energy flowing from the community's renewal of baptismal promises. Especially in light of the first reading today, parishes might focus on reigniting the call to serve, with planned "ministry fairs" and other invitations to sign up for a parish committee, group, or liturgical ministry.

Baptism indeed is a call to service, especially out in the world to be apostles and ambassadors for Christ. However, take care that you don't inadvertently communicate to the neophytes that their baptism is now the reason they should sign up for a ministry. That distorts both our understanding of baptism and ministry!

Baptism sends us out from the church walls to announce to others that Jesus has saved us and wants to heal the wounds of people's suffering. Ministry is a call given by the community of Christians and a communal, prayerful discernment of how best people can exercise their baptismal priesthood for the good of the community and the world.

For neophytes, their "ministry" to the community *is to be neophytes!* That is, they are to be living, breathing signs of Christ's resurrection. This neophyte year is intended for these new Christians to deepen their understanding of what Christ has done for them and to live out that joy in their daily lives. Some may be called to ministry in the community, but just as with all the baptized, the response to that call requires maturity of faith and careful discernment. Let neophytes grow in their discipleship and savor this special year in their lives.

About Liturgical Music

Suggestions: We have so many facets to choose from to highlight the focus of today's liturgy—the church; discipleship; Jesus as the way, truth, and life; service; home in God's house; mothering care and giving life—as well as the seasonal focus of Easter and the shift toward Pentecost and the Holy Spirit.

One song in particular gives us an image of God who "mothered us in wholeness" and "loved us into birth." Bernadette Farrell's gorgeous "God, Beyond All Names" (OCP) has powerful text that offers us another way to reflect on who God is. This would work well as a song during the preparation of gifts. Such a song is also a more appropriately liturgical way to mark Mother's Day than a Marian song that shifts the focus away from God and onto the Blessed Mother.

Another piece that is appropriate during Communion is *Psallite*'s "I Am the Way: Follow Me" (Liturgical Press). The antiphon text is "I am the Way: follow me. I am the Truth: believe in me. I am the Life: dwell in me, alleluia."

SPIRITUALITY

GOSPEL ACCLAMATION
John 14:23

℟. Alleluia, alleluia.
Whoever loves me will keep my word, says the Lord,
and my Father will love him and we will come to him.
℟. Alleluia, alleluia.

Gospel

John 14:15-21; L55A

Jesus said to his disciples:
"If you love me, you will keep my commandments.
And I will ask the Father,
and he will give you another Advocate to be with you always,
the Spirit of truth, whom the world cannot accept,
because it neither sees nor knows him.
But you know him, because he remains with you,
and will be in you.
I will not leave you orphans; I will come to you.
In a little while the world will no longer see me,
but you will see me, because I live and you will live.
On that day you will realize that I am in my Father
and you are in me and I in you.
Whoever has my commandments and observes them
is the one who loves me.
And whoever loves me will be loved by my Father,
and I will love him and reveal myself to him."

Reflecting on the Gospel

"If you're good at the restaurant, we can have dessert," the parents said to their children. It was one in a string of many negotiations they made to encourage good behavior. As it happened, behavior was good and everybody was able to order dessert. The next day, the parents said, "If your room is clean, you can go out to play." After some delay, all of the children cleaned their rooms enough to earn some outside time. These kinds of conditional promises may be familiar to parents, children, teacher, students, and more. We might be a bit surprised to hear one open the gospel passage today. Jesus says to his disciples, "If you love me, you will keep my commandments." While this is not exactly the same as the two examples above, the conditional nature of the statement is similar.

Another way to restate what Jesus said might be this: "When you keep my commandments, I know you love me." What precisely are Jesus' commandments? In the Gospel of John the commandments are as simple and profound as this: "[L]ove one another" (John 13:34; cf. John 15:12). Most of the other ethical demands Jesus cites in the Gospel of John are rooted in the Ten Commandments. So we might say that when we love one another, we demonstrate that we love Jesus. Put another way, when we do not love one another, we demonstrate that we are not loving Jesus. But loving one another can be challenging. It's like the comedian said: "I love humanity, just not human beings." We are called to love not only in the abstract, but in particularity.

The gospel passage closes with these words: "And whoever loves me will be loved by my Father, / and I will love him and reveal myself to him." When we continue to develop into loving human beings, who express that love in service to others, we experience the love of God. Christ himself is revealed in the loving relationships we have with one another, and for that reason these relationships may be considered "holy." The entire gospel can be summed up by this Johannine emphasis on the love of God, the love of Christ, and the command for us to love one another.

Living the Paschal Mystery

As Christians we seek to follow the example of Christ, who poured himself out in love for his friends. Especially in the Gospel of John, we hear the word "love" often. For example, "God so loved the world that he sent his only son" (John 3:16), the simple and straightforward "God is love" (1 John 4:8), and of course the command to "love one another" (John 13:34; 15:12). The command seems so simple but it is very difficult to carry out. Here we have no list of duties or acts to perform, such as going to church or saying certain prayers. Instead, we have the profound command to love. Love knows no limits and there is not a point when we say "enough." Love sees the other as another self, so that the needs of the other are as important as our own. When modern communication has made the world a global village, the needs of our neighbors can seem overwhelming.

Where do we stop? Yet, we are called to move beyond ourselves as Jesus did and to place our lives in service of the other, in imitation of him. Then we may merit the name "disciple," when we are known by our love.

Focusing the Gospel

Key words and phrases: "On that day you will realize that I am in my Father / and you are in me and I in you."

To the point: Today's gospel continues on with Jesus' Last Supper discourse, which we read from last Sunday. When he is speaking to his disciples the night before he dies, Jesus' mysterious words tell of the profound intimacy the disciples will share with God the Father, Son, and Holy Spirit. While they will share in the life of the Father and Son, they will also be given an "Advocate to be with you always / the Spirit of truth" who will remain with them. As Jesus prepares his disciples for the next stage of their faith journey when he will not be physically present in the same way he was before, it almost seems as if greater connection is being offered. While they might not be able to follow him on the roads of Israel or share conversations over breakfast, Jesus promises that he will continue to reveal himself to all those who love him.

Connecting the Gospel

to the first reading: The promised Advocate is not a gift for the first disciples alone, but for every believer who comes to faith in Jesus. In the Acts of the Apostles, Philip travels to Samaria, and after proclaiming "the Christ to them" the crowds "accepted the word of God." Having heard the news, Peter and John travel to Samaria to lay hands on these newest disciples so they might also receive the Holy Spirit.

to experience: Christianity is not a set of rules or a philosophy of life; rather it is a relationship with a person, the person of Christ and through him the triune God. Whereas rules and regulations are static and rigid, a living relationship is dynamic, requiring communication, trust, and faith. Through the outpouring of the Holy Spirit dwelling in us, we are invited into an ever-deepening relationship with God.

Connecting the Responsorial Psalm

to the readings: Our psalm for today is one of joy and praise, an apt response to the happenings in the first reading where Philip proclaims Christ to the people of Samaria and performs signs of God's power by healing the paralyzed, crippled, and possessed. The psalmist calls for us to "[c]ome and see the works of God, / his tremendous deeds among the children of Adam." From the central event in the Old Testament (mentioned in today's psalm) when the Israelites passed through the sea "on foot" to escape slavery in Egypt, we could say that God's greatest works are all oriented to freedom: freedom from slavery, freedom from brokenness in mind, body, or spirit, and freedom from sin. Freedom is necessary for prayer. True praise and worship cannot be coerced or demanded.

to psalmist preparation: As you lead today's psalm calling for "all the earth to cry out to God with joy," consider where you might need God's freeing action in your life so as to praise him even more fully.

PROMPTS FOR FAITH-SHARING

In the first reading, Philip goes to Samaria and "proclaimed the Christ to them." In your life who has proclaimed Christ to you, either in word or deed?

In the first letter of St. Peter the apostle urges his fellow disciples, "Always be ready to give an explanation / to anyone who asks you for a reason for your hope." What would be the reason you would offer?

Jesus tells his disciples, "If you love me, you will keep my commandments." How would you summarize the commandments of the Lord? How do you strive to keep them in your daily life?

Jesus promises his disciples that after his ascension, the Holy Spirit will remain with them. How have you experienced the Spirit's presence in your life?

Model Rite for the Blessing and Sprinkling of Water

Presider: In today's gospel Jesus tells us, "Whoever has my commandments and observes them / is the one who loves me." May this water strengthen us in the life of discipleship as we seek to follow Jesus' path of love and mercy . . . *[pause]*

[continue with The Roman Missal, *Appendix II]*

Homily Points

• In today's gospel, Jesus tells us twice that it is our actions that matter in the life of discipleship. We might speak or write pious things, or foster good intentions, but in the end it is how we keep the commandments of Christ that will determine if we are in true relationship with Jesus or not.

• This is not to say that we should reduce Christianity to a list of rules and regulations to be followed or a series of actions that can be checked off one by one. Instead, Jesus' commandments can be summed up in one word: "love." The simplicity of this command, however, does not make it easy to follow. To truly love another human being requires much from us—just ask the parents of an infant or the spouse of a person with Alzheimer's. In these instances, love cannot just be expressed in words. Words will not change a baby's diaper or keep a person with dementia safe. In these instances, as in so many others, only our actions will do.

• Jesus tells us plainly, "If you love me, you will keep my commandments." The life of discipleship that Jesus is calling us to is one that will stretch and challenge us. To truly keep Jesus' command to love God with all our heart, mind, soul, and strength and to love our neighbor as ourselves (Mark 12:30-31) is to be constantly drawn beyond ourselves. Jesus gives these words to his disciples on the night before he will make his complete gift of self on the cross. In the Eucharist, Jesus continues to give us his body and blood as nourishment. In the life of Christ, we see love poured out in action and we are called to do the same.

Model Universal Prayer (Prayer of the Faithful)

Presider: Let us bring our prayers before the Lord through the power of the Holy Spirit, our Advocate.

Response: Lord, hear our prayer.

For God's holy church, may the Holy Spirit purify, strengthen, and sustain it to teach and keep the commandments of the Lord . . .

For all the people who dwell on the earth, may God's Spirit animate us to be good stewards of the environment and to care for creation . . .

For all preparing for the sacrament of confirmation at Pentecost, may they be healed, nourished, and empowered by the Holy Spirit active in their lives . . .

For all gathered here, may we be always ready to proclaim the Christ in word and deed to those we meet . . .

Presider: God, our hope and our stronghold, in your love you have given us an Advocate, the Holy Spirit, who remains with us always. Hear our prayers that in your Spirit we might keep your commandments and devote ourselves to your praise. We ask this through Christ our Lord. **Amen.**

COLLECT

Let us pray.

Pause for silent prayer

Grant, almighty God,
that we may celebrate with heartfelt
devotion these days of joy,
which we keep in honor of the risen Lord,
and that what we relive in remembrance
we may always hold to in what we do.
Through our Lord Jesus Christ, your Son,
who lives and reigns with you in the unity
of the Holy Spirit,
one God, for ever and ever. **Amen.**

FIRST READING

Acts 8:5-8, 14-17

Philip went down to the city of Samaria
and proclaimed the Christ to them.
With one accord, the crowds paid attention
to what was said by Philip
when they heard it and saw the signs he
was doing.
For unclean spirits, crying out in a loud
voice,
came out of many possessed people,
and many paralyzed or crippled people
were cured.
There was great joy in that city.

Now when the apostles in Jerusalem
heard that Samaria had accepted the
word of God,
they sent them Peter and John,
who went down and prayed for them,
that they might receive the Holy Spirit,
for it had not yet fallen upon any of
them;
they had only been baptized in the
name of the Lord Jesus.
Then they laid hands on them
and they received the Holy Spirit.

RESPONSORIAL PSALM

Ps 66:1-3, 4-5, 6-7, 16, 20

℟. (1) Let all the earth cry out to God with joy.
or:
℟. Alleluia.

Shout joyfully to God, all the earth,
sing praise to the glory of his name;
proclaim his glorious praise.
Say to God, "How tremendous are your
deeds!"

℟. Let all the earth cry out to God with joy.
or:
℟. Alleluia.

"Let all on earth worship and sing praise
to you,
sing praise to your name!"
Come and see the works of God,
his tremendous deeds among the
children of Adam.

℟. Let all the earth cry out to God with joy.
or:
℟. Alleluia.

He has changed the sea into dry land;
through the river they passed on foot.
Therefore let us rejoice in him.
He rules by his might forever.

℟. Let all the earth cry out to God with joy.
or:
℟. Alleluia.

Hear now, all you who fear God, while I
declare
what he has done for me.
Blessed be God who refused me not
my prayer or his kindness!

℟. Let all the earth cry out to God with joy.
or:
℟. Alleluia.

SECOND READING
1 Pet 3:15-18

Beloved:
Sanctify Christ as Lord in your hearts.
Always be ready to give an explanation
to anyone who asks you for a reason for
your hope,
but do it with gentleness and reverence,
keeping your conscience clear,
so that, when you are maligned,
those who defame your good conduct
in Christ
may themselves be put to shame.
For it is better to suffer for doing good,
if that be the will of God, than for
doing evil.
For Christ also suffered for sins once,
the righteous for the sake of the
unrighteous,
that he might lead you to God.
Put to death in the flesh,
he was brought to life in the Spirit.

About Liturgy

First Communion: Easter season is also First Communion season in many parishes. Here are some best practices to keep in mind:

One community, one family in Christ: Underlying conflicts between parish and school sacramental preparation programs can intensify as First Communion days approach. Work now and throughout the year to improve the sense that your parish is one community that celebrates together even if formation happens separately. Schedule liturgies together during the year for the parish and school communities, and gather families together for meals and other social events.

Sunday is for sacraments: The Lord's Day is the most appropriate day for sacraments, especially the Eucharist. Encourage preparation program leaders and families to celebrate First Communion during the parish Sunday Masses.

Share the blessing: You don't have to celebrate everyone's First Communion in one Mass. If you have many candidates, spread them out over several weeks and over different Mass times. If having a group photo with all the candidates in their Communion finery is important, schedule a celebration at the end of the Easter season when all the candidates can get dressed up, have a party, and get their photo taken. This would be a great opportunity for a bit of mystagogy as well!

About Initiation

Give a reason for your hope: Thankfully, many parishes and dioceses have been focusing on evangelization as the responsibility of all the baptized. However, the structure and content of some of these efforts seem to equate evangelization with learning more about Catholicism. But evangelization is not head-knowledge about faith; it is heart-knowledge of Christ and what Christ has done for us.

Blessed Paul VI, in his apostolic exhortation On Evangelization in the Modern World, describes two steps of evangelization. First, there is a "wordless witness" that disciples make through their actions. Then comes the second step of evangelization, which Paul VI calls "explicit witness." This is beautifully summarized by today's second reading: "Always be ready to give an explanation to anyone who asks you for a reason for your hope" (1 Pet 3:15). For seekers who have never known Christ, the answer they're looking for is not an academic explanation of faith but the *reason* for our faith, which is God's love for us in Christ.

Pope Francis said in his own apostolic exhortation on evangelization: "[A]nyone who has truly experienced God's saving love does not need much time or lengthy training to go out and proclaim that love. Every Christian is a missionary to the extent that he or she has encountered the love of God in Christ Jesus . . . The Samaritan woman became a missionary immediately after speaking with Jesus and many Samaritans come to believe in him 'because of the woman's testimony' (Jn 4:39) . . . So what are we waiting for?" (Joy of the Gospel 120).

About Liturgical Music

Singing by heart: The communion procession calls for music that can be sung without need for printed or projected aids. Litanies and repeated refrains work well. One such piece that uses today's gospel text is *Psallite*'s "Live on in My Love" (Liturgical Press). Short verses are led by choir or cantor using the gospel text, and the assembly responds with a meditative short refrain, "Live on my love."

Other good options for this day are several settings of "Ubi Caritas," one by Laurence Rosania, another by Bob Hurd (both OCP), and the ostinato setting from the Taizé community (GIA).

SPIRITUALITY

GOSPEL ACCLAMATION
Matt 28:19a, 20b

℟. Alleluia, alleluia.
Go and teach all nations, says the Lord;
I am with you always, until the end of the world.
℟. Alleluia, alleluia.

Gospel

Matt 28:16-20; L58A

The eleven disciples went to Galilee,
to the mountain to which Jesus had ordered them.
When they saw him, they worshiped,
but they doubted.
Then Jesus approached and said to them,
"All power in heaven and on earth
has been given to me.
Go, therefore, and make disciples of all nations,
baptizing them in the name of the Father,
and of the Son, and of the Holy Spirit,
teaching them to observe all that I have commanded you.
And behold, I am with you always, until the end of the age."

Reflecting on the Gospel

The ascension of the Lord before his disciples is depicted graphically in the Acts of the Apostles, when Jesus is said to ascend physically into the sky, being taken away from their sight by a cloud (Acts 1:9). But our gospel reading today comes not from Acts of course, since it is not a gospel, nor from Luke, the author of Acts, but from the conclusion of the Gospel of Matthew. In this story, the last four verses of the gospel, there is no ascension! Instead, the eleven disciples (a sober reminder of Judas's absence) meet at the rendezvous point that had been relayed to them by the women in Jerusalem. The eleven, according to the Gospel of Matthew, now see the risen Lord for the first time; and the evangelist is not clear as to how long after Easter this episode in Galilee took place. The story is sometimes called the "Commissioning of the Disciples," or "The Great Commission," for Jesus commissions the disciples to spread the good news. But it is not called "The Ascension."

So, on this feast of the Ascension, we hear about the risen Lord commissioning his disciples to go out to all nations, making disciples, teaching, and baptizing them. Prior to the death and resurrection of Jesus, discipleship (again, according to the Gospel of Matthew) was limited to the twelve. Now, after the resurrection, all nations, all peoples are invited into discipleship. The Gentile mission prefigured by the magi visiting the child Jesus now comes to fruition. Now that Jesus has been raised from the dead, there is no limitation on who may be a disciple.

In Acts, the ascension serves as the final leave-taking of Jesus before his assembled disciples. In Matthew, the commissioning of the disciples serves the same function. As the gospel concludes, there is no further appearance of the risen Lord. Matthew has not written his own version of the Acts of the Apostles. Thus, this appearance is the (first and) final one. Even though there is no physically graphic ascension into the clouds, this is the ultimate, in the sense of last, appearance of the risen Lord to his disciples. And despite this last appearance, Jesus promises that he is with them. Earlier in the gospel Jesus spoke about how judgment will be based on how we treat the one who hungers or the one who thirsts, for in each encounter we see Jesus. When we serve the poor, we serve Jesus. When we neglect the poor, we neglect Jesus. Jesus is present among us always in the poor and lowly of the world. That is his promise.

Living the Paschal Mystery

The ascension is depicted so graphically in Acts that many of us read Matthew's story with Acts in the background. But the story of the ascension is not so much about Jesus magically rising into the air and being taken away by clouds, as it is about the last time he was seen by his disciples. Theologically, the important aspect is what he says, not how he leaves. In the Gospel of Matthew, he commissions the disciples to evangelize, to tell the good news, making disciples on their way by baptizing. Indeed, in the Gospel of Matthew this message is so significant that Matthew does not even narrate an ascension! For us, we are reminded that to live the paschal mystery is to die, rise, and go with Christ. We, like the disciples, are sent on mission—to live the gospel values that Jesus incarnated, to teach all nations, to make disciples. May our lives of service and sacrifice for others be such a witness that others are drawn to Christ. For then we may be assured that we are living the paschal mystery.

Focusing the Gospel

Key words and phrases: "And behold, I am with you always, until the end of the age."

To the point: In the first chapter of Matthew's gospel, an angel appears to Joseph in a dream to tell him the true identity of the child his betrothed is carrying, a savior who has been foretold by the prophets, "'Emmanuel,' which means 'God is with us'" (1:23; NABRE). Now in the final words of Matthew's gospel, Jesus again reaffirms that he is indeed, and forever will remain, "God with us." With his resurrection, the risen Lord is not bound by time and space; instead, since "[a]ll power in heaven and on earth has been given to [him]," he is able to be present to his disciples everywhere and in every age.

Connecting the Gospel

to the second reading: In Paul's letter to the Ephesians, he prays for "a Spirit of wisdom and revelation" to be given to the community. Paul, the great apostle, was not at the scene of the ascension or with the disciples on the mountain in Galilee when Jesus gave them their commission to "make disciples of all nations." But after his conversion to Christianity, this is what Paul dedicates his life to as he founds churches throughout the Mediterranean. For Paul and the disciples who join the church following the death, resurrection, and ascension of Jesus, the Spirit of wisdom and revelation is their way of coming to know their Lord who is now seated at God's "right hand in the heavens."

to experience: As disciples of Jesus, we are all in need of the Spirit of wisdom and revelation that St. Paul prays to come upon the Ephesians. How do you invite this Spirit into your own life so that you may come to know Jesus better?

Connecting the Responsorial Psalm

to the readings: Today's psalm is one of the most triumphant in the whole book of Psalms. It paints a picture we can clearly see in our minds as well as hear, with the sounds of trumpets blaring and the joyful shouts of the thronging crowds. Jesus' words to the disciples in Matthew's gospel are also triumphant. He tells them, "All power in heaven and on earth has been given to me." With the power he has been given, Jesus commissions the disciples to go out to all the nations and baptize "in the name of the Father, / and of the Son, and of the Holy Spirit." It is fitting that our psalm ends with the affirmation "[f]or king of all the earth is God . . . God reigns over all the nations."

to psalmist preparation: In the second verse of today's psalm, we are called to "[s]ing praise to God, sing praise; / sing praise to our king, sing praise." In your daily life, how do you offer praise to God the King?

PROMPTS FOR FAITH-SHARING

In the Acts of the Apostles, the disciples are shaken from their reverie by two men in white garments asking, "[W]hy are you standing there looking at the sky?" Where in your life do you feel God calling you from contemplation into action?

In his letter to the Ephesians, St. Paul prays that his readers will be given "a Spirit of wisdom and revelation / resulting in knowledge of [God]." Throughout your life how has your understanding and knowledge of God grown or changed?

In the gospel reading, despite all they have witnessed and experienced, the disciples "doubted." How do you deal with doubt in the life of faith?

How does your faith community carry on the great commission that Jesus gave the first apostles to "make disciples of all nations" through baptism and teaching?

Model Rite for the Blessing and Sprinkling of Water

Presider: Jesus commissions the apostles to go and "make disciples of all nations, / baptizing them in the name of the Father, / and of the Son, and of the Holy Spirit." May this water remind us of our own baptism and revitalize us to go forth and proclaim Christ to all we meet . . . *[pause]*

[continue with The Roman Missal, *Appendix II]*

Homily Points

• Jesus' words to the disciples in Matthew's gospel are ones of supreme triumph. He tells them, "All power in heaven and on earth has been given to me." The actual scene of the ascension from the Acts of the Apostles doesn't include these words. When Jesus is asked by the disciples, "Lord, are you at this time going to restore the kingdom to Israel?" Jesus replies, "It is not for you to know the times or seasons / that the Father has established by his own authority."

• It seems the disciples are in some way still longing for a show of power and might upon the earth that will grant them freedom from their Roman oppressors. But this is not God's plan. The Jesus who submitted to death on a cross has not risen from the dead in order to wage war.

• In Matthew's gospel, even though Jesus now has been given supreme authority over heaven and earth, his commission to the disciples shows that his mission remains the same. He invites them to "[g]o, therefore, and make disciples of all nations, / baptizing them . . . [and] teaching them to observe all that I have commanded you." From Jesus' preaching in the gospels, we know what his commandments center on—love of God and love of neighbor. It is impossible to teach love through violence or oppression. As disciples of Jesus, we believe in life that is stronger than death and love that is stronger than hatred. To evangelize the world, we must show the love of Jesus in word and deed to all we meet; only in this way can we "make disciples of all nations."

Model Universal Prayer (Prayer of the Faithful)

Presider: Before Jesus is taken up to heaven, he assures us, "I am with you always, until the end of the age." With faith in his word, let us bring our needs before the Lord.

Response: Lord, hear our prayer.

For the leaders of the church, with apostolic fervor may they carry out Jesus' commission to bring the gospel to the ends of the earth . . .

For those in elected office, may they be granted wisdom and discernment in making decisions for the common good . . .

For those who have been displaced from their homes due to war, violence, or natural disasters, may they find shelter and safety and welcome . . .

For all members of our parish community, may the eyes of our hearts be enlightened to Christ's presence among us in Word, sacrament, and one another . . .

Presider: God of salvation, your son, Jesus, ascends into heaven to sit at your right hand. Hear our prayers that all might come to know your merciful love and to live in the light of your presence. We ask this through Christ our Lord. **Amen.**

COLLECT

Let us pray.

Pause for silent prayer

Gladden us with holy joys, almighty God,
and make us rejoice with devout thanksgiving,
for the Ascension of Christ your Son
is our exaltation,
and, where the Head has gone before in glory,
the Body is called to follow in hope.
Through our Lord Jesus Christ, your Son,
who lives and reigns with you in the unity of the Holy Spirit,
one God, for ever and ever. **Amen.**

FIRST READING

Acts 1:1-11

In the first book, Theophilus,
I dealt with all that Jesus did and taught
until the day he was taken up,
after giving instructions through the Holy Spirit
to the apostles whom he had chosen.
He presented himself alive to them
by many proofs after he had suffered,
appearing to them during forty days
and speaking about the kingdom of God.
While meeting with them,
he enjoined them not to depart from Jerusalem,
but to wait for "the promise of the Father
about which you have heard me speak;
for John baptized with water,
but in a few days you will be baptized with the Holy Spirit."

When they had gathered together they asked him,
"Lord, are you at this time going to restore the kingdom to Israel?"
He answered them, "It is not for you to know the times or seasons
that the Father has established by his own authority.
But you will receive power when the Holy Spirit comes upon you,
and you will be my witnesses in Jerusalem,
throughout Judea and Samaria,
and to the ends of the earth."
When he had said this, as they were looking on,
he was lifted up, and a cloud took him from their sight.

While they were looking intently at the
sky as he was going,
suddenly two men dressed in white
garments stood beside them.
They said, "Men of Galilee,
why are you standing there looking at
the sky?
This Jesus who has been taken up from
you into heaven
will return in the same way as you have
seen him going into heaven."

RESPONSORIAL PSALM

Ps 47:2-3, 6-7, 8-9

℟. (6) God mounts his throne to shouts of joy: a blare of trumpets for the Lord.
or:
℟. Alleluia.

All you peoples, clap your hands,
shout to God with cries of gladness,
for the LORD, the Most High, the awesome,
is the great king over all the earth.

℟. God mounts his throne to shouts of joy: a blare of trumpets for the Lord.
or:
℟. Alleluia.

God mounts his throne amid shouts of joy;
the LORD, amid trumpet blasts.
Sing praise to God, sing praise;
sing praise to our king, sing praise.

℟. God mounts his throne to shouts of joy: a blare of trumpets for the Lord.
or:
℟. Alleluia.

For king of all the earth is God;
sing hymns of praise.
God reigns over the nations,
God sits upon his holy throne.

℟. God mounts his throne to shouts of joy: a blare of trumpets for the Lord.
or:
℟. Alleluia.

SECOND READING

Eph 1:17-23

See Appendix A, p. 294.

About Liturgy

Real absence: In each Lectionary year, we hear today's reading from the beginning of the Acts of the Apostles on ascension. In Cycle A, however, we might perceive echoes from the Third Sunday of Easter's gospel of the disciples on the road to Emmaus. In both, the risen Christ disappears from the disciples' sight and the witnesses return to Jerusalem. In both, this is where the true work of the church begins. Christ's presence is no longer confined to Jesus' body but is now embodied by an entire community, sent to be his presence in the world.

We are disciples in that long line of women and men whose ancestors in faith came from those followers of Christ on the road and in that upper room. In some way, at every Eucharist, we, too, are witnesses to the "absence" of Christ that reveals his ultimate and complete presence. In a sermon on the ascension, St. Leo the Great said it this way: "What was visible in our Savior has passed over into his mysteries" (*Catechism of the Catholic Church* 1115), that is, into the sacraments that we celebrate.

We have a choice every time we gather for the Eucharist. We can stay, looking up at the sky, looking for Christ. Or, having been nourished by Word and sacrament, we can go out, sent to announce the gospel of the Lord, and be his presence to those in need. That is when the real story of ascension begins.

About Initiation

The purpose of baptism: The end of Matthew's gospel, which we hear today, summarizes for us the very meaning of why we are baptized: "Go, therefore, and make disciples of all nations, baptizing them in the name of the Father, and of the Son, and of the Holy Spirit, teaching them to observe all that I have commanded you" (28:19-20).

The first command in this passage after "[g]o" is "make disciples." As initiation ministers, we must always remember that Jesus did not say to make Catholics but disciples. That nuance shapes how we understand the purpose of what we are doing in preparing people for baptism.

The purpose of baptism is neither to become a member of a community nor to get into heaven. It is to make disciples. Disciples learn discipline for the purpose of doing a mission. Therefore, the purpose of Christian initiation is "to bring us, the faithful of Christ, to his full stature and to enable us to carry out the mission of the entire people of God in the Church and in the world" (Christian Initiation: General Introduction, 2).

About Liturgical Music

Awaiting the Spirit: When Ascension is celebrated on the Thursday during the sixth week of Easter, it begins a novena of prayer from the day after Ascension to Pentecost. With most dioceses transferring Ascension to the Sunday before Pentecost, that sense of waiting for the Spirit is muted. But you can still help draw out this distinctive quality of these days before Pentecost.

Today (and on the Seventh Sunday of Easter, if your diocese celebrates Ascension on Thursday), incorporate songs of the Spirit. One simple way to connect the days from Ascension to Pentecost is to sing the Taizé chant "Veni, Sancte Spiritus" (GIA) without the accompanying Pentecost Sequence text and only with very simple musical accompaniment. Use it as a prelude or gathering song, as a conclusion to the distribution of Communion, or even as a sending forth song. Then at Pentecost, use the full setting and arrangement. You can do this with other Holy Spirit songs as well, such as Ken Canedo's "Holy Spirit" (OCP) or settings of Psalm 104.

SPIRITUALITY

GOSPEL ACCLAMATION
cf. John 14:18

℟. Alleluia, alleluia.
I will not leave you orphans, says the Lord.
I will come back to you, and your hearts will rejoice.
℟. Alleluia, alleluia.

Gospel John 17:1-11a; L59A

Jesus raised his eyes to heaven and said,
"Father, the hour has come.
Give glory to your son, so that your son may glorify you,
just as you gave him authority over all people,
so that your son may give eternal life to all you gave him.
Now this is eternal life,
that they should know you, the only true God,
and the one whom you sent, Jesus Christ.
I glorified you on earth
by accomplishing the work that you gave me to do.
Now glorify me, Father, with you,
with the glory that I had with you before the world began.

"I revealed your name to those whom you gave me out of the world.
They belonged to you, and you gave them to me,
and they have kept your word.
Now they know that everything you gave me is from you,
because the words you gave to me I have given to them,
and they accepted them and truly understood that I came from you,
and they have believed that you sent me.
I pray for them.
I do not pray for the world but for the ones you have given me,
because they are yours, and everything of mine is yours
and everything of yours is mine,
and I have been glorified in them.
And now I will no longer be in the world,
but they are in the world, while I am coming to you."

Reflecting on the Gospel

As we near the end of the Easter season, we hear a gospel reading from John. The setting is Jesus' final prayer to the Father prior to his being betrayed on the night before his death. The prayer is more than three chapters long (chapters 15–17)! Moreover, it concludes on a somewhat startling note with Jesus saying he is NOT praying for the world "but for the ones you have given me." He says he will no longer be in the world, but they are in the world.

In some ways this episode seems a far cry from some of Jesus' earlier words in this same gospel about how "God so loved the world he gave his only son." But these episodes together summarize one of the overarching themes of John's gospel. Jesus was with God from the beginning. God's love for the world meant he sent his only Son, who revealed the name of God to those chosen. Jesus prays for these chosen few who know the only true God. They know the one sent by God, Jesus Christ. And this knowledge is eternal life. Now Jesus prepares to return to the Father, departing this world. Those chosen few, who came to know God and the one he sent, Jesus, remain in the world with the assistance of another Advocate.

It's clear that this gospel and even its language is unlike the others. This Gospel of John reflects its own unique theological vision about Jesus and his identity.

Much later, a heresy known as "Gnosticism" arose, claiming among other things that knowledge was the way to eternal life. The Gospel of John was the favorite among Gnostics, and this gospel passage we read today might give us some indication as to why.

But for us two thousand years later, we may hear the passage proclaimed this week and nod approvingly. Even so, it would be good to listen carefully for the theological nuances of the text, recognizing the role of knowledge, eternal life, glory, prayer, and the world.

Jesus prays not only for the disciples in his day and time, but for us today. He is no longer in the world as he once was, but we are. His prayers for us strengthen us as we live in the midst of the world. We are the objects of his prayer. In the face of all we encounter in the world, we have an advocate in Jesus, and another advocate in the Spirit. On the night before he died, this prayer was for us.

Living the Paschal Mystery

We live in the world but are not of the world. Such is Christian identity, as it is rooted in Jesus' identity. God so loved the world that he gave his only son. But he called those who were his own in the world. The son came for us; we have been chosen.

When we feel called by the allure of the world, let us recall that the world is only a temporary home for us. A bright future awaits where love reigns and glory is resplendent.

The night before he died, Jesus prayed for us and for all those who were chosen by God. Rather than make us smug, this knowledge should humble us and cause us to emulate him who came to serve rather than be served.

For Jesus in the Gospel of John, the crucifixion is the lifting up, the exaltation of the Son of God. With eyes of faith, let us see anew and reorient our lives.

Focusing the Gospel

Key words and phrases: "Now this is eternal life, / that they should know you, the only true God, / and the one whom you sent, Jesus Christ."

To the point: Today's gospel offers us a new vision and definition of eternal life; it is knowing the one God and his son, Jesus. In these words, Jesus is not urging us to place emphasis on intellectual knowledge *about* God. Instead, we are invited to enter into a deep relationship with the one who calls us by name and made us for himself.

Connecting the Gospel

to the first: Today's first reading from the Acts of the Apostles picks up right where it left off on the feast of the Ascension. In his final words to the apostles before being lifted up to heaven, Jesus assures them, "[Y]ou will receive power when the Holy Spirit comes upon you." After Jesus is "lifted up" and taken "from their sight," the disciples return to the upper room in Jerusalem to devote themselves to prayer. In their time following Jesus during his ministry, the disciples have had numerous opportunities to observe the Lord at prayer. Many times they have seen him steal away to a deserted place to commune with God. They've also received and treasured the instruction he gave them after being asked, "Lord, teach us to pray" (Luke 11:1; NABRE). Today's gospel reading comes from a section in John known as the "High Priestly" prayer of Jesus. In it, Jesus prays for unity among his followers, their protection, and their joy. Near the end, he opens up this prayer to include not only the friends who sit before him but also "those who will believe in me through their word" (17:20; NABRE).

to experience: In our lives as disciples, we have also been initiated into the Christian tradition of prayer. Jesus himself offers us the model of communion with God in his prayer through both word and action. Following in his footsteps and those of the earliest disciples, how do you devote yourself to prayer?

Connecting the Responsorial Psalm

to the readings: While today's first reading and gospel lift up moments of prayer, the second reading from the first letter of St. Peter centers on a different theme, rejoicing in suffering. We know that the apostles who gather in the upper room to await the gift of the Holy Spirit will live boldly in witness to Christ. Most of their lives will end in violent death, and yet, even as they see their closest companions martyred, the apostles are not deterred from proclaiming Jesus to all they meet. We might ask, where did their tenacity in the face of death arise from? Our psalm response suggests an answer—unshakeable hope and trust in the God of life: "I believe that I shall see the good things of the Lord in the land of the living."

to psalmist preparation: As you prepare to lead the assembly in song and prayer, consider this question: What is the hope that you cling to even in the midst of suffering or fear?

PROMPTS FOR FAITH-SHARING

In the first reading the apostles return to the upper room along with "Mary the mother of Jesus, and his brothers" and devote themselves to prayer. Who are your companions in prayer at this moment in your life?

The psalmist sings, "The Lord is my light and my salvation; / whom should I fear?" Where has fear or anxiety crept into your life, and how might God be calling you to renew your trust in him?

In his epistle, St. Peter urges us to "rejoice to the extent that you share in the sufferings of Christ." Who has been a model for you in enduring suffering with grace and peace?

In the gospel Jesus prays, "I glorified you on earth / by accomplishing the work that you gave me to do." How does your work give glory to God?

Model Rite for the Blessing and Sprinkling of Water

Presider: In today's gospel Jesus prays to the Father, asking that he might give eternal life to his disciples. In the waters of baptism, we have died with Christ and risen as a new creation. May these waters remind us of our baptismal joy and bring us to fuller life in Christ . . . *[pause]*

[continue with The Roman Missal, *Appendix II]*

Homily Points

- Today we begin the seventh week of the Easter season. The mystery that we began to celebrate with the Holy Triduum will not be complete until the feast of Pentecost when God's own Spirit alights upon the apostles and they are emboldened to proclaim the good news of Jesus' triumph over death and invitation to all to share in his light and life. While we only receive the sacraments of baptism and confirmation once, each Easter season we recall in a particular way the moment we entered into the life of Christ and received the fullness of the Spirit, as we support and pray for those who are baptized, confirmed, and join us at the table of the Lord for the first time.

- Fittingly, in today's readings we are given images of deep and persistent prayer. The night he will be betrayed and handed over for crucifixion, Jesus gathers with his closest friends for one final meal. In John's gospel this meal concludes with prayer. Even as he anticipates his passion and death, Jesus remains focused on his mission from God: to bring all whom he has been given to the completeness of joy and unity in God's kingdom. Likewise, in the first reading the disciples, who have seen Jesus gathered up into heaven, return to Jerusalem to await the gift of the Holy Spirit with a single-minded devotion to prayer.

- Within the story of the earliest followers of Christ, we find a pattern for our own journeys of faith. We have been called to proclaim Christ to all nations, but we cannot do it without the fire of the Holy Spirit alive in our hearts. Over the next week, as we draw closer and closer to Pentecost, let us also enter into deep and fervent prayer, asking for the abundance of the Holy Spirit that we might boldly proclaim Christ in word and action to all we meet.

Model Universal Prayer (Prayer of the Faithful)

Presider: Trusting in the love of Jesus, our High Priest who never ceases to lift us up in prayer to the Father, let us bring our needs before the Lord.

Response: Lord, hear our prayer.

For God's holy church, with one accord may the people of God, spread throughout the world, pray ceaselessly in both word and action . . .

For leaders of nations, may they be inspired to work for the end of religious persecution and to establish the right of all people to worship in safety . . .

For all whose faith has been shaken or who have left the church due to scandal, may they find refuge in Jesus, the Good Shepherd . . .

For all gathered here around the table of the Lord, may we give glory to God in all that we say and do . . .

Presider: God, redeemer and savior, in your son, Jesus, we are called to fullness of life and promised life eternal. Hear our prayers that by the working of the Holy Spirit, we might grow in faith, hope, and love each day. We ask this through Christ our Lord. **Amen.**

COLLECT

Let us pray.

Pause for silent prayer

Graciously hear our supplications, O Lord,
so that we, who believe that the Savior of the human race
is with you in your glory,
may experience, as he promised,
until the end of the world,
his abiding presence among us.
Who lives and reigns with you in the unity of the Holy Spirit,
one God, for ever and ever. **Amen.**

FIRST READING

Acts 1:12-14

After Jesus had been taken up to heaven the apostles
returned to Jerusalem
from the mount called Olivet, which is near Jerusalem,
a sabbath day's journey away.

When they entered the city
they went to the upper room where they were staying,
Peter and John and James and Andrew,
Philip and Thomas, Bartholomew and Matthew,
James son of Alphaeus, Simon the Zealot,
and Judas son of James.
All these devoted themselves with one accord to prayer,
together with some women,
and Mary the mother of Jesus, and his brothers.

RESPONSORIAL PSALM
Ps 27:1, 4, 7-8

℟. (13) I believe that I shall see the good things of the Lord in the land of the living.
or:
℟. Alleluia.

The LORD is my light and my salvation;
whom should I fear?
The LORD is my life's refuge;
of whom should I be afraid?

℟. I believe that I shall see the good things of the Lord in the land of the living.
or:
℟. Alleluia.

One thing I ask of the LORD;
this I seek:
To dwell in the house of the LORD
all the days of my life,
that I may gaze on the loveliness of the LORD
and contemplate his temple.

℟. I believe that I shall see the good things of the Lord in the land of the living.
or:
℟. Alleluia.

Hear, O LORD, the sound of my call;
have pity on me, and answer me.
Of you my heart speaks; you my glance seeks.

℟. I believe that I shall see the good things of the Lord in the land of the living.
or:
℟. Alleluia.

SECOND READING
1 Pet 4:13-16

Beloved:
Rejoice to the extent that you share in the sufferings of Christ,
so that when his glory is revealed
you may also rejoice exultantly.
If you are insulted for the name of Christ, blessed are you,
for the Spirit of glory and of God rests upon you.
But let no one among you be made to suffer
as a murderer, a thief, an evildoer, or as an intriguer.
But whoever is made to suffer as a Christian should not be ashamed
but glorify God because of the name.

About Liturgy

The Lord's Day: Instead of the Seventh Sunday of Easter, most dioceses in the United States will mark Ascension Sunday today. Although we lose the historical tradition of a nine-day novena of prayer when Ascension is transferred to Sunday, this valid practice highlights the pride of place that Sunday holds in the way Christians mark time.

Sunday is the first day and the last, the day of resurrection and the sending of the Spirit. It is "the original feast day" (The Constitution on the Sacred Liturgy 106). St. John Paul II outlined some of its other titles in his apostolic letter *Dies Domini*: It is the day of the Creator's work; the weekly Easter; the day of Christ-Light, of faith; an indispensable day.

Whether today is the Seventh Sunday of Easter or Ascension, it is always and most importantly the Lord's Day, for all times and seasons belong to God.

Memorial Day: In the United States this year, May 25 is Memorial Day, a day when we remember those who have died in service to this country. Christian liturgy is by nature not tied to any country, since we are citizens of heaven. However, we do have a Christian responsibility to pray for the dead as a spiritual work of mercy. We also want to keep in mind our call to work toward the peace of God's kingdom so that we need train for war no longer, as Isaiah's vision gives us.

Be sure to include an intercession remembering those who have died in service to this country and an intercession for the end to war.

About Initiation

Fifty days or one year of mystagogy: As we near the close of the Easter season, we also near the end of the final period of the RCIA, the period of postbaptismal catechesis or mystagogy. RCIA 249 invites us to mark the close of this period with a celebration for the neophytes held near Pentecost Sunday. There are no specific guidelines for what this celebration looks like other than the inclusion of "festivities in keeping with local custom."

Note that the United States bishops also recommend that after Easter, "[T]he program for the neophytes should extend until the anniversary of Christian initiation, with at least monthly assemblies of the neophytes" (National Statutes for the Catechumenate 24).

About Liturgical Music

End of "choir season": Some choirs may be gearing up not only for Pentecost and the end of the Easter season next Sunday but also the end of the choir year when many of them take breaks from liturgical service for the summer. Rest is certainly important. Even God rested! But you might want to rethink this practice.

No other liturgical ministries are given annual breaks from service. If we do this with choirs, it may communicate that choral music—or even liturgical music in general—is nonessential albeit a nice addition at Mass. It may also poorly form music ministers in their first role as assembly members, such that some may think they aren't "doing anything" at Mass if they aren't in the choir singing in harmonies. Recall that the United States bishops' document Sing to the Lord says: "When the choir is not exercising its particular role, it joins the congregation in song. The choir's role in this case is not to lead congregational singing, but to sing with the congregation" (31). The choir indeed still serves the liturgy even if the members are singing in unison and are unrehearsed.

Instead of encouraging a break from service this summer, make it a break from weekly rehearsal. Prepare music that the assembly knows and loves, and have your choir members be a visible and audible support for the assembly's song.

SPIRITUALITY

GOSPEL ACCLAMATION

℟. Alleluia, alleluia.
Come, Holy Spirit, fill the hearts of your faithful
and kindle in them the fire of your love.
℟. Alleluia, alleluia.

Gospel

John 20:19-23; L63A

On the evening of that first day of the week,
when the doors were locked,
where the disciples were,
for fear of the Jews,
Jesus came and stood in their midst
and said to them, "Peace be with you."
When he had said this, he showed them his hands and his side.
The disciples rejoiced when they saw the Lord.
Jesus said to them again, "Peace be with you.
As the Father has sent me, so I send you."
And when he had said this, he breathed on them and said to them,
"Receive the Holy Spirit.
Whose sins you forgive are forgiven them,
and whose sins you retain are retained."

Reflecting on the Gospel

The church concludes the Easter season with the feast of Pentecost, fifty days after Passover. In so doing the church is following our "elder brother in faith" (the Jewish people, according to Pope St. John Paul II). The feast of Pentecost was a Jewish feast of new grain, new wine, the first fruits of the harvest. It was held fifty days after Passover, thus the (albeit Greek) name "Pentecost," which means fifty. The book of Acts tells us that it was on this feast that Peter was emboldened by the Holy Spirit to speak to the Jewish pilgrims who had assembled in Jerusalem that day. As Luke tells it in Acts, it was on that day that the Spirit was given to the disciples and also poured out onto the crowds who were listening to Peter preach. But our gospel reading is not from Acts (as it is not a gospel) nor is it from Luke (the author of Acts). Instead, we have a reading from the Gospel of John whereby Jesus gives the gift of the Holy Spirit.

The episode in the Gospel of John in today's reading happens on Easter Sunday evening. It is on that day that Jesus gives the disciples the gift of the Holy Spirit in a graphic, nearly sacramental way—by breathing on them. Jesus' presence brought joy to the disciples whose spirits needed revivification after the tragic events that had so recently transpired. Whether the handing on of the Spirit happened on Easter Sunday evening as John says, or on Pentecost as Luke says, the key theological point is that the Spirit was given to the early Christian community. The Spirit has been with the church, the community of disciples, ever since. In fact, the same spirit is alive in each of our congregations and parishes. Rather than a historical event trapped in the past, the handing on of the Spirit continues to happen quite regularly in the lives of believers, and that ultimately is what the feast of Pentecost celebrates: the presence of the Spirit in the lives of believers.

Living the Paschal Mystery

How many of us would like to have been present during the ministry of Jesus, or even during that of the early Christians? What would it have been like to hear the words of Peter at Pentecost? What would it have been like to have seen the risen Jesus and to have heard him say, "Peace be with you" before handing on the Holy Spirit? Yet, for those of us in the twenty-first century, we experience that same Holy Spirit. When we were baptized, we were given the gift of the Spirit, and then we were sealed by that same spirit in confirmation. The Holy Spirit lives in our parishes, families, friends, and relationships. Once we experience the dying and rising of Christ, we live in a newness of life accompanied and animated by the Holy Spirit.

After he rose from the dead, Jesus gave his Holy Spirit to be with us. In our daily lives, let us allow ourselves to be guided by the Spirit of Christ, whose disciples we are.

Focusing the Gospel

Key words and phrases: "Receive the Holy Spirit."

To the point: Earlier in John's gospel, during the Last Supper discourse, Jesus promised his disciples, "I will ask the Father, and he will give you another Advocate to be with you always, the Spirit of truth" (14:16-17; NABRE). In today's gospel this promise is fulfilled. An advocate is one who intercedes on another's behalf. In his letter to the Romans, St. Paul explains the Spirit's role in our lives: "[T]he Spirit too comes to the aid of our weakness; for we do not know how to pray as we ought, but the Spirit itself intercedes with inexpressible groaning" (8:26; NABRE). With the gift of the Holy Spirit, the life of God comes to make a home in every believer.

Connecting the Gospel

to the first and second readings: In the first reading and the gospel, we are given accounts of how the disciples first receive the gift of the Holy Spirit. The second reading from St. Paul's first letter to the Corinthians expounds upon this gift. Not only is the Holy Spirit given to each individual believer, but it is given for the benefit of the church. The spiritual gifts and abilities that we receive from the Holy Spirit are to be used in service to God and the Body of Christ.

to experience: The universal church includes a marvelous diversity of peoples. Our differences are a blessing but can also be a source of conflict. St. Paul lets us know that it is the spirit who unites us all just as a body that has many parts is united. When each individual member of Christ's body uses his or her gifts and talents for the good of all, we are able to function as Christ intended—in one body, intent on loving God and caring for each other.

Connecting the Responsorial Psalm

to the readings: Not only does the Spirit bless humans, it sustains and renews all of creation, as our psalm announces. From the first two verses of Genesis we hear how when "God created the heavens and the earth . . . the earth was formless and empty, darkness was over the surface of the deep, and the Spirit of God was hovering over the waters" (1:1-2; NIV). Just as God's Spirit created order in the cosmos and on our planet at the time of creation, it continues to bring beauty from chaos. The psalmist proclaims, "When you send forth your spirit, they are created, / and you renew the face of the earth."

to psalmist preparation: On the feast of Pentecost we ask in a particular way for the Holy Spirit to be poured out upon us and upon all of creation. Where are you most in need of the Spirit's renewing presence in your life?

PROMPTS FOR FAITH-SHARING

On the feast of Pentecost confirmations are often celebrated and, with this sacrament, the gifts of the Holy Spirit. Which of the seven gifts (wisdom, understanding, counsel, fortitude, knowledge, piety, and fear of the Lord) are you most in need of at this point in your life?

Our responsorial psalm is "Lord, send out your Spirit and renew the face of the earth." Where do you see the need for renewal in our world right now?

In the second reading, St. Paul writes, "To each individual the manifestation of the Spirit / is given for some benefit." Which gifts/talents have you been given by God and how do you use these gifts/talents to serve others?

In today's gospel, Jesus greets his disciples by offering them peace. How do you strive to bring Christ's peace to those you greet each day?

CELEBRATION

Model Rite for the Blessing and Sprinkling of Water

Presider: The Holy Spirit descends on the apostles like "tongues as of fire." May this water remind us of the waters of baptism, which gifted us with this same Spirit . . . *[pause]*

[continue with The Roman Missal, *Appendix II]*

Homily Points

- In the second story of creation from the book of Genesis, God forms "man out of the dust of the ground and [blows] into his nostrils the breath of life" (2:7; NABRE). In today's gospel reading, Jesus breathes upon his disciples while telling them, "Receive the Holy Spirit." In this way, the disciples are given a newness of life—the life of the risen Jesus that is stronger than death, and the life of the triune God in the gift of the Holy Spirit.

- In the first reading we find the apostles gathered together and waiting, as Jesus had asked them to do, "for the promise of the Father about which you have heard me speak . . . in a few days you will be baptized with the holy Spirit" (Acts 1:4-5; NABRE). The disciples had already received their commission to go forth and bear witness to the good news of Jesus' life, death, and resurrection, but they were not yet equipped to carry out their task. Only when they have been filled with the Holy Spirit are they enabled to "speak in different tongues" and to proclaim "the mighty acts of God."

- The Spirit that descends upon the apostles is described as a "strong driving wind" and "tongues of fire." Both wind and fire have the ability to form, shape, and transform matter. Today we gather to ask for this transforming power of God to be poured out upon us and upon all of creation. In the Holy Spirit we receive everything we need to carry out Jesus' mission of love in the world: to be the Body of Christ and to build the kingdom of God.

Model Universal Prayer (Prayer of the Faithful)

Presider: On this feast of Pentecost let us entrust our needs, and those of our world, to the Lord of life.

Response: Lord, hear our prayer.

For God's holy church, may the diverse gifts of the Spirit be celebrated in all of their manifestations . . .

For the earth and all who call this planet home, may an outpouring of the Holy Spirit bring renewal and peace . . .

For indigenous peoples and those whose cultures are threatened with extinction, may their languages and way of life be safeguarded . . .

For all gathered here, by living lives rooted in the Lord may the fruits of the Holy Spirit flourish in our community . . .

Presider: God of glory and might, you send out your Spirit to renew the face of the earth. Hear our prayers that by this same Spirit we might be refreshed and invigorated to proclaim your word of peace and joy through lives of devotion and grace. Through Christ our Lord. **Amen.**

COLLECT

Let us pray.

Pause for silent prayer

O God, who by the mystery of today's
great feast
sanctify your whole Church in every
people and nation,
pour out, we pray, the gifts of the Holy Spirit
across the face of the earth
and, with the divine grace that was at work
when the Gospel was first proclaimed,
fill now once more the hearts of believers.
Through our Lord Jesus Christ, your Son,
who lives and reigns with you in the unity
of the Holy Spirit,
one God, for ever and ever. **Amen.**

FIRST READING

Acts 2:1-11

When the time for Pentecost was fulfilled,
they were all in one place together.
And suddenly there came from the sky
a noise like a strong driving wind,
and it filled the entire house in which
they were.
Then there appeared to them tongues as
of fire,
which parted and came to rest on each
one of them.
And they were all filled with the Holy
Spirit
and began to speak in different tongues,
as the Spirit enabled them to proclaim.

Now there were devout Jews from every
nation under heaven
staying in Jerusalem.
At this sound, they gathered in a large
crowd,
but they were confused
because each one heard them speaking
in his own language.
They were astounded, and in amazement
they asked,
"Are not all these people who are
speaking Galileans?
Then how does each of us hear them in
his native language?
We are Parthians, Medes, and Elamites,
inhabitants of Mesopotamia, Judea and
Cappadocia,
Pontus and Asia, Phrygia and
Pamphylia,
Egypt and the districts of Libya near
Cyrene,
as well as travelers from Rome,
both Jews and converts to Judaism,
Cretans and Arabs,
yet we hear them speaking in our own
tongues
of the mighty acts of God."

RESPONSORIAL PSALM

Ps 104:1, 24, 29-30, 31, 34

℟. (cf. 30) Lord, send out your Spirit, and renew the face of the earth.
or: ℟. Alleluia.

Bless the LORD, O my soul!
O LORD, my God, you are great indeed!
How manifold are your works, O LORD!
The earth is full of your creatures.

℟. Lord, send out your Spirit, and renew the face of the earth.
or: ℟. Alleluia.

If you take away their breath, they perish
and return to their dust.
When you send forth your spirit, they are created,
and you renew the face of the earth.

℟. Lord, send out your Spirit, and renew the face of the earth.
or: ℟. Alleluia.

May the glory of the LORD endure forever;
may the LORD be glad in his works!
Pleasing to him be my theme;
I will be glad in the LORD.

℟. Lord, send out your Spirit, and renew the face of the earth.
or: ℟. Alleluia.

SECOND READING

1 Cor 12:3b-7, 12-13

Brothers and sisters:
No one can say, "Jesus is Lord," except by the Holy Spirit.

There are different kinds of spiritual gifts but the same Spirit;
there are different forms of service but the same Lord;
there are different workings but the same God
who produces all of them in everyone.
To each individual the manifestation of the Spirit
is given for some benefit.

As a body is one though it has many parts,
and all the parts of the body, though many, are one body,
so also Christ.
For in one Spirit we were all baptized into one body,
whether Jews or Greeks, slaves or free persons,
and we were all given to drink of one Spirit.

SEQUENCE

See Appendix A, p. 295.

CATECHESIS

About Liturgy

An extended Pentecost Vigil: By this time of year, most parishes are ready for the simplicity of Ordinary Time to resume! But more and more parishes are beginning to explore the option of an extended form of the Pentecost Vigil, newly included in the third edition of the Roman Missal. The structure of this extended vigil is similar to the Liturgy of the Word of the Easter Vigil, so it is a fitting bookend to the season.

The Pentecost Vigil, whether in the extended or simple form, is always used on the Saturday evening before Pentecost. Thus, it is a true vigil and not a Sunday Mass celebrated on Saturday evening.

For the extended vigil, there is an option to combine it with Evening Prayer. Most parishes will skip this option and begin the Vigil Mass as usual. In this extended format, after the *Kyrie*, the presider leads a collect; then all are seated for a series of four readings, psalms (or silence), and prayers. After the fourth prayer, the Gloria is sung concluding with the collect of the day. Then all are seated for the New Testament reading. From here, Mass continues as usual.

Note that the Pentecost Sequence is sung only at the Mass during the day, and both the vigil and the Sunday Masses conclude with the solemn dismissal last heard on the octave of Easter (Second Sunday of Easter).

About Initiation

Gathering with the bishop: In some dioceses, the local bishop gathers the newly initiated for a Mass at the cathedral. This often happens around Pentecost, although it may take place at another time during the year. The purpose is for the bishop to "show his pastoral concern for these new members of the Church . . . particularly if he was unable to preside at the sacraments of initiation himself" (RCIA 251).

Whether or not your bishop coordinates such a gathering for the neophytes, look for opportunities to help your bishop fulfill his responsibility of showing concern for the neophytes. Take your neophytes and their godparents to the cathedral during their neophyte year when your bishop is presiding. If your bishop comes to your parish for confirmation or other events, be sure to introduce your neophytes to him. If neither of these are possible, you can write a brief note to your bishop asking for his prayers. Include some photos and stories about your neophytes and their Easter celebration of the sacraments.

About Liturgical Music

Singing in different languages: Some choirs incorporate a diversity of music today from different cultures and languages. One such example is the Pentecost Sequence ("Veni Sancte Spiritus," GIA) from the Taizé community that has the ostinato refrain in Latin while the verses are sung in English and other languages. Another example is Ricky Manalo's four-part multilingual chant "Come, O Spirit of God" (OCP) in Latin, Tagalog, English, Vietnamese, and Spanish.

Especially if your community is diverse, with members who speak these languages, short sung refrains are excellent ways to help one another pray in a different tongue. However, be careful to ensure that you are respecting languages that are not your own. Invite native speakers to teach your choir proper pronunciation; better yet, invite native-speaking members of those language groups to lead the community in singing those pieces.

Remember that singing in another person's language should always be accompanied by a commitment to entering into relationship with those for whom that is their mother tongue. In this way, our sung prayer can become a truer expression of our communion in Christ and not simply a novelty or a performance done for its own sake.

ORDINARY TIME II

SPIRITUALITY

GOSPEL ACCLAMATION
cf. Rev 1:8

℟. Alleluia, alleluia.
Glory to the Father, the Son, and the Holy Spirit;
to God who is, who was, and who is to come.
℟. Alleluia, alleluia.

Gospel

John 3:16-18; L164A

God so loved the world that he gave his only Son,
so that everyone who believes in him might not perish
but might have eternal life.
For God did not send his Son into the world to condemn the world,
but that the world might be saved through him.
Whoever believes in him will not be condemned,
but whoever does not believe has already been condemned,
because he has not believed in the name of the only Son of God.

Reflecting on the Gospel

On this the feast of the Most Holy Trinity, we have one of the shortest gospel readings of the year, and this from the Gospel of John. The passage is only three verses and it is proclaimed at the Liturgy of the Eucharist often in less than a minute, no more than two. The opening line of this gospel reading will be familiar to many, as it may be used frequently to sum up Christian theology: "God so loved the world that he gave his only Son."

This pithy statement grounds God's action and motivation in love. God is not an angry parent waiting for wayward humanity to make inevitable mistakes, only so he can punish and dole out consequences. No, "God is love" (1 John 4:8) and God acts out of love. It is this same love that reflects God's desire to give (not merely to send) his only Son. The Son of God is given as a gift to the world out of love. As followers of this same Son, we ought to be motivated by love as well. We freely give without counting the cost; and we give not merely from our excess, but we give our very selves. That is the mark of a Christian disciple.

Finally, though we celebrate the feast of the Holy Trinity, there is nothing about the Holy Spirit, or the Advocate (to use a Johannine term), in these three verses. The gospel reading reflects a theological relationship between God and the Son. Later chapters in the Gospel of John will speak of the Spirit, who is sent after the resurrection. And, of course, other New Testament texts also have more to say about the Spirit and the relationship between God the Father, Jesus the Son, and the Spirit. Theologians will wrestle with these passages for centuries, struggling to articulate the triune relationship of the one Godhead in a way that expresses Christian belief accurately. But Christian identity is not only about believing, but perhaps even more fundamentally, it is about doing. So these three verses give us a model for action motivated by love. We are to be givers, disciples of the Son of God who was given to the world.

Living the Paschal Mystery

The mystery of the Trinity can be baffling to comprehend. Three persons, one God. We often state the intellectual proposition of faith without understanding it. And when attempting to understand the meaning of our words, we often fall back on that term: mystery. But what does the Trinity mean for us, beyond an intellectual proposition to which we nod assent?

As we read in the opening line of the gospel today, God is self-gift. God loves and God gives. Those attributes would mark our identity as Christians. If we want to live the paschal mystery, or even live the trinitarian mystery, it would behoove us to become like God and to love, to give to the point of giving our very selves. Doing the gospel, or living our faith, is much more a marker of Christian identity than merely parroting propositions we may or may not understand.

Focusing the Gospel

Key words and phrases: God so loved the world that he gave his only Son

To the point: Our God is the ultimate gift giver. From the first story of creation, God gifted humanity with plants and animals to steward and use. In time, God called a people with whom to form a covenant relationship, the people of Israel. And then, in the fullness of time, he gave his only son, Jesus, to open up this covenant to all who call upon the Lord. In all these gifts God calls us into relationship with himself, Father, Son, and Holy Spirit. What will be our response to the abundant gifts of God?

Connecting the Gospel

to the first reading: In the book of Exodus, Moses draws near to the Lord and receives the revelation that his God is one who is "merciful and gracious . . . slow to anger and rich in kindness and fidelity." Moses makes a request, that this good and gracious God might "come along in our company." After the people build a tabernacle according to God's instructions, the Lord indeed comes to dwell there (Exod 40:34). In the incarnation, God gives his son to be his living, breathing presence among the people. In Jesus we are gifted with God's very self, and when it is time for the risen Lord to ascend to the Father, we are given another gift—the presence of the Holy Spirit who dwells within Jesus' disciples.

to experience: Throughout the history of salvation, God has longed to be in communion with the people he has created. We are invited to make the heart of the Trinity our own dwelling place and to rest secure there in the love of God.

Connecting the Responsorial Psalm

to the readings: Today's responsorial psalm is not from the book of Psalms at all but from the book of Daniel. It is taken from the canticle of the three youths, cast into the fiery furnace by King Nebuchadnezzar who had demanded that they fall down in worship before a golden statue. Although the king has the fire stoked to seven times its usual heat (Dan 3:19), the young men are unharmed, for "the angel of the Lord went down . . . [and] drove the fiery flames out of the furnace" (Dan 3:49; NABRE). In response, the three young men sing to the glory of God the first four verses of which we sing today in our psalm. On this feast of the Holy Trinity we pronounce that our God, Father, Son, and Holy Spirit, is "praiseworthy and exalted above all for all forever."

to psalmist preparation: In your own life of faith, what helps you to give glory and praise to our triune God in the midst of struggle and hardship?

PROMPTS FOR FAITH-SHARING

In the first reading, Moses invites God to "come along in our company." How do you invite God into your daily life?

On this feast of the Holy Trinity, how does it change you or affect your perception of God to think of God-self as a relationship of three persons: Father, Son, and Holy Spirit?

In the second reading St. Paul urges the Corinthians to "encourage one another." Which individuals or groups within your community are in need of encouragement?

Our gospel today begins with one of the most well-known lines in Holy Scripture: "God so loved the world that he gave his only Son." What does this action tell us about the one we call Father?

CELEBRATION

Model Penitential Act

Presider: Our gospel for today tells us that "God did not send his Son into the world to condemn the world, / but that the world might be saved through him." With faith in God's loving kindness, let us pause to ask for his mercy and healing . . . *[pause]*

Lord Jesus, you are the only Son of the Father: Lord, have mercy.

Christ Jesus, you call us to live in peace with you and one another: Christ, have mercy.

Lord Jesus, in relationship with God the Father and the Holy Spirit, you are the Holy Trinity: Lord, have mercy.

Homily Points

• The catechism tells us that "the mystery of the Most Holy Trinity is the central mystery of Christian faith and life" (*Catechism of the Catholic Church* 234). Within our Catholic faith it is necessary for us to have a strong "theology of mystery." When we speak of mysteries within our faith, we are not talking about problems to be solved or even concepts that we can come to a definite answer or pronouncement on. The mystery of God and the Holy Trinity are always to some extent beyond us and our human capacities to comprehend fully.

• This doesn't mean that calling it a "mystery" excuses us from wading deeply into the theological richness of the Trinity. Mysteries instead call us into a relationship with the One who is our creator and Lord. By sitting with the mystery of the Trinity, by spending time in contemplation and prayer before it, we are led into deeper communion with God the Father, Son, and Holy Spirit.

• Rather than being a complete enigma to us, the nature of the Trinity is one we trace upon our bodies each time we make the sign of the cross. When we proclaim God as Father, Son, and Holy Spirit in prayer, we are entering into the dynamic life of the living God. As St. Paul makes clear in his letter to the Corinthians, our God is still active in "the grace of the Lord Jesus Christ / and the love of God / and the fellowship of the Holy Spirit." In embracing this mystery of one God in three persons, we are called beyond ourselves into the self-giving love of the Trinity, which provides us with a model for the Christian life.

Model Universal Prayer (Prayer of the Faithful)

Presider: In confidence and love, let us bring our prayers before God the Father, Son, and Holy Spirit.

Response: Lord, hear our prayer.

For all members of the universal church, through the sharing of gifts and respecting diversity, may we grow in unity . . .

For leaders of nations throughout the world, may they uphold the importance of civil discourse and collaborate together for the common good . . .

For those suffering from chronic illness, may they receive necessary medical attention, compassionate care, and support . . .

For all gathered here, as a community of faith, may we encourage one another in the life of discipleship . . .

Presider: Triune God, you reveal yourself to us as a community of persons living in dynamic and self-giving love. Hear our prayers that, made in the image of God, we might model communion with one another where all are valued and respected. We ask this through Christ our Lord. **Amen.**

COLLECT

Let us pray.

Pause for silent prayer

God our Father, who by sending into the world
the Word of truth and the Spirit of sanctification
made known to the human race your wondrous mystery,
grant us, we pray, that in professing the true faith,
we may acknowledge the Trinity of eternal glory
and adore your Unity, powerful in majesty.
Through our Lord Jesus Christ, your Son,
who lives and reigns with you in the unity of the Holy Spirit,
one God, for ever and ever. **Amen.**

FIRST READING

Exod 34:4b-6, 8-9

Early in the morning Moses went up Mount Sinai
as the LORD had commanded him,
taking along the two stone tablets.

Having come down in a cloud, the LORD stood with Moses there
and proclaimed his name, "LORD."
Thus the LORD passed before him and cried out,
"The LORD, the LORD, a merciful and gracious God,
slow to anger and rich in kindness and fidelity."
Moses at once bowed down to the ground in worship.
Then he said, "If I find favor with you, O LORD,
do come along in our company.
This is indeed a stiff-necked people; yet pardon our wickedness and sins,
and receive us as your own."

RESPONSORIAL PSALM
Dan 3:52, 53, 54, 55

℟. (52b) Glory and praise forever!

Blessed are you, O Lord, the God of our fathers,
praiseworthy and exalted above all forever;
and blessed is your holy and glorious name,
praiseworthy and exalted above all for all ages.

℟. Glory and praise forever!

Blessed are you in the temple of your holy glory,
praiseworthy and glorious above all forever.

℟. Glory and praise forever!

Blessed are you on the throne of your kingdom,
praiseworthy and exalted above all forever.

℟. Glory and praise forever!

Blessed are you who look into the depths
from your throne upon the cherubim,
praiseworthy and exalted above all forever.

℟. Glory and praise forever!

SECOND READING
2 Cor 13:11-13

Brothers and sisters, rejoice. Mend your ways, encourage one another,
agree with one another, live in peace,
and the God of love and peace will be with you.
Greet one another with a holy kiss.
All the holy ones greet you.

The grace of the Lord Jesus Christ
and the love of God
and the fellowship of the Holy Spirit be with all of you.

CATECHESIS

About Liturgy

A trinity of love: June often means weddings. However, the number of Catholic weddings celebrated in church has been falling dramatically over the last few decades. This can be a cause for despair, or it can strengthen our resolve to give more care to the couples who do ask the church to witness their wedding.

The revision of the Order of Celebrating Matrimony brought some new rituals. It also reiterated some old rubrics that have never been fully implemented. One is the entrance procession. The bride and groom process in together following the ministers and wedding party while the entrance song is sung by everyone as at Sunday Mass! This is quite different from what most couples expect: the groom waits for his bride at the altar as her father "gives her away" to him.

As liturgists, we might cringe. But here is our chance to help these couples see their love through the lens of Christian symbol. Through that perspective, the couple enters together because they are equals, choosing on their own accord to give themselves to one another. Following the cross and the Word, they begin their new vocation as spouses at the doors of the church where their life of faith began in baptism. Joining the assembly in giving God praise, they make their vows in the midst of that community of disciples, who themselves promise their love and support to the couple.

Our Christian rites strive to communicate clearly that marriage is not simply between a man and woman but is a trinity of love caught up in the love of the Most Holy Trinity that binds husband and wife to the Christian community through the love of Christ they encounter in this sacrament.

About Initiation

First consecration: The cross—not the shamrock—is our foremost symbol of the Trinity, encompassing the love bonded in the Spirit between the Father and the Son. One of the first things Catholic parents teach their children is how to make the sign of the cross. That is a reminder of the child's baptism when the Christian community claimed that infant for Christ with that same simple gesture.

For adults and children who have reached catechetical age, we claim them for Christ in the same way during the Rite of Acceptance. The seekers are marked by that cross on not only their foreheads but their entire body. This is their "first consecration" (RCIA 41) and the climax of the Rite of Acceptance itself. Prior to this, the seekers are called "candidates" (as in candidates for becoming catechumens). But at the end of the signing of the senses, they receive a new name: "catechumen." Now consecrated to Christ through the sign of the Trinity, they are "joined to the Church . . . and part of the household of Christ" (RCIA 47).

About Liturgical Music

Suggestions: Especially today, take care that you sing all the necessary stanzas of hymns if one verse addresses the Father, another the Son, and another the Spirit. Today of all days, we need to keep the Persons of the Trinity together!

Also, today and next Sunday are festal echoes of Easter in that they are solemnities in Ordinary Time. One way to highlight this connection is to use some of the same music from Pentecost on these two Sundays. One suggestion is *Psallite*'s "The Love of God" (Liturgical Press), which has specific verses for Pentecost and for Trinity Sunday and a refrain appropriate for both: "The love of God is poured into our hearts; the Spirit of Christ is dwelling within."

SPIRITUALITY

GOSPEL ACCLAMATION
John 6:51

℟. Alleluia, alleluia.
I am the living bread that came down from heaven,
says the Lord;
whoever eats this bread will live forever.
℟. Alleluia, alleluia.

Gospel

John 6:51-58; L167A

Jesus said to the Jewish crowds:
"I am the living bread that came down from heaven;
whoever eats this bread will live forever;
and the bread that I will give
is my flesh for the life of the world."

The Jews quarreled among themselves, saying,
"How can this man give us his flesh to eat?"
Jesus said to them,
"Amen, amen, I say to you,
unless you eat the flesh of the Son of Man and drink his blood,
you do not have life within you.
Whoever eats my flesh and drinks my blood
has eternal life,
and I will raise him on the last day.
For my flesh is true food,
and my blood is true drink.
Whoever eats my flesh and drinks my blood
remains in me and I in him.
Just as the living Father sent me
and I have life because of the Father,
so also the one who feeds on me
will have life because of me.
This is the bread that came down from heaven.
Unlike your ancestors who ate and still died,
whoever eats this bread will live forever."

Reflecting on the Gospel

Following Holy Trinity Sunday last week, we now celebrate the feast of the Most Holy Body and Blood of Christ, also known as Corpus Christi, which is Latin for "Body of Christ." What the church intends to celebrate at this feast is not the corpse of Jesus on the cross, his body during his earthly ministry, or even the Pauline sense of the church itself as the body of Christ. Instead, as we can tell from the gospel reading, the church celebrates the presence of Christ in the eucharistic species. The Body and Blood of Christ we celebrate is the consecrated bread and wine that has become Christ himself.

The gospel reading today is not from the Last Supper as we might expect. Instead, the reading is from part of the "bread of life discourse" of the Gospel of John. The eucharistic theology is up-front and paramount. Jesus proclaims that he is the living bread come down from heaven. And to be certain that his listeners understand, he states clearly that this is true food and true drink. The imagery is so stark that many stumble over this teaching. Still Jesus maintains that those who consume this bread will live forever.

Later theologians build on this to say that it is precisely because Christians consume the Eucharist that we have the hope of eternal life. The Eucharist is the guarantor or the seed of eternal life that will come to fruition on the last day. Irenaeus, for example, who flourished in the latter half of the second century, says that when we receive the Eucharist, our bodies are no longer corruptible but have the hope of the resurrection to eternity (Irenaeus, *Against Heresies*, 4.18.5).

Thus, the church gives us this feast day to reflect on the sacramental life by which we participate in the divine life. Our consumption of the Eucharist is itself a promise of eternal life. But rather than a mere magical elixir, the Eucharist nourishes us so that we may live as followers of Jesus and emulate the life he led. By our reception of the Eucharist we, too, are called to become bread for the world and nourishment for those in need. The Eucharist is a call to Christian action.

Living the Paschal Mystery

The eucharistic species (the bread and the wine) is more than a thing to be reified; it is a eucharistic process, a self-giving of Christ himself so that he is bread broken and wine poured out in service and in love. It is not enough merely to admire the eucharistic species, though there is certainly a history of eucharistic adoration in our church, and it has a place. To truly celebrate the feast of Corpus Christi, we must become an *alter Christus* (another Christ) in the midst of the world today, so that we are bread broken and wine poured out for the needs of humanity.

The challenge of the Eucharist is not about spending time in private prayer before the Blessed Sacrament, though that is certainly good. Rather, the Eucharist demands that, as followers of Christ, we, too, allow ourselves to be broken for others, to be poured out. In so doing, we will be emulating Christ and living the paschal mystery.

Focusing the Gospel

Key words and phrases: "[T]he bread that I will give / is my flesh for the life of the world."

To the point: The bread Jesus offers is not only for the crowds that followed him in the land of Israel, or only for the disciples who heard his words at the Last Supper over the bread and wine. Its purpose is not limited to bringing the faithful into communion with him and with each other. Rather, this living bread sent down from heaven is meant for "the life of the world." As those who are nourished at the table of the Lord, we must not hide this treasure away but instead, being the eucharistic people Christ has called us to be, take it out into the world to bless, heal, restore, and revive.

Connecting the Gospel

to the first reading: In the book of Deuteronomy, Moses reminds the people of how the Lord himself "fed you in the desert with manna." After letting the people be "afflicted with hunger" to help them understand that "not by bread alone does one live," God satisfies their hunger with manna. This miraculous food sustained the people through their forty years in the desert before entering the Promised Land. Now, in the gospels, Jesus proclaims that he, the incarnate Son of God, is "the living bread that came down from heaven."

to experience: Where are you hungering in your spiritual life and how might God be calling you to feed that hunger?

Connecting the Responsorial Psalm

to the readings: Psalm 147 illustrates the abundant blessings the God of Israel showers upon his people. They dwell secure because "he has strengthened the bars of [Jerusalem's] gates" and "granted peace within [Jerusalem's] borders." They are sustained "with the best of wheat" and shepherded by the very "statutes" and "ordinances" of the Lord, which "he has not made known to [other nations]." On this feast of Corpus Christi, we also celebrate the care God has bestowed upon us by feeding us at the table of the Lord and sustaining us with his Word and commandments. In these abundant blessings we are also called to be a blessing to others. In the first letter to the Corinthians, St. Paul asks, "The cup of blessing that we bless, / is it not a participation in the blood of Christ? / The bread that we break, / is it not a participation in the body of Christ?" We know that Jesus' blood was poured out and his body broken that it might redeem the world.

to psalmist preparation: How are you called to be poured out, blessed, broken, and shared for the life of the world as a participant in the Body and Blood of Christ?

PROMPTS FOR FAITH-SHARING

The first reading from Deuteronomy reminds us that "not by bread alone does one live." At this moment on your faith journey, which spiritual sources are nourishing you?

St. Paul tells the Corinthians that in receiving the Eucharist they become one body in Christ. Where is your parish community in need of healing or relationship building in order to more fully reflect this unity?

On the feast of Corpus Christi we revere the gift of the Eucharist in our lives. This past year, how has this gift of Christ's Body and Blood affected your life?

How does your parish community, in receiving Jesus, "the living bread," seek to be nourishment for others?

Model Penitential Act

Presider: On this feast of Corpus Christi, Jesus tells us, "I am the living bread that came down from heaven." As we prepare to meet the risen Lord in the word of God and in the Eucharist, let us recall our sins and ask for God's pardon and mercy . . . *[pause]*

Lord Jesus, you are the living bread sent down from heaven: Lord have mercy.

Christ Jesus, in the Eucharist you unite us into one body: Christ have mercy.

Lord Jesus, in your Body and Blood you offer us food for everlasting life: Lord have mercy.

Homily Points

• Recently we concluded the Easter season, the pinnacle celebration of our liturgical year when we remember and live in a particular way the paschal mystery of Jesus' life, death, and resurrection. Next Sunday we will return to the green vestments and cloths of Ordinary Time, a time of living and growing in our faith.

• As we live out our lives as Christians, we are not in the same position as the first disciples who could bodily follow Jesus as he traversed the countryside of Israel. But we do still touch the risen Lord, in his Body and Blood that comes to us through the bread and wine of the Eucharist. He remains present to us here, and also within the other sacraments of the church, each of which includes different tangible signs and elements that allow us to draw near to the Lord with all of our senses.

• In the first reading we are reminded that God gave the Israelites food for their journey through the desert to the Promised Land. Their daily bread is manna, rained down from heaven each morning (Exod 16:4-5). In his goodness God also provides daily bread for us in the eucharistic feast. This bread, sent from heaven, is Jesus' "flesh for the life of the world." We, who are nourished at the table of the Lord, have been strengthened to become bread that is broken and shared, and wine that is poured out for others. Throughout this coming year, let us return again and again to meet Jesus in the bread and wine, to receive the nourishment necessary to sustain us in the life of discipleship.

Model Universal Prayer (Prayer of the Faithful)

Presider: Our Lord gives himself to us as nourishment in the word of God and the bread and wine of the eucharistic feast. In thanksgiving let us turn to him in prayer.

Response: Lord, hear our prayer.

For God's holy church, fed by the Body and Blood of Christ, may it become bread broken and wine poured out for others . . .

For nations of the world facing famine and drought, may their suffering be assuaged by the care and assistance of nations with plenty . . .

For Catholics throughout the world who go without the Eucharist due to oppression or lack of vocations, may they be fed spiritually by the Lord himself . . .

For all gathered here around the table of the Lord, in partaking in the eucharistic feast may we be emboldened to carry Christ to the world . . .

Presider: God of abundance, through the bread and wine of the Eucharist, your son, Jesus, remains with us always. Hear our prayers that in gathering around this altar table and being nourished by the Lord, we might give flesh to the Body of Christ in the world. We ask this through Christ our Lord. **Amen.**

COLLECT

Let us pray.

Pause for silent prayer

O God, who in this wonderful Sacrament
have left us a memorial of your Passion,
grant us, we pray,
so to revere the sacred mysteries of your Body and Blood
that we may always experience in ourselves
the fruits of your redemption.
Who live and reign with God the Father
in the unity of the Holy Spirit,
one God, for ever and ever. **Amen.**

FIRST READING

Deut 8:2-3, 14b-16a

Moses said to the people:
"Remember how for forty years now the LORD, your God,
has directed all your journeying in the desert,
so as to test you by affliction
and find out whether or not it was your intention
to keep his commandments.
He therefore let you be afflicted with hunger,
and then fed you with manna,
a food unknown to you and your fathers,
in order to show you that not by bread alone does one live,
but by every word that comes forth from the mouth of the LORD.

"Do not forget the LORD, your God,
who brought you out of the land of Egypt,
that place of slavery;
who guided you through the vast and terrible desert
with its saraph serpents and scorpions,
its parched and waterless ground;
who brought forth water for you from the flinty rock
and fed you in the desert with manna,
a food unknown to your fathers."

RESPONSORIAL PSALM
Ps 147:12-13, 14-15, 19-20

℟. (12) Praise the Lord, Jerusalem.
or:
℟. Alleluia.

Glorify the LORD, O Jerusalem;
praise your God, O Zion.
For he has strengthened the bars of your gates;
he has blessed your children within you.

℟. Praise the Lord, Jerusalem.
or:
℟. Alleluia.

He has granted peace in your borders;
with the best of wheat he fills you.
He sends forth his command to the earth;
swiftly runs his word!

℟. Praise the Lord, Jerusalem.
or:
℟. Alleluia.

He has proclaimed his word to Jacob,
his statutes and his ordinances to Israel.
He has not done thus for any other nation;
his ordinances he has not made known to them.
Alleluia.

℟. Praise the Lord, Jerusalem.
or:
℟. Alleluia.

SECOND READING
1 Cor 10:16-17

Brothers and sisters:
The cup of blessing that we bless,
is it not a participation in the blood of Christ?
The bread that we break,
is it not a participation in the body of Christ?
Because the loaf of bread is one,
we, though many, are one body,
for we all partake of the one loaf.

OPTIONAL SEQUENCE

See Appendix A, p. 295.

About Liturgy

Communion minister basics: Today is an opportune time to remind your Communion ministers of some basics:

Focus on the right things: The Communion minister's attention should be on the two aspects of the Body of Christ—in the consecrated bread and wine and in the people of God. Both are sacred and should be revered. Be attentive to both.

Take time: The few seconds you have with each person can be profound and should not be rushed. If there is a worry that Communion is taking too long, rushing is not the solution. Instead, add more Communion ministers.

You are the body of Christ too: Use your body well in this ministry. Look people in the eye with kindness. Smile. Say in a clear, strong voice, "The Body/Blood of Christ." Don't turn your loving gaze away from anyone until that person leaves your station.

Use the purificator: This cloth is meant to be used and not remain neatly folded. Unfold the cloth fully, and wipe the rim of the chalice well inside and out after each person receives. Give the chalice a quarter turn before sharing it with the next person, and use a different part of the purificator to wipe the chalice after each communicant.

About Initiation

The tabernacle: As Catholics, we pray before the tabernacle, which is a venerable practice of devotion to Christ in the Blessed Sacrament. Catechumens and candidates should learn the relationship between the tabernacle and the celebration of the Eucharist. Two points are key: First, "[t]he reason for which the Church reserves the eucharist outside Mass is, primarily, the administration of viaticum to the dying and, secondarily, communion of the sick, communion outside Mass, and adoration of Christ present in the sacrament" (Holy Communion and Worship of the Eucharist outside Mass 5). Second, during the celebration of the Mass, our focus is toward the altar and Christ's presence there in the Eucharist, the ministers, and the assembly that gathers around it. The tabernacle is secondary to the primary action taking place at the altar during Mass.

Teach catechumens and candidates to genuflect to the tabernacle whenever they enter the church outside of Mass and to bow to the altar at the very beginning and end of Mass.

About Liturgical Music

When does the Communion song begin? The General Instruction of the Roman Missal (GIRM) is clear: "While the Priest is receiving the Sacrament, the Communion Chant is begun" (86). Yet often music ministers wait to begin the Communion song long after the priest has eaten the host and drunk from the chalice. The most common reason they give for doing this is that they feel it is irreverent to begin the music while the priest receives Communion.

However, the purpose of the song is "to express the spiritual union of the communicants by means of the unity of their voices, to show gladness of heart, and to bring out more clearly the 'communitarian' character of the procession to receive the Eucharist" (GIRM 86). The priest receiving Communion is part of the expression of spiritual union that all the communicants share. There is only *one* Communion, not two. Therefore, begin the song when Communion is begun—that is, when the priest receives.

GOSPEL ACCLAMATION
Matt 11:29ab

℟. Alleluia, alleluia.
Take my yoke upon you, says the Lord;
and learn from me, for I am meek and humble of heart.
℟. Alleluia, alleluia.

Gospel Matt 11:25-30; L170A

At that time Jesus exclaimed:
"I give praise to you, Father, Lord of heaven and earth,
for although you have hidden these things
from the wise and the learned
you have revealed them to little ones.
Yes, Father, such has been your gracious will.
All things have been handed over to me by my Father.
No one knows the Son except the Father,
and no one knows the Father except the Son
and anyone to whom the Son wishes to reveal him.

"Come to me, all you who labor and are burdened,
and I will give you rest.
Take my yoke upon you and learn from me,
for I am meek and humble of heart;
and you will find rest for yourselves.
For my yoke is easy, and my burden light."

See Appendix A, p. 296, for the other readings.

Reflecting on the Gospel

The feast of the Most Sacred Heart of Jesus commemorates and celebrates the mercy of God, often represented graphically by the image of a heart. And artistically this is no mere Valentine's Day heart, but a veristic human heart sometimes accompanied by thorns. This feast goes back centuries, to the time of St. Bernard of Clairveaux (1090–1153). In today's age, besides the Most Sacred Heart of Jesus, we also celebrate Divine Mercy Sunday (the Sunday after Easter), which was instituted under Pope St. John Paul II. So there are a number of opportunities for us to celebrate God's mercy, itself a favorite theme of Pope Francis.

The gospel reading for this feast is from Matthew, which begins with a prayer of Jesus to the Father. This prayer reflects "high Christology" of the sort that feels like it could be in the Gospel of John. But we are reminded that such high Christology is not restricted to that gospel alone. Matthew, too, gives us profound reflections (on the lips of Jesus) on the unique and intimate relationship that the Father and the Son have with one another.

Jesus praises the Father because he has hidden "these things from the wise and the learned." Instead, the revelation has been given to the "little ones," the poor, lowly, and outcast.

We might recall that the message of Jesus appealed to those who were on the outskirts of society and religious life. In a world where these "little ones" were kept away from power, wealth, privilege, and status by systemic oppression, Jesus proclaims that the structure has been (or will be) overturned. The wise and the learned now fail to understand. The "little ones" receive a revelation that has been hidden. Is it no wonder that Jesus found his end on a cross?

The mercy of God is revealed in the preaching and the person of Jesus. In the concluding lines of the gospel reading, Jesus encourages those who labor and are burdened to come to him. The lowest classes of society will find refuge in him. Their burden will be light, their yoke easy with him. The unjust systems of the world that keep the "little ones" oppressed, laboring, and burdened will be overturned by the mercy of God. This is good news! But for those who benefit from the system and keep the "little ones" oppressed, Jesus' words are anything but welcome.

Living the Paschal Mystery

On this feast day when we celebrate God's mercy, it is good to remind ourselves of the power of Jesus' message when it was first preached. This was a message of good news to those who had been locked out from the benefits of society: laborers who were cheated wages, slaves who by definition did not enjoy freedom, and those burdened by the affairs of others. Jesus chose to side with those who were the "little ones" rather than with the powerful. As disciples of Jesus, we must heed this call too. We are to champion those who are cheated and denied the benefits of society. When we place our lot with the "little ones" and accompany them on their way, our eyes will be exposed to the mercy of God. It's often said that Jesus came to comfort the afflicted rather than comfort the already comfortable. Who are those afflicted in our own time and day? Let us, as followers of Jesus, accompany them. In so doing, we will be living the paschal mystery.

Focusing the Gospel

Key words and phrases: "I am meek and humble of heart."

To the point: Earlier in Matthew's gospel, Jesus spoke the Beatitude "Blessed are the meek, / for they will inherit the land" (5:5; NABRE). In Jesus' own life we see this lived out—the one who humbles himself even to the point of death on a cross is also the one who is given "all power on heaven and on earth" (28:18; NABRE). As disciples of Christ, we are invited into this paradoxical way of living. Our leader, our master, our Lord, is meek and humble and invites us to be the same.

Model Penitential Act

Presider: On this feast of the Most Sacred Heart of Jesus, we commemorate and celebrate the mercy of God. Grateful for his never-ending love, let us turn to our Lord and ask for his healing and pardon . . . *[pause]*

Lord Jesus, you desire us to find rest in your Sacred Heart: Lord, have mercy.
Christ Jesus, your kindness and compassion are everlasting: Christ, have mercy.
Lord Jesus, you are meek and humble of heart: Lord, have mercy.

Model Universal Prayer (Prayer of the Faithful)

Presider: Through the intercession of Jesus' sacred heart, let us bring our needs, and those of our world, before the God of love.

Response: Lord, hear our prayer.

For God's holy church, may it align itself with the little ones, who are precious to the Lord, in every decision, policy, and campaign of social outreach . . .

For nations struggling under crushing debt and poverty, may they receive assistance that safeguards their dignity and provides for their most vulnerable citizens . . .

For all those who labor and are burdened with the worries of the world, may they find rest and peace within Jesus' sacred heart . . .

For each member of our parish community, confident in the loving kindness of our God, may we reach out in love to all we meet . . .

Presider: God, giver of every good gift, in Jesus' sacred heart you reveal your love for the world. Hear our prayers that day by day your love might be brought to perfection in us so that we might be a sign of it to others. We ask this through Christ our Lord. **Amen.**

About Liturgy

Parish name days: One parish I lived in was named Sacred Heart of Jesus. Each year, their name day came and went without acknowledgment. Today, it is their annual parish fiesta drawing thousands of people from all over the neighborhood.

Today's readings dwell on the love of God that binds us together in Christ as "a people sacred to the Lord" (Deut 7:6). Our parish's patronal feast day, or "name day" or titular day, is a special time for our community members to strengthen that bond of love that makes them a unique expression of the church.

A parish's name day is celebrated as a solemnity in that parish. On that day, the color white may be used and the Gloria sung. If desired and allowed by the liturgical calendar, the celebration of the parish's name day may be transferred to all Masses of a Sunday, if the Sunday is in Ordinary Time and if that Sunday is not a day on which any solemnity of the Lord, of Mary, or of the saints listed in the General Calendar falls.

Look up when your parish's name day happens in the liturgical calendar, and plan to celebrate it well as a community.

COLLECT

Let us pray.

Pause for silent prayer

Grant, we pray, almighty God,
that we, who glory in the Heart of your
beloved Son
and recall the wonders of his love for us,
may be made worthy to receive
an overflowing measure of grace
from that fount of heavenly gifts.
Through our Lord Jesus Christ, your Son,
who lives and reigns with you in the unity of
the Holy Spirit,
one God, for ever and ever. **Amen.**

or:

O God, who in the Heart of your Son,
wounded by our sins,
bestow on us in mercy
the boundless treasures of your love,
grant, we pray,
that, in paying him the homage of our devotion,
we may also offer worthy reparation.
Through our Lord Jesus Christ, your Son,
who lives and reigns with you in the unity of
the Holy Spirit,
one God, for ever and ever. **Amen.**

FOR REFLECTION

- In the first reading and the gospel we see God's preference for the small and little. Who are these "little ones" within your own community? How is God calling you to care for them?
- Today's second readings states plainly, "God is love" and so we are called to "love one another." What is an action of love you would like to commit to this week?
- From which labors or burdens is the Lord inviting you to find rest from in his sacred heart?

Homily Points

- "God is love." In order to know God, we must know love, and if we know love, we love one another. Perhaps this is why Jesus gives praise to God in the gospel for revealing things to the "little ones" that have eluded the "the wise and the learned."
- On this feast of the Sacred Heart of Jesus, we can look to the "little ones" in our midst to show us again the truth of the kingdom of God where love reigns.

SPIRITUALITY

GOSPEL ACCLAMATION
cf. John 15:26b, 27a

℟. Alleluia, alleluia.
The Spirit of truth will testify to me,
says the Lord;
and you also will testify.
℟. Alleluia, alleluia.

Gospel

Matt 10:26-33; L94A

Jesus said to the Twelve:
"Fear no one.
Nothing is concealed that will not be revealed,
nor secret that will not be known.
What I say to you in the darkness, speak in the light;
what you hear whispered, proclaim on the housetops.
And do not be afraid of those who kill the body but cannot kill the soul;
rather, be afraid of the one who can destroy
both soul and body in Gehenna.
Are not two sparrows sold for a small coin?
Yet not one of them falls to the ground without your Father's knowledge.
Even all the hairs of your head are counted.
So do not be afraid; you are worth more than many sparrows.
Everyone who acknowledges me before others
I will acknowledge before my heavenly Father.
But whoever denies me before others,
I will deny before my heavenly Father."

Reflecting on the Gospel

It's nearly the end of June and we are celebrating "Ordinary Time," the Twelfth Sunday of such. Easter is over; Pentecost and the feasts that follow have concluded. Now we enter the liturgical period wherein we will read primarily from the Gospel of Matthew (Cycle A), accompanying Jesus throughout this story, growing in our knowledge and awareness of him.

Matthew has long been known as the "church's gospel." We read the Sermon on the Mount, with its standard form of the Lord's Prayer (as opposed to the shorter version in Luke). Matthew tells us about the giving of the keys of the kingdom to Peter, and he uses the phrase "upon this rock I will build my church." In fact, the very term "church" appears in this gospel alone among the others. With an infancy narrative, resurrection narrative, and much material unique to Matthew, the gospel is twenty-eight chapters long. Compare that to the sixteen chapters of Mark, which was considered something of a "reader's digest" version of Matthew. So it's not surprising that the church placed this gospel first in the canon and preferred reading from it at liturgies. Now we settle in to hear Matthew's version of the Jesus story for much of the rest of the liturgical year.

In the reading we hear today, maybe it is fitting that Jesus says to his disciples three times some variation of "fear not" or "do not be afraid." The disciples (and that includes us) are to be fearless. The basis of this fearlessness is the Father, who knows all—even the most seemingly insignificant things that we do not know (e.g., the hairs on our head). The Father even knows each and every sparrow. We, each human being, is worth more than two sparrows (which themselves were worth only a small coin in antiquity). So the disciples can rest assured: they can be fearless in facing the world, as they are worth a great deal in the sight of God.

With this assurance, with this fearlessness, the disciples are emboldened to acknowledge Jesus and preach him to the ends of the earth (Matt 28:19-20). The danger is for those who know Jesus but choose not to acknowledge him before others. As far as they are concerned, Jesus will not acknowledge them before the Father.

Living the Paschal Mystery

Fearlessness ought to be a mark of Christian discipleship. It is a quality that motivated Jesus throughout his earthly ministry and allowed him to face threats and violence. Fearlessness accompanied him even as he went to his death. Not many of us will be called to make the ultimate sacrifice required for being a disciple of Jesus, though this does happen in parts of the world even today. Instead, our own attitude of fearlessness can manifest itself in caring for those in need and for those on the margins of society. When we overcome our own prejudices and implicit biases, we are dying to ourselves and allowing the spirit of Christ to rise up within us. So let us live as disciples of Jesus, facing the world in a fearless manner, knowing that we are worth a great deal in the sight of our loving God.

Focusing the Gospel

Key words and phrases: "Even all the hairs of your head are counted."

To the point: At the beginning of the tenth chapter of Matthew (from which today's gospel is taken), the twelve apostles are named and then sent out on mission by Jesus. After outlining what they should take (and not take) for the journey, he warns them of the dangers of their quest: "Behold, I am sending you like sheep in the midst of wolves" (10:16; NABRE). It is in this context, after delineating a series of possible persecutions they will undergo (beatings in the synagogues and general hatred from all corners), that Jesus tells them, "Fear no one" and "Do not be afraid." Even if they face death itself, God is with them.

Connecting the Gospel

to the first reading: Jeremiah is a prophet who faced his fair share of persecutions, including being imprisoned in a dungeon and then thrown into a muddy cistern (Jeremiah 38:6). The whisperings of denunciation by Jeremiah's foes are understandable, as Jeremiah was preaching a very unpopular message that the kingdom of Judah should capitulate to the attacking Babylonians. We could say that Jeremiah's outrage at his foes is understandable as well. It is not easy to be a prophet for God, and certainly not when the intended audience for God's prophecies are intent upon getting rid of the message by doing away with the messenger. Despite these hardships, Jeremiah is resolute in his decision to carry on. He has entrusted his cause to the Lord; he cannot fail.

to experience: Throughout the gospels Jesus makes it clear to his disciples that following him will entail hardships and maybe even persecution. And yet we have nothing to fear, for the God of life holds us in the palm of his hand and has counted every hair on our heads.

Connecting the Responsorial Psalm

to the readings: The psalmist sings, "[Z]eal for your house consumes me." This zeal leads to shame and insults, and even to being cast out from family and friends. As with the first reading from Jeremiah, even though this psalm begins with despair it ends in hope, for despite current difficulties, "the Lord hears the poor, / and his own who are in bonds he spurns not." For this reason, the psalmist will continue to praise the Lord. It is the same hope and joy that the apostles are called on to have in the gospel. Though they might face persecution, they are protected unto eternal life by the God of creation. They need not fear.

to psalmist preparation: Has there been a time in your life when you prayed with the conviction and desperation of today's psalm asking, "Lord, in your great love, answer me"? What did this time teach you about faith?

PROMPTS FOR FAITH-SHARING

In the first reading the prophet Jeremiah says to God, "[T]o you I have entrusted my cause." Which cause(s) is near to your heart at this moment in time? How might you entrust it to God's care?

In today's psalm we hear, "For your sake I bear insult, / and shame covers my face." Has there been a time in your life where you experienced insult or shame because of your faith? What helped you get through this time?

Jesus tells his disciples, "Fear no one," and twice he urges them, "[D]o not be afraid." How might you embrace this fearlessness in your life?

Jesus says to the twelve, "Even all the hairs on your head are counted." How have you experienced this abundant love of God in your life?

Model Penitential Act

Presider: In today's gospel Jesus tells his disciples three times that they are not to fear. With abounding trust in the mercy of God, let us turn to him and ask for pardon and peace . . . *[pause]*

Lord Jesus, you are the champion of the poor and downcast: Lord, have mercy.
Christ Jesus, through you we are given everlasting life: Christ, have mercy.
Lord Jesus, you call us to be courageous in faith: Lord, have mercy.

Homily Points

• We have entered into Ordinary Time again, a time of living and growing in our faith. Sometimes it is a relief to get back to "regular life" after a vacation or time of celebration. In a way, the stretch of the liturgical year between now and the first Sunday of Advent is our longest time of "regular life" within the church. We refocus on the everyday joys and challenges of living life in Christ.

• Today's readings seem to point to two great truths of discipleship. The first is that we are greatly loved. Our creator has counted all of the hairs on our heads and we are infinitely precious to him. Thus we know, as today's psalm proclaims, that the Lord hears us when we call out to him, "and his own who are in bonds he spurns not." Which leads us to the second great truth: sometimes we'll be "in bonds."

• Being a follower of Christ does not entitle us to comfort, luxury, and safety; in fact, sometimes it will lead us in the opposite direction. Jesus warns the twelve apostles before he sends them out on mission that they will very likely be met with derision, even stating, "You will be hated by all because of my name" (Matt 10:22). With such dire warnings, it's surprising the apostles didn't walk away at that moment. Perhaps without Jesus' assurances from today's gospel, they would have. Even if they face human hatred, they are to fear no one and nothing, for their souls are protected by the God of everlasting life. As we enter into this time of living and growing in Christ, we are called to sink deeply into these two truths: that discipleship will involve hardships *and* being deeply beloved of God.

Model Universal Prayer (Prayer of the Faithful)

Presider: Jesus tells his disciples of their preciousness to God, stating, "[A]ll the hairs on your head are counted." With trust in God's goodness, let us turn to him in prayer.

Response: Lord, hear our prayer.

For God's holy church, in justice and mercy may it preach God's light in the midst of darkness . . .

For civil authorities and those in elected office, may they wield their power with humility and dedicate themselves to the service of the vulnerable . . .

For those paralyzed by fear and phobias, may the reassurance of God's love and the support of community bring courage and peace . . .

For all gathered here, secure in God's abundant love for us, may we go forth to share this love with all we meet . . .

Presider: Good and gracious God, in the gospel Jesus urges us to be fearless in the life of discipleship. Hear our prayers that your peace may reign in the hearts of all who worship you and that this peace may be spread through all the world. We ask this through Christ our Lord. **Amen.**

COLLECT

Let us pray.

Pause for silent prayer

Grant, O Lord,
that we may always revere and love your holy name,
for you never deprive of your guidance
those you set firm on the foundation of your love.
Through our Lord Jesus Christ, your Son,
who lives and reigns with you in the unity of the Holy Spirit,
one God, for ever and ever. **Amen.**

FIRST READING

Jer 20:10-13

Jeremiah said:
"I hear the whisperings of many:
'Terror on every side!
Denounce! Let us denounce him!'
All those who were my friends
are on the watch for any misstep of mine.
'Perhaps he will be trapped; then we can prevail,
and take our vengeance on him.'
But the LORD is with me, like a mighty champion:
my persecutors will stumble, they will not triumph.
In their failure they will be put to utter shame,
to lasting, unforgettable confusion.
O LORD of hosts, you who test the just,
who probe mind and heart,
let me witness the vengeance you take on them,
for to you I have entrusted my cause.
Sing to the LORD,
praise the LORD,
for he has rescued the life of the poor
from the power of the wicked!"

RESPONSORIAL PSALM
Ps 69:8-10, 14, 17, 33-35

℟. (14c) Lord, in your great love, answer me.

For your sake I bear insult,
and shame covers my face.
I have become an outcast to my brothers,
a stranger to my children,
because zeal for your house consumes me,
and the insults of those who blaspheme
you fall upon me.

℟. Lord, in your great love, answer me.

I pray to you, O LORD,
for the time of your favor, O God!
In your great kindness answer me
with your constant help.
Answer me, O LORD, for bounteous is your
kindness;
in your great mercy turn toward me.

℟. Lord, in your great love, answer me.

"See, you lowly ones, and be glad;
you who seek God, may your hearts
revive!
For the LORD hears the poor,
and his own who are in bonds he spurns
not.
Let the heavens and the earth praise him,
the seas and whatever moves in them!"

℟. Lord, in your great love, answer me.

SECOND READING
Rom 5:12-15

Brothers and sisters:
Through one man sin entered the world,
and through sin, death,
and thus death came to all men,
inasmuch as all sinned—
for up to the time of the law, sin was in
the world,
though sin is not accounted when there
is no law.
But death reigned from Adam to Moses,
even over those who did not sin
after the pattern of the trespass of
Adam,
who is the type of the one who was to
come.

But the gift is not like the transgression.
For if by the transgression of the one the
many died,
how much more did the grace of God
and the gracious gift of the one man
Jesus Christ
overflow for the many.

About Liturgy

Transitions: This time of year sees us marking many different transitions in both family and parish life, with graduations, families moving into and out of the parish, and parish staff and pastors receiving new assignments or retiring from ministry.

For graduates, the United States bishops' *Catholic Household Blessings and Prayers*, revised edition, gives us a prayer before a child's graduation (part IV). The *Book of Blessings* gives us official blessings for welcoming new parishioners (chapter 66) and for departing parishioners (chapter 67). The *Book of Blessings* also includes an official order for the installation of a new pastor (appendix I). However, there is no blessing of a staff person or pastor leaving a parish. Here is a prayer you can adapt for your community:

Lord Jesus, from the beginning of creation you named and claimed us for yourself. Look with kindness upon your servant, N., who leaves this community, marked by your cross, fed by your word, filled with our care, and sent to be your presence to all she/he meets. Guide her/him on the way, and bless her/him with your wisdom, that she/he may be a word of hope for a world in need. We ask this through Christ our Lord. Amen.

About Initiation

Summer catechesis: Summer is meant for rest and recreation, and no one really wants to come to meetings if they don't have to. So how do you do year-round catechesis when everyone is in summer break mode?

This is the perfect time to reimagine catechesis and to remember that everything the parish does—because Christ is present whenever two or three are gathered in his name—can be an opportunity to encounter Christ and to deepen our intimacy with Christ through the community.

Instead of trying to schedule weekly RCIA sessions, look at what your parish has planned for the summer and recommend that your catechumens and candidates, with their sponsors, participate in a few of those activities. Look especially for social events and service opportunities. For example, the parish's summer picnic, the Knights of Columbus breakfast, the annual neighborhood cleanup day, the summer movie fest, building the parish float for the local parade—all these can become catechetical moments when your catechumens and candidates learn how to do what Catholics do to deepen their love of God's word, their sense of community, their prayer life, and their service to those in need.

About Liturgical Music

Singing our blessings: On various occasions at Sunday Mass, the community will want to bless a specific person or group of people. Although these don't usually require additional music, it would be a good practice to have a sung acclamation that the assembly can sing as part of the blessing.

There are short pieces that have been composed specifically as blessings sung by the assembly: "May the Road Rise Up" (Tom Kendzia, OCP); "May God Bless and Keep You" (Christopher Walker, OCP); "Irish Blessing" (Bob Fabing, SJ, OCP). You could also use a refrain or part of a refrain of a well-known song as a blessing acclamation. For example, the section that begins "Rejoice and be glad, yours is the kingdom of God" from "Blest Are They" (David Haas, GIA) or the entire refrain of Michael Joncas's "On Eagle's Wings" (OCP) could be immediately used within a blessing with little instruction to the assembly.

GOSPEL ACCLAMATION
cf. Luke 1:76

℟. Alleluia, alleluia.
You, child, will be called prophet of the Most High,
for you will go before the Lord to prepare his way.
℟. Alleluia, alleluia.

Gospel Luke 1:57-66, 80; L587

When the time arrived for Elizabeth to have her child
she gave birth to a son.
Her neighbors and relatives heard
that the Lord had shown his great mercy toward her,
and they rejoiced with her.
When they came on the eighth day to circumcise the child,
they were going to call him Zechariah after his father,
but his mother said in reply,
"No. He will be called John."
But they answered her,
"There is no one among your relatives who has this name."
So they made signs, asking his father what he wished him to be called.

Continued in Appendix A, p. 297.

See Appendix A, p. 297, for the other readings.

Reflecting on the Gospel

The birth of John the Baptist prefigured the birth of Jesus according to the Gospel of Luke. Perhaps surprisingly, Luke is the only New Testament author to give us this story about John the Baptist. And Luke is the only one to tell us that Jesus and John were cousins, as their mothers were sisters. The historicity and biological veracity of Luke's claim are generally not a matter for preaching, though they provide fertile ground for a rich imagination. Scholars of Scripture are dubious about these biological claims too, since no other New Testament author speaks to it. Still, the theological point at issue is something that all can accept: John the Baptist foreshadowed the way of Jesus.

In today's gospel reading, Zechariah, Elizabeth's husband and the father of the child, had earlier been struck dumb, literally speechless. It is up to Elizabeth to name the child and she does so with conviction. Even when she faces questioning, she does not relent. Zechariah himself supports her and the name for the child. After this act of solidarity, "his mouth was opened, his tongue freed, and he spoke blessing God." Luke writes a cinematic masterpiece filled with drama. It is apparent to all that this child is special, unique, called to some greater purpose.

Again, in pithy words worthy of a great storyteller, Luke informs us that "the child grew and became strong in spirit / and he was in the desert until the day / of his manifestation to Israel." We are left to imagine, if these wondrous events surrounded the nativity of John the Baptist, what will the nativity of Jesus reveal? Of course, we know the answer, as we are too familiar with the story. But it is a good exercise to read it as though we were reading it anew. The evangelist Luke is a theologian. And the theology he conveys through these short stories is profound, inspiring reflection for centuries.

Living the Paschal Mystery

When we encounter the birth of a child or attend a baptism, sometimes our thoughts wander to the future. What is in store for this child? What will she become? What decisions will he make? What will be her loves, his inspirations? Will this young child have children someday? Grandchildren? We might even wonder what end, or death, this person will face in the future. Will tragedy befall this person? Eventually our mind's attention turns back to the present, and we focus again on the child in our midst with all her potential.

John the Baptist (and Jesus) had births that were filled with wonder. The precious life of John caused the community to wonder, "What, then, will this child be?" We share this question with each new birth. And yet we know that John the Baptist (and Jesus) faced violent ends. The birth of a baby and the violent execution of that same person decades later is hard to fathom. Yet these events also happen in our midst all too often.

As Christians, we are to accompany those in our lives. We do not abandon one when the going gets tough. Instead, we witness the sacredness of life at all stages.

Focusing the Gospel

Key words and phrases: The child grew and became strong in spirit.

To the point: When someone becomes famous later on in life, oftentimes attention is then paid to his or her earlier, relatively unknown years. Luke offers us the background story of John's conception and birth. Even at the time of his circumcision there is wonder surrounding this child. He is set apart, for "the hand of the Lord was with him." Just as this child must have grown physically, mentally, and emotionally, we are told he grows "strong in spirit" as well. John remains a model for us of fidelity and single-mindedness in the service of God.

Model Penitential Act

Presider: On the nativity of John the Baptist we remember this great saint, so strong in spirit and devoted to the Lord. We pause to ask forgiveness for the times we have not lived up to his example . . . *[pause]*

Lord Jesus, you are the Light of the World of whom John the Baptist testifies: Lord, have mercy.

Christ Jesus, you are the Lamb of God who takes away the sins of the world: Christ, have mercy.

Lord Jesus, you call us to faithful discipleship: Lord, have mercy.

Model Universal Prayer (Prayer of the Faithful)

Presider: Through the intercession of John the Baptist who proclaimed the Christ even from the womb, let us bring our needs before the Lord.

Response: Lord, hear our prayer.

For leaders of the church, with the fidelity and devotion of John the Baptist may they testify to the truth in word and deed . . .

For nations endowed with wealth and luxury, may they find innovative ways to share resources with those in need . . .

For all those who are brought low by the enslaving power of sin, may they heed the Baptist's call to repentance and live in the freedom of Christ . . .

For all gathered here, may we grow strong in spirit, ready to answer the call of the Lord to service . . .

Presider: God of glory and might, in John the Baptist you have given us a model of single-minded love and devotion in the life of faith. Hear our prayers that we might also testify to the Lamb of God in word and action. We ask this through Christ our Lord. **Amen.**

About Liturgy

Delighting in the calendar: The marking of Christian time is a kind of sacramental encounter with the mystery of Christ. The way we observe the various memorials and seasons of the year is not linear or literal. We should not look for exactness in the calendar, as if Jesus' birthday were exactly December 25 and John's were June 24. Rather, these memorials and seasons are doorways into *kairos*, God's perfect time to encounter us in our human *chronos* time.

However, our spiritual tradition does delight in incorporating familiar human and cosmic elements into our time keeping. Thus, at the annunciation, the angel tells Mary that Elizabeth, John's mother, is already six months pregnant. Therefore, it is only fitting that John's birth is marked six months before Jesus'. We also see in the birth of Jesus the light of the world, thus his birth occurs near the winter solstice and the growing daylight in the Northern Hemisphere. In the birth of John, the forerunner of Christ, of whom John said, "He must increase; I must decrease" (John 3:30), his birth occurs near the summer solstice when the hours of daylight begin to wane.

COLLECT

Let us pray.

Pause for silent prayer

O God, who raised up Saint John the Baptist
to make ready a nation fit for Christ the Lord,
give your people, we pray,
the grace of spiritual joys
and direct the hearts of all the faithful
into the way of salvation and peace.
Through our Lord Jesus Christ, your Son,
who lives and reigns with you in the unity
of the Holy Spirit,
one God, for ever and ever. **Amen.**

FOR REFLECTION

- In the first reading God tells the prophet Isaiah, "I will make you a light to the nations." How does your family, parish, or the universal church strive to be a light in darkness?
- The psalmist sings, "I give thanks that I am fearfully, wonderfully made." How have you been "wonderfully made"? What are the gifts and talents you thank God for?
- In John the Baptist we find the last and greatest of the biblical prophets. On our baptism we were also anointed as priest, prophet, and king. How do you exercise prophetic ministry?

Homily Points

- Paul quotes the Old Testament where God testifies, "I have found David, son of Jesse, a man after my own heart." What an apt description of what it is to be a saint! We see this lived out in John the Baptist. From the womb, John leaps for joy when the Lord approaches. His every action and every word is intent upon testifying to the glory of God.

- The intervening years between John's birth and adulthood are spent in the desert becoming strong in the spirit. John's life in the desert reminds us of what is essential: to serve the Lord with single-minded integrity and love. In this way we become a person after God's own heart.

SPIRITUALITY

GOSPEL ACCLAMATION
1 Peter 2:9

℟. Alleluia, alleluia.
You are a chosen race, a royal priesthood, a holy nation;
announce the praises of him who called you out of darkness into his wonderful light.
℟. Alleluia, alleluia.

Gospel

Matt 10:37-42; L97A

Jesus said to his apostles:
"Whoever loves father or mother more than me is not worthy of me,
and whoever loves son or daughter more than me is not worthy of me;
and whoever does not take up his cross
and follow after me is not worthy of me.

"Whoever finds his life will lose it,
and whoever loses his life for my sake will find it.
Whoever receives you receives me,
and whoever receives me receives the one who sent me.
Whoever receives a prophet because he is a prophet
will receive a prophet's reward,
and whoever receives a righteous man
because he is a righteous man
will receive a righteous man's reward.
And whoever gives only a cup of cold water
to one of these little ones to drink
because the little one is a disciple—
amen, I say to you, he will surely not lose his reward."

Reflecting on the Gospel

The seemingly paradoxical saying "Youth is wasted on the young" is attributed to George Bernard Shaw. Deep wisdom is conveyed in this short statement, and it causes us to ponder not only our past but even our present, and none of us will be younger than we are today. The comedian George Carlin asked the paradoxical question, "If you try to fail and you succeed, which have you done?"

The Christian life is marked by paradox, the greatest of which is the God-human Jesus. But many more paradoxes abound: death leads to life, to give is to receive, and emptying oneself is the means to fulfillment.

The gospel reading today reflects some of these fundamental Christian paradoxes as well: "Whoever finds his life will lose it, and whoever loses his life for my sake will find it." This kind of teaching is fairly common among religious wisdom figures, and we shouldn't be surprised to hear it on the lips of Jesus.

Prior to this aphorism, Jesus claims that anyone who loves father or mother more than Jesus is not worthy of him. This may sound off-putting to modern ears. It's interesting to note that Matthew seems to have modified his source material for this passage, which likely read something like what we find in Luke (14:26): "If any one comes to me without hating his father and mother, wife and children, brothers and sisters, and even his own life, he cannot be my disciple." The term "hate" is much stronger than the "love more" we find in Matthew. The point of course is that Jesus ought to be the center and focus of one's life. Not even family relations should come first.

Those worthy of Jesus are the ones who take up their cross and follow him. This does not mean to seek out suffering and place oneself in harm's way merely for the sake of it. It certainly does not give license for Christians to act in obnoxious ways so they can consider the consequences of that behavior "suffering for Christ." Rather, taking up one's cross refers to managing any and all of the difficulties and challenges that come with following Jesus. The image of the cross calls to mind violent and public execution at the hands of the state. Moreover, it foreshadows Jesus' own end on a cross. His followers should not shy away from such duties that flow naturally from being a Christian. As Jesus did, to gain life we must give it away. This is the ultimate paradox.

Living the Paschal Mystery

The paschal mystery is a paradox par excellence. Suffering and death lead to new life and resurrection. There can be no resurrection without death. There is no new life without casting aside the old. When we listen to the words of Jesus in today's gospel, we might be especially attuned to the notion of paradox expressed in the saying about finding our lives—for to find our lives, we must lose them. We surrender ourselves to the will of God and thereby find ultimate meaning and purpose. As Augustine said, "[O]ur hearts are restless until they rest in you Lord."

When we busy ourselves with projects, deadlines, and goals that give us a sense of urgency and meaning, we might be missing the quintessential meaning of our lives, which may be found in stillness and quiet. It's the paradox reflected in the U2 song "Running to Stand Still." During this Thirteenth Sunday in Ordinary Time, we might pause to consider our ultimate purpose and meaning. Are we running to stand still? Are we restless until we rest in the Lord? Only by giving over our very selves will we receive even more. By embracing the cross, Christ experienced exaltation and new life, showing us the way to the same.

Focusing the Gospel

Key words and phrases: "Whoever receives you receives me."

To the point: Today's passage continues with chapter 10 from the Gospel of Matthew, which we heard last week. Jesus is continuing his instructions to the twelve apostles before sending them forth on mission. While warning of the persecutions they might face, Jesus also assures them of their preciousness in the sight of God. They are so closely connected to their Master that when any action (good or bad) is done to or for the disciples, it is as if it had been done to Jesus himself.

Connecting the Gospel

to the first reading: The second part of today's gospel focuses on hospitality and the reward for it. Jesus talks of the rewards of receiving a prophet, a "righteous man," and also of giving a "little one" a drink of water. In each instance the person who provides hospitality will be rewarded for his or her efforts. In today's first reading this is played out with the story of Elisha the prophet, who is offered a room by a woman who is childless. Wishing to repay her hospitality, Elisha promises her that in a year's time she will be "fondling a baby son." Although we don't hear about it in today's reading from the second book of Kings, Elisha's prophecy comes true and the woman does bear a son. Several years later Elisha will repay the woman's hospitality again when her son falls ill and dies. At the widow's insistence, Elisha returns to her house where he revives the child and gives him back to his mother (2 Kgs 4:36-37).

to experience: In the ancient world hospitality was a very important custom. Living in a harsh environment, if one turned away a wayfarer who was in need of food or water, it could lead to death. In today's society, with concerns over one's own personal safety, hospitality to strangers has become increasingly rare. What are some ways you, your family, or your parish community offers hospitality to others?

Connecting the Responsorial Psalm

to the readings: Today's psalm of joy and praise seems to be a fitting response from the childless woman who is promised a son. At that time, a woman who became widowed would rely on her sons for support. If a woman had no sons, she would be at the mercy of the community to provide for her. The woman of Shunem was in danger of this fate since "her husband was getting on in years." When Elisha prophesies that she will have a son, this not only meant that she would enjoy the blessings of children but also that she would be protected from destitution when her husband died.

to psalmist preparation: Today's psalm is a litany to God's goodness. In the Lord is found light, kindness, justice, strength, and protection. What would be your litany (list) of the blessings of the Lord in your life?

PROMPTS FOR FAITH-SHARING

In the first reading from the second book of Kings, we find an example of hospitality in the care given to Elisha. How does hospitality figure into the life of your family?

The psalmist proclaims, "Forever I will sing the goodness of the Lord." For which of God's blessings are you particularly thankful today?

St. Paul urges the Romans to think of themselves as "dead to sin / and living for God in Christ Jesus." Within your daily life what are the actions or habits that show you are a person "living for God"?

Jesus tells the apostles, "[W]hoever does not take up his cross / and follow after me is not worthy of me." What does the cross look like that you are called to carry?

Model Penitential Act

Presider: In the gospel Jesus tells his apostles, "[W]hoever does not take up his cross / and follow after me is not worthy of me." For the times we have failed in the life of discipleship, let us ask for mercy and healing . . . *[pause]*

Lord Jesus, you are the promised one of God: Lord, have mercy.
Christ Jesus, you are our shield, strength, and salvation: Christ, have mercy.
Lord Jesus, you call us to take up our crosses and follow you: Lord, have mercy.

Homily Points

• In today's challenging gospel, Jesus tells the twelve apostles, "[W]hoever does not take up his cross / and follow after me is not worthy of me." Later on in Matthew's gospel we'll hear this sentiment another way: "Whoever wishes to come after me must deny himself, take up his cross, and follow me" (16:24; NABRE). What a startling command to hear on the lips of the Lord of life—in order to be his follower, one must become comfortable with a symbol of torture and death, so comfortable as to carry it in one's arms on the journey of faith.

• Our second reading today is from St. Paul's letter to the Romans. It's the same epistle that we read each year on the Easter Vigil and it begins with Paul's question: "Are you unaware that we who were baptized into Christ Jesus / were baptized into his death?" Within the paschal mystery, life and death are irrevocably tied together. But it's not as one would think—that life inevitably leads to death. Instead, this logic is turned on its head, and *death* becomes the passageway to life everlasting.

• In chapter 10 of Matthew's gospel, Jesus is preparing the apostles to go out on their first mission without him. He warns them of the persecutions they will likely face and outlines what they should take and what they should leave behind on this journey. Today's gospel reading is the last segment of Jesus' rather lengthy instructions. In it, he sums up what the disciples should be prepared to lose as they follow him. They must love him more than family and more than life itself. Only in being willing to lose it all will they receive the abundant life he wishes to give them. Such is the life of discipleship.

Model Universal Prayer (Prayer of the Faithful)

Presider: Believing in the light of Christ, which banishes all darkness, let us bring our needs, and the needs of our world, before the Lord.

Response: Lord, hear our prayer.

For God's holy church, through practicing radical hospitality, may all people know they are welcome and loved in the sight of God . . .

For nations torn apart by the ravages of civil war, may civilians be protected and peace restored . . .

For young people seeking direction and lives of meaning, may they be emboldened to take up their crosses and follow the Lord of life . . .

For all gathered here, may our fidelity to and love of God ensure the passing on of the faith to future generations . . .

Presider: Creator God, you have made the world and all that is in it and proclaimed that it is good. Hear our prayers that as faithful disciples, we might take on the task of restoring and repairing creation through the work of our hands. We ask this through Christ our Lord. **Amen.**

COLLECT

Let us pray.

Pause for silent prayer

O God, who through the grace of adoption
chose us to be children of light,
grant, we pray,
that we may not be wrapped in the
darkness of error
but always be seen to stand in the bright
light of truth.
Through our Lord Jesus Christ, your Son,
who lives and reigns with you in the unity
of the Holy Spirit,
one God, for ever and ever. **Amen.**

FIRST READING

2 Kgs 4:8-11, 14-16a

One day Elisha came to Shunem,
where there was a woman of influence,
who urged him to dine with her.
Afterward, whenever he passed by, he
used to stop there to dine.
So she said to her husband, "I know that
Elisha is a holy man of God.
Since he visits us often, let us arrange a
little room on the roof
and furnish it for him with a bed, table,
chair, and lamp,
so that when he comes to us he can stay
there."
Sometime later Elisha arrived and stayed
in the room overnight.

Later Elisha asked, "Can something be
done for her?"
His servant Gehazi answered, "Yes!
She has no son, and her husband is
getting on in years."
Elisha said, "Call her."
When the woman had been called and
stood at the door,
Elisha promised, "This time next year
you will be fondling a baby son."

RESPONSORIAL PSALM
Ps 89:2-3, 16-17, 18-19

℟. (2a) Forever I will sing the goodness of the Lord.

The promises of the LORD I will sing forever,
through all generations my mouth shall proclaim your faithfulness.
For you have said, "My kindness is established forever";
in heaven you have confirmed your faithfulness.

℟. Forever I will sing the goodness of the Lord.

Blessed the people who know the joyful shout;
in the light of your countenance, O LORD, they walk.
At your name they rejoice all the day,
and through your justice they are exalted.

℟. Forever I will sing the goodness of the Lord.

You are the splendor of their strength,
and by your favor our horn is exalted.
For to the LORD belongs our shield,
and to the Holy One of Israel, our king.

℟. Forever I will sing the goodness of the Lord.

SECOND READING
Rom 6:3-4, 8-11

Brothers and sisters:
Are you unaware that we who were baptized into Christ Jesus
were baptized into his death?
We were indeed buried with him through baptism into death,
so that, just as Christ was raised from the dead
by the glory of the Father,
we too might live in newness of life.

If, then, we have died with Christ,
we believe that we shall also live with him.
We know that Christ, raised from the dead, dies no more;
death no longer has power over him.
As to his death, he died to sin once and for all;
as to his life, he lives for God.
Consequently, you too must think of yourselves as dead to sin
and living for God in Christ Jesus.

About Liturgy

Basic hospitality: To really know how welcoming your community is, you'll need to do a little test. Find a friend or two who have never been to your parish and do not know anyone there. If they're not Catholic, even better! Ask your friends to come to Mass one Sunday and experience it as a visitor would. Tell them just the name and city of your church and nothing else. They will need to rely on your parish's website or find your parish phone number to get your Mass schedule and address. Ask them not to seek you out when they're there but just to observe what it is like being a visitor looking for a church community to join.

After their visit, meet with them and ask them questions similar to a customer service survey: How easy was it to find Mass times, the church address, and other information you needed? How easy was it to find parking and the church door? Were you greeted at the door? How many people welcomed you? On a scale of 1 to 5, rate how welcomed you felt. Did the entryway and church space look inviting? Was it easy to find the music and responses for the Mass? Did someone greet you after Mass and invite you to return again? Could you find the restrooms easily? Were they clean? Would you recommend our church to a friend?

About Initiation

Welcoming seekers: Seekers come to your church every day. They'll show up at Sunday Mass or a wedding, funeral, or baptism. Maybe they're new to the neighborhood, or they're going through a rough time in their life and need a place to pray and maybe someone to talk to. Or their parent just died, and they don't know what to do. Or they're getting married and have always dreamt of a church wedding but haven't been attending church in a long time.

Whether or not these seekers are looking to be initiated, the role of the faithful is always the same: "[T]he supreme purpose of the apostolate is that Christ's message is made known to the world by word and deed and that his grace is communicated" (RCIA 9.1).

Try the test described in "Basic hospitality" above. Then look at RCIA 9.1 and read the "job description" of the faithful for when they encounter any seeker. Look for ways that your community members can "give [seekers] evidence of the spirit of the Christian community and to welcome them into their homes, into personal conversation, and into community gatherings."

About Liturgical Music

Patriotic songs: With next week being the Fourth of July, this is a good time to rephrase today's gospel: "Whoever loves nation more than me is not worthy of me."

The focus of Christian liturgy is always praise to the Father through Christ in the Spirit. Simply because a song mentions God does not mean the song is directed to God and gives praise for the gift of Jesus. "America the Beautiful" sings of our country's beauty, not God's. "God Bless America," although addressed to God, is primarily, again, about our nation and makes no mention of Christ or Christ's sacrifice.

The inclusion of patriotic songs in Catholic hymnals is not meant to encourage their use at the Mass but rather to offer people the option of singing these songs at other gatherings and events that specifically focus on our nation.

Catholics should pray for their nation, and we should be patriotic. When we gather as a nation for events about our nation, we should sing our patriotic songs. But when we gather as a people of God at the liturgical rituals of our faith, God and God's love in Christ should be at the center of our song.

GOSPEL ACCLAMATION
Matt 16:18

℟. Alleluia, alleluia.
You are Peter and upon this rock I will build my Church,
and the gates of the netherworld shall not prevail against it.
℟. Alleluia, alleluia.

Gospel Matt 16:13-19; L591

When Jesus went into the region of Caesarea Philippi
he asked his disciples,
"Who do people say that the Son of Man is?"
They replied, "Some say John the Baptist, others Elijah,
still others Jeremiah or one of the prophets."
He said to them, "But who do you say that I am?"
Simon Peter said in reply,
"You are the Christ, the Son of the living God."
Jesus said to him in reply, "Blessed are you, Simon son of Jonah.
For flesh and blood has not revealed this to you, but my heavenly Father.

Continued in Appendix A, p. 298.

See Appendix A, p. 298, for the other readings.

Reflecting on the Gospel

Companions are sometimes also friendly competitors. John Lennon and Paul McCartney wrote songs together and each said the other made him a better writer. Lennon wrote "Strawberry Fields Forever" and McCartney followed it with "Penny Lane." Lennon wrote the opening and closing of "A Day in the Life," with McCartney writing the middle section. That song in particular has been called one of the best. The Lennon-McCartney partnership had some creative tension that produced some of the most popular music of all time. Each made the other better. Perhaps something similar was at work with Peter and Paul.

Interestingly, each of the saints began life with a different name. Peter (the name means Rock) was initially known as Simon, son of Jonah. It was Jesus himself who gave Simon the name Peter as we learn in today's gospel. In Matthew's telling, Jesus gave him this name after Simon confessed Jesus as Messiah, the Christ. Matthew's version of the story also has Jesus giving Simon the keys to the kingdom and saying that he would build his church on this rock (a play on words, as "Peter" means "rock," as noted above). Matthew is the only gospel to even use the word "church" and it's clear that this is an important topic for him. The Gospel of John, on the other hand, never uses the word "church" and portrays Jesus naming Simon "Peter" before Simon ever does or says anything! (1:42)

Paul was earlier known as Saul. Nothing so dramatic as Simon's name-changing by Jesus happened with Paul. Instead, we are informed as an aside that Saul was also known as Paul (Acts 13:9). After that seemingly inconsequential comment, he is never referred to as Saul again! Of course, in his letters he refers to himself only as Paul. So if we had only his letters, we would not be aware that he was ever known as Saul. We need the Acts of the Apostles for that bit of information.

The renaming follows a biblical theme that appears occasionally in the Old Testament. Of the many examples, we recall that Abraham was first known as Abram and that Sarah was first known as Sarai.

We also know from the Acts of the Apostles and from some of Paul's letters that Peter and Paul knew each other and interacted occasionally. The two men had their differences, even though each was called by Christ. Paul was known as the Apostle to the Gentiles (or the uncircumcised) whereas Peter was the Apostle to the Jews (or the circumcised). Each had their own mission within a broader purpose. And it's likely that each made the other better. Paul spurred Peter to consider the full ramifications of baptizing Gentiles, and Peter shared stories of Jesus with Paul.

Let us recall that no one of us has everything it means to be a follower of Christ. If Peter and Paul complemented one another, our own ministry and identity will be complemented by others as well.

Living the Paschal Mystery

In the midst of summer when we celebrate the feast of Sts. Peter and Paul, we are reminded that discipleship is something we do together. It is not simply a "me and Jesus" relationship. Even Peter, who was named Rock upon which the church was built and who had spent years with Jesus, had Paul, someone who did not know Jesus and who was called after the resurrection. And Paul, a highly educated Pharisee, was complemented by an "uneducated, ordinary" fisherman, Peter (Acts 4:13).

As disciples of Jesus, we are called to be in community. Jesus chooses the community, not us. We might think a community of our own choosing would be better, but that is not the way Jesus would have it. Instead, we die to our own conceptions and desires, and open ourselves up to what Jesus would have.

Focusing the Gospel

Key words and phrases: "[W]ho do you say that I am?"

To the point: In today's gospel, Jesus asks the quintessential question of discipleship: "[W]ho do you say that I am?" In order to be a disciple, one must know that person deeply. Although Peter answers the question with his proclamation, "You are the [Christ], the Son of the living God," Peter and Paul both answered it even more profoundly with their lives. In their teaching and apostolic ministry, they gave witness to Jesus, the Light of the World, who had called them to spread this light to others. Their deaths testified to Jesus, the Lord of life, who conquered death once and for all and offers eternal life to his followers.

Model Penitential Act

Presider: In Sts. Peter and Paul we are given models of discipleship and apostolic vigor. As we celebrate this feast day, let us pause to call to mind the times we have fallen short in the life of discipleship and to ask for God's mercy . . . *[pause]*

Lord Jesus, you deliver us from all our fears: Lord, have mercy.
Christ Jesus, you are our strength and our salvation: Christ, have mercy.
Lord Jesus, you are the Christ, the Son of the living God: Lord, have mercy.

Model Universal Prayer (Prayer of the Faithful)

Presider: Through the intercession of Sts. Peter and Paul, who gave their lives for Christ and his church, let us bring our needs before the Lord.

Response: Lord, hear our prayer.

For bishops and priests, may they be animated by the apostolic vigor of Sts. Peter and Paul and be strengthened to lead selflessly and fearlessly . . .

For all nations of the world, may they work together to ensure freedom of religion and to offer safety to those enduring persecution . . .

For all those who are lacking or struggling in faith, may they persevere and never cease turning to Jesus, the way, the truth, and the life . . .

For all gathered here to celebrate the feast day of Sts. Peter and Paul, may we be delivered from our fears and nourished to continue the journey of faith . . .

Presider: God, our strength and salvation, through the blood of the martyrs your church was planted on the earth. Hear our prayers that through the intercession of Sts. Peter and Paul it might continue to flourish and grow. We ask this through Christ our Lord. **Amen.**

About Liturgy

Who do you say that I am? The way we speak about our faith in Jesus matters. We cannot let our "insider lingo" and doctrinal language get in the way of evangelization. Peter spoke plainly with passion that made him seem drunk to his hearers, but he inspired entire communities to conversion. Paul, though infamous for his one-page sentences, always made sure to let his deeds of service speak clearly about his love for Christ who saved him. Whether in eloquent, impassioned speech or in letters, both apostles had the goal of communicating *who* Jesus was for them and not merely facts and teachings *about* Jesus. Let us ask Sts. Peter and Paul to give us words that matter and inspire us to deeds that announce clearly our faith.

COLLECT

Let us pray.

Pause for silent prayer

O God, who on the Solemnity of the Apostles
Peter and Paul
give us the noble and holy joy of this day,
grant, we pray, that your Church
may in all things follow the teaching
of those through whom she received
the beginnings of right religion.
Through our Lord Jesus Christ, your Son,
who lives and reigns with you in the unity of
the Holy Spirit,
one God, for ever and ever. **Amen.**

FOR REFLECTION

- In the first reading we hear of Peter's miraculous escape from prison. Where are you in need of God's freeing power in your life?
- St. Paul writes on the brink of his execution, secure in what he has done and in God's faithfulness. When you think of the moment of your own death, what are the actions you have done (or would like to do) that will bring you comfort?
- Jesus asks his disciples, "[W]ho do you say that I am?" How would you answer this question in your own words of faith?

Homily Points

- In the readings we find Sts. Peter and Paul both in prison. Despite Peter's escape, we know that both will eventually undergo a martyr's death. While they both faced struggles in life (Peter denied Jesus three times and Paul violently persecuted the early church), their growth in discipleship and fidelity to the Lord is apparent. Neither Paul nor Peter express fear in the face of imprisonment and likely execution.
- Though most of us will not face a martyr's death, we will all face the end as Peter and Paul did. Today might be a good moment to pause and reflect on our own journey of faith. What corrections or changes might be necessary so that when we approach death we can say, as Paul did, "I have finished the race; / I have kept the faith"?

SPIRITUALITY

GOSPEL ACCLAMATION
cf. Matt 11:25

℟. Alleluia, alleluia.
Blessed are you, Father, Lord of heaven and earth;
you have revealed to little ones the mysteries of the kingdom.
℟. Alleluia, alleluia.

Gospel

Matt 11:25-30; L100A

At that time Jesus exclaimed:
"I give praise to you, Father, Lord of heaven and earth,
for although you have hidden these things
from the wise and the learned
you have revealed them to little ones.
Yes, Father, such has been your gracious will.
All things have been handed over to me by my Father.
No one knows the Son except the Father,
and no one knows the Father except the Son
and anyone to whom the Son wishes to reveal him.

"Come to me, all you who labor and are burdened,
and I will give you rest.
Take my yoke upon you and learn from me,
for I am meek and humble of heart;
and you will find rest for yourselves.
For my yoke is easy, and my burden light."

Reflecting on the Gospel

As we journey with Jesus in the Gospel of Matthew, we encounter him teaching, preaching, praying, and praising. In today's gospel, he seems to do all at once! The passage (which is the same gospel passage that was read at the feast of the Sacred Heart not long ago) opens with Jesus addressing God as "Father, Lord of Heaven and Earth." In some ways this prefigures the language later creeds will use and that we proclaim in the Nicene Creed when we say, "[O]ne God, Father almighty, creator of heaven and earth." The phrase "heaven and earth" may also call to mind the opening verse of Genesis, though there the first term is plural: "heavens and earth." The phrase is used to mean all of creation. The Father is the Lord of all creation. It is his handiwork and there is nothing that stands apart from it that is not under his dominion.

The relationship between the Father and Son is intimate and dynamic. Jesus beckons the disciples into this relationship with the invitation "come to me." The term "yoke" that follows would have conjured up the image of Mosaic Law. Of course, a yoke is a type of wooden harness, bar, or frame used to keep oxen (or cattle) driving in the same direction, at the urging of a master. Wisdom is sometimes referred to as a yoke (Sirach 51:26), as is the law, but not in a negative way. In the New Testament (not only in Matthew but elsewhere), Jesus' ways are also referred to as a yoke.

Jesus tells his disciples that he himself is the yoke, meek and humble of heart. The rest he promises comes from emulating his ways, his attitudes, his dispositions, and his general way of being in the world. The disciple is yoked to Jesus, and the disciple finds this to be a lightness in his or her way of being. The yoke is not burdening or overbearing.

When we are followers of Jesus, when we imbibe his attitudes, our lives will not be burdened but filled with joy or, as Pope Francis might refer to it, the joy of the gospel.

Living the Paschal Mystery

Bearing a yoke would not seem to be an enjoyable experience. But Jesus gives us this image in today's gospel reading and nearly subverts it. The yoke of Jesus, the one who is meek and humble of heart, is itself easy; the burden is light. This seems to be a different image than "take up your cross and follow me." In today's gospel, we learn that when we are true disciples of Christ, we conform to the person himself. So conformed, we find any burden not to be a burden at all.

To live the paschal mystery with Christ is to live with the knowledge that we are his. He has already won the victory. Secure in this relationship with him, we need only act as he would in the world, as another Christ to serve the needs of those around us. Any setback or death we experience will find new life due to the same Christ we serve. This is good news, and a spiritually rewarding way to live the paschal mystery.

Focusing the Gospel

Key words and phrases: "No one knows the Son except the Father, / and no one knows the Father except the Son / and anyone to whom the Son wishes to reveal him."

To the point: As Christians, we come to God the Father through his Son, Jesus Christ. In the person of Jesus we find the "Lord of heaven and earth" revealed. He is the humble carpenter, the son of Mary, who was born among animals in Bethlehem and died upon a cross. He is also the Son of God, whose birth was heralded by angels, whose life conquered death, and who now sits at the right hand of the Father. In Jesus we find God, truly glorious and powerful, and also perfectly meek and humble.

Connecting the Gospel

to the first reading: Our first reading from Zechariah paints a picture of the savior of Jerusalem, "a king," who will be "meek, and riding on an ass," banishing "the chariots from Ephraim, / and the horse from Jerusalem." By using the simpler and humbler transportation of riding on a mule, this figure distances himself from the trappings of the monarchy with their chariots and horses. Of course, this verse calls to mind Jesus' entry into Jerusalem on Palm Sunday, when "Jesus found an ass and sat upon it" (John 12:15; NABRE). In the gospel for today, Jesus praises God for revealing secrets to the "little ones" while concealing them from the "wise and the learned." As we so often see in the gospels and throughout the Bible, God is aligned with the humble and sides with the meek.

to experience: In life it is easy to let the trappings of wealth and power creep in, trappings which are so celebrated by the world. Jesus calls us to another way. Whereas building a life around the acquisition of money or prestige will never really satisfy our deepest longings as humans, in the Lord who is "meek and humble of heart" we can find rest and peace.

Connecting the Responsorial Psalm

to the readings: Today's psalm is one of praise to God, our king. Rather than lauding God's power and strength, the psalmist highlights the grace and mercy of the Lord who is "slow to anger and of great kindness" and "compassionate toward all his works." Within God, the Father, Son, and Holy Spirit, we find the "Lord of heaven and earth" whose concern is for the humble and the lowly.

to psalmist preparation: To honor and praise God well, we must hold both images of the Lord in our mind: the one who reigns over heaven and earth in glory and the one who came to dwell among the meek and the lowly and to identify himself among them. How do you balance these two truths in your prayer and life of discipleship?

PROMPTS FOR FAITH-SHARING

The prophecy of Zechariah reminds us of Jesus' entry into Jerusalem: "See, your king shall come to you; / a just savior is he, / meek and riding on an ass." Where are you being called to follow the example of Jesus and humble yourself?

Today's psalm concludes, "The Lord lifts up all who are falling / and raises up all who are bowed down." Within our world, who are the groups or individuals who are "bowed down"? How might God be calling us to care for them?

St. Paul reminds us that we are given life by "[God's] Spirit that dwells in you." Where have you noticed the Spirit working within you and leading you to greater life?

Jesus lifts up the "little ones" as a model for those who truly desire to understand the mystery of the kingdom of God. Who have been the "little ones" along your faith journey who have taught you the way of the kingdom?

Model Penitential Act

Presider: The truths of the kingdom of God are revealed to the humble. Let us turn to the Lord and ask for him to strip away the pride and vanity that clouds our vision so that we might draw closer to him . . . *[pause]*

Lord Jesus, you are the way, the truth, and the life: Lord, have mercy.
Christ Jesus, you are meek and humble of heart: Christ, have mercy.
Lord Jesus, you desire to give us rest: Lord, have mercy.

Homily Points

• Today's gospel reading seems to provide a stark contrast to the one we heard just last Sunday when Jesus told the disciples that only the one who was willing to take up his cross was worthy of following him. Today we hear Jesus proclaim, "[M]y yoke is easy, and my burden light." Which are we to believe? Is the life of discipleship one of hardship and drudgery or one of comfort and ease?

• Just as Jesus offers many parables to help his disciples understand the mystery of the kingdom of God, it seems he also gives us different images of what it means to be a disciple. As with the parables, no *one* image can completely capture and express what Jesus is trying to relate, but each contains truth.

• We could look at this from the perspective of our own faith journey. Within the life of faith, when have you faced hardship or heartbreak? When we open our hearts to love God and others, we also open ourselves up for pain, disappointment, and grief. And yet, our sure hope in the Lord is that light is stronger than darkness, love is stronger than hatred, and life is stronger than death. This hope eases the burden of the cross, transforming it to the yoke of Jesus. And perhaps it gives us insight into who really carries our crosses. When we are yoked together with the Lord of life, we shoulder the burden together, and as was revealed to St. Paul, Jesus tells us, "My grace is sufficient for you, for power is made perfect in weakness" (2 Cor 12:9; NABRE), another paradox in the life of faith.

Model Universal Prayer (Prayer of the Faithful)

Presider: In perfect trust, let us bring our prayers before the Lord who is meek and humble of heart.

Response: Lord, hear our prayer.

For leaders and ministers within the church, may they look to the humble and lowly for inspiration and understanding as they seek to follow Jesus . . .

For diplomats throughout the world, may they urge peace and work for unity among peoples . . .

For those who have suffered abuse at the hands of a family member or authority figure, may our tender Lord bind up their wounds . . .

For our parish and local community, may we work together to lift up the most vulnerable in our midst and to end all forms of oppression . . .

Presider: God who champions the lowly and lifts up all who are bowed down, you sent your son, Jesus, to teach us the way of humility. Hear our prayers that in following him we may give rest to the weary and build up the kingdom of God. We ask this through Christ our Lord. **Amen.**

COLLECT

Let us pray.

Pause for silent prayer

O God, who in the abasement of your Son
have raised up a fallen world,
fill your faithful with holy joy,
for on those you have rescued from slavery
to sin
you bestow eternal gladness.
Through our Lord Jesus Christ, your Son,
who lives and reigns with you in the unity
of the Holy Spirit,
one God, for ever and ever. **Amen.**

FIRST READING

Zech 9:9-10

Thus says the Lord:
Rejoice heartily, O daughter Zion,
shout for joy, O daughter Jerusalem!
See, your king shall come to you;
a just savior is he,
meek, and riding on an ass,
on a colt, the foal of an ass.
He shall banish the chariot from Ephraim,
and the horse from Jerusalem;
the warrior's bow shall be banished,
and he shall proclaim peace to the
nations.
His dominion shall be from sea to sea,
and from the River to the ends of the
earth.

RESPONSORIAL PSALM

Ps 145:1-2, 8-9, 10-11, 13-14

℟. (cf. 1) I will praise your name forever,
my king and my God.
or:
℟. Alleluia.

I will extol you, O my God and King,
and I will bless your name forever and
ever.
Every day will I bless you,
and I will praise your name forever and
ever.

℟. I will praise your name forever, my
king and my God.
or:
℟. Alleluia.

The LORD is gracious and merciful,
slow to anger and of great kindness.
The LORD is good to all
and compassionate toward all his works.

℟. I will praise your name forever, my king and my God.
or:
℟. Alleluia.

Let all your works give you thanks, O LORD,
and let your faithful ones bless you.
Let them discourse of the glory of your kingdom
and speak of your might.

℟. I will praise your name forever, my king and my God.
or:
℟. Alleluia.

The LORD is faithful in all his words
and holy in all his works.
The LORD lifts up all who are falling
and raises up all who are bowed down.

℟. I will praise your name forever, my king and my God.
or:
℟. Alleluia.

SECOND READING
Rom 8:9, 11-13

Brothers and sisters:
You are not in the flesh;
on the contrary, you are in the spirit,
if only the Spirit of God dwells in you.
Whoever does not have the Spirit of Christ
does not belong to him.
If the Spirit of the one who raised Jesus from the dead dwells in you,
the one who raised Christ from the dead
will give life to your mortal bodies also,
through his Spirit that dwells in you.
Consequently, brothers and sisters,
we are not debtors to the flesh,
to live according to the flesh.
For if you live according to the flesh, you will die,
but if by the Spirit you put to death the deeds of the body,
you will live.

About Liturgy

Praying for our nation: Whenever we gather at Mass, our focus is always directed toward the Father in praise and thanksgiving for the gift of Jesus, the Son. All the ritual gestures we make, the prayers we offer, and the music we sing must enable our contemplation of God.

When choosing music for this weekend, see the liturgical music section from last Sunday. Note, The Constitution on the Sacred Liturgy says, "[S]acred music is to be considered the more holy in proportion as it is more closely connected with the liturgical action, whether it adds delight to prayer, fosters unity of minds, or confers greater solemnity upon the sacred rites" (112). Music (and all the other artistic elements) should closely connect with the liturgical action.

We can use this principle to help us discern whether or not to incorporate any national elements into the liturgy today. There are currently no guidelines regarding the use of flags in the sanctuary. However, the United States bishops have encouraged pastors not to place them in the sanctuary so that the focus can remain on Christ. The use of non-ritual texts as prayers, such as the Pledge of Allegiance or the reading of national documents or speeches, has no place in the Mass. However, it would be very appropriate and necessary to pray for our nation in the universal prayer (intercessions).

Note that although there is a Mass in the Roman Missal for the USA that may be used for the Fourth of July, the usual Saturday evening Mass that day should use the readings and prayers for the Sunday.

About Initiation

Reception into the full Catholic communion: Today's gospel describing the easy yoke of Christ reminds us that we are called to require "no greater burden than necessary . . . for the establishment of communion and unity" (RCIA 473) with those Christians seeking to become Catholic. In fact, the process given to us in the RCIA is meant to allow Protestants to be received *as soon as they are ready*. The United States bishops state: "Those baptized persons who have lived as Christians and need only instruction in the Catholic tradition and a degree of probation with the Catholic community should not be asked to undergo a full program parallel to the catechumenate" (National Statutes 31). They should not need to wait until Easter, nor should they celebrate the optional Rite of Welcoming or any of the other optional rites for the baptized. Recall that RCIA 400 restricts those rites to those baptized "who did not receive further catechetical formation" after their baptism as infants. Christians who are living the Christian way of life who desire to become Catholic should be given appropriate instruction and then prepared quickly for the Rite of Reception.

About Liturgical Music

Hospitable music: Although many people listen to music, most today do not make music themselves either on their own or in a group. Music is typically performed *for* them. However, our liturgical experience must be different: "The congregation commonly sings unison melodies, which are more suitable for generally unrehearsed community singing. This is the primary song of the Liturgy" (Sing to the Lord 28). How can you make your music hospitable and enable the song of an assembly that probably does not read music or sing very often at home?

Start with music that has a simple range and natural tempo—not too high or low, too fast or slow to sing. Depending on your community, syncopations may be too difficult. Don't change music too often. Be sure your worship aids are readable, especially for aging eyes. Remember that the way you invite people to sing is often more important than what you sing.

SPIRITUALITY

GOSPEL ACCLAMATION

℟. Alleluia, alleluia.
The seed is the word of God, Christ is the sower.
All who come to him will have life forever.
℟. Alleluia, alleluia.

Gospel Matt 13:1-23; L103A

On that day, Jesus went out of the house and sat down by the sea.
Such large crowds gathered around him
that he got into a boat and sat down,
and the whole crowd stood along the shore.
And he spoke to them at length in parables, saying:
"A sower went out to sow.
And as he sowed, some seed fell on the path,
and birds came and ate it up.
Some fell on rocky ground, where it had little soil.
It sprang up at once because the soil was not deep,
and when the sun rose it was scorched,
and it withered for lack of roots.
Some seed fell among thorns, and the thorns grew up and choked it.
But some seed fell on rich soil, and produced fruit,
a hundred or sixty or thirtyfold.
Whoever has ears ought to hear."

The disciples approached him and said,
"Why do you speak to them in parables?"
He said to them in reply,
"Because knowledge of the mysteries of the kingdom of heaven
has been granted to you, but to them it has not been granted.
To anyone who has, more will be given and he will grow rich;
from anyone who has not, even what he has will be taken away.

Continued in Appendix A, p. 299, or
Matt 13:1-9 *in Appendix A, p. 299.*

Reflecting on the Gospel

In the middle of summer, we continue reading from the Gospel of Matthew (Cycle A). Today we begin chapter 13, sometimes referred to as the chapter on parables, for Matthew has Jesus teach seven parables in this chapter. The word "parable" reflects the Hebrew word *māshāl*, which in turn means wisdom-saying or proverb. This term could be used to mean anything from an aphorism to a lengthy allegorical tale. The latter is what we have today, with the parable of the sower, as Jesus himself calls it (Matt 13:18).

Matthew's story of the parable of the sower follows Mark's, which Matthew used as a source. In fact, there is little variation at all. Significantly, Matthew says that Jesus sat by the shore (Matt 13:1), but when the crowds grew too large he moved to a boat where he sat as well (Matt 13:2). That particular verb ("sat") recalls the Sermon on the Mount (Matt 5:1), where Jesus also sat to teach. The verb is used by Mark too, and it is an indication of a true teacher—one who sits to dispense wisdom. This is no peripatetic professor.

Fortunately for us (and for the early disciples), Jesus explained this parable himself. There is no need to discern the intended meaning. Those who read the longer gospel today have the advantage of that explanation. For those who read the shorter reading, it is recommended that the parable be explained in much the same words as Jesus used. So perhaps it's simply best to proclaim the longer version of the gospel.

The parable of the sower is rooted in antiquity with the image of scattering seed on the ground, which would have preceded plowing. Today even gardeners often sow seed by plowing first, planting the seed, then covering the seed with soil. But that is not the way those in the ancient world performed the task. It's for this reason that many seeds may be eaten by the birds or may fall on rocky soil. Not all the seed that is scattered takes root and bears fruit. Indeed, if those in the ancient world planted seeds the way a modern gardener does, it's highly unlikely that Jesus would have used this same parable! Instead, we might have a parable about the care with which the sower sows seed. But such is not the world of antiquity.

Jesus ends this simple allegorical tale with an injunction: "Whoever has ears ought to hear."

Living the Paschal Mystery

The parable in today's gospel may cause us to stop and consider several questions: What kind of seed are we? Were we scattered on rocky soil or fertile? Will we bear fruit? If so, how much—thirty, sixty, one hundred fold? Being viewed as seed scattered on the ground does not seem to leave much room for free will. The seed scattered on rocks can scarcely move itself to the fertile soil. Is it the fault of the seed for landing in an inhospitable environment? Then again, what about the seed that finds itself in fertile soil? Is there a responsibility to grow and produce fruit? That can hardly happen if it's eaten by a bird. Again, the question of free will seems to be outside the realm of this parable.

Today, we might pray for the grace to grow where we find ourselves and to produce as much fruit as possible. One day there will be a harvest and we shall experience new life. Such is the paschal mystery.

Focusing the Gospel

Key words and phrases: "Whoever has ears ought to hear."

To the point: These words, or ones almost exactly like it, are found seven times on the lips of Jesus within the gospels. Usually in connection with the parables, Jesus issues this command three times in Matthew's gospel (twice within the thirteenth chapter that we are currently reading) and twice in both Mark and Luke. Within our life of prayer, we might tend to focus on what words *we* are going to say, neglecting the more important aspect of communication—listening. Jesus' command to "hear" requires more than just taking in the words he speaks. To truly hear what Jesus is saying, especially within the context of the parables, we are required to profoundly ponder what Jesus wishes us to know. Only with ears attuned to the word of God and hearts open to receive him can we gain insight into the kingdom of God.

Connecting the Gospel

to the first reading: The first reading from the prophet Isaiah contains another image for the Word of God. It is sent forth like rain and snow "from the heavens" and does not return "until it has watered the earth," causing seeds to grow. Just so, we are told, "my word shall not return to me void, / but shall do my will, / achieving the end for which I sent it." In the first story of creation, the words spoken by God cause light and darkness, plants, animals, and humans to appear on the earth. Now in today's gospel, Jesus, the Word of God, sits in a boat to teach the gathered crowds in parables.

to experience: The first reading announces the effectiveness of God's words to bring about growth and life. How has time spent with the word of God nurtured growth in your own life?

Connecting the Responsorial Psalm

to the readings: Today's psalm refrain comes from the Gospel of Luke and Luke's version of the parable of the sower, "The seed that falls on good ground will yield a fruitful harvest." Within the psalm it is God who brings about fertile soil by watering the land and "breaking up its clods." God is the one who has "prepared the grain" and produced "a rich harvest." Just as fields need rich soil in order to produce crops, so it seems that we need "good ground" within ourselves in order to receive the word of God and bear its fruit. When God's word lands on this soil, the harvest will yield "a hundred or sixty or thirtyfold."

to psalmist preparation: Perhaps we have a role to play in developing this good soil within ourselves, or maybe it is the work of the Holy Spirit inside of us gently "breaking up the clods" within our hearts to make space for this word to take root. In either case, God's word "shall not return to [him] void" as the prophet Isaiah proclaims. How do you welcome God's transforming word into your life?

PROMPTS FOR FAITH-SHARING

Through the prophet Isaiah, God announces, "[M]y word shall not return to me void, but shall do my will, / achieving the end for which I sent it." How do you make room for God's word to form your life?

In his letter to the Romans, St. Paul uses the image of "labor pains" to describe the suffering or hardship that disciples must undergo leading to redemption. When have you suffered or undergone hardship for a goal or relationship?

Looking back on your life through the lens of today's parable, have you experienced environments that have been like rocky ground, thorny ground, or rich soil?

How can you cultivate rich soil within your life now so as to grow in faith?

Model Penitential Act

Presider: In today's gospel Jesus ends the parable of the sower by proclaiming, "Whoever has ears ought to hear." For the times we have ignored the word of God or closed our ears to the sound of his voice, let us ask for mercy and forgiveness . . . *[pause]*

Lord Jesus, you sow the seeds of everlasting life: Lord, have mercy.
Christ Jesus, you are the Word of God sent down from heaven: Christ, have mercy.
Lord Jesus, you are the true Teacher, calling us to life: Lord, have mercy.

Homily Points

• In today's parable Jesus gives four different scenarios for the seed scattered by the sower: some falls upon a path, some falls on rocky ground, some falls among thorns, and some lands on rich soil. When we enter into the parables of Jesus, it is best to keep an open mind. These mysterious sayings require much from us. They invite us to take the images and to relate them to our own experiences.

• In living the life of faith, we hear Jesus' words over and over again. Familiarity with the word of God is good, but it can also lead us to skim over or fail to take in the message contained. Perhaps this could be like the seed scattered along the path. Our preconceptions have packed down the soil so that it can't accept the gift God wishes to offer. The seed sown on rocky ground might be what we experience when the gospel message initially elicits joy and excitement, but we fail to accept the challenge inherent in Jesus' call to love and devotion. Unless we put down the roots of real life change, the word cannot bear fruit. Thorny ground could be what happens when the voices of the world choke out the voice of Jesus calling us to life.

• Undoubtedly, each of us has had experiences where we have heard God's word proclaimed, either in the Scriptures or in the preaching or testimony of another disciple, and this word has failed to flourish in our lives. Hopefully we also have had times where this word has fallen on fertile soil, when the gospel message has touched us deeply and caused us to grow more into the people Jesus calls us to be. In the life of discipleship, let us work to develop fertile ground for the word to take root.

Model Universal Prayer (Prayer of the Faithful)

Presider: Having been nourished by the word of God, let us now entrust to the Lord our needs and those of our world.

Response: Lord, hear our prayer.

For catechists and all who teach the faith, may they faithfully sow the seeds of God's word and tend to its growth . . .

For farmers throughout the world and all who work in the fields, may God prosper the work of their hands and bring about a bounteous harvest . . .

For those who will go to bed hungry tonight, especially children and the disabled, may their cries be heard and answered by all who enjoy abundance . . .

For all gathered here, may we nurture fertile soil within ourselves, our families, and our parish, so that the word of God might take root and flourish . . .

Presider: God of never failing love and compassion, you provide us with all we need to grow and thrive in the life of discipleship. Hear our prayers that in studying your Word and living lives of service to you and our neighbor, we might come to life everlasting. We ask this through Christ our Lord. **Amen.**

COLLECT

Let us pray.

Pause for silent prayer

O God, who show the light of your truth
to those who go astray,
so that they may return to the right path,
give all who for the faith they profess
are accounted Christians
the grace to reject whatever is contrary to
the name of Christ
and to strive after all that does it honor.
Through our Lord Jesus Christ, your Son,
who lives and reigns with you in the unity
of the Holy Spirit,
one God, for ever and ever. **Amen.**

FIRST READING

Isa 55:10-11

Thus says the LORD:
Just as from the heavens
the rain and snow come down
and do not return there
till they have watered the earth,
making it fertile and fruitful,
giving seed to the one who sows
and bread to the one who eats,
so shall my word be
that goes forth from my mouth;
my word shall not return to me void,
but shall do my will,
achieving the end for which I sent it.

CATECHESIS

RESPONSORIAL PSALM
Ps 65:10, 11, 12-13, 14

℟. (Luke 8:8) The seed that falls on good ground will yield a fruitful harvest.

You have visited the land and watered it;
greatly have you enriched it.
God's watercourses are filled;
you have prepared the grain.

℟. The seed that falls on good ground will yield a fruitful harvest.

Thus have you prepared the land:
drenching its furrows,
breaking up its clods,
softening it with showers,
blessing its yield.

℟. The seed that falls on good ground will yield a fruitful harvest.

You have crowned the year with your bounty,
and your paths overflow with a rich harvest;
the untilled meadows overflow with it,
and rejoicing clothes the hills.

℟. The seed that falls on good ground will yield a fruitful harvest.

The fields are garmented with flocks
and the valleys blanketed with grain.
They shout and sing for joy.

℟. The seed that falls on good ground will yield a fruitful harvest.

SECOND READING
Rom 8:18-23

Brothers and sisters:
I consider that the sufferings of this present time are as nothing
compared with the glory to be revealed for us.
For creation awaits with eager expectation
the revelation of the children of God;
for creation was made subject to futility,
not of its own accord but because of the one who subjected it,
in hope that creation itself
would be set free from slavery to corruption
and share in the glorious freedom of the children of God.
We know that all creation is groaning in labor pains even until now;
and not only that, but we ourselves,
who have the firstfruits of the Spirit,
we also groan within ourselves
as we wait for adoption, the redemption of our bodies.

About Liturgy

Lectors as seed-sowers: If, as we hear in the Alleluia verse today, the seed is the word of God and Christ is the sower, then those who proclaim the word in the midst of the assembly bear great responsibility. They are, in essence, seed-sowers, scattering the seed of God's word through the grace of Christ.

Although they cannot control the kind of ground the seed falls upon in the hearts of their hearers, they *can* be sure that the seed *lands* on the "ears of their hearts," as St. Benedict says in the opening lines of his rule. Here are some principles that all lectors (including deacons and priests) can work on:

This is proclamation: Lectoring is not reading in public. It is announcing good news. Getting the words right and making sure you are heard clearly is just the starting point. You have to *believe* what you are saying and desire with all your heart for others to believe too. A sense of proclamation comes mostly from your attitude about what you are announcing.

This is ritual: Ritual has a beginning, a middle, and an end. It tells a story. Know the structure of your reading, where the climax is, and how the pace and rhythm varies throughout to bring out the structure. Ritual involves not only words but also gesture, posture, music, and bearing. How you use your body, communicate with your eyes and your face, walk to the ambo and stand there matters.

This is not about you: The sower is Christ. Your words have power only through Christ. So don't make such a show of reading that the focus is no longer on Christ. On the other hand, don't make a big deal if you flub a word or a line here or there. Christ is in charge. Just do your best every time. Remember that Christ can change lives through you in this ministry of the Word.

About Initiation

"Catechumen": So many of the words we use in the RCIA come from Greek, and "catechumen" is one of them. This and the word "catechist" are derived from *katechein*, which implies a sound made in reply, a response, or an echo. In terms of instruction, it describes the back-and-forth dialogue between teacher and student. A catechumen, then, is one in whom the word of God echoes and is given in reply. The catechumen hears God's word and responds to it by both word and deed.

This is a good reminder for catechists. Catechesis is not a lecture. It's not a video that everyone watches. It's not a monologue. Catechesis is dialogue, everyone hearing God's word and responding to it, sharing reflections and wisdom (yes, catechumens have wisdom to share!), and putting it into practice in one's life. God's word is living and active, and shall not return to God void.

About Liturgical Music

Psalmists as seed-sowers: Those who lead the singing of the responsorial psalm serve more as a lector than a cantor in that the principal work they do in this part of the Mass is proclamation of the word through music. Take a look at the principles listed above, and remind your psalmists that they are seed-sowers of God's word.

Suggestions: *Psallite* has a lovely piece that would be an appropriate song during Communion today. When juxtaposed with the act of eating and drinking the Body and Blood of Christ, "As Seed for the Sowing" (Liturgical Press) connects the Word of God that feeds us with the Eucharist that sustains us. There are a variety of verses that can be sung, either superimposed on the assembly's refrain or antiphonally.

SPIRITUALITY

GOSPEL ACCLAMATION
cf. Matt 11:25

℟. Alleluia, alleluia.
Blessed are you, Father, Lord of heaven and earth;
you have revealed to little ones the mysteries of
the kingdom.
℟. Alleluia, alleluia.

Gospel Matt 13:24-43; L106A

Jesus proposed another parable
to the crowds, saying:
"The kingdom of heaven may be likened
to a man who sowed good seed in his field.
While everyone was asleep his enemy came
and sowed weeds all through the wheat, and then went off.
When the crop grew and bore fruit, the weeds appeared as well.
The slaves of the householder came to him and said,
'Master, did you not sow good seed in your field?
Where have the weeds come from?'
He answered, 'An enemy has done this.'
His slaves said to him,
'Do you want us to go and pull them up?'
He replied, 'No, if you pull up the weeds
you might uproot the wheat along with them.
Let them grow together until harvest;
then at harvest time I will say to the harvesters,
"First collect the weeds and tie them in bundles for burning;
but gather the wheat into my barn."'"

He proposed another parable to them.
"The kingdom of heaven is like a mustard seed
that a person took and sowed in a field.
It is the smallest of all the seeds,
yet when full-grown it is the largest of plants.

Continued in Appendix A, p. 300, or
Matt 13:24-30 *in Appendix A, p. 300.*

Reflecting on the Gospel

This Sunday we continue reading from Matthew 13, the chapter on parables. This is the primary chapter in the Gospel of Matthew where Jesus speaks in parables, and he speaks seven of them. That alone should tell us that we are dealing with Matthew's evangelical hand in editing and placing these parables where he does in his story about Jesus.

The shorter gospel reading today is about the weeds and the wheat, whereas the longer reading includes other parables. The parable of the weeds and the wheat occurs only in Matthew. No other gospel includes this parable, causing scholars to wonder whether Matthew had access to a special source, or perhaps he composed it himself. Even if that is so, the passage is still scriptural, still inspired, and still authoritative. One reason scholars query whether Matthew composed it is that so many of the stories that are unique to him fit a pattern of judgment followed by a fiery end. And this story certainly falls into that category.

The good sower expects a harvest of wheat but is unaware that his enemy cast weeds into the field. The precise term for the weed is "darnel," which is a plant that looks like wheat. Darnel is sometimes called "false wheat."

Rather than uproot the darnel, a process that would harm the wheat, both are allowed to grow together. In the end there will be a sorting, and the darnel is destined for the fire.

Such an apocalyptic image requires little imagination. This is hardly the sort of parable whose meaning is difficult to discern. Instead, we see clearly that the followers of Jesus, the "church" (Matthew is the only gospel to use that term), is a field of wheat and weeds, the good and the bad. The church does not (or should not) play God and determine who will be uprooted. Instead, uprooting is God's role and he will perform it . . . in the end.

For anyone whose life is bound up in the church (or any institution composed of human beings), today's gospel rings true. There are weeds in the church in every time and place. But it is not our role to uproot. At harvest time God will separate the weeds from the wheat. Our role is simply to produce for the harvest.

Living the Paschal Mystery

How many of us would like to be in charge, deciding what's best for the group, what's best for the church? When enemies get in the way, we would have the authority to uproot and be rid of them. Even if we are not the ones to be "in charge," how many of us would like someone else to do the uprooting or weeding? But such is not the way it is with God and the church. In today's gospel passage found only in Matthew, we learn from Jesus that God is aware that there are weeds growing within the wheat. God is content to let them grow together, only to be separated later, at harvest time.

It is our task to simply let God be God while we grow into the harvest we are meant to be. Our lives are not to be filled with judgmentalism but with mercy. We are reminded of Pope Francis's words, "[W]ho am I to judge," or Jesus' own words in the Gospel of John, "Let the one who is without sin cast the first stone." These are gentle reminders for us that as disciples, followers of the Son of God, we are content to allow God to act in his own time.

Focusing the Gospel

Key words and phrases: "The kingdom of heaven is like . . ."

To the point: There are many names that Jesus goes by in the gospels. He is known as Emmanuel, Christ, Son of God, Son of Man, Lamb of God, and many others. Perhaps given our readings from last Sunday, this Sunday, and the next we should add another title for Jesus: Storyteller. For these three weeks our gospel readings come from the thirteenth chapter of Matthew and are devoted to Jesus' teaching in parables. Parables are a particular genre of storytelling in which something that is well-known to the listener (a farmer sowing seeds, a shepherd caring for sheep, a woman baking bread) is used to shed light on something that is not well-known (the nature of the kingdom of God or who one might consider a neighbor). For this Sunday and the next, all the parables we read focus on one mystery, the kingdom of God (or kingdom of heaven, depending on your Bible translation). This mystery cannot be reduced to only one image and so Jesus offers us many parables to ponder. As a teller of parables, Jesus asks for our conscious participation as we consider how *is* the kingdom of God like the wheat and the weeds, or the mustard seed, or a woman baking bread.

Connecting the Gospel

to the first reading: Jesus' interpretation of the parable of the weeds and the wheat can seem a little harsh, especially when it mentions souls thrown into a "fiery furnace, / where there will be wailing and grinding of teeth." The first reading seems to balance out this picture by naming God as one who judges "with clemency" and who has given "your children good ground for hope / that you would permit repentance for their sins."

to experience: Gospel readings proclaiming "fire and brimstone" offer a word of warning to unrepentant sinners who do evil and "cause others to sin," but they can also have the unintended consequence of leading the faithful to fear or even to scrupulosity. In these cases, it is important to be grounded in the compassionate and merciful love of God who is always ready to take back the repentant sinner.

Connecting the Responsorial Psalm

to the readings: Like the first reading, today's psalm lifts up God as one who is "abounding in kindness" as well as "good and forgiving." In the second reading from St. Paul's letter to the Romans, we see these same traits in the Holy Trinity, who the apostle points to as our intercessor. When "we do not know how to pray as we ought," the Spirit of God comes "to the aid of our weakness" and "intercedes with inexpressible groanings."

to psalmist preparation: When was a particular time you experienced the forgiving and healing action of God? What brought this moment about and what fruits did it produce in your life?

PROMPTS FOR FAITH-SHARING

The Book of Wisdom proclaims, "[T]hose who are just must be kind." How do you try to balance justice and kindness in your own life?

The first reading announces that we have "good ground for hope / that [God] would permit repentance for [our] sins." Where in your own life are you in need of forgiving others or receiving forgiveness?

In the second reading St. Paul talks of the Holy Spirit's role in our prayer by interceding for us "with inexpressible groanings." How do you make space for the Holy Spirit within your life of prayer?

Of today's many parables, which one speaks to you the most about the mystery of the kingdom of God? What does it reveal?

Model Penitential Act

Presider: In today's gospel Jesus proposes many parables to describe the kingdom of God. As we prepare to greet the Lord in the Scriptures and the Eucharist, let us pause to ask forgiveness for the times we have failed to build up the kingdom in our words or in our actions . . . *[pause]*

Lord Jesus, you speak in parables to announce the mystery of your kingdom: Lord, have mercy.

Christ Jesus, you are the Son of Man sowing good seed in the world: Christ, have mercy.

Lord Jesus, you call us to fullness of life: Lord, have mercy.

Homily Points

• Jesus' parables always deal with real, everyday occurrences such as a farmer sowing grain, a shepherd searching for a lost sheep, or a merchant searching for pearls. Within the parables, though, there is usually something shocking that takes place such as the shepherd leaving ninety-nine of his sheep defenseless in the wilderness in order to go after one that was lost, or a Samaritan being the hero of the story instead of the villain. We find these surprising elements in our parables today as well.

• For instance, have you ever heard of a gardener who was against weeding? In the parable of the wheat and the weeds, the householder makes the unorthodox decision to let the wheat and the weeds all grow together. He doesn't want to risk anything harming the wheat and so decides he will leave it until the harvest when the two can be separated. We might ponder, along with Jesus' first listeners, what might this tell us about the kingdom of God and God's justice?

• In the parable of the leaven, the amount of flour used by the woman provides the element of surprise. Three measures of wheat flour would have been enough to feed a hundred people, and yet the yeast has the power to cause this flour to change and grow and become something that is nourishing for others. What might this parable tell us about the power, growth, and abundance of the kingdom of God? To fully enter into a parable, one must be willing to let go of the security offered by answers and definitions. Most of the parables Jesus offered did not come with explanations. Instead, just as Jesus' first listeners did, we are invited to ponder and wrestle with what this living word has to teach us today.

Model Universal Prayer (Prayer of the Faithful)

Presider: Trusting in the action of the Holy Spirit to intercede for us, let us bring our prayers before the Lord.

Response: Lord, hear our prayer.

For those who exercise the ministry of preaching, grounded in the life-giving word of God, may they speak words of compassion and hope . . .

For those who work in the judicial branch of government, in wisdom and mercy may they work for justice while protecting the dignity of all . . .

For those fleeing from violence, war, and poverty, may they find shelter, support, and safe passage . . .

For all gathered here, formed by the word of God and fed by his Body and Blood, may any sickness of mind, body, or spirit be healed . . .

Presider: God of creation, in you we place our hope and trust. Hear our prayers that in listening to your word and feasting at your table, we might be strengthened to do your will now and always. We ask this through Christ our Lord. **Amen.**

COLLECT

Let us pray.

Pause for silent prayer

Show favor, O Lord, to your servants
and mercifully increase the gifts of your grace,
that, made fervent in hope, faith, and charity,
they may be ever watchful in keeping your commands.
Through our Lord Jesus Christ, your Son,
who lives and reigns with you in the unity of the Holy Spirit,
one God, for ever and ever. **Amen.**

FIRST READING

Wis 12:13, 16-19

There is no god besides you who have the care of all,
that you need show you have not unjustly condemned.
For your might is the source of justice;
your mastery over all things makes you lenient to all.
For you show your might when the perfection of your power is disbelieved;
and in those who know you, you rebuke temerity.
But though you are master of might, you judge with clemency,
and with much lenience you govern us;
for power, whenever you will, attends you.
And you taught your people, by these deeds,
that those who are just must be kind;
and you gave your children good ground for hope
that you would permit repentance for their sins.

RESPONSORIAL PSALM
Ps 86:5-6, 9-10, 15-16

℟. (5a) Lord, you are good and forgiving.

You, O LORD, are good and forgiving,
abounding in kindness to all who call upon you.
Hearken, O LORD, to my prayer
and attend to the sound of my pleading.

℟. Lord, you are good and forgiving.

All the nations you have made shall come
and worship you, O LORD,
and glorify your name.
For you are great, and you do wondrous deeds;
you alone are God.

℟. Lord, you are good and forgiving.

You, O LORD, are a God merciful and gracious,
slow to anger, abounding in kindness and fidelity.
Turn toward me, and have pity on me;
give your strength to your servant.

℟. Lord, you are good and forgiving.

SECOND READING
Rom 8:26-27

Brothers and sisters:
The Spirit comes to the aid of our weakness;
for we do not know how to pray as we ought,
but the Spirit himself intercedes with inexpressible groanings.
And the one who searches hearts
knows what is the intention of the Spirit,
because he intercedes for the holy ones
according to God's will.

About Liturgy

Making changes: Especially if you've just come back from a music or liturgy conference this summer, you'll want to make many changes in your community's liturgy right away! But true, lasting change doesn't happen that way. Sure, you could come in and pull all the "weeds" in your community's liturgical practice overnight. But hearts won't be changed that way, and you'll just annoy everyone.

To get real liturgical change happening, start by sharing your vision—one grounded in the liturgical documents and the tradition of the church while also sensitive to the particular needs of the community. Tell everyone, and be passionate. Start with *why*—why this change is important, why it should happen, and why it would benefit the community. Gather a small coalition of people who get the vision and can communicate it to others. This communication won't be just a note in the bulletin or an announcement at Mass; it's a long-term dialogue with people in your community.

Next, pick just one thing to change. Make it big enough that it will make a difference, but not so out of reach that people lose energy. Determine the small steps you need to take to accomplish the change. Develop a reasonable schedule for those steps. Then communicate to everyone who will be affected by each of those steps. Be sure they understand the big vision, have heard your passion, know why it matters, and understand the timeline for the steps toward that change.

Then implement your steps. With each step, evaluate what happened and adjust as needed for the next steps. Don't be afraid to adjust the timeline if there's a lot of resistance from key people. If there is, go back to communicating the vision until everyone has felt heard and can agree on a next step toward change.

About Initiation

Who belongs in the RCIA and who doesn't? In "About Initiation" for the Fourteenth Sunday in Ordinary Time, we briefly noted that the RCIA is not meant for everyone who needs the sacraments of initiation. Paragraph 400, in regards to those who are baptized, is clear that the RCIA process is for those who received no further instruction or formation, or had any kind of connection with the Christian community after their baptism as infants. However, most of the people we find in the RCIA do not fit into this category. They are adults who were never confirmed, or they are Christians who have lived their entire life in their Christian community and practiced all the disciplines of being Christian and who now want to live that faith in the Catholic Church. They may be poorly catechized or under-catechized. At some point they received some sort of catechesis and formation; even so, they may need lots of catching up. They should be in an ongoing formation process for adults that is separate from the RCIA, which is for those who are unbaptized or those who are baptized but completely uncatechized.

About Liturgical Music

Suggestions: God's mercy is front and center this Sunday. With the near-distant Year of Mercy behind us, we received several useful compositions on this topic. One that stands out is Ed Bolduc's "There's a Wideness in God's Mercy: Be Merciful" (WLP). The verses use the text from the traditional hymn of the same name, while the refrain takes the message of mercy as a call for us to be merciful, just as God is merciful. It is an excellent piece that will stay in your assembly's hearts and on their lips.

Also bring back from last week *Psallite's* "As Seed for the Sowing" (Liturgical Press) for Communion this week, using the setting with verses from Psalm 111.

SPIRITUALITY

GOSPEL ACCLAMATION
cf. Matt 11:25

℟. Alleluia, alleluia.
Blessed are you, Father, Lord of heaven and earth;
you have revealed to little ones the mysteries of
the kingdom.
℟. Alleluia, alleluia.

Gospel Matt 13:44-52; L109A

Jesus said to his disciples:
"The kingdom of heaven is like a treasure buried in a field,
which a person finds and hides again,
and out of joy goes and sells all that he has and buys that field.
Again, the kingdom of heaven is like a merchant
searching for fine pearls.
When he finds a pearl of great price,
he goes and sells all that he has and buys it.
Again, the kingdom of heaven is like a net thrown into the sea,
which collects fish of every kind.
When it is full they haul it ashore
and sit down to put what is good into buckets.
What is bad they throw away.
Thus it will be at the end of the age.
The angels will go out and separate the wicked from the righteous
and throw them into the fiery furnace,
where there will be wailing and grinding of teeth.

"Do you understand all these things?"
They answered, "Yes."
And he replied,
"Then every scribe who has been instructed in the kingdom of heaven
is like the head of a household
who brings from his storeroom both the new and the old."

or Matt 13:44-46 *in Appendix A, p. 300.*

Reflecting on the Gospel

Today's reading gives us the third Sunday in a row where we hear from Matthew's chapter on parables. Seven parables of Jesus in the Gospel of Matthew appear in chapter 13. The setting is in the house, where Jesus continues to teach his disciples using this rhetorical device, often explaining the allegorical meaning to them. Though in today's reading Jesus asks them a simple question, "Do you understand all these things?" to which the disciples reply, "Yes." Of course, those at the liturgy today will only hear those words if the longer gospel reading is proclaimed.

This particular gospel reading preserves parables not found anywhere else in the New Testament. These parables either come from Matthew's special source or they are his own composition.

The reading begins with two parables: the treasure buried in the field, and the pearl of great price. Each is a side of the coin so to speak, with Jesus instructing his disciples that the kingdom of heaven is worth such a price. In other words, once one encounters the kingdom of heaven, a proper response is to reprioritize all else in favor of this. It is worth selling everything else to possess this one thing.

The longer gospel reading gives one more parable, but it has another point. Rather than reinforce the lesson of the first two parables, the third—the net cast into the sea which brings in a terrific catch—has another message. The net is returned with good fish, but also with things that are not so good. The latter is thrown away. This then becomes the image for the eschatological judgment, a topic that Matthew addresses quite often. At the judgment, some will be not merely cast aside or "thrown away," but the angels will throw the wicked into the "fiery furnace." As we saw last week, this is a favorite Matthean theme, and it causes some scholars to posit that the parable is a Matthean creation, though certainly canonical Scripture that is both authoritative and inspired.

Matthew is sure to tell us there will be a final, definitive judgment and an unfortunate end is possible based on the decisions we have made.

Living the Paschal Mystery

The Christian life ought to be a source of joy for us. Some of this joy is reflected in the first two parables. In each, people sell whatever they can to take possession of a prized object. This is what it ought to be like for us with respect to the kingdom of heaven. Once we realize what it is, what a prize we have, we joyfully reorient all of our priorities in light of it. We want that one prize above all else. And what's more, we have it! Thus, the source of joy.

When animated by Christian joy, we may be shocked at the inevitable suffering and death that Christ experiences. There is evil in the world and this evil impinges on our own reality. It certainly did for Jesus. But that terrible experience is not the end. Joy and love triumph as new life springs forth from humiliation and death. This new life itself is a cause of joy. And so as Christians our joy is foundational. It should be a hallmark of our witness in the world. It is an essential element of our living the paschal mystery.

Focusing the Gospel

Key words and phrases: "goes and sells all he has and buys it"

To the point: Today we are given more parables about the kingdom of heaven. The first two sound remarkably similar, each ending with the person who had discovered his heart's desire giving up everything else so as to possess it. And this is what the kingdom of heaven is like. Jesus' words point to the only thing in our lives that will bring us true fulfillment, joy, or peace: the kingdom which he proclaims.

Connecting the Gospel

to the second reading: The second reading begins with St. Paul's words to the Romans: "We know that all things work for good for those who love God." Within the parables today we see two figures at work. The merchant has devoted his life to finding and selling fine pearls. When his search turns up the greatest pearl of all, he doesn't hesitate to sell everything he owns to buy it. The other parable is a bit different. The person laboring in the field seems to find the treasure hidden there almost by mistake. He sort of stumbles upon it. But, like the merchant, he recognizes the value of what he has found and also gives up everything else to own the field with its treasure. It seems there might be different ways that people discover the kingdom that will be more valuable than anything else. In the end, though, for those who recognize it and are willing to sacrifice for it, "all things work for good."

to experience: In your own journey of faith, has your path to God been more like that of the merchant actively seeking, or has it surprised you like the experience of the person who finds treasure hidden in a field?

Connecting the Responsorial Psalm

to the readings: The kingdom of God is built on the commandments to love God and to love neighbor. These are the commandments that the psalmist sings in praise of, even proclaiming them "more precious / than thousands of gold and silver pieces." For the psalmist, the law of God is the "precious pearl" and the "hidden treasure" for which he would give up everything. The prayer of Solomon is similar. When the Lord tells him, "Ask something of me and I will give it to you," Solomon does not ask for "a long life . . . / nor for riches, / nor for the life of [his] enemies." Instead Solomon tells God his greatest desire is for "an understanding heart / to judge your people and to distinguish right from wrong." Solomon would also say that knowing and keeping the law of the Lord is worth more than any earthly riches.

to psalmist preparation: As you prepare to cantor this Sunday's psalm, take some time to consider how you reverence, make space for, and keep the word of God in your life. Would an outside observer looking in on your daily routine be able to tell this word is valuable and precious to you?

PROMPTS FOR FAITH-SHARING

In the first reading, when God invites Solomon to ask him for anything, Solomon asks for "an understanding heart." Which gift of the Holy Spirit or virtue are you most in need of right now in your life?

The psalmist sings, "The revelation of your words sheds light." How has the word of God been a light to show you the way?

St. Paul writes to the Romans that we are to be "conformed to the image of [God's] Son." What attributes of Jesus do you find the easiest (or the hardest) to emulate?

Considering the parables of the precious pearl and the hidden treasure, what do you think Jesus wants us to know about the kingdom of God?

Model Penitential Act

Presider: In the first reading King Solomon asks God to grant him "an understanding heart / to judge your people and to distinguish right from wrong." Let us turn to the giver of every good gift and ask for his pardon and mercy . . . *[pause]*

Lord Jesus, you are our joy, our hope, and our salvation: Lord, have mercy.
Christ Jesus, you came to show sinners the way to everlasting life: Christ, have mercy.
Lord Jesus, you are the font of wisdom and understanding: Lord, have mercy.

Homily Points

• Today's readings seem to ask us to consider what is the most important, most precious thing in our lives and what would we be willing to give up for it. In the first reading when God tells Solomon, "Ask something of me and I will give it to you," it's as if Solomon has been given a blank check by a person whose checking account has no limit. God himself seems to know full well what Solomon could ask for: riches, long life, the death of enemies. Instead, Solomon requests the one thing that will help him most to carry out the task God has given him. As the new king of the people of Israel, in order to rule the people fairly and justly, he asks for "an understanding heart / to judge your people and to distinguish right from wrong." This is Solomon's "precious pearl," the one thing his heart desires.

• While last Sunday's parables highlighted the growth and spread of the kingdom of God, the two we hear today point to its value above all else. Both the merchant and the man working in the field go and sell everything they have to buy the object they have found. As with last week's parables, we might be shocked by what we hear. What merchant would sell all he has to buy only one item?

• It seems that Jesus is telling us that when the kingdom of God is found, its value causes all else to diminish in comparison. It is worthy of all our time, our efforts, and our resources. Perhaps these parables call us to discern what is essential and what is superfluous in our lives. What is your "precious pearl" and what would you be willing to give up to possess it?

Model Universal Prayer (Prayer of the Faithful)

Presider: Trusting in the one who calls us by name and leads us to life, let us bring our prayers before the Lord.

Response: Lord, hear our prayer.

For those who exercise the ministries of confessor and spiritual director within the church, may they be granted the understanding heart of Solomon . . .

For leaders of the world, as a united front may they combat the scourge of terrorism and promote the values of justice and peace . . .

For family and friends of those who have died by suicide, may they be comforted in their grief and sorrow . . .

For all gathered here, in joy may we give up all that is superfluous and meaningless in order to embrace the fullness of the kingdom of God . . .

Presider: Gracious God, in you we find our heart's desires and fulfillment of every need. Hear our prayers that in being formed by the word of God and nourished at the table of the Lord, we might go forth to build your kingdom. We ask this through Christ our Lord. **Amen.**

COLLECT

Let us pray.

Pause for silent prayer

O God, protector of those who hope in you,
without whom nothing has firm foundation, nothing is holy,
bestow in abundance your mercy upon us
and grant that, with you as our ruler and guide,
we may use the good things that pass
in such a way as to hold fast even now
to those that ever endure.
Through our Lord Jesus Christ, your Son,
who lives and reigns with you in the unity of the Holy Spirit,
one God, for ever and ever. **Amen.**

FIRST READING

1 Kgs 3:5, 7-12

The LORD appeared to Solomon in a dream at night.
God said, "Ask something of me and I will give it to you."
Solomon answered:
"O LORD, my God, you have made me, your servant, king
to succeed my father David;
but I am a mere youth, not knowing at all how to act.
I serve you in the midst of the people whom you have chosen,
a people so vast that it cannot be numbered or counted.
Give your servant, therefore, an understanding heart
to judge your people and to distinguish right from wrong.
For who is able to govern this vast people of yours?"

The LORD was pleased that Solomon made this request.
So God said to him:
"Because you have asked for this—
not for a long life for yourself,
nor for riches,
nor for the life of your enemies,
but for understanding so that you may know what is right—
I do as you requested.
I give you a heart so wise and understanding
that there has never been anyone like you up to now,
and after you there will come no one to equal you."

RESPONSORIAL PSALM
Ps 119:57, 72, 76-77, 127-128, 129-130

℟. (97a) Lord, I love your commands.

I have said, O Lord, that my part
is to keep your words.
The law of your mouth is to me more precious
than thousands of gold and silver pieces.

℟. Lord, I love your commands.

Let your kindness comfort me
according to your promise to your servants.
Let your compassion come to me that I may live,
for your law is my delight.

℟. Lord, I love your commands.

For I love your commands
more than gold, however fine.
For in all your precepts I go forward;
every false way I hate.

℟. Lord, I love your commands.

Wonderful are your decrees;
therefore I observe them.
The revelation of your words sheds light,
giving understanding to the simple.

℟. Lord, I love your commands.

SECOND READING
Rom 8:28-30

Brothers and sisters:
We know that all things work for good for those who love God,
who are called according to his purpose.
For those he foreknew he also predestined
to be conformed to the image of his Son,
so that he might be the firstborn
among many brothers and sisters.
And those he predestined he also called;
and those he called he also justified;
and those he justified he also glorified.

About Liturgy

We've always done it that way!: A young boy watched his sister cut an inch off the dinner ham. "Why do you cut an inch off the ham before you put it in the oven?" he asked. His sister replied, "That's how Dad always does it. It makes the ham taste better." The next day, the two asked their father why he cut an inch off the ham. "That's how your grandmother always does it. It makes the ham juicier," he told them. The next day, the three of them called up Grandma and asked, "Why do you cut an inch off the ham? Is it to make it taste better?" "Oh no, dears," she laughed. "It's because I never have a pan big enough to fit the ham!"

It's inevitable that a community will pick up a liturgical practice or habit that is a bit out of the ordinary or doesn't quite fit but over the years has become "the way we've always done it." The psalmist leads the psalm from the choir instead of the ambo; the announcements happen during the second collection before the prayer after Communion; the First Communion children always sing a song for the assembly after Communion.

Things like these tend to happen simply because no one has stopped to ask *why* they happen that way and *if* that's the way they should happen. These summer Ordinary Time days are a good time to start asking "why?"

About Initiation

Discernment: Part of accompanying people toward deeper relationship with Christ in the sacraments is learning how to discern the action of the Spirit in their lives. Sometimes we think discernment is deciding who gets to be baptized and who doesn't, a kind of "who's in and who's out" mentality. But discernment is more like what we see in today's gospel. We look deeply and search for what is good in a person's life and help him or her discard what is destructive or not life-giving. For what is good, we give them ways to strengthen that grace and build upon it. For what needs to be discarded, we encourage them with prayer and support them by our own example of conversion.

Discernment is truly a pastoral help that points out the treasures in someone's life and guides that person to cherish these unique gifts from God.

About Liturgical Music

The new and the old: The longer version of today's gospel reading gives us the wonderful line about the scribe "who brings from his storeroom both the new and the old" (Matt 13:52).

Music leaders need to be like the scribe praised in the reading, taking from the rich storeroom of sacred music from our heritage that has shaped us as a church. The Constitution on the Sacred Liturgy says, "The treasure of sacred music is to be preserved and fostered with great care. Choirs must be diligently promoted, especially in cathedral churches; but bishops and other pastors of souls must be at pains to ensure that, whenever the sacred action is to be celebrated with song, the whole body of the faithful may be able to contribute that active participation which is rightly theirs" (114).

We also must seek out and cultivate new music to add to our treasury: "Composers, filled with the Christian spirit, should feel that their vocation is to cultivate sacred music and increase its store of treasures. Let them produce compositions which have the qualities proper to genuine sacred music, not confining themselves to works which can be sung only by large choirs, but providing also for the needs of small choirs and for the active participation of the entire assembly of the faithful" (121).

SPIRITUALITY

GOSPEL ACCLAMATION
Matt 4:4b

℟. Alleluia, alleluia.
One does not live on bread alone,
but on every word that comes forth from the mouth of God.
℟. Alleluia, alleluia.

Gospel Matt 14:13-21; L112A

When Jesus heard of the death of John the Baptist,
he withdrew in a boat to a deserted place by himself.
The crowds heard of this and followed him on foot from their towns.
When he disembarked and saw the vast crowd,
his heart was moved with pity for them, and he cured their sick.
When it was evening, the disciples approached him and said,
"This is a deserted place and it is already late;
dismiss the crowds so that they can go to the villages
and buy food for themselves."
Jesus said to them, "There is no need for them to go away;
give them some food yourselves."
But they said to him,
"Five loaves and two fish are all we have here."
Then he said, "Bring them here to me,"
and he ordered the crowds to sit down on the grass.
Taking the five loaves and the two fish, and looking up to heaven,
he said the blessing, broke the loaves,
and gave them to the disciples,
who in turn gave them to the crowds.
They all ate and were satisfied,
and they picked up the fragments left over—
twelve wicker baskets full.
Those who ate were about five thousand men,
not counting women and children.

Reflecting on the Gospel

After three weeks of hearing Jesus preach and teach in parables, we now move into the next chapter of Matthew's gospel, one in which Jesus performs the miracle of the multiplication of the loaves and fishes. Unlike some of the parables from last week and the week before, which are found only in Matthew, the story of the multiplication of the loaves and fishes is in each gospel, and in both Matthew and Mark the miracle happens twice! (Mark 6:32-44; 8:1-10; Matt 14:13-21; 15:32-39). Many scholars will posit that precisely because of the multiple attestation of this miracle, the event is rooted in some historical event in the life of Jesus (which cannot be said for every gospel story).

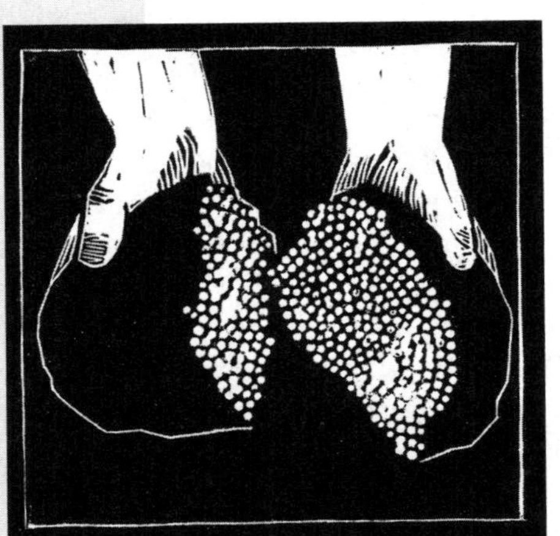

This event was retold a number of times, with various pieces of the story being accented or downplayed, as well as connections made with the Old Testament prophet Elisha and the Last Supper of Jesus with his disciples. Indeed the gospel story as we have it (or them) makes it nearly impossible to reconstruct the historical event, as the story had been the subject of theologizing for some time prior to being written down, and then again by those who wrote it down—the evangelists themselves.

For those who have a familiarity with the Old Testament, the connection to Elisha (2 Kgs 4:42-44) seems clear. In that story, the prophet tells his servant to give bread to the people so they can eat. The servant objects that the bread is not enough for the number of people who need to eat. Elisha merely repeats his command and says, "[F]or thus says the LORD: you will eat and have some left over" (2 Kgs 4:43). The connection between that story and what we have in Matthew seems crystal clear. The evangelist, or somebody who told the story before him, made the connection between Jesus' acts and those of Elisha.

And yet there is a connection to the Last Supper too. Four verbs serve as the link between the multiplication story and Jesus' actions the night before he died. In both settings, Jesus *takes* bread, *says a blessing*, *breaks* the bread, and *gives* it. Both the eucharistic tones and the allusions to Elisha are clear.

Jesus' actions are those of a prophet and so much more. The Gospel of John uses the story to launch into the bread of life discourse, but in Matthew, we have the narration of the miracle without any such extended discourse on the part of Jesus. We are reminded by this miracle story, a version of which appears six times in the gospels (!), that Jesus feeds the hungry and in so doing is a model for his followers to do the same.

Living the Paschal Mystery

Bread is such a simple but profound sign. It does not occur naturally, but requires human effort. Grain must be crushed to form flour. Flour is mixed with water or some other liquid to form dough, and the dough must be leavened with yeast to rise. Then the baking begins and we finally have a loaf of bread, sustenance that will fill us up and last. The human effort required to make bread is significant, and it involves time, all of which perhaps explains why so many of us simply buy bread today. Even so, there are not many things that taste better than a good loaf of homemade bread.

When we consider that Jesus multiplied the loaves so that all could eat, we recall that he acted as the prophet Elisha of old. He also foreshadowed his own Last Supper and the eucharistic gift he would leave his followers. As a result, even today we take bread, bless it, break it, and give it. In so doing we celebrate and consume Jesus himself, who was broken for us and given to us. As we are sustained on our earthly journey by the Eucharist, we live the paschal mystery.

Focusing the Gospel

Key words and phrases: "Five loaves and two fish are all we have here."

To the point: In today's gospel, though the disciples are in the company of the Bread of Life himself, they worry about the effects of hunger. Their protest that "[f]ive loaves and two fish are all we have" gives us an insight into their desire to be rid of the crowds. They are operating from a place of scarcity. This amount of food would hardly be enough to feed their small band of thirteen. If they share it, they will have nothing. But Jesus is not dissuaded; he blesses and distributes the meager feast and once everyone has eaten their fill, the leftovers total "twelve wicker baskets full." Another important number in the Bible, "twelve" can signal fullness and calls to mind the twelve tribes of Israel. In the Lord we do not need to fear scarcity—there is enough to satisfy the hunger of all.

Connecting the Gospel

to the second reading: The second reading from Paul's letter to the Romans tells us that we have nothing to fear. The abundance of the Lord, which satisfies our deepest hunger, is also found in his protective love. Paul begins his discourse with the question, "What will separate us from the love of Christ?" His answer? Nothing. Our bond to Jesus cannot be severed by "death, nor life, / nor angels, nor principalities, / nor present things, nor future things, /nor powers, nor height, nor depth, / nor any other creature."

to experience: Today's readings call us to let go of all fear. We do not need to worry that there is not enough to go around. We do not need to cower before any natural or supernatural force. We are protected and nourished by the infinite love of God. Under his care, fear melts away, leaving behind only love and the desire to serve him and our neighbor.

Connecting the Responsorial Psalm

to the readings: Today's psalm refrain, "The hand of the Lord feeds us; he answers all our needs," summarizes the actions of Jesus in the gospel. By his own hand, the Lord of life takes up the five loaves and two fish, "said the blessing, broke the loaves, / and gave them to the disciples, / who in turn gave them to the crowds." Fed by the hand of the Lord, "all ate and were satisfied." Jesus reveals the abundance of God who calls out to his people through the prophet Isaiah, "All you who are thirsty, / come to the water! / You who have no money, / come, receive grain and eat." Whereas the disciples want to send the crowds away so they can go and "buy food for themselves," this is not Jesus' way. Our Lord is one of supreme self-giving and he continues to feed us with himself in the bread and wine of the Eucharist.

to psalmist preparation: Throughout your own life of faith, how has Jesus fed you in his abundance? How are you being called through your ministry to be bread that is broken and shared for others?

PROMPTS FOR FAITH-SHARING

Through the prophet Isaiah, the Lord calls to all who hunger and thirst to come to him and be satisfied. How does your parish community reach out to those who hunger and thirst, either physically or spiritually?

In the letter to the Romans, St. Paul boldly proclaims that nothing can separate us from the love of God. Is there an individual in your life who is in need of this message? How might you express it to this person?

Many times in the gospels we hear of Jesus going off to a "deserted place by himself" in order to pray. Where do you find solace and quiet to pray?

Jesus' miracles show us what life is like in the kingdom of God. From today's miracle of feeding the five thousand from five loaves and two fish, what message do you receive about the kingdom?

Model Penitential Act

Presider: In a deserted place, Jesus feeds over five thousand people with five loaves and two fish. Trusting in the abundance of our Lord, let us turn to him and ask for mercy and healing . . . *[pause]*

Lord Jesus, you feed the hungry and care for the poor: Lord, have mercy.
Christ Jesus, your healing touch brings wholeness and life: Christ, have mercy.
Lord Jesus, you are just in all your ways, holy in all your works: Lord, have mercy.

Homily Points

• In today's gospel reading there is some discord between Jesus and his disciples. Although Jesus had been the one to leave the crowds and seek out a deserted place to mourn John the Baptist, when the crowds find him and interrupt his solitude, instead of irritation or annoyance, "his heart was moved with pity for them." The disciples seem to be the ones who are flustered by this turn of events and so take it upon themselves to tell Jesus when evening falls that it's time to dismiss the crowds so they can go and buy their own dinners.

• The crowds do not seem concerned about physical hunger. Perhaps the hunger Jesus was already filling, the hunger that initially drove them out of their familiar towns and into this deserted place, was deeper than any physical hunger pains could be.

• Jesus tells his disciples, "There is no need for them to go away; / give them some food yourselves." As with all his words and actions, Jesus is mentoring the disciples in what it really means to follow him. Instead of sending people away, they should be inviting them closer. Instead of telling them to go and take care of their own needs, they should be feeding them (both spiritually and physically) themselves. As followers of Christ, we are also the intended recipients of Jesus' words. We are not to hoard the bread of life or the word of God, but instead we are to invite all we meet to come to the feast. We should not be concerned with scarcity. At the table of the Lord, we find abundance and more than enough to satisfy the hunger of all.

Model Universal Prayer (Prayer of the Faithful)

Presider: In confidence that our God hears and answers prayer, let us bring our needs before him.

Response: Lord, hear our prayer.

For all who preach the word of God, in word and action may they boldly proclaim the never-failing, never-ending love of our Creator . . .

For elected officials and those who hold public office, may they keep the needs of the poor and vulnerable in mind as they shape public policy . . .

For those who have turned away from their faith, may they know the compassionate love of God and hear his voice calling them by name . . .

For all gathered here, may we never cease to hunger and thirst for righteousness . . .

Presider: God of abundance, in you we find nourishment that satisfies. Hear our prayers that your mercy and love might fill the earth so that all people would dwell in peace. We ask this through Christ our Lord. **Amen.**

COLLECT

Let us pray

Pause for silent prayer

Draw near to your servants, O Lord,
and answer their prayers with unceasing
kindness,
that, for those who glory in you as their
Creator and guide,
you may restore what you have created
and keep safe what you have restored.
Through our Lord Jesus Christ, your Son,
who lives and reigns with you in the unity
of the Holy Spirit,
one God, for ever and ever. **Amen.**

FIRST READING

Isa 55:1-3

Thus says the LORD:
All you who are thirsty,
come to the water!
You who have no money,
come, receive grain and eat;
come, without paying and without cost,
drink wine and milk!
Why spend your money for what is not
bread;
your wages for what fails to satisfy?
Heed me, and you shall eat well,
you shall delight in rich fare.
Come to me heedfully,
listen, that you may have life.
I will renew with you the everlasting
covenant,
the benefits assured to David.

CATECHESIS

RESPONSORIAL PSALM
Ps 145:8-9, 15-16, 17-18

℟. (cf. 16) The hand of the Lord feeds us; he answers all our needs.

The LORD is gracious and merciful,
slow to anger and of great kindness.
The LORD is good to all
and compassionate toward all his works.

℟. The hand of the Lord feeds us; he answers all our needs.

The eyes of all look hopefully to you,
and you give them their food in due season;
you open your hand
and satisfy the desire of every living thing.

℟. The hand of the Lord feeds us; he answers all our needs.

The LORD is just in all his ways
and holy in all his works.
The LORD is near to all who call upon him,
to all who call upon him in truth.

℟. The hand of the Lord feeds us; he answers all our needs.

SECOND READING
Rom 8:35, 37-39

Brothers and sisters:
What will separate us from the love of Christ?
Will anguish, or distress, or persecution, or famine,
or nakedness, or peril, or the sword?
No, in all these things we conquer overwhelmingly
through him who loved us.
For I am convinced that neither death, nor life,
nor angels, nor principalities,
nor present things, nor future things,
nor powers, nor height, nor depth,
nor any other creature will be able to separate us
from the love of God in Christ Jesus our Lord.

About Liturgy

A church that is poor for the poor: Hearing in God's word about comfort for those in need is one thing. Hearing in God's word any justification for complacency and apathy toward those in need is another. We must be careful. Today's Scriptures are not about our comfort. They are about what we are called to do as disciples of Jesus who says to us today: There is no need for them—the hungry, the poor, the immigrant, the outcast, the one you would rather not deal with—to go away; give them some food, some help, some welcome, some kindness, some mercy yourselves.

In previous weeks' gospels leading up to today, we heard about the word of God that, if planted into fertile hearts, grows abundantly. If we hear today's readings as an invitation to stay in a place of safety and comfort, for God will take care of us, then we've become the rocky soil into which the Word was sown but took no root. We've become the weeds secretly planted into the field by the enemy. Precisely because God takes care of our every need, we must go out and give others what they need.

Pope Francis said, "How I would like a church that is poor and for the poor" (March 16, 2013). His constant call for us to go to society's peripheries is not simply because it is a nice thing to do for people in need. If our hearts are to be changed into fertile soil, we must get out of our comfort zones and easy circle of friends and enter into relationship with those we may pray for but never interact with on a human level. Feed them yourselves. Become bread for others as Jesus has become the living bread for you. That is what we are commissioned to do every Sunday.

About Initiation

Come to the water: Today's first reading from Isaiah will be heard again at the Easter Vigil (presuming your community will proclaim more than the minimum number of two or three readings from the Old Testament that night). Take time with your catechumens (and with your neophytes baptized at the last Easter Vigil) to reflect deeply on this reading. What is their thirst? What do they value most? What have they wasted themselves on thinking it would satisfy? For neophytes: How have they experienced delight and fullness of life in these last few months?

This first reading is also a good opportunity to explore the significance of holy water and how we use it as a sacramental to bless ourselves as a reminder of and preparation for baptism.

About Liturgical Music

Getting out of our comfort zones: Most of us do this ministry because we love to make music. It's not primarily about being part of a faith-sharing or prayer group. Yet that has to be part of what we do if we are to be *ministers* and not just musicians. We can begin with learning to be ministers for those with whom we sing and make music each week.

If you are not already taking time at each rehearsal and gathering to pray, then make a commitment to help your music ministers and yourself get out of your comfort zones. Even a simple sign of the cross, silent prayer, or spontaneous intercessions for people we want to remember, concluding with the Lord's Prayer, is a good start to helping music ministers turn their attention toward the peripheries of the rehearsal room.

SPIRITUALITY

GOSPEL ACCLAMATION
cf. Ps 130:5

℟. Alleluia, alleluia.
I wait for the Lord;
my soul waits for his word.
℟. Alleluia, alleluia.

Gospel Matt 14:22-33; L115A

After he had fed the people, Jesus made the disciples get into a boat
and precede him to the other side,
while he dismissed the crowds.
After doing so, he went up on the mountain by himself to pray.
When it was evening he was there alone.
Meanwhile the boat, already a few miles offshore,
was being tossed about by the waves, for the wind was against it.
During the fourth watch of the night,
he came toward them walking on the sea.
When the disciples saw him walking on the sea they were terrified.
"It is a ghost," they said, and they cried out in fear.
At once Jesus spoke to them, "Take courage, it is I; do not be afraid."
Peter said to him in reply,
"Lord, if it is you, command me to come to you on the water."
He said, "Come."
Peter got out of the boat and began to walk on the water toward Jesus.
But when he saw how strong the wind was he became frightened;
and, beginning to sink, he cried out, "Lord, save me!"
Immediately Jesus stretched out his hand and caught Peter,
and said to him, "O you of little faith, why did you doubt?"
After they got into the boat, the wind died down.
Those who were in the boat did him homage, saying,
"Truly, you are the Son of God."

Reflecting on the Gospel

In the year 1300 the church in Rome celebrated one of the first "holy year" feasts that would come to mark each centenary, then each twenty-five years, and occasionally each year ending in 33 (the traditional age of Jesus) or even 83 (the traditional age of Jesus, plus 50!), as in 1833, 1933, 1983. In 1300, pilgrims descended on Rome for this holy year, as they would for centuries thereafter. As part of the commemoration, two years prior the mosaicist Giotto di Bondone was commissioned to create the *navicella* (the little boat) that depicts the scene we read in the gospel today for St. Peter's Basilica. Centuries after di Bondone, during the time that St. Peter's Basilica was completely renovated, the *navicella* was nearly destroyed. It was ultimately restored and moved to the portico of the renovated Basilica where it can still be seen today. Often visitors and pilgrims walk right under it without knowing it's there! When one stands under the portico, looking out to the piazza, the mosaic is directly overhead, on the inside panel of the exterior wall of the façade, facing the basilica.

The episode in the gospel (Jesus walking on the water) appears in two other gospel accounts, but Matthew has a unique version of the story. It is only Matthew that has Peter on the water with Jesus, and then sinking due to a lack of faith. Of course, Jesus rescues him and that is the moment depicted in di Bondone's mosaic at St. Peter's Basilica in Rome.

It doesn't take much imagination to see in this story that the boat represents the church (Matthew is the only gospel to use the term "church") and that Peter, as leader of the twelve himself, is reliant upon Jesus. In fact, the entire boat is buffeted by the storm but does not sink. When Jesus comes aboard, the storm subsides and the waters are calm.

We are told that this happened during the fourth watch of the night (between 3 a.m. and 6 a.m.). Modern folks might wonder what the twelve were doing on the water at that time of night, especially during a storm! The answer is that Jesus had commanded them to meet him at the other side. The Sea of Galilee is about thirteen miles long by eight miles wide. So even to traverse the shorter distance could have been treacherous, especially at night.

As for those of us in the boat today, we can expect turbulence much like the disciples themselves experienced. Though Peter was willing to step outside the boat, his faith was little, not enough for him to stand on his own. His immediate cry for help was heard and he was saved. We may take comfort in knowing that those in the ship will be safe even if the journey is bumpy. And the Lord is there to save us when we cry out.

Living the Paschal Mystery

We might wonder why Jesus commanded his disciples to set out by boat at dusk to meet him on the other side. It does not sound like a very wise or prudent request, and especially so after the storm arose. Nevertheless, the disciples follow the advice of their master. Rather than meet them on the other side, during the darkest part of the night, the disciples experience Jesus walking on the water in the midst of the wind and storm. Impetuous Peter seeks to walk on the water too, but he is unable to do so due to his lack of faith. In the end, the Lord calms the storm and joins the disciples in the boat.

When we experience turbulence and storms, we may be reassured that the Lord is near. When we call, he answers. He will join us and the storms will subside. Is it any wonder this story has been read for centuries as an allegory for the relationship between Christ and the church? The boat may protect us from the storm, but we still experience the effects of the storm. It is only Jesus himself who can calm the waters.

Focusing the Gospel

Key words and phrases: But when he saw how strong the wind was he became frightened.

To the point: Today's gospel begins with the disciples in a boat "a few miles offshore . . . being tossed about by the waves." When the men in the boat catch sight of Jesus walking on the water toward them, they become even more frightened. Instead of being overjoyed at the sight of their salvation, the disciples are terrified thinking this is a ghost. Jesus immediately tells them, "Take courage, it is I; do not be afraid." As a way of testing the identity of this being, Peter asks to be commanded to come out on the water in the same way. Jesus complies. While Peter keeps his focus on Jesus, he, too, walks on water, but as soon as he becomes aware of the strength of the wind, he flounders and begins to sink. He calls out in distress, "Lord, save me!" When our gaze is focused on Jesus, we also find the strength and resources to do things that frighten us. Even when our focus drifts and we become overwhelmed, we need not fear. The Lord is always ready to reach out a hand to stop us from sinking.

Connecting the Gospel

to the first reading: In the first reading, the prophet Elijah also receives a revelation of God. Standing outside of a cave where he has been told "the Lord will be passing by," Elijah witnesses a strong, heavy wind that crushes rocks and rends the mountains, an earthquake, and a fire, but God is not in any of these displays of force or power. It is only when he encounters "a tiny whispering sound" that Elijah hides his face in his cloak. The same calm seems to fall upon the disciples in the boat when the wind ceases. In the post-storm silence they do "him homage, saying, 'Truly, you are the Son of God.'"

to experience: In today's first reading and in the gospel, God and Jesus are not revealed in the storms that surround Elijah and the disciples. Instead, God is in the courage that Jesus offers to the disciples and in the quiet whispering sound following the wind, earthquake, and fire that shake the cave of Elijah. In our own lives of faith, do we find God in the quiet or is our gaze distracted by worldly shows of power and force?

Connecting the Responsorial Psalm

to the readings: The experiences of both Elijah and the disciples in today's gospel offer us opportunities to "see" God's kindness. As the psalmist states, "I will hear what God proclaims; / the Lord—for he proclaims peace." In the "tiny whispering sound" and the calm waters after the storm, God's peace is announced.

to psalmist preparation: Where do you find time and space to meet God in silence so as to be rooted in his kindness and salvation?

PROMPTS FOR FAITH-SHARING

In your life, where do you experience the quiet presence of God?

Today's psalm prays, "Lord, let us see your kindness, and grant us your salvation." Is there a situation in your life right now that would benefit from kindness?

St. Paul writes to the Romans, "I speak the truth in Christ, I do not lie." When has the truth spoken to you in love brought new growth and flourishing?

In the gospel reading Jesus calls out to the frightened disciples, "Take courage, it is I, do not be afraid." When have you needed courage to follow Jesus in the life of faith?

Model Penitential Act

Presider: In today's gospel when Peter begins to sink, Jesus catches him and asks, "O you of little, faith, why did you doubt?" For the times our own faith has faltered, let us ask for pardon and healing . . . *[pause]*

Lord Jesus, you are the Son of God and master of creation: Lord, have mercy.
Christ Jesus, in you we find courage and strength: Christ, have mercy.
Lord Jesus, you intercede for us at the right hand of the Father: Lord, have mercy.

Homily Points

• Have you ever wondered why Jesus chose fishermen to be his first disciples? They don't seem to be the obvious choice to help Jesus in his mission of proclaiming the kingdom of God. These men were most likely illiterate and their long days (and sometimes even nights) at sea, as well as the endless work of mending their nets, would have kept them from spending extra time in the synagogue studying the word of God. And yet, there are other things about fishermen that probably made them the ideal first disciples of the Lord. Their lives required hard, physical labor, patience, and trust. As anyone who has spent serious time devoted to fishing knows, there is no guarantee that a day's labors will produce results. Instead, one must be prepared to show up again and again in the hopes of a catch. Fishermen also need a healthy respect for the forces of creation and the humility to know when to turn back and call it a day.

• These first disciples of Jesus tell us a lot about what it takes to be a Christian and a "fisher of men." Peter's vocation to build the kingdom of God required all of the attributes he had honed as a fisherman: physical labor, patience, trust, and humility.

• We, too, are called to be fishermen—to put our muscle behind building a just and peaceful society, to cast out our nets again and again in hope, and, most important, to develop the tenacity to keep trying in the face of failure. Just like Peter, we are not alone in our efforts; walking on the stormy waves or sitting in the boat beside us, Jesus, the Lord of life continues to call out, "Take courage . . . Do not be afraid."

Model Universal Prayer (Prayer of the Faithful)

Presider: Jesus tells his disciples, "[D]o not be afraid." With perfect trust that banishes all fear, let us bring our needs before the Lord.

Response: Lord, hear our prayer.

For all members of the universal church, may they aid each other in holiness by speaking the truth in love . . .

For the nations of the world, may diverse peoples be brought together by mutual respect and goodwill to promote peace and justice for all . . .

For families who are separated due to work, military service, or travel, may they know the comfort of a supportive community . . .

For all gathered here, may we come to find God in the still, quiet moments of our days and bring his peace to all we meet . . .

Presider: Eternal God, in you we find courage and strength for the journey of faith. Hear our prayers that we might be a comforting presence to those who are suffering in our families and communities. We ask this through Christ our Lord. **Amen.**

COLLECT

Let us pray.

Pause for silent prayer

Almighty ever-living God,
whom, taught by the Holy Spirit,
we dare to call our Father,
bring, we pray, to perfection in our hearts
the spirit of adoption as your sons and daughters,
that we may merit to enter into the inheritance
which you have promised.
Through our Lord Jesus Christ, your Son,
who lives and reigns with you in the unity of the Holy Spirit,
one God, for ever and ever. **Amen.**

FIRST READING

1 Kgs 19:9a, 11-13a

At the mountain of God, Horeb,
Elijah came to a cave where he took shelter.
Then the LORD said to him,
"Go outside and stand on the mountain before the LORD;
the LORD will be passing by."
A strong and heavy wind was rending the mountains
and crushing rocks before the LORD—
but the LORD was not in the wind.
After the wind there was an earthquake—
but the LORD was not in the earthquake.
After the earthquake there was fire—
but the LORD was not in the fire.
After the fire there was a tiny whispering sound.
When he heard this,
Elijah hid his face in his cloak
and went and stood at the entrance of the cave.

RESPONSORIAL PSALM
Ps 85:9, 10, 11-12, 13-14

℟. (8) Lord, let us see your kindness, and grant us your salvation.

I will hear what God proclaims;
the LORD—for he proclaims peace.
Near indeed is his salvation to those who fear him,
glory dwelling in our land.

℟. Lord, let us see your kindness, and grant us your salvation.

Kindness and truth shall meet;
justice and peace shall kiss.
Truth shall spring out of the earth,
and justice shall look down from heaven.

℟. Lord, let us see your kindness, and grant us your salvation.

The LORD himself will give his benefits;
our land shall yield its increase.
Justice shall walk before him,
and prepare the way of his steps.

℟. Lord, let us see your kindness, and grant us your salvation.

SECOND READING
Rom 9:1-5

Brothers and sisters:
I speak the truth in Christ, I do not lie;
my conscience joins with the Holy Spirit in bearing me witness
that I have great sorrow and constant anguish in my heart.
For I could wish that I myself were accursed and cut off from Christ
for the sake of my own people,
my kindred according to the flesh.
They are Israelites;
theirs the adoption, the glory, the covenants,
the giving of the law, the worship, and the promises;
theirs the patriarchs, and from them,
according to the flesh, is the Christ,
who is over all, God blessed forever.
Amen.

About Liturgy

Church would be great if . . . : There's a joke that says, "Church would be great if it weren't for all the people." It's meant to be funny, but, unfortunately, I know we've met some people for whom it's serious. How often have we witnessed parents at Mass with squirmy children getting "the look" or an unkind word from people nearby? Or worse? Twice, I've heard a homilist stop his homily to publicly ask specific parents to take their child out because the child was being too noisy!

There is a beautiful nuance that we get in the juxtaposition of today's readings. In the first reading, we hear that the Lord was not in the wind, the quake, or the fire. Yet in the gospel, Jesus was indeed *right there* in the midst of the storm itself.

Whatever is happening around you does not determine God's presence. God is *always* present! The key is what you are paying attention to and what you are looking for. If you look only toward your own comfort and ease, and pay attention to your own quiet amid your storms, then you will miss the Lord right in front of you. You *will* be distracted by disruptions around you. However, if you look right into the very thing that is disrupting your life and seek out Christ's presence there, more than likely you will find the Lord and see God's kindness, as the psalmist today begs. The infant's cry will no longer be an intrusion but an invitation to give God thanks for the gift of life and the gift of this family who, in the midst of their own storms, have sought out Christ's presence in your midst.

Silences in the Mass: Even amid distractions, those who prepare the liturgy should attend to the assigned silences in the Mass. See more about this in the "About Liturgical Music" section for the Second Sunday of Lent.

About Initiation

When does RCIA begin? You're probably getting ready for the "beginning" of RCIA this year after a break during the summer. Even so, be careful that your language or announcements don't imply that there is a formal "start" to the RCIA process. Remember that the first period of the Rite of Christian Initiation of Adults is called the period of *evangelization* and precatechumenate (emphasis added). It would be silly to say, "Evangelization begins on September 6 with our first meeting for those who want to become Catholic." Evangelization is year-round, and it usually doesn't involve a meeting!

Instead of saying that RCIA begins on a particular date, just say every month or so, "If you want to learn more about becoming Catholic, let me know, and we'll get you started in the process." If your formal meetings don't begin for a while, simply take them to Mass and introduce them to folks each week. Look at RCIA 9.1 for some other ideas.

About Liturgical Music

Preventing distractions: Some music ministers serve from the loft. However, most music groups are found near the sanctuary. In fact, choirs should be placed so they are seen as part of the worshiping community and not separate from it (see Sing to the Lord 98).

Wherever your music ministers serve from in your worship space, be sure they keep their attention on the ritual focus and not on their music or their instruments in between songs. When lectors are proclaiming the reading or presiders are inviting us to pray, music ministers should internally and outwardly be focused on that ritual action, just as all members of the assembly are called to do. In this way, they will be examples of keeping our eyes on Christ.

GOSPEL ACCLAMATION
℟. Alleluia, alleluia.
Mary is taken up to heaven;
a chorus of angels exults.
℟. Alleluia, alleluia.

Gospel Luke 1:39-56; L622

Mary set out
and traveled to the hill country in haste
to a town of Judah,
where she entered the house of Zechariah
and greeted Elizabeth.
When Elizabeth heard Mary's greeting,
the infant leaped in her womb,
and Elizabeth, filled with the Holy Spirit,
cried out in a loud voice and said,
"Blessed are you among women,
and blessed is the fruit of your womb.
And how does this happen to me,
that the mother of my Lord should come to me?
For at the moment the sound of your greeting reached my ears,
the infant in my womb leaped for joy.
Blessed are you who believed
that what was spoken to you by the Lord
would be fulfilled."

And Mary said:

"My soul proclaims the greatness of the Lord;
my spirit rejoices in God my Savior
for he has looked with favor on his lowly servant.

Continued in Appendix A, p. 301.

See Appendix A, p. 301, for the other readings.

Reflecting on the Gospel

We hear Mary's voice in the Gospel of Luke today. Luke is the gospel writer who gives the largest role to Mary, from the annunciation where Mary said "yes," and the visitation, the nativity of Jesus, and even to her own presence at significant times in Jesus' ministry through Pentecost in Acts of the Apostles. As mother of Jesus, or "mother of my Lord," as Elizabeth calls her, Mary was in a unique position. But she was not passive, as her words from the gospel today indicate. She had a vision for justice that certainly would have inspired and informed Jesus. Indeed, many of the themes in the canticle today will be echoed by Jesus throughout the Gospel of Luke and even into the Acts of the Apostles by Jesus' disciples. Namely, Mary's claim that "he has cast down the mighty from their thrones / and has lifted up the lowly" finds fulfillment in Jesus' ministry, just as "he has filled the hungry with good things / and sent the rich away empty" foreshadows many of Jesus' own parables.

But today we are celebrating not the feast of the Visitation, but the feast of the Assumption, when Mary was taken (the Latin term *assumptio* means "taken") into heaven. Since this is a feast based on a Latin term, that is a signal that the feast itself developed later. Even the Eastern church celebrates the *Dormition* of Mary ("sleeping" of Mary), which is also a Latin term. We will search the Scriptures in vain to find any mention of either the "sleeping" of Mary or her being "taken" into heaven. These traditions arose independently as ways of explaining what happened to Mary.

In fact, the formal teaching of this church dogma was not done officially until 1950, though its roots certainly go much deeper than that.

When we consider Mary's role in the church today, we will likely find more to contemplate in her words in Scripture, which is why the church gives us this reading from Luke. So though we celebrate her assumption today, we hear her voice proclaiming justice to the downtrodden, a reversal of the present order of things. Let us not miss her voice by gazing into the heavens seeking to see where she went.

Living the Paschal Mystery

Marian doctrines can seem to be never ending sources of division with our Christian sisters and brothers. This is one reason why it is so important that the church gives us words from Mary in today's gospel.

When Mary spoke these words proclaimed today in the liturgy, Jesus had not even been born. She was a young woman who was motivated by justice. God was on her side and she foresaw a great reversal. How, then, did she react upon Jesus' death? We know she remained with the disciples up to and including Pentecost. Her faith never seems to have been shaken. She seems to have been prepared for the ultimate reversal from death to life during her entire life. Let us, too, live this paschal mystery as Mary did.

Focusing the Gospel

Key words and phrases: And Mary said: "My soul proclaims the greatness of the Lord."

To the point: Throughout the infancy narratives of Luke we find beloved prayers of the church. There is the canticle of Zechariah after John is born (1:68-79), the canticle of Simeon when the baby Jesus is presented in the temple (2:29-32), the Gloria the angels sing to announce Christ's birth (2:14), and at the visitation, portrayed in today's gospel, we find words from the Hail Mary and also the *Magnificat*. Within the gospels this is the longest proclamation Mary gives, and it offers us great insight into her theology and relationship with God. In the life of Mary, we find a model of discipleship and also an image of what God would like to do in the life of every believer. We are invited to bear Christ to the world through our words and actions, and rest in the hope of everlasting life with God, Mary, and all the saints.

Model Penitential Act

Presider: In today's gospel we hear Mary's words: "My soul proclaims the greatness of the Lord." We, too, have gathered to sing the Lord's praises. Let us pause to ask for his healing and mercy that we might worship him well . . . *[pause]*

Lord Jesus, you are Son of God and son of Mary: Lord, have mercy.
Christ Jesus, you are the one foretold by the prophets: Christ, have mercy.
Lord Jesus, you are the holy and anointed one: Lord, have mercy.

Model Universal Prayer (Prayer of the Faithful)

Presider: Through the intercession of Mary, Mother of God, let us bring our needs, and the needs of our world, before the Lord.

Response: Lord, hear our prayer.

For God's holy church, in word and deed may it proclaim along with Mary the saving power of God who feeds the hungry and lifts up the lowly . . .

For governments throughout the world, may the voices of all people, regardless of age, gender, race, or sexual orientation, be valued and welcomed in public discourse . . .

For persecuted Christians wherever they may be, may they be protected and strengthened in faith . . .

For all gathered here, like Mary, may we be devoted to the word of God and with joy proclaim it to others . . .

Presider: God of justice, along with Mary we praise your holy name and give you thanks for all you have done for us. Hear our prayers that following her example, we might also bear Christ to the world in our words and actions. We ask this through Christ our Lord. **Amen.**

About Liturgy

Holy days of obligation: When August 15 falls on Saturday, you will inevitably get the question, "Is today a holy day of obligation?" The real question they're probably asking is, "Do I have to go to Mass twice this weekend?"

In 1993 the United States bishops decreed for the Latin Rite US dioceses that when August 15 (and January 1 and November 1) falls on a Saturday, the obligation is repealed. However, it is always good to mark the day in some way through personal prayer or works of mercy.

Some curious minds might wonder, if it *were* an obligation, could they do a "two for one"—going to the Saturday evening Mass and getting both Sunday and the solemnity covered? Technically, no. Regardless of the readings or prayers used at the Saturday evening Mass, one fulfills only one obligation per Mass.

More important, determine which readings and prayers to use at your regular Saturday evening Mass. There is no hard guideline for this choice. Either Sunday or Assumption may be celebrated, though most parishioners will expect to hear the Sunday readings at the Saturday evening Mass.

COLLECT

Let us pray.

Pause for silent prayer

Almighty ever-living God,
who assumed the Immaculate Virgin Mary,
the Mother of your Son,
body and soul into heavenly glory,
grant, we pray,
that, always attentive to the things that are above,
we may merit to be sharers of her glory.
Through our Lord Jesus Christ, your Son,
who lives and reigns with you in the unity of
the Holy Spirit,
one God, for ever and ever. **Amen.**

FOR REFLECTION

- Elizabeth greets Mary, "Blessed are you who believed / that what was spoken to you by the Lord / would be fulfilled." How is Mary a model of belief and discipleship in your life?
- Mary begins the *Magnificat*, "My soul proclaims the greatness of the Lord." How do you seek to magnify the Lord with your life?
- We all need companions in the spiritual life. Who do you journey with along the road of discipleship?

Homily Points

- On this feast of the Assumption, we celebrate the end of Mary's life when she was bodily taken up to heaven to dwell with God. Our gospel for today comes from Mary's visitation to her kinswoman Elizabeth and gives us a glimpse into her prophetic understanding of God and his actions within the world. The words of the *Magnificat* call us to take stock of our own lives.
- In Mary we find the quintessential model of discipleship. English theologian Caryll Houselander tells us, "The one thing that she did and does is the one thing that we all have to do, namely, to bear Christ into the world. Christ must be born from every soul, formed in every life" (*The Reed of God*). In your own words and actions, how do you seek to "bear Christ into the world"?

SPIRITUALITY

GOSPEL ACCLAMATION
cf. Matt 4:23

℟. Alleluia, alleluia.
Jesus proclaimed the Gospel of the kingdom
and cured every disease among the people.
℟. Alleluia, alleluia.

Gospel

Matt 15:21-28; L118A

At that time, Jesus withdrew to the region of Tyre and Sidon.
And behold, a Canaanite woman of that district came and called out,
"Have pity on me, Lord, Son of David!
My daughter is tormented by a demon."
But Jesus did not say a word in answer to her.
Jesus' disciples came and asked him,
"Send her away, for she keeps calling out after us."
He said in reply,
"I was sent only to the lost sheep of the house of Israel."
But the woman came and did Jesus homage, saying, "Lord, help me."
He said in reply,
"It is not right to take the food of the children
and throw it to the dogs."
She said, "Please, Lord, for even the dogs eat the scraps
that fall from the table of their masters."
Then Jesus said to her in reply,
"O woman, great is your faith!
Let it be done for you as you wish."
And the woman's daughter was healed from that hour.

Reflecting on the Gospel

"We're not going to play with you!" the kids on the playground said to the new student. It was a shocking thing for the teachers to hear, as they had been speaking to the students about welcoming and creating an environment where we all "get along." The taunts certainly did not conform to the mission of the Catholic school. Clearly, more work would need to be done before the new student would feel welcome. The teachers hoped they could address the situation before the new student left and found a different school.

In today's gospel, a Canaanite woman comes up to Jesus and asks for his mercy, not for her but for her daughter. Now, Canaanites were people displaced a millennium before the time of Jesus, when the Israelites took possession of the land. The Israelites even enslaved some of the Canaanites in those early years. It was "easy" to look down on a Canaanite, as they were not considered part of God's chosen people. Jesus' behavior, like that of the disciples, can seem a bit shocking. Jesus initially refuses to acknowledge the woman, and the disciples seek to have her dismissed. Jesus finally does speak, only to say that he was "sent only to the lost sheep of the house of Israel." That is, he was not sent for a Canaanite, even if her daughter was suffering. At this point in the story, it's good for us to pause and not attempt to explain away this type of attitude. In fact, other times in the Gospel of Matthew, Jesus says that he was sent only to the lost sheep of the house of Israel. In this gospel, the message of Jesus goes out to all nations only after the resurrection (Matt 28:16-20). But during the earthly ministry of Jesus, it seems non-Israelites, non-Jews, were not part of his mission.

Even so, the woman persists. She does not back away. Jesus replies, effectively reiterating what he had said initially, though using a rather insulting term: "dogs." No matter, the woman continues, accepts the insulting metaphor, and says even dogs get the scraps. Finally, Jesus relents, and with a word the woman's daughter is healed. Many commentators focus their attention on Jesus' words and actions in this scene. But we may also consider this from the point of view of the woman—the outsider, the excluded. She persists and she ultimately receives what she sought, not something for herself but for her daughter.

Today, we are living in the post-resurrection world. Therefore, when we are in a position to include, to welcome, to invite, let us do so. This might mean welcoming a new child on the playground, an outsider who has moved to the neighborhood, or even a non-citizen or one who does not share our ethnic identity. The inclination to exclude and not to help is strong. It's overcome in the resurrection.

Living the Paschal Mystery

The resurrection gives power and new life. After the resurrection, Jesus tells his disciples to go to all nations, teaching and baptizing. The scene from today's gospel lets us know that the earthly ministry of Jesus was not characterized in that way, at least not as Matthew presents it. But now that Christ has been raised from the dead, all are welcome, and all may be disciples. No longer is God's chosen people limited to one group. Instead, by what God has done in Christ, all are chosen and called to be children of God.

The suffering and death of Jesus put an end to a way of thinking that saw God's favor bestowed on a limited group of people. With the resurrection, there has been a *metanoia*, a new way of thinking that embraces inclusion and invitation. Let us be guided by a resurrection way of life that seeks to welcome rather than create divisions. In so doing, we will be living the paschal mystery.

Focusing the Gospel

Key words and phrases: "O woman, great is your faith!"

To the point: In today's gospel we encounter something that may shock and startle us: it seems as though Jesus' own understanding of his identity and mission evolves. In proclaiming Jesus as true God and true man, sometimes it is easier to emphasize his divinity over his humanity. We know that as true God, Jesus did not sin, but in every other way he entered into the human experience, from being born in Bethlehem to the agony of death on the cross. As humans grow, our understanding of our self and others changes and develops. This seems to happen with Jesus in the course of his encounter with the Canaanite woman. Initially, he refuses her request, citing his understanding of his ministry as "only to the lost sheep of Israel." But the woman's persistence and faith leads him to eventually comply, telling her, "Let it be done for you as you wish."

Connecting the Gospel

to the first and second readings: Both the first and the second reading speak of inclusion within the people of God. God proclaims through Isaiah that "foreigners who join themselves to the Lord . . . I will bring to my holy mountain / and make joyful in my house of prayer." In Paul's letter to the Romans, we hear this expanded even further. With the coming of Jesus—his life, death, and resurrection—God's covenant with the Jewish people has been opened to include all people. Paul sees his main role as "apostle to the Gentiles" and will spend his years of active ministry spreading the word of God mainly amongst those who have no Jewish heritage.

to experience: As Christians, we are thankful for the opening of the covenant in Jesus to include us, and yet we must be careful not to believe or preach that we have taken the place of the Jewish people. As St. Paul states, "[T]he gifts and the call of God are irrevocable," and the Jewish people remain chosen by the Lord and precious in his sight.

Connecting the Responsorial Psalm

to the readings: Although the Old Testament is the story of God specifically joining himself to the people of Israel, all throughout the Hebrew Scriptures we find the understanding that their God is not the ruler of their people alone, but of the whole earth. Today's psalm refrain, "O God, let all the nations praise you!" speaks to this.

to psalmist preparation: The book of Psalms is sacred to both the Jewish and the Christian people. All over the world, Jews and Christians pray with the words of the psalms in their personal prayer and in communal liturgy. As a cantor, you have a role in proclaiming the psalms to the people of God that links you closely with our Jewish brothers and sisters. How do the psalms sustain and nourish you in faith?

PROMPTS FOR FAITH-SHARING

At the end of the first reading God proclaims, "[M]y house shall be called / a house of prayer for all peoples." What are the different ethnic groups within your parish? How are all included in worship and ministry?

Through the prophet Isaiah, the Lord urges his people to "[o]bserve what is right, do what is just." Where is justice lacking in your community or nation, and how might God be calling you to advocate for justice?

The Canaanite woman is persistent in her request that Jesus heal her daughter. Where are you being called to persistence in prayer?

Jesus tells her, "[W]oman, great is your faith!" Who has been a model of faith for you in your life?

Model Penitential Act

Presider: As we prepare to meet the risen Lord in his Word and at the altar, let us pause to call to mind our sins so that we might ask the Lord for his mercy . . . *[pause]*

Lord Jesus, you are our salvation and our hope: Lord, have mercy.
Christ Jesus, you guide us along the path of everlasting life: Christ, have mercy.
Lord Jesus, in justice and mercy you rule the nations: Lord, have mercy.

Homily Points

• Today's gospel passage can be difficult to reconcile with the Jesus we know from the rest of the Scriptures. In Luke, from the very beginning Jesus is proclaimed as a gift "for all the people" (2:10). And when he is presented at the temple, the prophet Simeon takes him in his arms, blessing God and saying, "[M]y eyes have seen your salvation, / which you prepared in the sight of all the peoples, / a light for revelation to the Gentiles, / and glory for your people Israel" (2:30-32). It is startling, then, to find Jesus in today's gospel initially refusing the Canaanite woman who begs for her daughter's healing.

• It is important to remember that the communities of faith that produced each gospel had a hand in shaping the narrative of Jesus' life, death, and resurrection. While Luke wrote for a largely Gentile community, Matthew's was Jewish. When looked at from the perspective of that audience, this gospel is startling in a different way. For Jewish Christians, it might have been difficult to welcome outsiders in. We can imagine these listeners possibly breathing a sigh of relief when they hear Jesus' response to the woman that he was sent "only to the lost sheep of the house of Israel."

• And then everything changes. The woman is not put off by Jesus' refusal or even by his comparison of her and her people to "dogs." Her persistence leads him to relent, healing her daughter and even exclaiming, "O woman, great is your faith!" For the people of Matthew's community, this gospel passage would be a reminder that in Jesus, God's covenant has been opened to all people of goodwill. Within our own communities it also holds a challenge: how willing are *we* to welcome the outsider and the foreigner?

Model Universal Prayer (Prayer of the Faithful)

Presider: Knowing the gracious love of God, let us bring to him all of our needs and those of our world.

Response: Lord, hear our prayer.

For the universal church, may it be strengthened through its diversity and become a place where all peoples of the world find welcome . . .

For those who have been entrusted with wealth and authority, may they humbly steward their resources for the good of their communities . . .

For those who are tormented by mental or spiritual illness and for their caretakers and loved ones, may Jesus' healing touch bring comfort and peace . . .

For all gathered here around the altar of the Lord, nourished by his Body and Blood may we go forth to proclaim the gospel to all we meet . . .

Presider: Creator God, in your mercy and goodness, you have called all people to yourself. Hear our prayers that by embracing diversity, we might build homes and parishes that welcome all. We ask this through Christ our Lord. **Amen.**

COLLECT

Let us pray.

Pause for silent prayer

O God, who have prepared for those who
love you
good things which no eye can see,
fill our hearts, we pray, with the warmth
of your love,
so that, loving you in all things and above
all things,
we may attain your promises,
which surpass every human desire.
Through our Lord Jesus Christ, your Son,
who lives and reigns with you in the unity
of the Holy Spirit,
one God, for ever and ever. **Amen.**

FIRST READING

Isa 56:1, 6-7

Thus says the LORD:
Observe what is right, do what is just;
for my salvation is about to come,
my justice, about to be revealed.

The foreigners who join themselves to the
LORD,
ministering to him,
loving the name of the LORD,
and becoming his servants—
all who keep the sabbath free from
profanation
and hold to my covenant,
them I will bring to my holy mountain
and make joyful in my house of prayer;
their burnt offerings and sacrifices
will be acceptable on my altar,
for my house shall be called
a house of prayer for all peoples.

RESPONSORIAL PSALM
Ps 67:2-3, 5, 6, 8

℟. (4) O God, let all the nations praise you!

May God have pity on us and bless us;
may he let his face shine upon us.
So may your way be known upon earth;
among all nations, your salvation.

℟. O God, let all the nations praise you!

May the nations be glad and exult
because you rule the peoples in equity;
the nations on the earth you guide.

℟. O God, let all the nations praise you!

May the peoples praise you, O God;
may all the peoples praise you!
May God bless us,
and may all the ends of the earth fear him!

℟. O God, let all the nations praise you!

SECOND READING
Rom 11:13-15, 29-32

Brothers and sisters:
I am speaking to you Gentiles.
Inasmuch as I am the apostle to the Gentiles,
I glory in my ministry in order to make my race jealous
and thus save some of them.
For if their rejection is the reconciliation of the world,
what will their acceptance be but life from the dead?

For the gifts and the call of God are irrevocable.
Just as you once disobeyed God
but have now received mercy because of their disobedience,
so they have now disobeyed in order that,
by virtue of the mercy shown to you,
they too may now receive mercy.
For God delivered all to disobedience,
that he might have mercy upon all.

CATECHESIS

About Liturgy

Second chances: Just imagine how difficult it must have been for the Canaanite woman to stand up as an outcast and as a woman to this group of men who obviously seem not to want her there. She must have known that it would be risky to show up, speak out, and make her request, much less talk back and persist if denied! If she were anything like me—knowing that I'd be the minority, the only woman in a roomful of men with authority—I would have been rehearsing all my lines, preparing what I would do, and rallying up all my courage. In the end, I would still doubt whether or not I should do it.

Now imagine how much courage it might have taken some people sitting in your pews today to decide to come to church, where they may feel uncomfortable because they don't know the rituals or anyone there. They might feel shame for some past sin they believe is written on their face. Perhaps they feel like the odd person out in a roomful of people who don't look or think like them or speak their language.

There is likely someone in your pews today who, though feeling unwanted, unnoticed, even rejected by the church, has nonetheless decided to persist and give the church a second chance. Will these individuals have to fight to be seen? Will they have to take a risk to be heard? Will the people they encounter and the words they hear from parishioners, from the music, from the homily say, "We see you. Great is your faith!"

Through her courage, persistence, and faith, the Canaanite woman gave Jesus a second chance to change his mind. For some people in our pews today, this is the last chance they are giving us to be a word of hope in their time of need.

About Initiation

Register of catechumens: The Rite of Acceptance ritualizes God's call to the seeker and the seeker's response to that call by accepting the way of the gospel. This call is irrevocable, and once answered and affirmed, the seeker receives a permanent place in the household of God and enters an official order (role) in the church: the order of catechumens.

Because their place in God's house can never be taken away, there must be a permanent record of their new order. RCIA 46 indicates that after the Rite of Acceptance, the parish should record the names of the catechumens, their sponsors, and the minister of the rite, along with the date and place of the rite, in a register of catechumens. This record book is similar to the parish's sacramental register and should be strictly kept and protected in the same way.

About Liturgical Music

Suggestions: God's mercy is once again at the forefront this Sunday, especially in the sense of mercy that is not limited but given to all. Bring back Ed Bolduc's "There's a Wideness in God's Mercy: Be Merciful" (WLP) that was suggested from the Sixteenth Sunday in Ordinary Time. This would be an excellent sending forth song with its refrain: "So be merciful just as our God is merciful. Be merciful just as our God is merciful to us. Let there be a wideness in God's mercy. Let there be a kindness in our hearts. Oh, may our lives be merciful."

Another song appropriate for today is *Psallite's* "The Mercy of God Is for All" (Liturgical Press). The antiphon for the assembly is easily memorized and sung. Interspersed within the chanted verses is a short response by the assembly taken from the antiphon. This makes it easily sung by all during the Communion procession.

SPIRITUALITY

GOSPEL ACCLAMATION
Matt 16:18

℟. Alleluia, alleluia.
You are Peter and upon this rock I will build my Church
and the gates of the netherworld shall not prevail against it.
℟. Alleluia, alleluia.

Gospel

Matt 16:13-20; L121A

Jesus went into the region of Caesarea Philippi and
he asked his disciples,
"Who do people say that the Son of Man is?"
They replied, "Some say John the Baptist, others Elijah,
still others Jeremiah or one of the prophets."
He said to them, "But who do you say that I am?"
Simon Peter said in reply,
"You are the Christ, the Son of the living God."
Jesus said to him in reply,
"Blessed are you, Simon son of Jonah.
For flesh and blood has not revealed this to you, but my heavenly Father.
And so I say to you, you are Peter,
and upon this rock I will build my church,
and the gates of the netherworld shall not prevail against it.
I will give you the keys to the kingdom of heaven.
Whatever you bind on earth shall be bound in heaven;
and whatever you loose on earth shall be loosed in heaven."
Then he strictly ordered his disciples to tell no one that he was the Christ.

Reflecting on the Gospel

The man came to the Scripture class seeking not only answers but ammunition. His Protestant friends were telling him that Peter was not the first pope. They had Scripture passages to back up their claims. He was sure there was something in the Bible he could use to counteract their arguments. Now the man was asking the instructor for three other Scripture passages he could use that would trump theirs! He was a bit disappointed when the instructor said that's not the way Catholics read Scripture—how he had wanted the equivalent of three aces to play during the next go-around with his Protestant interlocutors!

The story in today's gospel reading from Matthew is a favorite in Catholic-Protestant dialogue or even debates on the role of Peter and the development of the papacy. But the papacy is a long way from the setting of this particular story. Instead, if we read it on its terms, we see that Simon Bar-jonah confesses Jesus as the Christ. He recognizes Jesus for who he is, and Jesus responds by saying this insight was given to him by the heavenly Father. Jesus then names him "Peter," a Greek term meaning "Rock" (though in Aramaic the term is *Kephas*). Prior to this, no person in recorded history had been named "Rock." It's as though Jesus named someone "Window." For us today, who are so familiar with the name "Peter," it sounds standard. But in antiquity, this nickname would have sounded odd. And for that reason, most scholars believe the name "Peter" goes back to the historical Jesus.

Jesus then says that on this "rock" (whether "rock" in this instance refers to the person of Simon Bar-jonah or his confession of Jesus as Christ is debated) he will build his "church." The term "church" appears in the gospels only in Matthew, and only here and in Matthew 18:17. Historically, churches developed later, so it seems anachronistic for Matthew (or any evangelist) to use the term during the historical ministry of Jesus. It's partially for that reason that the phrase is thought to be a Matthean addition. Even so, Matthew is informing, or reminding, his audience that Peter was a spokesperson for the group, confessed Jesus as Christ, but even this was not due to his insight but from a gift of the Father.

As Catholics, we read Scripture holistically, not cherry-picking verses from here and there, and then applying them in a context divorced from their own. A Catholic approach to Scripture seeks to understand the context in which the book, letter, or verse was written; the intent of the author, as much as possible; and how it corresponds to other Scripture. If we are looking for Scripture verses to use in theological debate with other Christians, we are playing the wrong game.

Living the Paschal Mystery

There is a saying about the Bible, "Familiarity with Scripture is familiarity with Christ." Though Catholics have not had a long history of being familiar with Scripture, there are more and more Bible studies available today online and in parishes, from university level to adult faith formation. Commentaries abound and even the New American Bible is available for free with its footnotes on the USCCB website. Since Vatican II, Catholics have been encouraged to become familiar with Scripture, "the soul of theology" (according to Vatican II itself).

Jesus himself knew Scripture and often cited it. We would do well to do the same. When we learn about the Bible, read footnotes, examine commentaries, and pray with the text, we likely put to death ignorance and instead raise to life knowledge and understanding. To live the paschal mystery is to become familiar with Scripture, not so we can cite passages in theological debates, but so that the wisdom of sacred writ washes over us as waves on a beach. Over time, the waves shape the beach as the Scriptures shape us. Let us live the paschal mystery by embracing familiarity with Scripture, for in so doing, we will become familiar with Christ himself.

Focusing the Gospel

Key words and phrases: "But who do you say that I am?"

To the point: In today's gospel Jesus asks his disciples to report on the rumors and gossip of the crowd that follows him. He wants to know what they are saying about his identity. While the crowds posit that Jesus might be Elijah or John the Baptist or one of the prophets come back to life, they haven't made the startling conclusion that Peter has come to: that this man is in fact the anointed one they have been waiting for, the Messiah, "the Son of the living God." This question of faith remains one that is asked of each disciple today. We have met Jesus in the word of God and in the sacraments of the church. We have heard him proclaimed to us by catechists, evangelists, and preachers. Still, Jesus wants to know, "Who do *you* say that I am?"

Connecting the Gospel

to the first reading: In the first reading the person of Eliakim, who will be given the "key of the house of David," seems to be foreshadowing the role Peter will play in establishing the church. Just as God promises to "fix [Eliakim] like a peg in a sure spot," Peter is named "Rock." Throughout the history of salvation, God calls on humans to be his collaborators. Eliakim is called to take over authority from Shebna, who it seems had abused his station as master of the palace. Unfortunately, Eliakim will also prove an unfit leader, for only a few verses later in Isaiah we read that "the peg fixed in a firm place shall give way, break off and fall" (Isa 22:25; NABRE). From the gospels we know that Peter will also have his moments of failure.

to experience: Throughout the history of the church there have been times when our leaders have failed us. Despite this, Jesus' promise remains: the church he founded shall stand firm and "the gates of the netherworld shall not prevail against it." In the end, our faith is in Jesus, our true leader and Lord.

Connecting the Responsorial Psalm

to the readings: Today's psalm refrain speaks to the one in whom our hope lies: "Lord, your love is eternal; do not forsake the work of your hands." Despite the many times the people of Israel turn away from God in the Old Testament, God continues to call them back into relationship with him. This is true with the disciples and the early church in the New Testament as well. In the verses immediately following today's gospel (which will be proclaimed next Sunday), Peter protests Jesus' revelation that he will be killed and then raised, which leads to the harsh rebuke, "Get behind me, Satan! You are an obstacle to me."

to psalmist preparation: In your own life of faith, when have you stumbled and fallen? In these moments have you perceived God at your side with his eternal love, ready to redeem and restore?

PROMPTS FOR FAITH-SHARING

God says of his servant Eliakim, "I will fix him like a peg in a sure spot." Which spiritual leaders do you look to for their constancy and steady guidance?

The psalmist sings, "[W]hen I called, you answered me." When have you had an experience of being answered by the Lord?

St. Paul writes to the Romans, "Oh, the depth of the riches and wisdom / and knowledge of God!" How do you continue to grow in your faith intellectually?

In today's gospel Peter answers Jesus' question, "Who do you say that I am?" by proclaiming, "You are the Christ, the Son of the living God." How do you announce who you believe Jesus to be through your words and actions?

Model Penitential Act

Presider: In today's gospel, Jesus asks the disciples, "Who do you say that I am?" We claim Jesus as Lord and savior, and so let us turn to him seeking forgiveness for the times we have failed in the life of discipleship . . . *[pause]*

Lord Jesus, you are the Christ, the Son of the living God: Lord, have mercy.

Christ Jesus, in you we find freedom from sin and fullness of redemption: Christ, have mercy.

Lord Jesus, you call us to live in the truth: Lord, have mercy.

Homily Points

• After Peter confesses that Jesus is "the Christ, the Son of the living God," Jesus makes his own profession about Peter, "[Y]ou are Peter, / and upon this rock I will build my church." As Catholics, we treasure this verse as the biblical foundation of the ministry of the pope who leads from the chair of St. Peter. Within our church, the role of the pope is a unifying force that draws us into communion with each other.

• Despite Jesus' elevation of Peter, he is not a perfect disciple. In only a few more verses, after he protests Jesus' prediction of his passion and death, Jesus will issue a startling rebuke: "Get behind me, Satan! You are an obstacle to me." Never in the gospels has Jesus' proverb that the exalted shall be humbled (Matt 23:12) taken effect so quickly! Despite denying Jesus three times during his passion, Peter is forgiven and restored by the risen Lord and continues to lead the early church until his martyrdom in Rome. In many ways the story of Peter should bring us hope. We also are not perfect disciples. We, too, will stumble and fall at times, and yet if we remain faithful, Jesus can use our lives to build up and strengthen his church.

• Our history as a church is made up of saints and sinners. At certain times in history the people of God have suffered greatly under the leadership of corrupt ministers. In today's gospel Jesus makes a promise we can cling to even today, saying of the church, "[T]he gates of the netherworld shall not prevail against it." Because the church is made up of humans, it is sinful and always in need of purification and renewal. Because it is the spouse of Christ, it is beloved and redeemed, and shall not be overcome by evil.

Model Universal Prayer (Prayer of the Faithful)

Presider: Through the intercession of St. Peter, the first pope and rock upon which the church was built, let us entrust our needs to the Lord.

Response: Lord, hear our prayer.

For the pope, bishops, and priests, may they grow in faith and love each day for Christ and his church . . .

For leaders of nations, may they enact legislation and uphold laws that protect the dignity of life in all its stages . . .

For all married couples, may their unions be built upon the sure foundation of God's love and Jesus' call to service . . .

For all gathered here, as baptized Christians may we exercise the ministry of priest, prophet, and king in serving the church and others . . .

Presider: Almighty and ever-living God, you sent your son, Jesus, to dwell amongst us and to reveal to us your face. Hear our prayers that in following the footsteps of the first disciples, we might proclaim him to the world with joy and apostolic fervor. We ask this through Christ our Lord. **Amen.**

COLLECT

Let us pray.

Pause for silent prayer

O God, who cause the minds of the
faithful
to unite in a single purpose,
grant your people to love what you
command
and to desire what you promise,
that, amid the uncertainties of this world,
our hearts may be fixed on that place
where true gladness is found.
Through our Lord Jesus Christ, your Son,
who lives and reigns with you in the unity
of the Holy Spirit,
one God, for ever and ever. **Amen.**

FIRST READING

Isa 22:19-23

Thus says the LORD to Shebna, master of
the palace:
"I will thrust you from your office
and pull you down from your station.
On that day I will summon my servant
Eliakim, son of Hilkiah;
I will clothe him with your robe,
and gird him with your sash,
and give over to him your authority.
He shall be a father to the inhabitants of
Jerusalem,
and to the house of Judah.
I will place the key of the House of David
on Eliakim's shoulder;
when he opens, no one shall shut;
when he shuts, no one shall open.
I will fix him like a peg in a sure spot,
to be a place of honor for his family."

RESPONSORIAL PSALM
Ps 138:1-2, 2-3, 6, 8

℟. (8bc) Lord, your love is eternal; do not forsake the work of your hands.

I will give thanks to you, O Lord, with all my heart,
for you have heard the words of my mouth;
in the presence of the angels I will sing your praise;
I will worship at your holy temple.

℟. Lord, your love is eternal; do not forsake the work of your hands.

I will give thanks to your name,
because of your kindness and your truth:
when I called, you answered me;
you built up strength within me.

℟. Lord, your love is eternal; do not forsake the work of your hands.

The Lord is exalted, yet the lowly he sees,
and the proud he knows from afar.
Your kindness, O Lord, endures forever;
forsake not the work of your hands.

℟. Lord, your love is eternal; do not forsake the work of your hands.

SECOND READING
Rom 11:33-36

Oh, the depth of the riches and wisdom and knowledge of God!
How inscrutable are his judgments and how unsearchable his ways!
For who has known the mind of the Lord
or who has been his counselor?
Or who has given the Lord anything
that he may be repaid?
For from him and through him and for him are all things.
To him be glory forever. Amen.

CATECHESIS

About Liturgy

Blessing liturgical ministers: This time of year, you might want to plan a blessing for your liturgical ministers as they begin another term of service for your parish. In the *Book of Blessings,* you can find orders for the Blessing of Readers (chapter 61), the Blessing of Altar Servers, Sacristans, Musicians, and Ushers (chapter 62), and the Commissioning of Extraordinary Ministers of Holy Communion (chapter 63).

Communion ministers who are not ordained are the only people of these ministries to be officially commissioned rather than just given a blessing. This is because they require approval by the diocesan bishop since they are not the ordinary ministers of Communion. (Contact your diocesan worship office or your bishop's office to learn about the process for requesting that your Communion ministers be commissioned.) For all your liturgical ministers, you might reserve one of the upcoming Sundays when they may be formally blessed and Communion ministers commissioned for service to the community.

About Initiation

Who do you say that I am? It's easy to simply respond to an inquirer's question, "Who is Jesus?" with a prepared lesson plan from a reputable publisher, or an excerpt from the catechism, or a well-produced video by a dynamic speaker on the topic. In a way, that's what the disciples did today, responding to Jesus' question with what others have said about him.

But who do *you* say Jesus is? That's a lot harder question to answer because it has to come from our heart and not from a textbook or resource. An authentic answer requires *our own* words, coming from *our own* personal relationship with Christ.

A good catechist doesn't just mimic other people's answers about our faith. They study and read, they pray and question, they reflect for themselves from their heart on what they truly believe, and then they speak in their own words. We catechize not to infuse information into other people but to help them enter into an intimate relationship with Christ: "[T]he definitive aim of catechesis is to put people not only in touch but in communion, in intimacy, with Jesus Christ" (*Catechesi Tradendae* 5). Only if we have that intimate relationship with Jesus ourselves can we teach others well about our faith in Christ.

About Liturgical Music

Making the words we sing our own: For Jesus, as a devout Jew, the psalms were his songbook. Surely these musical prayers influenced his own faith in God and shaped the way he lived that faith, especially in the face of doubt and persecution. Recall the psalms that came from his lips as he was dying on the cross. These texts were embedded in his heart and became his own words at the very moments he needed them.

We, too, should develop an intimate relationship with the psalms. Even if we are not the psalmist leading the responsorial psalm, we can take time with the psalms each week and pray with them. Here's an easy daily process:

Day 1: Read the entire psalm for the following Sunday as it appears in the Lectionary. Look for words and phrases that speak to you. Day 2: Sing the psalm setting for Sunday. Imagine Jesus singing that psalm with you. Day 3: Look up the psalm in the Bible and read the entire chapter. Find background material about that psalm. Day 4: Put yourself in the psalm. What does the psalm mean to you? Day 5: Reflect on what is happening in the world or in your life that connects with this psalm. Day 6: Memorize one or two lines of the psalm that you want to keep in your heart. Day 7: Sing it anew with the assembly.

SPIRITUALITY

GOSPEL ACCLAMATION
See Eph 1:17-18

℟. Alleluia, alleluia.
May the Father of our Lord Jesus Christ
enlighten the eyes of our hearts,
that we may know what is the hope
that belongs to our call.
℟. Alleluia, alleluia.

Gospel

Matt 16:21-27; L124A

Jesus began to show his disciples
that he must go to Jerusalem and suffer greatly
from the elders, the chief priests, and the scribes,
and be killed and on the third day be raised.
Then Peter took Jesus aside and began to rebuke him,
"God forbid, Lord! No such thing shall ever happen to you."
He turned and said to Peter,
"Get behind me, Satan! You are an obstacle to me.
You are thinking not as God does, but as human beings do."

Then Jesus said to his disciples,
"Whoever wishes to come after me must deny himself,
take up his cross, and follow me.
For whoever wishes to save his life will lose it,
but whoever loses his life for my sake will find it.
What profit would there be for one to gain the whole world
and forfeit his life?
Or what can one give in exchange for his life?
For the Son of Man will come with his angels in his Father's glory,
and then he will repay all according to his conduct."

Reflecting on the Gospel

This Sunday's gospel reading from Matthew immediately follows last week's, which is not always the case in the Lectionary. In other words, the episode about Jesus rebuking Peter today comes immediately after the story of Peter proclaiming Jesus the Christ and Jesus in turn saying he will build his church upon this "rock." In some ways, this is a good reminder of the unintended life of discipleship when we can experience extreme highs one moment and fall into such depths the next. For all Peter's exuberance in proclaiming Jesus the Christ, it is only a few verses later that Jesus is rebuking him for thinking not as God does, but as human beings do.

And what precisely is the cause of the rebuke? How is Peter thinking as human beings do? It's because Peter does not comprehend or understand the necessity of suffering and how it is a constitutive element of Jesus' identity as Messiah. Though the Old Testament does not say it, Jesus certainly does. The Messiah will suffer and die. Peter, informed by the Scriptures, has good justification for telling Jesus that he has it all wrong. When Peter proclaimed Jesus Messiah, he did not have in mind suffering and death, but triumph and jubilation. This is the source of the misunderstanding. But Jesus, ever the teacher, takes the time to explain how and why Peter has it wrong. Jesus will encounter opposition that will lead to his death. The same can be said for the disciples.

As the meaning of discipleship becomes more clear, we can wonder how Jesus had any remaining disciples! If the cost of discipleship is one's very life, perhaps it's better not to be a disciple? In the gospels it's clear that "would-be disciples" do in fact leave Jesus—they cease to follow him. But Peter and the others maintain their relationship with him, allowing it to go deeper, into a more full and complete understanding. By seeking to save one's life, it will be lost. By giving away one's life, it will be saved. To be the reigning, victorious Messiah means a life that ends in suffering and death. The paradoxical notions of Jesus' teaching are central to his wisdom.

Living the Paschal Mystery

The paradoxical sayings of Jesus are on full display today, following Peter's proclamation of him as Messiah. The paradoxes come to the fore because of Peter's misunderstanding of what it means to be the Messiah. Rather than victory and a glorious reign (which apparently is what Peter had in mind), Jesus rebukes him to say that his Messiahship will lead to his death. Only then will he be raised.

As disciples, we are to take on the mind of God, to think not as human beings do. Our human priorities are often misplaced, focused on temporal well-being and the accolades of our peers. Instead, Jesus reminds Peter (and us) that God is one's true audience. Our ways of thinking need to be inverted, or even turned inside out. When we think as God does, we will know that loss means finding, denial of oneself is ultimate fulfillment, and death leads to life. To think in these ways requires extra effort because it does not come naturally. But once we do think as God does, we are on our way to living the paschal mystery.

Focusing the Gospel

Key words and phrases: Jesus began to show his disciples / that he must suffer greatly . . . and be killed and on the third day be raised.

To the point: When Peter rebukes Jesus for predicting his passion, it's almost as if he stopped listening after hearing Jesus reveal that he would suffer and die. It is normal to protest when thinking of a loved one going through pain and even death. But Jesus' prediction doesn't stop with pain and death; he goes on to say he will also be raised. Jesus' response to Peter is to exclaim, "Get behind me, Satan!" Earlier in Matthew's gospel when tempted in the desert, Jesus refuses to give in to the devil's suggestions that he turn rock into bread, test God's love for him, or bow down in worship in return for power and authority. At the end he yells, "Get away, Satan!" (4:10; NABRE). As a human being, Jesus can be tempted, though as God he does not give in to temptation. In Peter's protest that "[n]o such thing shall happen to you," he is tempting Jesus to turn away from the cross. But Jesus knows that the only way to risen life is through death.

Connecting the Gospel

to the second reading: St. Paul's words to the Romans today also have a paschal bent. He urges them to "offer your bodies as a living sacrifice, / holy and pleasing to God, your spiritual worship." Scholars believe this letter was written between AD 56 and 58. At this time the temple in Jerusalem still stood where sacrificial worship was enacted. For Christians, Jesus' death upon the cross took away the need for sacrifice, for "we have been consecrated through the offering of the body of Jesus Christ once for all" (Heb 10:10). Instead of animal sacrifice, Paul proposes that the Romans offer their bodies as a living sacrifice. This doesn't mean that they can only please God through a martyr's death but that everything they do, every moment of their lives, can be an act of love for God.

to experience: How do you offer your life up to God as an act of worship?

Connecting the Responsorial Psalm

to the readings: The question could be asked, if this is the way of God that suffering, struggle, and ultimately death are all a part of the package, what has kept Jews and Christians faithful throughout the ages? Today's psalm refrain seems to hold an answer: "My soul is thirsting for you, O Lord my God." Just as we need water to live, our longing for God is innate and undeniable. We may try to satisfy the thirst in our souls with many other things, but ultimately true peace is only found in our Creator.

to psalmist preparation: How do you experience the thirst for God in your life?

PROMPTS FOR FAITH-SHARING

Jeremiah says his call to prophesy is like "fire burning in my heart." What work has God called you to that sparks this kind of passion?

The psalmist proclaims to God, "You are my help . . . My soul clings fast to you." Where are you most in need of God's assistance right now in your life?

St. Paul invites the Romans to "discern what is the will of God, / what is good and pleasing and perfect." How do you practice discernment in your life when faced with a big decision?

In the gospel Jesus says, "Whoever wishes to come after me must deny himself, / take up his cross, and follow me." What is the cross you have been given to bear?

Model Penitential Act

Presider: In today's gospel Jesus calls us to deny ourselves, take up our crosses, and follow him. As we begin our celebration, let us turn to the Lord seeking healing and pardon for the times we have failed in the life of faith . . . *[pause]*

Lord Jesus, you humbled yourself to face death on a cross: Lord, have mercy.
Christ Jesus, in your resurrection you are exalted above all others: Christ, have mercy.
Lord Jesus, your kingdom will have no end: Lord, have mercy.

Homily Points

• For the second time in Matthew's gospel Jesus tells his disciples that "[w]hoever wishes to come after me must deny himself, / take up his cross, and follow me." At the time of Jesus, the cross was a method of torture and execution used by the Roman government. It was a particularly brutal and humiliating way to die, as death by crucifixion was used mainly on slaves and foreigners, and not often on Roman citizens.

• Slowly, over the first few centuries following Jesus' death and resurrection, the cross became the symbol of triumph over death that we are familiar with today. We hang crosses in our homes, churches, and around our necks. We begin and end prayer with this sign. When we consider Jesus' call today that his disciples must take up their crosses and follow him, we might wonder, was Jesus calling them to carry an instrument of death or the promise of their resurrection?

• Perhaps it is possible to answer "both." In St. Paul's letter to the Romans he urges them to "offer your bodies as a living sacrifice." In everything they do, every moment of every day, they are to live for Christ. And eventually living will result in dying. It could be martyrdom, or an act of courage that saves a friend, or a quiet, slow shutting down of the body, but one way or another, as human beings we will exit this life. And yet, this is not cause for despair. Today's gospel acclamation asks, "May the Father of our Lord Jesus Christ enlighten the eyes of our hearts, that we may know what is the hope that belongs to our call." We hope and glory in the cross of Christ, the cause of his death and the symbol of the risen life that he desires to share with us.

Model Universal Prayer (Prayer of the Faithful)

Presider: Firm in our commitment to follow the Lord, let us bring our prayers before our loving God.

Response: Lord, hear our prayer.

For God's holy church, in humility and faith, may it align itself with the poor, vulnerable, and suffering wherever they may be . . .

For those who are held captive or unjustly imprisoned throughout the world, may their hope remain strong and their freedom soon be secured . . .

For those who have become impoverished due to medical expenses, may they receive the assistance necessary to provide for themselves and their families . . .

For all gathered here, may we be strengthened in our commitment to deny ourselves, pick up our crosses, and lead lives of true discipleship . . .

Presider: God, our light and our salvation, in the lives of the prophets, apostles, and saints we find models of fidelity to you. Hear our prayers that we might serve you always with integrity and love. We ask this through Christ our Lord. **Amen.**

COLLECT

Let us pray.

Pause for silent prayer

God of might, giver of every good gift,
put into our hearts the love of your name,
so that, by deepening our sense of
reverence,
you may nurture in us what is good
and, by your watchful care,
keep safe what you have nurtured.
Through our Lord Jesus Christ, your Son,
who lives and reigns with you in the unity
of the Holy Spirit,
one God, for ever and ever. **Amen.**

FIRST READING

Jer 20:7-9

You duped me, O LORD, and I let myself
be duped;
you were too strong for me, and you
triumphed.
All the day I am an object of laughter;
everyone mocks me.

Whenever I speak, I must cry out,
violence and outrage is my message;
the word of the LORD has brought me
derision and reproach all the day.

I say to myself, I will not mention him,
I will speak in his name no more.
But then it becomes like fire burning in
my heart,
imprisoned in my bones;
I grow weary holding it in, I cannot endure
it.

CATECHESIS

About Liturgy

The cross and the gospel way: Our primary symbols reflect facets of the same reality—the paschal mystery. Take, for example, the washing of the feet and the Eucharist. At Holy Thursday, the day when we imitate Jesus' example by washing one another's feet, we proclaim John's version of the Last Supper, which makes no mention of the words of institution: "This is my body. This is my blood. Do this in memory of me." Instead, we are given Jesus' instruction: "This is my example given for you. As I have done, so you must do." In liturgical juxtaposition, we see that washing feet and sharing the Body and Blood of Christ are the same mystery.

So, too, is the acceptance of the gospel way of life and taking up one's cross to follow Christ. In the Rite of Acceptance, which begins an adult's formal preparation for baptism, a primary symbol is the cross. The presider asks the seekers if they are ready to follow the way of the gospel, which is ultimately the way of the cross. We then sign their forehead and all their senses with that cross, indicating that their entire being is now oriented toward Jerusalem and to the cross of Christ. From then on, they are fed by the Word and live that Word by taking up their cross each day.

Highlight this symbolic connection by using the same cross that you will venerate on Good Friday during your celebrations of the Rite of Acceptance. You can take it one step further and highlight that cross prominently during infant baptisms as well.

About Initiation

Times for the Rite of Acceptance: RCIA 18 indicates that the Rite of Acceptance should be scheduled two or more times during the year, so that a parish will be ready to celebrate it as seekers become ready to enter the order of catechumens. Today would be a good Sunday to celebrate this important rite.

Be sure that there are no other major additional rites, blessings, or announcements taking place at the Mass that would detract from the significance of this rite. This will be the first homily the new catechumens will hear as members of the household of God. Scheduling the mission appeals talk by a guest homilist today, for example, competes with the rite and does a disservice to both the guest and the catechumen.

About Liturgical Music

Let the assembly hear their voice: Once I had to be out of town for the weekend and would not be able to lead the music at my parish for one of their Masses. Before I left, I made sure an accompanist and a cantor were going to be there in my place. When I returned, I discovered that the cantor had shown up, but there was no accompanist! His car had died along the way, and he just couldn't make it or find anyone else at the last minute to help.

The quick-thinking cantor wasn't fazed. She found another person in the assembly who she knew was a strong singer, and the two of them joyfully led that assembly in song without any accompaniment. To their surprise (and the pastor's), the assembly sang even louder and with more exuberance than they had ever heard! It was a wonderful Spirit-led celebration.

Sometimes, we might be drowning out the assembly's voice with our instruments. It's good every so often, perhaps for one song or even just one refrain, to let the assembly hear their own voice without any accompaniment so that they can clearly exercise their role as the primary music minister of the Mass.

RESPONSORIAL PSALM
Ps 63:2, 3-4, 5-6, 8-9

℟. (2b) My soul is thirsting for you, O Lord my God.

O God, you are my God whom I seek;
for you my flesh pines and my soul thirsts
like the earth, parched, lifeless and without water.

℟. My soul is thirsting for you, O Lord my God.

Thus have I gazed toward you in the sanctuary
to see your power and your glory,
for your kindness is a greater good than life;
my lips shall glorify you.

℟. My soul is thirsting for you, O Lord my God.

Thus will I bless you while I live;
lifting up my hands, I will call upon your name.
As with the riches of a banquet shall my soul be satisfied,
and with exultant lips my mouth shall praise you.

℟. My soul is thirsting for you, O Lord my God.

You are my help,
and in the shadow of your wings I shout for joy.
My soul clings fast to you;
your right hand upholds me.

℟. My soul is thirsting for you, O Lord my God.

SECOND READING
Rom 12:1-2

I urge you, brothers and sisters, by the mercies of God,
to offer your bodies as a living sacrifice,
holy and pleasing to God, your spiritual worship.
Do not conform yourselves to this age
but be transformed by the renewal of your mind,
that you may discern what is the will of God,
what is good and pleasing and perfect.

SPIRITUALITY

GOSPEL ACCLAMATION
2 Cor 5:19

℟. Alleluia, alleluia.
God was reconciling the world to himself in Christ
and entrusting to us the message of
reconciliation.
℟. Alleluia, alleluia.

Gospel

Matt 18:15-20; L127A

Jesus said to his disciples:
"If your brother sins against you,
go and tell him his fault between you and him alone.
If he listens to you, you have won over your brother.
If he does not listen,
take one or two others along with you,
so that 'every fact may be established
on the testimony of two or three witnesses.'
If he refuses to listen to them, tell the church.
If he refuses to listen even to the church,
then treat him as you would a Gentile or a tax collector.
Amen, I say to you,
whatever you bind on earth shall be bound in heaven,
and whatever you loose on earth shall be loosed in heaven.
Again, amen, I say to you,
if two of you agree on earth
about anything for which they are to pray,
it shall be granted to them by my heavenly Father.
For where two or three are gathered together in my name,
there am I in the midst of them."

Reflecting on the Gospel

Conflict resolution is a hot topic in management manuals, business leadership books, and of course familial relations. Even though we may all approach an issue with good intent, since we are human beings, conflict will naturally arise. As hard as it may be to believe (tongue in cheek), even in churches—communities dedicated to the love of God and the service of neighbor—we experience conflict. Such conflict in the church is unfortunately nothing new. Matthew's gospel today tells us how conflict resolution is to take place in a community of believers. Generally, he is reflecting the rule of subsidiarity, which is, handle the issue at the lowest, or closest, level possible, as opposed to bringing it to a central authority. In modern terms, it's as though Matthew is telling us that each conflict at the parish level need not go to the bishop, much less to the Vatican!

It should be noted that the conflict resolution pattern is to be applied to a member of the community ("a brother"). Matthew is not giving instructions on how to resolve conflicts with outsiders. These rules apply only to fellow Christians, members of the church. Each disciple is empowered to correct any other when there is the occasion of sin. But this correction is to be done privately as a way to honor the reputation of the one being corrected and in light of the familial relationships that are the model for this community of disciples (cf. Matt 12:46-50).

Only if this one-on-one correction fails does the circle widen to include others, echoing Mosaic Law (Deut 19:15). If this, too, fails, the matter comes to the "church." Significantly, this and Matthew 16:18 are the only verses in the gospels (Matthew and otherwise) where the term "church" appears. Interestingly, there seems to be no role for a leader, whether that be a Petrine figure (cf. Matt 16:18) or a "bishop," as Paul will reference in some of his letters. Instead, Matthew envisions the church acting collectively and punishing a sinner by treating him "as you would a Gentile or a tax collector." That is to say, the sinner is to be excommunicated, or cast outside the community. This advice might sound odd to us, but it reflects the Jewish roots of the Matthean community. Similar advice is found in Paul (1 Cor 5:1-8).

Thus, when we join a community of believers, it's not that we've found heaven on earth, or a community of perfection. Instead, we have a community of human beings—with faults, failings, and even sin. The church, and even individual believers, has an obligation to act when faced with sinful actions.

Living the Paschal Mystery

Wouldn't it be so much better if we could all get along? Our lives would be happy, and joy would mark our existence. But the church is not like that. Even the most secure and safe nuclear families—individuals raised in the same household, for whom love may be a given—have challenges with one another. As long as we are living in the period before the coming of Christ, we will experience sin and the fragmentation and fracturing of relationships. How do we respond when this inevitably happens? Certainly not in kind. Matthew gives us some practical steps to follow.

Only when we experience the new life of the resurrection will every tear be wiped away and relationships restored. Until that time, we do the best we can, motivated by love and guided by the wisdom of Christ.

Focusing the Gospel

Key words and phrases: "[G]o and tell him his fault between you and him alone."

To the point: While Jesus' teaching in today's gospel makes sense, it's also really difficult! When someone hurts us, it's so much easier to fume to others about what this person has done than to go and talk to the one who has wronged us. Often when our egos or feelings have been bruised, there is a deep desire to get others on our side. Their support makes us feel better about ourselves and justified in our grievance. Though this may seem easier and safer than going to the one who has hurt us directly, it's no way to build a community. As Jesus recounts the process, if meeting one-on-one doesn't work, only then should other members of the community be brought in. This first step of direct communication is the foundation for living in the world as a reconciling community, intent on building peace.

Connecting the Gospel

to the first reading: In the first reading, God tells Ezekiel he has made him "watchman of the house of Israel." He is to be the mouthpiece for God and to speak God's word to the people. This might include some unpleasant messages like telling the wicked, "O wicked one, you shall surely die." But these prophecies are necessary, and God warns Ezekiel that if he does not "speak out to dissuade the wicked from his way, / the wicked shall die for his guilt, / but I will hold you responsible for his death." The first reading and the gospel seem to hearken back to the words of Cain when God asks him where his brother Abel is and he replies, "I do not know. Am I my brother's keeper?" (Gen 4:9; NABRE). The answer from today's readings is a resounding "yes!"

to experience: Not only are we to care for our brothers and sisters physically, we are to look after them spiritually. The *Catechism of the Catholic Church* states that "charity demands beneficence and fraternal correction" (1829). Of course, as members of the Body of Christ we also must be prepared to receive correction from others with the same goodwill that we offer it to our brothers and sisters.

Connecting the Responsorial Psalm

to the readings: Today's psalm tells us what is needed in order to live well in a community of peace and reconciliation. Sometimes God's messages of correction and encouragement will come from the mouths of our brothers and sisters in Christ. When this happens our psalm refrain urges us, "[H]arden not your hearts." A heart that is filled up with pride and vanity, or is fearful of being cast out, cannot open and soften to accept correction. When we are secure in God's love and our own preciousness in his sight, we can let go of pride and anger. Only then can we take feedback with the goodwill it was intended and strive to be better as we continue on the journey of faith.

to psalmist preparation: How do you keep your heart open and accepting to God's correcting word?

PROMPTS FOR FAITH-SHARING

God tells the prophet Ezekiel that he will be God's spokesperson in dissuading the wicked. What should be the role of the church or individual members of the Body of Christ in being a prophetic voice against evil?

Not only are we called to offer correction, sometimes correction will be offered to us. When this happens, today's psalm tells us, "[H]arden not your hearts." What helps you when you are on the receiving end of correction?

St. Paul tells the Romans, "[L]ove is the fulfillment of the law." How would you apply this to one of the political debates taking place in society?

In today's gospel Jesus outlines the way to resolve conflicts between disciples. What has been your own experience when facing conflicts within your parish community?

Model Penitential Act

Presider: In his letter to the Romans, St. Paul pronounces, "[L]ove is the fulfillment of the law." For all the times our words and actions have been lacking in love, let us ask for pardon and mercy . . . *[pause]*

Lord Jesus, you came to lead sinners to the path of righteousness: Lord, have mercy.
Christ Jesus, in you we find peace: Christ, have mercy.
Lord Jesus, you are the rock of our salvation: Lord, have mercy.

Homily Points

• In today's gospel Jesus lays out the nuts and bolts of what it means to be a community intent on living out God's message of peace and forgiveness. The gospel acclamation tells us how important our witness to reconciliation is, for "God was reconciling the world to himself in Christ and entrusting to us the message of his reconciliation." In this context, when Christian families or communities of faith are overcome by bickering, resentment, and lack of respect for each other, it is a scandal. If we are serious about building the kingdom of God on earth, we must be intentional about how we resolve conflict.

• One of the most difficult things about conflict, and especially about conflict within communities of faith, is that we have been conditioned to think of conflict itself as inherently evil. If we become motivated by this belief, we become conflict avoiders. Unfortunately, buried conflict does not go away; it festers and eventually poisons relationships. In today's gospel Jesus does not tell us to avoid or cover up conflict, but instead to face it head-on. We are to go to the one who has wronged us directly and speak to that person with goodwill and compassion. Jesus tells us, "If he listens to you, you have won over your brother." Only if this first step of direct communication fails should others become involved.

• In order to live as a sign of reconciliation in the world, we must become comfortable with healthy conflict. We are human beings attempting, to the best of our ability, to be the people God has called us to be. We will fail at times. But with God's love and the help of our brothers and sisters, we can forgive ourselves and each other and try again.

Model Universal Prayer (Prayer of the Faithful)

Presider: Confident in Jesus' words that "where two or three are gathered together in my name, / there I am in the midst of them," let us bring our prayers before the Lord.

Response: Lord, hear our prayer.

For all ministers within the church, may they serve as humble mediators in resolving conflicts amongst the people of God . . .

For diplomats and peacekeepers throughout the world, may their work bring safety and security to all people, especially the most vulnerable of society . . .

For those in need of forgiveness for sins against God and neighbor, may their hearts be turned toward repentance and mercy be upon them . . .

For all gathered here, in truth and mercy may we correct each other when necessary and humbly accept correction when it is offered to us . . .

Presider: God of perfect kindness and compassion, through your son, Jesus, you revealed to us your law of love. Hear our prayers that we might follow your commands with faithfulness and joy. We ask this through Christ our Lord. **Amen.**

COLLECT

Let us pray.

Pause for silent prayer

O God, by whom we are redeemed and
receive adoption,
look graciously upon your beloved sons
and daughters,
that those who believe in Christ
may receive true freedom
and an everlasting inheritance.
Through our Lord Jesus Christ, your Son,
who lives and reigns with you in the unity
of the Holy Spirit,
one God, for ever and ever. **Amen.**

FIRST READING

Ezek 33:7-9

Thus says the LORD:
You, son of man, I have appointed
watchman for the house of Israel;
when you hear me say anything, you
shall warn them for me.
If I tell the wicked, "O wicked one, you
shall surely die,"
and you do not speak out to dissuade
the wicked from his way,
the wicked shall die for his guilt,
but I will hold you responsible for his
death.
But if you warn the wicked,
trying to turn him from his way,
and he refuses to turn from his way,
he shall die for his guilt,
but you shall save yourself.

RESPONSORIAL PSALM
Ps 95:1-2, 6-7, 8-9

℟. (8) If today you hear his voice, harden not your hearts.

Come, let us sing joyfully to the LORD;
let us acclaim the rock of our salvation.
Let us come into his presence with thanksgiving;
let us joyfully sing psalms to him.

℟. If today you hear his voice, harden not your hearts.

Come, let us bow down in worship;
let us kneel before the LORD who made us.
For he is our God,
and we are the people he shepherds, the flock he guides.

℟. If today you hear his voice, harden not your hearts.

Oh, that today you would hear his voice:
"Harden not your hearts as at Meribah,
as in the day of Massah in the desert,
where your fathers tempted me;
they tested me though they had seen my works."

℟. If today you hear his voice, harden not your hearts.

SECOND READING
Rom 13:8-10

Brothers and sisters:
Owe nothing to anyone, except to love one another;
for the one who loves another has fulfilled the law.
The commandments, "You shall not commit adultery;
you shall not kill; you shall not steal;
you shall not covet,"
and whatever other commandment there may be,
are summed up in this saying, namely,
"You shall love your neighbor as yourself."
Love does no evil to the neighbor;
hence, love is the fulfillment of the law.

About Liturgy

Liturgical ministry sponsors: New liturgical ministers can benefit from having a "sponsor" or mentor during their formation and training. By using liturgical ministry sponsors, you can recruit new ministers throughout the year as people inquire about serving, and you can provide more personalized formation and genuine discernment for readiness. Serving as a liturgical ministry sponsor also encourages veteran ministers to continue improving their own skills.

The sponsor serves in a similar way as a sponsor for a catechumen. They accompany their companion throughout their formation and act as an example of excellence in ministry. They regularly meet with them for prayer and faith-sharing. They help the new liturgical minister prepare for the upcoming Mass and sit with them during it for support. After Mass, they meet with their companion to provide suggestions for improvement. They can also inform the liturgical ministry coordinator of any concerns they may have that they cannot resolve with their companion. Together with their companion and with others in the community, ministry sponsors discern their companion's readiness for ongoing service in that ministry. Once new liturgical ministers are on the regular schedule, their sponsors can continue to meet with them to share faith and be a support throughout their ministry.

About Initiation

Training in Christian community: RCIA 75 outlines four areas of discipleship that catechumens must be trained in to prepare for initiation. The second area of training is in Christian community.

The RCIA group is not meant to be a small, enclosed faith community, separate from the wider parish or even diocesan community. If your catechumens and candidates never interact with parishioners outside of the RCIA and participate in the life of the wider community during their formation, then their formation is insufficient.

True Christian community is a company of believers, each with their own concerns and worries, their own sinfulness and weakness. Some may even annoy or offend us. And still we are called to love them. The mark of Christian community is not perfection or the absence of conflict, but the enduring love that is given even to the point of self-renunciation and sacrifice.

About Liturgical Music

How to gracefully accept criticism: Receiving a negative comment about some aspect of our music ministry can be difficult to hear. When such comments come your way, keep the following things in mind. If the comment is made anonymously, it is best to ignore it. Don't waste energy on anonymous complaints.

If they do give you their name and a way to connect with them, and if their complaint is reasonable, then reach out to them and just listen. For most people, they simply want to feel heard. You don't need to agree with them or to defend your perspective; just try to listen for the deeper value that they desire to uphold. You may find that you share the same value or goal, but not the methodology for achieving it. In all things, do not demonize them. Assume that, like you, they love the church and the liturgy and want the best for the community. At the very least, thank them for sharing their concern. Then take all this to prayer, dialogue, and discernment with a trusted colleague.

SPIRITUALITY

GOSPEL ACCLAMATION
John 13:34

℟. Alleluia, alleluia.
I give you a new commandment, says the Lord;
love one another as I have loved you.
℟. Alleluia, alleluia.

Gospel

Matt 18:21-35; L130A

Peter approached Jesus and
asked him,
"Lord, if my brother sins
against me,
how often must I forgive?
As many as seven times?"
Jesus answered, "I say to
you, not seven times but
seventy-seven times.
That is why the kingdom of
heaven may be likened to
a king
who decided to settle
accounts with his servants.
When he began the accounting,
a debtor was brought before him who
owed him a huge amount.
Since he had no way of paying it back,
his master ordered him to be sold,
along with his wife, his children, and
all his property,
in payment of the debt.
At that, the servant fell down, did him
homage, and said,
'Be patient with me, and I will pay
you back in full.'
Moved with compassion the master of
that servant
let him go and forgave him the loan.
When that servant had left, he found
one of his fellow servants
who owed him a much smaller
amount.

Continued in Appendix A, p. 301.

Reflecting on the Gospel

Though chapter 13 in Matthew is commonly known as the "parables chapter," for the seven parables Jesus speaks, we find parables in a few other places in the gospel; and today's gospel reading is one example. The story of the unrepentant debtor is unique to Matthew. Though the opening verses of today's gospel find an echo in Luke 17:4, the parable is unparalleled.

The story is simple but profound. One who owed the king an inordinate sum (10,000 talents is hyperbole equivalent to our saying "a hundred million dollars") has no chance of paying it off. He will never earn that much and therefore he is essentially placed in debtors' prison, after all his assets, his very person, and his family were sold for cash value. The king, hearing the pleas of mercy, relents and releases the man from his debts and from prison. The king was moved by pity.

Then, the same man finds one who is in debt to him (a denarius was about a day's wage for a laborer). This debtor appeals to the man who was just forgiven, using language that sounds eerily familiar. But rather than be moved by pity as the king was and emulate the forgiveness he was shown, the man who now finds himself in a position of power casts the poor debtor in prison.

The king's servants report all this to the king, who is infuriated at the aborted forgiveness. "Should you not have had pity?" is the terrifying question that sends the man not merely to prison but to the torturer for what is effectively eternity.

The lesson for us could not be clearer. We who have been forgiven are to forgive others. It is the Lord's Prayer that is found in this gospel as well: "forgive us as we forgive those . . ." The Lord's forgiveness is freely given, but it may be taken back if we do not emulate this same forgiveness in our own lives.

The final words of the gospel are a haunting reminder that we may face the same fate as the one handed over to torturers if we do not forgive "from the heart."

Living the Paschal Mystery

Grudges are awful things. They can gnaw away at the one harboring them. We may hear "forgive but don't forget" as a way to remind ourselves of past transgressions we've suffered. But today's gospel calls us to a higher standard. The forgiveness we've experienced (worth a hundred million dollars—something we cannot repay) should motivate us to be free with forgiveness when others wrong us. We cannot dole out forgiveness in infinitesimal pieces only to those we deem worthy once some rectification has been made. Instead, forgiveness ought to be given freely.

We must die to the grudges, slights, rudeness, and other transgressions we've suffered and rise to a sense of freedom that comes through forgiving as we've been forgiven. Jesus himself warns us in a negative way (*via negativa*) that if we withhold forgiveness, it will be withheld from us. And the consequences of that are severe indeed.

Focusing the Gospel

Key words and phrases: "Lord, if my brother sins against me, / how often must I forgive?"

To the point: Peter comes to Jesus with a question about forgiveness. He seems to have already figured out an answer that might satisfy his query about how many times to forgive and suggests seven as a reasonable number. In Peter's scenario, forgiveness is abundant (after all, forgiving seven times after someone has harmed us intentionally seems generous) but limited. It also requires careful record keeping on the part of the one being wronged. Jesus does away with Peter's carefully doled out justice by responding, "[N]ot seven times but seventy-seven times." Jesus isn't offering another arbitrary number (albeit a much bigger one) but requiring forgiveness that is limitless. As followers of Christ, we are not in a position to judge if another is worthy of forgiveness; we are simply to grant it.

Connecting the Gospel

to the first reading: Jesus' teaching on forgiveness is not new but firmly rooted in the Scriptures. In the book of Sirach we are told, "The vengeful will suffer the Lord's vengeance." Perhaps this is another way of looking at the golden rule. But instead of treating others as we would like to be treated, we can expect to be treated by God as we treat others. If we hold onto grudges and "nourish anger against another," the psalmist asks, how can we "expect healing from the Lord?"

to experience: Just as we have been freely forgiven and compassionately loved by God we are called to forgive and love. This is not easy. Sometimes hurts are so deep that the best we can do in any given moment is to ask God to give us the desire to forgive, and then to wait patiently for the grace to do so.

Connecting the Responsorial Psalm

to the readings: We have been created in the image and likeness of God and are called to be like him. Today's psalm refrain proclaims, "The Lord is kind and merciful, slow to anger, and rich in compassion." This is the ideal to which we are all to aspire. To become "rich in compassion," we must first experience and sit in the compassionate love of God, the one who "pardons all your iniquities, / heals all your ills, / redeems your life from destruction," and "crowns you with kindness and compassion." In today's parable it seems that the debtor who was forgiven "a huge amount" did not let the experience of the king's generosity to him pierce his soul. When he is called upon to be generous and compassionate, he responds instead with anger and revenge.

to psalmist preparation: In order to proclaim God's mercy and kindness to others, take a moment in prayer to consider how you have experienced this mercy and compassion in your own life. Where might God be calling you to exercise forgiveness in your relationships with others?

PROMPTS FOR FAITH-SHARING

The first reading from Sirach begins, "Wrath and anger are hateful things, / yet the sinner hugs them tight." Is there wrath or anger you have been hanging onto that you're ready to let go of with God's help?

Sirach also prompts us to "remember your last days, set enmity aside." Where is there a relationship in your life that you would like to heal or strengthen?

Jesus ends the parable today, "So will my heavenly Father do to you, / unless each of you forgives your brother from your heart." How do you understand Jesus' words, to forgive "from the heart"?

What has helped you when you found it difficult to forgive others for the harm they had done?

Model Penitential Act

Presider: In today's gospel Jesus tells us we are to forgive "not seven times, but seventy-seven times." For the times we have failed in mercy to those who have harmed us, let us ask the Lord for healing and pardon . . . *[pause]*

Lord Jesus, you show us the way of compassion: Lord, have mercy.
Christ Jesus, you heal our ills and free us from sin: Christ, have mercy.
Lord Jesus, you sustain us with the bread of life: Lord, have mercy.

Homily Points

• We know that Jesus came to bring forgiveness and fullness of life to his followers. But it seems that this forgiveness and fullness of life cannot be received by us if we are caught up in thoughts of revenge, bitterness, hatred, and resentment. When these feelings toward another take over, we are no longer living in the freedom of the children of God, but instead in a prison of our own making that insulates us from the mercy and kindness our creator desires to bestow.

• There is a well-known saying that "resentment is like drinking poison and hoping your enemy will die." When we withhold from another the mercy and compassion that we have been shown by God, we inflict more harm upon ourselves. Instead of growing in kindness, we nourish the seeds of anger and hatred within us and, as the book of Sirach tells us, "Wrath and anger are hateful things." Full of our own righteous grief and bitterness, we slowly crowd out the love of God, until there is no room for anything else in our lives.

• All of this is not to suggest that forgiveness is easy. Some hurts are so deep that the path of forgiveness is long and twisty instead of the work of a moment. In these instances, simply getting on the path to forgiveness is a triumph that requires prayer to ask God to even plant the desire for forgiveness within our hearts. When this is the case, we need not despair or give up. St. Paul reminds us that God's strength is made perfect in human weakness (2 Cor 12:9). He will help us to escape the prison we have constructed out of pain and lead us again into the fullness of life.

Model Universal Prayer (Prayer of the Faithful)

Presider: Knowing the depths of God's mercy, let us bring our prayers before the Lord.

Response: Lord, hear our prayer.

For God's holy church, may it be a fountain of mercy and a beacon of forgiveness, illuminating the darkness of sin and calling sinners home . . .

For elected officials and those who hold public office, may they safeguard the rights of prisoners, offering opportunities for restorative justice and rehabilitation . . .

For those who have been victims of violent crimes and for their families, may they receive the necessary support to heal from trauma and grace to forgive . . .

For all gathered here, formed by the word of God, may we resolve to bring God's mercy and love to the areas of our society where it is most needed . . .

Presider: Good and gracious God, you desire to bring all people to yourself that your mercy and forgiveness might redeem the world. Hear our prayers that having received the gift of your compassion, we might go forth to bring it to others. We ask this through Christ our Lord. **Amen.**

COLLECT

Let us pray.

Pause for silent prayer

Look upon us, O God,
Creator and ruler of all things,
and, that we may feel the working of your mercy,
grant that we may serve you with all our heart.
Through our Lord Jesus Christ, your Son,
who lives and reigns with you in the unity of the Holy Spirit,
one God, for ever and ever. **Amen.**

FIRST READING

Sir 27:30–28:7

Wrath and anger are hateful things,
yet the sinner hugs them tight.
The vengeful will suffer the LORD's vengeance,
for he remembers their sins in detail.
Forgive your neighbor's injustice;
then when you pray, your own sins will be forgiven.
Could anyone nourish anger against another
and expect healing from the LORD?
Could anyone refuse mercy to another like himself,
can he seek pardon for his own sins?
If one who is but flesh cherishes wrath,
who will forgive his sins?
Remember your last days, set enmity aside;
remember death and decay, and cease from sin!
Think of the commandments, hate not your neighbor;
remember the Most High's covenant, and overlook faults.

RESPONSORIAL PSALM
Ps 103:1-2, 3-4, 9-10, 11-12

℟. (8) The Lord is kind and merciful, slow to anger, and rich in compassion.

Bless the LORD, O my soul;
  and all my being, bless his holy name.
Bless the LORD, O my soul,
  and forget not all his benefits.

℟. The Lord is kind and merciful, slow to anger, and rich in compassion.

He pardons all your iniquities,
  heals all your ills.
He redeems your life from destruction,
  he crowns you with kindness and compassion.

℟. The Lord is kind and merciful, slow to anger, and rich in compassion.

He will not always chide,
  nor does he keep his wrath forever.
Not according to our sins does he deal with us,
  nor does he requite us according to our crimes.

℟. The Lord is kind and merciful, slow to anger, and rich in compassion.

For as the heavens are high above the earth,
  so surpassing is his kindness toward those who fear him.
As far as the east is from the west,
  so far has he put our transgressions from us.

℟. The Lord is kind and merciful, slow to anger, and rich in compassion.

SECOND READING
Rom 14:7-9

Brothers and sisters:
None of us lives for oneself, and no one dies for oneself.
For if we live, we live for the Lord,
  and if we die, we die for the Lord;
  so then, whether we live or die, we are the Lord's.
For this is why Christ died and came to life,
  that he might be Lord of both the dead and the living.

About Liturgy

Is your liturgy "working"? The Constitution on the Sacred Liturgy says that the liturgy, especially the Eucharist, "is the outstanding means whereby the faithful may express in their lives, and manifest to others, the mystery of Christ and the real nature of the true Church" (2). This is our measuring stick for how well our liturgy is working. Are the faithful of your community expressing in their daily lives who Christ is through their own words and actions? Are they showing clearly to others the best of what the church is called to be? Good liturgy is not measured by the quality of hospitality, preaching, music, or any other aspect of the Mass. Attendance numbers cannot be the judge of the success of our liturgies. And our purpose is not to create more relevant or entertaining or attractive worship, but to become more and more like Christ in the world.

Recall Pope John Paul II's words: "[B]y our concern for those in need we will be recognized as true followers of Christ. This will be the criterion by which the authenticity of our Eucharistic celebrations is judged" (*Mane nobiscum Domine* 28).

Excellent liturgical ministry and quality preaching, music, and hospitality are not enough. They are starting points through which the faithful learn how to manifest the mystery of Christ and the real nature of the church. Remember to constantly call your community to greater visible works of mercy in their lives and stronger words of compassion to those in need.

About Initiation

Learning to forgive: One of the hallmarks of being Christian is embodied in today's gospel reading. Showing mercy and offering forgiveness—that goes beyond simple fairness or equity—is a mandate from Jesus himself. To prepare our catechumens and candidates well for being true disciples of Christ, we must do more than just teach them *about* forgiveness. We need to invite them to *do* forgiveness and encounter Christ's mercy through their own practice of offering forgiveness to those who have hurt them and asking for forgiveness when they have harmed another.

The Rite of Christian Initiation of Adults says that part of their formation is to "practice love of neighbor, even at the cost of self-renunciation" (75.2). Furthermore, it says that when they do this consistently, there will be social consequences to their actions.

Be sure that your catechesis on forgiveness is not merely scholastic or intellectual understanding but actual practice that leads to self-sacrifice and mercy that does not count the cost.

About Liturgical Music

Suggestions: Music about mercy should abound this day. "My People, What Do I Require?" (GIA) is a hymn text by Herman Stuempfle Jr. paired to the tune LAND OF REST. The text is inspired from the prophet Micah describing what the Lord requires: "Be merciful and just to all; walk humbly with the Lord. Love mercy: let your hand be swift to serve a neighbor's need. Let good intent and gracious word be matched by loving deed." Another recommendation is from *Psallite* called "If You Will Love Each Other" (Liturgical Press). The refrain reads, "If you will love each other, forgiving from the heart, then my Father will heal and forgive you." A third suggestion reflects the beautiful text from today's second reading. "*Pues Si Vivimos*/When We Are Living" (Abingdon Press) is a traditional Spanish song with text by Robert Escamilla that has been translated into English. The first verse reads, "When we are living, we are in Christ Jesus, and when we die, we remain in him. Both in our living, and in our dying, we are the Lord's, we belong to him."

SPIRITUALITY

GOSPEL ACCLAMATION
cf. Acts 16:14b

℟. Alleluia, alleluia.
Open our hearts, O Lord,
to listen to the words of your Son.
℟. Alleluia, alleluia.

Gospel Matt 20:1-16a; L133A

Jesus told his disciples this parable:
"The kingdom of heaven is like a landowner
who went out at dawn to hire laborers for his vineyard.
After agreeing with them for the usual daily wage,
he sent them into his vineyard.
Going out about nine o'clock,
the landowner saw others standing idle in the marketplace,
and he said to them, 'You too go into my vineyard,
and I will give you what is just.'
So they went off.
And he went out again around noon,
and around three o'clock, and did likewise.
Going out about five o'clock,
the landowner found others standing around, and said to them,
'Why do you stand here idle all day?'
They answered, 'Because no one has hired us.'
He said to them, 'You too go into my vineyard.'
When it was evening the owner of the vineyard said to his foreman,
'Summon the laborers and give them their pay,
beginning with the last and ending with the first.'
When those who had started about five o'clock came,
each received the usual daily wage.
So when the first came, they thought that they would receive more,
but each of them also got the usual wage.

Continued in Appendix A, p. 302.

Reflecting on the Gospel

There is an old joke about a Protestant being led around heaven by St. Peter. They pass a room and St. Peter says, "Be quiet around this room." To which the Protestant asks, "Why?" Peter responds, "In that room are the Catholics, and they think they're the only ones here."

Jesus was a master teacher. His parables inspired and they were remembered in part because they were simple stories that conveyed multiple layers of meaning. Each story seems to have a variety of possible entry points, as does today's gospel. Is the landowner truly just when he gives all the workers the same wage? What would unionized workers say about this practice? Why does the landowner distribute wages in the manner he does, with those who worked the longest receiving their pay last? Is he trying to incite a riot, or maybe inspire jealousy and envy?

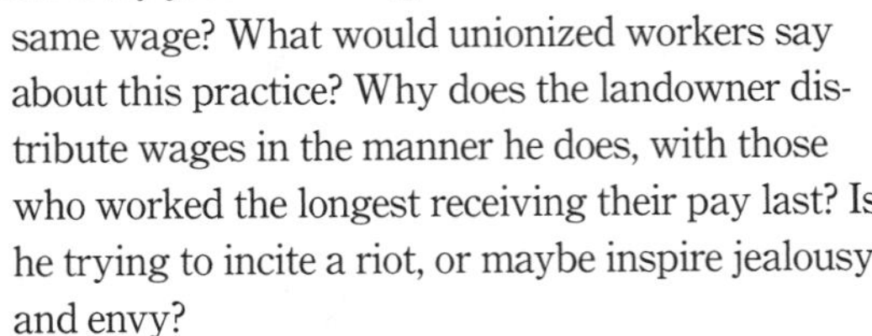

All of these questions and more may be conjured up by a quick reading of the parable.

Not only was Jesus a master teacher, but we recall that he taught two thousand years ago! One challenge is that some of his stories are set deeply in the milieu of his context. The parable is not in fact making statements about modern labor law or the role of unions or day laborers. Instead, landowners in Jesus' time had incredible power over workers and over their property. Perhaps because there were no labor unions, guest worker programs, or labor laws to protect workers, the landowner was able to act with impunity. This kind of power makes for an apt image of a powerful and unaccountable God!

So Jesus uses the character of the landowner in the parable to say that God gives each his or her due at the very least, and he is generous. It is not up to us to tell God how and in what way he is to be generous with his resources. God gives to each what he will, though not less than what he promised.

In the early church this parable was often interpreted in terms of Jews and Gentiles, with Jews being the early workers and Gentiles being those who came late. God gives each a share of his kingdom. All will likely be surprised by the generosity of God and by who appears at the heavenly banquet. Ideally, no one group will think its members are the only ones to share in God's goodness.

Living the Paschal Mystery

It's probably the case that none of us enjoy being supplicants. We all tend to work for a wage we consider just (if and when possible) and expect to be paid for our labor. When we see acts of generosity, it can be natural to expect that we might receive some of that generosity as well. It sounds strange to hear it said that someone is generous only with one group and not another. And such is the seeming riddle of today's parable.

God is a just and generous giver. When we receive what we have from God, there is no room for complaint, jealousy, or envy. The gifts of God are given to whom he will. Let us die to our own sense of who is just and worthy in God's sight and leave room to be surprised by his generosity. None of us can predict the actions of God.

Focusing the Gospel

Key words and phrases: "Thus, the last will be first, and the first will be last."

To the point: It seems that God's justice turns everything on its head. The words Jesus speaks at the end of today's parable could be considered nonsense. The very definition of first is that it comes before all others. And yet, in today's parable God makes the ones who have worked the longest in his vineyard equal to the ones who have just begun their labor. To add insult to injury, the first hired are the last paid. Jesus warns us against our innate human proclivity to demand what is "fair." God is generous. He forgives sinners, seeks out the lost, and desires to bring everyone to the joys of everlasting life. As disciples, we are called to embrace this as good news and not as a cause for resentment.

Connecting the Gospel

to the first reading: In the first reading, God, speaking through Isaiah, tells us, "[M]y thoughts are not your thoughts, / nor are your ways my ways." Within the gospels we will oftentimes encounter sayings or parables that seem to go against our very notion of commonsense. Jesus tells us earlier in Matthew's gospel, "[L]ove your enemies and pray for those who persecute you" (5:44; NABRE). Instead of exacting revenge, we are to turn the other cheek (5:39). And in today's gospel reading we are warned against trying to impose our human ideas of fairness onto God's generosity. After all, we are not the measure of righteousness and truth—God is.

to experience: In dedicating our lives to Christ, we have chosen to follow one whose ways and thoughts are above ours, "as high as the heavens are above the earth." Therefore, discipleship will demand that we grow and stretch to become more like our heavenly Father and to resist the temptation to try and make God more like us.

Connecting the Responsorial Psalm

to the readings: Today's psalm refrain proclaims, "The Lord is near to all who call upon him." There is an inherent gift and challenge within this line. We are reassured of God's help and nearness to us at all times, especially when we are in need. And we also must proclaim with words and actions that this is true for everyone else too. For God, there is no "us and them." Each person he has created is beloved and precious in his sight, including those who have hurt us. Our greatest prayer should be that those who do evil will be converted. As Isaiah says in our first reading, "Let the scoundrel forsake his way, / and the wicked his thoughts; / let him turn to the Lord for mercy."

to psalmist preparation: Sometimes it seems much easier to desire the downfall or condemnation of those who wreak havoc on the world. But this is not God's dream. Instead, he desires to gather all people to himself. Let us take time to pray this week that all people would turn toward the Lord and enter into the kingdom of God.

PROMPTS FOR FAITH-SHARING

Today's psalm proclaims, "The Lord is near to all who call upon him." In your life of faith, when have you needed to call upon the Lord the most fervently?

St. Paul writes to the Philippians, "For me life is Christ, and death is gain." Do you identify with this statement? Why or why not?

How do you feel about God's justice as portrayed in the parable of the laborers in the vineyard?

In what ways do you try to live out Jesus' proverb, "The last will be first, and the first will be last"?

Model Penitential Act

Presider: In today's second reading we are urged to "conduct yourselves in a way worthy of the gospel of Christ." For the times we have failed to act in a Christlike manner, let us turn to the Lord and ask for forgiveness . . . *[pause]*

Lord Jesus, in your kingdom the first shall be last and the last shall be first: Lord, have mercy.

Christ Jesus, you will not forsake those who turn to you in need: Christ, have mercy.

Lord Jesus, you are just in all your ways and abounding in compassion: Lord, have mercy.

Homily Points

- The adjective "daily" is found four times in the Gospel of Matthew. Once in the Lord's Prayer (6:11) and three times in today's parable. Perhaps it can be a key to help us discover the secret of God's generosity and justice. In the Lord's Prayer, Jesus teaches us to ask only for "our daily bread." We are not to ask for more than we need, but enough to see us through that day. We are to trust in God's providence to provide again for what we will require tomorrow.

- In today's parable, the owner of the vineyard goes out and hires laborers five times throughout the day: dawn, nine o'clock, noon, three o'clock, and five o'clock. Twice we are told what he will pay. To those hired at dawn he promises "the usual daily wage." At nine o'clock he offers to pay "what is just." In Jesus' time it was normal for workers to receive their pay at the end of each day. In the book of Deuteronomy the people are told they must pay their hired servants each day "before the sun goes down, since the servant is poor and is counting on them."

- In the end, what the landowner decides is "just" is to pay all the laborers the daily wage needed to support themselves and their families. There is a fullness and abundance in God's mercy and care that will provide what is enough, what is satisfying, for each. As children of the living God, we are to rejoice in his bounty, what is given both to us and to everyone.

Model Universal Prayer (Prayer of the Faithful)

Presider: Trusting in the boundless generosity of our God, let us bring our needs before the Lord.

Response: Lord, hear our prayer.

For those who have dedicated themselves to consecrated life, may they be renewed in their ministry and strengthened in communal life . . .

For governments all over the world, may they look out for the common good and be transparent to the people whom they serve . . .

For all who labor, may they have safe working conditions and receive a just wage . . .

For all gathered here, with joy may we work tirelessly in the vineyard of the Lord to build his kingdom of truth and love . . .

Presider: God of life, you have made us in your image and given us work to do in caring for and stewarding creation. Hear our prayers that we might respond to your call in our lives to serve you and others. We ask this through Christ our Lord. **Amen.**

COLLECT

Let us pray.

Pause for silent prayer

O God, who founded all the commands of
your sacred Law
upon love of you and of our neighbor,
grant that, by keeping your precepts,
we may merit to attain eternal life.
Through our Lord Jesus Christ, your Son,
who lives and reigns with you in the unity
of the Holy Spirit,
one God, for ever and ever. **Amen.**

FIRST READING

Isa 55:6-9

Seek the LORD while he may be found,
call him while he is near.
Let the scoundrel forsake his way,
and the wicked his thoughts;
let him turn to the LORD for mercy;
to our God, who is generous in
forgiving.
For my thoughts are not your thoughts,
nor are your ways my ways, says the
LORD.
As high as the heavens are above the
earth,
so high are my ways above your ways
and my thoughts above your thoughts.

RESPONSORIAL PSALM
Ps 145:2-3, 8-9, 17-18

℟. (18a) The Lord is near to all who call upon him.

Every day will I bless you,
and I will praise your name forever and ever.
Great is the LORD and highly to be praised;
his greatness is unsearchable.

℟. The Lord is near to all who call upon him.

The LORD is gracious and merciful,
slow to anger and of great kindness.
The LORD is good to all
and compassionate toward all his works.

℟. The Lord is near to all who call upon him.

The LORD is just in all his ways
and holy in all his works.
The LORD is near to all who call upon him,
to all who call upon him in truth.

℟. The Lord is near to all who call upon him.

SECOND READING
Phil 1:20c-24, 27a

Brothers and sisters:
Christ will be magnified in my body,
whether by life or by death.
For to me life is Christ, and death is gain.
If I go on living in the flesh,
that means fruitful labor for me.
And I do not know which I shall choose.
I am caught between the two.
I long to depart this life and be with Christ,
for that is far better.
Yet that I remain in the flesh
is more necessary for your benefit.

Only, conduct yourselves in a way worthy of the gospel of Christ.

CATECHESIS

About Liturgy

Opportunities to serve: Notice that in today's gospel the landowner not only paid each person a full day's wage but also gave everyone an opportunity to serve. In parish life, it is not unusual to see the same people serving in liturgical ministry year after year. When such assignments seemingly become permanent, others have fewer chances to serve in that ministry. Sometimes we might even see one minister performing multiple liturgical roles in the same Mass—serving as a lector, altar server, intercessions reader, and Communion minister! Whether this is done because of lack of volunteers or simply out of habit, limiting such assignments to a few does not reflect a primary goal of Vatican II, which was to show more clearly the diversity and necessity of all the members of the Body of Christ.

Regarding serving in multiple ministries during the Mass, the Constitution on the Sacred Liturgy states: "In liturgical celebrations each person, minister or layman, who has an office to perform, should do all of, but only, those parts which pertain to his office by the nature of the rite and the principles of liturgy" (28). Regarding length of service, extraordinary ministers of Holy Communion are commissioned for a limited number of years designated by each bishop. There is no similar stipulation for other liturgical ministries. However, it is good practice to regularly invite new ministers to serve and veteran ministers to explore other ministries or focus for a while on their primary ministry of being a member of the assembly.

About Initiation

Christian generosity: As children, we are taught not to take more than our fair share. This is a good lesson, and it applies to adults as well! But what about the giver? Is it possible for the one who gives to give more than a fair share? With God it certainly is, for God's ways are not our ways. God gives not out of a sense of fairness or merit; indeed, God may give more than a fair share—God gives generously to all. Though each laborer in today's gospel deserved a wage, God gave the same amount to each, regardless of how long that person worked.

This model of generosity applies to our catechumens and candidates as well. Rather than giving merely a fair share, let's overwhelm them with generosity that comes from God. In so doing, our hope is that they, too, become generous givers in an endless forward cycle of charity.

About Liturgical Music

Just wages: You won't find many full-time paid music directors in parishes today. Most will be part-time, in charge of one or two liturgies. Still others may be working for free. Some parishes want to pay just wages for competent, professional music directors, but the money simply isn't available. However, I would guess that some parishes do not prioritize providing excellent musical leadership for every liturgy, so they use whomever they can find. This creates a disjointed approach to music ministry, harms the quality of the liturgy, and leaves gaps in leadership for the more important liturgies of the year. It also prevents qualified, skilled music ministers from earning a living wage.

The liturgy is the most important thing we do each week. Those who provide professional work at the service of the liturgy—people who have spent years developing their skills—should be given reasonable and just pay.

SPIRITUALITY

GOSPEL ACCLAMATION
John 10:27

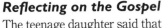

℟. Alleluia, alleluia.
My sheep hear my voice, says the Lord;
I know them, and they follow me.
℟. Alleluia, alleluia.

Gospel

Matt 21:28-32; L136A

**Jesus said to the chief priests
and elders of the people:
"What is your opinion?
A man had two sons.
He came to the first and said,
'Son, go out and work in the
vineyard today.'
He said in reply, 'I will not,'
but afterwards changed his
mind and went.
The man came to the other son
and gave the same order.
He said in reply, 'Yes, sir,' but
did not go.
Which of the two did his father's will?"
They answered, "The first."
Jesus said to them, "Amen, I say to you,
tax collectors and prostitutes
are entering the kingdom of God
before you.
When John came to you in the way of
righteousness,
you did not believe him;
but tax collectors and prostitutes did.
Yet even when you saw that,
you did not later change your minds
and believe him."**

Reflecting on the Gospel

The teenage daughter said that she was staying out late and not to expect her home until midnight. Her parents told her to be home by ten, to which she replied, "Whatever." Later that night, around five minutes to ten, she came home. The parents were a bit puzzled and said, "Home already?" She replied, "Well, you said be home by ten." There is a difference between saying and doing, as reflected in today's gospel.

The parable (cf. Matt 21:33, 45) Jesus utters today is in the Jerusalem temple in the context of a dialogue, or verbal jousting match really, between Jesus and the chief priests and the elders of the people. In the story we are approaching Holy Week, though liturgically we are in the twenty-sixth week of Ordinary Time. This section of the gospel is the first of three parables, which we will read liturgically in successive weeks: the two sons, the evil tenants, and the royal wedding feast.

As with all of Jesus' parables, the meaning of the "two sons" parable today is polyvalent. We can understand it in numerous ways, and this is precisely why the device of "parable" is so effective as a teaching tool. One apparent meaning is the favorite Matthean theme of doing versus saying (cf. Matt 7:21-23; 12:50; 23:3-4). Matthew's contention throughout the gospel is that not everyone who says "Lord, Lord" will enter the kingdom of heaven, but only those who do the will of the Father, which is to act mercifully particularly to those in need.

It's unfortunate that throughout history and even into the present day, there are many adherents of religion (this is not limited to Jews or Christians) who will talk a good game, but their actions indicate something else. We have many phrases in English that speak to this: "Actions speak louder than words," "By their actions you shall know them," "I don't believe what you say. I believe what you do," or "People lie, actions don't." All of these maxims get at one of the fundamental meanings of this parable.

True, our words and actions should match one another. But as Jesus makes clear, our actions—most especially how we care for those on the margins—matter much more than our good intentions.

Living the Paschal Mystery

Have you ever met a flatterer, or people pleaser? Those who say what you want to hear but have no intention of following through? Or those who over-promise and under-deliver? It can be challenging to hear the words of Jesus in the parable today about such behaviors. Despite our best intentions, it is our actions that truly mean more than our words. Without actions, our words are a "clanging gong," to use a term from St. Paul. There are many reasons why we might over-promise, but we are reminded of another saying in the gospels: "Let your 'Yes' mean 'Yes' and your 'No' mean No'" (Matt 5:37). At some level, this is simply good advice from Jesus the teacher.

As we go about our lives, let us make an extra effort to think carefully before we commit ourselves or say we will do something. Simply modifying a commitment with the words "I intend to . . ." or "I'll make my best effort to . . ." may be all we need to temper expectations. By avoiding the trap of being a people-pleaser, flatterer, or one who over-promises, and instead being a person of action and doing on behalf of others, we will be living the gospel message.

Focusing the Gospel

Key words and phrases: "[Y]ou did not later change your minds"

To the point: With today's gospel we enter the last week of Jesus' earthly life as he speaks with his disciples, preaches to the crowds, and spars with the chief priests and elders. These events take place in Jerusalem and the surrounding area just before and during the feast of Passover. Today Jesus confronts the chief priests and elders about their inability to change their position even after hearing the preaching of John the Baptist. By remaining entrenched in their own way of doing things, they are missing the work of God in their midst. It seems there is good news in today's parable as well, however: even if one originally refuses the request of God, there is still time to turn to him and do what is just.

Connecting the Gospel

to the first reading: This message of hope is also found in the first reading, where God, speaking through the prophet Ezekiel, says that if a person bent on evil "turns from the wickedness he has committed, / and does what is right and just, / he shall preserve his life." Of course, the opposite is also true—just as a wicked person who has turned from evil is no longer counted among the lost, a virtuous person who "turns away from virtue to commit iniquity" is not saved by his or her previous virtue.

to experience: As with last Sunday's readings we are reminded that we cannot comprehend God's justice through our normal human lens. In the first reading God tells us, "Is it my way that is unfair, or rather, are not your ways unfair?" In seeking to pronounce judgment of others, we inevitably fail—for this is not our role, but God's.

Connecting the Responsorial Psalm

to the readings: Today's psalm is one of a repentant sinner who begs for God to forget "the sins of my youth and my frailties." It reminds us that we are all repentant sinners who turn to the Lord, humbly seeking mercy. Only in emptying ourselves of our pride and sureness (the same things that block the chief priests and elders of today's gospel in recognizing Jesus' identity) can we become the humble who can learn the ways of God. We find our greatest model of humility in Jesus. St. Paul's letter to the Philippians reminds us of how "he emptied himself, / taking the form of a slave, / coming in human likeness; / and found human in appearance, / he humbled himself, / becoming obedient to the point of death, / even death on a cross."

to psalmist preparation: Just as the psalmist asks for God to "[r]emember your mercies, O Lord," let us also take time this week in prayer to contemplate the compassion God has shown throughout our lives.

PROMPTS FOR FAITH-SHARING

Today's psalm proclaims, "[God] teaches the humble his way." How do you adopt an attitude of humility in your daily life?

St. Paul urges the church in Philippi to be "united in heart, thinking one thing." Where is your parish community the most united? What divides you?

The apostle asks the community members to reject "selfishness" and "vainglory" by regarding "others as more important than yourself." In your life, who has been a model of placing others above self?

Considering today's parable, which son are you more likely to be (the one who commits but doesn't follow through, or the one who refuses but in the end complies)?

Model Penitential Act

Presider: In today's second reading, St. Paul urges us to "[d]o nothing out of selfishness or out of vainglory; / rather, humbly regard others as more important than yourselves." For the times we have placed our needs above the needs of others, let us ask for pardon and mercy . . . *[pause]*

Lord Jesus, you are the way, the truth, and the life: Lord, have mercy.

Christ Jesus, you call us to fidelity in word and deed: Christ, have mercy.

Lord Jesus, you humbled yourself on the cross and are exalted at the right hand of the Father: Lord, have mercy.

Homily Points

• Today's parable about the two sons should make us all squirm a little. How many times have we found it easier to tell someone what he or she wanted to hear with no intention of following through, rather than entering into a difficult conversation? We could think of tired parents who tell their child, "I'll play with you after dinner," only to have that time come and be ready with another excuse. Or children who promise to clean their room, never intending to keep their word and hoping their parents will become distracted by something else.

• In today's gospel there are two sons and neither is perfect. One refuses his father's request but then does it; the other accepts the request but doesn't follow through. In the end, it seems that virtuous actions are more important than virtuous words. In our daily lives people make many requests of us. Some are important, and others we could probably politely refuse. One meaning for today's parable might be the importance of knowing our limits and being honest about what we can and can't (or will and won't) do.

• The parable also points to something else though—our relationship with God and our commitment to the life of discipleship. God has asked us to work in his vineyard, caring for the poor, working for justice, and bringing peace to others. As Christians, we are called to love God and others, not simply through the words we say but, more important, in the ways we give of ourselves for the good of all. In your life, where is God calling you to more action and fewer words?

Model Universal Prayer (Prayer of the Faithful)

Presider: Knowing the compassionate love of the Father, let us turn to him in prayer.

Response: Lord, hear our prayer.

For God's holy church, in word and deed may it proclaim God's boundless mercy to the world . . .

For leaders of nations, may they work together to safeguard the environment and to aid those most affected by climate change . . .

For those who have lost their way and wandered far from God's love, may they return to the Lord of mercy who is always ready to forgive and restore . . .

For all gathered here around the table of the Lord, may we always strive to follow him with fidelity by keeping our baptismal promises and living as children of light . . .

Presider: God of creation, you have called us to serve you by loving our neighbor as our self. Hear our prayers that with acts of sacrifice and self-giving, we might place others' needs before our own. We ask this through Christ our Lord. **Amen.**

COLLECT

Let us pray.

Pause for silent prayer

O God, who manifest your almighty power
above all by pardoning and showing mercy,
bestow, we pray, your grace abundantly upon us
and make those hastening to attain your promises
heirs to the treasures of heaven.
Through our Lord Jesus Christ, your Son,
who lives and reigns with you in the unity of the Holy Spirit,
one God, for ever and ever. **Amen.**

FIRST READING

Ezek 18:25-28

Thus says the LORD:
You say, "The LORD's way is not fair!"
Hear now, house of Israel:
Is it my way that is unfair, or rather, are not your ways unfair?
When someone virtuous turns away from virtue to commit iniquity, and dies,
it is because of the iniquity he committed that he must die.
But if he turns from the wickedness he has committed,
and does what is right and just,
he shall preserve his life;
since he has turned away from all the sins that he has committed,
he shall surely live, he shall not die.

RESPONSORIAL PSALM

Ps 25:4-5, 6-7, 8-9

℟. (6a) Remember your mercies, O Lord.

Your ways, O LORD, make known to me;
teach me your paths,
guide me in your truth and teach me,
for you are God my savior.

℟. Remember your mercies, O Lord.

Remember that your compassion, O LORD,
and your love are from of old.
The sins of my youth and my frailties remember not;
in your kindness remember me,
because of your goodness, O LORD.

℟. Remember your mercies, O Lord.

Good and upright is the Lord;
thus he shows sinners the way.
He guides the humble to justice,
and teaches the humble his way.

℟. Remember your mercies, O Lord.

SECOND READING
Phil 2:1-11

Brothers and sisters:
If there is any encouragement in Christ,
any solace in love,
any participation in the Spirit,
any compassion and mercy,
complete my joy by being of the same mind, with the same love,
united in heart, thinking one thing.
Do nothing out of selfishness or out of vainglory;
rather, humbly regard others as more important than yourselves,
each looking out not for his own interests,
but also for those of others.

Have in you the same attitude
that is also in Christ Jesus,
Who, though he was in the form of God,
did not regard equality with God
something to be grasped.
Rather, he emptied himself,
taking the form of a slave,
coming in human likeness;
and found human in appearance,
he humbled himself,
becoming obedient to the point of death,
even death on a cross.
Because of this, God greatly exalted him
and bestowed on him the name
which is above every name,
that at the name of Jesus
every knee should bend,
of those in heaven and on earth
and under the earth,
and every tongue confess that
Jesus Christ is Lord,
to the glory of God the Father.

or Phil 2:1-5

See Appendix A, p. 302.

CATECHESIS

About Liturgy

More than the liturgy is required: As liturgists and liturgical ministers, we deal with many ritual words and actions. When I was immersed in full-time parish work, overseeing several liturgies every weekend, I thought to myself that praying at Mass was enough. Wasn't I doing more than what was required by giving thanks and praise to God multiple times every week?

Then I heard today's gospel, and I had to wonder: Is doing church ministry the same as doing the Father's will? More often than I'd like to admit, I have been content to sing and pray week after week about the hungry being fed, yet I have done very little to feed the hungry poor I drive past every day on the way to church.

Godfrey Diekmann, OSB, a monk of St. John's Abbey and renowned liturgist, was known to ask his liturgy students, "What good is it if the bread and wine are changed [into the Body and Blood of Christ] but we are not?"

At the end of the Mass, one of the formulas for the dismissal commissions us with these words: "Go in peace, glorifying the Lord by your lives." Ritual words and actions at the liturgy are not enough. They are rehearsal for how we are to live and act in our daily lives.

About Initiation

The ongoing, gradual process of conversion: Author Anne Lamott wrote, "The opposite of faith is not doubt, but certainty." The chief priests' sin that Jesus names in today's parable may be generally described as the inability to change one's mind—to be so certain of one's opinion, direction, or perspective that no amount of evidence can sway them to change. Now Christian faith is not something we analyze with a microscope. However, we are called to learn how to see behind the "signs of the times" to the mystery of God contained in them (see General Directory for Catechesis 108). RCIA 75.2 describes it as learning to "follow supernatural inspiration in their deeds."

Conversion is changing one's mind evidenced by one's deeds. This is a gradual process, and Christians are called to constant conversion as they look for the mystery of God all around them in the particular circumstance they find themselves. Two questions you can ask your catechumens and candidates (and one another) that can help them follow supernatural inspiration are "Where did you see God today?" and "So what?" In other words, how will you live differently today because of what God has revealed to you?

About Liturgical Music

Doing what we sing: As music ministers, we are saturated with words in the performance of our ministry, and it can become very easy to gloss over the meaning of those words as we focus on getting the music right. Today's gospel is a reminder for us that words aren't important if we don't live them in our actions.

For instance, today you might sing "Eye Has Not Seen" by Marty Haugen (GIA) in connection with the second reading verse, "Have in you the same attitude that is also in Christ Jesus" (Phil 2:5). When you sing, "Spirit of love, come, give us the mind of Jesus, teach us the wisdom of God," what implications do those words have for your life? If we are to have the same attitude as Christ, then how do you live out these words from Philippians: "Do nothing out of selfishness or out of vainglory" (2:3)? In your mind, heart, and actions, do you harbor any resentment of your fellow music ministers who might be given a solo or asked to lead the psalm? What consequences do the words you sing have in your life?

SPIRITUALITY

GOSPEL ACCLAMATION
cf. John 15:16

℟. Alleluia, alleluia.
I have chosen you from the world, says the Lord,
to go and bear fruit that will remain.
℟. Alleluia, alleluia.

Gospel Matt 21:33-43; L139A

Jesus said to the chief priests
and the elders of the people:
"Hear another parable.
There was a landowner who planted a vineyard,
put a hedge around it, dug a wine press in it, and built a tower.
Then he leased it to tenants and went on a journey.
When vintage time drew near,
he sent his servants to the tenants to obtain his produce.
But the tenants seized the servants and one they beat,
another they killed, and a third they stoned.
Again he sent other servants, more numerous than the first ones,
but they treated them in the same way.
Finally, he sent his son to them, thinking,
'They will respect my son.'
But when the tenants saw the son, they said to one another,
'This is the heir.
Come, let us kill him and acquire his inheritance.'
They seized him, threw him out of the vineyard, and killed him.
What will the owner of the vineyard do to those tenants when he comes?"
They answered him,
"He will put those wretched men to a wretched death
and lease his vineyard to other tenants
who will give him the produce at the proper times."

Continued in Appendix A, p. 302.

Reflecting on the Gospel

The second of three parables in as many weeks greets us on the Twenty-Seventh Sunday in Ordinary Time. Matthew has inherited this parable from Mark and edited it slightly. Most scholars agree that the parable goes back to the historical Jesus, even if they differ on where the story "originally" ended. Often it is maintained that Jesus' words ended with "they seized him, threw him out of the vineyard, and killed him." That is, Jesus' words end with the narration of the story. The question and what comes later was developed by the early tradition, especially the citation of Psalm 118:22-23 with its saying that the stone which the builders rejected has become the cornerstone. This psalm was popular in the early church and we hear it in Acts 4:11 and 1 Peter 2:7. Moreover, it's thought that Jesus' words ended with "and killed him" as they are so stark. There is no resurrection or exaltation imagined. Instead, it is the tradition that adds the psalm citation that was so popular among early believers.

The image of the vineyard itself is rooted (so to speak) in Isaiah 7, which is the first reading this Sunday. Jesus was familiar with Scripture and often used images from the sacred text in his teachings.

Often this parable is read in a way that reflects relations (and tensions) between Christians and Jews of Matthew's time. It's clear from Matthew's telling (though today's gospel ends before we read this section) that the chief priests and Pharisees certainly had no misunderstanding—they saw themselves in this parable and did not take kindly to this verbal dagger. They tried to arrest Jesus. But in the story proclaimed today, we do not hear the reaction of the chief priests and Pharisees.

From the early Christians' point of view, articulated in the Gospel of Matthew, the Jews had Jesus killed and the Father had effectively opened up the vineyard (the kingdom of God) to the nations (Gentiles). The church today is clear that this reading does not mean the Jewish people were rejected (e.g., Pontifical Biblical Commission, The Jewish People and Their Sacred Scriptures in the Christian Bible [2002] 71). This parable and others like it in the Gospel of Matthew must be read with care, especially in light of both historical and modern Jewish-Christian relations.

Living the Paschal Mystery

Though the gospel was written two thousand years ago, it unfortunately has been misused throughout history as justification for Christians to persecute Jews. The church tells us that the words here echo words of the prophets and their critiques of the people of God. But when Christians definitively separated from Jews, the words were understood differently, not as an internal critique between members of a family but as a forceful condemnation of the "other."

> But it must be admitted that many of these passages are capable of providing a pretext for anti-Jewish sentiment and have in fact been used in this way. To avoid mistakes of this kind, it must be kept in mind that the New Testament polemical texts, even those expressed in general terms, have to do with concrete historical contexts and are never meant to be applied to Jews of all times and places merely because they are Jews. (Pontifical Biblical Commission, Jewish People 87)

Now in the modern world, especially in light of the holocaust, we must do all we can to put away any anti-Jewish reading of the text. In so doing, we will walk in the newness of life.

Focusing the Gospel

Key words and phrases: "[T]he kingdom of God will be taken away from you / and given to a people that will produce its fruit."

To the point: Jesus has harsh words today for the chief priests and elders. As a faithful Jew, Jesus was not confronting them about their Jewish religion, but about their practice of it. The chief priests and elders were the authority figures within the religious community. In the *Magnificat* we are told who our God is. He champions the lowly and casts down the mighty. It seems the chief priests and elders had grown comfortable with where they were and did not like Jesus' teachings that challenged their authority. Jesus' words remain as shocking and challenging today. Especially now, where Christians might find themselves as the majority religion in many parts of the world, and enjoying the power that comes with being able to influence laws and culture, we must always ask ourselves: With whom are we aligned? Are we producing the fruits of the kingdom of God where the lowly are lifted up, or have we become the new keepers of the status quo—a status quo that benefits us?

Connecting the Gospel

to the first reading: The first reading from the prophet Isaiah is in the form of an allegory. God plants a vineyard and tends it lovingly, but instead of producing good fruit it yields wild (also translated as "rotten"; NABRE) grapes. At the end of the reading we are told what these "rotten grapes" are: "bloodshed" and the outcry of the oppressed. Despite the teachings of the Law and the prophets, the people of God have turned their back on God's commandments. In the rest of this chapter from Isaiah, the prophet outlines the many sins of the people, including debauchery, corruption, and depriving the innocent of justice (5:22-23).

to experience: In today's gospel, the chief priests and elders listening to Jesus' parable of the vineyard would have been very familiar with "The Song of the Vineyard," in the book of the prophet Isaiah. Each makes reference to the fruits that the vineyard produces. Within our own lives as Christians, we might ask ourselves, within our families, parish communities, and the church as a whole, what kind of fruit are we producing?

Connecting the Responsorial Psalm

to the readings: Today's psalm could be seen as a direct response to the devastating first reading from the prophet Isaiah where God vows to let his vineyard ("the house of Israel") be "overgrown with thorns and briars." The psalmist pleads, "Once again, O Lord of hosts, / look down from heaven, and see; / take care of this vine, / and protect what your right hand has planted."

to psalmist preparation: The writings of the prophets, like the parables of Jesus, are meant to shake us from our complacency and cause us to take stock of life. In the psalms we find prayers for every emotion, from triumphant and praising, to pleading and invoking. Which psalms speak to you most at this time in your life?

PROMPTS FOR FAITH-SHARING

St. Paul writes to the Philippians, "Have no anxiety at all." Where have worries or anxiety crept into your life and how might you turn these over to the Lord?

When in your life have you encountered the "peace of God that surpasses all understanding"?

St. Paul urges the Corinthians to only think about things that are honorable, just, pure, lovely, gracious, excellent, and worthy of praise. What are your favorite books, movies, or music that emulate these values?

In the gospel Jesus quotes the Scripture passage, "The stone that the builders rejected / has become the cornerstone." Can you think of an example in your life where this proved to be the case?

Model Penitential Act

Presider: As we prepare to meet the Lord in the Holy Scriptures and the bread and wine of the Eucharist, let us call to mind our sins and ask for God's pardon and peace . . . *[pause]*

Lord Jesus, you are the stone rejected by the builders that has become the cornerstone: Lord, have mercy.
You call us to produce good fruit for the kingdom of God: Christ, have mercy.
Lord Jesus, you offer us peace that surpasses understanding: Lord, have mercy.

Homily Points

• In a little less than two months we will celebrate the First Sunday of Advent. As we approach the feast of Christ the King and the end of this liturgical year, our readings turn to the parables and preaching of Jesus' final week in Jerusalem before his crucifixion. We might notice an increased intensity to the gospel stories that we are given. Jesus knows he has little time left, and as he prepares himself and his disciples for what lies ahead, his words take on a harsher tone.

• In today's gospel, Jesus gives the parable of the vineyard that a landowner leases to tenants. Instead of handing over produce to the landowner's servants, the tenants beat and kill them. Jesus foreshadows his own death when he says, "Finally [the landowner] sent his son to them, thinking, / 'They will respect my son.' . . . They seized him, threw him out of the vineyard, and killed him."

• In reading this parable we remember it is addressed to us now, just as much as it was addressed to the chief priests and elders in the time of Jesus. Jesus tells them (us), "[T]he kingdom of God will be taken away from you / and given to a people that will produce its fruit." What is this fruit that Jesus speaks of? A little later on in Matthew's gospel Jesus will spell it out clearly; when the Son of Man returns, we will be judged on how we cared for the poor and vulnerable, for "whatever you did for one of the least brothers of mine, you did for me" (25:40). If we desire to be the people of God and to tend the vineyard of the Lord, we must put our faith into action and produce the fruits of the kingdom.

Model Universal Prayer (Prayer of the Faithful)

Presider: With faith in our God, the giver of every good gift, let us bring our needs before the Lord.

Response: Lord, hear our prayer.

For bishops, priests, and deacons, may they be faithful stewards of the church and serve the people of God with integrity . . .

For those in government authority, may they practice civil discourse, advocating for truthful and transparent leadership . . .

For those lacking access to education, especially girls and women, may they find resources and discover avenues to pursue their goals . . .

For all members of this parish community, may each of us use our gifts and talents to build up the church and to care for those in need . . .

Presider: God of wisdom and love, in you we find peace that surpasses all understanding. Hear our prayers that the work of our hands might build up the kingdom of God and help to spread your peace throughout the world. We ask this through Christ our Lord. **Amen.**

COLLECT

Let us pray.

Pause for silent prayer

Almighty ever-living God,
who in the abundance of your kindness
surpass the merits and the desires of
those who entreat you,
pour out your mercy upon us
to pardon what conscience dreads
and to give what prayer does not dare to
ask.
Through our Lord Jesus Christ, your Son,
who lives and reigns with you in the unity
of the Holy Spirit,
one God, for ever and ever. **Amen.**

FIRST READING

Isa 5:1-7

Let me now sing of my friend,
my friend's song concerning his vineyard.
My friend had a vineyard
on a fertile hillside;
he spaded it, cleared it of stones,
and planted the choicest vines;
within it he built a watchtower,
and hewed out a wine press.
Then he looked for the crop of grapes,
but what it yielded was wild grapes.

Now, inhabitants of Jerusalem and people
of Judah,
judge between me and my vineyard:
What more was there to do for my vineyard
that I had not done?
Why, when I looked for the crop of grapes,
did it bring forth wild grapes?
Now, I will let you know
what I mean to do with my vineyard:
take away its hedge, give it to grazing,
break through its wall, let it be trampled!
Yes, I will make it a ruin:
it shall not be pruned or hoed,
but overgrown with thorns and briers;
I will command the clouds
not to send rain upon it.
The vineyard of the LORD of hosts is the
house of Israel,
and the people of Judah are his
cherished plant;
he looked for judgment, but see,
bloodshed!
for justice, but hark, the outcry!

RESPONSORIAL PSALM

Ps 80:9, 12, 13-14, 15-16, 19-20

℟. (Isaiah 5:7a) The vineyard of the Lord is the house of Israel.

A vine from Egypt you transplanted;
you drove away the nations and planted it.
It put forth its foliage to the Sea,
its shoots as far as the River.

℟. The vineyard of the Lord is the house of Israel.

Why have you broken down its walls,
so that every passer-by plucks its fruit,
the boar from the forest lays it waste,
and the beasts of the field feed upon it?

℟. The vineyard of the Lord is the house of Israel.

Once again, O LORD of hosts,
look down from heaven, and see;
take care of this vine,
and protect what your right hand has planted,
the son of man whom you yourself made strong.

℟. The vineyard of the Lord is the house of Israel.

Then we will no more withdraw from you;
give us new life, and we will call upon your name.
O LORD, God of hosts, restore us;
if your face shine upon us, then we shall be saved.

℟. The vineyard of the Lord is the house of Israel.

SECOND READING
Phil 4:6-9

Brothers and sisters:
Have no anxiety at all, but in everything,
by prayer and petition, with thanksgiving,
make your requests known to God.
Then the peace of God that surpasses all understanding
will guard your hearts and minds in Christ Jesus.

Finally, brothers and sisters,
whatever is true, whatever is honorable,
whatever is just, whatever is pure,
whatever is lovely, whatever is gracious,
if there is any excellence
and if there is anything worthy of praise,
think about these things.
Keep on doing what you have learned and received
and heard and seen in me.
Then the God of peace will be with you.

CATECHESIS

About Liturgy

Praying during election season: We're coming up to a major election next month, and certainly there will already have been lots of campaigning and maybe even some ugly comments tossed about over social media, TV, and the news. Some of these comments might even come from "good Christians" passionate about their chosen candidate or public policy.

In the liturgy, whether in introductory comments, homilies, the universal prayers, or announcements, we must be careful to remember the church's teaching on the relationship between the political community and the church: "The Church, by reason of her role and competence, is not identified in any way with the political community nor bound to any political system. She is at once a sign and a safeguard of the transcendent character of the human person" (Pastoral Constitution on the Church in the Modern World 76). Moreover, "[Christians] must recognize the legitimacy of different opinions with regard to temporal solutions, and respect citizens, who, even as a group, defend their points of view by honest methods" (75). Above all, "[a]ll citizens . . . should be mindful of the right and also the duty to use their free vote to further the common good" (75).

We should encourage everyone to work for the common good and exercise their duty to vote. In all things, we must keep one another accountable in the tone of our words toward those with whom we disagree. We cannot allow "wild" or rotten fruit to come out of the vineyard of the Lord, but we can strive to cultivate a generosity of spirit and goodwill toward one another.

In this election season, let all Christians dwell on today's words from Philippians and use them as a barometer for measuring how our words and actions advance the common good.

About Initiation

Make your requests known: Today's reading from Philippians invites us to make our requests known to God "by prayer and petition, with thanksgiving" (4:6). Paul then describes the result of this kind of prayer: "[T]he peace of God . . . will guard your hearts and minds" (4:7). Notice that the result of prayer is not getting what we ask for but, rather, peace in Christ.

As we continue to accompany our catechumens and candidates on their journey of conversion, let us help them develop a mature prayer life, one that does not treat prayer as a way to get what we want but rather as a way to build a relationship with God through the Spirit that leads to peace in Christ. Take care of the words you use when you speak about your prayer life. God will not always answer our prayers the way we desire. Let us not be distracted by our expectations, which prevent us from receiving God's peace.

About Liturgical Music

The fruit of liturgical music: In their document on liturgical music, the United States bishops said, "Charity, justice, and evangelization are thus the normal consequences of liturgical celebration. Particularly inspired by sung participation, the body of the Word Incarnate goes forth to spread the Gospel with full force and compassion" (Sing to the Lord 9).

Music ministers have a role to play in cultivating the fruits of liturgical celebration, which are "charity, justice, and evangelization." Through our work within the liturgy and, more important, through our example of charity, justice, and spreading the gospel "with full force and compassion," we will be good stewards of the vineyard God has given us to tend.

SPIRITUALITY

GOSPEL ACCLAMATION
cf. Eph 1:17-18

℟. Alleluia, alleluia.
May the Father of our Lord Jesus Christ
enlighten the eyes of our hearts,
so that we may know what is the hope
that belongs to our call.
℟. Alleluia, alleluia.

Gospel Matt 22:1-14; L142A

Jesus again in reply spoke to the chief priests and elders of the people
in parables, saying,
"The kingdom of heaven may be likened to a king
who gave a wedding feast for his son.
He dispatched his servants
to summon the invited guests to the feast,
but they refused to come.
A second time he sent other servants, saying,
'Tell those invited: "Behold, I have prepared my banquet,
my calves and fattened cattle are killed,
and everything is ready; come to the feast."'
Some ignored the invitation and went away,
one to his farm, another to his business.
The rest laid hold of his servants,
mistreated them, and killed them.
The king was enraged and sent his troops,
destroyed those murderers, and burned their city.
Then he said to his servants, 'The feast is ready,
but those who were invited were not worthy to come.
Go out, therefore, into the main roads
and invite to the feast whomever you find.'
The servants went out into the streets
and gathered all they found, bad and good alike,
and the hall was filled with guests.

Continued in Appendix A, p. 303, or
Matt 22:1-10 *in Appendix A, p. 303.*

Reflecting on the Gospel

Now we come to the third of three parables in three weeks. After learning about the two sons and the evil tenants, we now hear about the royal wedding feast. This parable, like the one from last week, is addressed to the chief priests and elders. Care should be exercised to remember that Jesus is not talking about all Jews; he speaks to the leaders in a particular time and place. And the parable he speaks to them is harsh, especially the end. If we choose the shorter gospel reading, the last four verses will not be read—and it might be easier for the preacher if they weren't! Many problematic issues are avoided by simply reading the shorter version of this gospel.

In the shorter reading, the parable is fairly straightforward. The king sets a banquet, but the guests do not come. The first servants (prophets) are ignored, as are the second set (the apostles). Indeed, the invitees kill the messengers! The king enacts his vengeance on these people, killing them and burning their city before extending the invitation to others. (The fact that the king burns a city between setting a table for guests and serving the dinner tells us clearly that we are in the realm of story.)

This parable, then, is read like last week's, in Christian-Jewish terms. The people whom God had chosen ignored his invitation both when the prophets announced it and when the apostles were sent. We recall that Matthew is writing at a time after the destruction of Jerusalem. So the parable's mentioning of the people being killed and the city burned quite literally happened when Jerusalem was destroyed by the Romans in AD 70. The original audience of Matthew's gospel did not need much imagination to get the point.

The last four verses conclude on a troubling note. When the new guests arrive, the king sees someone not properly dressed. For that he is bound and thrown out. Again, we might wonder what kind of king this is! But the image of a king in Jesus' time certainly had the power of life and death over his subjects. It makes for an apt image of God, even if the behaviors of the king in this particular parable sound off-putting. We recall earlier Matthean parables like the weeds and wheat. Matthew knows the church is a collection of the good and bad. Some quite literally need to be tossed out. (These Matthean themes of violence are often seen as problematic today and the subject of many scholarly works.)

Those invited to the feast, and those who attend, should not be smug. There is no guarantee. An invitation does not necessarily mean attendance, and attendance does not necessarily mean celebration. There are expectations that need to be met. "Many are invited but few are chosen" is a sober reminder for us all.

Living the Paschal Mystery

In a story filled with such violence as we have today, it might be easy to forget we are dealing with a merciful God! God calls a people to himself and desires that they come to him. The destruction of the city of Jerusalem with its temple was interpreted at the time by Christians as God's judgment on Judah. A violent world saw stories of violence. Though we may wish to minimize the violence, unfortunately it has been part of human history from the beginning and continues to this day.

It might be difficult to strip away the violent imagery and focus instead on the kernel underneath it all. Matthew's church has the wisdom and experience of decades since the death and resurrection of Jesus. It has learned that there are some in the church who do not belong, as indicated in several parables. Sadly, our modern experience reflects this too. Simply being in the church does not make one holy, God's chosen, or a paragon of virtue. There are weeds within the wheat. Only God has the authority to definitively and eternally expel such a person. The sobering reminder that "many are invited but few are chosen" should cause us to pause, reflect, and reexamine our lives.

Focusing the Gospel

Key words and phrases: "[C]ome to the feast."

To the point: In today's parable a king issues an invitation to come to the wedding feast for his son. After those initially invited refuse, he sends his servants out "into the main roads" telling them "invite to the feast whomever you find." The invitation to be part of the kingdom of God is not reserved for a select group but is a blanket invitation to all people. Despite the generosity of the invitation, there are some things we must do as invited guests. The most important one seems to be to simply to show up. But after that we must also come clothed "in a wedding garment," as today's gospel tells us. Multiple meanings could be deduced about what this wedding garment might symbolize. One could be that if we are invited to the greatest feast of all, we can't just wander in because the door was open; we must be ready to truly enter into the celebration.

Connecting the Gospel

to the first reading: Despite the harshness of today's gospel, the first reading from the prophet Isaiah joyfully lifts up how God desires to "provide for all peoples / a feast of rich food and choice wines." These words hearken to the king's invitation in today's parable: "Behold, I have prepared my banquet, / my calves and fattened cattle are killed, / and everything is ready; come to the feast."

to experience: We know that our God is an abundant giver of gifts who provided manna for the Hebrew people when they wandered in the desert, fed the five thousand through the miracles of Jesus in the gospels, and even to this day feeds us in the Eucharist. The invitation of the gospel is issued to each of us: "[C]ome to the feast."

Connecting the Responsorial Psalm

to the readings: In today's psalm, God again is the host of a sumptuous banquet. The psalmist sings, "You spread a table before me / in the sight of my foes; / you anoint my head with oil; / my cup overflows." We see this imagery in the feast God invites all people to in the first reading and again in the banquet prepared by the king in Jesus' parable. The Bible often lifts up the virtue of hospitality. But it is important, too, to consider the duties expected of a guest. In the gospel parable the first set of guests ignore the invitation and refuse to attend. In contrast, not only does the psalmist gratefully sit at the table of the Lord, he also anticipates dwelling "in the house of the Lord for years to come."

to psalmist preparation: How do you experience the abundant gifts of God in your own life?

PROMPTS FOR FAITH-SHARING

Isaiah prophesies, "The Lord God will wipe away / the tears from every face." Where is there suffering or sadness in your community? How might God be calling you to be a source of comfort for others?

St. Paul tells the Philippians, "I know how to live in humble circumstances; / I know also how to live with abundance." What do you think is the key to living well in differing situations?

St. Paul writes, "I can do all things in him who strengthens me." Where are you in need of God's strength to take on a new challenge?

In today's parable, Jesus likens the kingdom of God to a wedding feast. In what ways do you think this might be an apt description of heaven?

Model Penitential Act

Presider: In today's gospel parable the guests initially invited to a wedding feast refuse to come. For the times we have not answered the invitation of the Lord in our own lives, let us pause to ask for pardon and mercy . . . *[pause]*

Lord Jesus, you comfort those who mourn, and weep with those who weep: Lord, have mercy.

Christ Jesus, you call us to fullness of life: Christ, have mercy.

Lord Jesus, you are the Son of the living God: Lord, have mercy.

Homily Points

• In today's parable, the kingdom of heaven is compared to a wedding feast. Before looking at the particular course of the wedding feast, we could say, what a joyful image! For the bride and groom, their wedding day will hopefully be one of the happiest of their lives. Not only are they stepping into a new future with their beloved, but their family and friends have gathered to support their union. There are many ways we could think of a wedding feast as a fitting comparison to the kingdom of heaven. In today's parable Jesus focuses on the invitation.

• A king is throwing a wedding feast for his son and on the day of the banquet sends his servants out twice to bid the invited guests to come. In a shocking display of bad manners, twice the guests refuse. We might consider, how could this be like the kingdom of heaven?

• It is good to note that before flying into a rage, the king offers his guests multiple chances—there's the initial invitation before the wedding day and then twice personal summons are given. The second time the king even sends the message, "Behold, I have prepared my banquet, / my calves and fattened cattle are killed, / and everything is ready; come to the feast." Throughout our lives God offers many invitations to us to be part of his kingdom and to be fed at his table. Even though we have been invited, we also know that God honors our free will. If we refuse the invitation to the feast, we won't be forced to join. As we journey closer to the end of our liturgical year, now is a good time to ponder, over this past year, how have we responded to the invitations God has issued in our lives?

Model Universal Prayer (Prayer of the Faithful)

Presider: Trusting in the Lord of life who calls us by name, let us turn to God in prayer.

Response: Lord, hear our prayer.

For all members of the church, may we answer the call of the Lord in our lives to serve him and others in love and humility . . .

For nations that are overwhelmed by outbreaks of infectious disease and epidemics, may they receive necessary medications and support to care for the ill . . .

For the elderly and their caregivers, may they know the care and compassion of God and live in dignity and comfort . . .

For all gathered here, may we have hope in Christ's promises and perseverance to meet the challenges of each day . . .

Presider: God, our shepherd and guide, through the parables your son, Jesus, teaches us the secrets of your kingdom. Hear our prayers that in meditating on your word, we might grow ever closer to you. We ask this through Christ our Lord. **Amen.**

COLLECT

Let us pray.

Pause for silent prayer

May your grace, O Lord, we pray,
at all times go before us and follow after
and make us always determined
to carry out good works.
Through our Lord Jesus Christ, your Son,
who lives and reigns with you in the unity
of the Holy Spirit,
one God, for ever and ever. **Amen.**

FIRST READING

Isa 25:6-10a

On this mountain the LORD of hosts
will provide for all peoples
a feast of rich food and choice wines,
juicy, rich food and pure, choice wines.
On this mountain he will destroy
the veil that veils all peoples,
the web that is woven over all nations;
he will destroy death forever.
The Lord GOD will wipe away
the tears from every face;
the reproach of his people he will remove
from the whole earth; for the LORD has
spoken.
On that day it will be said:
"Behold our God, to whom we looked to
save us!
This is the LORD for whom we looked;
let us rejoice and be glad that he has
saved us!"
For the hand of the LORD will rest on this
mountain.

RESPONSORIAL PSALM
Ps 23:1-3a, 3b-4, 5, 6

℟. (6cd) I shall live in the house of the Lord all the days of my life.

The LORD is my shepherd; I shall not want.
In verdant pastures he gives me repose;
beside restful waters he leads me;
he refreshes my soul.

℟. I shall live in the house of the Lord all the days of my life.

He guides me in right paths
for his name's sake.
Even though I walk in the dark valley
I fear no evil; for you are at my side
with your rod and your staff
that give me courage.

℟. I shall live in the house of the Lord all the days of my life.

You spread the table before me
in the sight of my foes;
you anoint my head with oil;
my cup overflows.

℟. I shall live in the house of the Lord all the days of my life.

Only goodness and kindness follow me
all the days of my life;
and I shall dwell in the house of the LORD
for years to come.

℟. I shall live in the house of the Lord all the days of my life.

SECOND READING
Phil 4:12-14, 19-20

Brothers and sisters:
I know how to live in humble circumstances;
I know also how to live with abundance.
In every circumstance and in all things
I have learned the secret of being well fed and of going hungry,
of living in abundance and of being in need.
I can do all things in him who strengthens me.
Still, it was kind of you to share in my distress.

My God will fully supply whatever you need,
in accord with his glorious riches in Christ Jesus.
To our God and Father, glory forever and ever. Amen.

CATECHESIS

About Liturgy

Appropriate dress: Chapter VI of the General Instruction of the Roman Missal gives us a thorough description of appropriate dress for liturgical ministers. First, it says that "diversity of offices is shown outwardly in the celebration of the Eucharist by the diversity of sacred vestments, which must therefore be a sign of the function proper to each minister" (335). The United States bishops have allowed that "acolytes, altar servers, readers, and other lay ministers may wear the alb or other appropriate and dignified clothing" (339).

When multiple people serve within an office, ideally their vestments should be the same for each person in that office. For example, if there are two deacons assisting at a Mass, their vestments should be the same to show that they both serve in the office of deacon. Similarly, all altar servers assisting within a Mass should wear the same style vestment. If they are in alb, they should all wear the same color and style. There should be no differences in vestment for altar servers, or any other liturgical ministers, because of age or gender. Note that cassock and surplice are specifically reserved for clerics, so should not be worn by laypersons.

The choice whether to vest lay liturgical ministers in albs is dependent on each parish. The decision should be consistently applied to all the Masses but may also change throughout the year according to a celebration's degree of solemnity.

About Initiation

Vestments for the RCIA: Some parishes ask catechumens to wear a liturgical vestment for the RCIA rites. For example, they might invite catechumens to wear purple or dark-colored albs for the scrutinies. There is no requirement for this, and doing so may confuse the purpose of liturgical vestments, which is to show one's liturgical function and office.

However, liturgical vestments are appropriately used for catechumens at the Easter Vigil. There, those to be baptized might wear a non-white or dark-colored robe for their baptism. This allows them to wear clothing under their robe that can get wet, especially in full-immersion baptisms. After they are baptized, they can put on more formal clothing in preparation for receiving a white garment. This white garment should be more than a small piece of fabric, and it should not look like a stole. Albs or white choir robes work best.

Although not required, neophytes might be invited to wear this white garment at Mass throughout the Easter season.

If those already baptized are invited to wear a liturgical garment for their Rite of Reception or for their celebration of confirmation and Eucharist, it should be a white garment in remembrance of their baptism.

About Liturgical Music

Choir robes: The same principles outlined in the General Instruction of the Roman Missal on proper attire for liturgical ministers apply for music ministers as well. The United States bishops speak specifically to liturgical vesture for music ministers in "Sing to the Lord." There, they state that "[c]hoir and ensemble members may dress in albs or choir robes, but always in clean, presentable, and modest clothing. Cassock and surplice, being clerical attire, are not recommended as choir vesture" (33). They give the same recommendation for the psalmist (36) and the cantor (40).

Different ensembles might choose different attire when serving at their proper Masses. However, whenever a parish's various music ministers gather together to assist at the same Mass, they should all be vested similarly to show their unity of liturgical function.

SPIRITUALITY

GOSPEL ACCLAMATION
Phil 2:15d, 16a

℟. Alleluia, alleluia.
Shine like lights in the world
as you hold on to the word of life.
℟. Alleluia, alleluia.

Gospel

Matt 22:15-21; L145A

The Pharisees went off
and plotted how they might entrap Jesus in speech.
They sent their disciples to him, with the Herodians, saying,
"Teacher, we know that you are a truthful man
and that you teach the way of God in accordance with the truth.
And you are not concerned with anyone's opinion,
for you do not regard a person's status.
Tell us, then, what is your opinion:
Is it lawful to pay the census tax to Caesar or not?"
Knowing their malice, Jesus said,
"Why are you testing me, you hypocrites?
Show me the coin that pays the census tax."
Then they handed him the Roman coin.
He said to them, "Whose image is this and whose inscription?"
They replied, "Caesar's."
At that he said to them,
"Then repay to Caesar what belongs to Caesar
and to God what belongs to God."

Reflecting on the Gospel

As we continue to follow and witness Jesus' activities as events in Jerusalem march closer to that fateful end, we have today not a parable (we had three in a row in as many weeks). Instead, we hear about a verbal sparring match between Jesus and the Herodians and Pharisees, adversaries themselves. But a common threat (Jesus) has united these two competitors. The Herodians and the Pharisees (or at least their disciples) scheme together to ensnare (which is another meaning of the Greek term translated as "entrap") Jesus with a clever riddle.

The puzzle posed is sublime. When asked whether to pay the tax, Jesus might say to pay it, in which case he can be said to endorse the political system. Or Jesus might say not to pay the tax, in which case he can be said to endorse the overthrow of the political system. Either answer seemingly dooms him. But their insincerity and their plotting are plain to see. Instead of falling into the "either/or" trap, Jesus does something more cunning. After addressing them directly as "hypocrites," he asks for a coin, something which he does not have. They produce the coin, thereby demonstrating that they essentially endorse the system. He asks them whose image and whose inscription is on this coin they bear. With their reply, their fate is sealed. "Then repay to Caesar what belongs to Caesar and to God what belongs to God."

Jesus is not issuing a dissertation on the intersection of politics, religion, and the economy. He is not endorsing or condemning an economic system. But by his reply he has indicted the Pharisees and the Herodians for their inordinate concern about money versus what ought to be a concern for the things of God.

His indictment should strike us too. Where are our concerns? Are we focused on money or on God? Are we sincere of heart, or are we scheming? It's likely too flippant on our part to say with a sincere heart that we are focused only on God. Jesus' words to his verbal opponents are addressed to us too: "Repay to Caesar what belongs to Caesar and to God what belongs to God."

Living the Paschal Mystery

In the modern, rather individualistic world in which we live, there is a temptation to believe that what we have, we have earned. My possessions are mine, a result of my own hard work or that of others, such as family. But today's gospel is a good reminder that all we have is from God. As such, we should not and cannot be hoarders of God's good gifts. Even money itself should not be thought of as ours.

Jesus calls us to an entirely new way of thinking. We return to be fed at the table of his word and at the table of his Eucharist so often in part because we need to be reminded of this way of thinking when we are so immersed in the world with its ways.

Any resources we have are truly not our own. Even what we acquired through our own labor and efforts cannot be taken with us when we pass on from this life. Let us die to the notion of possessions—what is mine versus yours—and let us instead engage in a lifestyle of discipleship, which shares what we have with the least among us. In that way we will be living the paschal mystery.

Focusing the Gospel

Key words and phrases: The Pharisees went off / and plotted how they might entrap Jesus in speech.

To the point: If the Pharisees and Herodians were upset by Jesus before, by the opening of today's gospel reading, they are incensed. Jesus has just finished telling three very pointed parables all aimed at them. At the end of the parable of the two sons, he told the religious leaders, "[T]ax collectors and prostitutes are entering the kingdom of God before you" (21:31; NABRE). After the parable of the tenants he warned, "[T]he kingdom of God will be taken away from you and given to a people that will produce its fruit" (21:43; NABRE). And then, finally, in the parable of the wedding feast, it seems the chief priests and Pharisees are associated with the invited guests who refuse to attend. After the king in the parable becomes enraged, not only are these guests killed, their city is also burnt (22:7). We might wonder, didn't Jesus know he was poking a hornets' nest? Jesus' message is too important to blunt or water down to avoid offending others. He "speaks truth to power" and though his life will soon be forfeited, his voice is not silenced.

Connecting the Gospel

to the first reading: The Pharisees and Herodians try to entrap Jesus by asking him whether it is "lawful to pay the census tax to Caesar." Of course, Caesar was the emperor of the Roman government and had control of the land of Israel at the time of Jesus. As a harsh oppressor, Caesar was not well liked, to say the least. In the first reading we encounter a foil for Caesar, another foreign king, Cyrus. Though we are told Cyrus does not know God, he becomes God's instrument in finally releasing the Israelites from the Babylonian exile. When Cyrus, the king of Persia, is victorious in his uprising against Babylon, he sends the Israelites home. Of Cyrus, God says through the prophet Isaiah, "He carries out my every wish, / saying of Jerusalem, 'Let it be rebuilt,' / and of the temple, 'Lay its foundations'" (44:28; NABRE).

to experience: Throughout the Scriptures we find examples of people outside of the Jewish or Christian community acting with goodwill and forwarding God's dream for the world, even if this is not their explicit intention. In our own day we are encouraged to be aware of how those who are not Christians can still "reflect a ray of that truth which enlightens all men and women" (*Nostra Aetate* 2).

Connecting the Responsorial Psalm

to the readings: Psalm 96 urges us to "[s]ing to the Lord a new song." This new song comes to life as the Israelites are freed from exile in Babylon and allowed to return to their homeland to begin the process of rebuilding and restoring what was lost.

to psalmist preparation: Where is God calling you to embrace a new song in your life of faith?

PROMPTS FOR FAITH-SHARING

Today's psalm prompts us to "[s]ing to the Lord a new song." Where is God calling you to newness in your life?

St. Paul begins his letter to the Thessalonians by giving thanks for their faith and "endurance in hope." Who are the people who inspire you with their faith and hope?

The Pharisees say to Jesus, "[Y]ou are not concerned with anyone's opinion." Would you agree with this statement? How do the opinions of others affect you?

Jesus tells the Pharisees, "[R]epay to Caesar what belongs to Caesar / and to God what belongs to God." What do you think he means by this teaching?

Model Penitential Act

Presider: In Jesus we find the words of everlasting life and the way of salvation. As we begin our celebration, let us pause to ask for our ears to be opened to hear and follow the word of God . . . *[pause]*

Lord Jesus, you are the way, the truth, and the life: Lord, have mercy.
Christ Jesus, you call us to walk as children of light: Christ, have mercy.
Lord Jesus, your glory fills all creation: Lord, have mercy.

Homily Points

- In today's gospel Jesus responds to the Pharisees' question, "Is it lawful to pay the census tax to Caesar?" with a clever rejoinder. He asks the Pharisees to produce a coin for him. This, in and of itself, proves problematic for Jesus' questioners. Money was a tricky issue for the Jews of Jesus' day. While they needed coinage to go about the business of daily life, the coins, with their image of Caesar and the inscription "son of god," went against the first commandment to "have no other gods beside me" (Exod 20:3; NABRE) and to possess no "likeness of anything in the heavens above or on the earth below or in the waters beneath the earth" (20:4; NABRE).

- When the Pharisees show Jesus the coin, he points out its blasphemy by asking, "Whose image is this and whose inscription?" Of course, they must reply "Caesar's," leading into Jesus' line: "Then repay to Caesar what belongs to Caesar / and to God what belongs to God."

- It is interesting that Jesus asks the question of whose image is on the coin. In considering Jesus' injunction to the Pharisees, if the census tax can be paid to Caesar who has issued money in his own image, what should be repaid to God? The first creation story tells us, "God created mankind in his image; / in the image of God he created them; / male and female he created them." So perhaps the answer could be "us." We are the repayment to God for the great gift of life and love—each moment of each day, every word and action, all to be given to our creator. It is up to us to live out Jesus' words in our own day, to give to the world what belongs to the world and "to God what belongs to God."

Model Universal Prayer (Prayer of the Faithful)

Presider: With trust in God's love and care for all his creatures, let us bring our needs before the Lord.

Response: Lord, hear our prayer.

For leaders of the church, in joy may they dedicate their lives to serving God in truth and to caring for his people, especially the most vulnerable . . .

For governments of the world, may they serve their people with integrity and honesty . . .

For those burdened by financial hardship, may they be given opportunities and assistance in supporting themselves and their families . . .

For all gathered here, may we steward our gifts of time, talent, and treasure to build up the church of God and to help those in need . . .

Presider: Almighty God, in your Word and the Eucharist you provide us with nourishment for the journey of faith. Hear our prayers that we might be filled with peace and strengthened in hope to go forth and proclaim you're the gospel. We ask this through Christ our Lord. **Amen.**

COLLECT

Let us pray.

Pause for silent prayer

Almighty ever-living God,
grant that we may always conform our will to yours
and serve your majesty in sincerity of heart.
Through our Lord Jesus Christ, your Son,
who lives and reigns with you in the unity of the Holy Spirit,
one God, for ever and ever. **Amen.**

FIRST READING

Isa 45:1, 4-6

Thus says the LORD to his anointed, Cyrus,
whose right hand I grasp,
subduing nations before him,
and making kings run in his service,
opening doors before him
and leaving the gates unbarred:
For the sake of Jacob, my servant,
of Israel, my chosen one,
I have called you by your name,
giving you a title, though you knew me not.
I am the LORD and there is no other,
there is no God besides me.
It is I who arm you, though you know me not,
so that toward the rising and the setting of the sun
people may know that there is none besides me.
I am the LORD, there is no other.

RESPONSORIAL PSALM
Ps 96:1, 3, 4-5, 7-8, 9-10

℟. (7b) Give the Lord glory and honor.

Sing to the LORD a new song;
sing to the LORD, all you lands.
Tell his glory among the nations;
among all peoples, his wondrous deeds.

℟. Give the Lord glory and honor.

For great is the LORD and highly to be praised;
awesome is he, beyond all gods.
For all the gods of the nations are things of nought,
but the LORD made the heavens.

℟. Give the Lord glory and honor.

Give to the LORD, you families of nations,
give to the LORD glory and praise;
give to the LORD the glory due his name!
Bring gifts, and enter his courts.

℟. Give the Lord glory and honor.

Worship the LORD, in holy attire;
tremble before him, all the earth;
say among the nations: The LORD is king,
he governs the peoples with equity.

℟. Give the Lord glory and honor.

SECOND READING
1 Thess 1:1-5b

Paul, Silvanus, and Timothy to the church of the Thessalonians
in God the Father and the Lord Jesus Christ:
grace to you and peace.
We give thanks to God always for all of you,
remembering you in our prayers,
unceasingly calling to mind your work of faith and labor of love
and endurance in hope of our Lord Jesus Christ,
before our God and Father,
knowing, brothers and sisters loved by God,
how you were chosen.
For our gospel did not come to you in word alone,
but also in power and in the Holy Spirit and with much conviction.

CATECHESIS

About Liturgy

Citizens of both cities: The last major document from the Second Vatican Council was *Gaudium et Spes*, the Pastoral Constitution on the Church in the Modern World. Although this document does not speak of the church's liturgical life, it has implications for the relationship between our liturgical life and our secular activities. Namely, it calls us to connect our liturgical practice of faith and our acts of worship with our civic responsibilities and the practice of our daily lives. Because Christians are "citizens of both cities," the council encouraged them "to perform their duties faithfully in the spirit of the Gospel" (43). In both our religious and civic duties, Christians "by our faith are bound all the more to fulfill these responsibilities according to the vocation of each one" (43). Therefore, as citizens of a nation, we cannot ignore our duty to follow its laws or to participate in the act of voting. Nor can we, as citizens of the heavenly kingdom, "immerse ourselves in earthly activities as if these latter were utterly foreign to religion, and religion were nothing more than the fulfillment of acts of worship and the observance of a few moral obligations" (43). We must align the concrete, public practices of our daily lives with the faith that we profess.

To this end, the Universal Prayer calls us to pray for our civic as well as religious leaders. Also, in the homily and in other parish activities, we might encourage citizens to work publicly for justice by participating in secular efforts that promote the common good.

About Initiation

Faith is not a refuge from the world: It can become too easy for a person new to faith to imagine that what Christians do on Sunday is disconnected from what they do in their daily life, especially in their secular activities. However, part of the formation of catechumens is to help them connect their life of faith with their actions in the world. The spiritual life of Christians "should become manifest by means of its social consequences" (RCIA 75.2) such that those who encounter them in their daily life outside of the parish notice in them a countercultural way of living. Furthermore, catechumens are to learn how to live the church's apostolic life "through the witness of their lives" (75.4). Apostolic life means going out into the world to bring the message of the gospel to every corner of society.

Thus, what we do on Sunday is a rehearsal for how we are to live throughout the week. To do this well, we bring to our Sunday celebration the needs and concerns of the world so that we may see clearly, through the lens of the gospel, how to connect the faith we profess with the daily life we live.

About Liturgical Music

Song suggestions: Fred Kaan's familiar text "For the Healing of the Nations," set to ST THOMAS (Hope Publishing), would be a good song for sending that connects our Christian faith to our call to exercise it in concrete ways in our daily life. Another excellent sending forth text that calls us to live our faith is Marin Willett's "Go, Be Justice," which is set to the familiar hymn BEACH SPRING (WLP).

Though we may be citizens of both heaven and earth, our first loyalty is to God. The antiphon text of *Psallite*'s "You Alone Are Lord" (Liturgical Press) builds on today's first reading from Isaiah: "You alone are Lord, there is no other; we belong to you, chosen in love."

SPIRITUALITY

GOSPEL ACCLAMATION
John 14:23

℟. Alleluia, alleluia.
Whoever loves me will keep my word, says the Lord,
and my Father will love him and we will come to him.
℟. Alleluia, alleluia.

Gospel

Matt 22:34-40; L148A

When the Pharisees heard
that Jesus had silenced
the Sadducees,
they gathered together, and
one of them,
a scholar of the law, tested
him by asking,
"Teacher, which
commandment in the
law is the greatest?"
He said to him,
"You shall love the Lord,
your God,
with all your heart,
with all your soul,
and with all your mind.
This is the greatest and the first
commandment.
The second is like it:
You shall love your neighbor as
yourself.
The whole law and the prophets
depend on these two
commandments."

Reflecting on the Gospel

There's a Texas saying, "When you boil the pot dry," meant to refer to what's left after all else goes away. For example, "When you boil the pot dry, it was a misunderstanding that caused all the fuss." It's akin to getting to the gist of the matter, without superfluous details. "What's the bottom line?" is another expression that captures the sentiment.

In Jesus' day—when over 600 particular laws made up the totality of Mosaic Law, and a violation of one effectively meant a violation of the totality—the 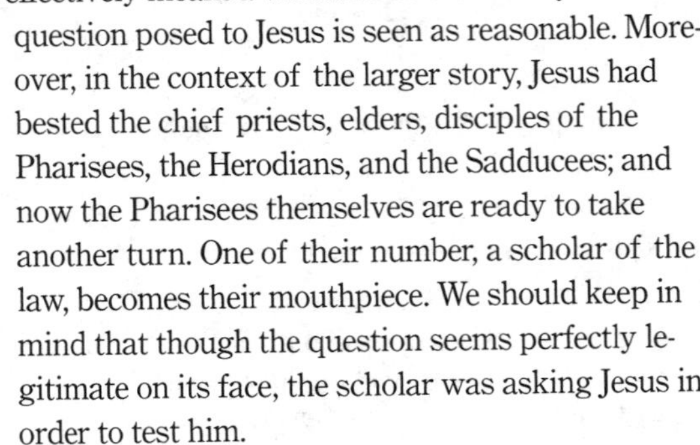 question posed to Jesus is seen as reasonable. Moreover, in the context of the larger story, Jesus had bested the chief priests, elders, disciples of the Pharisees, the Herodians, and the Sadducees; and now the Pharisees themselves are ready to take another turn. One of their number, a scholar of the law, becomes their mouthpiece. We should keep in mind that though the question seems perfectly legitimate on its face, the scholar was asking Jesus in order to test him.

That test doesn't seem to bother Jesus, who responds by quoting Mosaic Law, first Deuteronomy 6:5 followed by Leviticus 19:18. It's quite likely that Jesus himself was the first to combine these two commandments. For him, and for his disciples, these two commandments are the foundation of the law and the prophets. It's what we have when we boil the pot dry. It's the bottom line.

When we love God and love our neighbor, we are fulfilling the law. All of the law, the entirety of the more than 600 particular laws, are summed up in these two. For us today, we might think of something similar if one were to ask which is the most important teaching in the catechism, or which is the most important precept of the church. Perhaps a comparable question might be whether it is more important to tend to a sick relative or attend Mass? The answer sidesteps all these questions by saying the most important law is twofold: Love God and love your neighbor. With these as our guiding light, all else comes into focus.

Living the Paschal Mystery

Getting to the crux of the matter can be an important exercise. Pruning away extraneous detail to reveal the core issue is essential in many cases. For Christians, we recall that Jesus' teachings were rooted in Mosaic Law and the prophets. Yet he emphasized or combined aspects of each that made them seem to come alive, or to be read and understood in a new way. It's certainly true that loving God and loving one's neighbor were commandments in Mosaic Law. But who had ever combined them like this before? Ultimately, it's a good reminder of the core of the religious message. All of our actions ought to flow from this twofold love. Loving God and loving neighbor go together, and they cannot be reduced one to the other or one over the other. When we live by this guiding principle, we are living the paschal mystery.

Focusing the Gospel

Key words and phrases: "The second is like it"

To the point: When Jesus is asked which is the greatest commandment, he quickly responds with the second half of the *Shema,* the great Jewish prayer that begins "Hear, O Israel!" (Deut 6:5; NABRE). In saying that the greatest commandment is to love God with your whole being, Jesus effectively answers the question posed to him by the scholar of the law. But Jesus doesn't stop there; he adds a bonus answer, also saying what the second greatest commandment is: "You shall love your neighbor as yourself." By pairing together these two commandments from the Old Testament, Jesus reveals how we live out the first by doing the second. To love God with our whole heart, mind, and soul can be difficult to quantify or see, but in our actions of caring for our neighbor, God's beloved sons and daughters, we show our devotion to God.

Connecting the Gospel

to the first reading: The first reading from the book of Exodus lays out in part how God expects us to love our neighbors as ourselves. In particular, God lifts up the needs of the refugee, widow, orphan, and the poor. It is as if hurting one of these beloved ones of God is hurting God himself. God tells the people that if they harm another and "he cries out to me, I will hear him; for I am compassionate."

to experience: We cannot say we love God and remain indifferent to the plight of those whom God loves. In today's gospel, Jesus summarizes all the teachings of the law and the prophets in a single statement: love God and love neighbor. These two are intertwined in such a way that we cannot do one without the other. If we truly love God, we will be compelled to ease suffering wherever we find it. And when we reach out in compassion to those in need, we are serving God, even if we don't know it.

Connecting the Responsorial Psalm

to the readings: Today the psalmist praises God as his "strength," "rock," "fortress," "deliverer," and "stronghold." In giving us his summary of the law and the prophets in today's gospel reading, Jesus provides us with a firm foundation for faith. Earlier in the Gospel of Matthew, Jesus tells us, "Everyone who listens to these words of mine and acts on them will be like a wise man who built his house on rock" (Matt 7:24; NABRE). Despite the many questions and challenges that can arise in the life of discipleship, if we are actively loving God and loving our neighbor we know we are not being steered in the wrong direction.

to psalmist preparation: How does your faith in God provide you with a firm foundation when faced with difficult decisions?

PROMPTS FOR FAITH-SHARING

The first reading from Exodus exhorts the people to be merciful to foreigners seeking refuge. How does your family or parish minister to immigrants or refugees?

Today's psalm refrain is "I love you, Lord, my strength." How has God given you strength in the life of discipleship?

In his first letter to the Thessalonians, St. Paul writes, "[Y]ou became imitators of us and of the Lord." What saint or person of faith do you hope to imitate?

Jesus tells us the greatest and first commandment is "You shall love the Lord, your God." How do you keep your life centered around this commandment?

CELEBRATION

Model Penitential Act

Presider: In today's gospel Jesus proclaims the greatest commandment is to love God and the second is to love our neighbor as ourselves. For the times we have failed in keeping these commands, let us ask the Lord for pardon . . . *[pause]*

Lord Jesus, you hear the cry of the poor: Lord, have mercy.
Christ Jesus, you are our rock, fortress, and deliverer: Christ, have mercy.
Lord Jesus, you call us to walk in God's light: Lord, have mercy.

Homily Points

• Jesus gives us a mission statement in today's gospel for how we are to live our lives as Christians. If we truly want to follow him, we must love God with our whole being and love our neighbor as ourselves. With these two commandments Jesus tells us how to evaluate and discern between the minutiae that make up everyday life. In all things we can ask, by doing this would I be loving God and loving my neighbor?

• As with all mission statements, if we simply post it on the wall but don't act on it, it won't make any difference in our lives. The sentiments of these two statements—to love God and love neighbor—*sound* appealing, but what does this really look like when it is lived out? To love God with our whole mind, heart, and soul requires more than a fleeting thought every now and then. We are called to make God our top priority and to put time and effort into this relationship. We come to know God through reading his Word, meeting him in the sacraments, and listening to and talking to him in prayer.

• The second part of the commandment has sometimes been read "love your neighbor *as much as* you love yourself." This interpretation requires that we first love ourselves before we can extend this love to others. While it is true that we can't pass on what we don't have, it does not get to the crux of Jesus' meaning. We are called to love our neighbor *as* another self. This requires us to recognize that when our neighbor is suffering, we are suffering, and if we hurt a neighbor we are hurting our very selves. Jesus has laid out for us the path of discipleship; now it's up to us to put his words into practice.

Model Universal Prayer (Prayer of the Faithful)

Presider: Knowing God's compassionate love for all those in need, let us turn to him in prayer.

Response: Lord, hear our prayer.

For God's holy church, may all ministries serving orphans and vulnerable adults be prospered . . .

For leaders of nations, may they work together to offer safe refuge to those fleeing violence, persecution, and war in their home countries . . .

For people who have been outcast from society, may they find welcoming, supportive communities and know the love of God . . .

For all gathered here around the table of the Lord, may we be knit together as a dynamic community of faith and strengthened in keeping God's commandments . . .

Presider: God of mercy and kindness, you call us to care for the vulnerable and to serve those in need. Hear our prayers that we might always follow your commandments to love you and to love our neighbor as ourselves. We ask this through Christ our Lord. **Amen.**

COLLECT

Let us pray.

Pause for silent prayer

Almighty ever-living God,
increase our faith, hope and charity,
and make us love what you command,
so that we may merit what you promise.
Through our Lord Jesus Christ, your Son,
who lives and reigns with you in the unity
of the Holy Spirit,
one God, for ever and ever. **Amen.**

FIRST READING

Exod 22:20-26

Thus says the LORD:
"You shall not molest or oppress an alien,
for you were once aliens yourselves in
the land of Egypt.
You shall not wrong any widow or orphan.
If ever you wrong them and they cry out
to me,
I will surely hear their cry.
My wrath will flare up, and I will kill you
with the sword;
then your own wives will be widows,
and your children orphans.

"If you lend money to one of your poor
neighbors among my people,
you shall not act like an extortioner
toward him
by demanding interest from him.
If you take your neighbor's cloak as a
pledge,
you shall return it to him before sunset;
for this cloak of his is the only covering
he has for his body.
What else has he to sleep in?
If he cries out to me, I will hear him; for I
am compassionate."

RESPONSORIAL PSALM
Ps 18:2-3, 3-4, 47, 51

℟. (2) I love you, Lord, my strength.

I love you, O LORD, my strength,
O LORD, my rock, my fortress, my deliverer.

℟. I love you, Lord, my strength.

My God, my rock of refuge,
my shield, the horn of my salvation, my stronghold!
Praised be the LORD, I exclaim,
and I am safe from my enemies.

℟. I love you, Lord, my strength.

The LORD lives and blessed be my rock!
Extolled be God my savior.
You who gave great victories to your king
and showed kindness to your anointed.

℟. I love you, Lord, my strength.

SECOND READING
1 Thess 1:5c-10

Brothers and sisters:
You know what sort of people we were among you for your sake.
And you became imitators of us and of the Lord,
receiving the word in great affliction, with joy from the Holy Spirit,
so that you became a model for all the believers
in Macedonia and in Achaia.
For from you the word of the Lord has sounded forth
not only in Macedonia and in Achaia,
but in every place your faith in God has gone forth,
so that we have no need to say anything.
For they themselves openly declare about us
what sort of reception we had among you,
and how you turned to God from idols
to serve the living and true God
and to await his Son from heaven,
whom he raised from the dead,
Jesus, who delivers us from the coming wrath.

About Liturgy

Do Catholic piety and social justice go together? That is a question some devout Catholics actually have. However, in light of today's readings, it seems the answer is quite obvious! Catholic piety without social justice is neither Catholic nor pious. Devotion in prayer and acts of worship without concrete works of mercy is simply abstract and empty ritualism. The greatest commandment, which we hear today in the gospel, combines both love of God and love of neighbor. One without the other negates both. Recall, too, that Luke's version of this same gospel passage includes the parable of the Good Samaritan as Jesus' response to the scholar's question, "And who is my neighbor?" (Luke 10:29).

Homilists today cannot responsibly preach the gospel without helping their listeners understand that ritual devotion and practice, no matter how pious, are never complete until they are reflected by acts of justice for immigrants, migrants, refugees, and strangers. Knowing the laws of our faith and its dogmas is insufficient unless we practice them by caring for the widow, the orphan, and the least among our society. And piety in prayer is empty until it is filled with concern and protection for those exploited by unjust systems and societal attitudes.

About Initiation

The greatest commandment: In the past, the way we have taught inquirers seeking to become baptized may have implied that being Catholic is simply about following various laws and regulations, and memorizing a prescribed set of doctrines. However, the church's contemporary documents on evangelization and catechesis, statements made by recent popes, and the Rite of Christian Initiation of Adults give us a more holistic view of what it means to be a disciple of Christ.

Everything we teach—and the way we teach—needs to communicate not a legalistic approach to faith but one that is a response to God's love. As Pope Francis has said: "On the lips of the catechist the first proclamation must ring out over and over: 'Jesus Christ loves you; he gave his life to save you; and now he is living at your side every day to enlighten, strengthen and free you.' . . . We must not think that in catechesis the kerygma gives way to a supposedly more 'solid' formation. Nothing is more solid, profound, secure, meaningful and wisdom-filled than that initial proclamation" (Joy of the Gospel 164–65.)

About Liturgical Music

Preparing for the new liturgical year: As November approaches, you are probably beginning to prepare your choirs for the Advent and Christmas seasons. In these last few weeks before the new liturgical year, do not overlook spiritual preparation for your music ministers as well.

Take some time at each upcoming rehearsal to invite music ministers to reflect on the past liturgical year and to prepare their hearts for the new year. Where have they encountered God's presence in their ministry? What do they need from the Spirit in order to become more faithful disciples in the new liturgical year? Each week you might write down their responses in a journal.

Then at the rehearsal for the Thanksgiving Day liturgy or for Christ the King, you might incorporate these responses as part of the prayer you use to begin or end that rehearsal. These can become a "litany of thanksgiving" interspersed with a sung refrain from an appropriate psalm or acclamation.

Alternatively, if you are able, consider hosting a retreat for music ministers near the feast of St. Cecilia (November 22), which is Christ the King Sunday this year. Use that time for spiritual preparation, reflection, and prayer.

SPIRITUALITY

GOSPEL ACCLAMATION
Matt 11:28

℟. Alleluia, alleluia.
Come to me, all you who labor and are burdened,
and I will give you rest, says the Lord.
℟. Alleluia, alleluia.

Gospel

Matt 5:1-12a; L667

When Jesus saw the crowds, he went up the mountain,
and after he had sat down, his disciples came to him.
He began to teach them, saying:

"Blessed are the poor in spirit,
for theirs is the Kingdom of heaven.
Blessed are they who mourn,
for they will be comforted.
Blessed are the meek,
for they will inherit the land.
Blessed are they who hunger and thirst for righteousness,
for they will be satisfied.
Blessed are the merciful,
for they will be shown mercy.
Blessed are the clean of heart,
for they will see God.
Blessed are the peacemakers,
for they will be called children of God.
Blessed are they who are persecuted for the sake of righteousness,
for theirs is the Kingdom of heaven.
Blessed are you when they insult you and persecute you
and utter every kind of evil against you falsely because of me.
Rejoice and be glad,
for your reward will be great in heaven."

Reflecting on the Gospel

The popular book *My Life with the Saints*, by the Jesuit James Martin, is an introduction to certain saints told through memoir. Some of the most famous and most well-recognized saints are there, including St. Peter, Mary, the mother of Jesus, St. Ignatius of Loyola (the founder of the Jesuits), even Joan of Arc, Mother Teresa, and more, as well as some of the lesser known saints. Most of the saints he discusses, as reflected in the sample selection above, and as has been true throughout Christian history, were celibates.

But the fact that most saints were celibates does not mean that one needs to be celibate to be a saint, or that those who are not celibate have a more difficult time becoming a saint. Instead, it's a reflection of the kinds of people with whom the church is familiar. Even when married people are recognized as saints by the church, it's most often because they lived as celibates after having children (e.g., Luigi and Maria Beltrame Quattrocchi) or one spouse lived as a celibate after the other died (e.g., Elizabeth Ann Seton). This can make it seem like the only way to become a saint is to become celibate!

Because so many whom the church names as saints were priests, religious, or consecrated people, it can make these people seem far removed from the daily life of a vast majority of people. One estimate, for example, lists a total of ten married couples who have been recognized as saints in the two thousand years of Christian history. And the Quattrochis, mentioned above, led a family life almost as if it were a small monastery with daily Mass, daily rosary, and regular theology classes at the Gregorian (Jesuit university in Rome). Not many of us maintain that kind of home life, and it certainly is not the only way to sanctity.

So it's critically important that we have the words of the Beatitudes in today's gospel to remind us of what holiness looks like. Nowhere in the Beatitudes is a word about celibacy or, frankly, about sexuality at all. There is certainly nothing about one's vocational state (priest, sister, etc.). Instead, we have attributes such as "poor in spirit," "meek," and "merciful." These are the hallmarks of sanctity. And they can be practiced by anybody, religious or lay, Catholic or Protestant, even Christian or non-Christian. We recall that the Gospel of Matthew is much more about actions than words. And those actions have to do with mercy rather than celibacy.

Living the Paschal Mystery

Holiness and sanctity can seem so out of reach when we have as examples those whose lives are so different from the vast majority. Sanctity is not a prize given to those who complete a marathon, something most people cannot do. Instead, sanctity is something each of us is called to. Holiness is something each Christian can live. It is nothing more than living the paschal mystery, a daily dying to self so that we put others before us. Family members practice this daily! (Or at least they have many chances to practice this each day.) When parents sacrifice their own wants for the sake of their children, or when siblings put the needs of their brothers or sisters before their own, these are acts of sanctity. It is through such acts that we live the gospel passage today as "peacemakers." Division and strife are not marks of sanctity; unity and peace are. Let us live the gospel message today and, in so doing, live the paschal mystery into our own sanctity.

Focusing the Gospel

Key words and phrases: He began to teach them

To the point: Away from the crowds, Jesus sits down with his disciples and teaches them the path to holiness. These are the ones who have already decided that they will follow Jesus and have left family and livelihoods to do just that. Now, before they go farther, Jesus will lay out what it means to join him on this journey. In his apostolic exhortation Rejoice and Be Glad, Pope Francis tells us, "The Beatitudes are like a Christian's identity card. So if anyone asks: 'What must one do to be a good Christian?' the answer is clear" (63). Like the initial twelve disciples, we are to embrace and live the Beatitudes. On the journey of faith we will mourn, face persecution and insult, be called to align ourselves with the poor, hunger and thirst for righteousness, exercise mercy, be purified of heart, and bring peace. In these Christian attitudes, we proclaim our identity as followers of the Lord of life.

Connecting the Gospel

to the first reading: From the small group of twelve disciples who join Jesus at the top of the mountain two millennia ago and receive the Beatitudes from his lips, the number of Christians has grown and grown. In the book of Revelation, the picture painted of those who have "washed their robes / and made them white in the Blood of the Lamb" are too numerous to count and hail from "every nation, race, people and tongue."

to experience: Throughout the church year we celebrate the lives of the saints whose names are known to us. In a particular way, today's feast is for the saints whose names we do not know, but who are in heaven and joined to us in the mystical Body of Christ. From the book of Revelation, we know that these holy men and women are not isolated to a particular "nation, race, people [or] tongue"; instead they reflect the beautiful diversity of God's creation.

Connecting the Responsorial Psalm

to the readings: Today's psalm refrain connects us to the holy ones in heaven by our same desire to see the face of God. The middle verse asks, "Who can ascend the mountain of the Lord? / or who may stand in his holy place? / One whose hands are sinless, whose heart is clean, / who desires not what is in vain." In the Beatitudes, Jesus gives us the formula for this holiness that brings us close to God.

to psalmist preparation: On the earth we find revelations of God's presence in creation, the people around us, the word of God, and the sacraments. Each nourishes our hunger for the living God, and yet, we long for the fullness of time when "we shall see him as he is," as the first letter of St. John tells us. In your own life of faith, how do you foster and live out this desire to see the face of God?

PROMPTS FOR FAITH-SHARING

The second reading from St. John tells us, "Beloved, we are God's children now; / what we shall be has not yet been revealed." What do you think God's dream is for your life?

On this feast of All Saints' Day, how have you been inspired by the lives and example of the saints?

How do you strive to embrace the Beatitudes in your life of faith?

Which beatitude is the most difficult for you to live out? Which is the easiest?

CELEBRATION

Model Penitential Act

Presider: On this feast day, let us pray with all the saints that we might be brought to holiness and cleansed from sin . . . *[pause]*

Lord Jesus, you are our strength and our salvation: Lord, have mercy.

Christ Jesus, you are the Lamb of God who takes away the sins of the world: Christ, have mercy.

Lord Jesus, you intercede for us at the right hand of the Father: Lord, have mercy.

Homily Points

• The gospel for All Saints' Day is always taken from the beginning of Jesus' Sermon on the Mount where, through the Beatitudes, he introduces his disciples to what it truly means to live in his kingdom. In his apostolic exhortation Rejoice and Be Glad: On the Call to Holiness in Today's World, Pope Francis meditates on each of the Beatitudes individually. He warns us, "Even if we find Jesus' message attractive, the world pushes us towards another way of living" (65).

• We could say the same about the lives of the saints. Within their stories we find much that attracts us—their light, joy, kindness, and sometimes even miraculous works inspire us on the journey of faith. But their path to holiness also inevitably included hardship, struggle, and great self-denial. In the martyrs we find saints who so pushed against and frightened the world that, like Jesus, they ended up giving their very lives in service of God.

• Many of the Beatitudes provide us with a dichotomy: those who mourn shall be comforted, the persecuted should be glad, and the meek and poor will receive true riches. As Christians, we also embrace a dichotomy by turning away from what the world calls "good" and devoting our lives instead to the path of holiness. In resisting the excesses of the world, we enter into the fullness of life Jesus promised to his followers (John 10:10). Pope Francis tells us that "[i]n the Beatitudes, we find a portrait of the Master, which we are called to reflect in our daily lives" (Rejoice and Be Glad 63). By meditating on the words of Jesus may we embrace the path of holiness trod by the saints throughout history.

Model Universal Prayer (Prayer of the Faithful)

Presider: Through the intercession of all the saints, let us make our needs known to our loving God.

Response: Lord, hear our prayer.

For God's holy church, may it continue to be a school of holiness and a refuge for sinners who long to see God's face . . .

For leaders of nations, may they embrace mercy, compassion, and humility as they exercise authority and leadership . . .

For those who are persecuted due to their religion, creed, or culture, may they find safe refuge and be granted freedom of expression . . .

For all gathered here, may we answer the call to holiness and may our lives proclaim God's love and peace . . .

Presider: God of everlasting love, in the lives of your saints your mercy and compassion are revealed. Hear our prayers that in embracing the Beatitudes, we might build your kingdom here on earth. We ask this through Christ our Lord. **Amen.**

COLLECT

Let us pray.

Pause for silent prayer

Almighty ever-living God,
by whose gift we venerate in one celebration
the merits of all the Saints,
bestow on us, we pray,
through the prayers of so many intercessors,
an abundance of the reconciliation with you
for which we earnestly long.
Through our Lord Jesus Christ, your Son,
who lives and reigns with you in the unity of the Holy Spirit,
one God, for ever and ever. **Amen.**

FIRST READING

Rev 7:2-4, 9-14

I, John, saw another angel come up from the East,
holding the seal of the living God.
He cried out in a loud voice to the four angels
who were given power to damage the land and the sea,
"Do not damage the land or the sea or the trees
until we put the seal on the foreheads of the servants of our God."
I heard the number of those who had been marked with the seal,
one hundred and forty-four thousand marked
from every tribe of the children of Israel.

After this I had a vision of a great multitude,
which no one could count,
from every nation, race, people, and tongue.
They stood before the throne and before the Lamb,
wearing white robes and holding palm branches in their hands.
They cried out in a loud voice:

"Salvation comes from our God,
who is seated on the throne,
and from the Lamb."

All the angels stood around the throne
and around the elders and the four living creatures.
They prostrated themselves before the throne,
worshiped God, and exclaimed:

"Amen. Blessing and glory, wisdom and thanksgiving,
honor, power, and might
be to our God forever and ever. Amen."

Then one of the elders spoke up and said
to me,
"Who are these wearing white robes,
and where did they come from?"
I said to him, "My lord, you are the one
who knows."
He said to me,
"These are the ones who have survived
the time of great distress;
they have washed their robes
and made them white in the Blood of
the Lamb."

RESPONSORIAL PSALM

Ps 24:1bc-2, 3-4ab, 5-6

℟. (cf. 6) Lord, this is the people that longs
to see your face.

The LORD's are the earth and its fullness;
the world and those who dwell in it.
For he founded it upon the seas
and established it upon the rivers.

℟. Lord, this is the people that longs to
see your face.

Who can ascend the mountain of the
LORD?
or who may stand in his holy place?
One whose hands are sinless, whose heart
is clean,
who desires not what is vain.

℟. Lord, this is the people that longs to
see your face.

He shall receive a blessing from the LORD,
a reward from God his savior.
Such is the race that seeks him,
that seeks the face of the God of Jacob.

℟. Lord, this is the people that longs to
see your face.

SECOND READING

1 John 3:1-3

Beloved:
See what love the Father has bestowed
on us
that we may be called the children of
God.
Yet so we are.
The reason the world does not know us
is that it did not know him.
Beloved, we are God's children now;
what we shall be has not yet been
revealed.
We do know that when it is revealed we
shall be like him,
for we shall see him as he is.
Everyone who has this hope based on him
makes himself pure,
as he is pure.

About Liturgy

Middle-class holiness: This year we have the great blessing of celebrating the Solemnity of All Saints on Sunday. Homilists—and all who want to prepare well for this celebration—will certainly want to read or reread Pope Francis's apostolic exhortation on the call to holiness in today's world, Rejoice and Be Glad (Rejoice and Be Glad). It is a beautiful and accessible reflection on what it means to be holy.

In chapter 3, Francis explores the meaning of each line of the Beatitudes from Matthew's gospel, which we hear today. For Francis, the Beatitudes coupled with the "Great Criterion" from chapter 25 of Matthew's gospel are what shaped the lives of the saints. When we take these two passages to heart, Francis says, we, too, can become "genuinely happy" (109).

Francis also reminds us that holiness is not something reserved only for those who live exemplary lives of faith. Rather, it is "present in the patience of God's people: in those parents who raise their children with immense love, in those men and women who work hard to support their families, in the sick, in elderly religious who never lose their smile . . . Very often it is a holiness found in our next-door neighbors, those who, living in our midst, reflect God's presence. We might call them 'the middle class of holiness'" (7).

All who serve the liturgy will also want to pay attention to paragraphs 57–59, in which Francis describes a heretical "new pelagianism" that is often expressed in "a punctilious concern for the Church's liturgy" (57).

About Initiation

Patron saints: In "About Initiation" for the Fourth Sunday of Advent, we looked at how choosing a saint's name for baptism (and confirmation) is no longer a requirement. Although catechumens and candidates need not select a saint's name for initiation, we can still encourage them to know the stories of the saints and to model their lives after these holy women and men. Begin by helping them learn about the patron saints of your parish, city, diocese, or country. Also help them discover the stories of the saints who share their name or whose feast days fall on their birthday or other important personal anniversaries.

If, after learning more about a saint, a catechumen or candidate desires to be baptized or confirmed with that saint's name, encourage that person to use both his or her birth name and chosen saint name during the ceremony—for example, "Alyssa Catherine."

About Liturgical Music

Litany of Saints: In addition to using it at baptismal liturgies, ordinations, and the First Sunday of Lent, today is the premier day for singing the Litany of the Saints. Whether the traditional chant found in the Roman Missal (see also the appendix in the Rite of Baptism) or another contemporary setting, the litany can be appropriate in several different places during the Mass.

As a gathering song, it recalls that it is not only we from this parish community but all the saints who gather to give praise to God. As a song during the preparation of gifts, it extends the intercessions just prayed. At Communion, we remember that in the Eucharist we join with the saints and angels now rejoicing at the heavenly banquet of the Lamb. When it's used as a sending forth song, the saints remind us that at our baptism we each were given a unique mission that we are to live out in works of mercy so that our lives, like theirs, may be witnesses of God's mercy.

Whatever setting you use, be sure to include your parish's patron saint. Also, omit any intercessory verses that are specific for other liturgical rites, such as baptism.

GOSPEL ACCLAMATION
See John 6:40

This is the will of my Father, says the Lord,
that everyone who sees the Son and believes in
him
may have eternal life.

Gospel

John 6:37-40; L668

Jesus said to the crowds:
"Everything that the Father gives me
will come to me,
and I will not reject anyone who
comes to me,
because I came down from heaven
not to do my own will
but the will of the one who sent me.
And this is the will of the one who sent
me,
that I should not lose anything of
what he gave me,
but that I should raise it on the last
day.
For this is the will of my Father,
that everyone who sees the Son and
believes in him
may have eternal life,
and I shall raise him on the last day."

See Appendix A., p. 303, for the other readings.

Additional reading choices are in the Lectionary for Mass *(L668) or those given in the Masses for the Dead (L1011–1016).*

Reflecting on the Gospel

Land developers were surveying what was to be a new subdivision on the far outskirts of the town, close to some of the most arid land in the state. One civil engineer asked where the water would come from. "There's an aquifer here that will last fifty years. That's what code requires." The civil engineer asked, "What happens after fifty years?" "I won't be here to find out! Not my problem" was the reply.

Yesterday we celebrated All Saints, whereas today it is All Souls. The capital "S" saints were yesterday's focus. These were people like Sts. Clare and Francis of Assisi, St. Catherine of Siena, Sts. Peter and Paul, and many others. Today we commemorate all those holy souls, whether they were recognized officially as saints or not, who came before us. We might think of these people when, in the Litany of the Saints that we sing in the liturgy, we hear "all those holy men and women . . ."

It is significant that the church gives us this day, as it connects us with our ancestors in faith, such as deceased grandparents, great-grandparents, uncles, aunts, and extended family. We recall that together we form a "cloud of witnesses" (Heb 12:1) whose faith has been handed from one generation to the next. As St. Paul says, "So we preach, and so you believed" (1 Cor 15:11). Now in our present day, so many of us share the faith with others, who will in turn pass it down to others. It's hardly likely that we ourselves will be recognized by the church as a capital "S" saint, but due to our identity as disciples of Christ, one day we, too, may be remembered on this day fifty, or one hundred, or more years from now. Let us hope we built our homes on good ground, with access to clean water, clean air, and the like. We think not merely of ourselves but of generations to come.

The gospel passage the church uses to commemorate this feast is from John, with its universal character of salvation. In sum, God desires all to be saved. And Jesus himself will be the cause of the resurrection. Then we shall be one family united in Christ. All those who have come before us, and all those yet to come, will be together. For it is the will of the Father that all those who come to Christ will never be driven away.

Living the Paschal Mystery

We live with markers of the past all around us. Our lives are built on the good work of others. The homes we purchase, roads we drive on, monuments, churches, and cathedrals were likely all built before us. We owe much to those who came before us. We owe not only our material blessings but our spiritual blessing as well. We are connected to those ancestors in faith. The world is about so much more than us. And after we depart this earthly life, there will be others who come after us, whose faith might even be built upon our own.

This passing down the faith from generation to generation began with the first disciples and apostles, and continues into our own day. The death and resurrection of the Lord becomes the message we share with others. Death is not the end; new life awaits. For centuries past and centuries still to come, a "cloud of witnesses" (Heb 12:1) proclaims the glory of God.

Focusing the Gospel

Key words and phrases: "[T]his is the will of the one who sent me, / that I should not lose anything of what he gave me"

To the point: The Gospel of John conveys the essential core of Jesus' mission. As we hear earlier in John's gospel, Jesus was not sent into the world to condemn but rather to save (3:17). It is God's will that we might be saved from death and destruction and kept safe in the hand of God all the days of our life, and unto eternal life as well. This is the hope that we celebrate on All Souls' Day as we celebrate the "souls of the just," including those belonging to our own family and those whom we have counted as friends and companions on the way of discipleship.

Model Penitential Act

Presider: Today's first reading tells us, "[T]he souls of the just are in the hand of God." Let us turn to the Lord and ask for pardon and healing that we may be counted among the just . . . *[pause]*

Lord Jesus, you are our salvation and hope: Lord, have mercy.
Christ Jesus, you call all people to yourself: Christ, have mercy.
Lord Jesus, you bestow upon us peace that passes all understanding: Lord, have mercy.

Model Universal Prayer (Prayer of the Faithful)

Presider: Together with all the holy men and women who have praised God throughout the ages, let us turn to the Lord in prayer.

Response: Lord, hear our prayer.

For the people of God spread throughout the world, may we lead lives of justice and peace, proclaiming the Lord in word and deed . . .

For peacekeepers and diplomats, in wisdom and with concern for the common good may they work for fruitful cooperation among nations . . .

For those who mourn and grieve for loved ones who have died, may they know the hope of resurrection and be comforted in their sorrow . . .

For this parish community, may we be a house of welcome and a place of refuge for all who seek the face of God . . .

Presider: God of mercy, who shepherds us from death into life, you care for and protect the souls of the just. Hear our prayers that we might be beacons of your light shining in the dark places of the world. We ask this through Christ our Lord. **Amen.**

About Liturgy

Remembering all holy women and men: Today we recall our ancestors in faith who have died and recognize them as yet-to-be-named saints awaiting the resurrection.

Today, why not also include a sung litany of saints? Bernadette Farrell's "Saints of God in Glory" (OCP) would be an excellent gathering song. This is the refrain: "Saints of God in glory, be with us, rejoice with us, sing praise with us, and pray with us now." The verses have no sung text but include suggested lists of saints and other holy people that are spoken by a cantor or reader.

Use the suggested verses, or prepare your own verses of saints important to your community. For one of the verses, invite the assembly to speak out loud the names of their beloved dead. Or if you gather such names from your parishioners throughout the year, the cantor might read a prepared list of these names as one of the verses. If you use this as a gathering song, you can also invite the assembly to bring forward a picture of their beloved dead and place it upon a separate altar space near the sanctuary during the song.

COLLECT (from the first Mass)
Let us pray.

Pause for silent prayer

Listen kindly to our prayers, O Lord,
and, as our faith in your Son,
raised from the dead, is deepened,
so may our hope of resurrection for your departed servants
also find new strength.
Through our Lord Jesus Christ, your Son,
who lives and reigns with you in the unity of the Holy Spirit,
one God, for ever and ever. **Amen.**

FOR REFLECTION

- On All Souls' Day, who are the family or friends that have died who you celebrate and remember on this day?
- What has helped you most when going through a time of grief or sorrow in your life?

Homily Points

- Today's liturgy is one of hope and joy. We gather to proclaim again that "the souls of the just are in the hand of God, / and no torment shall touch them." Those who have died in the friendship of God have not been lost, but are held fast in the love of our Creator.
- Not only is there hope for our own beloved dead, but for us as well. In the gospel passage, Jesus proclaims the will of God that "I should not lose anything of what he gave me." If we cling to Christ, there is nothing that can remove us from his hand.

SPIRITUALITY

GOSPEL ACCLAMATION
Matt 24:42a, 44

℟. Alleluia, alleluia.
Stay awake and be ready!
For you do not know on what day your Lord will come.
℟. Alleluia, alleluia.

Gospel Matt 25:1-13; L154A

Jesus told his disciples this parable:
"The kingdom of heaven will be like ten virgins
who took their lamps and went out to meet the bridegroom.
Five of them were foolish and five were wise.
The foolish ones, when taking their lamps,
brought no oil with them,
but the wise brought flasks of oil with their lamps.
Since the bridegroom was long delayed,
they all became drowsy and fell asleep.
At midnight, there was a cry,
'Behold, the bridegroom! Come out to meet him!'
Then all those virgins got up and trimmed their lamps.
The foolish ones said to the wise,
'Give us some of your oil,
for our lamps are going out.'
But the wise ones replied,
'No, for there may not be enough for us and you.
Go instead to the merchants and buy some for yourselves.'
While they went off to buy it,
the bridegroom came
and those who were ready went into the wedding feast with him.
Then the door was locked.
Afterwards the other virgins came and said,
'Lord, Lord, open the door for us!'
But he said in reply,
'Amen, I say to you, I do not know you.'
Therefore, stay awake,
for you know neither the day nor the hour."

Reflecting on the Gospel

Robert Baden Powell founded the Boy Scouts over one hundred years ago. The motto he chose for the organization was, "Be prepared." This motto happened to have the same initials (B.P.) as his own name, Baden Powell, and this was no accident. Once he was asked about the motto, "Be prepared for what?" "Anything!" was the answer. This motto has guided scouts in the organization for more than a century, and it is similar to the gist of the gospel today.

The parable Jesus tells in today's gospel may seem at first glance to be un-Christian. Why wouldn't the five who have oil share theirs with the five who do not have oil? But that's the wrong question. A better question would be, why weren't the five who have no extra oil prepared? They knew enough to bring their lamps, but they did not bring reserve flasks of oil. They had not anticipated that they would need more oil than what their lamp could hold. Rather than share, leading to a situation where nobody would have enough oil, the "wise" ones told the "foolish" to go get their own oil. And when they were gone, doing just that, the groom appeared, the guests entered, and the doors were locked. When the "foolish" ones returned, the master said he did not know them and they were not allowed in. Their cry of "Lord, Lord" calls to mind other passages in this gospel where people cry "Lord, Lord," only to hear the master reply that he does not know them (7:21-23; 25:31-46).

The motto "Be prepared" seems particularly apt here, and it reflects the attitude of many other parables in the Gospel of Matthew. Though Christians often imagine a forgiving God, that concept needs to be squared with the parables we read, such as the one we have today. Why didn't the master simply let the "foolish" ones in? Is it really that important that they forgot to bring extra oil? Does the punishment fit the crime, so to speak? Again, these questions come readily to mind, but they are not the focus of the story. Instead, the point of the parable is "preparedness" with respect to the coming of the "Lord." And this likely reflects the situation in the Matthean community. This is the same gospel that gives us the parable of the weeds and the wheat growing together. Matthew seems to be aware that the church is a mixed bag of the wise and the foolish, those prepared for the Lord's coming and those who are unprepared. It's not for one group to throw out the other. God will allow those to enter whom he will. The ill-prepared, hoping on that day for someone else to bail them out, will not be allowed to enter.

Living the Paschal Mystery

The meaning of Jesus' parables can be difficult to discern. And the meaning is polyvalent. One can read into them almost anything. The parable we read today should be a clarion call to "be prepared" for the coming of Jesus at the end times. And even if we think the end times are far, far away, my own personal end (death) may come when I least expect it. So it can be a fruitful exercise to read these parables in terms of my own death: Am I prepared for that? How would I live on this earth if today were my last? Or if this week were my last? Would my priorities shift? This kind of exercise can clarify our own priorities and behaviors. Jesus reminds us that the fools are the ones who were not prepared for the coming of the master. Let us be like the wise ones, attentive to the coming of the Lord, for we know not when that day might be.

Focusing the Gospel

Key words and phrases: Since the bridegroom was long delayed, / they all became drowsy and fell asleep.

To the point: As we near the end of the liturgical year, Jesus gives us another parable relating to the end of times and also our own personal ends. At the time of Jesus, and in the early church when this gospel was written, there had been a great expectation that Jesus' second coming was imminent and that it would likely happen during the lifetimes of the first disciples. Today's parable brings up the possibility that the bridegroom might be "delayed." As those in the early church came to accept that the timeline for Jesus' return might be much different from what they had originally expected and hoped, they saw the need to keep up the urgency that first accompanied the task Jesus had given them: to go out and spread the gospel to all nations. In today's gospel we are reminded of the need to be prepared and "stay awake." We do not know the hour of our Lord's return, nor do we know the hour when our lives will end. As we read every Ash Wednesday in St. Paul's second letter to the Corinthians, we do not need to wait for a more "acceptable time" to fully give our lives to Christ, for "now is the day of salvation."

Connecting the Gospel

to the first reading: In the gospel parable, the ten virgins are divided into those who are wise and those who are foolish. In today's first reading we have a hymn to divine wisdom who "is readily perceived by those who love her, / and found by those who seek her." The parable of the ten virgins might cause us to feel sorry for the bridesmaids who run out of oil, only to have those who brought extra refuse to share. However, from the first reading, we could say that wisdom was available to all. It appears that the foolish refused to seek her out before they began their vigil for the bridegroom.

to experience: In the first reading, Wisdom is personified as a woman, who graciously appears and attends to all who seek her. Even before the person who desires wisdom has begun his quest, "he shall find her sitting by his gate." Where do you find wisdom in your own life?

Connecting the Responsorial Psalm

to the readings: In today's responsorial psalm we find images of seeking and keeping vigil. The psalmist sings, "O God, you are my God whom I seek" and "through the night-watches I will meditate on you." Thirst for the living God motivates the psalmist's ardent searching and patient waiting. No ordinary thirst, this spiritual need is "like the earth, parched, lifeless and without water."

to psalmist preparation: When in your life have you experienced this depth of thirst for God? In the spiritual life, we are to cultivate the longing for God as well as to find the sources that truly quench our desire. Only God can fill the ache within, and so, like the psalmist, we are content to search and wait for him to reveal himself.

PROMPTS FOR FAITH-SHARING

The first reading is a hymn to wisdom, who is "found by those who seek her." How do you search out and immerse yourself in wisdom?

St. Paul's words urge us to "not grieve like the rest, who have no hope." As Christians, we still do grieve when a loved one dies, even as we hope in the resurrection. How does your family or parish community help others in the passage of grief?

In today's parable the bridesmaids need oil so that their lamps might burn brightly at the arrival of the bridegroom. What is the oil that keeps your lamp of faith burning?

Today's gospel could be seen as a call to be ready for the hour of our own death, when we meet the heavenly Bridegroom. How does living with death in mind shape your life and decisions?

Model Penitential Act

Presider: In today's gospel, Jesus calls us to "stay awake" for we do not know "the day nor the hour" of his return. Let us pause to ask forgiveness for the times we have failed to be persistent in faith . . . *[pause]*

Lord Jesus, you are the light of the world: Lord, have mercy.
Christ Jesus, you are the wisdom that we seek: Christ, have mercy.
Lord Jesus, you desire to lead us to life everlasting: Lord, have mercy.

Homily Points

• Today's parable of the ten virgins gives us an opportunity to ponder the second coming of Christ and the time when we will meet the Lord of life at the end of our own lives. Its imagery also might remind us of how we began our lives as Christians with new life through the baptismal waters and by receiving the light of Christ from the paschal candle. If we were baptized as infants, our parents and godparents were told, "[T]his light is entrusted to you to be kept burning brightly. This child of yours has been enlightened by Christ. He is to walk always as a child of light. May he keep the flame of faith alive in his heart. When the Lord comes, may he go out to meet him with all the saints in the heavenly kingdom" (Rite of Baptism for Children 100).

• As we grow, this responsibility to keep the flame of faith alive is transferred more and more to each of us. We are always to remember that we are children of the light and to nourish the flame received at baptism so it will be burning brightly until the last breath we take.

• In today's parable, the foolish virgins have not brought enough oil to keep their lamps lit, and when the bridegroom finally arrives they are not waiting joyfully to greet him. As we contemplate this parable we might wonder, what is this oil that keeps the light of Christ alive within us? We might also ponder, is this oil something that another can give to us, or is it something that we must find on our own? We have received the light of Christ in baptism; now our task is to keep it burning brightly until we meet the Lord.

Model Universal Prayer (Prayer of the Faithful)

Presider: Trusting in our God whose "kindness is a greater good than life," let us bring our prayers before the Lord.

Response: Lord, hear our prayer.

For those who exercise authority within the church, may they be steeped in wisdom so as to guide the people of God with prudent leadership . . .

For health care workers throughout the world, may they be protected from disease as they care for the ill and dying . . .

For the mentally disabled, may their lives be cherished and their wisdom and gifts to society recognized and lauded . . .

For all gathered here, especially those who grieve the loss of a loved one, may we be sustained and comforted in the hope of the resurrection . . .

Presider: God of wisdom, in the parables Jesus reveals to us the ways of your kingdom. Hear our prayers that when Christ, the heavenly bridegroom returns, we will be waiting to meet him with lamps lit. We ask this through Christ our Lord. **Amen.**

COLLECT

Let us pray.

Pause for silent prayer

Almighty and merciful God,
graciously keep from us all adversity,
so that, unhindered in mind and body
alike,
we may pursue in freedom of heart
the things that are yours.
Through our Lord Jesus Christ, your Son,
who lives and reigns with you in the unity
of the Holy Spirit,
one God, for ever and ever. **Amen.**

FIRST READING

Wis 6:12-16

Resplendent and unfading is wisdom,
and she is readily perceived by those
who love her,
and found by those who seek her.
She hastens to make herself known in
anticipation of their desire;
whoever watches for her at dawn shall
not be disappointed,
for he shall find her sitting by his gate.
For taking thought of wisdom is the
perfection of prudence,
and whoever for her sake keeps vigil
shall quickly be free from care;
because she makes her own rounds,
seeking those worthy of her,
and graciously appears to them in the
ways,
and meets them with all solicitude.

RESPONSORIAL PSALM

Ps 63:2, 3-4, 5-6, 7-8

℟. (2b) My soul is thirsting for you, O Lord my God.

O God, you are my God whom I seek;
for you my flesh pines and my soul
thirsts
like the earth, parched, lifeless and
without water.

℟. My soul is thirsting for you, O Lord my God.

Thus have I gazed toward you in the
sanctuary
to see your power and your glory,
for your kindness is a greater good than
life;
my lips shall glorify you.

℟. My soul is thirsting for you, O Lord my God.

Thus will I bless you while I live;
lifting up my hands, I will call upon your name.
As with the riches of a banquet shall my soul be satisfied,
and with exultant lips my mouth shall praise you.

℟. My soul is thirsting for you, O Lord my God.

I will remember you upon my couch,
and through the night-watches I will meditate on you:
you are my help,
and in the shadow of your wings I shout for joy.

℟. My soul is thirsting for you, O Lord my God.

SECOND READING
1 Thess 4:13-18

We do not want you to be unaware,
brothers and sisters,
about those who have fallen asleep,
so that you may not grieve like the rest,
who have no hope.
For if we believe that Jesus died and rose,
so too will God, through Jesus,
bring with him those who have fallen asleep.
Indeed, we tell you this, on the word of the Lord,
that we who are alive,
who are left until the coming of the Lord,
will surely not precede those who have fallen asleep.
For the Lord himself, with a word of command,
with the voice of an archangel and with the trumpet of God,
will come down from heaven,
and the dead in Christ will rise first.
Then we who are alive, who are left,
will be caught up together with them in the clouds
to meet the Lord in the air.
Thus we shall always be with the Lord.
Therefore, console one another with these words.

or 1 Thess 4:13-14

See Appendix A, p. 304.

CATECHESIS

About Liturgy

Preparing for the new liturgical year: For those who serve the liturgical life of a community, what do you need to do to prepare for the coming liturgical year? By now you should already have a common calendar accessible by all the parish and school staff, liturgical minister coordinators, catechetical leaders, and parish committees and groups. The calendar should show all the major liturgical days and seasons for the new liturgical year, holy days of obligation, parish patron saint days, the parish's anniversary of dedication, and liturgical days proper for your diocese.

Next, mark days for specific major rites or blessings, such as RCIA rites and sacraments. On these days, include a note that no additional secondary rites, blessings, special announcements, or guest homilists should be scheduled for that Mass so that the focus can be on the rite.

Now, add any non-liturgical events that affect the entire parish, such as public holidays, vacation or in-service days for the pastor and other key parish leaders, parish fiesta days, or fundraising appeal days. Other than civic holidays, unrelated, non-liturgical events should not be scheduled on significant liturgical days, whenever possible. For example, the parish's annual fiesta should not be scheduled during Lent.

Finally, add meeting dates for liturgical planning when presiders, homilists, music coordinators, and any other liturgical leaders should be present for seasonal planning, evaluation, and retreats.

About Initiation

An RCIA calendar: Some RCIA teams like to prepare a calendar for team members, sponsors, and potential catechumens and candidates. While this can be a good idea, it can have some drawbacks if you use it incorrectly. If your calendar infers, even slightly, that there is a "beginning" or "end" to RCIA, then your calendar will be counterproductive. It makes RCIA a scheduled program rather than the parish's method of evangelization and discipleship, which we do every day, all year long. Instead of listing topics to be covered, simply note on the calendar that there will be an RCIA gathering.

Be sure that dates for the major rites are included in the calendar. However, when sharing the calendar with inquirers, be clear that each person's schedule for the major rites is determined by his or her readiness for each rite. Assure them that there is no "normal" pace, deadline, or timeframe and that individuals celebrate these rites as they are ready.

About Liturgical Music

Being prepared and agile: What is a good timeframe for having music selected and prepared for Mass? Many effective music directors plan out the music for an entire liturgical season. Several months in advance, they dedicate a full day or two to read through all the readings for that season, study music planning guides and liturgical resources, review what had been sung by the parish in the past, and finally pray and discern what should be sung this year for that season. A benefit to doing this is that you get a full view of how you can unify and develop the focus of each season through your liturgical music choices. You can also be sure that you are not scheduling the same music or new music too often.

Though you want to be prepared in advance, you also want to be flexible enough to make last-minute changes in order to connect with a current event or issue affecting the parish.

SPIRITUALITY

GOSPEL ACCLAMATION
John 15:4a, 5b

℟. Alleluia, alleluia.
Remain in me as I remain in you, says the Lord.
Whoever remains in me bears much fruit.
℟. Alleluia, alleluia.

Gospel Matt 25:14-30; L157A

Jesus told his disciples this parable:
"A man going on a journey
called in his servants and entrusted his possessions to them.
To one he gave five talents; to another, two; to a third, one—
to each according to his ability.
Then he went away.
Immediately the one who received five talents went and traded with them,
and made another five.
Likewise, the one who received two made another two.
But the man who received one went off and dug a hole in the ground
and buried his master's money.

"After a long time
the master of those servants came back
and settled accounts with them.
The one who had received five talents came forward
bringing the additional five.
He said, 'Master, you gave me five talents.
See, I have made five more.'
His master said to him, 'Well done, my good and faithful servant.
Since you were faithful in small matters,
I will give you great responsibilities.
Come, share your master's joy.'
Then the one who had received two talents also came forward and said,
'Master, you gave me two talents.
See, I have made two more.'
His master said to him, 'Well done, my good and faithful servant.

Continued in Appendix A, p. 304, or
Matt 25:14-15, 19-21 *in Appendix A, p. 304.*

Reflecting on the Gospel

The parable in today's gospel follows immediately upon the parable we read last week. Both the parable of the wise and foolish virgins and the parable of the talents speak to the coming of the Lord on the last day. In each case there is a delay or an intervening time during which different characters in the story respond and react differently. In today's story, the master entrusts money with three servants according to their ability. One receives five, another two, and the last, one. The first two invest the funds in a variety of activities and they both double the money entrusted to them. The third, however, buries the sole talent in the ground, depriving the master of the simple interest it would have earned if it had been deposited in a bank. Not surprisingly, the master is furious with the third servant.

Jesus concludes the parable with some folk wisdom, reflecting common attitudes of the day (and even today), with a phrase akin to "the rich get richer and poor get poorer." It would be a mistake to read this parable as somehow endorsing a political and economic system whereby the wealthy receive a majority of benefits while the poor suffer. Instead, that economic condition, which characterized the time of Jesus (and perhaps even our own!), becomes the folk wisdom reinforced by the parable.

The lesson from the parable has to do with the intervening time between the resurrection and the coming of Christ. How will the disciples (the servants) invest their own talents in service of the master? One must risk oneself to earn a reward. The investment of talent, skills, and gifts will generate returns. The miserable disciple who invests nothing of himself, but instead uses the time prior to the coming of the Lord merely to loaf around, will be punished. He is hardly worthy of the name servant (disciple). Interestingly, the reward for the first two is the same, "Come, share your master's joy." But the third is exiled.

Like last week's parable, and many before, today's story is an echo of the Matthean church, which had both weeds and wheat in its midst. There were industrious Christians, investing their talents and skills in the service of the Lord, and there were freeloaders, who risked nothing of themselves for God. It would be a mistake to read this parable in economic terms, endorsing a particular system or class of people. Instead, this parable is speaking to life in the church prior to the coming of Jesus: Am I a disciple who invests myself, my skills, and my talents for God? Or am I content to let others do that work? To those who invest themselves, Jesus says, "Come, share your master's joy."

Living the Paschal Mystery

Life in a community can be a gift. We join others who share a common purpose. We combine effort to achieve a common goal. But in these cases, much like "group work" assigned to schoolchildren, there can be freeloaders who live off the largesse of others' efforts while contributing little to no effort of their own. The parable today reminds us that there will come a time when God will take stock of each person's efforts. This is not our work to do, but God's.

When we hear this parable and others like it, we can be moved to action, investing ourselves more fully in the Christian life. And for the Gospel of Matthew that means service of others, especially the less fortunate. May this gospel motivate us to continue serving without counting the cost, investing fully of ourselves and our talents. There will be an accounting, and when there is, we want to hear the words, "Come, share your master's joy."

Focusing the Gospel

Key words and phrases: "Since you were faithful in small matters, / I will give you great responsibilities."

To the point: Among other lessons, today's parable reinforces the importance of every action in the life of discipleship. The small tasks of care and love that we do (or neglect to do) every day are what make up the life of faith. In Jesus' own life, the majority of his time on the earth was spent not in active ministry, but as a "carpenter's son" in Nazareth. For thirty years, our Lord's life revolved around his family, community, and his work. We could say that in his hidden life in Nazareth, Jesus redeemed and glorified the everyday events and happenings of human existence. Though we don't have many gospel accounts of Jesus' early years, meditating on them can lead us to greater faithfulness in "small matters" and help us to see how every action, no matter how mundane, can be a way of worshiping God.

Connecting the Gospel

to the second reading: Today's reading from Paul's first letter to the Thessalonians reflects the same sense of urgency that we find in Jesus' parables dealing with his second coming. Today's parable of the talents and last Sunday's of the ten virgins both include a figure (associated with Jesus) who will arrive at an unknown time. The ten virgins are waiting for the bridegroom who has been "delayed," while the servants in today's gospel have been given talents to use while their master is away on a journey for "a long time."

to experience: For people who are motivated by deadlines, having a big project and unlimited time to do it in can be a recipe for disaster. With no set date for completion, the procrastinator can easily fritter away time with any number of less important tasks or unnecessary activities. Paul warns the Thessalonians to not be dissuaded from the work of discipleship due to the unknown time of Jesus' return. He tells them, "[T]he day of the Lord will come / like a thief at night . . . let us stay alert and sober." Discipleship isn't a test we can cram for the night before, but a daily living out of Jesus' commandments to love God and love our neighbor as ourselves.

Connecting the Responsorial Psalm

to the readings: Today's psalm refrain proclaims, "Blessed are those who fear the Lord." In some ways this can seem contrary to the gospel, where the servant given one talent goes and buries it "out of fear." God does not desire that we fear him in a way that paralyzes us from taking risks and using the gifts we have been given. The term "fear of the Lord" in the Bible is also sometimes translated as having "wonder and awe in the Lord's presence." Instead of paralyzing us, this wonder and awe can draw us forward with delight to seek to serve God in all we do.

to psalmist preparation: How do you experience wonder and awe in God's presence?

PROMPTS FOR FAITH-SHARING

The first reading describes a woman who "works with loving hands." How do you work with your hands to serve others?

St. Paul writes to the Thessalonians, "[Y]ou are children of the light." How do you strive to be light in places or times of darkness?

The servant who buries his talent cites fear as the reason he hid it. Have you had to battle fear in using your God-given talents?

What is one gift or talent that you have received from the hand of God and are using to serve God's people?

Model Penitential Act

Presider: Today's parable of the talents encourages us to use our gifts for the good of others. For the times we have not done this, let us ask for mercy and forgiveness . . . *[pause]*

Lord Jesus, you show us the way to life everlasting: Lord, have mercy.
Christ Jesus, you reveal the kingdom in parables: Christ, have mercy.
Lord Jesus, you call us to serve you with joy: Lord, have mercy.

Homily Points

• Jesus offers us yet another parable about being prepared for the day when we will meet him at the end of our lives. In today's parable servants are given differing amounts of "talents" to steward for their master as he is away on a long journey. Though there is no set amount for what a talent would be equivalent to in today's currency, biblical scholars agree that it was a large amount of money. On the master's return, the servants who used their talents to earn more are rewarded, while the servant who buried his talent in the ground is sent away from the master's presence.

• In considering this parable, our first question could be, what does a talent stand for in the life of faith? What have we been given by God that we are to steward wisely? We could answer in many ways, for the gifts of God in our life are numerous—including health, material goods, and abilities. One thing the parable seems to make clear is that we are not to guard these treasures jealously by burying them in the ground. Instead, they are to be invested and used.

• It is interesting that the servant who buries his talent cites "fear" as the reason. It seems that he is so concerned about losing what he has been given that burying it is the only safe option. The master doesn't buy this excuse, instead calling the man a "wicked, lazy servant." As we continue to ponder how we are to live lives of discipleship, today's parable asks us to examine our conscience. Which gifts of God have we "buried" out of fear or laziness? Now is the time to dig them back up and start using them to build the kingdom of God.

Model Universal Prayer (Prayer of the Faithful)

Presider: With confidence in God's goodness, let us turn to the Lord in prayer.

Response: Lord, hear our prayer.

For God's holy church, may it recognize and welcome the talents of all the faithful in building up the Body of Christ . . .

For leaders of nations, may they show a preferential option for the poor in implementing just economic systems . . .

For all unemployed and underemployed adults, may they find work that matches their talents and provides a living wage . . .

For all gathered here, may we offer our gifts of time, talent, and treasure in service of others and of the church . . .

Presider: God of life and love, you call us to serve you joyfully with the gifts and talents we have received from your hand. Hear our prayers that we might dedicate our lives to the path of discipleship. We ask this through Christ our Lord. **Amen.**

COLLECT

Let us pray.

Pause for silent prayer

Grant us, we pray, O Lord our God,
the constant gladness of being devoted
to you,
for it is full and lasting happiness
to serve with constancy
the author of all that is good.
Through our Lord Jesus Christ, your Son,
who lives and reigns with you in the unity
of the Holy Spirit,
one God, for ever and ever. **Amen.**

FIRST READING

Prov 31:10-13, 19-20, 30-31

When one finds a worthy wife,
her value is far beyond pearls.
Her husband, entrusting his heart to her,
has an unfailing prize.
She brings him good, and not evil,
all the days of her life.
She obtains wool and flax
and works with loving hands.
She puts her hands to the distaff,
and her fingers ply the spindle.
She reaches out her hands to the poor,
and extends her arms to the needy.
Charm is deceptive and beauty fleeting;
the woman who fears the LORD is to be
praised.
Give her a reward for her labors,
and let her works praise her at the city
gates.

RESPONSORIAL PSALM
Ps 128:1-2, 3, 4-5

℟. (cf. 1a) Blessed are those who fear the Lord.

Blessed are you who fear the LORD,
who walk in his ways!
For you shall eat the fruit of your handiwork;
blessed shall you be, and favored.

℟. Blessed are those who fear the Lord.

Your wife shall be like a fruitful vine
in the recesses of your home;
your children like olive plants
around your table.

℟. Blessed are those who fear the Lord.

Behold, thus is the man blessed
who fears the LORD.
The LORD bless you from Zion:
may you see the prosperity of Jerusalem
all the days of your life.

℟. Blessed are those who fear the Lord.

SECOND READING
1 Thess 5:1-6

Concerning times and seasons, brothers and sisters,
you have no need for anything to be written to you.
For you yourselves know very well that the day of the Lord will come
like a thief at night.
When people are saying, "Peace and security,"
then sudden disaster comes upon them,
like labor pains upon a pregnant woman,
and they will not escape.

But you, brothers and sisters, are not in darkness,
for that day to overtake you like a thief.
For all of you are children of the light
and children of the day.
We are not of the night or of darkness.
Therefore, let us not sleep as the rest do,
but let us stay alert and sober.

About Liturgy

You have more power than you think: Shortly after the sex abuse crisis in the church re-emerged in 2018, many called for more participation by laypersons, especially women, in the reforms of the church and in its management. This call is absolutely necessary, not because there is a crisis but because it is the rightful duty of all the baptized.

For too long, we have equated leadership and authority with ordination, making those "in the pews" second-class citizens less responsible for sanctifying the world to Christ because they did not have the gifts given by ordination. In other words, we've left "real discipleship" to clergy while laypersons merely "help Father."

This does a disservice to laypersons *and* to clergy because it minimizes the dignity, mission, and gifts given by our common baptism. Baptism gives us gifts, and we each are mandated and authorized to use them in service of the reign of God. The members of the common priesthood of Christ cannot leave all the work of growing the kingdom to those who share in Christ's ministerial priesthood. That would be like burying our talents.

When we each recognize that baptism in Christ Jesus is the source of our power, we will have a chance—both women and men, lay and ordained—to reform and reshape the church, where all belong, all are needed, and all are called to use their gifts.

About Initiation

Rite of Welcome: For baptized adults and children of catechetical age who were baptized as infants but never received any further Christian formation, they may celebrate an optional rite at the beginning of their formation called the Rite of Welcoming the Candidates. Although this rite may look similar to the Rite of Acceptance for unbaptized persons, there is a significant difference. The Rite of Welcome recognizes that the person is already baptized and thus a full member of the household of God because of that baptism. It matters not that they have never been formed or have not celebrated any other sacraments in the Catholic Church. Baptism gives them the gifts of God's Spirit, making them children of God.

Today's gospel appropriately reflects how these candidates will begin learning how to put the gifts they received at their baptism to good use for the sake of God's kingdom.

At the beginning of the rite, be sure to follow the rubric at RCIA 416, which states: "Because they are already numbered among the baptized, the candidates are seated in a prominent place among the faithful." They should not begin the rite outside or at the doors of the church, as you would with an unbaptized person.

About Liturgical Music

Song suggestions: Look for music that speaks of putting your gifts to use for the mission of Christ. Some suggestions are "Come and See the Many Wonders," a hymn text by Harry Hagan, OSB, set to HYFRYDOL (St. Meinrad's Archabbey). This would be a fitting song for sending forth. "We Are Called" by David Haas (GIA) is also a good option for the end of Mass. Another suggestion is James Seddon's text "Church of God, Elect and Glorious" (Hope Publishing). This can be set to HYFRYDOL or NETTLETON and works wells as a gathering hymn.

In these last Sundays of Ordinary Time, you might also use music that looks toward the coming of Christ. An excellent, joyful example is "Soon and Very Soon" by Andraé Crouch. You can also bring this back toward the end of the Advent season.

SPIRITUALITY

GOSPEL ACCLAMATION
Mark 11:9, 10

℟. Alleluia, alleluia.
Blessed is he who comes in the name of the Lord!
Blessed is the kingdom of our father David that is to come!
℟. Alleluia, alleluia.

Gospel Matt 25:31-46; L160A

Jesus said to his disciples:
"When the Son of Man comes in his glory,
and all the angels with him,
he will sit upon his glorious throne,
and all the nations will be assembled before him.
And he will separate them one from another,
as a shepherd separates the sheep from the goats.
He will place the sheep on his right and the goats on his left.
Then the king will say to those on his right,
'Come, you who are blessed by my Father.
Inherit the kingdom prepared for you from the foundation of the world.
For I was hungry and you gave me food,
I was thirsty and you gave me drink,
a stranger and you welcomed me,
naked and you clothed me,
ill and you cared for me,
in prison and you visited me.'
Then the righteous will answer him and say,
'Lord, when did we see you hungry and feed you,
or thirsty and give you drink?
When did we see you a stranger and welcome you,
or naked and clothe you?
When did we see you ill or in prison, and visit you?'
And the king will say to them in reply,
'Amen, I say to you, whatever you did for one of the least brothers of mine,
you did for me.'

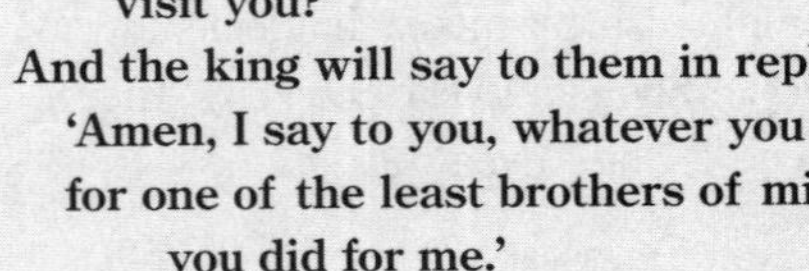

Continued in Appendix A, p. 305.

Reflecting on the Gospel

Like climbing to the top of Mt. Everest, today's gospel reading is the pinnacle of Jesus' teachings in the Gospel of Matthew. This is not a parable, but instead the interpretive key to Jesus' teachings earlier in the gospel. Now what Jesus said in the Sermon on the Mount (7:21-23), that "not all who call Lord, Lord will enter the kingdom of heaven," becomes clear. This story also foreshadows his resurrection appearance and promise in the closing line of the gospel, "And behold, I am with you always, until the end of the age" (28:20).

In the gospel story, we are two days from Passover when Jesus will be handed over to be crucified (26:1-2). All that remains between this teaching and the Passover meal Jesus will celebrate with his disciples is his anointing at Bethany by the woman with an alabaster jar of perfumed oil (26:6-13). So this teaching about how we will be judged is the crescendo of Jesus' message.

Jesus' promise to be with us always is fulfilled in that he is present in the hungry, thirsty, naked, ill, imprisoned, and in the stranger. Though some who claim to know Jesus are surprised that they did not see him in the face of the poor, this is to their own perdition. Even more, those who did not or do not know Jesus receive their heavenly reward precisely because they did the will of God; they fed the hungry and in so doing they were feeding Jesus. They gave drink to the thirsty and in so doing they were giving drink to Jesus. Jesus does not say that it is as though he is present in these people. No, he is them: "I was hungry and you gave me no food." "What you did not do for one of these least ones, you did not do for me." Again, Jesus does not say, "It's as though you did not do for me." He identifies with the poor and the lowly, for he is them.

There are no excuses on the part of those who claim to have known Jesus. They cannot say that the poor were not working, or they deserved to be poor, or they should get a job. Those who claim to know Jesus but have not acted on behalf of the poor are sent off to eternal punishment. "Depart from me, you accursed." We now see clearly how not everyone who cries Lord, Lord will enter the kingdom, but only those who do the will of my father (7:21-23). Indeed, this chapter and this particular teaching is at the root of the Catholic Church's "social gospel." It is why the church established hospitals, schools, food pantries, social services, and so many other ministries. Faith in action, rather than faith alone, is the church's credo. And it is not enough to rely on others, the church at large, to perform this ministry. It is the obligation of anyone who dares to call himself or herself a disciple of Christ. Indeed, those who do not know Christ but still perform these actions will inherit eternal life. These sober words conclude Jesus' teaching ministry and are a clarion call to all who would seek to follow him.

Living the Paschal Mystery

It is a bold thing to identify with Christ. From the Sermon on the Mount with the Beatitudes, to this concluding teaching of Jesus on judgment, being a follower of Christ is not for the faint of heart. Self-sacrifice, love of the other, and service are central to the identity of a Christian. How mortally dangerous it is, then, to call oneself Christian, to claim the role of disciple, without performing the actions required by one. It would be better not to claim the title at all.

Essential Matthean themes are expressed in this story: doing versus merely saying, is one. Doing the will of God—caring for the poor and for the stranger—is not merely about performing kind acts but is the basis of salvation, for Christian and non-Christian alike. As we live the paschal mystery, let us keep before us the awesome call and responsibility to express our faith in action, not merely words.

Focusing the Gospel

Key words and phrases: "[W]hatever you did for one of the least brothers of mine, you did for me."

To the point: In the golden rule, Jesus tells us we must care for our neighbor as ourselves. Today this commandment is expanded: we are to care for those in need as we would care for the Lord himself. For whether we are serving another or turning our gaze and walking away, we are comforting or rejecting the Lord.

Connecting the Gospel

to the first reading: In the beginning of chapter 34 of Ezekiel, where our first reading is taken from today, God commands Isaiah to "prophesy against the shepherds of Israel" (34:2; NABRE). God accuses them that by not caring for the flock of the Lord, "my sheep became plunder . . . my sheep became food for wild beasts" (34:8; NABRE). This is the context for God to say at the beginning of the first reading, "I myself will look after and tend my sheep." Because the kings and leaders have failed so miserably in their role as protector and shepherd, God will be the one to bring back the strayed, bind up the injured, and heal the sick.

to experience: Though both the first reading and the gospel talk about "sheep," the metaphors used are very different. In one, God condemns the corrupt leaders of Israel for failing to care for his sheep. In the other, Jesus separates the sheep from the goats, with the former being those who have kept his commandments and the latter having neglected to care for the poor and suffering. There is a similar message in both readings, however: God identifies himself with the weak and the downtrodden, and he calls us to do the same.

Connecting the Responsorial Psalm

to the readings: Once again our psalm for today is Psalm 23. This is the third time this psalm has been proclaimed at the liturgy in the past two months. We prayed with it on the Twenty-Eighth Sunday in Ordinary Time, as well as on All Souls' Day. It is fitting for today, given the "sheep" present in both the first reading and the gospel; it is particularly hearkening to the reading from Ezekiel where God proclaims that he will be the one to tend the scattered sheep of the house of Israel. Our psalm reminds us that with the Lord as our shepherd, we will dwell in security and safety. This psalm could also be seen as another model for how we are to care for others. In John's gospel Jesus tells his disciples, "As I have loved you, so you also should love one another" (13:34; NABRE). Psalm 23 gives us a portrait of Jesus, the Good Shepherd, who guides his sheep and abundantly fulfills their needs. This is the generosity that we are to emulate in serving others.

to psalmist preparation: Just as the Lord shepherds you, how do you seek to be a good shepherd for those who have been given into your care?

PROMPTS FOR FAITH-SHARING

In the first reading from the prophet Ezekiel, God says, "I will rescue [my sheep] from every place where they were scattered." Thinking about your parish community, who is missing? How might you reach out to them?

How have you experienced God's shepherding care most recently?

In this past year, how have you practiced the corporal works of mercy?

How would you like to incorporate the corporal works of mercy into your life in the coming year?

Model Penitential Act

Presider: In today's gospel Jesus tells us that we will be judged on how we have treated others. For the times we have failed to provide and care for the poor and the vulnerable, let us ask for forgiveness . . . *[pause]*

Lord Jesus, you are the Good Shepherd who calls us to life: Lord, have mercy.
Christ Jesus, you are the first fruits of creation: Christ, have mercy.
Lord Jesus, you came to show sinners the way: Lord, have mercy.

Homily Points

• In the 2018 documentary *Won't You Be My Neighbor?* Joanne Rogers, the wife of famous children's television host Fred Rogers (though many of us probably know him better as "Mr. Rogers"), recalls one of the last conversations she shared with her husband as he lay dying from stomach cancer. He asked her, "Do you think I'm a sheep?" In the documentary, Joanne says she knew just what Fred was referring to, as he'd been meditating on the same gospel reading that we have for today.

• Today we celebrate Christ the King Sunday, our final Sunday of the church year and, fittingly, our gospel speaks to us of what will happen at the end of time "when the Son of Man comes in his glory." He will sit in judgment of the nations, and if we were wondering how we will be judged, Jesus spells it out. Those who enter into the kingdom of heaven will be the ones who fed the hungry, gave water to the thirsty, welcomed the stranger, clothed the naked, cared for the ill, and visited the imprisoned. These are the nonnegotiable actions of discipleship. When we show love and care for others, we are loving and caring for Christ, and when we insulate ourselves from suffering and turn away, we are rejecting Christ.

• Joanne Rogers answered the question of her husband (who had been ordained to the Presbyterian church as "an evangelist to television" and dedicated his career to standing up for and nourishing the lives of young children) in this way: "If there ever were a sheep, Fred, you're one." Let's take some time this Sunday to consider, if someone were to look objectively at the actions that have made up our life, would we be identified as a sheep or a goat?

Model Universal Prayer (Prayer of the Faithful)

Presider: Trusting in God to provide for all our needs, let us turn to him in prayer.

Response: Lord, hear our prayer.

For bishops and priests, may they shepherd God's flock with wisdom and compassion, always aligning themselves with the poor and vulnerable . . .

For law enforcement officers throughout the world, as they protect and care for the people they serve, may their own lives be protected . . .

For those who lack food, water, shelter, and clothing, may those who have an abundance willingly share with those who have nothing . . .

For all gathered here around the table of the Lord, nourished by God's word and the Eucharist, may we go forth to be Christ's hands and feet in the world . . .

Presider: God of perfect justice and perfect mercy, at the end of time, your son, Jesus, will come to judge the nations. Hear our prayers that we might dedicate our lives to serving you in all those who need our care. We ask this through Christ our Lord. **Amen.**

COLLECT

Let us pray.

Pause for silent prayer

Almighty ever-living God,
whose will is to restore all things
in your beloved Son, the King of the
universe,
grant, we pray,
that the whole creation, set free from
slavery,
may render your majesty service
and ceaselessly proclaim your praise.
Through our Lord Jesus Christ, your Son,
who lives and reigns with you in the unity
of the Holy Spirit,
one God, for ever and ever. **Amen.**

FIRST READING

Ezek 34:11-12, 15-17

Thus says the Lord God:
I myself will look after and tend my
sheep.
As a shepherd tends his flock
when he finds himself among his
scattered sheep,
so will I tend my sheep.
I will rescue them from every place where
they were scattered
when it was cloudy and dark.
I myself will pasture my sheep;
I myself will give them rest, says the
Lord God.
The lost I will seek out,
the strayed I will bring back,
the injured I will bind up,
the sick I will heal,
but the sleek and the strong I will
destroy,
shepherding them rightly.

As for you, my sheep, says the Lord God,
I will judge between one sheep and
another,
between rams and goats.

RESPONSORIAL PSALM

Ps 23:1-2, 2-3, 5-6

℟. (1) The Lord is my shepherd; there is nothing I shall want.

The Lord is my shepherd; I shall not want.
In verdant pastures he gives me repose.

℟. The Lord is my shepherd; there is nothing I shall want.

Beside restful waters he leads me;
he refreshes my soul.
He guides me in right paths
for his name's sake.

℟. The Lord is my shepherd; there is nothing I shall want.

You spread the table before me
in the sight of my foes;
you anoint my head with oil;
my cup overflows.

℟. The Lord is my shepherd; there is nothing I shall want.

Only goodness and kindness follow me
all the days of my life;
and I shall dwell in the house of the LORD
for years to come.

℟. The Lord is my shepherd; there is nothing I shall want.

SECOND READING

1 Cor 15:20-26, 28

Brothers and sisters:
Christ has been raised from the dead,
the firstfruits of those who have fallen asleep.
For since death came through man,
the resurrection of the dead came also through man.
For just as in Adam all die,
so too in Christ shall all be brought to life,
but each one in proper order:
Christ the firstfruits;
then, at his coming, those who belong to Christ;
then comes the end,
when he hands over the kingdom to his God and Father,
when he has destroyed every sovereignty
and every authority and power.
For he must reign until he has put all his enemies under his feet.
The last enemy to be destroyed is death.
When everything is subjected to him,
then the Son himself will also be subjected
to the one who subjected everything to him,
so that God may be all in all.

CATECHESIS

About Liturgy

Living the liturgy: How fitting in this year when we celebrated All Saints on a Sunday and proclaimed the Beatitudes that we hear on this Christ the King Sunday what Pope Francis calls its companion reading—the "Great Criterion" from the end of the twenty-fifth chapter of Matthew's gospel (see Rejoice and Be Glad 95). From the saints who gave us real human examples of discipleship, to Jesus' own words describing what makes us recognized by God *as* disciples, we conclude the liturgical year with a clear message: "Jesus affirms that mercy is not only an action of the Father, it becomes a criterion for ascertaining who his true children are . . . Love, after all, can never be just an abstraction. By its very nature, it indicates something concrete: intentions, attitudes, and behaviors that are shown in daily living" (*Misericordiae Vultus* 9).

This gospel is the key that interprets the entire liturgical year we have just celebrated. We have no clearer image for what true faith looks like. As we prepare to enter a new liturgical year, with all its seasons, solemnities, and feasts, let us remember that the liturgy must be lived in our daily lives through concrete acts. Living the liturgy we celebrate each week is not a metaphor but rehearsal for daily life: "We may think that we give glory to God only by our worship and prayer, or simply by following certain ethical norms. It is true that the primacy belongs to our relationship with God, but we cannot forget that the ultimate criterion on which our lives will be judged is what we have done for others. Prayer is most precious, for it nourishes a daily commitment to love. Our worship becomes pleasing to God when we devote ourselves to living generously, and allow God's gift, granted in prayer, to be shown in our concern for our brothers and sisters" (Rejoice and Be Glad 104).

About Initiation

Endings and beginnings: You might think today or the First Sunday of Advent are good days to celebrate the Rite of Acceptance with unbaptized adults and children of catechetical age. However, celebrating this first catechumenal rite now might imply that with the beginning of the new year also comes the "beginning" of the RCIA. Remember that there is no "start" or "end" to the RCIA. Because we are called to evangelize constantly, we are always in the first period of the RCIA, the period of evangelization and precatechumenate. Rather, schedule the Rite of Acceptance for a different Sunday in Ordinary Time or for a weekday Ordinary Time gathering. Recall that the rite may be celebrated outside of Mass and that a deacon may preside if it is outside of Mass.

About Liturgical Music

Suggestions: We have many songs that build upon today's gospel passage, and your music today should have at least one in addition to some of the traditional hymns for the solemnity.

One beautiful bilingual setting is "*Para Amar Como Tú*" (which means "to love like you") by Jesse Manibusan and Santiago Fernandez (OCP). The simple refrain reads, "O God, great is your love, everlasting and true. *Señor, danos tu amor para amar como tú.*" The bilingual verses describe acts of mercy that reveal what true discipleship looks like. Interspersed within the verses is a short acclamation: *"y amar como tú."* This would be appropriate for preparation of gifts or Communion.

Because this is the last Sunday before Advent, enhance the Gloria by adding more to the instrumentation. Today is also a good day to sing a song of praise with the assembly after Communion. If you do, you can send the assembly out with a grand instrumental or choral piece for the closing procession.

GOSPEL ACCLAMATION
See Matthew 11:25

℟. Alleluia, alleluia.
Blessed are you, Father, Lord of heaven and earth;
you have revealed to little ones the mysteries of
the Kingdom.
℟. Alleluia, alleluia.

Gospel

Luke 17:11-19; L947.6

As Jesus continued his journey to Jerusalem,
he traveled through Samaria and Galilee.
As he was entering a village, ten lepers met him.
They stood at a distance from him and raised their voices, saying,
"Jesus, Master! Have pity on us!"
And when he saw them, he said,
"Go show yourselves to the priests."
As they were going they were cleansed.
And one of them, realizing he had been healed,
returned, glorifying God in a loud voice;
and he fell at the feet of Jesus and thanked him.
He was a Samaritan.
Jesus said in reply,
"Ten were cleansed, were they not?
Where are the other nine?
Has none but this foreigner returned to give thanks to God?"
Then he said to him, "Stand up and go;
your faith has saved you."

See Appendix A, p. 305, for the other readings.

Additional reading choices are in the Lectionary for Mass, *vol. IV, "In Thanksgiving to God," nos. 943–947.*

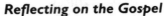

Reflecting on the Gospel

The Greek term "eucharist" means Thanksgiving. This quintessential American holiday, proclaimed officially by President Abraham Lincoln in the midst of the Civil War, has something in common with our faith.

It's been said that the best prayer of all is the prayer of gratitude. When we express thanks for our blessings, we are implicitly admitting that they are gifts. We did not, and we do not, "deserve" our blessings, which is why we say thank you. Even if we believe we have earned the physical resources we have at our disposal, the means to work and to earn are themselves gifts. One's health, wellness, family, friends are all gifts. The multitude of gifts (some have more than others) is not a marker of God's love, as though God loves the wealthy more than the poor or the healthy more than the sick. Instead, gifts are a cause of gratitude and recognition that they are not deserved, but by definition, freely given.

We recall, too, that Jesus tells us, to whom much is given much will be expected (cf. Luke 12:48). On global terms, the United States has much more than many other nations combined. And on this our national holiday, we consider how much is expected of us in light of how much we have been given. Our resources are not owed to us, and we do not have them because we are particularly favored by God.

The gospel reading given to us today speaks of Jerusalem surrounded by armies and preparing for its siege and ultimate downfall. Jesus spoke this decades before the Romans razed the city and its temple to the ground. The people thought they were insulated from such destruction because of God's favor. But the city, the land, and the temple itself were not saved from annihilation. Even the resources of God's chosen people were not earned or deserved.

Let us be thankful for the spiritual and material blessings we enjoy in our lives and as a nation. But let us also be humble enough to share these blessings, for they were given freely to be shared. We ought not hoard what was given to us as a gift, but instead react with humility, gratitude, and praise.

Living the Paschal Mystery

It's easy to become comfortable with the lifestyles we have created or try to create for ourselves. Then, tragedy can come in an instant. Loss of life—whether spouse, child, parent, or friend—can happen unexpectedly. Loss of job, income, or wealth may also loom as a specter just out of range of our awareness. When catastrophe strikes, we can be unprepared. One reminder of how fleeting our lives and possessions are is the reality of death. We cannot take it with us.

So it is good to develop an attitude of detachment toward material things or, better, an attitude of gratitude. When we recognize that everything we have is a gift, we come closer to living the paschal mystery where death and loss lead to new life and gain.

Focusing the Gospel

Key words and phrases: "[T]hey will see the Son of Man / coming in a cloud with power and great glory."

To the point: Today's gospel reading from Luke prophesies what will happen in the last days before the Lord returns. The imagery comes from the fate of Jerusalem in AD 70 when the Roman army came in and razed the city in response to a Jewish revolt. All throughout the world, unfortunately, calamities and tragedies like this happen. The good news within our gospel today comes in the last few lines. No matter how dark the times might look, death and destruction will not triumph, for the Son of Man will return "coming in a cloud with power and great glory." Therefore, we are not to fear or panic; Jesus has already conquered sin and death—our redemption is at hand.

Model Penitential Act

Presider: Today we gather in thanksgiving for all God has done in our lives. Let us pause to ask for his healing and mercy for times we have not served him well . . . *[pause]*

Lord Jesus, you are the Lamb of God who takes away the sins of the world: Lord, have mercy.
Christ Jesus, your mercy endures forever: Christ, have mercy.
Lord Jesus, you are the way, the truth, and the life: Lord, have mercy.

Model Universal Prayer (Prayer of the Faithful)

Presider: Knowing that our God is the giver of every good gift, let us turn to him in prayer.

Response: Lord, hear our prayer.

For God's holy church, may it grow in holiness, peace, and humility . . .

For nations of the world blessed with abundance, may they share what they have been given so that all might prosper . . .

For those who are hungry and homeless within our own nation, may they be granted safe shelter and nourishing food this day and all days . . .

For all gathered here, in thanking God for all that we have received, may we be blessed with generosity to use our gifts and talents for the good of others . . .

Presider: Almighty and ever-living God, in you we live and move and have our being. Hear our prayers that as citizens of this nation, members of the church, and your beloved sons and daughters, we might always do what is pleasing in your sight. We ask this through Christ our Lord. **Amen.**

About Liturgy

Setting the table: The dinner table is the domestic church's "altar" around which the household community gathers. It is often where we recount the moments of our day and retell the stories of our ancestors. Here, whether over a meager meal or feast, we find hospitality, mercy, and forgiveness. Strangers welcomed here become friends, and estranged loved ones reconcile. It is truly a sacred place.

Help your community recognize the connection between their dinner table and the eucharistic altar. At today's liturgy, honor the altar table in simple but familiar ways. As part of the preparation of gifts procession, invite community members of various ages to "set" the altar table. Some carry forward a beautiful cloth and place it on the altar. Others bring flowers and light candles. Invite community members to carry the Communion vessels in procession to place them on the altar. Then highlight the procession of bread and wine with candles, cross, and incense.

At the invitation to Communion, the presider might offer some words that connect what we do at the church's altar table with what we will do at our Thanksgiving meals around our tables at home.

COLLECT

Let us pray.

Pause for silent prayer

Father all-powerful,
your gifts of love are countless
and your goodness infinite;
as we come before you on Thanksgiving Day
with gratitude for your kindness,
open our hearts to have concern
for every man, woman, and child,
so that we may share your gifts in loving service.
Through our Lord Jesus Christ your Son,
who lives and reigns with you in the unity of
the Holy Spirit,
One God, for ever and ever. **Amen.**

FOR REFLECTION

- Which gift of God are you most thankful for this year?
- Today's psalm refrain comes from the book of Revelation: "Blessed are they who are called to the wedding feast of the Lamb." How do you experience yourself as "blessed"?
- Where is God calling you to use your gifts to build his kingdom?

Homily Points

- Though Thanksgiving isn't a liturgical holiday, it's very fitting that in the life of the American church it usually falls on one of the last days of the church year. As we prepare ourselves to enter into Advent and begin anew our cyclical living out of the life of Christ, now is a good time to pause for a moment and take stock.

- Our God, the great gift-giver, reveals himself to us by the gifts he gives, from creation to the gift of his very own son. He also reveals to us who *we* are by gifts. The talents and passions each of us has are uniquely endowed to us by our creator, and through using them well we are invited to help build his kingdom here on earth. How are you being called to use your gifts this coming year?

Readings *(continued)*

Second Sunday of Advent, December 8, 2019

Gospel (cont.)

Matt 3:1-12; L4A

Even now the ax lies at the root of the trees.
Therefore every tree that does not bear good fruit
will be cut down and thrown into the fire.
I am baptizing you with water, for repentance,
but the one who is coming after me is mightier than I.
I am not worthy to carry his sandals.
He will baptize you with the Holy Spirit and fire.
His winnowing fan is in his hand.
He will clear his threshing floor
and gather his wheat into his barn,
but the chaff he will burn with unquenchable fire."

SECOND READING (cont.)

Rom 15:4-9

Welcome one another, then, as Christ welcomed you,
for the glory of God.
For I say that Christ became a minister of the circumcised
to show God's truthfulness,
to confirm the promises to the patriarchs,
but so that the Gentiles might glorify God for his mercy.
As it is written:
Therefore, I will praise you among the Gentiles
and sing praises to your name.

The Immaculate Conception of the Blessed Virgin Mary, December 9, 2019

Gospel (cont.)

Luke 1:26-38; L689

He will be great and will be called Son of the Most High,
and the Lord God will give him the throne of David his father,
and he will rule over the house of Jacob forever,
and of his Kingdom there will be no end."
But Mary said to the angel,
"How can this be,
since I have no relations with a man?"
And the angel said to her in reply,
"The Holy Spirit will come upon you,
and the power of the Most High will overshadow you.
Therefore the child to be born
will be called holy, the Son of God.
And behold, Elizabeth, your relative,
has also conceived a son in her old age,
and this is the sixth month for her who was called barren;
for nothing will be impossible for God."
Mary said, "Behold, I am the handmaid of the Lord.
May it be done to me according to your word."
Then the angel departed from her.

FIRST READING

Gen 3:9-15, 20

After the man, Adam, had eaten of the tree,
the LORD God called to the man and asked him, "Where are you?"
He answered, "I heard you in the garden;
but I was afraid, because I was naked,
so I hid myself."
Then he asked, "Who told you that you were naked?
You have eaten, then,
from the tree of which I had forbidden you to eat!"
The man replied, "The woman whom you put here with me—
she gave me fruit from the tree, and so I ate it."
The LORD God then asked the woman,
"Why did you do such a thing?"
The woman answered, "The serpent tricked me into it, so I ate it."

Then the LORD God said to the serpent:
"Because you have done this, you shall be banned
from all the animals
and from all the wild creatures;
on your belly shall you crawl,
and dirt shall you eat
all the days of your life.
I will put enmity between you and the woman,
and between your offspring and hers;
he will strike at your head,
while you strike at his heel."

The man called his wife Eve,
because she became the mother of all the living.

The Immaculate Conception of the Blessed Virgin Mary, December 9, 2019

RESPONSORIAL PSALM
Ps 98:1, 2-3ab, 3cd-4

℟. (1a) Sing to the Lord a new song, for he has done marvelous deeds.

Sing to the LORD a new song,
for he has done wondrous deeds;
His right hand has won victory for him,
his holy arm.

℟. Sing to the Lord a new song, for he has done marvelous deeds.

The LORD has made his salvation known:
in the sight of the nations he has revealed his justice.
He has remembered his kindness and his faithfulness
toward the house of Israel.

℟. Sing to the Lord a new song, for he has done marvelous deeds.

All the ends of the earth have seen
the salvation by our God.
Sing joyfully to the LORD, all you lands;
break into song; sing praise.

℟. Sing to the Lord a new song, for he has done marvelous deeds.

SECOND READING
Eph 1:3-6, 11-12

Brothers and sisters:
Blessed be the God and Father of our Lord Jesus Christ,
who has blessed us in Christ
with every spiritual blessing in the heavens,
as he chose us in him, before the foundation of the world,
to be holy and without blemish before him.
In love he destined us for adoption to himself through Jesus Christ,
in accord with the favor of his will,
for the praise of the glory of his grace
that he granted us in the beloved.

In him we were also chosen,
destined in accord with the purpose of the One
who accomplishes all things according to the intention of his will,
so that we might exist for the praise of his glory,
we who first hoped in Christ.

The Nativity of the Lord, December 25, 2019 (Vigil Mass)

Gospel (cont.)
Matt 1:1-25; L13ABC

Asaph became the father of Jehoshaphat,
Jehoshaphat the father of Joram,
Joram the father of Uzziah.
Uzziah became the father of Jotham,
Jotham the father of Ahaz,
Ahaz the father of Hezekiah.
Hezekiah became the father of Manasseh,
Manasseh the father of Amos,
Amos the father of Josiah.
Josiah became the father of Jechoniah and his brothers
at the time of the Babylonian exile.

After the Babylonian exile,
Jechoniah became the father of Shealtiel,
Shealtiel the father of Zerubbabel,
Zerubbabel the father of Abiud.
Abiud became the father of Eliakim,
Eliakim the father of Azor,
Azor the father of Zadok.
Zadok became the father of Achim,
Achim the father of Eliud,
Eliud the father of Eleazar.
Eleazar became the father of Matthan,
Matthan the father of Jacob,
Jacob the father of Joseph, the husband of Mary.
Of her was born Jesus who is called the Christ.

Thus the total number of generations
from Abraham to David
is fourteen generations;
from David to the Babylonian exile,
fourteen generations;
from the Babylonian exile to the Christ,
fourteen generations.

Now this is how the birth of Jesus Christ came about.
When his mother Mary was betrothed to Joseph,
but before they lived together,
she was found with child through the Holy Spirit.
Joseph her husband, since he was a righteous man,
yet unwilling to expose her to shame,
decided to divorce her quietly.
Such was his intention when, behold,
the angel of the Lord appeared to him in a dream and said,
"Joseph, son of David,
do not be afraid to take Mary your wife into your home.
For it is through the Holy Spirit
that this child has been conceived in her.
She will bear a son and you are to name him Jesus,
because he will save his people from their sins."
All this took place to fulfill
what the Lord had said through the prophet:
Behold, the virgin shall conceive and bear a son,
and they shall name him Emmanuel,
which means "God is with us."
When Joseph awoke,
he did as the angel of the Lord had commanded him
and took his wife into his home.
He had no relations with her until she bore a son,
and he named him Jesus.

Gospel

or Matt 1:18-25

This is how the birth of Jesus Christ came about.
When his mother Mary was betrothed to Joseph,
but before they lived together,
she was found with child through the Holy Spirit.
Joseph her husband, since he was a righteous man,
yet unwilling to expose her to shame,
decided to divorce her quietly.
Such was his intention when, behold,
the angel of the Lord appeared to him in a dream and said,
"Joseph, son of David,
do not be afraid to take Mary your wife into your home.
For it is through the Holy Spirit
that this child has been conceived in her.
She will bear a son and you are to name him Jesus,
because he will save his people from their sins."
All this took place to fulfill
what the Lord had said through the prophet:

Behold, the virgin shall conceive and bear a son,
and they shall name him Emmanuel,
which means "God is with us."
When Joseph awoke,
he did as the angel of the Lord had commanded him
and took his wife into his home.
He had no relations with her until she bore a son,
and he named him Jesus.

FIRST READING

Isa 62:1-5

For Zion's sake I will not be silent,
for Jerusalem's sake I will not be quiet,
until her vindication shines forth like the dawn
and her victory like a burning torch.

Nations shall behold your vindication,
and all the kings your glory;
you shall be called by a new name
pronounced by the mouth of the Lord.
You shall be a glorious crown in the hand of the Lord,
a royal diadem held by your God.
No more shall people call you "Forsaken,"
or your land "Desolate,"
but you shall be called "My Delight,"
and your land "Espoused."
For the Lord delights in you
and makes your land his spouse.
As a young man marries a virgin,
your Builder shall marry you;
and as a bridegroom rejoices in his bride
so shall your God rejoice in you.

RESPONSORIAL PSALM

Ps 89:4-5, 16-17, 27, 29

℟. (2a) For ever I will sing the goodness of the Lord.

I have made a covenant with my chosen one,
I have sworn to David my servant:
forever will I confirm your posterity
and establish your throne for all generations.

℟. For ever I will sing the goodness of the Lord.

Blessed the people who know the joyful shout;
in the light of your countenance, O Lord, they walk.
At your name they rejoice all the day,
and through your justice they are exalted.

℟. For ever I will sing the goodness of the Lord.

He shall say of me, "You are my father,
my God, the rock, my savior."
Forever I will maintain my kindness toward him,
and my covenant with him stands firm.

℟. For ever I will sing the goodness of the Lord.

SECOND READING

Acts 13:16-17, 22-25

When Paul reached Antioch in Pisidia and entered the synagogue,
he stood up, motioned with his hand, and said,
"Fellow Israelites and you others who are God-fearing, listen.
The God of this people Israel chose our ancestors
and exalted the people during their sojourn in the land of Egypt.
With uplifted arm he led them out of it.
Then he removed Saul and raised up David as king;
of him he testified,
'I have found David, son of Jesse, a man after my own heart;
he will carry out my every wish.'
From this man's descendants God, according to his promise,
has brought to Israel a savior, Jesus.
John heralded his coming by proclaiming a baptism of repentance
to all the people of Israel;
and as John was completing his course, he would say,
'What do you suppose that I am? I am not he.
Behold, one is coming after me;
I am not worthy to unfasten the sandals of his feet.'"

Gospel (cont.)

Luke 2:1-14; L14ABC

She wrapped him in swaddling clothes and laid him in a manger,
because there was no room for them in the inn.

Now there were shepherds in that region living in the fields
and keeping the night watch over their flock.
The angel of the Lord appeared to them
and the glory of the Lord shone around them,
and they were struck with great fear.
The angel said to them,
"Do not be afraid;
for behold, I proclaim to you good news of great joy
that will be for all the people.
For today in the city of David
a savior has been born for you who is Christ and Lord.
And this will be a sign for you:
you will find an infant wrapped in swaddling clothes
and lying in a manger."

And suddenly there was a multitude of the heavenly host with the angel,
praising God and saying:
"Glory to God in the highest
and on earth peace to those on whom his favor rests."

FIRST READING

Isa 9:1-6

The people who walked in darkness
have seen a great light;
upon those who dwelt in the land of gloom
a light has shone.
You have brought them abundant joy
and great rejoicing,
as they rejoice before you as at the harvest,
as people make merry when dividing spoils.
For the yoke that burdened them,
the pole on their shoulder,
and the rod of their taskmaster
you have smashed, as on the day of Midian.
For every boot that tramped in battle,
every cloak rolled in blood,
will be burned as fuel for flames.
For a child is born to us, a son is given us;
upon his shoulder dominion rests.
They name him Wonder-Counselor, God-Hero,
Father-Forever, Prince of Peace.
His dominion is vast
and forever peaceful,
from David's throne, and over his kingdom,
which he confirms and sustains
by judgment and justice,
both now and forever.
The zeal of the LORD of hosts will do this!

RESPONSORIAL PSALM

Ps 96:1-2, 2-3, 11-12, 13

℟. (Luke 2:11) Today is born our Savior,
Christ the Lord.

Sing to the LORD a new song;
sing to the LORD, all you lands.
Sing to the LORD; bless his name.

℟. Today is born our Savior, Christ the Lord.

Announce his salvation, day after day.
Tell his glory among the nations;
among all peoples, his wondrous deeds.

℟. Today is born our Savior, Christ the Lord.

Let the heavens be glad and the earth rejoice;
let the sea and what fills it resound;
let the plains be joyful and all that is in them!
Then shall all the trees of the forest exult.

℟. Today is born our Savior, Christ the Lord.

They shall exult before the LORD, for he comes;
for he comes to rule the earth.
He shall rule the world with justice
and the peoples with his constancy.

℟. Today is born our Savior, Christ the Lord.

SECOND READING

Titus 2:11-14

Beloved:
The grace of God has appeared, saving all
and training us to reject godless ways and worldly desires
and to live temperately, justly, and devoutly in this age,
as we await the blessed hope,
the appearance of the glory of our great God
and savior Jesus Christ,
who gave himself for us to deliver us from all lawlessness
and to cleanse for himself a people as his own,
eager to do what is good.

The Nativity of the Lord, *December 25, 2019 (Mass at Dawn)*

FIRST READING
Isa 62:11-12

See, the LORD proclaims
to the ends of the earth:
say to daughter Zion,
your savior comes!
Here is his reward with him,
his recompense before him.
They shall be called the holy people,
the redeemed of the LORD,
and you shall be called "Frequented,"
a city that is not forsaken.

RESPONSORIAL PSALM
Ps 97:1, 6, 11-12

℟. A light will shine on us this day: the Lord is born for us.

The LORD is king; let the earth rejoice;
let the many isles be glad.
The heavens proclaim his justice,
and all peoples see his glory.

℟. A light will shine on us this day: the Lord is born for us.

Light dawns for the just;
and gladness, for the upright of heart.
Be glad in the LORD, you just,
and give thanks to his holy name.

℟. A light will shine on us this day: the Lord is born for us.

SECOND READING
Titus 3:4-7

Beloved:
When the kindness and generous love
of God our savior appeared,
not because of any righteous deeds we had done
but because of his mercy,
he saved us through the bath of rebirth
and renewal by the Holy Spirit,
whom he richly poured out on us
through Jesus Christ our savior,
so that we might be justified by his grace
and become heirs in hope of eternal life.

The Nativity of the Lord, *December 25, 2019 (Mass During the Day)*

Gospel (cont.)
John 1:1-18; L16ABC

And the Word became flesh
and made his dwelling among us,
and we saw his glory,
the glory as of the Father's only Son,
full of grace and truth.
John testified to him and cried out, saying,
"This was he of whom I said,
'The one who is coming after me ranks ahead of me
because he existed before me.'"
From his fullness we have all received,
grace in place of grace,
because while the law was given through Moses,
grace and truth came through Jesus Christ.
No one has ever seen God.
The only Son, God, who is at the Father's side,
has revealed him.

or John 1:1-5, 9-14

In the beginning was the Word,
and the Word was with God,
and the Word was God.
He was in the beginning with God.
All things came to be through him,
and without him nothing came to be.
What came to be through him was life,
and this life was the light of the human race;
the light shines in the darkness,
and the darkness has not overcome it.
The true light, which enlightens everyone,
was coming into the world.
He was in the world,
and the world came to be through him,
but the world did not know him.
He came to what was his own,
but his own people did not accept him.

But to those who did accept him
he gave power to become children of God,
to those who believe in his name,
who were born not by natural generation
nor by human choice nor by a man's decision
but of God.
And the Word became flesh
and made his dwelling among us,
and we saw his glory,
the glory as of the Father's only Son,
full of grace and truth.

The Nativity of the Lord, December 25, 2019 (Mass During the Day)

FIRST READING
Isa 52:7-10

How beautiful upon the mountains
are the feet of him who brings glad tidings,
announcing peace, bearing good news,
announcing salvation, and saying to Zion,
"Your God is King!"

Hark! Your sentinels raise a cry,
together they shout for joy,
for they see directly, before their eyes,
the LORD restoring Zion.
Break out together in song,
O ruins of Jerusalem!
For the LORD comforts his people,
he redeems Jerusalem.
The LORD has bared his holy arm
in the sight of all the nations;
all the ends of the earth will behold
the salvation of our God.

RESPONSORIAL PSALM
Ps 98:1, 2-3, 3-4, 5-6

℟. (3c) All the ends of the earth have seen the saving power of God.

Sing to the LORD a new song,
for he has done wondrous deeds;
his right hand has won victory for him,
his holy arm.

℟. All the ends of the earth have seen the saving power of God.

The LORD has made his salvation known:
in the sight of the nations he has revealed his justice.
He has remembered his kindness and his faithfulness
toward the house of Israel.

℟. All the ends of the earth have seen the saving power of God.

All the ends of the earth have seen
the salvation by our God.
Sing joyfully to the LORD, all you lands;
break into song; sing praise.

℟. All the ends of the earth have seen the saving power of God.

Sing praise to the LORD with the harp,
with the harp and melodious song.
With trumpets and the sound of the horn
sing joyfully before the King, the LORD.

℟. All the ends of the earth have seen the saving power of God.

SECOND READING
Heb 1:1-6

Brothers and sisters:
In times past, God spoke in partial and various ways
to our ancestors through the prophets;
in these last days, he has spoken to us through the Son,
whom he made heir of all things
and through whom he created the universe,
who is the refulgence of his glory,
the very imprint of his being,
and who sustains all things by his mighty word.
When he had accomplished purification from sins,
he took his seat at the right hand of the Majesty on high,
as far superior to the angels
as the name he has inherited is more excellent than theirs.

For to which of the angels did God ever say:
You are my son; this day I have begotten you?
Or again:
I will be a father to him, and he shall be a son to me?
And again, when he leads the firstborn into the world, he says:
Let all the angels of God worship him.

The Holy Family of Jesus, Mary, and Joseph, December 29, 2019

SECOND READING
Col 3:12-17

Brothers and sisters:
Put on, as God's chosen ones, holy and beloved,
heartfelt compassion, kindness, humility, gentleness, and patience,
bearing with one another and forgiving one another,
if one has a grievance against another;
as the Lord has forgiven you, so must you also do.
And over all these put on love,
that is, the bond of perfection.
And let the peace of Christ control your hearts,
the peace into which you were also called in one body.
And be thankful.
Let the word of Christ dwell in you richly,
as in all wisdom you teach and admonish one another,
singing psalms, hymns, and spiritual songs
with gratitude in your hearts to God.
And whatever you do, in word or in deed,
do everything in the name of the Lord Jesus,
giving thanks to God the Father through him.

Solemnity of Mary, the Holy Mother of God, January 1, 2020

FIRST READING
Num 6:22-27

The LORD said to Moses:
"Speak to Aaron and his sons and tell them:
This is how you shall bless the Israelites.
Say to them:
The LORD bless you and keep you!
The LORD let his face shine upon
you, and be gracious to you!
The LORD look upon you kindly and
give you peace!
So shall they invoke my name upon the
Israelites,
and I will bless them."

RESPONSORIAL PSALM
Ps 67:2-3, 5, 6, 8

℟. (2a) May God bless us in his mercy.

May God have pity on us and bless us;
may he let his face shine upon us.
So may your way be known upon earth;
among all nations, your salvation.

℟. May God bless us in his mercy.

May the nations be glad and exult
because you rule the peoples in equity;
the nations on the earth you guide.

℟. May God bless us in his mercy.

May the peoples praise you, O God;
may all the peoples praise you!
May God bless us,
and may all the ends of the earth fear him!

℟. May God bless us in his mercy.

SECOND READING
Gal 4:4-7

Brothers and sisters:
When the fullness of time had come, God sent
his Son,
born of a woman, born under the law,
to ransom those under the law,
so that we might receive adoption as sons.
As proof that you are sons,
God sent the Spirit of his Son into our
hearts,
crying out, "Abba, Father!"
So you are no longer a slave but a son,
and if a son then also an heir, through God.

The Epiphany of the Lord, January 5, 2020

Gospel (cont.)
Matt 2:1-12; L20ABC

After their audience with the king they set out.
And behold, the star that they had seen at its rising preceded them,
until it came and stopped over the place where the child was.
They were overjoyed at seeing the star,
and on entering the house
they saw the child with Mary his mother.
They prostrated themselves and did him homage.
Then they opened their treasures
and offered him gifts of gold, frankincense, and myrrh.
And having been warned in a dream not to return to Herod,
they departed for their country by another way.

Third Sunday in Ordinary Time, January 26, 2020

Gospel (cont.)
Matt 4:12-23; L67A

They were in a boat, with their father Zebedee, mending their nets.
He called them, and immediately they left their boat and their father
and followed him.
He went around all of Galilee,
teaching in their synagogues, proclaiming the gospel of the
kingdom,
and curing every disease and illness among the people.

or Matt 4:12-17

When Jesus heard that John had been arrested,
he withdrew to Galilee.
He left Nazareth and went to live in Capernaum by the sea,
in the region of Zebulun and Naphtali,
that what had been said through Isaiah the prophet
might be fulfilled:
Land of Zebulun and land of Naphtali,
the way to the sea, beyond the Jordan,
Galilee of the Gentiles,
the people who sit in darkness have seen a great light,
on those dwelling in a land overshadowed by death
light has arisen.
From that time on, Jesus began to preach and say,
"Repent, for the kingdom of heaven is at hand."

The Presentation of the Lord, February 2, 2020

Gospel (cont.)
Luke 2:22-40; L524

The child's father and mother were amazed at what was said about
him;
and Simeon blessed them and said to Mary his mother,
"Behold, this child is destined
for the fall and rise of many in Israel,
and to be a sign that will be contradicted
—and you yourself a sword will pierce—
so that the thoughts of many hearts may be revealed."
There was also a prophetess, Anna,
the daughter of Phanuel, of the tribe of Asher.
She was advanced in years,
having lived seven years with her husband after her marriage,
and then as a widow until she was eighty-four.
She never left the temple,
but worshiped night and day with fasting and prayer.
And coming forward at that very time,
she gave thanks to God and spoke about the child
to all who were awaiting the redemption of Jerusalem.

When they had fulfilled all the prescriptions
of the law of the Lord,
they returned to Galilee, to their own town of Nazareth.
The child grew and became strong, filled with wisdom;
and the favor of God was upon him.

or Luke 2:22-32

When the days were completed for their purification
according to the law of Moses,
Mary and Joseph took Jesus up to Jerusalem
to present him to the Lord,
just as it is written in the law of the Lord,
Every male that opens the womb shall be consecrated to the Lord,
and to offer the sacrifice of
a pair of turtledoves or two young pigeons,
in accordance with the dictate in the law of the Lord.

Now there was a man in Jerusalem whose name was Simeon.
This man was righteous and devout,
awaiting the consolation of Israel,
and the Holy Spirit was upon him.
It had been revealed to him by the Holy Spirit
that he should not see death
before he had seen the Christ of the Lord.
He came in the Spirit into the temple;
and when the parents brought in the child Jesus
to perform the custom of the law in regard to him,
he took him into his arms and blessed God, saying:
"Now, Master, you may let your servant go
in peace, according to your word,
for my eyes have seen your salvation,
which you prepared in sight of all the peoples,
a light for revelation to the Gentiles,
and glory for your people Israel."

Sixth Sunday in Ordinary Time, February 16, 2020

Gospel (cont.)
Matt 5:17-37; L76A

Therefore, if you bring your gift to the altar,
and there recall that your brother
has anything against you,
leave your gift there at the altar,
go first and be reconciled with your brother,
and then come and offer your gift.
Settle with your opponent quickly while on the way to court.
Otherwise your opponent will hand you over to the judge,
and the judge will hand you over to the guard,
and you will be thrown into prison.
Amen, I say to you,
you will not be released until you have paid the last penny.

"You have heard that it was said,
You shall not commit adultery.
But I say to you,
everyone who looks at a woman with lust
has already committed adultery with her in his heart.
If your right eye causes you to sin,
tear it out and throw it away.
It is better for you to lose one of your members
than to have your whole body thrown into Gehenna.
And if your right hand causes you to sin,
cut it off and throw it away.
It is better for you to lose one of your members
than to have your whole body go into Gehenna.

"It was also said,
Whoever divorces his wife must give her a bill of divorce.
But I say to you,
whoever divorces his wife—unless the marriage is unlawful—
causes her to commit adultery,
and whoever marries a divorced woman commits adultery.

"Again you have heard that it was said to your ancestors,
Do not take a false oath,
but make good to the Lord all that you vow.
But I say to you, do not swear at all;
not by heaven, for it is God's throne;
nor by the earth, for it is his footstool;
nor by Jerusalem, for it is the city of the great King.
Do not swear by your head,
for you cannot make a single hair white or black.
Let your 'Yes' mean 'Yes,' and your 'No' mean 'No.'
Anything more is from the evil one."

Sixth Sunday in Ordinary Time, February 16, 2020

Gospel

or Matt 5:20-22a, 27-28, 33-34a, 37

Jesus said to his disciples:
"I tell you, unless your righteousness surpasses
that of the scribes and Pharisees,
you will not enter the kingdom of heaven.

"You have heard that it was said to your ancestors,
You shall not kill; and whoever kills will be liable to judgment.
But I say to you,
whoever is angry with his brother
will be liable to judgment.

"You have heard that it was said,
You shall not commit adultery.
But I say to you,
everyone who looks at a woman with lust
has already committed adultery with her in his heart.

"Again you have heard that it was said to your ancestors,
Do not take a false oath,
but make good to the Lord all that you vow.
But I say to you, do not swear at all.
Let your 'Yes' mean 'Yes,' and your 'No' mean 'No.'
Anything more is from the evil one."

Ash Wednesday, February 26, 2020

FIRST READING

Joel 2:12-18

Even now, says the LORD,
return to me with your whole heart,
with fasting, and weeping, and mourning;
Rend your hearts, not your garments,
and return to the LORD, your God.
For gracious and merciful is he,
slow to anger, rich in kindness,
and relenting in punishment.
Perhaps he will again relent
and leave behind him a blessing,
Offerings and libations
for the LORD, your God.

Blow the trumpet in Zion!
proclaim a fast,
call an assembly;
Gather the people,
notify the congregation;
Assemble the elders,
gather the children
and the infants at the breast;
Let the bridegroom quit his room
and the bride her chamber.
Between the porch and the altar
let the priests, the ministers of the LORD, weep,
And say, "Spare, O LORD, your people,
and make not your heritage a reproach,
with the nations ruling over them!
Why should they say among the peoples,
'Where is their God?'"

Then the LORD was stirred to concern for his land
and took pity on his people.

RESPONSORIAL PSALM

Ps 51:3-4, 5-6ab, 12-13, 14, and 17

℟. (see 3a) Be merciful, O Lord, for we have sinned.

Have mercy on me, O God, in your goodness;
in the greatness of your compassion wipe out my offense.
Thoroughly wash me from my guilt
and of my sin cleanse me.

℟. Be merciful, O Lord, for we have sinned.

For I acknowledge my offense,
and my sin is before me always:
"Against you only have I sinned,
and done what is evil in your sight."

℟. Be merciful, O Lord, for we have sinned.

A clean heart create for me, O God,
and a steadfast spirit renew within me.
Cast me not out from your presence,
and your Holy Spirit take not from me.

℟. Be merciful, O Lord, for we have sinned.

Give me back the joy of your salvation,
and a willing spirit sustain in me.
O Lord, open my lips,
and my mouth shall proclaim your praise.

℟. Be merciful, O Lord, for we have sinned.

SECOND READING

2 Cor 5:20–6:2

Brothers and sisters:
We are ambassadors for Christ,
as if God were appealing through us.
We implore you on behalf of Christ,
be reconciled to God.
For our sake he made him to be sin who did not know sin,
so that we might become the righteousness of God in him.

Working together, then,
we appeal to you not to receive the grace of God in vain.
For he says:

In an acceptable time I heard you,
and on the day of salvation I helped you.

Behold, now is a very acceptable time;
behold, now is the day of salvation.

Gospel (cont.)

Matt 4:1-11; L22A

Then the devil took him up to a very high mountain,
and showed him all the kingdoms of the world in their magnificence,
and he said to him, "All these I shall give to you,
if you will prostrate yourself and worship me."
At this, Jesus said to him,
"Get away, Satan!
It is written:
The Lord, your God, shall you worship
and him alone shall you serve."

Then the devil left him and, behold,
angels came and ministered to him.

SECOND READING (cont.)

Rom 5:12-19

But the gift is not like the transgression.
For if by the transgression of the one, the many died,
how much more did the grace of God
and the gracious gift of the one man Jesus Christ
overflow for the many.
And the gift is not like the result of the one who sinned.
For after one sin there was the judgment that brought condemnation;
but the gift, after many transgressions, brought acquittal.
For if, by the transgression of the one,
death came to reign through that one,
how much more will those who receive the abundance of grace
and of the gift of justification
come to reign in life through the one Jesus Christ.
In conclusion, just as through one transgression
condemnation came upon all,
so, through one righteous act,
acquittal and life came to all.
For just as through the disobedience of the one man
the many were made sinners,
so, through the obedience of the one,
the many will be made righteous.

or Rom 5:12, 17-19

Brothers and sisters:
Through one man sin entered the world,
and through sin, death,
and thus death came to all men, inasmuch as all sinned.

For if, by the transgression of the one,
death came to reign through that one,
how much more will those who receive the abundance of grace
and of the gift of justification
come to reign in life through the one Jesus Christ.
In conclusion, just as through one transgression
condemnation came upon all,
so, through one righteous act,
acquittal and life came to all.
For just as through the disobedience of the one man
the many were made sinners,
so, through the obedience of the one,
the many will be made righteous.

Gospel (cont.)

John 4:5-42; L28A

Jesus answered and said to her,
"Everyone who drinks this water will be thirsty again;
but whoever drinks the water I shall give will never thirst;
the water I shall give will become in him
a spring of water welling up to eternal life."
The woman said to him,
"Sir, give me this water, so that I may not be thirsty
or have to keep coming here to draw water."

Jesus said to her,
"Go call your husband and come back."
The woman answered and said to him,
"I do not have a husband."
Jesus answered her,
"You are right in saying, 'I do not have a husband.'
For you have had five husbands,
and the one you have now is not your husband.
What you have said is true."
The woman said to him,
"Sir, I can see that you are a prophet.
Our ancestors worshiped on this mountain;
but you people say that the place to worship is in Jerusalem."
Jesus said to her,
"Believe me, woman, the hour is coming
when you will worship the Father
neither on this mountain nor in Jerusalem.
You people worship what you do not understand;
we worship what we understand,
because salvation is from the Jews.
But the hour is coming, and is now here,
when true worshipers will worship the Father in Spirit and truth;
and indeed the Father seeks such people to worship him.
God is Spirit, and those who worship him
must worship in Spirit and truth."
The woman said to him,
"I know that the Messiah is coming, the one called the Christ;
when he comes, he will tell us everything."
Jesus said to her,
"I am he, the one speaking with you."

At that moment his disciples returned,
and were amazed that he was talking with a woman,
but still no one said, "What are you looking for?"
or "Why are you talking with her?"
The woman left her water jar
and went into the town and said to the people,
"Come see a man who told me everything I have done.
Could he possibly be the Christ?"
They went out of the town and came to him.
Meanwhile, the disciples urged him, "Rabbi, eat."
But he said to them,
"I have food to eat of which you do not know."
So the disciples said to one another,
"Could someone have brought him something to eat?"
Jesus said to them,
"My food is to do the will of the one who sent me
and to finish his work.
Do you not say, 'In four months the harvest will be here'?
I tell you, look up and see the fields ripe for the harvest.
The reaper is already receiving payment
and gathering crops for eternal life,
so that the sower and reaper can rejoice together.
For here the saying is verified that 'One sows and another reaps.'
I sent you to reap what you have not worked for;
others have done the work,
and you are sharing the fruits of their work."

Many of the Samaritans of that town began to believe in him
because of the word of the woman who testified,
"He told me everything I have done."
When the Samaritans came to him,
they invited him to stay with them;
and he stayed there two days.
Many more began to believe in him because of his word,
and they said to the woman,
"We no longer believe because of your word;
for we have heard for ourselves,
and we know that this is truly the savior of the world."

Gospel (cont.)

or John 4:5-15, 19b-26, 39a, 40-42; L28A

Jesus came to a town of Samaria called Sychar,
near the plot of land that Jacob had given to his son Joseph.
Jacob's well was there.
Jesus, tired from his journey, sat down there at the well.
It was about noon.

A woman of Samaria came to draw water.
Jesus said to her,
"Give me a drink."
His disciples had gone into the town to buy food.
The Samaritan woman said to him,
"How can you, a Jew, ask me, a Samaritan woman, for a drink?"
—For Jews use nothing in common with Samaritans.—
Jesus answered and said to her,
"If you knew the gift of God
and who is saying to you, 'Give me a drink,'
you would have asked him
and he would have given you living water."
The woman said to him,
"Sir, you do not even have a bucket and the cistern is deep;
where then can you get this living water?
Are you greater than our father Jacob,
who gave us this cistern and drank from it himself
with his children and his flocks?"
Jesus answered and said to her,
"Everyone who drinks this water will be thirsty again;
but whoever drinks the water I shall give will never thirst;
the water I shall give will become in him
a spring of water welling up to eternal life."
The woman said to him,
"Sir, give me this water, so that I may not be thirsty
or have to keep coming here to draw water."

"I can see that you are a prophet.
Our ancestors worshiped on this mountain;
but you people say that the place to worship is in Jerusalem."
Jesus said to her,
"Believe me, woman, the hour is coming
when you will worship the Father
neither on this mountain nor in Jerusalem.
You people worship what you do not understand;
we worship what we understand,
because salvation is from the Jews.
But the hour is coming, and is now here,
when true worshipers will worship the Father in Spirit and truth;
and indeed the Father seeks such people to worship him.
God is Spirit, and those who worship him
must worship in Spirit and truth."
The woman said to him,
"I know that the Messiah is coming, the one called the Christ;
when he comes, he will tell us everything."
Jesus said to her,
"I am he, the one speaking with you."

Many of the Samaritans of that town began to believe in him.
When the Samaritans came to him,
they invited him to stay with them;
and he stayed there two days.
Many more began to believe in him because of his word,
and they said to the woman,
"We no longer believe because of your word;
for we have heard for ourselves,
and we know that this is truly the savior of the world."

Gospel
Luke 2:41-51a; L543

Each year Jesus' parents went to Jerusalem for the feast of Passover,
and when he was twelve years old,
they went up according to festival custom.
After they had completed its days, as they were returning,
the boy Jesus remained behind in Jerusalem,
but his parents did not know it.
Thinking that he was in the caravan,
they journeyed for a day
and looked for him among their relatives and acquaintances,
but not finding him,
they returned to Jerusalem to look for him.
After three days they found him in the temple,
sitting in the midst of the teachers,
listening to them and asking them questions,
and all who heard him were astounded
at his understanding and his answers.
When his parents saw him,
they were astonished,
and his mother said to him,
"Son, why have you done this to us?
Your father and I have been looking for you with great anxiety."
And he said to them,
"Why were you looking for me?
Did you not know that I must be in my Father's house?"
But they did not understand what he said to them.
He went down with them and came to Nazareth,
and was obedient to them.

FIRST READING
2 Sam 7:4-5a, 12-14a, 16

The LORD spoke to Nathan and said:
"Go, tell my servant David,
'When your time comes and you rest with your ancestors,
I will raise up your heir after you, sprung from your loins,
and I will make his kingdom firm.
It is he who shall build a house for my name.
And I will make his royal throne firm forever.
I will be a father to him,
and he shall be a son to me.
Your house and your kingdom shall endure forever before me;
your throne shall stand firm forever.'"

RESPONSORIAL PSALM
Ps 89:2-3, 4-5, 27 and 29

℟. (37) The son of David will live for ever.

The promises of the LORD I will sing forever,
through all generations my mouth will proclaim your faithfulness,
For you have said, "My kindness is established forever";
in heaven you have confirmed your faithfulness.

℟. The son of David will live for ever.

"I have made a covenant with my chosen one;
I have sworn to David my servant:
Forever will I confirm your posterity
and establish your throne for all generations."

℟. The son of David will live for ever.

"He shall say of me, 'You are my father,
my God, the Rock, my savior.'
Forever I will maintain my kindness toward him,
and my covenant with him stands firm."

℟. The son of David will live for ever.

SECOND READING
Rom 4:13, 16-18, 22

Brothers and sisters:
It was not through the law
that the promise was made to Abraham and his descendants
that he would inherit the world,
but through the righteousness that comes from faith.
For this reason, it depends on faith,
so that it may be a gift,
and the promise may be guaranteed to all his descendants,
not to those who only adhere to the law
but to those who follow the faith of Abraham,
who is the father of all of us, as it is written,
I have made you father of many nations.
He is our father in the sight of God,
in whom he believed, who gives life to the dead
and calls into being what does not exist.
He believed, hoping against hope,
that he would become *the father of many nations,*
according to what was said, *Thus shall your descendants be.*
That is why *it was credited to him as righteousness.*

Gospel (long form cont.)

John 9:1-41; L31A

So they said to him, "How were your eyes opened?"
He replied,
"The man called Jesus made clay and anointed my eyes
and told me, 'Go to Siloam and wash.'
So I went there and washed and was able to see."
And they said to him, "Where is he?"
He said, "I don't know."

They brought the one who was once blind to the Pharisees.
Now Jesus had made clay and opened his eyes on a sabbath.
So then the Pharisees also asked him how he was able to see.
He said to them,
"He put clay on my eyes, and I washed, and now I can see."
So some of the Pharisees said,
"This man is not from God,
because he does not keep the sabbath."
But others said,
"How can a sinful man do such signs?"
And there was a division among them.
So they said to the blind man again,
"What do you have to say about him,
since he opened your eyes?"
He said, "He is a prophet."

Now the Jews did not believe
that he had been blind and gained his sight
until they summoned the parents of the one who had gained his sight.
They asked them,
"Is this your son, who you say was born blind?
How does he now see?"
His parents answered and said,
"We know that this is our son and that he was born blind.
We do not know how he sees now,
nor do we know who opened his eyes.
Ask him, he is of age;
he can speak for himself."
His parents said this because they were afraid of the Jews,
for the Jews had already agreed
that if anyone acknowledged him as the Christ,
he would be expelled from the synagogue.
For this reason his parents said,
"He is of age; question him."

So a second time they called the man who had been blind
and said to him, "Give God the praise!
We know that this man is a sinner."
He replied,
"If he is a sinner, I do not know.
One thing I do know is that I was blind and now I see."
So they said to him,
"What did he do to you?
How did he open your eyes?"
He answered them,
"I told you already and you did not listen.
Why do you want to hear it again?
Do you want to become his disciples, too?"
They ridiculed him and said,
"You are that man's disciple;
we are disciples of Moses!
We know that God spoke to Moses,
but we do not know where this one is from."
The man answered and said to them,
"This is what is so amazing,
that you do not know where he is from, yet he opened my eyes.
We know that God does not listen to sinners,
but if one is devout and does his will, he listens to him.
It is unheard of that anyone ever opened the eyes of a person born
blind.
If this man were not from God,
he would not be able to do anything."
They answered and said to him,
"You were born totally in sin,
and are you trying to teach us?"
Then they threw him out.

When Jesus heard that they had thrown him out,
he found him and said, "Do you believe in the Son of Man?"
He answered and said,
"Who is he, sir, that I may believe in him?"
Jesus said to him,
"You have seen him,
and the one speaking with you is he."
He said,
"I do believe, Lord," and he worshiped him.
Then Jesus said,
"I came into this world for judgment,
so that those who do not see might see,
and those who do see might become blind."

Some of the Pharisees who were with him heard this
and said to him, "Surely we are not also blind, are we?"
Jesus said to them,
"If you were blind, you would have no sin;
but now you are saying, 'We see,' so your sin remains."

Fourth Sunday of Lent, March 22, 2020

Gospel (short form)

John 9:1, 6-9, 13-17, 34-38; L31A

As Jesus passed by he saw a man blind from birth.
He spat on the ground and made clay with the saliva,
and smeared the clay on his eyes, and said to him,
"Go wash in the Pool of Siloam"—which means Sent—.
So he went and washed, and came back able to see.

His neighbors and those who had seen him earlier as a beggar said,
"Isn't this the one who used to sit and beg?"
Some said, "It is,"
but others said, "No, he just looks like him."
He said, "I am."

They brought the one who was once blind to the Pharisees.
Now Jesus had made clay and opened his eyes on a sabbath.
So then the Pharisees also asked him how he was able to see.
He said to them,
"He put clay on my eyes, and I washed, and now I can see."
So some of the Pharisees said,
"This man is not from God,
because he does not keep the sabbath."
But others said,
"How can a sinful man do such signs?"
And there was a division among them.
So they said to the blind man again,
"What do you have to say about him,
since he opened your eyes?"
He said, "He is a prophet."

They answered and said to him,
"You were born totally in sin,
and are you trying to teach us?"
Then they threw him out.

When Jesus heard that they had thrown him out,
he found him and said, "Do you believe in the Son of Man?"
He answered and said,
"Who is he, sir, that I may believe in him?"
Jesus said to him,
"You have seen him,
and the one speaking with you is he."
He said,
"I do believe, Lord," and he worshiped him.

Gospel (cont.)
Luke 1:26-38; L545

But Mary said to the angel,
"How can this be,
since I have no relations with a man?"
And the angel said to her in reply,
"The Holy Spirit will come upon you,
and the power of the Most High will overshadow you.
Therefore the child to be born
will be called holy, the Son of God.
And behold, Elizabeth, your relative,
has also conceived a son in her old age,
and this is the sixth month for her who was called barren;
for nothing will be impossible for God."
Mary said, "Behold, I am the handmaid of the Lord.
May it be done to me according to your word."
Then the angel departed from her.

FIRST READING
Isa 7:10-14; 8:10

The LORD spoke to Ahaz, saying:
Ask for a sign from the LORD, your God;
let it be deep as the nether world, or high as the sky!
But Ahaz answered,
"I will not ask! I will not tempt the LORD!"
Then Isaiah said:
Listen, O house of David!
Is it not enough for you to weary people,
must you also weary my God?
Therefore the Lord himself will give you this sign:
the virgin shall be with child, and bear a son,
and shall name him Emmanuel,
which means "God is with us!"

RESPONSORIAL PSALM
Ps 40:7-8a, 8b-9, 10, 11

℟. (8a and 9a) Here I am, Lord; I come to do your will.

Sacrifice or offering you wished not,
but ears open to obedience you gave me.
Holocausts and sin-offerings you sought not;
then said I, "Behold, I come."

℟. Here I am, Lord; I come to do your will.

"In the written scroll it is prescribed for me,
To do your will, O God, is my delight,
and your law is within my heart!"

℟. Here I am, Lord; I come to do your will.

I announced your justice in the vast assembly;
I did not restrain my lips, as you, O LORD, know.

℟. Here I am, Lord; I come to do your will.

Your justice I kept not hid within my heart;
your faithfulness and your salvation I have spoken of;
I have made no secret of your kindness and your truth
in the vast assembly.

℟. Here I am, Lord; I come to do your will.

SECOND READING
Heb 10:4-10

Brothers and sisters:
It is impossible that the blood of bulls and goats
takes away sins.
For this reason, when Christ came into the world, he said:

"Sacrifice and offering you did not desire,
but a body you prepared for me;
in holocausts and sin offerings you took no delight.
Then I said, 'As is written of me in the scroll,
behold, I come to do your will, O God.'"

First Christ says, "Sacrifices and offerings,
holocausts and sin offerings,
you neither desired nor delighted in."
These are offered according to the law.
Then he says, "Behold, I come to do your will."
He takes away the first to establish the second.
By this "will," we have been consecrated
through the offering of the Body of Jesus Christ once for all.

Gospel (cont.)

John 11:1-45; L34A

But if one walks at night, he stumbles,
because the light is not in him."
He said this, and then told them,
"Our friend Lazarus is asleep,
but I am going to awaken him."
So the disciples said to him,
"Master, if he is asleep, he will be saved."
But Jesus was talking about his death,
while they thought that he meant ordinary sleep.
So then Jesus said to them clearly,
"Lazarus has died.
And I am glad for you that I was not there,
that you may believe.
Let us go to him."
So Thomas, called Didymus, said to his fellow disciples,
"Let us also go to die with him."

When Jesus arrived, he found that Lazarus
had already been in the tomb for four days.
Now Bethany was near Jerusalem, only about two miles away.
And many of the Jews had come to Martha and Mary
to comfort them about their brother.
When Martha heard that Jesus was coming,
she went to meet him;
but Mary sat at home.
Martha said to Jesus,
"Lord, if you had been here,
my brother would not have died.
But even now I know that whatever you ask of God,
God will give you."
Jesus said to her,
"Your brother will rise."
Martha said to him,
"I know he will rise,
in the resurrection on the last day."
Jesus told her,
"I am the resurrection and the life;
whoever believes in me, even if he dies, will live,
and everyone who lives and believes in me will never die.
Do you believe this?"
She said to him, "Yes, Lord.
I have come to believe that you are the Christ, the Son of God,
the one who is coming into the world."

When she had said this,
she went and called her sister Mary secretly, saying,
"The teacher is here and is asking for you."
As soon as she heard this,
she rose quickly and went to him.
For Jesus had not yet come into the village,
but was still where Martha had met him.
So when the Jews who were with her in the house comforting her
saw Mary get up quickly and go out,
they followed her,
presuming that she was going to the tomb to weep there.
When Mary came to where Jesus was and saw him,
she fell at his feet and said to him,
"Lord, if you had been here,
my brother would not have died."
When Jesus saw her weeping and the Jews who had come with her
weeping,
he became perturbed and deeply troubled, and said,
"Where have you laid him?"
They said to him, "Sir, come and see."
And Jesus wept.
So the Jews said, "See how he loved him."
But some of them said,
"Could not the one who opened the eyes of the blind man
have done something so that this man would not have died?"

So Jesus, perturbed again, came to the tomb.
It was a cave, and a stone lay across it.
Jesus said, "Take away the stone."
Martha, the dead man's sister, said to him,
"Lord, by now there will be a stench;
he has been dead for four days."
Jesus said to her,
"Did I not tell you that if you believe
you will see the glory of God?"
So they took away the stone.
And Jesus raised his eyes and said,
"Father, I thank you for hearing me.
I know that you always hear me;
but because of the crowd here I have said this,
that they may believe that you sent me."
And when he had said this,
he cried out in a loud voice,
"Lazarus, come out!"
The dead man came out,
tied hand and foot with burial bands,
and his face was wrapped in a cloth.
So Jesus said to them,
"Untie him and let him go."

Now many of the Jews who had come to Mary
and seen what he had done began to believe in him.

Gospel (cont.)

or John 11:3-7, 17, 20-27, 33b-45; L34A

The sisters of Lazarus sent word to Jesus saying,
"Master, the one you love is ill."
When Jesus heard this he said,
"This illness is not to end in death,
but is for the glory of God,
that the Son of God may be glorified through it."
Now Jesus loved Martha and her sister and Lazarus.
So when he heard that he was ill,
he remained for two days in the place where he was.
Then after this he said to his disciples,
"Let us go back to Judea."

When Jesus arrived, he found that Lazarus
had already been in the tomb for four days.
When Martha heard that Jesus was coming,
she went to meet him;
but Mary sat at home.
Martha said to Jesus,
"Lord, if you had been here,
my brother would not have died.
But even now I know that whatever you ask of God,
God will give you."
Jesus said to her,
"Your brother will rise."
Martha said,
"I know he will rise,
in the resurrection on the last day."
Jesus told her,
"I am the resurrection and the life;
whoever believes in me, even if he dies, will live,
and everyone who lives and believes in me will never die.
Do you believe this?"
She said to him, "Yes, Lord.
I have come to believe that you are the Christ, the Son of God,
the one who is coming into the world."

He became perturbed and deeply troubled, and said,
"Where have you laid him?"
They said to him, "Sir, come and see."
And Jesus wept.
So the Jews said, "See how he loved him."
But some of them said,
"Could not the one who opened the eyes of the blind man
have done something so that this man would not have died?"

So Jesus, perturbed again, came to the tomb.
It was a cave, and a stone lay across it.
Jesus said, "Take away the stone."
Martha, the dead man's sister, said to him,
"Lord, by now there will be a stench;
he has been dead for four days."
Jesus said to her,
"Did I not tell you that if you believe
you will see the glory of God?"
So they took away the stone.
And Jesus raised his eyes and said,
"Father, I thank you for hearing me.
I know that you always hear me;
but because of the crowd here I have said this,
that they may believe that you sent me."
And when he had said this,
he cried out in a loud voice,
"Lazarus, come out!"
The dead man came out,
tied hand and foot with burial bands,
and his face was wrapped in a cloth.
So Jesus said to them,
"Untie him and let him go."

Now many of the Jews who had come to Mary
and seen what he had done began to believe in him.

Gospel at the Procession with Palms (cont.)

Matt 21:1-11; L37A

The crowds preceding him and those following
kept crying out and saying:
"Hosanna to the Son of David;
blessed is he who comes in the name of the Lord;
hosanna in the highest."
And when he entered Jerusalem
the whole city was shaken and asked, "Who is this?"
And the crowds replied,
"This is Jesus the prophet, from Nazareth in Galilee."

Gospel at Mass

Matt 26:14–27:66; L38A

One of the Twelve, who was called Judas Iscariot, went to the chief priests and said, "What are you willing to give me if I hand him over to you?" They paid him thirty pieces of silver, and from that time on he looked for an opportunity to hand him over.

On the first day of the Feast of Unleavened Bread, the disciples approached Jesus and said, "Where do you want us to prepare for you to eat the Passover?" He said, "Go into the city to a certain man and tell him, 'The teacher says, "My appointed time draws near; in your house I shall celebrate the Passover with my disciples."'" The disciples then did as Jesus had ordered, and prepared the Passover.

When it was evening, he reclined at table with the Twelve. And while they were eating, he said, "Amen, I say to you, one of you will betray me." Deeply distressed at this, they began to say to him one after another, "Surely it is not I, Lord?" He said in reply, "He who has dipped his hand into the dish with me is the one who will betray me. The Son of Man indeed goes, as it is written of him, but woe to that man by whom the Son of Man is betrayed. It would be better for that man if he had never been born." Then Judas, his betrayer, said in reply, "Surely it is not I, Rabbi?" He answered, "You have said so."

While they were eating, Jesus took bread, said the blessing, broke it, and giving it to his disciples said, "Take and eat; this is my body." Then he took a cup, gave thanks, and gave it to them, saying, "Drink from it, all of you, for this is my blood of the covenant, which will be shed on behalf of many for the forgiveness of sins. I tell you, from now on I shall not drink this fruit of the vine until the day when I drink it with you new in the kingdom of my Father." Then, after singing a hymn, they went out to the Mount of Olives.

Then Jesus said to them, "This night all of you will have your faith in me shaken, for it is written: / *I will strike the shepherd, / and the sheep of the flock will be dispersed;* / but after I have been raised up, I shall go before you to Galilee." Peter said to him in reply, "Though all may have their faith in you shaken, mine will never be." Jesus said to him, "Amen, I say to you, this very night before the cock crows, you will deny me three times." Peter said to him, "Even though I should have to die with you, I will not deny you." And all the disciples spoke likewise.

Then Jesus came with them to a place called Gethsemane, and he said to his disciples, "Sit here while I go over there and pray." He took along Peter and the two sons of Zebedee, and began to feel sorrow and distress. Then he said to them, "My soul is sorrowful even to death. Remain here and keep watch with me." He advanced a little and fell prostrate in prayer, saying, "My Father, if it is possible, let this cup pass from me; yet, not as I will, but as you will." When he returned to his disciples he found them asleep. He said to Peter, "So you could not keep watch with me for one hour? Watch and pray that you may not undergo the test. The spirit is willing, but the flesh is weak." Withdrawing a second time, he prayed again, "My Father, if it is not possible that this cup pass without my drinking it, your will be done!" Then he returned once more and found them asleep, for they could not keep their eyes open. He left them and withdrew again and prayed a third time, saying the same thing again. Then he returned to his disciples and said to them, "Are you still sleeping and taking your rest? Behold, the hour is at hand when the Son of Man is to be handed over to sinners. Get up, let us go. Look, my betrayer is at hand."

While he was still speaking, Judas, one of the Twelve, arrived, accompanied by a large crowd, with swords and clubs, who had come from the chief priests and the elders of the people. His betrayer had arranged a sign with them, saying, "The man I shall kiss is the one; arrest him." Immediately he went over to Jesus and said, "Hail, Rabbi!" and he kissed him. Jesus answered him, "Friend, do what you have come for." Then stepping forward they laid hands on Jesus and arrested him. And behold, one of those who accompanied Jesus put his hand to his sword, drew it, and struck the high priest's servant, cutting off his ear. Then Jesus said to him, "Put your sword back into its sheath, for all who take the sword will perish by the sword. Do you think that I cannot call upon my Father and he will not provide me at this moment with more than twelve legions of angels? But then how would the Scriptures be fulfilled which say that it must come to pass in this way?" At that hour Jesus said to the crowds, "Have you come out as against a robber, with swords and clubs to seize me? Day after day I sat teaching in the temple area, yet you did not arrest me. But all this has come to pass that the writings of the prophets may be fulfilled." Then all the disciples left him and fled.

Those who had arrested Jesus led him away to Caiaphas the high priest, where the scribes and the elders were assembled. Peter was following him at a distance as far as the high priest's courtyard, and going inside he sat down with the servants to see the outcome. The chief priests and the entire Sanhedrin kept trying to obtain false testimony against Jesus in order to put him to death, but they found none, though many false witnesses came forward. Finally two came forward who stated, "This man said, 'I can destroy the temple of God and within three days rebuild it.'" The high priest rose and addressed him, "Have you no answer? What are these men testifying against you?" But Jesus was silent. Then the high priest said to him, "I order you to tell us under oath before the living God whether you are the Christ, the Son of God." Jesus said to him in reply, "You have said so. But I tell you: / From now on you will see 'the Son of Man / seated at the right hand of the Power' / and 'coming on the clouds of heaven.'" / Then the high priest tore his robes and said, "He has blasphemed! What further need have we of witnesses? You have now heard the blasphemy; what is your opinion?" They said in reply, "He deserves to die!" Then they spat in his face and struck him, while some slapped him, saying, "Prophesy for us, Christ: who is it that struck you?"

Now Peter was sitting outside in the courtyard. One of the maids came over to him and said, "You too were with Jesus the Galilean." But he denied it in front of everyone, saying, "I do not know what you are talking about!" As he went out to the gate, another girl saw him and said to those who were there, "This man was with Jesus the Nazorean." Again he denied it with an oath, "I do not know the man!" A little later the bystanders came over and said to Peter, "Surely you too are one of them; even your speech gives you away." At that he began to curse and to swear, "I do not know the man." And immediately a cock crowed. Then Peter remembered the word that Jesus had spoken: "Before the cock crows you will deny me three times." He went out and began to weep bitterly.

When it was morning, all the chief priests and the elders of the people took counsel against Jesus to put him to death. They bound him, led him away, and handed him over to Pilate, the governor.

Then Judas, his betrayer, seeing that Jesus had been condemned, deeply regretted what he had done. He returned the thirty pieces of silver to the chief priests and elders, saying, "I have sinned in betraying innocent blood." They said, "What is that to us? Look to it yourself." Flinging the money into the temple, he departed and went off and hanged himself. The chief priests gathered up the money, but said, "It is not lawful to deposit this in the temple treasury, for it is the price of blood." After consultation, they used it to buy the potter's field as a burial place for foreigners. That is why that field even today is called the Field of Blood. Then was fulfilled what had been said through Jeremiah the prophet, *And they took the thirty pieces of silver, the value of a man with a price on his head, a price set by some of the Israelites, and they paid it out for the potter's field just as the Lord had commanded me.*

Now Jesus stood before the governor, and he questioned him, "Are you the king of the Jews?" Jesus said, "You say so." And when he was accused by the chief priests and elders, he made no answer. Then Pilate said to him, "Do you not hear how many things they are testifying against you?" But he did not answer him one word, so that the governor was greatly amazed.

Now on the occasion of the feast the governor was accustomed to release to the crowd one prisoner whom they wished. And at that time they had a notorious prisoner called Barabbas. So when they had assembled, Pilate said to them, "Which one do you want me to release to you, Barabbas, or Jesus called Christ?" For he knew that it was out of envy that they had handed him over. While he was still seated on the bench, his wife sent him a message, "Have nothing to do with that righteous man. I suffered much in a dream today because of him." The chief priests and the elders persuaded the crowds to ask for Barabbas but to destroy Jesus. The governor said to them in reply, "Which of the two do you want me to release to you?" They answered, "Barabbas!" Pilate said to them, "Then what shall I do with Jesus called Christ?" They all said, "Let him be crucified!" But he said, "Why? What evil has he done?" They only shouted the louder, "Let him be crucified!" When Pilate saw that he was not succeeding at all, but that a riot was breaking out instead, he took water and washed his hands in the sight of the crowd, saying, "I am innocent of this man's blood. Look to it yourselves." And the whole people said in reply, "His blood be upon us and upon our children." Then he released Barabbas to them, but after he had Jesus scourged, he handed him over to be crucified.

Then the soldiers of the governor took Jesus inside the praetorium and gathered the whole cohort around him. They stripped off his clothes and threw a scarlet military cloak about him. Weaving a crown out of thorns, they placed it on his head, and a reed in his right hand. And kneeling before him, they mocked him, saying, "Hail, King of the Jews!" They spat upon him and took the reed and kept striking him on the head. And when they had mocked him, they stripped him of the cloak, dressed him in his own clothes, and led him off to crucify him.

As they were going out, they met a Cyrenian named Simon; this man they pressed into service to carry his cross.

And when they came to a place called Golgotha—which means Place of the Skull—, they gave Jesus wine to drink mixed with gall. But when he had tasted it, he refused to drink. After they had crucified him, they divided his garments by casting lots; then they sat down and kept watch over him there. And they placed over his head the written charge against him: This is Jesus, the King of the Jews. Two revolutionaries were crucified with him, one on his right and the other on his left. Those passing by reviled him, shaking their heads and saying, "You who would destroy the temple and rebuild it in three days, save yourself, if you are the Son of God, and come down from the cross!" Likewise the chief priests with the scribes and elders mocked him and said, "He saved others; he cannot save himself. So he is the king of Israel! Let him come down from the cross now, and we will believe in him. He trusted in God; let him deliver him now if he wants him. For he said, 'I am the Son of God.'" The revolutionaries who were crucified with him also kept abusing him in the same way.

From noon onward, darkness came over the whole land until three in the afternoon. And about three o'clock Jesus cried out in a loud voice, *"Eli, Eli, lema sabachthani?"* which means, "My God, my God, why have you forsaken me?" Some of the bystanders who heard it said, "This one is calling for Elijah." Immediately one of them ran to get a sponge; he soaked it in wine, and putting it on a reed, gave it to him to drink. But the rest said, "Wait, let us see if Elijah comes to save him." But Jesus cried out again in a loud voice, and gave up his spirit.

(Here all kneel and pause for a short time.)

And behold, the veil of the sanctuary was torn in two from top to bottom. The earth quaked, rocks were split, tombs were opened, and the bodies of many saints who had fallen asleep were raised. And coming forth from their tombs after his resurrection, they entered the holy city and appeared to many. The centurion and the men with him who were keeping watch over Jesus feared greatly when they saw the earthquake and all that was happening, and they said, "Truly, this was the Son of God!" There were many women there, looking on from a distance, who had followed Jesus from Galilee, ministering to him. Among them were Mary Magdalene and Mary the mother of James and Joseph, and the mother of the sons of Zebedee.

When it was evening, there came a rich man from Arimathea named Joseph, who was himself a disciple of Jesus. He went to Pilate and asked for the body of Jesus; then Pilate ordered it to be handed over. Taking the body, Joseph wrapped it in clean linen and laid it in his new tomb that he had hewn in the rock. Then he rolled a huge stone across the entrance to the tomb and departed. But Mary Magdalene and the other Mary remained sitting there, facing the tomb.

The next day, the one following the day of preparation, the chief priests and the Pharisees gathered before Pilate and said, "Sir, we remember that this impostor while still alive said, 'After three days I will be raised up.' Give orders, then, that the grave be secured until the third day, lest his disciples come and steal him and say to the people, 'He has been raised from the dead.' This last imposture would be worse than the first." Pilate said to them, "The guard is yours; go, secure it as best you can." So they went and secured the tomb by fixing a seal to the stone and setting the guard.

or Matt 27:11-54; L38A

Jesus stood before the governor, Pontius Pilate, who questioned him,
"Are you the king of the Jews?"
Jesus said, "You say so."
And when he was accused by the chief priests and elders,
he made no answer.
Then Pilate said to him,
"Do you not hear how many things they are testifying against you?"
But he did not answer him one word,
so that the governor was greatly amazed.

Now on the occasion of the feast
the governor was accustomed to release to the crowd
one prisoner whom they wished.

And at that time they had a notorious prisoner called Barabbas.
So when they had assembled, Pilate said to them,
"Which one do you want me to release to you,
Barabbas, or Jesus called Christ?"
For he knew that it was out of envy
that they had handed him over.
While he was still seated on the bench,
his wife sent him a message,
"Have nothing to do with that righteous man.
I suffered much in a dream today because of him."
The chief priests and the elders persuaded the crowds
to ask for Barabbas but to destroy Jesus.
The governor said to them in reply,
"Which of the two do you want me to release to you?"
They answered, "Barabbas!"
Pilate said to them,
"Then what shall I do with Jesus called Christ?"
They all said,
"Let him be crucified!"
But he said,
"Why? What evil has he done?"
They only shouted the louder,
"Let him be crucified!"
When Pilate saw that he was not succeeding at all,
but that a riot was breaking out instead,
he took water and washed his hands in the sight of the crowd,
saying, "I am innocent of this man's blood.
Look to it yourselves."
And the whole people said in reply,
"His blood be upon us and upon our children."
Then he released Barabbas to them,
but after he had Jesus scourged,
he handed him over to be crucified.

Then the soldiers of the governor took Jesus inside the praetorium
and gathered the whole cohort around him.
They stripped off his clothes
and threw a scarlet military cloak about him.
Weaving a crown out of thorns, they placed it on his head,
and a reed in his right hand.
And kneeling before him, they mocked him, saying,
"Hail, King of the Jews!"
They spat upon him and took the reed
and kept striking him on the head.
And when they had mocked him,
they stripped him of the cloak,
dressed him in his own clothes,
and led him off to crucify him.

As they were going out, they met a Cyrenian named Simon;
this man they pressed into service
to carry his cross.

And when they came to a place called Golgotha
—which means Place of the Skull—,
they gave Jesus wine to drink mixed with gall.
But when he had tasted it, he refused to drink.
After they had crucified him,
they divided his garments by casting lots;
then they sat down and kept watch over him there.
And they placed over his head the written charge against him:
This is Jesus, the King of the Jews.

Two revolutionaries were crucified with him,
one on his right and the other on his left.
Those passing by reviled him, shaking their heads and saying,
"You who would destroy the temple and rebuild it in three days,
save yourself, if you are the Son of God,
and come down from the cross!"
Likewise the chief priests with the scribes and elders mocked him and said,
"He saved others; he cannot save himself.
So he is the king of Israel!
Let him come down from the cross now,
and we will believe in him.
He trusted in God;
let him deliver him now if he wants him.
For he said, 'I am the Son of God.'"
The revolutionaries who were crucified with him
also kept abusing him in the same way.

From noon onward, darkness came over the whole land
until three in the afternoon.
And about three o'clock Jesus cried out in a loud voice,
"Eli, Eli, lema sabachthani?"
which means, "My God, my God, why have you forsaken me?"
Some of the bystanders who heard it said,
"This one is calling for Elijah."
Immediately one of them ran to get a sponge;
he soaked it in wine, and putting it on a reed,
gave it to him to drink.
But the rest said,
"Wait, let us see if Elijah comes to save him."
But Jesus cried out again in a loud voice,
and gave up his spirit.

(Here all kneel and pause for a short time.)

And behold, the veil of the sanctuary
was torn in two from top to bottom.
The earth quaked, rocks were split, tombs were opened,
and the bodies of many saints who had fallen asleep were raised.
And coming forth from their tombs after his resurrection,
they entered the holy city and appeared to many.
The centurion and the men with him who were keeping watch over Jesus
feared greatly when they saw the earthquake
and all that was happening, and they said,
"Truly, this was the Son of God!"

Gospel (cont.)
John 13:1-15; L39ABC

For he knew who would betray him;
for this reason, he said, "Not all of you are clean."

So when he had washed their feet
and put his garments back on and reclined at table again,
he said to them, "Do you realize what I have done for you?
You call me 'teacher' and 'master,' and rightly so, for indeed I am.
If I, therefore, the master and teacher, have washed your feet,
you ought to wash one another's feet.
I have given you a model to follow,
so that as I have done for you, you should also do."

FIRST READING
Exod 12:1-8, 11-14

The LORD said to Moses and Aaron in the land of Egypt,
"This month shall stand at the head of your calendar;
you shall reckon it the first month of the year.
Tell the whole community of Israel:
On the tenth of this month every one of your families
must procure for itself a lamb, one apiece for each household.
If a family is too small for a whole lamb,
it shall join the nearest household in procuring one
and shall share in the lamb
in proportion to the number of persons who partake of it.
The lamb must be a year-old male and without blemish.
You may take it from either the sheep or the goats.
You shall keep it until the fourteenth day of this month,
and then, with the whole assembly of Israel present,
it shall be slaughtered during the evening twilight.
They shall take some of its blood
and apply it to the two doorposts and the lintel
of every house in which they partake of the lamb.
That same night they shall eat its roasted flesh
with unleavened bread and bitter herbs.

"This is how you are to eat it:
with your loins girt, sandals on your feet and your staff in hand,
you shall eat like those who are in flight.
It is the Passover of the LORD.
For on this same night I will go through Egypt,
striking down every firstborn of the land, both man and beast,
and executing judgment on all the gods of Egypt—I, the LORD!
But the blood will mark the houses where you are.
Seeing the blood, I will pass over you;
thus, when I strike the land of Egypt,
no destructive blow will come upon you.

"This day shall be a memorial feast for you,
which all your generations shall celebrate
with pilgrimage to the LORD, as a perpetual institution."

RESPONSORIAL PSALM
Ps 116:12-13, 15-16bc, 17-18

℟. (cf. 1 Cor 10:16) Our blessing-cup is a communion with the Blood of Christ.

How shall I make a return to the LORD
for all the good he has done for me?
The cup of salvation I will take up,
and I will call upon the name of the LORD.

℟. Our blessing-cup is a communion with the Blood of Christ.

Precious in the eyes of the LORD
is the death of his faithful ones.
I am your servant, the son of your handmaid;
you have loosed my bonds.

℟. Our blessing-cup is a communion with the Blood of Christ.

To you will I offer sacrifice of thanksgiving,
and I will call upon the name of the LORD.
My vows to the LORD I will pay
in the presence of all his people.

℟. Our blessing-cup is a communion with the Blood of Christ.

SECOND READING
1 Cor 11:23-26

Brothers and sisters:
I received from the Lord what I also handed on to you,
that the Lord Jesus, on the night he was handed over,
took bread, and, after he had given thanks,
broke it and said, "This is my body that is for you.
Do this in remembrance of me."
In the same way also the cup, after supper, saying,
"This cup is the new covenant in my blood.
Do this, as often as you drink it, in remembrance of me."
For as often as you eat this bread and drink the cup,
you proclaim the death of the Lord until he comes.

Gospel (cont.)

John 18:1–19:42; L40ABC

So the band of soldiers, the tribune, and the Jewish guards seized Jesus,
bound him, and brought him to Annas first.
He was the father-in-law of Caiaphas,
who was high priest that year.
It was Caiaphas who had counseled the Jews
that it was better that one man should die rather than the people.

Simon Peter and another disciple followed Jesus.
Now the other disciple was known to the high priest,
and he entered the courtyard of the high priest with Jesus.
But Peter stood at the gate outside.
So the other disciple, the acquaintance of the high priest,
went out and spoke to the gatekeeper and brought Peter in.
Then the maid who was the gatekeeper said to Peter,
"You are not one of this man's disciples, are you?"
He said, "I am not."
Now the slaves and the guards were standing around a charcoal fire
that they had made, because it was cold,
and were warming themselves.
Peter was also standing there keeping warm.

The high priest questioned Jesus
about his disciples and about his doctrine.
Jesus answered him,
"I have spoken publicly to the world.
I have always taught in a synagogue
or in the temple area where all the Jews gather,
and in secret I have said nothing. Why ask me?
Ask those who heard me what I said to them.
They know what I said."
When he had said this,
one of the temple guards standing there struck Jesus and said,
"Is this the way you answer the high priest?"
Jesus answered him,
"If I have spoken wrongly, testify to the wrong;
but if I have spoken rightly, why do you strike me?"
Then Annas sent him bound to Caiaphas the high priest.

Now Simon Peter was standing there keeping warm.
And they said to him,
"You are not one of his disciples, are you?"
He denied it and said,
"I am not."
One of the slaves of the high priest,
a relative of the one whose ear Peter had cut off, said,
"Didn't I see you in the garden with him?"
Again Peter denied it.
And immediately the cock crowed.

Then they brought Jesus from Caiaphas to the praetorium.
It was morning.
And they themselves did not enter the praetorium,
in order not to be defiled so that they could eat the Passover.
So Pilate came out to them and said,
"What charge do you bring against this man?"
They answered and said to him,
"If he were not a criminal,
we would not have handed him over to you."
At this, Pilate said to them,
"Take him yourselves, and judge him according to your law."
The Jews answered him,
"We do not have the right to execute anyone,"
in order that the word of Jesus might be fulfilled
that he said indicating the kind of death he would die.
So Pilate went back into the praetorium
and summoned Jesus and said to him,
"Are you the King of the Jews?"
Jesus answered,
"Do you say this on your own
or have others told you about me?"
Pilate answered,
"I am not a Jew, am I?
Your own nation and the chief priests handed you over to me.
What have you done?"
Jesus answered,
"My kingdom does not belong to this world.
If my kingdom did belong to this world,
my attendants would be fighting
to keep me from being handed over to the Jews.
But as it is, my kingdom is not here."
So Pilate said to him,
"Then you are a king?"
Jesus answered,
"You say I am a king.
For this I was born and for this I came into the world,
to testify to the truth.
Everyone who belongs to the truth listens to my voice."
Pilate said to him, "What is truth?"

When he had said this,
he again went out to the Jews and said to them,
"I find no guilt in him.
But you have a custom that I release one prisoner to you at Passover.
Do you want me to release to you the King of the Jews?"
They cried out again,
"Not this one but Barabbas!"
Now Barabbas was a revolutionary.

Then Pilate took Jesus and had him scourged.
And the soldiers wove a crown out of thorns and placed it on his head,
and clothed him in a purple cloak,
and they came to him and said,
"Hail, King of the Jews!"
And they struck him repeatedly.
Once more Pilate went out and said to them,
"Look, I am bringing him out to you,
so that you may know that I find no guilt in him."
So Jesus came out,
wearing the crown of thorns and the purple cloak.
And he said to them, "Behold, the man!"
When the chief priests and the guards saw him they cried out,
"Crucify him, crucify him!"
Pilate said to them,
"Take him yourselves and crucify him.
I find no guilt in him."
The Jews answered,
"We have a law, and according to that law he ought to die,
because he made himself the Son of God."
Now when Pilate heard this statement,

he became even more afraid,
and went back into the praetorium and said to Jesus,
"Where are you from?"
Jesus did not answer him.
So Pilate said to him,
"Do you not speak to me?
Do you not know that I have power to release you
and I have power to crucify you?"
Jesus answered him,
"You would have no power over me
if it had not been given to you from above.
For this reason the one who handed me over to you
has the greater sin."
Consequently, Pilate tried to release him; but the Jews cried out,
"If you release him, you are not a Friend of Caesar.
Everyone who makes himself a king opposes Caesar."

When Pilate heard these words he brought Jesus out
and seated him on the judge's bench
in the place called Stone Pavement, in Hebrew, Gabbatha.
It was preparation day for Passover, and it was about noon.
And he said to the Jews,
"Behold, your king!"
They cried out,
"Take him away, take him away! Crucify him!"
Pilate said to them,
"Shall I crucify your king?"
The chief priests answered,
"We have no king but Caesar."
Then he handed him over to them to be crucified.

So they took Jesus, and, carrying the cross himself,
he went out to what is called the Place of the Skull,
in Hebrew, Golgotha.
There they crucified him, and with him two others,
one on either side, with Jesus in the middle.
Pilate also had an inscription written and put on the cross.
It read,
"Jesus the Nazorean, the King of the Jews."
Now many of the Jews read this inscription,
because the place where Jesus was crucified was near the city;
and it was written in Hebrew, Latin, and Greek.
So the chief priests of the Jews said to Pilate,
"Do not write 'The King of the Jews,'
but that he said, 'I am the King of the Jews.'"
Pilate answered,
"What I have written, I have written."

When the soldiers had crucified Jesus,
they took his clothes and divided them into four shares,
a share for each soldier.
They also took his tunic, but the tunic was seamless,
woven in one piece from the top down.
So they said to one another,
"Let's not tear it, but cast lots for it to see whose it will be,"
in order that the passage of Scripture might be fulfilled that says:
They divided my garments among them,
and for my vesture they cast lots.
This is what the soldiers did.

Standing by the cross of Jesus were his mother
and his mother's sister, Mary the wife of Clopas,
and Mary of Magdala.
When Jesus saw his mother and the disciple there whom he loved
he said to his mother, "Woman, behold, your son."
Then he said to the disciple,
"Behold, your mother."
And from that hour the disciple took her into his home.

After this, aware that everything was now finished,
in order that the Scripture might be fulfilled,
Jesus said, "I thirst."
There was a vessel filled with common wine.
So they put a sponge soaked in wine on a sprig of hyssop
and put it up to his mouth.
When Jesus had taken the wine, he said,
"It is finished."
And bowing his head, he handed over the spirit.

Here all kneel and pause for a short time.

Now since it was preparation day,
in order that the bodies might not remain
on the cross on the sabbath,
for the sabbath day of that week was a solemn one,
the Jews asked Pilate that their legs be broken
and that they be taken down.
So the soldiers came and broke the legs of the first
and then of the other one who was crucified with Jesus.
But when they came to Jesus and saw that he was already dead,
they did not break his legs,
but one soldier thrust his lance into his side,
and immediately blood and water flowed out.
An eyewitness has testified, and his testimony is true;
he knows that he is speaking the truth,
so that you also may come to believe.
For this happened so that the Scripture passage might be fulfilled:
Not a bone of it will be broken.
And again another passage says:
They will look upon him whom they have pierced.

After this, Joseph of Arimathea,
secretly a disciple of Jesus for fear of the Jews,
asked Pilate if he could remove the body of Jesus.
And Pilate permitted it.
So he came and took his body.
Nicodemus, the one who had first come to him at night,
also came bringing a mixture of myrrh and aloes
weighing about one hundred pounds.
They took the body of Jesus
and bound it with burial cloths along with the spices,
according to the Jewish burial custom.
Now in the place where he had been crucified there was a garden,
and in the garden a new tomb, in which no one had yet been buried.
So they laid Jesus there because of the Jewish preparation day;
for the tomb was close by.

FIRST READING
Isa 52:13–53:12

See, my servant shall prosper,
he shall be raised high and greatly exalted.
Even as many were amazed at him—
so marred was his look beyond human semblance
and his appearance beyond that of the sons of man—
so shall he startle many nations,
because of him kings shall stand speechless;
for those who have not been told shall see,
those who have not heard shall ponder it.

Who would believe what we have heard?
To whom has the arm of the LORD been revealed?
He grew up like a sapling before him,
like a shoot from the parched earth;
there was in him no stately bearing to make us look at him,
nor appearance that would attract us to him.
He was spurned and avoided by people,
a man of suffering, accustomed to infirmity,
one of those from whom people hide their faces,
spurned, and we held him in no esteem.

Yet it was our infirmities that he bore,
our sufferings that he endured,
while we thought of him as stricken,
as one smitten by God and afflicted.
But he was pierced for our offenses,
crushed for our sins;
upon him was the chastisement that makes us whole,
by his stripes we were healed.
We had all gone astray like sheep,
each following his own way;
but the LORD laid upon him
the guilt of us all.

Though he was harshly treated, he submitted
and opened not his mouth;
like a lamb led to the slaughter
or a sheep before the shearers,
he was silent and opened not his mouth.
Oppressed and condemned, he was taken away,
and who would have thought any more of his destiny?
When he was cut off from the land of the living,
and smitten for the sin of his people,
a grave was assigned him among the wicked
and a burial place with evildoers,
though he had done no wrong
nor spoken any falsehood.
But the LORD was pleased
to crush him in infirmity.

If he gives his life as an offering for sin,
he shall see his descendants in a long life,
and the will of the LORD shall be accomplished through him.

Because of his affliction
he shall see the light
in fullness of days;
through his suffering, my servant shall justify many,
and their guilt he shall bear.
Therefore I will give him his portion among the great,
and he shall divide the spoils with the mighty,
because he surrendered himself to death
and was counted among the wicked;
and he shall take away the sins of many,
and win pardon for their offenses.

RESPONSORIAL PSALM
Ps 31:2, 6, 12-13, 15-16, 17, 25

℟. (Luke 23:46) Father, into your hands I commend my spirit.

In you, O LORD, I take refuge;
let me never be put to shame.
In your justice rescue me.
Into your hands I commend my spirit;
you will redeem me, O LORD, O faithful God.

℟. Father, into your hands I commend my spirit.

For all my foes I am an object of reproach,
a laughingstock to my neighbors, and a dread to my friends;
they who see me abroad flee from me.
I am forgotten like the unremembered dead;
I am like a dish that is broken.

℟. Father, into your hands I commend my spirit.

But my trust is in you, O LORD;
I say, "You are my God.
In your hands is my destiny; rescue me
from the clutches of my enemies and my persecutors."

℟. Father, into your hands I commend my spirit.

Let your face shine upon your servant;
save me in your kindness.
Take courage and be stouthearted,
all you who hope in the LORD.

℟. Father, into your hands I commend my spirit.

SECOND READING
Heb 4:14-16; 5:7-9

Brothers and sisters:
Since we have a great high priest who has passed through the heavens,
Jesus, the Son of God,
let us hold fast to our confession.
For we do not have a high priest
who is unable to sympathize with our weaknesses,
but one who has similarly been tested in every way,
yet without sin.
So let us confidently approach the throne of grace
to receive mercy and to find grace for timely help.

In the days when Christ was in the flesh,
he offered prayers and supplications with loud cries and tears
to the one who was able to save him from death,
and he was heard because of his reverence.
Son though he was, he learned obedience from what he suffered;
and when he was made perfect,
he became the source of eternal salvation
for all who obey him.

FIRST READING

Gen 1:1–2:2

In the beginning, when God created the heavens and the earth,
the earth was a formless wasteland, and darkness covered the abyss,
while a mighty wind swept over the waters.

Then God said,
"Let there be light," and there was light.
God saw how good the light was.
God then separated the light from the darkness.
God called the light "day," and the darkness he called "night."
Thus evening came, and morning followed—the first day.

Then God said,
"Let there be a dome in the middle of the waters,
to separate one body of water from the other."
And so it happened:
God made the dome,
and it separated the water above the dome from the water below it.
God called the dome "the sky."
Evening came, and morning followed—the second day.

Then God said,
"Let the water under the sky be gathered into a single basin,
so that the dry land may appear."
And so it happened:
the water under the sky was gathered into its basin,
and the dry land appeared.
God called the dry land "the earth,"
and the basin of the water he called "the sea."
God saw how good it was.
Then God said,
"Let the earth bring forth vegetation:
every kind of plant that bears seed
and every kind of fruit tree on earth
that bears fruit with its seed in it."
And so it happened:
the earth brought forth every kind of plant that bears seed
and every kind of fruit tree on earth
that bears fruit with its seed in it.
God saw how good it was.
Evening came, and morning followed—the third day.

Then God said:
"Let there be lights in the dome of the sky,
to separate day from night.
Let them mark the fixed times, the days and the years,
and serve as luminaries in the dome of the sky,
to shed light upon the earth."
And so it happened:
God made the two great lights,
the greater one to govern the day,
and the lesser one to govern the night;
and he made the stars.
God set them in the dome of the sky,
to shed light upon the earth,
to govern the day and the night,
and to separate the light from the darkness.
God saw how good it was.
Evening came, and morning followed—the fourth day.

Then God said,
"Let the water teem with an abundance of living creatures,
and on the earth let birds fly beneath the dome of the sky."
And so it happened:
God created the great sea monsters
and all kinds of swimming creatures with which the water teems,
and all kinds of winged birds.
God saw how good it was, and God blessed them, saying,
"Be fertile, multiply, and fill the water of the seas;
and let the birds multiply on the earth."
Evening came, and morning followed—the fifth day.

Then God said,
"Let the earth bring forth all kinds of living creatures:
cattle, creeping things, and wild animals of all kinds."
And so it happened:
God made all kinds of wild animals, all kinds of cattle,
and all kinds of creeping things of the earth.
God saw how good it was.
Then God said:
"Let us make man in our image, after our likeness.
Let them have dominion over the fish of the sea,
the birds of the air, and the cattle,
and over all the wild animals
and all the creatures that crawl on the ground."
God created man in his image;
in the image of God he created him;
male and female he created them.
God blessed them, saying:
"Be fertile and multiply;
fill the earth and subdue it.
Have dominion over the fish of the sea, the birds of the air,
and all the living things that move on the earth."
God also said:
"See, I give you every seed-bearing plant all over the earth
and every tree that has seed-bearing fruit on it to be your food;
and to all the animals of the land, all the birds of the air,
and all the living creatures that crawl on the ground,
I give all the green plants for food."
And so it happened.
God looked at everything he had made, and he found it very good.
Evening came, and morning followed—the sixth day.

Thus the heavens and the earth and all their array were completed.
Since on the seventh day God was finished
with the work he had been doing,
he rested on the seventh day from all the work he had undertaken.

or

Gen 1:1, 26-31a

In the beginning, when God created the heavens and the earth,
God said: "Let us make man in our image, after our likeness.
Let them have dominion over the fish of the sea,
the birds of the air, and the cattle,
and over all the wild animals
and all the creatures that crawl on the ground."
God created man in his image;
in the image of God he created him;
male and female he created them.
God blessed them, saying:
"Be fertile and multiply;
fill the earth and subdue it.
Have dominion over the fish of the sea, the birds of the air,
and all the living things that move on the earth."
God also said:
"See, I give you every seed-bearing plant all over the earth
and every tree that has seed-bearing fruit on it to be your food;
and to all the animals of the land, all the birds of the air,
and all the living creatures that crawl on the ground,
I give all the green plants for food."
And so it happened.
God looked at everything he had made, and found it very good.

RESPONSORIAL PSALM
Ps 104:1-2, 5-6, 10, 12, 13-14, 24, 35

℟. (30) Lord, send out your Spirit, and renew the face of the earth.

Bless the LORD, O my soul!
O LORD, my God, you are great indeed!
You are clothed with majesty and glory,
robed in light as with a cloak.

℟. Lord, send out your Spirit, and renew the face of the earth.

You fixed the earth upon its foundation,
not to be moved forever;
with the ocean, as with a garment, you covered it;
above the mountains the waters stood.

℟. Lord, send out your Spirit, and renew the face of the earth.

You send forth springs into the watercourses
that wind among the mountains.
Beside them the birds of heaven dwell;
from among the branches they send forth their song.

℟. Lord, send out your Spirit, and renew the face of the earth.

You water the mountains from your palace;
the earth is replete with the fruit of your works.
You raise grass for the cattle,
and vegetation for man's use,
producing bread from the earth.

℟. Lord, send out your Spirit, and renew the face of the earth.

How manifold are your works, O LORD!
In wisdom you have wrought them all—
the earth is full of your creatures.
Bless the LORD, O my soul!

℟. Lord, send out your Spirit, and renew the face of the earth.

or

Ps 33:4-5, 6-7, 12-13, 20 and 22

℟. (5b) The earth is full of the goodness of the Lord.

Upright is the word of the LORD,
and all his works are trustworthy.
He loves justice and right;
of the kindness of the LORD the earth is full.

℟. The earth is full of the goodness of the Lord.

By the word of the LORD the heavens were made;
by the breath of his mouth all their host.
He gathers the waters of the sea as in a flask;
in cellars he confines the deep.

℟. The earth is full of the goodness of the Lord.

Blessed the nation whose God is the LORD,
the people he has chosen for his own inheritance.
From heaven the LORD looks down;
he sees all mankind.

℟. The earth is full of the goodness of the Lord.

Our soul waits for the LORD,
who is our help and our shield.
May your kindness, O LORD, be upon us
who have put our hope in you.

℟. The earth is full of the goodness of the Lord.

SECOND READING
Gen 22:1-18

God put Abraham to the test.
He called to him, "Abraham!"
"Here I am," he replied.
Then God said:
"Take your son Isaac, your only one, whom you love,
and go to the land of Moriah.
There you shall offer him up as a holocaust
on a height that I will point out to you."
Early the next morning Abraham saddled his donkey,
took with him his son Isaac and two of his servants as well,
and with the wood that he had cut for the holocaust,
set out for the place of which God had told him.

On the third day Abraham got sight of the place from afar.
Then he said to his servants:
"Both of you stay here with the donkey,
while the boy and I go on over yonder.
We will worship and then come back to you."
Thereupon Abraham took the wood for the holocaust
and laid it on his son Isaac's shoulders,
while he himself carried the fire and the knife.
As the two walked on together, Isaac spoke to his father Abraham:
"Father!" Isaac said.
"Yes, son," he replied.
Isaac continued, "Here are the fire and the wood,
but where is the sheep for the holocaust?"
"Son," Abraham answered,
"God himself will provide the sheep for the holocaust."
Then the two continued going forward.

When they came to the place of which God had told him,
Abraham built an altar there and arranged the wood on it.
Next he tied up his son Isaac,
and put him on top of the wood on the altar.
Then he reached out and took the knife to slaughter his son.
But the LORD's messenger called to him from heaven,
"Abraham, Abraham!"
"Here I am," he answered.
"Do not lay your hand on the boy," said the messenger.
"Do not do the least thing to him.
I know now how devoted you are to God,
since you did not withhold from me your own beloved son."
As Abraham looked about,
he spied a ram caught by its horns in the thicket.
So he went and took the ram
and offered it up as a holocaust in place of his son.
Abraham named the site Yahweh-yireh;
hence people now say, "On the mountain the LORD will see."

Again the LORD's messenger called to Abraham from heaven and said:
"I swear by myself, declares the LORD,
that because you acted as you did
in not withholding from me your beloved son,
I will bless you abundantly
and make your descendants as countless
as the stars of the sky and the sands of the seashore;
your descendants shall take possession
of the gates of their enemies,
and in your descendants all the nations of the earth
shall find blessing—
all this because you obeyed my command."

or

Gen 22:1-2, 9a, 10-13, 15-18

God put Abraham to the test.
He called to him, "Abraham!"
"Here I am," he replied.
Then God said:
"Take your son Isaac, your only one, whom you love,
and go to the land of Moriah.
There you shall offer him up as a holocaust
on a height that I will point out to you."

When they came to the place of which God had told him,
Abraham built an altar there and arranged the wood on it.
Then he reached out and took the knife to slaughter his son.

But the LORD's messenger called to him from heaven,
"Abraham, Abraham!"
"Here I am," he answered.
"Do not lay your hand on the boy," said the messenger.
"Do not do the least thing to him.
I know now how devoted you are to God,
since you did not withhold from me your own beloved son."
As Abraham looked about,
he spied a ram caught by its horns in the thicket.
So he went and took the ram
and offered it up as a holocaust in place of his son.

Again the LORD's messenger called to Abraham from heaven and said:
"I swear by myself, declares the LORD,
that because you acted as you did
in not withholding from me your beloved son,
I will bless you abundantly
and make your descendants as countless
as the stars of the sky and the sands of the seashore;
your descendants shall take possession
of the gates of their enemies,
and in your descendants all the nations of the earth
shall find blessing—
all this because you obeyed my command."

RESPONSORIAL PSALM
Ps 16:5, 8, 9-10, 11

℟. (1) You are my inheritance, O Lord.

O LORD, my allotted portion and my cup,
you it is who hold fast my lot.
I set the LORD ever before me;
with him at my right hand I shall not be disturbed.

℟. You are my inheritance, O Lord.

Therefore my heart is glad and my soul rejoices,
my body, too, abides in confidence;
because you will not abandon my soul to the netherworld,
nor will you suffer your faithful one to undergo corruption.

℟. You are my inheritance, O Lord.

You will show me the path to life,
fullness of joys in your presence,
the delights at your right hand forever.

℟. You are my inheritance, O Lord.

THIRD READING
Exod 14:15–15:1

The LORD said to Moses, "Why are you crying out to me?
Tell the Israelites to go forward.
And you, lift up your staff and, with hand outstretched over the sea,
split the sea in two,
that the Israelites may pass through it on dry land.
But I will make the Egyptians so obstinate
that they will go in after them.
Then I will receive glory through Pharaoh and all his army,
his chariots and charioteers.
The Egyptians shall know that I am the LORD,
when I receive glory through Pharaoh
and his chariots and charioteers."

The angel of God, who had been leading Israel's camp,
now moved and went around behind them.
The column of cloud also, leaving the front,
took up its place behind them,
so that it came between the camp of the Egyptians
and that of Israel.
But the cloud now became dark, and thus the night passed
without the rival camps coming any closer together all night long.
Then Moses stretched out his hand over the sea,
and the LORD swept the sea
with a strong east wind throughout the night
and so turned it into dry land.
When the water was thus divided,
the Israelites marched into the midst of the sea on dry land,
with the water like a wall to their right and to their left.

The Egyptians followed in pursuit;
all Pharaoh's horses and chariots and charioteers went after them
right into the midst of the sea.
In the night watch just before dawn
the LORD cast through the column of the fiery cloud
upon the Egyptian force a glance that threw it into a panic;
and he so clogged their chariot wheels
that they could hardly drive.
With that the Egyptians sounded the retreat before Israel,
because the LORD was fighting for them against the Egyptians.

Then the LORD told Moses, "Stretch out your hand over the sea,
that the water may flow back upon the Egyptians,
upon their chariots and their charioteers."
So Moses stretched out his hand over the sea,
and at dawn the sea flowed back to its normal depth.
The Egyptians were fleeing head on toward the sea,
when the LORD hurled them into its midst.
As the water flowed back,
it covered the chariots and the charioteers of Pharaoh's whole army
which had followed the Israelites into the sea.
Not a single one of them escaped.
But the Israelites had marched on dry land
through the midst of the sea,
with the water like a wall to their right and to their left.
Thus the LORD saved Israel on that day
from the power of the Egyptians.
When Israel saw the Egyptians lying dead on the seashore
and beheld the great power that the LORD
had shown against the Egyptians,
they feared the LORD and believed in him
and in his servant Moses.

Then Moses and the Israelites sang this song to the LORD:
I will sing to the LORD, for he is gloriously triumphant;
horse and chariot he has cast into the sea.

RESPONSORIAL PSALM
Exod 15:1-2, 3-4, 5-6, 17-18

℟. (1b) Let us sing to the Lord; he has covered himself in glory.

I will sing to the LORD, for he is gloriously triumphant;
horse and chariot he has cast into the sea.
My strength and my courage is the LORD,
and he has been my savior.
He is my God, I praise him;
the God of my father, I extol him.

℟. Let us sing to the Lord; he has covered himself in glory.

The LORD is a warrior,
LORD is his name!
Pharaoh's chariots and army he hurled into the sea;
the elite of his officers were submerged in the Red Sea.

℟. Let us sing to the Lord; he has covered himself in glory.

The flood waters covered them,
they sank into the depths like a stone.
Your right hand, O LORD, magnificent in power,
your right hand, O LORD, has shattered the enemy.

℟. Let us sing to the Lord; he has covered himself in glory.

You brought in the people you redeemed
and planted them on the mountain of your inheritance—
the place where you made your seat, O LORD,
the sanctuary, LORD, which your hands established.
The LORD shall reign forever and ever.

℟. Let us sing to the Lord; he has covered himself in glory.

FOURTH READING
Isa 54:5-14

The One who has become your husband is your Maker;
his name is the LORD of hosts;
your redeemer is the Holy One of Israel,
called God of all the earth.
The LORD calls you back,
like a wife forsaken and grieved in spirit,
a wife married in youth and then cast off,
says your God.
For a brief moment I abandoned you,
but with great tenderness I will take you back.
In an outburst of wrath, for a moment
I hid my face from you;
but with enduring love I take pity on you,
says the LORD, your redeemer.
This is for me like the days of Noah,
when I swore that the waters of Noah
should never again deluge the earth;
so I have sworn not to be angry with you,
or to rebuke you.
Though the mountains leave their place
and the hills be shaken,
my love shall never leave you
nor my covenant of peace be shaken,
says the LORD, who has mercy on you.
O afflicted one, storm-battered and unconsoled,
I lay your pavements in carnelians,
and your foundations in sapphires;
I will make your battlements of rubies,
your gates of carbuncles,
and all your walls of precious stones.
All your children shall be taught by the LORD,
and great shall be the peace of your children.
In justice shall you be established,
far from the fear of oppression,
where destruction cannot come near you.

RESPONSORIAL PSALM
Ps 30:2, 4, 5-6, 11-12, 13

℟. (2a) I will praise you, Lord, for you have rescued me.

I will extol you, O LORD, for you drew me clear
and did not let my enemies rejoice over me.
O LORD, you brought me up from the netherworld;
you preserved me from among those going down into the pit.

℟. I will praise you, Lord, for you have rescued me.

Sing praise to the LORD, you his faithful ones,
and give thanks to his holy name.
For his anger lasts but a moment;
a lifetime, his good will.
At nightfall, weeping enters in,
but with the dawn, rejoicing.

℟. I will praise you, Lord, for you have rescued me.

Hear, O LORD, and have pity on me;
O LORD, be my helper.
You changed my mourning into dancing;
O LORD, my God, forever will I give you thanks.

℟. I will praise you, Lord, for you have rescued me.

FIFTH READING
Isa 55:1-11

Thus says the LORD:
All you who are thirsty,
come to the water!
You who have no money,
come, receive grain and eat;
come, without paying and without cost,
drink wine and milk!
Why spend your money for what is not bread,
your wages for what fails to satisfy?
Heed me, and you shall eat well,
you shall delight in rich fare.
Come to me heedfully,
listen, that you may have life.
I will renew with you the everlasting covenant,
the benefits assured to David.
As I made him a witness to the peoples,
a leader and commander of nations,
so shall you summon a nation you knew not,
and nations that knew you not shall run to you,
because of the LORD, your God,
the Holy One of Israel, who has glorified you.

Seek the LORD while he may be found,
call him while he is near.
Let the scoundrel forsake his way,
and the wicked man his thoughts;
let him turn to the LORD for mercy;
to our God, who is generous in forgiving.
For my thoughts are not your thoughts,
nor are your ways my ways, says the LORD.
As high as the heavens are above the earth,
so high are my ways above your ways
and my thoughts above your thoughts.

For just as from the heavens
the rain and snow come down
and do not return there
till they have watered the earth,
making it fertile and fruitful,
giving seed to the one who sows
and bread to the one who eats,
so shall my word be
that goes forth from my mouth;
my word shall not return to me void,
but shall do my will,
achieving the end for which I sent it.

RESPONSORIAL PSALM
Isa 12:2-3, 4, 5-6

℟. (3) You will draw water joyfully from the springs of salvation.

God indeed is my savior;
I am confident and unafraid.
My strength and my courage is the LORD,
and he has been my savior.
With joy you will draw water
at the fountain of salvation.

℟. You will draw water joyfully from the springs of salvation.

Give thanks to the LORD, acclaim his name;
among the nations make known his deeds,
proclaim how exalted is his name.

℟. You will draw water joyfully from the springs of salvation.

Sing praise to the LORD for his glorious achievement;
let this be known throughout all the earth.
Shout with exultation, O city of Zion,
for great in your midst
is the Holy One of Israel!

℟. You will draw water joyfully from the springs of salvation.

SIXTH READING
Bar 3:9-15, 32–4:4

Hear, O Israel, the commandments of life:
listen, and know prudence!
How is it, Israel,
that you are in the land of your foes,
grown old in a foreign land,
defiled with the dead,
accounted with those destined for the netherworld?
You have forsaken the fountain of wisdom!
Had you walked in the way of God,
you would have dwelt in enduring peace.
Learn where prudence is,
where strength, where understanding;
that you may know also
where are length of days, and life,
where light of the eyes, and peace.
Who has found the place of wisdom,
who has entered into her treasuries?

The One who knows all things knows her;
he has probed her by his knowledge—
the One who established the earth for all time,
and filled it with four-footed beasts;
he who dismisses the light, and it departs,
calls it, and it obeys him trembling;
before whom the stars at their posts
shine and rejoice;
when he calls them, they answer, "Here we are!"
shining with joy for their Maker.
Such is our God;
no other is to be compared to him:
he has traced out the whole way of understanding,
and has given her to Jacob, his servant,
to Israel, his beloved son.

Since then she has appeared on earth,
and moved among people.
She is the book of the precepts of God,
the law that endures forever;
all who cling to her will live,
but those will die who forsake her.
Turn, O Jacob, and receive her:
walk by her light toward splendor.
Give not your glory to another,
your privileges to an alien race.
Blessed are we, O Israel;
for what pleases God is known to us!

RESPONSORIAL PSALM
Ps 19:8, 9, 10, 11

℟. (John 6:68c) Lord, you have the words of everlasting life.

The law of the LORD is perfect,
refreshing the soul;
the decree of the LORD is trustworthy,
giving wisdom to the simple.

℟. Lord, you have the words of everlasting life.

The precepts of the LORD are right,
rejoicing the heart;
the command of the LORD is clear,
enlightening the eye.

℟. Lord, you have the words of everlasting life.

The fear of the LORD is pure,
enduring forever;
the ordinances of the LORD are true,
all of them just.

℟. Lord, you have the words of everlasting life.

They are more precious than gold,
than a heap of purest gold;
sweeter also than syrup
or honey from the comb.

℟. Lord, you have the words of everlasting life.

SEVENTH READING
Ezek 36:16-17a, 18-28

The word of the LORD came to me, saying:
Son of man, when the house of Israel lived in their land,
they defiled it by their conduct and deeds.
Therefore I poured out my fury upon them
because of the blood that they poured out on the ground,
and because they defiled it with idols.
I scattered them among the nations,
dispersing them over foreign lands;
according to their conduct and deeds I judged them.
But when they came among the nations wherever they came,
they served to profane my holy name,
because it was said of them: "These are the people of the LORD,
yet they had to leave their land."
So I have relented because of my holy name
which the house of Israel profaned
among the nations where they came.
Therefore say to the house of Israel: Thus says the Lord GOD:
Not for your sakes do I act, house of Israel,
but for the sake of my holy name,
which you profaned among the nations to which you came.
I will prove the holiness of my great name,
profaned among the nations,
in whose midst you have profaned it.
Thus the nations shall know that I am the LORD, says the Lord GOD,
when in their sight I prove my holiness through you.
For I will take you away from among the nations,
gather you from all the foreign lands,
and bring you back to your own land.
I will sprinkle clean water upon you
to cleanse you from all your impurities,
and from all your idols I will cleanse you.
I will give you a new heart and place a new spirit within you,
taking from your bodies your stony hearts
and giving you natural hearts.
I will put my spirit within you and make you live by my statutes,
careful to observe my decrees.
You shall live in the land I gave your fathers;
you shall be my people, and I will be your God.

RESPONSORIAL PSALM
Ps 42:3, 5; 43:3, 4

℟. (42:2) Like a deer that longs for running streams, my soul longs for you, my God.

Athirst is my soul for God, the living God.
When shall I go and behold the face of God?

℟. Like a deer that longs for running streams, my soul longs for you, my God.

I went with the throng
and led them in procession to the house of God,
amid loud cries of joy and thanksgiving,
with the multitude keeping festival.

℟. Like a deer that longs for running streams, my soul longs for you, my God.

Send forth your light and your fidelity;
they shall lead me on
and bring me to your holy mountain,
to your dwelling-place.

℟. Like a deer that longs for running streams, my soul longs for you, my God.

Then will I go in to the altar of God,
the God of my gladness and joy;
then will I give you thanks upon the harp,
O God, my God!

℟. Like a deer that longs for running streams, my soul longs for you, my God.

or

Isa 12:2-3, 4bcd, 5-6

℟. (3) You will draw water joyfully from the springs of salvation.

God indeed is my savior;
I am confident and unafraid.
My strength and my courage is the LORD,
and he has been my savior.
With joy you will draw water
at the fountain of salvation.

℟. You will draw water joyfully from the springs of salvation.

Give thanks to the LORD, acclaim his name;
among the nations make known his deeds,
proclaim how exalted is his name.

℟. You will draw water joyfully from the springs of salvation.

Sing praise to the LORD for his glorious achievement;
let this be known throughout all the earth.
Shout with exultation, O city of Zion,
for great in your midst
is the Holy One of Israel!

℟. You will draw water joyfully from the springs of salvation.

or

Ps 51:12-13, 14-15, 18-19

℟. (12a) Create a clean heart in me, O God.

A clean heart create for me, O God,
and a steadfast spirit renew within me.
Cast me not out from your presence,
and your Holy Spirit take not from me.

℟. Create a clean heart in me, O God.

Give me back the joy of your salvation,
and a willing spirit sustain in me.
I will teach transgressors your ways,
and sinners shall return to you.

℟. Create a clean heart in me, O God.

For you are not pleased with sacrifices;
should I offer a holocaust, you would not accept it.
My sacrifice, O God, is a contrite spirit;
a heart contrite and humbled, O God, you will not spurn.

℟. Create a clean heart in me, O God.

EPISTLE
Rom 6:3-11

Brothers and sisters:
Are you unaware that we who were baptized into Christ Jesus
were baptized into his death?
We were indeed buried with him through baptism into death,
so that, just as Christ was raised from the dead
by the glory of the Father,
we too might live in newness of life.

For if we have grown into union with him through a death like his,
we shall also be united with him in the resurrection.
We know that our old self was crucified with him,
so that our sinful body might be done away with,
that we might no longer be in slavery to sin.
For a dead person has been absolved from sin.
If, then, we have died with Christ,
we believe that we shall also live with him.
We know that Christ, raised from the dead, dies no more;
death no longer has power over him.
As to his death, he died to sin once and for all;
as to his life, he lives for God.
Consequently, you too must think of yourselves as being dead to sin
and living for God in Christ Jesus.

RESPONSORIAL PSALM
Ps 118:1-2, 16-17, 22-23

℟. Alleluia, alleluia, alleluia.

Give thanks to the LORD, for he is good,
for his mercy endures forever.
Let the house of Israel say,
"His mercy endures forever."

℟. Alleluia, alleluia, alleluia.

The right hand of the LORD has struck with power;
the right hand of the LORD is exalted.
I shall not die, but live,
and declare the works of the LORD.

℟. Alleluia, alleluia, alleluia.

The stone which the builders rejected
has become the cornerstone.
By the LORD has this been done;
it is wonderful in our eyes.

℟. Alleluia, alleluia, alleluia.

Gospel

Matt 28:1-10; L41ABC

After the sabbath, as the first day of the week was dawning,
Mary Magdalene and the other Mary came to see the tomb.
And behold, there was a great earthquake;
for an angel of the Lord descended from heaven,
approached, rolled back the stone, and sat upon it.
His appearance was like lightning
and his clothing was white as snow.
The guards were shaken with fear of him
and became like dead men.
Then the angel said to the women in reply,
"Do not be afraid!
I know that you are seeking Jesus the crucified.
He is not here, for he has been raised just as he said.
Come and see the place where he lay.
Then go quickly and tell his disciples,
'He has been raised from the dead,
and he is going before you to Galilee;
there you will see him.'
Behold, I have told you."
Then they went away quickly from the tomb,
fearful yet overjoyed,
and ran to announce this to his disciples.
And behold, Jesus met them on their way and greeted them.
They approached, embraced his feet, and did him homage.
Then Jesus said to them, "Do not be afraid.
Go tell my brothers to go to Galilee,
and there they will see me."

or, at an afternoon or evening Mass

Gospel

Luke 24:13-35; L46A

That very day, the first day of the week,
two of Jesus' disciples were going
to a village seven miles from Jerusalem called Emmaus,
and they were conversing about all the things that had occurred.
And it happened that while they were conversing and debating,
Jesus himself drew near and walked with them,
but their eyes were prevented from recognizing him.
He asked them,
"What are you discussing as you walk along?"
They stopped, looking downcast.
One of them, named Cleopas, said to him in reply,
"Are you the only visitor to Jerusalem
who does not know of the things
that have taken place there in these days?"
And he replied to them, "What sort of things?"
They said to him,
"The things that happened to Jesus the Nazarene,
who was a prophet mighty in deed and word
before God and all the people,
how our chief priests and rulers both handed him over
to a sentence of death and crucified him.
But we were hoping that he would be the one to redeem Israel;
and besides all this,
it is now the third day since this took place.
Some women from our group, however, have astounded us:
they were at the tomb early in the morning
and did not find his body;
they came back and reported
that they had indeed seen a vision of angels
who announced that he was alive.
Then some of those with us went to the tomb
and found things just as the women had described,
but him they did not see."
And he said to them, "Oh, how foolish you are!
How slow of heart to believe all that the prophets spoke!
Was it not necessary that the Christ should suffer these things
and enter into his glory?"
Then beginning with Moses and all the prophets,
he interpreted to them what referred to him
in all the Scriptures.
As they approached the village to which they were going,
he gave the impression that he was going on farther.
But they urged him, "Stay with us,
for it is nearly evening and the day is almost over."
So he went in to stay with them.
And it happened that, while he was with them at table,
he took bread, said the blessing,
broke it, and gave it to them.
With that their eyes were opened and they recognized him,
but he vanished from their sight.
Then they said to each other,
"Were not our hearts burning within us
while he spoke to us on the way and opened the Scriptures to us?"
So they set out at once and returned to Jerusalem
where they found gathered together
the eleven and those with them who were saying,
"The Lord has truly been raised and has appeared to Simon!"
Then the two recounted
what had taken place on the way
and how he was made known to them in the breaking of bread.

FIRST READING
Acts 10:34a, 37-43

Peter proceeded to speak and said:
"You know what has happened all over Judea,
beginning in Galilee after the baptism
that John preached,
how God anointed Jesus of Nazareth
with the Holy Spirit and power.
He went about doing good
and healing all those oppressed by the devil,
for God was with him.
We are witnesses of all that he did
both in the country of the Jews and in Jerusalem.
They put him to death by hanging him on a tree.
This man God raised on the third day and granted that he be visible,
not to all the people, but to us,
the witnesses chosen by God in advance,
who ate and drank with him after he rose from the dead.
He commissioned us to preach to the people
and testify that he is the one appointed by God
as judge of the living and the dead.
To him all the prophets bear witness,
that everyone who believes in him
will receive forgiveness of sins through his name."

RESPONSORIAL PSALM
Ps 118:1-2, 16-17, 22-23

℟. (24) This is the day the Lord has made; let us rejoice and be glad.
or:
℟. Alleluia.

Give thanks to the LORD, for he is good,
for his mercy endures forever.
Let the house of Israel say,
"His mercy endures forever."

℟. This is the day the Lord has made; let us rejoice and be glad.
or:
℟. Alleluia.

"The right hand of the LORD has struck with power;
the right hand of the LORD is exalted.
I shall not die, but live,
and declare the works of the LORD."

℟. This is the day the Lord has made; let us rejoice and be glad.
or:
℟. Alleluia.

The stone which the builders rejected
has become the cornerstone.
By the LORD has this been done;
it is wonderful in our eyes.

℟. This is the day the Lord has made; let us rejoice and be glad.
or:
℟. Alleluia.

SECOND READING

Col 3:1-4

Brothers and sisters:
If then you were raised with Christ, seek what is above,
where Christ is seated at the right hand of God.
Think of what is above, not of what is on earth.
For you have died, and your life is hidden with Christ in God.
When Christ your life appears,
then you too will appear with him in glory.

or
1 Cor 5:6b-8

Brothers and sisters:
Do you not know that a little yeast leavens all the dough?
Clear out the old yeast,
so that you may become a fresh batch of dough,
inasmuch as you are unleavened.
For our paschal lamb, Christ, has been sacrificed.
Therefore, let us celebrate the feast,
not with the old yeast, the yeast of malice and wickedness,
but with the unleavened bread of sincerity and truth.

SEQUENCE

Victimae paschali laudes
Christians, to the Paschal Victim
Offer your thankful praises!
A Lamb the sheep redeems;
Christ, who only is sinless,
Reconciles sinners to the Father.
Death and life have contended in that combat stupendous:
The Prince of life, who died, reigns immortal.
Speak, Mary, declaring
What you saw, wayfaring.
"The tomb of Christ, who is living,
The glory of Jesus' resurrection;
Bright angels attesting,
The shroud and napkin resting.
Yes, Christ my hope is arisen;
To Galilee he goes before you."
Christ indeed from death is risen, our new life obtaining.
Have mercy, victor King, ever reigning!
Amen. Alleluia.

Second Sunday of Easter (or of Divine Mercy), April 19, 2020

Gospel (cont.)
John 20:19-31; L43A

Then he said to Thomas, "Put your finger here and see my hands,
and bring your hand and put it into my side,
and do not be unbelieving, but believe."
Thomas answered and said to him, "My Lord and my God!"
Jesus said to him, "Have you come to believe because you have seen me?
Blessed are those who have not seen and have believed."

Now Jesus did many other signs in the presence of his disciples
that are not written in this book.
But these are written that you may come to believe
that Jesus is the Christ, the Son of God,
and that through this belief you may have life in his name.

Third Sunday of Easter, *April 26, 2020*

Gospel (cont.)

Luke 24:13-35; L46A

But we were hoping that he would be the one to redeem Israel;
and besides all this,
it is now the third day since this took place.
Some women from our group, however, have astounded us:
they were at the tomb early in the morning
and did not find his body;
they came back and reported
that they had indeed seen a vision of angels
who announced that he was alive.
Then some of those with us went to the tomb
and found things just as the women had described,
but him they did not see."
And he said to them, "Oh, how foolish you are!
How slow of heart to believe all that the prophets spoke!
Was it not necessary that the Christ should suffer these things
and enter into his glory?"
Then beginning with Moses and all the prophets,
he interpreted to them what referred to him
in all the Scriptures.
As they approached the village to which they were going,
he gave the impression that he was going on farther.
But they urged him, "Stay with us,
for it is nearly evening and the day is almost over."
So he went in to stay with them.
And it happened that, while he was with them at table,
he took bread, said the blessing,
broke it, and gave it to them.
With that their eyes were opened and they recognized him,
but he vanished from their sight.
Then they said to each other,
"Were not our hearts burning within us
while he spoke to us on the way and opened the Scriptures to us?"
So they set out at once and returned to Jerusalem
where they found gathered together
the eleven and those with them who were saying,
"The Lord has truly been raised and has appeared to Simon!"
Then the two recounted
what had taken place on the way
and how he was made known to them in the breaking of bread.

SECOND READING

1 Pet 1:17-21

Beloved:
If you invoke as Father him who judges impartially
according to each one's works,
conduct yourselves with reverence during the time of your sojourning,
realizing that you were ransomed from your futile conduct,
handed on by your ancestors,
not with perishable things like silver or gold
but with the precious blood of Christ
as of a spotless unblemished lamb.

He was known before the foundation of the world
but revealed in the final time for you,
who through him believe in God
who raised him from the dead and gave him glory,
so that your faith and hope are in God.

Fifth Sunday of Easter, *May 10, 2020*

Gospel (cont.)

John 14:1-12; L52A

The words that I speak to you I do not speak on my own.
The Father who dwells in me is doing his works.
Believe me that I am in the Father and the Father is in me,
or else, believe because of the works themselves.
Amen, amen, I say to you,
whoever believes in me will do the works that I do,
and will do greater ones than these,
because I am going to the Father."

The Ascension of the Lord, *May 21 (Thursday) or May 24, 2020*

SECOND READING Eph 1:17-23

Brothers and sisters:
May the God of our Lord Jesus Christ, the Father of glory,
give you a Spirit of wisdom and revelation
resulting in knowledge of him.
May the eyes of your hearts be enlightened,
that you may know what is the hope that belongs to his call,
what are the riches of glory
in his inheritance among the holy ones,
and what is the surpassing greatness of his power
for us who believe,
in accord with the exercise of his great might,
which he worked in Christ,
raising him from the dead
and seating him at his right hand in the heavens,
far above every principality, authority, power, and dominion,
and every name that is named
not only in this age but also in the one to come.
And he put all things beneath his feet
and gave him as head over all things to the church,
which is his body,
the fullness of the one who fills all things in every way.

Pentecost Sunday, *May 31, 2020*

SEQUENCE

Veni, Sancte Spiritus

Come, Holy Spirit, come!
And from your celestial home
  Shed a ray of light divine!
Come, Father of the poor!
Come, source of all our store!
  Come, within our bosoms shine.
You, of comforters the best;
You, the soul's most welcome guest;
  Sweet refreshment here below;
In our labor, rest most sweet;
Grateful coolness in the heat;
  Solace in the midst of woe.
O most blessed Light divine,
Shine within these hearts of yours,
  And our inmost being fill!
Where you are not, we have naught,
Nothing good in deed or thought,
  Nothing free from taint of ill.
Heal our wounds, our strength renew;
On our dryness pour your dew;
  Wash the stains of guilt away:
Bend the stubborn heart and will;
Melt the frozen, warm the chill;
  Guide the steps that go astray.
On the faithful, who adore
And confess you, evermore
  In your sevenfold gift descend;
Give them virtue's sure reward;
Give them your salvation, Lord;
  Give them joys that never end. Amen.
  Alleluia.

The Solemnity of the Most Holy Body and Blood of Christ, *June 14, 2020*

OPTIONAL SEQUENCE

Lauda Sion

Laud, O Zion, your salvation,
Laud with hymns of exultation,
  Christ, your king and shepherd true:

Bring him all the praise you know,
He is more than you bestow.
  Never can you reach his due.

Special theme for glad thanksgiving
Is the quick'ning and the living
  Bread today before you set:

From his hands of old partaken,
As we know, by faith unshaken,
  Where the Twelve at supper met.

Full and clear ring out your chanting,
Joy nor sweetest grace be wanting,
  From your heart let praises burst:

For today the feast is holden,
When the institution olden
  Of that supper was rehearsed.

Here the new law's new oblation,
By the new king's revelation,
  Ends the form of ancient rite:

Now the new the old effaces,
Truth away the shadow chases,
  Light dispels the gloom of night.

What he did at supper seated,
Christ ordained to be repeated,
  His memorial ne'er to cease:

And his rule for guidance taking,
Bread and wine we hallow, making
  Thus our sacrifice of peace.

This the truth each Christian learns,
Bread into his flesh he turns,
  To his precious blood the wine:

Sight has fail'd, nor thought conceives,
But a dauntless faith believes,
  Resting on a pow'r divine.

Here beneath these signs are hidden
Priceless things to sense forbidden;
  Signs, not things are all we see:

Blood is poured and flesh is broken,
Yet in either wondrous token
  Christ entire we know to be.

Whoso of this food partakes,
Does not rend the Lord nor breaks;
  Christ is whole to all that taste:

Thousands are, as one, receivers,
One, as thousands of believers,
  Eats of him who cannot waste.

Bad and good the feast are sharing,
Of what divers dooms preparing,
  Endless death, or endless life.

Life to these, to those damnation,
See how like participation
  Is with unlike issues rife.

When the sacrament is broken,
Doubt not, but believe 'tis spoken,
  That each sever'd outward token
    doth the very whole contain.

Nought the precious gift divides,
Breaking but the sign betides
  Jesus still the same abides,
    still unbroken does remain.

The shorter form of the sequence begins here.

Lo! the angel's food is given
To the pilgrim who has striven;
  See the children's bread from heaven,
    which on dogs may not be spent.

Truth the ancient types fulfilling,
Isaac bound, a victim willing,
  Paschal lamb, its lifeblood spilling,
  manna to the fathers sent.

Very bread, good shepherd, tend us,
Jesu, of your love befriend us,
  You refresh us, you defend us,
  Your eternal goodness send us
In the land of life to see.

You who all things can and know,
Who on earth such food bestow,
  Grant us with your saints, though lowest,
  Where the heav'nly feast you show,
Fellow heirs and guests to be. Amen. Alleluia.

FIRST READING
Deut 7:6-11

Moses said to the people:
"You are a people sacred to the LORD, your God;
he has chosen you from all the nations on the face of the earth
to be a people peculiarly his own.
It was not because you are the largest of all nations
that the LORD set his heart on you and chose you,
for you are really the smallest of all nations.
It was because the LORD loved you
and because of his fidelity to the oath he had sworn to your fathers,
that he brought you out with his strong hand
from the place of slavery,
and ransomed you from the hand of Pharaoh, king of Egypt.
Understand, then, that the LORD, your God, is God indeed,
the faithful God who keeps his merciful covenant
down to the thousandth generation
toward those who love him and keep his commandments,
but who repays with destruction a person who hates him;
he does not dally with such a one,
but makes them personally pay for it.
You shall therefore carefully observe the commandments,
the statutes and the decrees that I enjoin on you today."

RESPONSORIAL PSALM
Ps 103:1-2, 3-4, 6, 8, 10

℟. (cf. 17) The Lord's kindness is everlasting to those who fear him.

Bless the LORD, O my soul;
all my being, bless his holy name.
Bless the LORD, O my soul;
and forget not all his benefits.

℟. The Lord's kindness is everlasting to those who fear him.

He pardons all your iniquities,
heals all your ills.
He redeems your life from destruction,
crowns you with kindness and compassion.

℟. The Lord's kindness is everlasting to those who fear him.

Merciful and gracious is the LORD,
slow to anger and abounding in kindness.
Not according to our sins does he deal with us,
nor does he requite us according to our crimes.

℟. The Lord's kindness is everlasting to those who fear him.

SECOND READING
1 John 4:7-16

Beloved, let us love one another,
because love is of God;
everyone who loves is begotten by God and knows God.
Whoever is without love does not know God,
for God is love.
In this way the love of God was revealed to us:
God sent his only Son into the world
so that we might have life through him.
In this is love:
not that we have loved God, but that he loved us
and sent his Son as expiation for our sins.
Beloved, if God so loved us,
we also must love one another.
No one has ever seen God.
Yet, if we love one another, God remains in us,
and his love is brought to perfection in us.

This is how we know that we remain in him and he in us,
that he has given us of his Spirit.
Moreover, we have seen and testify
that the Father sent his Son as savior of the world.
Whoever acknowledges that Jesus is the Son of God,
God remains in him and he in God.
We have come to know and to believe in the love God has for us.

God is love, and whoever remains in love
remains in God and God in him.

Gospel (cont.)

Luke 1:57-66, 80; L587

He asked for a tablet and wrote, "John is his name,"
and all were amazed.
Immediately his mouth was opened, his tongue freed,
and he spoke blessing God.
Then fear came upon all their neighbors,
and all these matters were discussed
throughout the hill country of Judea.
All who heard these things took them to heart, saying,
"What, then, will this child be?"
For surely the hand of the Lord was with him.

The child grew and became strong in spirit,
and he was in the desert until the day
of his manifestation to Israel.

FIRST READING

Isa 49:1-6

Hear me, O coastlands,
listen, O distant peoples.
The LORD called me from birth,
from my mother's womb he gave me my name.
He made of me a sharp-edged sword
and concealed me in the shadow of his arm.
He made me a polished arrow,
in his quiver he hid me.
You are my servant, he said to me,
Israel, through whom I show my glory.

Though I thought I had toiled in vain,
and for nothing, uselessly, spent my strength,
yet my reward is with the LORD,
my recompense is with my God.
For now the LORD has spoken
who formed me as his servant from the womb,
that Jacob may be brought back to him
and Israel gathered to him;
and I am made glorious in the sight of the LORD,
and my God is now my strength!
It is too little, he says, for you to be my servant,
to raise up the tribes of Jacob,
and restore the survivors of Israel;
I will make you a light to the nations,
that my salvation may reach to the ends of the earth.

RESPONSORIAL PSALM

Ps 139:1b-3, 13-14ab, 14c-15

℟. (14a) I praise you, for I am wonderfully made.

O LORD, you have probed me, you know me;
you know when I sit and when I stand;
you understand my thoughts from afar.
My journeys and my rest you scrutinize,
with all my ways you are familiar.

℟. I praise you, for I am wonderfully made.

Truly you have formed my inmost being;
you knit me in my mother's womb.
I give you thanks that I am fearfully, wonderfully made;
wonderful are your works.

℟. I praise you, for I am wonderfully made.

My soul also you knew full well;
nor was my frame unknown to you
When I was made in secret,
when I was fashioned in the depths of the earth.

℟. I praise you, for I am wonderfully made.

SECOND READING

Acts 13:22-26

In those days, Paul said:
"God raised up David as their king;
of him God testified,
I have found David, son of Jesse, a man after my own heart;
he will carry out my every wish.
From this man's descendants God, according to his promise,
has brought to Israel a savior, Jesus.
John heralded his coming by proclaiming a baptism of repentance
to all the people of Israel;
and as John was completing his course, he would say,
'What do you suppose that I am? I am not he.
Behold, one is coming after me;
I am not worthy to unfasten the sandals of his feet.'

"My brothers, sons of the family of Abraham,
and those others among you who are God-fearing,
to us this word of salvation has been sent."

Gospel (cont.)

Matt 16:13-19; L591

And so I say to you, you are Peter,
and upon this rock I will build my Church,
and the gates of the netherworld shall not prevail against it.
I will give you the keys to the Kingdom of heaven.
Whatever you bind on earth shall be bound in heaven;
and whatever you loose on earth shall be loosed in heaven."

FIRST READING

Acts 12:1-11

In those days, King Herod laid hands upon some members of the Church to harm them.
He had James, the brother of John, killed by the sword,
and when he saw that this was pleasing to the Jews
he proceeded to arrest Peter also.
—It was the feast of Unleavened Bread.—
He had him taken into custody and put in prison
under the guard of four squads of four soldiers each.
He intended to bring him before the people after Passover.
Peter thus was being kept in prison,
but prayer by the Church was fervently being made
to God on his behalf.

On the very night before Herod was to bring him to trial,
Peter, secured by double chains,
was sleeping between two soldiers,
while outside the door guards kept watch on the prison.
Suddenly the angel of the Lord stood by him,
and a light shone in the cell.
He tapped Peter on the side and awakened him, saying,
"Get up quickly."
The chains fell from his wrists.
The angel said to him, "Put on your belt and your sandals."
He did so.
Then he said to him, "Put on your cloak and follow me."
So he followed him out,
not realizing that what was happening through the angel was real;
he thought he was seeing a vision.
They passed the first guard, then the second,
and came to the iron gate leading out to the city,
which opened for them by itself.
They emerged and made their way down an alley,
and suddenly the angel left him.
Then Peter recovered his senses and said,
"Now I know for certain
that the Lord sent his angel
and rescued me from the hand of Herod
and from all that the Jewish people had been expecting."

RESPONSORIAL PSALM

Ps 34:2-3, 4-5, 6-7, 8-9

℟. (8) The angel of the Lord will rescue those who fear him.

I will bless the LORD at all times;
his praise shall be ever in my mouth.
Let my soul glory in the LORD;
the lowly will hear me and be glad.

℟. The angel of the Lord will rescue those who fear him.

Glorify the LORD with me,
let us together extol his name.
I sought the LORD, and he answered me
and delivered me from all my fears.

℟. The angel of the Lord will rescue those who fear him.

Look to him that you may be radiant with joy,
and your faces may not blush with shame.
When the poor one called out, the LORD heard,
and from all his distress he saved him.

℟. The angel of the Lord will rescue those who fear him.

The angel of the LORD encamps
around those who fear him, and delivers them.
Taste and see how good the LORD is;
blessed the man who takes refuge in him.

℟. The angel of the Lord will rescue those who fear him.

SECOND READING

2 Tim 4:6-8, 17-18

I, Paul, am already being poured out like a libation,
and the time of my departure is at hand.
I have competed well; I have finished the race;
I have kept the faith.
From now on the crown of righteousness awaits me,
which the Lord, the just judge,
will award to me on that day, and not only to me,
but to all who have longed for his appearance.

The Lord stood by me and gave me strength,
so that through me the proclamation might be completed
and all the Gentiles might hear it.
And I was rescued from the lion's mouth.
The Lord will rescue me from every evil threat
and will bring me safe to his heavenly Kingdom.
To him be glory forever and ever. Amen.

Gospel (cont.)

Matt 13:1-23; L103A

This is why I speak to them in parables, because
they look but do not see and hear but do not listen or understand.

Isaiah's prophecy is fulfilled in them, which says:
You shall indeed hear but not understand,
you shall indeed look but never see.
Gross is the heart of this people,
they will hardly hear with their ears,
they have closed their eyes,
lest they see with their eyes
and hear with their ears
and understand with their hearts and be converted,
and I heal them.

"But blessed are your eyes, because they see,
and your ears, because they hear.
Amen, I say to you, many prophets and righteous people
longed to see what you see but did not see it,
and to hear what you hear but did not hear it.

"Hear then the parable of the sower.
The seed sown on the path is the one
who hears the word of the kingdom without understanding it,
and the evil one comes and steals away
what was sown in his heart.
The seed sown on rocky ground
is the one who hears the word and receives it at once with joy.
But he has no root and lasts only for a time.
When some tribulation or persecution comes because of the word,
he immediately falls away.
The seed sown among thorns is the one who hears the word,
but then worldly anxiety and the lure of riches choke the word
and it bears no fruit.
But the seed sown on rich soil
is the one who hears the word and understands it,
who indeed bears fruit and yields a hundred or sixty or thirtyfold."

or Matt 13:1-9

On that day, Jesus went out of the house and sat down by the sea.
Such large crowds gathered around him
that he got into a boat and sat down,
and the whole crowd stood along the shore.
And he spoke to them at length in parables, saying:
"A sower went out to sow.
And as he sowed, some seed fell on the path,
and birds came and ate it up.
Some fell on rocky ground, where it had little soil.
It sprang up at once because the soil was not deep,
and when the sun rose it was scorched,
and it withered for lack of roots.
Some seed fell among thorns, and the thorns grew up and choked it.
But some seed fell on rich soil, and produced fruit,
a hundred or sixty or thirtyfold.
Whoever has ears ought to hear."

Sixteenth Sunday in Ordinary Time, *July 19, 2020*

Gospel (cont.)

Matt 13:24-43; L106A

It becomes a large bush,
and the 'birds of the sky come and dwell in its branches.'"

He spoke to them another parable.
"The kingdom of heaven is like yeast
that a woman took and mixed with three measures of wheat flour
until the whole batch was leavened."

All these things Jesus spoke to the crowds in parables.
He spoke to them only in parables,
to fulfill what had been said through the prophet:
I will open my mouth in parables,
I will announce what has lain hidden from the foundation of the world.

Then, dismissing the crowds, he went into the house.
His disciples approached him and said,
"Explain to us the parable of the weeds in the field."
He said in reply, "He who sows good seed is the Son of Man,
the field is the world, the good seed the children of the kingdom.
The weeds are the children of the evil one,
and the enemy who sows them is the devil.
The harvest is the end of the age, and the harvesters are angels.
Just as weeds are collected and burned up with fire,
so will it be at the end of the age.
The Son of Man will send his angels,
and they will collect out of his kingdom
all who cause others to sin and all evildoers.
They will throw them into the fiery furnace,
where there will be wailing and grinding of teeth.
Then the righteous will shine like the sun
in the kingdom of their Father.
Whoever has ears ought to hear."

or Matt 13:24-30

Jesus proposed another parable to the crowds, saying:
"The kingdom of heaven may be likened
to a man who sowed good seed in his field.
While everyone was asleep his enemy came
and sowed weeds all through the wheat, and then went off.
When the crop grew and bore fruit, the weeds appeared as well.
The slaves of the householder came to him and said,
'Master, did you not sow good seed in your field?
Where have the weeds come from?'
He answered, 'An enemy has done this.'
His slaves said to him,
'Do you want us to go and pull them up?'
He replied, 'No, if you pull up the weeds
you might uproot the wheat along with them.
Let them grow together until harvest;
then at harvest time I will say to the harvesters,
"First collect the weeds and tie them in bundles for burning;
but gather the wheat into my barn."'"

Seventeenth Sunday in Ordinary Time, *July 26, 2020*

Gospel

Matt 13:44-46

Jesus said to his disciples:
"The kingdom of heaven is like a treasure buried in a field,
which a person finds and hides again,
and out of joy goes and sells all that he has and buys that field.
Again, the kingdom of heaven is like a merchant
searching for fine pearls.
When he finds a pearl of great price,
he goes and sells all that he has and buys it."

The Assumption of the Blessed Virgin Mary, August 15, 2020

Gospel (cont.)
Luke 1:39-56; L622

From this day all generations will call me blessed:
the Almighty has done great things for me,
and holy is his Name.
He has mercy on those who fear him
in every generation.
He has shown the strength of his arm,
and has scattered the proud in their conceit.
He has cast down the mighty from their thrones,
and has lifted up the lowly.
He has filled the hungry with good things,
and the rich he has sent away empty.
He has come to the help of his servant Israel
for he has remembered his promise of mercy,
the promise he made to our fathers,
to Abraham and his children forever."

Mary remained with her about three months
and then returned to her home.

FIRST READING
Rev 11:19a; 12:1-6a, 10ab

God's temple in heaven was opened,
and the ark of his covenant could be seen in the temple.

A great sign appeared in the sky, a woman clothed with the sun,
with the moon under her feet,
and on her head a crown of twelve stars.
She was with child and wailed aloud in pain
as she labored to give birth.
Then another sign appeared in the sky;
it was a huge red dragon, with seven heads and ten horns,
and on its heads were seven diadems.
Its tail swept away a third of the stars in the sky
and hurled them down to the earth.
Then the dragon stood before the woman about to give birth,
to devour her child when she gave birth.
She gave birth to a son, a male child,
destined to rule all the nations with an iron rod.
Her child was caught up to God and his throne.
The woman herself fled into the desert
where she had a place prepared by God.

Then I heard a loud voice in heaven say:
"Now have salvation and power come,
and the Kingdom of our God
and the authority of his Anointed One."

RESPONSORIAL PSALM
Ps 45:10, 11, 12, 16

℟. (10bc) The queen stands at your right hand, arrayed in gold.

The queen takes her place at your right hand in gold of Ophir.

℟. The queen stands at your right hand, arrayed in gold.

Hear, O daughter, and see; turn your ear,
forget your people and your father's house.

℟. The queen stands at your right hand, arrayed in gold.

So shall the king desire your beauty;
for he is your lord.

℟. The queen stands at your right hand, arrayed in gold.

They are borne in with gladness and joy;
they enter the palace of the king.

℟. The queen stands at your right hand, arrayed in gold.

SECOND READING
1 Cor 15:20-27

Brothers and sisters:
Christ has been raised from the dead,
the firstfruits of those who have fallen asleep.
For since death came through man,
the resurrection of the dead came also through man.
For just as in Adam all die,
so too in Christ shall all be brought to life,
but each one in proper order:
Christ the firstfruits;
then, at his coming, those who belong to Christ;
then comes the end,
when he hands over the Kingdom to his God and Father,
when he has destroyed every sovereignty
and every authority and power.
For he must reign until he has put all his enemies under his feet.
The last enemy to be destroyed is death,
for "he subjected everything under his feet."

Twenty-Fourth Sunday in Ordinary Time, September 13, 2020

Gospel (cont.)
Matt 18:21-35; L130A

He seized him and started to choke him, demanding,
'Pay back what you owe.'
Falling to his knees, his fellow servant begged him,
'Be patient with me, and I will pay you back.'
But he refused.
Instead, he had the fellow servant put in prison
until he paid back the debt.
Now when his fellow servants saw what had happened,
they were deeply disturbed, and went to their master
and reported the whole affair.
His master summoned him and said to him, 'You wicked servant!
I forgave you your entire debt because you begged me to.
Should you not have had pity on your fellow servant,
as I had pity on you?'
Then in anger his master handed him over to the torturers
until he should pay back the whole debt.
So will my heavenly Father do to you,
unless each of you forgives your brother from your heart."

Twenty-Fifth Sunday in Ordinary Time,
September 20 2020

Gospel (cont.)
Matt 20:1-16a; L133A

And on receiving it they grumbled against the landowner, saying,
'These last ones worked only one hour,
and you have made them equal to us,
who bore the day's burden and the heat.'
He said to one of them in reply,
'My friend, I am not cheating you.
Did you not agree with me for the usual daily wage?
Take what is yours and go.
What if I wish to give this last one the same as you?
Or am I not free to do as I wish with my own money?
Are you envious because I am generous?'
Thus, the last will be first, and the first will be last."

Twenty-Sixth Sunday in Ordinary Time,
September 27 2020

SECOND READING
Phil 2:1-5

Brothers and sisters:
If there is any encouragement in Christ,
any solace in love,
any participation in the Spirit,
any compassion and mercy,
complete my joy by being of the same mind, with the same love,
united in heart, thinking one thing.
Do nothing out of selfishness or out of vainglory;
rather, humbly regard others as more important than yourselves,
each looking out not for his own interests,
but also for those of others.

Have in you the same attitude
that is also in Christ Jesus.

Twenty-Seventh Sunday in Ordinary Time,
October 48, 2020

Gospel (cont.)
Matt 21:33-43; L139A

Jesus said to them, "Did you never read in the Scriptures:
The stone that the builders rejected
has become the cornerstone;
by the Lord has this been done,
and it is wonderful in our eyes?
Therefore, I say to you,
the kingdom of God will be taken away from you
and given to a people that will produce its fruit."

Gospel (cont.)

Matt 22:1-14; L142A

But when the king came in to meet the guests,
he saw a man there not dressed in a wedding garment.
The king said to him, 'My friend, how is it
that you came in here without a wedding garment?'
But he was reduced to silence.
Then the king said to his attendants, 'Bind his hands and feet,
and cast him into the darkness outside,
where there will be wailing and grinding of teeth.'
Many are invited, but few are chosen."

or Matt 22:1-10

Jesus again in reply spoke to the chief priests and elders of the people
in parables, saying,
"The kingdom of heaven may be likened to a king
who gave a wedding feast for his son.
He dispatched his servants
to summon the invited guests to the feast,
but they refused to come.
A second time he sent other servants, saying,
'Tell those invited: "Behold, I have prepared my banquet,
my calves and fattened cattle are killed,
and everything is ready; come to the feast."'
Some ignored the invitation and went away,
one to his farm, another to his business.
The rest laid hold of his servants,
mistreated them, and killed them.
The king was enraged and sent his troops,
destroyed those murderers, and burned their city.
Then he said to his servants, 'The feast is ready,
but those who were invited were not worthy to come.
Go out, therefore, into the main roads
and invite to the feast whomever you find.'
The servants went out into the streets
and gathered all they found, bad and good alike,
and the hall was filled with guests."

All Souls, November 2, 2020

FIRST READING

Dan 12:1-3; L1011.7

In those days, I, Daniel, mourned
and heard this word of the Lord:
At that time there shall arise
Michael, the great prince,
guardian of your people;
It shall be a time unsurpassed in distress
since nations began until that time.
At that time your people shall escape,
everyone who is found written in the book.

Many of those who sleep in the dust of the earth shall awake;
Some shall live forever,
others shall be an everlasting horror and disgrace.
But the wise shall shine brightly
like the splendor of the firmament,
And those who lead the many to justice
shall be like the stars forever.

RESPONSORIAL PSALM

Ps 27:1, 4, 7, and 8b, and 9a, 13-14; L1013.3

℟. (1a) The Lord is my light and my salvation.
or:
℟. (13) I believe that I shall see the good things of the Lord in the land of the living.

The LORD is my light and my salvation;
whom should I fear?
The LORD is my life's refuge;
of whom should I be afraid?

℟. The Lord is my light and my salvation.
or:
℟. I believe that I shall see the good things of the Lord in the land of the living.

One thing I ask of the LORD;
this I seek:
To dwell in the house of the LORD
all the days of my life,
That I may gaze on the loveliness of the LORD
and contemplate his temple.

℟. The Lord is my light and my salvation.
or:
℟. I believe that I shall see the good things of the Lord in the land of the living.

Hear, O LORD, the sound of my call;
have pity on me and answer me.
Your presence, O LORD, I seek.
Hide not your face from me.

℟. The Lord is my light and my salvation.
or:
℟. I believe that I shall see the good things of the Lord in the land of the living.

I believe that I shall see the bounty of the LORD
in the land of the living.
Wait for the LORD with courage;
be stouthearted, and wait for the LORD.

℟. The Lord is my light and my salvation.
or:
℟. I believe that I shall see the good things of the Lord in the land of the living.

SECOND READING

Rom 6:3-9; L1014.3

Brothers and sisters:
Are you unaware that we who were baptized into Christ Jesus
were baptized into his death?
We were indeed buried with him through baptism into death,
so that, just as Christ was raised from the dead
by the glory of the Father,
we too might live in newness of life.

For if we have grown into union with him through a death like his,
we shall also be united with him in the resurrection.
We know that our old self was crucified with him,
so that our sinful body might be done away with,
that we might no longer be in slavery to sin.
For a dead person has been absolved from sin.
If, then, we have died with Christ,
we believe that we shall also live with him.
We know that Christ, raised from the dead,
dies no more;
death no longer has power over him.

Thirty-Second Sunday in Ordinary Time, *November 8, 2020*

SECOND READING

1 Thess 4:13-14

We do not want you to be unaware, brothers and sisters,
about those who have fallen asleep,
so that you may not grieve like the rest, who have no hope.
For if we believe that Jesus died and rose,
so too will God, through Jesus,
bring with him those who have fallen asleep.

Thirty-Third Sunday in Ordinary Time, *November 15, 2020*

Gospel (cont.)

Matt 25:14-30; L157A

Since you were faithful in small matters,
I will give you great responsibilities.
Come, share your master's joy.'
Then the one who had received the one talent came forward and said,
'Master, I knew you were a demanding person,
harvesting where you did not plant
and gathering where you did not scatter;
so out of fear I went off and buried your talent in the ground.
Here it is back.'
His master said to him in reply, 'You wicked, lazy servant!
So you knew that I harvest where I did not plant
and gather where I did not scatter?
Should you not then have put my money in the bank
so that I could have got it back with interest on my return?
Now then! Take the talent from him and give it to the one with ten.
For to everyone who has,
more will be given and he will grow rich;
but from the one who has not,
even what he has will be taken away.
And throw this useless servant into the darkness outside,
where there will be wailing and grinding of teeth.'"

or Matt 25:14-15, 19-21

Jesus told his disciples this parable:
"A man going on a journey
called in his servants and entrusted his possessions to them.
To one he gave five talents; to another, two; to a third, one—
to each according to his ability.
Then he went away.

After a long time
the master of those servants came back
and settled accounts with them.
The one who had received five talents came forward
bringing the additional five.
He said, 'Master, you gave me five talents.
See, I have made five more.'
His master said to him, 'Well done, my good and faithful servant.
Since you were faithful in small matters,
I will give you great responsibilities.
Come, share your master's joy.'"

Gospel (cont.)

Matt 25:31-46; L160A

Then he will say to those on his left,
'Depart from me, you accursed,
into the eternal fire prepared for the devil and his angels.
For I was hungry and you gave me no food,
I was thirsty and you gave me no drink,
a stranger and you gave me no welcome,
naked and you gave me no clothing,
ill and in prison, and you did not care for me.'
Then they will answer and say,
'Lord, when did we see you hungry or thirsty
or a stranger or naked or ill or in prison,
and not minister to your needs?'
He will answer them, 'Amen, I say to you,
what you did not do for one of these least ones,
you did not do for me.'
And these will go off to eternal punishment,
but the righteous to eternal life."

Thanksgiving Day, November 26, 2020

(Other options can be found in the Lectionary for Mass, L943–947.)

FIRST READING

Sir 50:22-24; L943.2

And now, bless the God of all,
who has done wondrous things on earth;
Who fosters people's growth from their mother's womb,
and fashions them according to his will!
May he grant you joy of heart
and may peace abide among you;
May his goodness toward us endure in Israel
to deliver us in our days.

RESPONSORIAL PSALM

Ps 138:1-2a, 2bc-3, 4-5; L945.3

℟. (2bc) Lord, I thank you for your faithfulness and love.

I will give thanks to you, O Lord, with all of my heart,
for you have heard the words of my mouth;
in the presence of the angels I will sing your praise;
I will worship at your holy temple.

℟. Lord, I thank you for your faithfulness and love.

I will give thanks to your name,
Because of your kindness and your truth.
When I called, you answered me;
you built up strength within me.

℟. Lord, I thank you for your faithfulness and love.

All the kings of the earth shall give thanks to you, O Lord,
when they hear the words of your mouth;
And they shall sing of the ways of the Lord:
"Great is the glory of the Lord."

℟. Lord, I thank you for your faithfulness and love.

SECOND READING

1 Cor 1:3-9; L944.1

Brothers and sisters:
Grace to you and peace from God our Father
and the Lord Jesus Christ.

I give thanks to my God always on your account
for the grace of God bestowed on you in Christ Jesus,
that in him you were enriched in every way,
with all discourse and all knowledge,
as the testimony to Christ was confirmed among you,
so that you are not lacking in any spiritual gift
as you wait for the revelation of our Lord Jesus Christ.
He will keep you firm to the end,
irreproachable on the day of our Lord Jesus Christ.
God is faithful,
and by him you were called to fellowship
with his Son, Jesus Christ our Lord.

APPENDIX B

Lectionary Pronunciation Guide

Lectionary Word	Pronunciation
Aaron	EHR-uhn
Abana	AB-uh-nuh
Abednego	uh-BEHD-nee-go
Abel-Keramin	AY-b'l-KEHR-uh-mihn
Abel-meholah	AY-b'l-mee-HO-lah
Abiathar	uh-BAI-uh-ther
Abiel	AY-bee-ehl
Abiezrite	ay-bai-EHZ-rait
Abijah	uh-BAI-dzhuh
Abilene	ab-uh-LEE-neh
Abishai	uh-BIHSH-ay-ai
Abiud	uh-BAI-uhd
Abner	AHB-ner
Abraham	AY-bruh-ham
Abram	AY-br'm
Achaia	uh-KAY-yuh
Achim	AY-kihm
Aeneas	uh-NEE-uhs
Aenon	AY-nuhn
Agrippa	uh-GRIH-puh
Ahaz	AY-haz
Ahijah	uh-HAI-dzhuh
Ai	AY-ee
Alexandria	al-ehg-ZAN-dree-uh
Alexandrian	al-ehg-ZAN-dree-uhn
Alpha	AHL-fuh
Alphaeus	AL-fee-uhs
Amalek	AM-uh-lehk
Amaziah	am-uh-ZAI-uh
Amminadab	ah-MIHN-uh-dab
Ammonites	AM-uh-naitz
Amorites	AM-uh-raits
Amos	AY-muhs
Amoz	AY-muhz
Ampliatus	am-plee-AY-tuhs
Ananias	an-uh-NAI-uhs
Andronicus	an-draw-NAI-kuhs
Annas	AN-uhs
Antioch	AN-tih-ahk
Antiochus	an-TAI-uh-kuhs
Aphiah	uh-FAI-uh
Apollos	uh-PAH-luhs
Appius	AP-ee-uhs
Aquila	uh-KWIHL-uh
Arabah	EHR-uh-buh
Aram	AY-ram
Arameans	ehr-uh-MEE-uhnz
Areopagus	ehr-ee-AH-puh-guhs
Arimathea	ehr-uh-muh-THEE-uh
Aroer	uh-RO-er
Asaph	AY-saf
Asher	ASH-er
Ashpenaz	ASH-pee-naz
Assyria	a-SIHR-ee-uh
Astarte	as-TAHR-tee
Attalia	at-TAH-lee-uh
Augustus	uh-GUHS-tuhs
Azariah	az-uh-RAI-uh
Azor	AY-sawr
Azotus	uh-ZO-tus
Baal-shalishah	BAY-uhl-shuh-LAI-shuh
Baal-Zephon	BAY-uhl-ZEE-fuhn
Babel	BAY-bl
Babylon	BAB-ih-luhn
Babylonian	bab-ih-LO-nih-uhn
Balaam	BAY-lm
Barabbas	beh-REH-buhs
Barak	BEHR-ak
Barnabas	BAHR-nuh-buhs
Barsabbas	BAHR-suh-buhs
Bartholomew	bar-THAHL-uh-myoo
Bartimaeus	bar-tih-MEE-uhs
Baruch	BEHR-ook
Bashan	BAY-shan
Becorath	bee-KO-rath
Beelzebul	bee-EHL-zee-buhl
Beer-sheba	BEE-er-SHEE-buh
Belshazzar	behl-SHAZ-er
Benjamin	BEHN-dzhuh-mihn
Beor	BEE-awr
Bethany	BEHTH-uh-nee
Bethel	BETH-el
Bethesda	beh-THEHZ-duh
Bethlehem	BEHTH-leh-hehm
Bethphage	BEHTH-fuh-dzhee
Bethsaida	behth-SAY-ih-duh
Beth-zur	behth-ZER
Bildad	BIHL-dad
Bithynia	bih-THIHN-ih-uh
Boanerges	bo-uh-NER-dzheez
Boaz	BO-az
Caesar	SEE-zer
Caesarea	zeh-suh-REE-uh
Caiaphas	KAY-uh-fuhs
Cain	kayn
Cana	KAY-nuh
Canaan	KAY-nuhn
Canaanite	KAY-nuh-nait
Canaanites	KAY-nuh-naits
Candace	kan-DAY-see
Capernaum	kuh-PERR-nay-uhm
Cappadocia	kap-ih-DO-shee-u
Carmel	KAHR-muhl
carnelians	kahr-NEEL-yuhnz
Cenchreae	SEHN-kree-ay
Cephas	SEE-fuhs
Chaldeans	kal-DEE-uhnz
Chemosh	KEE-mahsh
Cherubim	TSHEHR-oo-bihm
Chislev	KIHS-lehv
Chloe	KLO-ee
Chorazin	kor-AY-sihn
Cilicia	sih-LIHSH-ee-uh
Cleopas	KLEE-o-pas
Clopas	KLO-pas
Corinth	KAWR-ihnth
Corinthians	kawr-IHN-thee-uhnz
Cornelius	kawr-NEE-lee-uhs
Crete	kreet
Crispus	KRIHS-puhs
Cushite	CUHSH-ait
Cypriot	SIH-pree-at
Cyrene	sai-REE-nee
Cyreneans	sai-REE-nih-uhnz
Cyrenian	sai-REE-nih-uhn
Cyrenians	sai-REE-nih-uhnz
Cyrus	SAI-ruhs
Damaris	DAM-uh-rihs
Damascus	duh-MAS-kuhs
Danites	DAN-aits
Decapolis	duh-KAP-o-lis
Derbe	DER-bee
Deuteronomy	dyoo-ter-AH-num-mee
Didymus	DID-I-mus
Dionysius	dai-o-NIHSH-ih-uhs
Dioscuri	dai-O-sky-ri
Dorcas	DAWR-kuhs
Dothan	DO-thuhn
dromedaries	DRAH-muh-dher-eez
Ebed-melech	EE-behd-MEE-lehk
Eden	EE-dn
Edom	EE-duhm
Elamites	EE-luh-maitz
Eldad	EHL-dad
Eleazar	ehl-ee-AY-zer
Eli	EE-lai
Eli Eli Lema Sabachthani	AY-lee AY-lee luh-MAH sah-BAHK-tah-nee

Lectionary Word	Pronunciation
Eliab	ee-LAI-ab
Eliakim	ee-LAI-uh-kihm
Eliezer	ehl-ih-EE-zer
Elihu	ee-LAI-hyoo
Elijah	ee-LAI-dzhuh
Elim	EE-lihm
Elimelech	ee-LIHM-eh-lehk
Elisha	ee-LAI-shuh
Eliud	ee-LAI-uhd
Elizabeth	ee-LIHZ-uh-bth
Elkanah	el-KAY-nuh
Eloi Eloi Lama Sabechthani	AY-lo-ee AY-lo-ee LAH-mah sah-BAHK-tah-nee
Elymais	ehl-ih-MAY-ihs
Emmanuel	eh-MAN-yoo-ehl
Emmaus	eh-MAY-uhs
Epaenetus	ee-PEE-nee-tuhs
Epaphras	EH-puh-fras
ephah	EE-fuh
Ephah	EE-fuh
Ephesians	eh-FEE-zhuhnz
Ephesus	EH-fuh-suhs
Ephphatha	EHF-uh-thuh
Ephraim	EE-fray-ihm
Ephrathah	EHF-ruh-thuh
Ephron	EE-frawn
Epiphanes	eh-PIHF-uh-neez
Erastus	ee-RAS-tuhs
Esau	EE-saw
Esther	EHS-ter
Ethanim	EHTH-uh-nihm
Ethiopian	ee-thee-O-pee-uhn
Euphrates	yoo-FRAY-teez
Exodus	EHK-so-duhs
Ezekiel	eh-ZEE-kee-uhl
Ezra	EHZ-ruh
frankincense	FRANGK-ihn-sehns
Gabbatha	GAB-uh-thuh
Gabriel	GAY-bree-ul
Gadarenes	GAD-uh-reenz
Galatian	guh-LAY-shih-uhn
Galatians	guh-LAY-shih-uhnz
Galilee	GAL-ih-lee
Gallio	GAL-ih-o
Gamaliel	guh-MAY-lih-ehl
Gaza	GAH-zuh
Gehazi	gee-HAY-zai
Gehenna	geh-HEHN-uh
Genesis	DZHEHN-uh-sihs
Gennesaret	gehn-NEHS-uh-reht
Gentiles	DZHEHN-tailz
Gerasenes	DZHEHR-uh-seenz
Gethsemane	gehth-SEHM-uh-ne
Gideon	GIHD-ee-uhn
Gilead	GIHL-ee-uhd
Gilgal	GIHL-gal
Golgotha	GAHL-guh-thuh
Gomorrah	guh-MAWR-uh
Goshen	GO-shuhn
Habakkuk	huh-BAK-uhk
Hadadrimmon	hay-dad-RIHM-uhn
Hades	HAY-deez
Hagar	HAH-gar
Hananiah	han-uh-NAI-uh
Hannah	HAN-uh
Haran	HAY-ruhn
Hebron	HEE-bruhn
Hermes	HER-meez
Herod	HEHR-uhd
Herodians	hehr-O-dee-uhnz
Herodias	hehr-O-dee-uhs
Hezekiah	heh-zeh-KAI-uh
Hezron	HEHZ-ruhn
Hilkiah	hihl-KAI-uh
Hittite	HIH-tait
Hivites	HAI-vaitz
Hophni	HAHF-nai
Hor	HAWR
Horeb	HAWR-ehb
Hosea	ho-ZEE-uh
Hur	her
hyssop	HIH-suhp
Iconium	ai-KO-nih-uhm
Isaac	AI-zuhk
Isaiah	ai-ZAY-uh
Iscariot	ihs-KEHR-ee-uht
Ishmael	ISH-may-ehl
Ishmaelites	ISH-mayehl-aits
Israel	IHZ-ray-ehl
Ituraea	ih-TSHOOR-ree-uh
Jaar	DZHAY-ahr
Jabbok	DZHAB-uhk
Jacob	DZHAY-kuhb
Jairus	DZH-hr-uhs
Javan	DZHAY-van
Jebusites	DZHEHB-oo-zaits
Jechoniah	dzhehk-o-NAI-uh
Jehoiakim	dzhee-HOI-uh-kihm
Jehoshaphat	dzhee-HAHSH-uh-fat
Jephthah	DZHEHF-thuh
Jeremiah	dzhehr-eh-MAI-uh
Jericho	DZHEHR-ih-ko
Jeroham	dzhehr-RO-ham
Jerusalem	dzheh-ROU-suh-lehm
Jesse	DZHEH-see
Jethro	DZHEHTH-ro
Joakim	DZHO-uh-kihm
Job	DZHOB
Jonah	DZHO-nuh
Joppa	DZHAH-puh
Joram	DZHO-ram
Jordan	DZHAWR-dn
Joseph	DZHO-zf
Joses	DZHO-seez
Joshua	DZHAH-shou-ah
Josiah	dzho-SAI-uh
Jotham	DZHO-thuhm
Judah	DZHOU-duh
Judas	DZHOU-duhs
Judea	dzhou-DEE-uh
Judean	dzhou-DEE-uhn
Junia	dzhou-nih-uh
Justus	DZHUHS-tuhs
Kephas	KEF-uhs
Kidron	KIHD-ruhn
Kiriatharba	kihr-ee-ath-AHR-buh
Kish	kihsh
Laodicea	lay-o-dih-SEE-uh
Lateran	LAT-er-uhn
Lazarus	LAZ-er-uhs
Leah	LEE-uh
Lebanon	LEH-buh-nuhn
Levi	LEE-vai
Levite	LEE-vait
Levites	LEE-vaits
Leviticus	leh-VIH-tih-kous
Lucius	LOO-shih-uhs
Lud	luhd
Luke	look
Luz	luhz
Lycaonian	lihk-ay-O-nih-uhn
Lydda	LIH-duh
Lydia	LIH-dih-uh
Lysanias	lai-SAY-nih-uhs
Lystra	LIHS-truh
Maccabees	MAK-uh-beez
Macedonia	mas-eh-DO-nih-uh
Macedonian	mas-eh-DO-nih-uhn
Machir	MAY-kihr
Machpelah	mak-PEE-luh
Magdala	MAG-duh-luh
Magdalene	MAG-duh-lehn
magi	MAY-dzhai
Malachi	MAL-uh-kai
Malchiah	mal-KAI-uh
Malchus	MAL-kuhz
Mamre	MAM-ree
Manaen	MAN-uh-ehn
Manasseh	man-AS-eh
Manoah	muh-NO-uh
Mark	mahrk
Mary	MEHR-ee
Massah	MAH-suh
Mattathias	mat-uh-THAI-uhs

Lectionary Word	Pronunciation
Matthan	MAT-than
Matthew	MATH-yoo
Matthias	muh-THAI-uhs
Medad	MEE-dad
Mede	meed
Medes	meedz
Megiddo	mee-GIH-do
Melchizedek	mehl-KIHZ-eh-dehk
Mene	MEE-nee
Meribah	MEHR-ih-bah
Meshach	MEE-shak
Mespotamia	mehs-o-po-TAY-mih-uh
Micah	MAI-kuh
Midian	MIH-dih-uhn
Milcom	MIHL-kahm
Miletus	mai-LEE-tuhs
Minnith	MIHN-ihth
Mishael	MIHSH-ay-ehl
Mizpah	MIHZ-puh
Moreh	MO-reh
Moriah	maw-RAI-uh
Mosoch	MAH-sahk
myrrh	mer
Mysia	MIH-shih-uh
Naaman	NAY-uh-muhn
Nahshon	NAY-shuhn
Naomi	NAY-o-mai
Naphtali	NAF-tuh-lai
Nathan	NAY-thuhn
Nathanael	nuh-THAN-ay-ehl
Nazarene	NAZ-awr-een
Nazareth	NAZ-uh-rehth
nazirite	NAZ-uh-rait
Nazorean	naz-aw-REE-uhn
Neapolis	nee-AP-o-lihs
Nebuchadnezzar	neh-byoo-kuhd-NEHZ-er
Negeb	NEH-gehb
Nehemiah	nee-hee-MAI-uh
Ner	ner
Nicanor	nai-KAY-nawr
Nicodemus	nih-ko-DEE-muhs
Niger	NAI-dzher
Nineveh	NIHN-eh-veh
Noah	NO-uh
Nun	nuhn
Obed	O-behd
Olivet	AH-lih-veht
Omega	o-MEE-guh
Onesimus	o-NEH-sih-muhs
Ophir	O-fer
Orpah	AWR-puh
Pamphylia	pam-FIHL-ih-uh
Paphos	PAY-fuhs

Lectionary Word	Pronunciation
Parmenas	PAHR-mee-nas
Parthians	PAHR-thee-uhnz
Patmos	PAT-mos
Peninnah	pee-NIHN-uh
Pentecost	PEHN-tee-kawst
Penuel	pee-NYOO-ehl
Perez	PEE-rehz
Perga	PER-guh
Perizzites	PEHR-ih-zaits
Persia	PER-zhuh
Peter	PEE-ter
Phanuel	FAN-yoo-ehl
Pharaoh	FEHR-o
Pharisees	FEHR-ih-seez
Pharpar	FAHR-pahr
Philemon	fih-LEE-muhn
Philippi	fil-LIH-pai
Philippians	fih-LIHP-ih-uhnz
Philistines	fih-LIHS-tihnz
Phinehas	FEHN-ee-uhs
Phoenicia	fee-NIHSH-ih-uh
Phrygia	FRIH-dzhih-uh
Phrygian	FRIH-dzhih-uhn
phylacteries	fih-LAK-ter-eez
Pi-Hahiroth	pai-huh-HAI-rahth
Pilate	PAI-luht
Pisidia	pih-SIH-dih-uh
Pithom	PAI-thahm
Pontius	PAHN-shus
Pontus	PAHN-tus
Praetorium	pray-TAWR-ih-uhm
Priscilla	PRIHS-kill-uh
Prochorus	PRAH-kaw-ruhs
Psalm	Sahm
Put	puht
Puteoli	pyoo-TEE-o-lai
Qoheleth	ko-HEHL-ehth
qorban	KAWR-bahn
Quartus	KWAR-tuhs
Quirinius	kwai-RIHN-ih-uhs
Raamses	ray-AM-seez
Rabbi	RAB-ai
Rabbouni	ra-BO-nai
Rahab	RAY-hab
Ram	ram
Ramah	RAY-muh
Ramathaim	ray-muh-THAY-ihm
Raqa	RA-kuh
Rebekah	ree-BEHK-uh
Rehoboam	ree-ho-BO-am
Rephidim	REHF-ih-dihm
Reuben	ROO-b'n
Revelation	reh-veh-LAY-shuhn
Rhegium	REE-dzhee-uhm
Rufus	ROO-fuhs

Lectionary Word	Pronunciation
Sabbath	SAB-uhth
Sadducees	SAD-dzhoo-seez
Salem	SAY-lehm
Salim	SAY-lim
Salmon	SAL-muhn
Salome	suh-LO-mee
Salu	SAYL-yoo
Samaria	suh-MEHR-ih-uh
Samaritan	suh-MEHR-ih-tuhn
Samothrace	SAM-o-thrays
Samson	SAM-s'n
Samuel	SAM-yoo-uhl
Sanhedrin	san-HEE-drihn
Sarah	SEHR-uh
Sarai	SAY-rai
saraph	SAY-raf
Sardis	SAHR-dihs
Saul	sawl
Scythian	SIH-thee-uihn
Seba	SEE-buh
Seth	sehth
Shaalim	SHAY-uh-lihm
Shadrach	SHAY-drak
Shalishah	shuh-LEE-shuh
Shaphat	Shay-fat
Sharon	SHEHR-uhn
Shealtiel	shee-AL-tih-ehl
Sheba	SHEE-buh
Shebna	SHEB-nuh
Shechem	SHEE-kehm
shekel	SHEHK-uhl
Shiloh	SHAI-lo
Shinar	SHAI-nahr
Shittim	sheh-TEEM
Shuhite	SHOO-ait
Shunammite	SHOO-nam-ait
Shunem	SHOO-nehm
Sidon	SAI-duhn
Silas	SAI-luhs
Siloam	sih-LO-uhm
Silvanus	sihl-VAY-nuhs
Simeon	SIHM-ee-uhn
Simon	SAI-muhn
Sin *(desert)*	sihn
Sinai	SAI-nai
Sirach	SAI-rak
Sodom	SAH-duhm
Solomon	SAH-lo-muhn
Sosthenes	SAHS-thee-neez
Stachys	STAY-kihs
Succoth	SUHK-ahth
Sychar	SI-kar
Syene	sai-EE-nee
Symeon	SIHM-ee-uhn
synagogues	SIHN-uh-gahgz

Lectionary Word	Pronunciation
Syrophoenician	SIHR-o fee-NIHSH-ih-uhn
Tabitha	TAB-ih-thuh
Talitha koum	TAL-ih-thuh-KOOM
Tamar	TAY-mer
Tarshish	TAHR-shihsh
Tarsus	TAHR-suhs
Tekel	TEH-keel
Terebinth	TEHR-ee-bihnth
Thaddeus	THAD-dee-uhs
Theophilus	thee-AH-fih-luhs
Thessalonians	theh-suh-LO-nih-uhnz
Theudas	THU-duhs
Thyatira	thai-uh-TAI-ruh
Tiberias	tai-BIHR-ih-uhs
Timaeus	tai-MEE-uhs
Timon	TAI-muhn
Titus	TAI-tuhs
Tohu	TO-hyoo
Trachonitis	trak-o-NAI-tis
Troas	TRO-ahs
Tubal	TYOO-b'l
Tyre	TAI-er
Ur	er
Urbanus	er-BAY-nuhs
Uriah	you-RAI-uh
Uzziah	yoo-ZAI-uh
Wadi	WAH-dee
Yahweh-yireh	YAH-weh-yer-AY
Zacchaeus	zak-KEE-uhs
Zadok	ZAY-dahk
Zarephath	ZEHR-ee-fath
Zebedee	ZEH-beh-dee
Zebulun	ZEH-byoo-luhn
Zechariah	zeh-kuh-RAI-uh
Zedekiah	zeh-duh-KAI-uh
Zephaniah	zeh-fuh-NAI-uh
Zerah	ZEE-ruh
Zeror	ZEE-rawr
Zerubbabel	zeh-RUH-buh-behl
Zeus	zyoos
Zimri	ZIHM-rai
Zion	ZAI-uhn
Ziph	zihf
Zoar	ZO-er
Zorah	ZAWR-uh
Zuphite	ZUHF-ait